AI-Powered Solutions for Bilingual Proficiency and Communication

Ali Sorayyaei Azar
https://orcid.org/0000-0003-3539-8250
University of Malaya, Malaysia

Sedigheh Shakib Kotamjani
https://orcid.org/0000-0001-6249-0293
Central Asian University, Uzbekistan

Marine Milad
https://orcid.org/0009-0000-0703-3604
Arab Open University, Kuwait

Shanina Sharatol Ahmad Shah
University of Malaya, Malaysia

IGI Global
Scientific Publishing
Publishing Tomorrow's Research Today

Vice President of Editorial Melissa Wagner
Director of Acquisitions Mikaela Felty
Director of Book Development Jocelynn Hessler
Production Manager Mike Brehm
Cover Design Jose Rosado

Published in the United States of America by
IGI Global Scientific Publishing
701 East Chocolate Avenue
Hershey, PA, 17033, USA
Tel: 717-533-8845 | Fax: 717-533-7115
Website: https://www.igi-global.com E-mail: cust@igi-global.com

Library of Congress Cataloging-in-Publication Data

Names: Sorayyaei Azar, Ali, 1967- editor | Shakib Kotamjani, Sedigheh, 1979- | Milad, Marine, 1973- editor | Sharatol Ahmad Shah, Shanina, 1975- editor

Title: AI-powered solutions for bilingual proficiency and communication / edited by Ali Sorayyaei Azar, Sedigheh Shakib Kotamjani, Marine Milad, Shanina Sharatol Ahmad Shah.

Description: Hershey, PA : IGI Global Scientific Publishing, 2026. | Includes bibliographical references and index. | Summary: "This book critically analyzes the role of AI in enhancing bilingual proficiency and communication across various contexts"-- Provided by publisher.

Identifiers: LCCN 2025003891 (print) | LCCN 2025003892 (ebook) | ISBN 9798337302751 hardcover | ISBN 9798337302768 paperback | ISBN 9798337302775 ebook

Subjects: LCSH: Bilingualism http://id.loc.gov/authorities/subjects/sh85014030 | Artificial intelligence--Educational applications http://id.loc.gov/authorities/subjects/sh87006783 | Language and languages--Study and teaching http://id.loc.gov/authorities/subjects/sh85074536 | Intercultural communication http://id.loc.gov/authorities/subjects/sh85067222 | LCGFT: Essays http://id.loc.gov/authorities/genreForms/gf2014026094

Classification: LCC P115 .A38 2025 (print) | LCC P115 (ebook) | DDC 404/.2028563--dc23/eng/20250314

LC record available at https://lccn.loc.gov/2025003891

LC ebook record available at https://lccn.loc.gov/2025003892

British Cataloguing in Publication Data
A Cataloguing in Publication record for this book is available from the British Library.

Table of Contents

Detailed Table of Contents

The objective of this chapter is to provide the readers with a foundational understanding of how AI-driven tools are being leveraged to facilitate bilingual proficiency. It addresses the various dimensions of bilingual language learning, focusing on the efficiency, personalization, and cultural adaptability AI brings to the field. The chapter offers insights into the present state of AI technologies in L2 learning and communication while projecting future innovations and challenges in this rapidly evolving landscape. By demystifying the use of AI in bilingual language learning and communication, this chapter aims to provide both a theoretical and practical framework for integrating AI tools into bilingual education programs. The chapter will impart to the readers a deeper understanding of how to use these technologies to improve their own or others' language proficiency and communication skills, ultimately contributing to greater linguistic and cultural exchange in an increasingly globalized world.

This chapter examines the evolution of language acquisition, transitioning from conventional grammar-translation techniques to the incorporation of advanced technology like Artificial Intelligence (AI). It underscores the crucial function of AI-driven tools—such as chatbots, virtual tutors, and customized learning platforms—in improving engagement, accessibility, and individualized education. The paper also examines problems such as technological obstacles, ethical implications, and AI's constraints in comprehending cultural context and complexity. Additionally, emerging technologies such as augmented reality (AR) and virtual reality (VR) are analyzed for their capacity to foster immersive educational settings. This research underscores the necessity for equitable implementation and the ongoing significance of educators in cultivating empathy and critical thinking. By appropriately adopting these developments, language acquisition can transcend cultural barriers and equip learners for a globally networked environment.

As artificial intelligence reshapes classrooms worldwide, this chapter explores how EFL educators navigate the promises and challenges of AI integration, revealing not only their readiness and strategies through the TPACK framework but also the transformative potential of AI adoption measured by the SAMR model. A descriptive quantitative case study was conducted with 32 EFL university educators using a structured questionnaire to assess familiarity with AI tools, perceptions of pedagogical impact, and adoption challenges. Findings reveal 78% of educators feel technologically competent, 75% report AI automation benefits, and 68% observe increased student motivation. However, 40% identify insufficient training and 35% cite a lack of EFL-specific AI tools as challenges. The study concludes that AI can transform EFL education when integrated through TPACK and SAMR. To maximize AI's effectiveness, structured professional development programs should be implemented to equip teachers with AI literacy, and collaborative AI tools should be designed specifically for language learning needs.

Abstract This chapter examines the role of Artificial Intelligence (AI) in Second Language Acquisition (SLA), exploring the opportunities and challenges associated with its integration into language education. Drawing on foundational SLA theories, the chapter analyzes how AI technologies, such as transformer-based NLP models, speech recognition tools, intelligent tutoring systems, and gamified applications, can enhance learner engagement, provide personalized feedback, support multilingual learners, and improve language instruction across different contexts. Ethical issues, such as algorithmic bias, lack of cultural awareness, threats to data privacy, and diminished human interaction, underscore the importance of developing AI systems

vocabulary. In this quasi-experimental study, data were collected from 32 secondary school students through a background questionnaire and a vocabulary test. The findings revealed that AI had a significant impact on vocabulary learning, particularly in terms of vocabulary retention levels.

The evolution of Artificial Intelligence (AI) in education offers new possibilities for supporting plurilingual students within Canada's varied linguistic landscape, where learners balance official and community languages while developing academic proficiency and negotiating identities. AI tools, such as adaptive learning platforms, natural language processing technologies, and real-time translation software, provide inclusive, personalized environments. Grounded in plurilingualism and inclusive education, this chapter outlines AI's potential to support language acquisition, foster cultural inclusivity, and promote identity negotiation. It also explores systemic barriers, presenting case studies from Canadian classrooms that illustrate AI's impact on student engagement and learning. Although AI offers innovative opportunities, concerns regarding equitable access, algorithmic bias, and data privacy must be addressed. Strategies for ethical application are proposed, along with context-sensitive plurilingual practices to foster metalinguistic awareness and equitable learning spaces.

Bilingual and multilingual education integrated with artificial intelligence (AI) has fundamentally altered conventional education paradigms, increasing the engagement

Preface

INTRODUCTION

The exponential growth of Artificial Intelligence (AI) has redefined many dimensions of modern society, and language learning stands at the forefront of this transformation. In an increasingly globalized world where bilingual and multilingual proficiency is essential for academic, professional, and cultural exchange, AI-powered solutions provide both unprecedented opportunities and complex challenges. This volume, *AI-Powered Solutions for Bilingual Proficiency and Communication*, brings together leading scholars and practitioners to explore how emerging technologies are reshaping language education and communication across diverse contexts.

As editors, our intent has been to curate a collection that balances theoretical rigor with practical application. Each chapter offers unique insights into the pedagogical, technological, and ethical dimensions of AI integration in language learning. Together, the contributions illustrate how AI can enhance bilingual proficiency through adaptive learning, immersive environments, intelligent tutoring, gamification, and data-driven instructional strategies. At the same time, they also acknowledge the limitations and risks of these technologies, from algorithmic bias and cultural insensitivity to data privacy concerns.

We envision this book as a valuable reference for educators, researchers, policymakers, and technology developers who seek to understand not only the current landscape but also the evolving potential of AI in bilingual education. By highlighting global perspectives, case studies, and conceptual analyses, the chapters aim to inspire future research and inform the responsible adoption of AI technologies in fostering multilingual communication.

CHAPTER OVERVIEW

Chapter 1 provides a comprehensive overview of AI applications in bilingual education, offering readers both theoretical foundations and practical strategies for integrating AI into learning environments.

Chapter 2 traces the transformation of language learning methodologies, showing how traditional techniques have evolved into AI-driven, interactive approaches that leverage chatbots, AR/VR, and virtual tutors.

Chapter 3 presents a case study applying the TPACK and SAMR models to assess educators' readiness, highlighting both the transformative potential and the challenges of AI integration in English language teaching.

Chapter 4 focuses on Second Language Acquisition (SLA), linking AI technologies with SLA theories, while also emphasizing ethical and cultural considerations in global implementation.

Chapter 5 explores immersive technologies such as AR/VR, emotional AI, and large language models (LLMs), presenting practical recommendations alongside ethical considerations for bilingual education.

Chapter 6 discusses intelligent tutoring systems, NLP, and immersive technologies, analyzing how personalized pathways can enhance bilingual mastery while addressing equity and privacy issues.

Chapter 7 highlights the use of AI tools within the Trifecta model, emphasizing gamification, conversational AI, and translation systems to enhance bilingual communication and cultural exchange.

Chapter 8 investigates AI-enhanced gamification in vocabulary learning, presenting empirical evidence on its effectiveness for vocabulary retention in EFL learners.

Chapter 9 offers a conceptual analysis of AI in teaching bilingual skills to children with autism, assessing both the potential benefits and the ethical, accessibility, and implementation challenges.

Chapter 10 examines adaptive assessments and AI-driven systems that personalize learning and feedback, highlighting both opportunities and risks in promoting cultural competence.

Chapter 11 provides practical guidelines for managing AI integration in bilingual education, outlining systematic frameworks and best practices for effective and ethical adoption.

Chapter 12 traces the historical evolution of language learning methodologies, situating AI within a broader continuum of educational transformation.

CONCLUSION

Collectively, the chapters in this book reveal how AI is not merely an auxiliary tool but a transformative force in the domain of bilingual education and communication. From immersive learning experiences to adaptive assessments, the technologies examined throughout the volume underscore how AI can personalize education, expand access, and facilitate cross-cultural understanding. Yet they also serve as a reminder that technology must remain grounded in ethical principles and guided by human-centered values.

Our contributors have highlighted both success stories and ongoing challenges, offering a realistic yet optimistic vision of the future of bilingual education. Their perspectives demonstrate that AI's impact is most profound when integrated thoughtfully, with sensitivity to learners' diverse needs and global contexts. This approach ensures that AI does not replace the human element in education but instead enhances and enriches it.

As editors, we extend our deepest gratitude to the authors whose expertise shaped this volume, and to the institutions and colleagues who supported their work. We hope this book will serve as both a scholarly reference and a practical guide, inspiring educators, researchers, and innovators to harness the transformative potential of AI responsibly. By doing so, we can create a future where bilingual proficiency and communication flourish as bridges between cultures, societies, and generations.

Ali Sorayyaei Azar
University of Malaya, Malaysia

Sedigheh Shakib Kotamjani
Central Asian University, Uzbekistan & Marine Milad Arab Open University, Kuwait

Shanina Sharatol Ahmad Shah
University of Malaya, Malaysia

Chapter 1
Harnessing Artificial Intelligence for Language Learning:
A Comprehensive Overview

Fareeha Javed
https://orcid.org/0000-0003-4455-047X
Lahore College for Women University, Pakistan

ABSTRACT

The objective of this chapter is to provide the readers with a foundational understanding of how AI-driven tools are being leveraged to facilitate bilingual proficiency. It addresses the various dimensions of bilingual language learning, focusing on the efficiency, personalization, and cultural adaptability AI brings to the field. The chapter offers insights into the present state of AI technologies in L2 learning and communication while projecting future innovations and challenges in this rapidly evolving landscape. By demystifying the use of AI in bilingual language learning and communication, this chapter aims to provide both a theoretical and practical framework for integrating AI tools into bilingual education programs. The chapter will impart to the readers a deeper understanding of how to use these technologies to improve their own or others' language proficiency and communication skills, ultimately contributing to greater linguistic and cultural exchange in an increasingly globalized world.

DOI: 10.4018/979-8-3373-0275-1.ch001

INTRODUCTION

Technology integration has grown in popularity in the fast-changing field of education, upending conventional wisdom and providing creative methods of instruction and learning (Wark, 2018). Artificial Intelligence (AI) is one important development that has attracted significant interest in education. AI has the potential to alter educational innovation, especially in second language (L2) learning. AI technologies, such as adaptive learning systems, natural language processing (NLP), and machine learning (ML), can greatly improve the customization and efficiency of L2 learning experiences. AI can provide rapid feedback, adapt to the learner's speed, and create interactive, engaging environments based on individual skill levels and learning styles (Chang et al., 2021; Choukaier, 2024; Kim & Gilman, 2021). Research is focusing on AI's potential to transform educational methods, especially in the context of L2 learning, as it develops and permeates numerous industries (Javed, 2024; Manire et al., 2023).

For bilinguals, the interaction of two languages can influence cognitive processes, emotional expression, and self-perception. Research has revealed that bilingualism improves cognitive flexibility, problem-solving ability, and may prevent neurological disorders such as dementia. However, it complicates identity formation as people navigate multiple cultural contexts. The introduction of AI-powered language tools has created opportunities for analyzing and understanding these processes. AI has provided deeper insights into how bi/multilingual people think, communicate, and relate to their identities using NLP models such as GPT and BERT, as well as real-time translation technologies. These technologies not only simulate linguistic activity but also reflect and enhance cognitive tendencies linked with bilingualism. However, their design and implementation must be approached with caution to ensure they respect and promote users' cultural and linguistic diversity (Anderson, 2024).

The objective of this chapter is to provide a foundational understanding of how the evolving role of AI and AI-driven tools are being leveraged to facilitate L2 learning and bilingual proficiency. It addresses various dimensions of bilingual language learning, focusing on the efficiency, personalization, and cultural adaptability AI brings to the field. The chapter offers insights into the present state of AI technologies in L2 learning and communication while projecting future innovations and challenges in this evolving landscape. By demystifying the use of AI in bilingual language learning and communication, this chapter provides a theoretical and practical framework for integrating AI tools into bilingual education programs. It imparts to readers a deeper understanding of how to use these technologies to improve language proficiency and communication skills, ultimately contributing to greater linguistic and cultural exchange in an increasingly globalized world.

AI in Language Learning

The traditional method of teaching languages has included classroom instruction, textbooks, and language exchange programs. Even though these approaches are commonly used and fairly effective, they often have disadvantages, such as limiting curriculum designs, lack of real-time feedback, and limited personalized instruction (Knox, 2020). In contrast, the advancement of AI has paved the way for cutting-edge L2 learning methodologies that employ technologies such as speech recognition, ML, and NLP. AI-powered solutions enable personalized, flexible, and immersive language learning experiences (Frith, 2019). AI language systems can provide immediate feedback and analyze learner progress, resulting in more efficient and effective learning. These technologies can also be tailored to the learner's pace and style, making language learning more engaging and enjoyable (Dhanapal et al., 2024).

In recent years, significant advancements in AI integration into L2 education have demonstrated how innovative technology and pedagogy can work together. AI is causing a major shift in the field of L2 learning (Dhanapal et al., 2024). Millions of people are learning English for academic, professional, and personal purposes, making L2 learning vital for global communication and educational progress. AI integration in L2 learning holds promise for resolving persistent issues, customizing educational experiences, and improving overall proficiency. However, research is ongoing into AI's effectiveness in L2 learning, its impact on students, and the methodological strategies used in related studies (Choukaier, 2024; Manire et al., 2023; Weng & Chiu, 2023).

Computer-assisted language learning (CALL) first appeared in the 1960s as a system for language training that allowed students to drill and rehearse. CALL's rise has been strongly linked to digital technology advancements, with L2 learning playing an increasingly important role. CALL development is split into three stages: behavioristic, communicative, and integrative. These represent evolving educational theories and technological progress. CALL has become a key component of L2 teaching. It uses a variety of tools, such as social media, mobile games, virtual reality (VR), and machine learning-based platforms, to provide contextualized interactive education (Fazal et al., 2024).

Numerous studies show that AI positively impacts language proficiency. Learners exposed to AI-driven methods improved their outcomes significantly (Chen et al., 2022). The versatility and personalized nature of AI enhance language skill development (Baker et al., 2021). AI-enhanced L2 environments have shown potential for increasing learner motivation and engagement (Kilag et al., 2023). Gamification, personalized content, and interactive features built into AI systems help make language learning more engaging and learner-centered (Anis, 2023).

Natural Language Processing (NLP) for Bilingual Proficiency

To promote language practice and interaction, NLP applications—such as chatbots and language assessment tools—have been used into L2 learning settings (Woo & Choi, 2021). By allowing students to participate in authentic language challenges, these technologies promote language production and communication ability (Yang et al., 2020). Because they offer real-time feedback on pronunciation and intonation, speech recognition systems are essential for L2 learning (Kilag et al., 2023). Research shows that adding speech recognition to language training might increase students' confidence and speaking abilities (Bakhodirov & Rahmanova, 2023). By using NLP to comprehend spoken and written words and reply to them in a human-like manner, for instance, natural language models (NLMs) are made to solve problems and tasks.

NLP involves three primary tasks: first, comprehending the user-provided written or spoken words; second, using the information to reply; and third, responding to the user in a human-like manner (Håkansson & Hartung, 2020). For a full working model, the AI must be able to handle a variety of languages and input variations in addition to the three primary tasks of NLP. This is because different languages have different grammar and syntax, and each user has a unique writing style. Language variability, which refers to the fact that different languages have different grammatical structures, vocabularies, and idiomatic expressions, or ambiguity, which can make it difficult for an AI to execute a program written in Java with natural language, are examples of linguistic challenges (Jurafsky & Martin, 2024). NLP makes AI a useful tool for L2 learning by enabling machines to comprehend human language.

Adaptive Learning and Personalization

Higher education has seen a considerable transformation since the introduction of customized adaptive learning, which combines adaptive learning technologies with personalized learning principles. AI-driven adaptive learning routes provide for individual learner variances by altering the difficulty and pace of education based on progress (Aggarwal, 2023). This technique is consistent with the ideas of individualized education, catering to L2 learners' unique requirements (Manire et al., 2023; Smets & Struyven, 2018).

Personalized adaptive learning, defined as "a technology-empowered effective pedagogy which can adaptively adjust teaching strategies timely based on real-time monitored (enabled by smart technology) learners' differences and changes in individual characteristics, performance, and personal development" (Peng et al., 2019, p. 2), has the potential to address long-standing challenges in higher education. These include the scalability of tailored education, participation in online learning environments, and accommodating different learner groups. Personalized adaptive learning pathways can be designed and delivered using a variety of single or multimodal data sources, such as pre-test questionnaires (Adewumi, 2020), student confidence levels (Jang et al., 2017), and activity logs from learning management systems. Learning paths have also been devised to tailor information delivery formats to student learning styles (Alsobhi & Alyoubi, 2019).

Conversational AI

The purpose of AI is to solve tasks or problems by using intelligent devices or software (McCarthy, 2007). A subtype of AI known as conversational AI makes use of deep learning models and language processing to produce natural language writing. In order to facilitate realistic, human-like discussions between humans and computers, conversational AI can leverage massive amounts of data, ML, and NLP (Kulkarni et al., 2019). In addition to using language processing, ChatGPT is a deep learning model that produces natural language writing. Decision-making, problem-solving, image processing, prediction, and language handling are just a few of the jobs and issues that an AI may handle. To solve a particular issue, these skills can be merged (Håkansson & Hartung, 2020).

Conversational AI, sometimes referred to as conversational agents, are intelligent software programs that learn by communicating like people. Initially providing standardized responses to common questions, these programs have since advanced into more complex ones with the help of deep learning technologies, neural networks, and Natural Language Understanding (NLU). They make up a sophisticated dialog system that mimics written and/or spoken communication with human users, usually via the Internet. They can respond with speech, visuals, virtual gestures, or haptica-assisted physical gestures, and they can be text-based or read from. Furthermore, some of them, also referred to as Intelligent Personal Assistants (IPAs), have received training to carry out certain jobs. Examples of these are Amazon Alexa, Apple Siri, Samsung Bixby, and IBM Watson (de Barcelos et al., 2020). In situations and environments where formal education and access to native speakers are not options, conversational AI may prove to be helpful tools as language-learning partners and constant instructors available at any time and any place (Belda-Medina & Calvo-Ferrer, 2022).

Chatbots

Modern developments in machine learning and NLP have contributed to the rapid evolution of chatbot technology over the past few decades (Caldarini et al., 2022; Luo et al., 2022). NLP-based AI English chatbots have become a potential method for L2 learning (Liu et al., 2021). AI-powered chatbots are also capable of having human-like conversations, which allows L2 learners to practice in a relaxed setting. Such interactive, adaptable technology may have a lot of promise to improve L2 learning in terms of resolving numerous issues that a traditional classroom environment just cannot effectively manage. It is also commonly known that non-native English speakers have a number of challenges when learning the language, including a lack of practice opportunities, a dearth of peers who speak the language, and an active dread of making mistakes in front of their peers. All of that could lead to language anxiety, which is thought to be one of the biggest obstacles to learning a language. Learners who sense dread or concern when speaking a L2 are said to have language anxiety. This is particularly true in the conventional classroom, where the majority are motivated by feelings of inadequacy and a generalized dread of being judged by their peers and teachers. Chatbots for language learning driven by AI (Crowder, 2024) seek to mitigate these problems by giving students access to a stable, accessible, and non-critical practice environment.

Because of their potential to enhance L2 learning in novel ways, chatbots are gaining popularity (Wang et al., 2021). Huang et al. (2018) created GenieTutor, a dialogue-based chatbot for English as a second/foreign language instruction, to focus on certain language learning interests, such as placing food orders, or to simply have open discussions about any subject. The Mondly chatbot was created as an extra feature of a language learning platform to help people learn a variety of languages. A chatbot can focus on particular topics and areas of interest, has infinite patience, can respond to requests instantly using natural language, can reduce learners' anxiety, which promotes willingness to communicate and self-correction if mistakes are made, and doesn't need a human teacher or interlocutor (Bibauw et al., 2019; Fryer et al., 2020). Students can practice newly learned language or linguistic skills they would not feel comfortable exercising with a human (Fryer et al., 2020). Recently, ChatGPT has attracted a lot of interest from a variety of sectors. It uses extensive databases to generate thorough written answers to information requests.

Automatic Speech Recognition

Automatic speech recognition (ASR) is a system that comprehends and generates written and spoken language using AI and machine learning approaches. It is frequently utilized in software programs that use speech-to-text and voice recognition, including note-taking apps, automated transcribers, and IPAs (Evers & Chen, 2022). When a user dictates a message into a smartphone, the device recognizes the language and uses it to carry out an operation. This is another example of ASR in action. Over the past ten years, ASR has advanced quickly, becoming increasingly precise and extensively used across numerous industries (Daniels & Iwago, 2017).

According to Golonka et al. (2014), who reviewed the many types of technology and their efficacy, research on ASR was a major source of the quantifiable influence of technology on L2 learning.

In the field of CALL, ASR has sparked a lot of attention (e.g., Ahn & Lee, 2016; de Vries et al., 2015; van Doremalen et al., 2016). The literature indicates that IPAs have a lot of promise for use as a L2 learning tool (Chen et al., 2023; Moussalli & Cardoso, 2020; Tai & Chen, 2023). In a less stressful setting, students are free to practice as much as they wish (Tai & Chen, 2023). In an evaluation study of an IPA, Dizon (2020) discovered that using Alexa improved L2 speaking capacity. Similarly, Google Assistant may be helpful for speaking and listening (Chen et al., 2023).

IPAs can comprehend user commands with a high degree of accuracy (Daniels & Iwago, 2017; Dizon et al., 2022). Because of its natural language usage and instant feedback, ASR in IPAs is advantageous for L2 development and enhancement. Since users receive instantaneous, customized, and independent feedback, the application of ASR in messaging apps, software, and websites helps users improve their L2 pronunciation (Chen, 2011; Dai & Wu, 2023; Dizon, 2017; McCrocklin, 2016, 2019). Apps and software that incorporate ASR make learning more dynamic, interesting, and pleasurable, which boosts L2 motivation (Moussalli & Cardoso, 2020; Tai & Chen, 2023). Students can have conversations with IPAs like Google Assistant and Alexa (Chen et al., 2023; Dizon, 2017).

MACHINE TRANSLATION AND CROSS-LANGUAGE COMMUNICATION

The automatic process of translating speech or text from one language—referred to as the source language—to another—referred to as the target language—is called machine translation (MT). In order to assess and comprehend the input in the source language and provide an equivalent representation in the target language, computational models and algorithms are used. The goal of MT is to make it easier for people who speak various languages to communicate and comprehend one another, allowing knowledge, concepts, and information to be shared across linguistic borders. To produce precise and contextually relevant translations, MT uses a variety of methods and strategies, such as rule-based systems, statistical models, and neural networks (Cheng et al., 2021).

MT Applications and Platforms

Individuals, businesses, and organizations widely use several popular machine translation applications and platforms:

Google Translate.

One of the most popular and extensively utilized MT tools is Google Translate. Along with many other functions including text translation, website translation, document translation, and real-time speech translation, it allows translation between a wide range of languages. Because Google Translate is available on both mobile and online platforms, it may be used on a variety of devices (Trzaskawka, 2020).

Microsoft Translator

Another popular MT tool is Microsoft Translator. It offers multilingual text, document, website, and speech translation services. A web-based translation, mobile apps, API services, and connection with Microsoft Office and other Microsoft products are just a few of the applications and integration choices that Microsoft translation provides (McGeachie & Dingel, 2007).

DeepL

DeepL is a well-known machine translation tool that produces translations of excellent quality. For precise and fluid translations, it makes use of neural machine translation technology. In addition to offering functionality like document and web page translation and API connection with other apps, DeepL facilitates translation between a variety of language pairs (DeepL, 2025).

Amazon Translate

Amazon Web Services (AWS) offers a machine translation service called Amazon Translate. It supports a variety of use cases, including content localization, real-time chat translation, and customer service translation, and provides automatic text translation in various languages. Neural machine translation models are used by Amazon Translate to deliver high-quality translations (aws, 2025).

Yandex Translate

The Russian technology company Yandex offers a machine translation service called Yandex Translate. It offers functions including text translation, document translation, and website translation, and it can translate between many language pairs. Additional capabilities like dictionary lookup, pronunciation help, and language identification are provided by Yandex Translate, which is accessible as a web-based application (Yandex Translate, 2025).

SYSTRAN

SYSTRAN is a company that offers machine translation services. Neural machine translation models, adaptable translation engines, and translation API services are among the translation solutions it provides to companies and organizations. SYSTRAN serves a number of industries, including localization, customer service, and e-commerce (SYSTRAN, 2025).

These are but a handful of well-known platforms and applications for MT. Users can select the platform that best suits their unique needs and requirements from among those that may offer varying functionality, language support, and integration choices.

Challenges in Generating Contextually Appropriate Translations

In MT, producing translations that are appropriate for the context is a difficult task. Most of the main challenges are caused due to ambiguity. Ambiguous words or phrases with numerous meanings depending on the context are common in languages. Accurately addressing ambiguity is essential to producing translations that are suitable for the context. In order to disambiguate and choose the appropriate translation, MT systems need to have a thorough understanding of the context and the surrounding words or sentences. Homonyms, polysemous terms, colloquial idioms, and cultural references can all lead to ambiguity (Chang & Krulee, 1991). Because language is inherently complex, words or phrases in the original language may have more than one meaning, which can cause ambiguity in translation. These are a few typical causes of ambiguity in translations:

Homonyms

Words that have different meanings but the same spelling or pronunciation are called homonyms. For instance, “bank” might be used to describe a river’s margin or a financial institution. The context plays a crucial role in identifying the correct meaning when translating a statement that contains a homonym. However, the translation system could find it difficult to distinguish and select the right translation if the context is unclear or insufficient.

Polysemy

When a term has multiple related meanings, it is referred to as polysemy. To connect these ideas, metaphorical or figurative extensions are commonly employed. For instance, “bright” can describe high light or cognitive levels. Understanding the precise meaning meant in the context is necessary when translating polysemous terms. MT systems could have trouble choosing the best translation choice if they don't have enough contextual knowledge (Pedersen, 1999).

Idiomatic Expressions

Phrases or sentences that are idiomatic are ones whose meaning cannot be deduced from the words alone. These idioms frequently have culturally or linguistically specific figurative or metaphorical implications. Accurate understanding of the underlying linguistic and cultural nuances is necessary when translating colloquial idioms. When dealing with idiomatic terms, MT systems may confront challenges because a literal translation could result in inaccurate or nonsensical translations (Serban et al., 2017).

Ambiguous Syntax

Ambiguity may be introduced by a sentence's syntactic structure. When a sentence structure permits more than one interpretation, it is said to have ambiguous syntax. Take, for instance, the statement, "Time flies like an arrow". Here, the phrase "like an arrow" might mean either that time is being compared to an arrow or that time is being compared to an arrow that is in motion. Understanding the context and intended meaning is necessary to resolve syntactic ambiguity and produce a suitable translation (Borsotti et al., 2021).

Cultural References

Because cultural allusions might not have exact translation equivalents in other languages, they can present translation difficulties. Names, sayings, slang, and culturally particular ideas are a few examples of these references. Localization, or adjusting the translation to the target culture, is typically necessary when translating cultural allusions. Without the required contextual and cultural information, MT systems could have trouble understanding cultural references (Alfaify & Pinto, 2022).

Contextual Ambiguity

When it comes to separating words or sentences, context is essential. The meaning of a word might vary based on the words, sentences, or speech that surround it. MT algorithms could find it difficult to understand the intended meaning and select the correct translation if there is insufficient context. Resolving ambiguity and producing translations that are appropriate for the context require an understanding of the larger context (Qin et al., 2021).

Resolving translation ambiguity is a challenging process that calls for contextual knowledge, the use of language models, and consideration of linguistic and cultural elements. In order to provide more accurate and contextually relevant translations, MT research is always being conducted to enhance systems' comprehension and disambiguation of the original text. Disambiguating polysemous words based on context and domain knowledge remains an important field of research in MT. Disambiguation accuracy is increased by developments in neural network topologies, large-scale corpora, NLP, and domain-specific resources. By correctly disambiguating polysemous terms, MT systems can improve their ability to provide reliable translations by utilizing context, statistical models, domain-specific information, and user feedback.

Cultural and Sociolinguistic Factors

Culture and sociolinguistic norms are closely linked to language. To be contextually suitable, translations must take sociolinguistic considerations and cultural sensitivity into consideration. This characteristic includes taking into account regional dialects, cultural quirks, politeness levels, and formal versus informal language. According to Procter and Joshi (2022), MT systems ought to be cognizant of these elements and provide translations that conform to the target language's sociolinguistic and cultural norms.

Contextual Disambiguation

Producing accurate translations requires an understanding of the context. For MT systems to generate translations that are acceptable for the context, they must be able to understand the meaning and intent of the original text. However, context might encompass information from earlier and later text segments in addition to specific sentences. Complex contextual modeling is needed to resolve pronoun references, capture anaphora and cataphora, and preserve coherence across the translated text (Kandasamy & Cherukuri, 2020).

Domain-Specific Knowledge

Translations in specialist professions, like medicine, law, or technology, frequently call for domain-specific expertise. Without access to pertinent domain-specific information, MT systems may find it difficult to translate technical phrases, jargon, or domain-specific terms accurately. For MT systems to produce contextually relevant translations in specialized fields, domain-specific information must be acquired and integrated (Asplund et al., 2022).

Rare and Low-Resource Languages

Additional difficulties arise when translating rare or low-resource languages in a contextually acceptable manner. MT systems' performance may be hampered by a lack of bilingual corpora, linguistic resources, and training data. In these situations, it becomes essential to modify current models or use transfer learning strategies in order to get around the lack of data and provide translations that are appropriate for the context (Maimaiti et al., 2022).

Stylistic Variations

Depending on the genre, formality, or intended audience, different languages display different stylistic patterns. It might be difficult to translate a text while maintaining its stylistic subtleties. For MT systems to produce contextually relevant translations and preserve the intended style, they must be able to adjust to various writing styles, such as formal versus casual, technical versus literary, or persuading versus informative (Qassem, 2020).

Improvements in machine learning methods, NLP, and access to vast amounts of varied training data are necessary to meet these problems. By creating more context-aware models, utilizing pre-training strategies, integrating domain-specific knowledge, and investigating ways to capture cultural and sociolinguistic aspects, researchers and developers are constantly striving to enhance MT systems. In order to get closer to machine translation solutions that are more accurate and contextually relevant, the objective is to improve the quality and contextuality of translations.

Integration of AI in Academic Writing

One significant development in the way students interact with the writing process is the integration of AI into academic writing. Grammarly, an AI-powered tool with advanced capabilities to help writers, is at the forefront of this innovation.

Grammarly

Grammarly is a useful writing tool that helps students write their theses and papers by providing them with detailed criticism and suggestions on how to improve their work. Grammarly is a sophisticated grammar checker that does more than just check for spelling errors. It also addresses other aspects of writing, such as grammar, punctuation, spelling, clarity, and writing style. Grammarly helps students to improve the caliber of their writing in many ways:

Correction of Spelling and Grammar

The main function of Grammarly is to identify and fix spelling and grammar mistakes in written material. Using a vast collection of language patterns and rules, it also detects and corrects frequent typos, grammatical faults, and spelling issues to guarantee compliance with accepted linguistic norms.

Improvement in Punctuation Usage

This application helps students improve the precision and suitability of punctuation usage in their writing task, going beyond spell and grammar checks. It highlights punctuation errors or omissions, provides recommendations for appropriate corrections, and guarantees consistent punctuation use across the page.

Enhancement of Clarity

In academic writing, especially when writing a thesis, where complex ideas must be expressed clearly and effectively, good communication is crucial. Grammarly offers recommendations to improve readability, remove ambiguity, and strengthen sentence structure, all of which increase the content's clarity.

Refinement of Writing Style

Grammarly examines the text's writing style and provides comments on things like sentence variety, tone, and coherence. It provides suggestions for improving the writing style, guaranteeing that the writing keeps a steady and polished tone while successfully communicating the desired point to the audience.

Enrichment of Vocabulary

Grammarly suggests synonyms and alternate word choices to improve the written work's overall quality by enhancing the text's vocabulary's depth and diversity. This helps learners express themselves more clearly and avoid using the same words over and over again.

Consistency Verification

Grammarly examines the content for spelling, grammar, punctuation, and writing style consistency. It helps to produce a polished and expert final product by pointing out any inconsistencies and offering recommendations to maintain consistency and coherence across the content.

Analysis of Writing Patterns

Grammarly uses advanced AI algorithms to evaluate enormous databases of writing samples, enabling it to derive insights from varied writing styles and effective communication patterns. Grammarly's recommendations are informed by this abundance of data, which helps students follow widely accepted writing standards in a variety of academic fields.

Tailored Feedback

Grammarly's AI technology provides each user with customized feedback. It provides personalized recommendations based on user interaction by absorbing information from each user's writing preferences and habits. Encouraging learners to develop their unique writing styles while maintaining academic requirements requires this individualized assistance.

Real-Time Support

Grammarly gives quick corrections and recommendations as students write, considerably easing the revision process. This immediacy not only protects the writing flow but also permits immediate learning from mistakes, a fundamental part of good writing enhancement.

Accessibility

Grammarly and other AI tools are available on multiple platforms and may be easily integrated into writing environments via programs and plugins. Whether they are writing an email, a thesis, or taking part in online conversations, students may hone their writing abilities from anywhere, thanks to this accessibility.

But even with all of its advantages, Grammarly has drawbacks. It might not always correctly understand the text's context, which could result in inaccurate recommendations. Furthermore, Grammarly's free edition has less features than its premium version, which can discourage some students from taking use of everything that it has to offer. Overall, even if Grammarly helps students write better writing tasks, they should be aware of its limits and use caution when putting its recommendations into practice.

Automatic Written Corrective Feedback

Teachers can use computers, specialized software, and applications to provide corrective feedback (CF) while taking the context and language learning objectives into account. In language lessons, teachers are now aware of computer-mediated corrective feedback (CMCF), sometimes known as computer-based written corrective feedback (WCF). While some writing aids, like "Wordtune", assist students in the writing process by producing context-based sentences and making suggestions, others, like "InstaText" and "QuillBot", provide feedback after the writing process by making precise suggestions and fixing mistakes. Actually, in addition to aiding in the learning process, CMCF can speed up the feedback process and free up instructor time to concentrate on more important topics in language sessions. With the help of CMCF, which offers instant, customized, and automatic feedback, students may discover where they have strayed from language standards, including spelling, grammar, punctuation, and capitalization mistakes.

The emergence of AI-based text generators has brought about "the biggest change in writing since the invention of the word processor" (Floridi & Chiriatti, 2020, p.69). With the use of text prediction technology, AI systems are becoming more and more capable of producing texts in response to prompts. According to Kasirzadeh and Gabriel (2023), large language models, which are AI systems that rely on large datasets and are trained on next word prediction, have improved their ability to generate grammatical, well-formed English text. However, it should be noted that the popularity of such tools may increase the potential of misuse, as they can be used to generate content directly rather than having students produce it themselves. Because the rise of such tools makes it inevitable that learners will use them, it is critical to direct them appropriately. The main challenge is to find a way to use the functionality of these tools to improve writing skills rather than to do it for them, and it is also critical to avoid plagiarism and cheating by incorporating such tools as a type of language learning material and an advantage in achieving ultimate learning goals.

Four categories are used by Alharbi (2023) to group AI-based writing aid tools: 1) AI-based machine translation (AMT); 2) automated writing evaluation tools (AWE); 3) automated writing corrective feedback providers (AWCF); and 4) GPT-3 automatic text generators (GPT-3). While the writer is creating the text, some popular AWCF applications, including Grammarly, Ginger, and ProWritingAid, may offer comments continually and concurrently (Dale & Viethen, 2021). AWCF tools like Wordtune and Grammarly have the following advantages: they provide quick feedback and are available in both free and paid versions (Huang et al., 2021; Nova, 2018); they improve writing quality (Ghufron, 2019); they increase lexical diversity (Dizon & Gayed, 2021); they categorize errors based on their nature and provide personalized feedback (O'Neill & Russell, 2020); and they prevent plagiarism by identifying textual borrowing (Dodigovic & Tovmasyan, 2021). Furthermore, according to Dale and Viethen (2021), one of the most significant breakthroughs brought to the writing domain by AI is the automatic completion of sentences and phrases, as well as the suggestion of alternative language. Furthermore, such AI-powered solutions are based on huge linguistic models, providing a comprehensive bundle of language aid services ranging from machine translation to sentence synthesis (Dale & Viethen, 2021).

L2 learners certainly require more tools to be integrated into schooling in order to accelerate the learning process, particularly in terms of writing abilities. As a result of the issues described above, implementing innovative tactics, utilizing technology breakthroughs, and incorporating AI into education might effectively assist L2 learners in the process of language acquisition, particularly in the development of writing skills. However, it has been debated how AWCF should be utilized, with some researchers offering it to learners with lower proficiency levels (Nova, 2018) and others recommending it for English learners with advanced proficiency levels (Koltovskaia, 2020).

The impact of such tools on the writing process appears to require further analysis in order to realize their full potential for different tasks and levels of student ability and to implement them appropriately in writing classrooms (Grimes & Warschauer, 2010; Huang & Wilson, 2021; Vinall & Hellmich, 2022). Moreover, only a few studies have examined the impact of AI writing assistants on various aspects of writing-task fulfillment, organization, lexis, grammar, and mechanics--with the suggestion that AWCF may fail to assist in areas such as organization, argumentation strength, and coherence (Al Mahmud, 2023; Rad et al., 2024). Since writing improvement is likely to be connected with the amount of time spent working on texts, the time spent using writing tools must be considered in any experimental study attempting to demonstrate the efficacy of the tools themselves in increasing students' writing abilities (Etaat, 2024).

Overall, as Chiu et al., (2023) point out, the scope of AIEd is too broad, and the majority of the studies have focused on engineering issues such as building new algorithms and machine learning approaches, leaving the influence of AI on education uncertain. Clearly, additional research is needed to determine whether and how these developing technologies might help education in general, and language learning in L2 and bilingual situations in particular. Furthermore, further research is needed on the various available AI-based tools, how they work, how they might be integrated into bilingual L2 learning contexts, and which aspects of language skills are most likely to be impacted by them. According to Godwin-Jones (2019), teachers must construct assignments that combine automatic text generators with student labor. In other words, students should not grow overly reliant on such technologies, which can divert them from the primary goals of learning. In fact, the usage of AI-based writing tools should be integrated into a comprehensive language curriculum that emphasizes communication (Link et al. 2022).

The Role of AI in Cultural Contextualization

Bilingualism is more than just the ability to converse in two languages; it has a profound impact on cognitive development, cultural identity, and self-perception. The use of AI in language processing has expanded the study of bilingualism's cognitive impacts. AI systems, particularly those developed for multilingual environments, provide tools for exploring how language use influences thought, memory, and identity (Anderson, 2024).

Cultural Sensitivity in AI

More lately, some researchers have begun to look into how we can culturally adjust AI models. Cultural sensitivity in AI refers to models that are culturally responsive and provide culturally acceptable responses. A language model that reflects how polite language functions across cultures, for example, can aid in language acquisition by directing learners to use the appropriate level of formality and politeness in diverse settings. Adding cultural understanding to AI models recognizes that language encompasses not only words but also the societal context (Boztemir & Calıskan, 2024). By conditioning AI models for these aspects, we may shift our focus away from syntactic words and toward practical language use. However, incorporating cultural information into AI-based systems is a problem; it is critical to understand the cultural variance that influences language use (Wei, 2023).

AI systems are rapidly being created to incorporate cultural nuances using a variety of ways, ensuring that they respect and comprehend different languages, traditions, and social norms. Here are some important ways this is being accomplished:

Multilingual and Dialect Support

AI models are now being trained on diverse linguistic datasets that include regional dialects, informal speech, and localized language patterns, enabling them to better understand and generate culturally relevant content. Translation tools such as Google Translate and DeepL are advancing by learning contextual meanings rather than relying solely on direct word-for-word translations, resulting in more accurate and natural outputs. Additionally, speech recognition and text-to-speech systems are increasingly adapting to a wide range of accents and pronunciation variations, making them more accessible and effective for users from different linguistic backgrounds.

Culturally Aware Content Moderation

AI moderation systems are increasingly being trained to recognize culturally specific expressions, enabling them to avoid unnecessary censorship of content that may be contextually appropriate within certain communities. In parallel, social media platforms are refining their content policies to reflect regional sensitivities, allowing for a more nuanced distinction between genuinely offensive material and culturally accepted forms of expression.

Bias Reduction and Ethical AI Development

To promote cultural fairness and inclusivity, developers audit datasets to identify and eliminate biases and stereotypes that may distort representation. AI models are fine-tuned using diverse and representative datasets to avoid privileging one cultural perspective over others. Additionally, researchers often collaborate with local communities to validate AI-generated content, ensuring its cultural accuracy and contextual relevance.

Personalized User Experience

AI-driven systems, such as those used by platforms like Netflix and Spotify, personalize content recommendations by analyzing regional trends and individual user preferences. Similarly, chatbots and virtual assistants are designed to modify their tone and communication styles to align with the cultural norms and expectations of their users, enhancing relevance and user experience across diverse contexts.

Cultural Context in Visual and Creative AI

AI-generated art and imagery are increasingly fine-tuned to accurately reflect the cultural aesthetics, symbols, and visual traditions of specific communities. Likewise, AI-powered storytelling tools are designed to incorporate folklore, myths, and historical narratives from various cultures, ensuring that the content they produce resonates with diverse cultural identities and preserves heritage.

AI's Role in Teaching Non-Verbal Cues, Idioms & Cultural Norms

Non-verbal communication plays a critical role in human interaction, influencing everything from social engagement to emotional exchange and learning. AI has become a pivotal tool in enhancing our understanding and interpretation of non-verbal communication, offering profound capabilities especially valuable in contexts involving individuals with communication impairments such as hearing loss. AI technologies like machine learning, natural language processing, and computer vision provide a framework through which non-verbal cues can be analysed with a degree of precision and consistency unmatched by human observers. AI is becoming an increasingly valuable tool in teaching non-verbal cues, idioms, and cultural norms, particularly for language learners, neurodivergent individuals, and those adapting to new cultural environments. Here's how AI contributes to these areas:

Teaching Non-Verbal Cues

AI technologies are increasingly enhancing the ability to understand and respond to non-verbal communication through tools like computer vision and emotion recognition. AI-powered facial recognition and gesture analysis can help users interpret key social cues such as facial expressions, eye contact, and body language. Applications like Affectiva offer feedback by analyzing emotional responses, helping learners recognize and respond to emotions appropriately. Additionally, AI-driven virtual avatars and chatbots can simulate realistic conversations, providing opportunities to practice interpreting non-verbal signals in various cultural and social contexts. The integration of augmented and virtual reality (AR/VR) further deepens this experience by immersing users in lifelike environments where they can engage with gestures, tone of voice, and posture, ultimately refining their interpersonal and cross-cultural communication skills.

Understanding Idioms & Figurative Language

AI language models, such as ChatGPT, are increasingly capable of performing contextual analysis by breaking down idioms, metaphors, and slang through clear explanations, real-world usage examples, and relevant cultural context. Interactive learning tools, including AI chatbots, enhance this process by engaging learners in natural conversations that introduce idiomatic expressions organically and provide instant feedback when misunderstandings or misuses occur. Additionally, AI enables personalized learning by adapting to each learner's proficiency level, identifying specific idioms they struggle with, and offering customized exercises to strengthen their understanding and usage. This targeted, context-rich approach makes mastering idiomatic language more accessible and effective.

Cultural Norms & Etiquette Training

AI-driven language learning platforms are gradually incorporating cross-cultural simulations to help users navigate real-world social interactions. These platforms can present culturally specific scenarios—such as how to greet someone in Japan versus the United States—enhancing learners' understanding of etiquette and communication styles. Conversational AI and role-playing tools further enrich this experience by acting as virtual partners, guiding users through appropriate responses in diverse social and professional contexts. Additionally, advanced AI systems can provide real-time behavioral feedback by analyzing speech patterns, gestures, and etiquette, offering corrective suggestions and explanations that illuminate important cultural differences. This integration of cultural awareness into language learning fosters more authentic and effective communication across global contexts.

Ethical Concerns in AI-Driven Language Learning

Beyond utility, AI poses risks when not designed with transparency and fairness. Biases in training data can marginalize non-native accents or dialects. Tools like speech recognition often underperform for underrepresented groups. Developers must conduct fairness audits, ensure data privacy, and support user agency over personal data. AI-driven language learning offers numerous benefits, but it also raises several ethical concerns that must be addressed to ensure fair, secure, and inclusive access. The three key issues include data privacy, bias in language representation, and accessibility.

Data Privacy

AI-powered language learning platforms collect extensive user data, including speech patterns, text inputs, and learning progress, which raises important ethical and privacy concerns. One major issue is user consent—learners may not always be fully aware of what data is being collected or how it is being used. Data security is another critical concern, as sensitive information must be securely stored and protected against breaches. Additionally, there is growing apprehension about third-party usage, where companies might share or monetize user data without explicit permission. To address these challenges, developers and providers should implement robust encryption measures, establish transparent and accessible data policies, and empower users with control over their personal information, including options to manage, delete, or restrict data sharing.

Bias in Language Representation

AI models are trained on vast datasets, which, while enabling powerful language learning capabilities, also carry the risk of embedded biases. These biases can manifest in various ways, including cultural and linguistic favoritism, where dominant languages and dialects are prioritized, marginalizing less common or indigenous languages. Stereotypical representations may also emerge in AI-generated translations or educational content, potentially reinforcing harmful or reductive views of certain cultures. Additionally, assessment tools that rely on accent detection or automated proficiency scoring can unfairly disadvantage non-native speakers with diverse accents. To address these concerns, it is essential for developers to train models on diverse, representative datasets, collaborate with linguists and cultural experts from varied backgrounds, and conduct ongoing audits of AI outputs to ensure fairness, accuracy, and inclusivity in language learning applications.

Accessibility and Inclusion

While AI language learning tools hold great promise for expanding educational access, they also present several challenges that must be addressed to ensure equity. The digital divide remains a significant barrier, as not all learners have reliable access to the internet or advanced technological devices required to use these tools effectively. Affordability is another concern, with many premium AI-based language learning services priced beyond the reach of low-income users. Additionally, disability inclusion is often overlooked; many AI platforms still lack essential features that accommodate learners with visual, auditory, or cognitive impairments. Addressing these issues is crucial to making AI-assisted language education truly inclusive and universally accessible.

Ensuring accessibility means offering free or low-cost versions, optimizing for low-bandwidth environments, and integrating assistive technologies like text-to-speech and customizable learning interfaces. AI-driven language learning must prioritize ethical responsibility to create a fair, unbiased, and inclusive learning environment. Addressing data privacy concerns, mitigating bias, and improving accessibility are crucial steps toward making AI language tools a force for good in education.

AI's Potential: AI's Role in Language Learning and Cross-Cultural Communication

AI automation and human expertise both play essential roles in fostering language proficiency and cross-cultural communication. Striking the right balance between the two enhances learning efficiency, accuracy, and cultural understanding. AI-driven language applications such as Duolingo and Babbel personalize lessons by adapting to learners' progress, while tools like Grammarly and speech recognition software offer real-time feedback to improve pronunciation and grammar. Instant translation and interpretation tools, including Google Translate and DeepL, facilitate seamless communication across languages. Moreover, AI can support the development of cross-cultural awareness by offering contextual insights into cultural nuances, idiomatic expressions, and appropriate social etiquette, thereby enriching the overall learning experience.

Challenges Facing AI: The Necessity of Human Expertise

While AI offers valuable support in language learning, it often struggles with contextual understanding, particularly when interpreting idioms, humor, and culturally specific references—areas where human intuition remains essential. Human interaction also plays a crucial role in developing emotional intelligence, such as empathy, tone recognition, and the ability to navigate emotional nuances, which AI currently lacks. Although AI can effectively assist with basic dialogues, complex conversations involving negotiations or culturally sensitive topics require the depth and adaptability of human expertise. Furthermore, native speakers and cultural experts offer a level of cultural authenticity and insight that AI cannot fully replicate, making their involvement indispensable for a truly immersive and accurate learning experience.

Future Directions: Achieving the Right Balance

AI should be viewed as a supplement rather than a replacement in language learning, effectively handling repetitive tasks, offering instant feedback, and enhancing practice opportunities, while human instructors guide deeper understanding and critical thinking. A blended learning approach that combines AI tools with live tutors, discussion groups, and cultural immersion experiences can create a more engaging and holistic learning environment. It is essential, however, to use AI responsibly, ensuring it does not reinforce stereotypes or propagate inaccuracies. To maintain ethical integrity and cultural relevance, AI systems should be continuously updated with human input to enhance their accuracy and sensitivity. By integrating

AI's efficiency with the depth of human expertise, learners can develop both strong language proficiency and meaningful cross-cultural communication skills.

CONCLUSION

This chapter emphasized that for AI to support equitable L2 learning, it must integrate interdisciplinary knowledge and reflect ethical, inclusive design. Future research should explore culturally adaptive systems and long-term learner engagement in underrepresented contexts. AI integration in language learning marks a transformative shift in cultivating bilingual proficiency. Technologies like adaptive systems, natural language processing, and machine learning offer personalized, efficient, and interactive experiences tailored to individual needs. These tools enable precise feedback, immersive engagement, and adaptability, enhancing second language acquisition. As AI evolves, its role in language education will expand, driving innovations that refine methodologies and optimize skill development.

Moreover, AI's role extends beyond language acquisition, fostering deeper understanding of cognitive and cultural aspects of multilingualism. Research highlights the cognitive benefits of bilingualism, including problem-solving and neurological resilience. AI tools provide insights into how bilingual individuals process language and navigate cultural identities. With AI-powered models and real-time translation, educators and learners can better understand the interplay between language and cognition, promoting effective communication across linguistic landscapes. Despite these advances, AI implementation requires careful consideration of ethical, cultural, and accessibility factors. Developers and educators must ensure inclusivity, respect linguistic diversity, and promote equitable access to quality education. Addressing algorithmic biases and prioritizing user-centric design are essential to maximizing benefits and mitigating challenges.

Looking ahead, AI holds immense potential to revolutionize language education. From virtual tutors to advanced language models, opportunities for enhancing bilingual learning abound. However, ongoing research, interdisciplinary collaboration, and ethical guidance must shape its responsible development. Ultimately, AI in bilingual education fosters greater linguistic and cultural exchange. By harnessing AI's power, learners, educators, and researchers can unlock new paths for acquisition, cognitive growth, and cross-cultural communication in an increasingly interconnected world.

REFERENCES

Adewumi, A. E. B. (2020). *The Impact of Using Adaptive Learning in a Remedial Mathematics Course at an Urban University*. New Jersey City University.

Aggarwal, D. (2023). Integration of innovative technological developments and AI with education for an adaptive learning pedagogy. *China Petroleum Processing and Petrochemical Technology*, *23*(2).

Ahn, T. Y., & Lee, S.-M. (2016). User experience of a mobile speaking application with automatic speech recognition for EFL learning. *British Journal of Educational Technology*, *47*(4), 778–786. DOI: 10.1111/bjet.12354

Al Mahmud, F. (2023). Investigating EFL Students' Writing Skills Through Artificial Intelligence: Wordtune Application as a Tool. *Journal of Language Teaching and Research*, *14*(5), 1395–1404. DOI: 10.17507/jltr.1405.28

Alfaify, A., & Ramos Pinto, S. (2022). Cultural references in films: An audience reception study of subtitling into Arabic. *Translator*, *28*(1), 112–131. DOI: 10.1080/13556509.2021.1898714

Alharbi, W. (2023). *AI in the Foreign Language Classroom: A Pedagogical Overview of Automated Writing Assistance Tools*. Hindawi Education Research International.

Alsobhi, A. Y., & Alyoubi, K. H. (2019). Adaptation algorithms for selecting personalised learning experience based on learning style and dyslexia type. *Data Technologies and Applications*, *53*(2), 189–200. DOI: 10.1108/DTA-10-2018-0092

Anderson, J. (2024). Cultural and Linguistic Dynamics in Bilingual AI Systems: Balancing Personal Identity and Global Connectivity. Anis, M. (2023).

Asplund, F., Björk, J., & Magnusson, M. (2022). Knowing too much? On bias due to domain-specific knowledge in internal crowdsourcing for explorative ideas. *R & D Management*, *52*(4), 720–734. DOI: 10.1111/radm.12517

aws (2025). The leading cloud. Retrieved from https://aws.amazon.com/what-is-aws/?nc1=f_cc

Baker, R. S., Gašević, D., & Karumbaiah, S. (2021). Four paradigms in learning analytics: Why paradigm convergence matters. *Computers and Education: Artificial Intelligence*, *2*, 100021. DOI: 10.1016/j.caeai.2021.100021

Bakhodirov, O., & Rahmanova, G. (2023). AI and language learning disabilities. *Innovative research in modern education, 1*(9), 7-10.

Belda-Medina, J., & Calvo-Ferrer, J. R. (2022). Using chatbots as AI conversational partners in language learning. *Applied Sciences (Basel, Switzerland)*, *12*(17), 8427. DOI: 10.3390/app12178427

Bibauw, S., François, T., & Desmet, P. (2019). Discussing with a computer to practice a foreign language: Research synthesis and conceptual framework of dialogue-based CALL. *Computer Assisted Language Learning*, *32*(8), 1–51. DOI: 10.1080/09588221.2018.1535508

Borsotti, A., Breveglieri, L., Crespi Reghizzi, S., & Morzenti, A. (2021). A deterministic parsing algorithm for ambiguous regular expressions. *Acta Informatica*, *58*(3), 195–229. DOI: 10.1007/s00236-020-00366-7

Boztemir, Y., & Calıskan, N. (2024). Analyzing and mitigating cultural hallucinations of commercial language models in Turkish. *Authorea Preprints*. DOI: 10.36227/techrxiv.171504678.80895811/v1

Caldarini, G., Jaf, S., & McGarry, K. (2022). A literature survey of recent advances in chatbots. *Information (Basel)*, *13*(1), 41. DOI: 10.3390/info13010041

Chang, C. H., & Krulee, G. K. (1991). Resolution of ambiguity in Chinese and its application to machine translation. *Machine Translation*, *6*(4), 279–315. DOI: 10.1007/BF00417653

Chang, W., Yuan, Y., & Lee, C. Y. (2021). Natural Language Processing in AI: Rethinking its role in language learning. *AI & Society*, *36*(3), 709–721.

Chen, H. H.-J. (2011). Developing and evaluating an oral skills training website supported by automatic speech recognition technology. *ReCALL*, *23*(1), 59–78. DOI: 10.1017/S0958344010000285

Chen, H. H.-J., Yang, C. T. Y., & Lai, K. K. W. (2023). Investigating college EFL learners' perceptions toward the use of Google Assistant for foreign language learning. *Interactive Learning Environments*, *31*(3), 1335–1350. DOI: 10.1080/10494820.2020.1833043

Chen, X., Zou, D., Xie, H., Cheng, G., & Liu, C. (2022). Two decades of artificial intelligence in education. *Journal of Educational Technology & Society*, *25*(1), 28–47.

Cheng, L., Varshney, K. R., & Liu, H. (2021). Socially responsible ai algorithms: Issues, purposes, and challenges. *Journal of Artificial Intelligence Research*, *71*, 1137–1181. DOI: 10.1613/jair.1.12814

Choukaier, D. (2024). Integrating AI In English Language Pedagogy: Innovations and Outcomes In Teaching English As Second/Foreign Language. *Educational Administration: Theory and Practice*, *30*(5), 3311–3822.

Crowder, J. (2024). *AI chatbots: The good, the bad, and the ugly*. Springer Nature. DOI: 10.1007/978-3-031-45509-4

Dai, Y., & Wu, Z. (2023). Mobile-assisted pronunciation learning with feedback from peers and/or automatic speech recognition: A mixed-methods study. *Computer Assisted Language Learning*, *36*(5–6), 861–884. DOI: 10.1080/09588221.2021.1952272

Dale, R., & Viethen, J. (2021). The automated writing assistance landscape in 2021. *Natural Language Engineering*, *27*(4), 511–518. DOI: 10.1017/S1351324921000164

Daniels, P., & Iwago, K. (2017). The suitability of cloud-based speech recognition engines for language learning. *The JALT CALL Journal*, *13*(3), 229–239. DOI: 10.29140/jaltcall.v13n3.j220

de Barcelos Silva, A., Gomes, M. M., da Costa, C. A., da Rosa Righi, R., Barbosa, J. L. V., Pessin, G., De Doncker, G., & Federizzi, G. (2020). Intelligent personal assistants: A systematic literature review. *Expert Systems with Applications*, *147*, 113193. DOI: 10.1016/j.eswa.2020.113193

de Vries, B. P., Cucchiarini, C., Bodnar, S., Strik, H., & van Hout, R. (2015). Spoken grammar practice and feedback in an ASR-based CALL system. *Computer Assisted Language Learning*, *28*(6), 550–576. DOI: 10.1080/09588221.2014.889713

Deep, L. (2025). DeepL Blog. Retrieved from https://www.deepl.com/en/blog

Dhanapal, C., Asharudeen, N., & Alfaruque, S. Y. (2024). Impact of Artificial Intelligence Versus Traditional Instruction for Language Learning: A Survey. *World Journal of English Language*, *14*(2), 182–182. DOI: 10.5430/wjel.v14n2p182

Dizon, G. (2017). Using intelligent personal assistants for second language learning: A case study of Alexa. *TESOL Journal*, *8*(4), 811–830. DOI: 10.1002/tesj.353

Dizon, G. (2020). Evaluating intelligent personal assistants for L2 listening and speaking development. *Language Learning & Technology*, *24*(1), 16–26. DOI: 10.64152/10125/44705

Dizon, G., Tang, D., & Yamamoto, Y. (2022). A case study of using Alexa for out-of-class, self-directed Japanese language learning. *Computers and Education: Artificial Intelligence*, *3*, 100088. DOI: 10.1016/j.caeai.2022.100088

Dodigovic, M., & Tovmasyan, A. (2021). Automated writing evaluation: The accuracy of Grammarly's feedback on form. *International Journal of TESOL Studies*, *3*(2), 71–87.

Etaat, F. (2024). The Effect of AI-Based Applications on EFL Writing Skill Development: An Inquiry into Integration of AI into Language Learning. Master's thesis, UiT Norges arktiske universitet.

Evers, K., & Chen, S. (2022). Effects of an automatic speech recognition system with peer feedback on pronunciation instruction for adults. *Computer Assisted Language Learning*, *35*(8), 1869–1889. DOI: 10.1080/09588221.2020.1839504

Fazal, N., Tahir, M. S., Chaudhary, M., & Abbasi, M. (2024). Effectiveness of AI Integration into Computer-Assisted Language Learning (CALL) on Student Writing Skills Based on Gender. *Pakistan Journal of Humanities and Social Sciences*, *12*(1), 224–230. DOI: 10.52131/pjhss.2024.v12i1.1974

Floridi, L., & Chiriatti, M. (2020). GPT-3: Its nature, scope, limits, and consequences. *Minds and Machines*, *30*(4), 681–694. DOI: 10.1007/s11023-020-09548-1

Frith, K. H. (2019). Artificial Intelligence. *Nursing Education Perspectives*, *40*(4), 261. DOI: 10.1097/01.NEP.0000000000000543 PMID: 31232902

Fryer, L. K., Coniam, D., Carpenter, R., & Lăpu neanu, D. (2020). Bots for language learning now: Current and future directions. *Language Learning & Technology*, *24*(2), 8–22. DOI: 10.64152/10125/44719

Ghufron, M. A. (2019). Exploring an automated feedback program 'Grammarly' and teacher corrective feedback in EFL writing assessment: modern vs. traditional assessment. The 3rd English Language and Literature International Conference, ELLiC, Semarang, Indonesia.

Godwin-Jones, R. (2019). Future directions in informal language learning. *The handbook of informal language learning*, 457-470.

Grimes, D., & Warschauer, M. (2010). Utility in a fallible tool: A multi-site case study of automated writing evaluation. *The Journal of Technology, Learning, and Assessment*, *8*(6), 1–43.

Håkansson, A., & Hartung, R. L. (2020). *Artificial Intelligence-Concepts, Areas, Techniques and Applications*. Studentlitteratur.

Huang, J.-X., Kwon, O.-W., Lee, K.-S., & Kim, Y.-K. (2018). Improve the chatbot performance for the DB-CALL system using a hybrid method and a domain corpus. In P. Taalas, J. Jalkanen, L. Bradley & S. Thouësny (Eds.), *Future-proof CALL: Language learning as exploration and encounters – short papers from EUROCALL 2018* (pp. 100–105). Research-publishing.net. DOI: 10.14705/rpnet.2018.26.820

Huang, Y., & Wilson, J. (2021). Using automated feedback to develop writing proficiency. *Computers and Composition*, *62*, 102675. DOI: 10.1016/j.compcom.2021.102675

Jang, E. E., Lajoie, S. P., Wagner, M., Xu, Z., Poitras, E., & Naismith, L. (2017). Person-oriented approaches to profiling learners in technology-rich learning environments for ecological learner modeling. *Journal of Educational Computing Research*, *55*(4), 552–597. DOI: 10.1177/0735633116678995

Javed, F. (2024). The Evolution of Artificial Intelligence in Teaching and Learning of English Language in Higher Education: Challenges, Risks, and Ethical Considerations. In *The Evolution of Artificial Intelligence in Higher Education: Challenges, Risks, and Ethical Considerations* (pp. 249-276). Emerald Publishing Limited.

Jurafsky, D., & Martin, J. H. (2024). Speech and Language Processing: An Introduction to Natural Language Processing, Computational Linguistics, and Speech Recognition. Retrieved from https://web.stanford.edu/~jurafsky/slp3/ed3book.pdf

Kandasamy, S., & Cherukuri, A. K. (2020). Query expansion using named entity disambiguation for a question-answering system. *Concurrency and Computation*, *32*(4), e5119. DOI: 10.1002/cpe.5119

Kasirzadeh, A., & Gabriel, I. (2023). In conversation with artificial intelligence: Aligning language models with human values. *Philosophy & Technology*, *36*(2), 27. DOI: 10.1007/s13347-023-00606-x

Kilag, O. K., Marquita, J., & Laurente, J. (2023). Teacher-Led Curriculum Development: Fostering Innovation in Education. *Excellencia: International Multidisciplinary. Journal of Education*, *1*(4), 223–237.

Kim, D., & Gilman, E. (2021). Implementing AI tools in the classroom: Teacher perspectives and experiences. *Educational Technology Research and Development*, *69*, 409–428.

Knox, J. (2020). Artificial Intelligence and education in China. *Learning, Media and Technology*, *45*(3), 1–14. DOI: 10.1080/17439884.2020.1754236

Koltovskaia, S. (2020). Student engagement with automated written corrective feedback (AWCF) provided by Grammarly: A multiple case study. *Assessing Writing, 44*, 100450. DOI: 10.1016/j.asw.2020.100450

Kulkarni, P., Mahabaleshwarkar, A., Kulkarni, M., Sirsikar, N., & Gadgil, K. (2019). Conversational AI: An overview of methodologies, applications & future scope. 2019 5th International Conference on Computing, Communication, Control and Automation, pp. 1-7.

Link, S., Mehrzad, M., & Rahimi, M. (2022). Impact of automated writing evaluation on teacher feedback, student revision, and writing improvement. *Computer Assisted Language Learning, 35*(4), 605–634. DOI: 10.1080/09588221.2020.1743323

Liu, Y., Sahagun, J., & Sun, Y. (2021). An adaptive and interactive educational game platform for english learning enhancement using AI and chatbot techniques. In 10th international conference on natural language processing (NLP 2021). Academy and Industry Research Collaboration Center (AIRCC). DOI: 10.5121/csit.2021.112308

Luo, B., Lau, R. Y., Li, C., & Si, Y. W. (2022). A critical review of state-of-the-art chatbot designs and applications. *Wiley Interdisciplinary Reviews. Data Mining and Knowledge Discovery, 12*(1), e1434. DOI: 10.1002/widm.1434

Maimaiti, M., Liu, Y., Luan, H., & Sun, M. (2022). Data augmentation for low-resource languages NMT guided by constrained sampling. *International Journal of Intelligent Systems, 37*(1), 30–51. DOI: 10.1002/int.22616

Manire, E., Kilag, O. K., Cordova Jr, N., Tan, S. J., Poligrates, J., & Omaña, E. (2023). Artificial Intelligence and English Language Learning: A Systematic Review. *Excellencia: International Multi-disciplinary Journal of Education (2994-9521), 1*(5), 485-497.

McCarthy, J. (2007). What is artificial intelligence? Retrieved from https://www-formal.stanford.edu/jmc/whatisai.pdf

McCrocklin, S. (2019). Learners' feedback regarding ASR-based dictation practice for pronunciation learning. *CALICO Journal, 36*(2), 119–137. DOI: 10.1558/cj.34738

McCrocklin, S. M. (2016). Pronunciation learner autonomy: The potential of automatic speech recognition. *System, 57*, 25–42. DOI: 10.1016/j.system.2015.12.013

McGeachie, J., & Dingel, J. (2007). Translate One, Analyze Many: Leveraging the Microsoft Intermediate Language and Source Code Transformation for Model Checking. *Electronic Notes in Theoretical Computer Science, 190*(1), 3–18. DOI: 10.1016/j.entcs.2007.02.057

Moussalli, S., & Cardoso, W. (2020). Intelligent personal assistants: Can they understand and be understood by accented L2 learners? *Computer Assisted Language Learning, 33*(8), 865–890. DOI: 10.1080/09588221.2019.1595664

Nova, M. (2018). Utilizing Grammarly in evaluating academic writing: Narrative research on EFL students' experience. *Premise: Journal of English Education and Applied Linguistics, 7*(1), 80–96.

O'Neill, R., & Russell, A. M. T. (2020). Grammarly: Help or hindrance? Academic learning advisors' perceptions of an online grammar checker. *Journal of Academic Language and Learning, 13*(1), A88–A107.

Pedersen, B. S. (1999). Systematic Verb Polysemy in MT: A Study of Danish Motion Verbs with Comparisons with Spanish. *Machine Translation, 14*(1), 35–82. DOI: 10.1023/A:1008183205171

Peng, H., Ma, S., & Spector, J. M. (2019). Personalized adaptive learning: An emerging pedagogical approach enabled by a smart learning environment. *Smart Learning Environments, 6*(1), 1–14. DOI: 10.1186/s40561-019-0089-y

Procter, T., & Joshi, A. (2022). Cultural Competency in Voice Evaluation: Considerations of Normative Standards for Sociolinguistically Diverse Voices. *Journal of Voice, 36*(6), 793–801. DOI: 10.1016/j.jvoice.2020.09.025 PMID: 33060004

Qassem, M. (2020). Translations of Stylistic Variations in the Noble Qur'an into English: Stylistic and Exegetical Perspectives. *Journal of Intercultural Communication Research, 50*, 1–19.

Qin, L., Che, W., Ni, M., Li, Y., & Liu, T. (2021). Knowing Where to Leverage: Context-Aware Graph Convolutional Network with an Adaptive Fusion Layer for Contextual Spoken Language Understanding. In *IEEE/ACM Trans. Audio Speech Lang. Process., 29* (pp. 1280–1289). IEEE. DOI: 10.1109/TASLP.2021.3053400

Rad, H. S., Alipour, R., & Jafarpour, A. (2024). Using artificial intelligence to foster students' writing feedback literacy, engagement, and outcome: A case of Wordtune application. *Interactive Learning Environments, 32*(9), 5020–5040. DOI: 10.1080/10494820.2023.2208170

Serban, I. V., Sankar, C., Germain, M., Zhang, S., Lin, Z., Subramanian, S., Bengio, Y. (2017). A deep reinforcement learning chatbot. *arXiv preprint arXiv:1709.02349*.

Smets, W., & Struyven, K. (2018). Aligning with Complexity: System-Theoretical Principles for Research on Differentiated Instruction. *Frontline Learning Research, 6*(2), 66–80. DOI: 10.14786/flr.v6i2.340

SYSTRAN. (2025). Our history. Retrieved from https://www.systransoft.com/systran/

Tai, T. Y., & Chen, H. H. J. (2023). The impact of Google Assistant on adolescent EFL learners' willingness to communicate. *Interactive Learning Environments, 31*(3), 1485–1502. DOI: 10.1080/10494820.2020.1841801

Trzaskawka, P. (2020). Selected Clauses of a Copyright Contract in Polish and English in Translation by Google Translate: A Tentative Assessment of Quality. *International Journal for the Semiotics of Law*, *33*(3), 689–705. DOI: 10.1007/s11196-020-09680-2

van Doremalen, J., Boves, L., Colpaert, J., Cucchiarini, C., & Strik, H. (2016). Evaluating automatic speech recognition-based language learning systems: A case study. *Computer Assisted Language Learning*, *29*(4), 833–851. DOI: 10.1080/09588221.2016.1167090

Vinall, K., & Hellmich, E. A. (2022). Do you speak translate? Reflections on the nature and role of translation. *Journal of Linguistics and Language Teaching*, *14*(1), 4–25.

Wang, J., Hwang, G.-W., & Chang, C.-Y. (2021). Directions of the 100 most cited chatbot-related human behavior research: A review of academic publications. *Computers and Education: Artificial Intelligence*, *2*, 100023. DOI: 10.1016/j.caeai.2021.100023

Wark, N. (2018). Shifting paradigms: A critical pragmatic evaluation of key factors affecting learner-empowered emergent technology integration.

Wei, L. (2023). Artificial intelligence in language instruction: Impact on English learning achievement, L2 motivation, and self-regulated learning. *Frontiers in Psychology*, *14*, 1261955. DOI: 10.3389/fpsyg.2023.1261955 PMID: 38023040

Weng, X., & Chiu, T. K. F. (2023). Instructional design and learning outcomes of intelligent computer assisted language learning: Systematic review in the field. *Computers and Education: Artificial Intelligence, 4.*

Woo, J. H., & Choi, H. (2021). Systematic review for AI-based language learning tools. *arXiv preprint arXiv:2111.04455.*

Yandex Translate. (2025). Translator for 100+ languages. Retrieved from https://translate.yandex.com/en/

Yang, F. C. O., Lo, F. Y. R., Hsieh, J. C., & Wu, W. C. V. (2020). Facilitating communicative ability of EFL learners via high-immersion virtual reality. *Journal of Educational Technology & Society*, *23*(1), 30–49.

Chapter 2
From Chalkboards to Chatbots:
The Transformation of Language Learning Through AI

Andi Asrifan
https://orcid.org/0000-0002-9934-6129
Universitas Negeri Makassar, Indonesia

Raveenthiran Vivekanantharasa
The Open University of Sri Lanka, Sri Lanka

Nurul Aini
https://orcid.org/0009-0007-7929-0512
IAIN Kediri, Indonesia

Ali Sorayyaei Azar
https://orcid.org/0000-0003-3539-8250
University of Malaya, Malaysia

Juvrianto Chrissunday Jakob
https://orcid.org/0000-0002-5267-3448
Politeknik Negeri Ambon, Indonesia

ABSTRACT

This chapter examines the evolution of language acquisition, transitioning from conventional grammar-translation techniques to the incorporation of advanced technology like Artificial Intelligence (AI). It underscores the crucial function of AI-driven tools—such as chatbots, virtual tutors, and customized learning platforms—in improving engagement, accessibility, and individualized education. The paper

DOI: 10.4018/979-8-3373-0275-1.ch002

also examines problems such as technological obstacles, ethical implications, and AI's constraints in comprehending cultural context and complexity. Additionally, emerging technologies such as augmented reality (AR) and virtual reality (VR) are analyzed for their capacity to foster immersive educational settings. This research underscores the necessity for equitable implementation and the ongoing significance of educators in cultivating empathy and critical thinking. By appropriately adopting these developments, language acquisition can transcend cultural barriers and equip learners for a globally networked environment.

1. THE EVOLUTION OF LANGUAGE LEARNING

1.1 Historical Perspectives

Language acquisition has experienced considerable changes throughout the centuries, influenced by cultural, social, and technical factors (Akour & Alenezi, 2022; Darder et al., 2023). Historically, two principal strategies prevailed: grammar-translation and communicative approaches.

The grammar-translation technique, dominant in the 19th and early 20th centuries, prioritized the explicit instruction of grammatical rules and vocabulary. This methodology was founded on the examination of classical languages, including Latin and Greek, wherein students concentrated on text translation and syntactic mastery. Instruction generally focused on the rote memorization of vocabulary lists and verb conjugation, with minimal attention given to speaking or listening proficiency (Nurfauziah et al., 2024). This strategy established a robust foundation in reading and writing; however, it frequently rendered learners inadequately equipped for practical communication. Critics contended that the absence of practical application constrained pupils' capacity to utilize the language in quotidian situations.

The communicative approach arose in the second part of the 20th century as a response to the constraints of the grammar-translation method. This approach emphasized contact as the principal technique of language acquisition. It underscored the significance of context, fluency, and the capacity to communicate meaning in practical scenarios. Lessons integrated role-playing, collaborative activities, and realistic materials, enabling learners to hone language skills in a more dynamic and engaging setting. The communicative approach acknowledges the importance of cultural context, urging students to comprehend not just the language but also the subtleties of the linked cultures (Hossain, 2024).

Notwithstanding its benefits, the communicative approach had difficulties, especially regarding consistency and evaluation. Educators frequently had difficulties reconciling fluency with accuracy, resulting in disparate outcomes in language proficiency. Moreover, the dependence on unplanned interactions occasionally caused less confident learners to feel inundated or inadequately equipped.

As the 20th century advanced, technological innovations impacted language acquisition approaches. The incorporation of audio-visual aids, language laboratories, and, subsequently, computer-assisted language learning (CALL) tools commenced the transformation of the educational landscape (Zhu et al., 2024). These developments provide novel chances for learners to interact with language in immersive and dynamic manners, facilitating the forthcoming significant transformation in language instruction.

Language acquisition has evolved from inflexible, rule-based approaches to more interactive, conversational methods. This historical backdrop establishes the foundation for comprehending the influence of artificial intelligence and digital tools on language acquisition, signifying a new epoch in the transition from chalkboards to chatbots.

1.2 The Role of Technology in Education

The use of technology in education has profoundly altered the realm of language acquisition, providing novel tools and methods that improve the instructional and learning experience (Akram et al., 2022; Timotheou et al., 2023). Technology has been instrumental in transforming language instruction and acquisition, from the introduction of audio-visual aids to the emergence of computer-assisted language learning (CALL).

During the mid-20th century, audio-visual aids were introduced into schools, enhancing the learning environment with more immersion (Shareef & Nithyanantham, 2022; Nwakaego, 2024). Instruments like projectors, film strips, and audio recordings facilitated educators in showcasing authentic language situations, permitting pupils to listen to native speakers and observe language in practice. This transition represented a change from conventional rote memory, including learners through visual and auditory cues. Utilizing these aids enhanced pronunciation and listening skills while aiding pupils in understanding cultural nuances related to the language.

The advancement of technology in the 1980s and 1990s marked the advent of computers, initiating a new epoch in language instruction. Computer-assisted language learning (CALL) was developed as a discipline focused on investigating the use of computers to enhance language acquisition (Idrissi et al., 2024). CALL programs included interactive exercises, allowing learners to practice grammar, vocabulary, and pronunciation at their own pace. This autonomous method enabled students to manage their education, accommodating various learning styles and preferences.

The internet has transformed language learning by offering abundant resources beyond conventional classrooms. Online platforms, language exchange websites, and educational applications have evolved, linking learners with native speakers and promoting authentic communication (Martyushev et al., 2021). This global connectivity enabled students to engage with the language and culture, dismantling geographical obstacles and facilitating possibilities for genuine practice.

Furthermore, the emergence of multimedia resources, including podcasts, movies, and interactive games, enhanced the language acquisition experience. These materials enhanced the learning experience, making it more engaging and pleasant for a generation familiar with dynamic digital content. Educators began integrating these tools into their courses, establishing blended learning environments that fused in-person instruction with online activities (Singh et al., 2022; Zagouras et al., 2022).

Nonetheless, the incorporation of technology in language acquisition presents certain obstacles. Educators must address challenges like technological access, digital literacy, and the need for proficient training to effectively employ these technologies. Moreover, the excessive quantity of accessible information may result in confusion and inconsistencies in language training.

In conclusion, technology has significantly influenced the development of language acquisition, augmenting established methods and offering novel opportunities for engagement and practice. Transitioning from chalkboards to chatbots necessitates a grasp of the historical background of technology in education to fully appreciate the revolutionary potential of artificial intelligence in language acquisition.

1.3 The Shift to Digital Learning

The shift from conventional physical classrooms to online platforms is a pivotal advancement in the progression of language acquisition. The transition, propelled by technological improvements and the pervasive presence of the internet, has revolutionized language education engagement, resulting in the emergence of e-learning and mobile applications.

The early 2000s witnessed the rise of e-learning as a legitimate substitute for traditional classroom education (Oda et al., 2022). Online courses and platforms have proliferated, enabling learners to study at their own pace and convenience. The democratization of education enabled individuals from varied backgrounds and locales to access previously inaccessible language learning resources. Consequently, learners could customize their educational experiences to accommodate their schedules, rendering language acquisition more accessible than before.

E-learning platforms like Duolingo, Rosetta Stone, and Babbel have transformed language acquisition through interactive and gamified methodologies (Khuman, 2024; Rafikha et al., 2024). These platforms employed algorithms to adjust to each learner's progress, guaranteeing that teachings were tailored to their specific requirements. The integration of multimedia components, including films, quizzes, and interactive activities, rendered learning captivating and pleasurable. This transition to personalized learning experiences signifies a change from the uniform approach of conventional classrooms.

Mobile applications significantly expedited the shift to digital education. The spread of smartphones and tablets enables learners to access language resources at any time and from any location. Applications such as Memrise and HelloTalk enabled language practice via flashcards, chat functionalities, and community interaction, permitting users to engage with native speakers worldwide (Kessler et al., 2025). This mobility enabled learners to incorporate language practice into their daily activities, strengthening skills through brief, manageable sessions.

Furthermore, the COVID-19 epidemic served as a spur for the extensive implementation of online education. With the closure of physical classrooms, educators and institutions rapidly transitioned to virtual educational environments. Video conferencing platforms such as Zoom and Microsoft Teams were indispensable for enabling real-time communication between educators and learners (Garlinska et al., 2023). This swift shift underscored the capability of digital platforms to sustain educational continuity, especially under adverse conditions.

Nonetheless, the transition to digital education presents certain challenges. Concerns include digital literacy, technological accessibility, and the risk of reduced interpersonal engagement must be resolved to guarantee good language learning experiences. Furthermore, dependence on displays may result in fatigue and disengagement, requiring inventive strategies to sustain student motivation.

The transition from physical classrooms to digital learning platforms has radically altered language instruction. E-learning and mobile applications have rendered language acquisition more accessible, individualized, and enjoyable. As we further investigate the convergence of technology and language acquisition, it is crucial to acknowledge the ramifications of this digital evolution on the future of education.

2. UNDERSTANDING AI AND ITS APPLICATIONS IN LANGUAGE LEARNING

2.1 What is Artificial Intelligence?

Artificial Intelligence (AI) denotes the emulation of human cognitive functions by computers, especially computer systems (Sarker, 2022; Zhang & Lu, 2021). These processes include many capabilities such as learning, thinking, problem solving, perception, and language understanding. In recent years, AI has gained prominence across multiple domains, particularly in education, where it is revolutionizing conventional teaching methods and improving learning experiences.

Machine learning, a subtype of artificial intelligence, is fundamental to AI, allowing systems to learn from data and enhance their performance autonomously over time without explicit programming. Machine learning algorithms examine extensive datasets to discern patterns and provide predictions (Sarker, 2021). In language acquisition, machine learning can be employed to customize educational materials, tailor to individual learners' requirements, and deliver specific feedback. Language learning platforms may monitor a student's progress and modify class difficulty according to their competence, so providing a customized learning experience that enhances engagement and retention.

A vital element of AI is natural language processing (NLP), which emphasizes the connection between computers and human language. Natural Language Processing (NLP) empowers robots to comprehend, interpret, and produce human language in a manner that is both significant and contextually pertinent (Nath et al., 2022). This technology is essential in language learning applications, enabling communication between learners and AI-powered tools like chatbots and virtual instructors. Utilizing NLP, these tools can interact with users in dialogue, respond to inquiries, and offer immediate feedback, mimicking authentic language exchanges that improve learners' speaking and comprehension abilities.

AI's significance in education is beyond simple automation; it provides creative remedies for enduring issues in language acquisition (Dong, 2024). AI can facilitate interaction between learners and native speakers by offering practice chances through conversational bots that simulate human dialogue. Moreover, AI-driven evaluations can assess students' performance instantaneously, pinpointing areas needing enhancement and recommending tailored learning trajectories.

Furthermore, AI's capacity to handle and analyze extensive datasets enables educators to obtain significant insights into student performance and learning practices. This data-centric methodology can guide instructional tactics, allowing educators to make educated choices that improve the overall learning experience.

In summary, artificial intelligence, including machine learning and natural language processing, is transforming language acquisition by offering personalized, adaptive, and interactive educational experiences. Upon further exploration of AI applications in language education, it is clear that these technologies not only improve learning outcomes but also transform the roles of educators and learners in the digital era.

2.2 AI-Powered Language Learning Tools

The emergence of artificial intelligence (AI) has created many language-learning systems that improve the educational experience (Kuddus, 2022). AI-driven technologies, such as chatbots, language applications, and virtual tutors, are revolutionizing language acquisition by offering personalized and interactive methods tailored to individual need.

A significant application of AI in language acquisition is the utilization of chatbots. These conversational agents replicate human interaction, enabling learners to practice speaking and writing in a low-stress setting. Chatbots can interact with users, offer immediate feedback on grammar and vocabulary, and adjust their responses according to the learner's competence level (Zhai & Wibowo, 2023). Platforms such as Duolingo employ chatbots to enhance conversational practice, allowing users to implement their acquired knowledge in real-time situations. This interactive component improves linguistic proficiency and fosters learners' self-assurance in their capabilities.

Language learning applications have achieved significant popularity by utilizing AI to develop entertaining and effective educational experiences (Zhai & Wibowo, 2023). Applications like Babbel and Memrise employ algorithms to customize learning trajectories, tailoring content to align with the learner's pace and preferences. These applications frequently integrate gamification components, like incentives and challenges, to engage users and enhance the learning experience. Through the analysis of user data, these systems can discern strengths and shortcomings, facilitating targeted practice that enhances language acquisition (Weng & Chiu, 2023).

Virtual tutors exemplify a novel application of AI in language instruction. These AI-driven solutions offer tailored education and assistance, emulating the function of a human tutor. Virtual instructors can evaluate a learner's advancement, deliver customized activities, and provide comprehensive pronunciation and grammar feedback (Mahmood & Bui, 2024). Platforms like Elsa Speak employ sophisticated speech recognition technology to assess a learner's spoken language, providing immediate corrections and recommendations for enhancement. This prompt feedback aids learners in honing their speaking abilities and enhancing their fluency.

Moreover, AI-driven tools are progressively included in conventional classroom environments, augmenting the teacher's function rather than supplanting it. Educators can employ AI analytics to obtain insights about student performance, allowing them to customize their instruction to address the varied requirements of their pupils (Dwivedi et al., 2024). This data-centric methodology facilitates enhanced lesson preparation and precise interventions, hence augmenting educational achievements.

In summary, AI-driven language learning tools, such as chatbots, language applications, and virtual tutors, are transforming language instruction and acquisition methodologies. These technologies improve engagement and efficacy in language learning by offering personalized, interactive, and adaptable experiences. As we further investigate the capabilities of AI in education, it is evident that these technologies will be important in transforming language acquisition, closing gaps, and enhancing communication in a progressively interconnected world.

2.3 Personalization Through AI

A significant transformational feature of artificial intelligence (AI) in language acquisition is its capacity to deliver customized educational experiences aligned with the specific needs of individual learners (Sajja et al., 2024). Conventional language education frequently adopts a uniform methodology, perhaps resulting in student disengagement or feelings of being overwhelmed. Conversely, AI algorithms utilize data analytics to adjust to individual learners' styles, speeds, and preferences, thereby generating personalized routes for language acquisition.

AI-powered language learning programs gather and evaluate extensive data from users, encompassing their interactions, workout performance, and quiz responses (Wei, 2023). This data enables algorithms to discern patterns in learning behaviors, strengths, and shortcomings. For example, if a student persistently encounters difficulties with verb conjugations, the system can autonomously modify the curriculum to offer more practice and resources concentrated on that aspect. This focused method enhances learners' skills and elevates their confidence as they observe measurable advancement.

Furthermore, AI systems can adapt to various learning methods. Certain learners may find visual assistance advantageous, whilst others may favor aural or tactile approaches. Through the examination of user interactions, AI can deliver knowledge in several formats—such as films, interactive activities, or text-based lessons—customized to the learner's chosen style (Lokare & Jadhav, 2024). This adaptability guarantees that students stay engaged and motivated, as they are more inclined to relate to content that aligns with their unique learning preferences.

The adaptability of AI also includes pace. Conventional classroom environments can operate at a predetermined pace, posing difficulties for students who want additional time to comprehend specific subjects. AI-driven systems facilitate self-paced learning for students, permitting them to review difficult subjects or advance quickly through simpler content (Chakraborty et al., 2024). This autonomous learning cultivates a sense of ownership and agency, enabling learners to manage their educational path.

Furthermore, AI can augment motivation via gamification and tailored feedback. These platforms promote learner engagement by establishing personalized objectives and offering incentives for achievements. Immediate feedback aids students in seeing their errors and learning from them promptly, thereby reinforcing concepts and fostering a growth attitude.

The personalized features of AI in language learning are transforming the educational experience. AI algorithms tailor learning routes to accommodate individual learning styles and paces, hence improving engagement and efficacy. Integrating AI in education will significantly enhance tailored learning experiences, which are essential for effective language acquisition and empowering learners in a varied and interconnected society.

3. THE ROLE OF CHATBOTS IN LANGUAGE ACQUISITION

3.1 Introduction to Chatbots

Chatbots have emerged as a dynamic and novel instrument in language learning, transforming the manner in which learners engage with new languages (Ouald et al. 2024). Chatbots, defined as AI-driven conversational agents, are engineered to replicate human communication via text or voice interactions. They employ natural language processing (NLP) technology to comprehend and respond to user inputs, rendering them an essential resource for language learners desiring practice and interaction in a low-stress setting.

The usefulness of chatbots is based on their capacity to enable interactive interaction. Students can communicate with chatbots instantaneously, honing their language abilities through dialogues that replicate genuine exchanges (Hew et al., 2023). This function is especially advantageous for language acquisition, enabling pupils to utilize vocabulary and grammar in context, so improving their speaking and writing skills. A learner can engage a chatbot in dialogue with commonplace subjects, such as travel, cuisine, or pastimes, obtaining prompt feedback on their linguistic application.

Chatbots are engineered with diverse interaction functionalities, offering consumers a spectrum of conversational experiences (Borsci et al., 2022). Certain chatbots are designed to adhere to particular scripts, directing learners through organized lessons or activities. Others utilize machine learning algorithms that allow them to adjust their responses according to the learner's skill level and preferences. This versatility guarantees that dialogues stay pertinent and captivating, addressing the distinct requirements of every user.

Furthermore, chatbots can integrate gamification components, rendering the learning experience engaging and stimulating. Chatbots promote consistent practice and reinforce language abilities through the integration of quizzes, challenges, and prizes, facilitating playful interaction (González-González et al., 2023). This gamified methodology not only improves retention but also cultivates a sense of accomplishment as learners advance through varying levels of difficulty.

A notable characteristic of chatbots is their accessibility. In contrast to conventional language courses with rigid timetables, chatbots are available around the clock, enabling learners to practice at their convenience. This flexibility is especially beneficial for busy individuals or those residing in several time zones, as it allows them to incorporate language practice into their everyday routines effortlessly.

In conclusion, chatbots serve as a potent instrument in the realm of language acquisition, providing interactive, adaptable, and engaging experiences for learners. Their capacity to enable real-time dialogue, tailor to specific requirements, and ensure constant accessibility renders them a vital asset in contemporary language instruction. As we explore the function of chatbots in language acquisition, it is evident that their incorporation into educational methodologies is transforming the manner in which learners obtain and refine new languages.

3.2 Benefits of Using Chatbots for Language Learning

Incorporating chatbots in language learning presents various benefits that markedly improve the educational experience (Huang et al., 2022). These AI-driven solutions offer learners options for ongoing practice, prompt feedback, and immersive conversational interaction, all enhancing language acquisition efficacy.

A primary advantage of chatbots is their round-the-clock availability. In contrast to conventional language courses that adhere to rigid timetables, chatbots are always available, enabling learners to practice at their convenience. This adaptability is especially beneficial for busy persons, students with fluctuating schedules, or those residing in different time zones. Chatbots facilitate continuous language practice, prompting learners to interact with the language more often, so strengthening their skills and fostering regular learning habits (Rafikha et al., 2024).

A significant benefit of employing chatbots is the immediate input they offer. Students engaging with chatbots obtain prompt replies to their inquiries and language applications (Hew et al., 2023). This immediate feedback is essential for language acquisition, enabling learners to recognize and rectify errors as they arise. For instance, if a learner employs erroneous grammar or vocabulary, the chatbot can swiftly identify the mistake and propose the correct version. This prompt correction reinforces learning, enabling learners to comprehend their errors and make real-time modifications, resulting in a more profound comprehension of language norms and structures.

Conversational practice constitutes another essential advantage of chatbots. Interacting with a chatbot enables learners to replicate authentic discussions inside a secure and nurturing setting. This activity is crucial for cultivating speaking and listening skills, as it allows learners to utilize vocabulary and grammar in context. Chatbots can engage users in many themes, prompting them to articulate their thoughts and opinions, so fostering confidence in their language skills (Hew et al., 2023). Moreover, the low-pressure dynamics of these exchanges alleviate the anxiety typically linked to speaking a new language, so encouraging learners to engage in practice more readily.

Moreover, chatbots can be configured with a diverse array of subjects and complexity levels, enabling learners to customize their practice according to their interests and skill levels. This customization guarantees that discussions stay pertinent and stimulating, encouraging learners to persist in their practice. Gamification components are frequently used in chatbot conversations, including prizes for accomplishing challenges or attaining milestones, hence augmenting motivation and engagement (Madan and Lohani, 2024).

In conclusion, the advantages of utilizing chatbots for language acquisition are extensive and significant. Their round-the-clock availability, immediate feedback, and opportunities for conversational practice foster an interesting and productive learning atmosphere. In examining the function of chatbots in language acquisition, it is evident that these technologies serve not merely as supplementary resources but as integral elements of contemporary language teaching, enabling learners to attain their linguistic objectives with assurance and simplicity.

3.3 Case Studies of Successful Chatbot Implementations

The use of chatbots in language instruction has been effectively evidenced in numerous educational establishments and linguistic initiatives globally (Belda-Medina & Calvo-Ferrer, 2022; Annamalai et al., 2023). These projects demonstrate the capacity of chatbots to improve the learning experience, aid language acquisition, and foster student engagement.

The University of Michigan created a chatbot called "M-Chat" to aid students in improving their language abilities in a conversational setting (Varghese et al., 2024; Bayat, 2023). M-Chat was developed to facilitate interactions that mirror real-life situations, enabling students to practice speaking and writing within a supportive context. The chatbot delivered immediate feedback on grammar and vocabulary, assisting learners in recognizing areas for enhancement. Preliminary assessments revealed that students engaging with M-Chat had enhanced confidence in their linguistic skills and a heightened readiness to partake in discussions. This effort demonstrated how chatbots can enhance conventional language education by offering supplementary practice opportunities beyond the classroom.

Duolingo, a prominent language learning website, successfully integrates chatbots into its curriculum. The chatbot function of Duolingo enables users to converse about diverse subjects, offering a pragmatic application of the vocabulary and grammar they have acquired. The chatbot adjusts to the learner's skill level, guaranteeing that interactions are pertinent and stimulating. Duolingo's gamified methodology and the chatbot's interactive characteristics have demonstrated efficacy in maintaining user engagement and motivation (Renacido & Biray, 2025). The site boasts millions of global users, illustrating the scalability and efficacy of chatbot integration in language acquisition.

In Asia, the language acquisition application “HelloTalk” utilizes a chatbot to enable linguistic communication among users. HelloTalk facilitates connections between learners and native speakers, enabling practice of the target language via text, voice, and video communication. The application's chatbot aids users by offering translation assistance and rectifying linguistic problems instantaneously. This interactive method allows learners to participate in genuine discussions while obtaining valuable assistance, so improving their language proficiency in a practical setting. HelloTalk's achievement in cultivating a worldwide community of language learners exemplifies the efficacy of chatbots in bridging persons from diverse cultures (Eswaran et al., 2025).

Additionally, the European Commission's “Chatbot for Language Learning” initiative sought to enhance linguistic proficiency among migrants and refugees. The chatbot was created to offer linguistic assistance and materials customized for these learners' need. The chatbot facilitated users' adaptation to their new environs by providing conversational practice and key language pertinent to daily living and integration (Allouch et al., 2021). This effort showcased the capability of chatbots to meet certain educational requirements and foster inclusion in language acquisition.

In conclusion, effective case studies of chatbot applications in language learning demonstrate the revolutionary capabilities of these AI-driven instruments. Chatbots have improved the educational experience across institutions and global language learning platforms by offering individualized, engaging, and interactive options for learners. The exploration of chatbots in language education reveals that their integration can profoundly influence language teaching and learning, facilitating more effective and inclusive acquisition methodologies.

4. CHALLENGES AND LIMITATIONS OF AI IN LANGUAGE LEARNING

4.1 Technological Barriers

The incorporation of artificial intelligence (AI) in language acquisition offers various advantages, although it also introduces considerable obstacles and constraints (Darwin et al. 2024). Technological obstacles significantly influence the accessibility and efficacy of AI-driven language teaching. Challenges include access to technology, digital literacy, and the digital divide must be resolved to guarantee equitable educational opportunities for all pupils.

Access to technology is a critical issue in the use of AI in language education (Mageira et al., 2022). In numerous areas, especially in developing nations or marginalized populations, students may be deprived of essential devices—such as smartphones, tablets, or computers—to utilize AI-driven instructional resources. This absence of access can impede students from reaping the advantages of chatbots and language applications' tailored and engaging experiences. In a more digital environment, the inequity in technological access can intensify pre-existing educational disparities, placing specific demographics at a disadvantage in developing crucial linguistic competencies.

Digital literacy is a crucial determinant affecting the efficacy of AI in language acquisition. Despite having access to technology, learners' proficiency in navigating digital platforms and utilizing AI tools can differ markedly. Numerous learners may lack the requisite skills to navigate intricate interfaces or resolve technological problems, resulting in frustration and disengagement (Lin & Chen, 2024). Moreover, educators must possess digital literacy abilities to incorporate AI tools into their instructional methodologies properly. Inadequate training and support may hinder both learners and educators from fully utilizing AI-driven language learning resources.

The digital gap exacerbates the complexities of AI in education. This word denotes the disparity between individuals with convenient access to digital technology and the internet and others lacking such access. Factors contributing to the digital gap encompass socioeconomic level, geographic location, and infrastructural deficiencies (Vassilakopoulou & Hustad, 2023). Students in rural areas may encounter difficulties due to poor internet connections, hindering their access to online language learning programs. Consequently, these learners may forfeit significant educational possibilities, so perpetuating cycles of disadvantage.

Furthermore, the swift progression of technological innovation can marginalize certain learners, especially older persons or those who did not have exposure to technology throughout their formative years. This age split may engender reluctance to embrace new tools, so exacerbating the disparity.

In summary, although AI can transform language acquisition, technological obstacles such as access to technology, digital literacy, and the digital divide present considerable problems. Resolving these challenges is crucial for guaranteeing that all learners can take advantage of the advancements introduced by AI. Educators and policymakers may establish a more inclusive language learning environment that enables all children to succeed in an increasingly linked world by promoting equitable access to technology and improving digital literacy.

4.2 Limitations of AI in Understanding Context and Nuance

Despite substantial advancements in language acquisition, artificial intelligence (AI) continues to encounter major constraints, especially in comprehending context and nuance (Xiao et al., 2024). These problems can impede the efficacy of AI-driven solutions, such as chatbots and language applications, in delivering learners a thorough and genuine language acquisition experience.

A significant problem faced by AI is understanding cultural context. Language is intricately connected to society, with numerous words, idioms, and expressions possessing meanings that transcend their literal interpretations (Naveen & Trojovský, 2024). The expression "kick the bucket" in English is an idiom signifying "to die," a meaning that may not be readily discernible to a non-native speaker. AI systems frequently have difficulties in accurately recognizing and interpreting idioms, resulting in possible misconceptions and confusion for learners. Without a comprehensive understanding of cultural context, learners may misuse terms, so impeding their capacity for successful communication in practical scenarios.

Likewise, AI's constraints in comprehending emotional tone pose considerable obstacles in language acquisition. Language encompasses more than mere words and grammar; it also communicates emotions, intentions, and nuances that can alter the meaning of a statement. The phrase "That is just great!" may signify either sincere commendation or scathing reproach, contingent upon the context and intonation. Although AI can assess text sentiment through machine learning algorithms, it frequently fails to grasp the complexities of human emotions, resulting in misinterpretations that may impair the quality of interactions between learners and AI tools (Liu-Thompkins et al., 2022).

Moreover, AI systems generally depend on extensive datasets to acquire language patterns; nevertheless, these datasets may insufficiently reflect the diversity of language usage across many cultures and circumstances (Liang et al., 2022). Consequently, AI may encounter difficulties in adapting to regional dialects, slang, or culturally particular references, thereby constraining its efficacy in delivering pertinent and meaningful language exercise. This deficiency in flexibility may result in learners feeling estranged from the language and culture they seek to master.

Furthermore, the static characteristics of numerous AI-driven technologies indicate that they may not adapt to the dynamic nature of language. New slang, idiomatic idioms, and cultural allusions continuously arise, and without regular updates, AI systems may become obsolete, hence diminishing their relevance in language acquisition (Tian, 2024).

In conclusion, although AI can improve language acquisition, its deficiencies in comprehending context and nuance present considerable obstacles. Resolving these difficulties is crucial for creating more successful AI-driven language learning systems that provide learners a more enriching and authentic experience. By integrating cultural insights and emotional intelligence into AI systems, educators and developers can establish more responsive and adaptive language learning environments that effectively equip learners for real-world communication.

4.3 Ethical Considerations

The growing integration of artificial intelligence (AI) in language learning has heightened ethical concerns around privacy, data security, and the larger consequences of dependence on AI in education (Adams et al., 2023; Akgun & Greenhow, 2022). These issues must be resolved to guarantee that the advantages of AI are achieved without jeopardizing the rights and safety of learners.

A fundamental ethical issue pertains to privacy concerns. AI-powered language learning applications frequently gather extensive data on users, encompassing personal details, learning behaviors, and performance indicators. This data collection prompts inquiries regarding the utilization of this information, the individuals with access to it, and the duration of its retention. Students may be oblivious to the degree of data collection and analysis occurring, resulting in possible breaches of privacy. Educational institutions and developers must prioritize transparency in data practices, ensuring users are informed about data-gathering methods and have the choice to opt-out if requested (Alzahrani et al., 2023).

Data security represents a significant challenge with the application of AI in language learning (Ahmad et al., 2022). The escalating volume of personal data storage and processing heightens the danger of data breaches and illegal access. Educational institutions and technology providers must establish stringent security protocols to safeguard sensitive information from cyber threats. Neglecting this responsibility endangers learners' privacy and may result in considerable reputational harm to companies engaged in language instruction.

Furthermore, the dependence on AI in education prompts inquiries into the function of human educators. Although AI tools can augment educational experiences, they must not supplant the essential contributions of educators. Educators are essential in cultivating critical thinking, emotional intelligence, and interpersonal skills—attributes that AI cannot emulate (Lin & Chen, 2024; Yu, 2024). Excessive dependence on AI may reduce focus on these fundamental elements of education, potentially affecting students' comprehensive development.

Moreover, AI algorithms are susceptible to bias, thereby reinforcing stereotypes and injustices. If the data utilized to train AI systems embodies existing prejudices, the resultant tools may yield distorted outputs that penalize specific groups of learners. Developers must diligently strive to create inclusive and egalitarian AI systems that identify and rectify these biases (Hanna et al., 2024).

The ethical implications of AI in language acquisition are intricate and diverse. Privacy issues, data protection, the consequences of depending on AI instead of human instructors, and the risk of bias must be meticulously addressed to guarantee that AI integration improves rather than undermines the educational experience. By emphasizing ethical practices and promoting openness, educational institutions, and technology companies can establish a more responsible and equitable environment for language learning in the digital era.

5. THE FUTURE OF LANGUAGE LEARNING WITH AI

5.1 Emerging Trends and Innovations

As artificial intelligence (AI) advances, the domain of language acquisition is set for substantial change due to new technology and innovative approaches (Marques-Cobeta, 2024). Notable breakthroughs include augmented reality (AR) and virtual reality (VR), which provide immersive and interactive experiences that can significantly improve language acquisition in unprecedented ways.

Augmented reality superimposes digital information onto the physical world, allowing learners to concurrently engage with tangible and virtual components. Augmented reality (AR) can foster immersive environments for students to practice language skills contextually (Qiu et al., 2023). For instance, learners might utilize AR applications to annotate things in their environment with the target language, so enhancing vocabulary retention by visual association. Furthermore, augmented reality can enhance interactive storytelling, enabling learners to interact with characters and situations that necessitate active language use. This immersive method enhances the enjoyment of learning and fosters a more profound comprehension and retention of language topics.

Conversely, virtual reality offers completely immersive experiences that transport learners to diverse places, allowing them to practice language skills in authentic contexts. Virtual reality language learning systems can replicate authentic scenarios, such as ordering food in a restaurant, traversing a foreign city, or engaging in a cultural event. Through the immersion of learners in these circumstances, virtual reality promotes genuine communication and motivates them to utilize their language abilities in practical contexts (Tang, 2024). This experiential learning methodology can substantially augment learners' confidence and proficiency as they speak and listen in a secure, regulated setting.

Furthermore, the amalgamation of AI with AR and VR technologies might enhance the personalization of the learning experience. AI algorithms can assess learners' performance in real-time, adjusting scenarios and challenges according to their competence levels and learning styles (Gligorea et al., 2023). This dynamic adaptability guarantees that each student obtains a customized experience that addresses their specific needs, hence enhancing engagement and efficacy.

Alongside AR and VR, further creative approaches are arising in the field of language acquisition. The implementation of gamification is increasingly prevalent, integrating game-like components into language teaching to stimulate motivation and improve engagement among learners. AI-powered analytics can monitor progress and offer feedback, enabling learners to establish objectives and acknowledge accomplishments.

Moreover, social learning systems are gaining popularity by linking learners with peers and native speakers for collaborative practice. These platforms utilize AI to pair users according to language objectives, hobbies, and competence levels, promoting significant interactions that enhance the learning experience.

In summary, the future of language acquisition using AI is promising, marked by new trends and developments that aim to improve engagement, customization, and efficacy. Technologies like augmented and virtual reality, integrated with AI-driven approaches, will transform language acquisition, making it more immersive and engaging. These innovations can potentially revolutionize language instruction, equipping learners for a globalized environment where successful communication is crucial.

5.2 The Role of Educators in an AI-Driven Landscape

As artificial intelligence (AI) progressively transforms the language learning domain, the role of educators is concurrently transforming. Although AI systems provide creative resources that can improve the educational experience, educators are essential for promoting human contact, critical thinking, and emotional intelligence. To prosper in an AI-driven landscape, educators must modify their pedagogical approaches to integrate new tools efficiently while preserving their fundamental position as facilitators of learning (Yadav, 2025).

Educators in an AI-enhanced classroom must attain proficiency in utilizing these tools. Educators want to acquaint themselves with diverse AI-powered resources, including language learning applications, chatbots, and virtual reality platforms, to comprehend their functionalities and educational advantages. By actively utilizing these tools, instructors can more effectively assist their students in their application, ensuring that learners fully capitalize on the benefits provided by AI (Kim et al., 2022). Professional development programs and training seminars equip educators with the essential skills to integrate AI into their curricula properly.

Furthermore, educators should utilize AI tools to customize learning experiences for their pupils (Srinivasa et al., 2022). AI technologies can assess individual learners' progress, strengths, and shortcomings, enabling educators to develop customized instructional plans. Educators can leverage data-driven insights to pinpoint areas requiring supplementary student support and modify their teaching tactics accordingly. This tailored method improves student involvement and cultivates a sense of ownership of their educational experience.

Nonetheless, although AI tools can enhance language practice and deliver immediate feedback, they cannot substitute the human connection provided by educators. Educators are essential in establishing relationships with pupils and building a secure and supportive atmosphere for language acquisition (Lau & Shea, 2024). They may foster open communication, attend to the emotional and social dimensions of learning, and offer mentorship that artificial intelligence cannot emulate. By cultivating robust interpersonal relationships, educators can inspire pupils and foster confidence in their linguistic capabilities.

Moreover, educators ought to promote collaborative learning experiences that include AI tools. Teachers can enhance peer relationships by promoting group activities and debates while employing AI-driven platforms for practice (Kim et al., 2022). Students can collaborate on language exercises via chatbots or participate in virtual reality scenarios that necessitate teamwork and communication. Integrating technology and human interaction enhances the educational experience and equips students for practical language application.

In summary, educators' function in an AI-driven environment is complex and vital. Educators can adeptly address the difficulties and opportunities posed by adopting AI technologies, customizing educational experiences, and promoting interpersonal relationships. As language acquisition progresses, instructors will lead, facilitating students' learning of new languages while maintaining empathy, teamwork, and critical thinking. Through this balanced approach, educators may cultivate a dynamic and effective language learning environment that equips students for success in an increasingly interconnected world.

5.3 Vision for Language Learning in 2030 and Beyond

Advancements in artificial intelligence (AI) and upcoming technologies (Tegon, 2021; Rajaram, 2023) are set to significantly influence the future of language learning in 2030 and beyond. As these advances progress, they will provide a landscape in which language instruction is increasingly accessible, individualized, and internationally integrated. This vision includes both learning methodologies and the wider consequences for intercultural communication and collaboration.

A major transformation expected by 2030 is the extensive incorporation of AI-facilitated individualized learning experiences. Language learners will gain advantages from adaptable platforms that assess their unique progress, preferences, and obstacles in real time (Sajja et al., 2024). These technologies will provide personalized lesson plans, practice tasks, and feedback, guaranteeing that each learner obtains a bespoke educational experience corresponding to their requirements. Consequently, language acquisition will become more efficient, enabling learners to advance at their speed while receiving tailored assistance.

Furthermore, the integration of augmented reality (AR) and virtual reality (VR) technology is expected to become prevalent in language instruction. Augmented Reality (AR) and Virtual Reality (VR) will offer chances for genuine language practice by immersing learners in realistic environments that replicate real-world interactions (Lee et al., 2024). For instance, students could travel virtually to a foreign nation, connecting with native speakers and managing quotidian scenarios in the target language. This immersive method will improve language proficiency and cultivate cultural awareness and empathy, vital elements of effective communication in a globalized context.

The prospects for international communication and collaboration will likewise increase substantially. AI-driven platforms will establish linkages between learners and native speakers from various backgrounds, facilitating real-time language exchanges and collaborative initiatives (Eswaran et al., 2025). This connection will facilitate cross-cultural discussion, enabling learners to hone their language abilities while acquiring insights into diverse cultures and views. These connections will dismantle language barriers and cultivate a feeling of global community.

Furthermore, progress in natural language processing (NLP) will facilitate the development of increasingly advanced translation systems, promoting effortless communication among speakers of diverse languages (Gupta et al., 2024). This technology will enable users to converse without the apprehension of miscommunication, thus enhancing collaboration across multiple domains, including business, education, and diplomacy.

As language teaching progresses, it is essential to confront ethical issues, including data privacy and the possibility of prejudice in AI systems. Guaranteeing equitable access to technology and resources is crucial to avert the exacerbation of inequities in language instruction (Gallegos-Rejas et al., 2023).

In summary, the vision for language acquisition in 2030 and beyond encompasses innovation, accessibility, and global interconnectedness. AI, AR, and VR technologies will provide learners with personalized, immersive, and collaborative language teaching, equipping them for effective communication in a progressively interconnected world. As we adopt these improvements, it is crucial to consider ethical implications and pursue inclusive practices that benefit all learners, promoting a future where language serves as a conduit for understanding and collaboration across cultures.

CONCLUSION

The progression of language acquisition, from conventional methods to incorporating advanced technologies, highlights humanity's persistent quest for more efficient and captivating educational experiences. Historically, grammar-translation and communicative approaches established the groundwork for systematic and pragmatic language acquisition. Technology has transformed this domain, bringing instruments such as audio-visual assistance, computer-assisted language learning (CALL), and, more recently, artificial intelligence (AI).

The revolutionary influence of AI on language acquisition is indisputable. Utilizing tools like chatbots, virtual tutors, and personalized learning platforms, learners now benefit from adaptive, engaging, and efficacious approaches tailored to their requirements. These advances facilitate learners in practicing language skills within authentic circumstances, getting immediate feedback, and advancing at their speed. Natural language processing (NLP) and machine learning augment the interactivity and authenticity of language teaching, closing gaps in cultural comprehension and conversational proficiency.

Nonetheless, the incorporation of AI also poses difficulties. Challenges such as technological access, digital literacy, and the digital divide underscore the necessity for equal and inclusive execution. Moreover, the existing constraints of AI in comprehending context and nuance underscore the vital function of educators in cultivating empathy, critical thinking, and cultural sensitivity.

The future of language learning is set to become increasingly immersive and interconnected. Emerging technologies like augmented reality (AR) and virtual reality (VR) are poised to transform language learning by generating situations that integrate practicality with innovation. By addressing ethical problems and utilizing these developments judiciously, educators and technologists can cultivate a future in which language functions as a conduit for global understanding and collaboration.

The transition from chalkboards to chatbots represents advancements in education and the relentless capacity of human ingenuity to address intricate learning obstacles.

REFERENCES

Adams, C., Pente, P., Lemermeyer, G., & Rockwell, G. (2023). Ethical principles for artificial intelligence in K-12 education. [sciencedirect.com]. *Computers and Education: Artificial Intelligence*, *4*, 100131. DOI: 10.1016/j.caeai.2023.100131

Ahmad, K., Maabreh, M., Ghaly, M., Khan, K., Qadir, J., & Al-Fuqaha, A. (2022). Developing future human-centered smart cities: Critical analysis of smart city security, Data management, and Ethical challenges. [HTML]. *Computer Science Review*, *43*, 100452. DOI: 10.1016/j.cosrev.2021.100452

Akgun, S. & Greenhow, C. (2022). Artificial intelligence in education: Addressing ethical challenges in K-12 settings. AI and Ethics. springer.com

Akour, M. & Alenezi, M. (2022). Higher education future in the era of digital transformation. Education Sciences. mdpi.com

Akram, H., Abdelrady, A. H., Al-Adwan, A. S., & Ramzan, M. (2022). Teachers' perceptions of technology integration in teaching-learning practices: A systematic review. [frontiersin.org]. *Frontiers in Psychology*, *13*, 920317. DOI: 10.3389/fpsyg.2022.920317 PMID: 35734463

Allouch, M., Azaria, A., & Azoulay, R. (2021). Conversational agents: Goals, technologies, vision and challenges. Sensors. mdpi.com

Alzahrani, A. S., Tsai, Y. S., Aljohani, N., Whitelock-Wainwright, E., & Gasevic, D. (2023). Do teaching staff trust stakeholders and tools in learning analytics? A mixed methods study. [springer.com]. *Educational Technology Research and Development*, *71*(4), 1471–1501. DOI: 10.1007/s11423-023-10229-w PMID: 37359481

Annamalai, N., Ab Rashid, R., Hashmi, U. M., Mohamed, M., Alqaryouti, M. H., & Sadeq, A. E. (2023). Using chatbots for English language learning in higher education. [sciencedirect.com]. *Computers and Education: Artificial Intelligence*, *5*, 100153. DOI: 10.1016/j.caeai.2023.100153

Bayat, M. (2023). Teaching Exceptional Children: Foundations and Best Practices in Early Childhood Special Education. [HTML]

Belda-Medina, J. & Calvo-Ferrer, J. R. (2022). Using chatbots as AI conversational partners in language learning. Applied Sciences. mdpi.com

Borsci, S., Malizia, A., Schmettow, M., Van Der Velde, F., Tariverdiyeva, G., Balaji, D., & Chamberlain, A. (2022). The chatbot usability scale: The design and pilot of a usability scale for interaction with AI-based conversational agents. [springer.com]. *Personal and Ubiquitous Computing*, *26*(1), 95–119. DOI: 10.1007/s00779-021-01582-9

Chakraborty, S., Misra, B., & Dey, N. (2024). AI-Empowered Knowledge [HTML]. *Management in Education.*

Darder, A., Hernandez, K., Lam, K. D., & Baltodano, M. (2023). Critical pedagogy: An introduction. In *The critical pedagogy reader* (pp. 1–30). Routledge. [HTML] DOI: 10.4324/9781003286080-1

Darwin, R., Rusdin, D., Mukminatien, N., Suryati, N., Laksmi, E. D., & Marzuki, . (2024). Critical thinking in the AI era: An exploration of EFL students' perceptions, benefits, and limitations. [tandfonline.com]. *Cogent Education*, *11*(1), 2290342. DOI: 10.1080/2331186X.2023.2290342

Dong, C. (2024). Educational concepts and methodologies in the AI era: Challenges and responses. Frontiers of Digital Education. [HTML]

Dwivedi, D. N., Mahanty, G., & nath Dwivedi, V. (2024). The Role of Predictive Analytics in Personalizing Education: Tailoring Learning Paths for Individual Student Success. In Enhancing Education With Intelligent Systems and Data-Driven Instruction (pp. 44-59). IGI Global. [HTML]

Eswaran, U., Eswaran, V., Murali, K., & Eswaran, V. (2025). AI-Powered Language Teaching and Learning: Innovations and Challenges. In Reimagining Intelligent Computer-Assisted Language Education (pp. 55-92). IGI Global. [HTML]

Gallegos-Rejas, V. M., Thomas, E. E., Kelly, J. T., & Smith, A. C. (2023). A multi-stakeholder approach is needed to reduce the digital divide and encourage equitable access to telehealth. [sagepub.com]. *Journal of Telemedicine and Telecare*, *29*(1), 73–78. DOI: 10.1177/1357633X221107995 PMID: 35733379

Garlinska, M., Osial, M., Proniewska, K., & Pregowska, A. (2023). The influence of emerging technologies on distance education. Electronics. mdpi.com

Gligorea, I., Cioca, M., Oancea, R., Gorski, A. T., Gorski, H., & Tudorache, P. (2023). Adaptive learning using artificial intelligence in e-learning: A literature review. [mdpi.com]. *Education Sciences*, *13*(12), 1216. DOI: 10.3390/educsci13121216

González-González, C. S., Muñoz-Cruz, V., Toledo-Delgado, P. A., & Nacimiento-García, E. (2023). Personalized gamification for learning: A reactive chatbot architecture proposal. [mdpi.com]. *Sensors (Basel), 23*(1), 545. DOI: 10.3390/s23010545 PMID: 36617143

Gupta, R., Agarwal, U., & Helen Victoria, A. (2024, January). Multilingual Communication: NMT-Based On-Call Speech Translation for Indian Languages. In International Conference on Multi-Strategy Learning Environment (pp. 113-127). Singapore: Springer Nature Singapore. [HTML] DOI: 10.1007/978-981-97-1488-9_9

Hanna, M., Pantanowitz, L., Jackson, B., Palmer, O., Visweswaran, S., Pantanowitz, J., & Rashidi, H. (2024). Ethical and Bias Considerations in Artificial Intelligence (AI)/Machine Learning. [sciencedirect.com]. *Modern Pathology*, •••, 100686. PMID: 39694331

Hew, K. F., Huang, W., Du, J., & Jia, C. (2023). Using chatbots to support student goal setting and social presence in fully online activities: learner engagement and perceptions. Journal of Computing in Higher Education. springer.com

Hossain, K. I. (2024). Reviewing the role of culture in English language learning: Challenges and opportunities for educators. Social Sciences & Humanities Open. sciencedirect.com

Huang, W., Hew, K. F., & Fryer, L. K. (2022). Chatbots for language learning—Are they really useful? A systematic review of chatbot-supported language learning. [wiley.com]. *Journal of Computer Assisted Learning, 38*(1), 237–257. DOI: 10.1111/jcal.12610

Idrissi, M., El Morabit, N., & El Kandoussi, M. (2024). Bridging Technology and Language Learning: A Comprehensive Analysis of CALL Integration within Second Language Acquisition. International Journal of Linguistics [al-kindipublisher.com]. *Literature and Translation, 7*(4), 60–65.

Kessler, M., Marino, F., & Farrell, S. (2025). Computer-Assisted Language Learning and Teaching: Emerging trends, challenges, and solutions in ELT. Adaptable English Language Teaching, 228-244. [HTML]

Khuman, P. (2024). The Navigation Of The English Language Teaching And Learning Ecosystem Using Digital Tools. HEMCHANDRACHARYA INTERNATIONAL E JOURNAL OF RESEARCH. hemchandracharyaejournal.com

Kim, J., Lee, H., & Cho, Y. H. (2022). Learning design to support student-AI collaboration: Perspectives of leading teachers for AI in education. Education and Information Technologies. springer.com

Kuddus, K. (2022). *Artificial intelligence in language learning: Practices and prospects*. Advanced Analytics and Deep Learning Models. [HTML]

Lau, W. S., & Shea, M. (2024). Empowering English learners in the classroom through culturally responsive social-emotional teaching practices. [HTML]. *Journal of Multilingual and Multicultural Development*, *45*(7), 2880–2897. DOI: 10.1080/01434632.2022.2078337

Lee, S. M., Yang, Z., & Wu, J. G. (2024). Live, play, and learn: Language learner engagement in the immersive VR environment. [HTML]. *Education and Information Technologies*, *29*(9), 10529–10550. DOI: 10.1007/s10639-023-12215-4

Liang, W., Tadesse, G. A., Ho, D., Fei-Fei, L., Zaharia, M., Zhang, C., & Zou, J. (2022). Advances, challenges and opportunities in creating data for trustworthy AI. [HTML]. *Nature Machine Intelligence*, *4*(8), 669–677. DOI: 10.1038/s42256-022-00516-1

Lin, H. & Chen, Q. (2024). Artificial intelligence (AI)-integrated educational applications and college students' creativity and academic emotions: students and teachers' perceptions and attitudes. BMC psychology. springer.com

Liu-Thompkins, Y., Okazaki, S., & Li, H. (2022). Artificial empathy in marketing interactions: Bridging the human-AI gap in affective and social customer experience. [springer.com]. *Journal of the Academy of Marketing Science*, *50*(6), 1198–1218. DOI: 10.1007/s11747-022-00892-5

Lokare, V. T., & Jadhav, P. M. (2024). An AI-based learning style prediction model for personalized and effective learning. [HTML]. *Thinking Skills and Creativity*, *51*, 101421. DOI: 10.1016/j.tsc.2023.101421

Madan, A., & Lohani, V. J. (2024). Leveraging Event Gamification for Event Planning and Creating a Memorable Experience. In *New Technologies in Virtual and Hybrid Events* (pp. 198–227). IGI Global. [HTML] DOI: 10.4018/979-8-3693-2272-7.ch011

Mageira, K., Pittou, D., Papasalouros, A., Kotis, K., Zangogianni, P., & Daradoumis, A. (2022). Educational AI chatbots for content and language integrated learning. [mdpi.com]. *Applied Sciences (Basel, Switzerland)*, *12*(7), 3239. DOI: 10.3390/app12073239

Mahmood, R. Q., & Bui, H. P. (2024). EFL learners' perceptions of pronunciation corrective feedback: insights from synchronous high variability phonetic training. In *Innovations in technologies for language teaching and learning* (pp. 95–119). Springer Nature Switzerland. [HTML] DOI: 10.1007/978-3-031-63447-5_6

Marques-Cobeta, N. (2024). Artificial Intelligence in Education: Unveiling Opportunities and Challenges. Innovation and Technologies for the Digital Transformation of Education: European and Latin American Perspectives, 33-42. [HTML]

Martyushev, N., Shutaleva, A., Malushko, E., Nikonova, Z., & Savchenko, I. (2021). Online communication tools in teaching foreign languages for education sustainability. [mdpi.com]. *Sustainability (Basel)*, *13*(19), 11127. DOI: 10.3390/su131911127

Nath, S., Marie, A., Ellershaw, S., Korot, E., & Keane, P. A. (2022). New meaning for NLP: The trials and tribulations of natural language processing with GPT-3 in ophthalmology. *The British Journal of Ophthalmology*, *106*(7), 889–892. ucl.ac.uk. DOI: 10.1136/bjophthalmol-2022-321141 PMID: 35523534

Naveen, P. & Trojovský, P. (2024). Overview and challenges of machine translation for contextually appropriate translations. Iscience. cell.com

Nurfauziah, D. H., Murtiningsih, T., & Al Farhan, M. (2024). Learning English Vocabulary Strategies for Non-English Department Students at Intensive English Class. IALLTEACH (Issues In Applied Linguistics & Language Teaching), 6(2), 210-218. uib.ac.id

Nwakaego, A. M. (2024). Selection of Instructional Materials for Efficiency in Teaching and Learning English Language. Educational Research (IJMCER). ijmcer.com

Ouald Chaib, S., Merrahi, M., & Khoulji, S. (2024, April). Enhancing Language Learning Personalization Through Deep Learning-Driven Chatbot Assistance. In International Conference On Big Data and Internet of Things (pp. 837-851). Cham: Springer Nature Switzerland. [HTML] DOI: 10.1007/978-3-031-74491-4_65

Qiu, X. Y., Chiu, C. K., Zhao, L. L., Sun, C. F., & Chen, S. J. (2023). Trends in VR/AR technology-supporting language learning from 2008 to 2019: A research perspective. [HTML]. *Interactive Learning Environments*, *31*(4), 2090–2113. DOI: 10.1080/10494820.2021.1874999

Rafikha, H., Ula, N., Rahmah, H., Khaira, N., Fitri, K., Ulfa, P. R., & Rasikhah, P. A. (2024). *Seven Innovative Ways to Learn English for Non-Native Speaker*. USK Press. [HTML]

Rafikha, H., Ula, N., Rahmah, H., Khaira, N., Fitri, K., Ulfa, P. R., & Rasikhah, P. A. (2024). *Seven Innovative Ways to Learn English for Non-Native Speaker*. USK Press. [HTML]

Rajaram, K. (2023). Future of learning: Teaching and learning strategies. In Learning Intelligence: Innovative and Digital Transformative Learning Strategies: Cultural and Social Engineering Perspectives (pp. 3-53). Singapore: Springer Nature Singapore. [HTML]

Renacido, J. M. D., & Biray, E. T. (2025). Enhancing Peer Engagement and Student Motivation Through AI-Gamified Interactive Learning Tools. In Advancing Sustainable Development Goals With Educational Technology (pp. 277-342). IGI Global Scientific Publishing. [HTML]

Sajja, R., Sermet, Y., Cikmaz, M., Cwiertny, D., & Demir, I. (2024). Artificial intelligence-enabled intelligent assistant for personalized and adaptive learning in higher education. Information. mdpi.com

Sarker, I. H. (2021). Machine learning: Algorithms, real-world applications and research directions. SN computer science. springer.com

Sarker, I. H. (2022). AI-based modeling: techniques, applications and research issues towards automation, intelligent and smart systems. SN Computer Science. springer.com

Shareef, S. M. & Nithyanantham, V. (2022). Fundamentals of educational technology. [HTML]

Singh, J., Evans, E., Reed, A., Karch, L., Qualey, K., Singh, L., & Wiersma, H. (2022). Online, hybrid, and face-to-face learning through the eyes of faculty, students, administrators, and instructional designers: Lessons learned and directions for the post-vaccine and post-pandemic/COVID-19 world. [sagepub.com]. *Journal of Educational Technology Systems*, *50*(3), 301–326. DOI: 10.1177/00472395211063754

Srinivasa, K. G., Kurni, M., & Saritha, K. (2022). Harnessing the Power of AI to Education. In *Learning, teaching, and assessment methods for contemporary learners: pedagogy for the digital generation* (pp. 311–342). Springer Nature Singapore. [HTML] DOI: 10.1007/978-981-19-6734-4_13

Tang, F. (2024). … technology in educating the students of english language: does it promote critical thinking and self-directed learning for achieving sustainability in education with the …. BMC psychology. springer.com

Tegon, R. (2021). Toward the 4th Agenda 2030 Goal: AI Support to Executive Functions for Inclusions. In Handbook of Research on Teaching With Virtual Environments and AI (pp. 591-615). IGI Global. [HTML]

Tian, X. (2024). Personalized translator training in the era of digital intelligence: Opportunities, challenges, and prospects. Heliyon. cell.com

Timotheou, S., Miliou, O., Dimitriadis, Y., Sobrino, S. V., Giannoutsou, N., Cachia, R., Monés, A. M., & Ioannou, A. (2023). Impacts of digital technologies on education and factors influencing schools' digital capacity and transformation: A literature review. [springer.com]. *Education and Information Technologies*, *28*(6), 6695–6726. DOI: 10.1007/s10639-022-11431-8 PMID: 36465416

Varghese, E. B., Qaraqe, M., & Al-Thani, D. (2024). Utilizing Artificial Intelligence to Support Autism Research. In The Impact of Artificial Intelligence on Societies: Understanding Attitude Formation Towards AI (pp. 87-108). Cham: Springer Nature Switzerland. [HTML]

Vassilakopoulou, P. & Hustad, E. (2023). Bridging digital divides: A literature review and research agenda for information systems research. Information Systems Frontiers. springer.com

Wei, L. (2023). Artificial intelligence in language instruction: impact on English learning achievement, L2 motivation, and self-regulated learning. Frontiers in Psychology. frontiersin.org

Weng, X. & Chiu, T. K. F. (2023). Instructional design and learning outcomes of intelligent computer assisted language learning: Systematic review in the field. Computers and Education: Artificial Intelligence. sciencedirect.com

Xiao, Y., Zhang, T., & He, J. (2024). A Review of Promises and Challenges of AI-Based Chatbots in Language Education through the Lens of Learner Emotions. Heliyon. cell.com

Yadav, S. (2025). *Advancing Education With AI-Driven Education for Diverse Learners: Integrating AI Into Pedagogical Practices*. Integrating AI Into Pedagogical Education. [HTML]

Yu, H. (2024). The application and challenges of ChatGPT in educational transformation: New demands for teachers' roles. Heliyon. cell.com

Zagouras, C., Egarchou, D., Skiniotis, P., & Fountana, M. (2022). Face to face or blended learning? A case study: Teacher training in the pedagogical use of ICT. [springer.com]. *Education and Information Technologies*, *27*(9), 12939–12967. DOI: 10.1007/s10639-022-11144-y PMID: 35729873

Zhai, C. & Wibowo, S. (2023). A systematic review on artificial intelligence dialogue systems for enhancing English as foreign language students' interactional competence in the university. Computers and Education: Artificial Intelligence. sciencedirect.com

Zhang, C., & Lu, Y. (2021). Study on artificial intelligence: The state of the art and future prospects. [HTML]. *Journal of Industrial Information Integration*, *23*, 100224. DOI: 10.1016/j.jii.2021.100224

Zhu, J., Zhang, X., & Li, J. (2024). Using AR filters in L2 pronunciation training: Practice, perfection, and willingness to share. [HTML]. *Computer Assisted Language Learning*, *37*(5-6), 1364–1396. DOI: 10.1080/09588221.2022.2080716

ADDITIONAL READING

Anderson, L. W., & Krathwohl, D. R. (Eds.). (2001). *A taxonomy for learning, teaching, and assessing: A revision of Bloom's taxonomy of educational objectives*. Longman.

Dede, C. (2010). Comparing frameworks for 21st century skills. In J. Bellanca & R. Brandt (Eds.), *21st century skills: Rethinking how students learn* (pp. 51–76). Solution Tree Press.

Fullan, M., & Langworthy, M. (2014). *A rich seam: How new pedagogies find deep learning*. Pearson.

Mishra, P., & Koehler, M. J. (2006). Technological pedagogical content knowledge: A framework for teacher knowledge. *Teachers College Record*, *108*(6), 1017–1054. DOI: 10.1111/j.1467-9620.2006.00684.x

Voogt, J., & Roblin, N. P. (2012). A comparative analysis of international frameworks for 21st century competences: Implications for national curriculum policies. *Journal of Curriculum Studies*, *44*(3), 299–321. DOI: 10.1080/00220272.2012.668938

KEY TERMS AND DEFINITIONS

21st-Century Skills: A collection of skills and capabilities, such as critical thinking, creativity, teamwork, and communication, deemed vital for success in the contemporary information economy.

Blended Learning: A pedagogical style that integrates in-person classroom techniques with online digital resources, providing flexibility and customization in educational experiences.

Collaborative Learning: A pedagogical approach in which students collaborate in groups to attain learning objectives, fostering peer interaction and collective knowledge creation.

Critical Thinking: The methodical process of critically studying, synthesizing, and assessing information to arrive at rational conclusions.

Digital Literacy: The capacity to identify, assess, and utilize digital information proficiently, ethically, and responsibly across diverse situations.

Learning Innovation: The implementation of innovative tactics, tools, or technologies in education to improve teaching efficacy and student involvement.

Pedagogical Shift: A shift in pedagogical methods or philosophy, frequently incorporating innovative strategies that correspond with technological progress or the requirements of learners.

Reflective Practice: A method wherein educators rigorously analyze their teaching experiences to enhance instructional choices and foster professional development.

Student Agency: The ability of learners to operate autonomously, make decisions, and assume responsibility for their own educational journey.

Technology Integration: The efficient utilization of digital technologies and platforms to enhance curriculum delivery and improve learning outcomes.

Chapter 3
Integrating Artificial Intelligence in English Language Teaching Based on TPACK and SAMR Model Insights: A Case Study of EFL Educators' Perspectives

Amal Abdelsattar Metwally
https://orcid.org/0000-0001-9067-3273
King Khalid University, Saudi Arabia

ABSTRACT

As artificial intelligence reshapes classrooms worldwide, this chapter explores how EFL educators navigate the promises and challenges of AI integration, revealing not only their readiness and strategies through the TPACK framework but also the transformative potential of AI adoption measured by the SAMR model. A descriptive quantitative case study was conducted with 32 EFL university educators using a structured questionnaire to assess familiarity with AI tools, perceptions of pedagogical impact, and adoption challenges. Findings reveal 78% of educators feel technologically competent, 75% report AI automation benefits, and 68% observe increased student motivation. However, 40% identify insufficient training and 35% cite a lack of EFL-specific AI tools as challenges. The study concludes that AI can transform EFL education when integrated through TPACK and SAMR. To maxi-

DOI: 10.4018/979-8-3373-0275-1.ch003

mize AI's effectiveness, structured professional development programs should be implemented to equip teachers with AI literacy, and collaborative AI tools should be designed specifically for language learning needs.

INTRODUCTION

The integration of Artificial Intelligence (AI) in English as a Foreign Language (EFL) instruction is transforming language education by enhancing student engagement, personalizing learning, and improving teaching effectiveness. In particular, as AI technologies continue to evolve, they provide innovative ways to augment traditional pedagogical methods and redefine instructional strategies. To provide a systematic understanding of this shift, this study examines AI's impact on EFL classrooms through the Technological Pedagogical Content Knowledge (TPACK) and Substitution, Augmentation, Modification, and Redefinition (SAMR) models, offering a structured framework to assess AI's role in language learning.

The TPACK model underscores the importance of educators possessing technological literacy alongside pedagogical and content expertise to effectively integrate AI tools. Meanwhile, the SAMR model categorizes AI adoption levels, ranging from simple substitution (e.g., using AI grammar checkers) to redefinition through immersive AI applications, such as intelligent tutoring systems and speech recognition software. Through these models, AI has the potential to personalize learning experiences, enabling adaptive platforms to adjust instructional content based on student proficiency levels. Furthermore, AI-powered chatbots, virtual tutors, and speech recognition technologies provide real-time feedback, helping students improve speaking, writing, and comprehension skills. In addition to supporting students, AI automates routine tasks, allowing educators to focus on critical thinking instruction and student mentorship, thereby enhancing classroom efficiency and learner autonomy.

Nevertheless, despite these advantages, AI integration in EFL instruction also presents challenges related to accessibility, teacher training, cultural inclusivity, and ethical considerations. To navigate these complexities, educators can strategically implement AI by leveraging frameworks like TPACK and SAMR, thereby maximizing its benefits while addressing potential obstacles. Ultimately, this study explores how AI can personalize learning, enhance language acquisition, and support teachers in creating dynamic, engaging, and effective EFL learning environments.

BACKGROUND

The rapid progression of AI technologies is revolutionizing education, introducing advanced tools that support individualized and adaptive learning experiences. In the context of language education, in EFL instruction, AI-powered applications such as Duolingo, Grammarly, chatbots, and speech recognition software provide learners with real-time feedback, interactive exercises, and autonomous learning pathways (Shengquan & Yu, 2021). Importantly, these AI-driven tools can analyze student performance, adapt content based on individual proficiency levels, and support skill development in areas such as grammar, pronunciation, and writing fluency. Additionally, AI assists educators by automating routine administrative tasks, such as grading assignments, generating lesson plans, and monitoring student progress, allowing teachers to focus on more interactive and student-centered instructional strategies.

However, despite the advantages of AI in language learning, its effective integration into EFL instruction requires a structured approach that aligns technology with pedagogical best practices. The Technological Pedagogical Content Knowledge (TPACK) model, developed by Mishra and Koehler (2006), provides a comprehensive framework for understanding how technology interacts with pedagogical methodologies and subject-matter expertise. By applying this model, educators can make informed decisions about which AI tools to implement and how to use them to enhance language instruction while maintaining a strong pedagogical foundation.

Complementing TPACK, the Substitution, Augmentation, Modification, and Redefinition (SAMR) model, developed by Puentedura (2006), offers another lens through which AI's impact on EFL teaching and learning can be evaluated. The SAMR model categorizes AI integration into four levels, ranging from basic substitution (where AI replaces traditional methods without significant change) to redefinition (where AI enables entirely new ways of learning that were previously impossible). As a result, this model helps educators determine whether AI tools are merely replacing existing practices or truly transforming teaching methodologies and student engagement.

Taken together, the integration of AI into EFL education presents both opportunities and challenges, particularly for educators navigating the complex interplay of pedagogy, content, and technology. While established models like TPACK and SAMR offer valuable frameworks for understanding technology integration, each has limitations when used in isolation. TPACK emphasizes the knowledge domains teachers need but often lacks practical guidance on implementation, whereas SAMR provides a clear trajectory for technology use but does not sufficiently address pedagogical depth or content alignment.

To address these limitations, this study responds to the urgent need for a more holistic and actionable approach by critically combining TPACK and SAMR. The combination allows educators to not only understand the components of effective integration but also to visualize the transformation of teaching practices through AI. Through this integration, the hybrid framework supports EFL teachers in making informed, context-sensitive decisions, thus addressing the current disconnect between instructional theory and classroom reality.

THEORETICAL FRAMEWORK

AI has become a transformative force across numerous sectors, including education. Historically, early applications of AI, such as the Intelligent Tutoring System (ITS), introduced personalized learning environments that catered to individual learning needs (Shengquan & Yu, 2021). The ITS was an early example of AI leveraging behavioral psychology principles to promote efficient learning through repeated practice and feedback. Over time, AI has evolved to include Natural Language Processing (NLP) for language learning, enabling real-time feedback, speech recognition, and personalized learning paths.

Building on this foundation, the use of AI in education aligns with the concept of Intelligent Education Systems (IES), which aim to support personalized, adaptive learning by responding dynamically to student input (Woolf et al., 2013). AI applications like Duolingo, Google Translate, and Grammarly are widely used in language education to assist students in honing their reading, writing, listening, and speaking skills (Dewi et al., 2021). Nevertheless, the success of these tools depends on their integration with pedagogical strategies that address individual learners' needs, making the role of teachers in AI-enhanced classrooms essential.

Consequently, the integration of AI in EFL instruction is transforming traditional language teaching, making it more adaptive, personalized, and data driven. However, the extent to which AI can enhance or redefine language learning experiences largely depends on educators' ability to integrate technology effectively. To support this effort, two dominant pedagogical frameworks—the TPACK model (Mishra & Koehler, 2006) and the SAMR model (Puentedura, 2006)- offer structured approaches to analyzing the depth and impact of AI integration in EFL instruction.

More specifically, the TPACK model, as outlined by Mishra and Koehler (2006), emphasizes that effective technology integration requires a balance of technological, pedagogical, and content knowledge. It provides educators with a framework to align AI tools with meaningful instructional goals.

Significantly, a study by Drugova et al. (2021) employed the TPACK-SAMR framework to examine the integration of AI-driven platforms such as Skyes in

Russian universities. The study highlighted how AI is used at different SAMR levels, progressing from basic substitution (i.e., AI replacing traditional methods) to redefinition (i.e., AI enabling novel learning experiences). In a related analysis, Falloon (2020) critiqued the hierarchical nature of the SAMR model, arguing that while it provides a roadmap for AI integration, it lacks pedagogical depth. He suggested that combining SAMR with TPACK ensures not just technological adoption but pedagogically meaningful integration, making AI more instructionally effective.

Furthermore, AI-powered adaptive learning platforms and chatbots are increasingly being used to personalize language instruction. Niess et al. (2013) introduced a Technology-Based Instruction (TbI) model, which aligns with TPACK principles and highlights AI's ability to provide real-time feedback, automate grading, and tailor lesson plans to students' learning needs. Their research found that adaptive AI tools enhance engagement by catering to individual learning styles. Similarly, Tang & Chaw (2016) explored the relationship between digital literacy and AI adoption, finding that students with higher digital competence are better able to engage with AI-based learning platforms. This aligns with the technological knowledge (TK) component of TPACK, emphasizing that both teachers and students must have adequate digital literacy to fully leverage AI in English language teaching (ELT).

Despite these promising developments, AI integration faces multiple challenges, particularly concerning teacher training, infrastructure, and accessibility. Sadeghi & Richards (2021) highlighted that many teachers lack AI-related training, making it difficult to implement AI tools effectively. Their study recommends comprehensive professional development programs aligned with TPACK and SAMR to help educators become digitally competent and pedagogically adaptive.

In addition to training, another significant barrier is the digital gap, particularly between urban and rural educational institutions. Bahri et al. (2022) conducted a comparative study of digital literacy among teachers and students in Indonesia and found that urban schools have greater access to AI-driven learning tools, while rural schools struggle with infrastructure limitations. This aligns with TPACK's technological component, suggesting that digital literacy initiatives should be prioritized alongside AI implementation efforts. Moreover, Farahani and Ghasemi (2024) emphasized the necessity of infrastructure improvements, ongoing professional development for educators, and strategic alignment of AI technologies with pedagogical objectives to ensure their effective and equitable integration into EFL classrooms.

Equally important, the ability of teachers to integrate AI into instruction is closely tied to their digital competence. Ramadhan et al. (2019) analyzed teacher proficiency in AI-driven digital literacy, revealing that while most educators are familiar with basic digital tools, they lack the pedagogical strategies to incorporate AI effectively. This reinforces findings from Falloon (2020), who stressed the need for professional development programs to equip educators with AI-focused instructional strategies.

Hassan & Mirza (2021) also assessed the digital competence of Indian EFL teachers, finding that lack of training in AI-enhanced instruction is a major barrier. Their study highlighted that while AI tools are becoming more prevalent in ELT, many teachers remain hesitant due to limited digital skills. Therefore, this highlights the need for teacher training programs that focus not just on technology adoption but also on pedagogical applications.

Beyond classroom instruction, AI is reshaping professional development for EFL teachers. Sadeghi & Richards (2021) examined AI-driven professional development programs, noting that AI can provide personalized training modules, facilitate peer learning through AI-powered networks, and automate assessment of teacher competencies. Their study suggests that institutions should integrate AI into teacher education programs, making continuous professional development more accessible and data driven.

In a broader context, AI is not only enhancing ELT practices but also redefining the learning environment. Altınay et al. (2016) discussed how AI fosters globalized learning communities, enabling collaborative online classrooms and AI-powered student interactions. Their study aligns with SAMR's redefinition stage, illustrating how AI is transforming traditional teacher-centered models into interactive, AI-driven ecosystems.

From a theoretical standpoint, Ouyang and Jiao (2021) analyzed the evolution of AI in education by categorizing it into three paradigms: AI-directed, AI-supported, and AI-empowered learning. The AI-directed paradigm, rooted in behaviorism, positions the learner as a passive recipient, with AI guiding the learning process through structured, pre-defined paths. This model mirrors early Intelligent Tutoring Systems (ITSs) that deliver content and feedback without adapting to individual learner needs. By contrast, the AI-supported paradigm follows a more interactive, constructivist approach where learners collaborate with AI systems. Here, AI dynamically adapts to learner progress, offering personalized and evolving feedback. This model is seen in adaptive learning platforms that adjust instruction based on student engagement, comprehension, and performance data.

At its most mature stage, the AI-empowered paradigm reflects a transformative level of integration, where learners take an active leadership role in their own education. As such, Ouyang and Jiao' study (2021) made a significant contribution by providing a structured framework that illustrates the shift from passive AI-directed learning to more interactive and autonomous AI-supported and AI-empowered models. This framework served as both a conceptual guide for educators and a practical roadmap for AI implementation in educational settings, helping stakeholders understand how AI can enhance learner engagement and autonomy. However, their study has certain limitations. While it presents theoretical paradigms, it lacks empirical validation across diverse educational contexts. Additionally, although it briefly discusses ethical concerns, data privacy, and algorithmic biases, these challenges are not explored in depth.

Expanding on the empirical evidence, Zhang and Aslan (2021) provided a comprehensive review of empirical studies on artificial intelligence in education (AIEd) from 1993 to 2020, analyzing 40 eligible studies from the Web of Science and specialized AIEd journals. The review highlighted AI's transformative potential in education, especially in customized learning, dynamic assessments, and interaction facilitation. Nonetheless, it noted a critical gap between AI innovations and their implementation in educational settings. The study further called for more interdisciplinary research, addressing AI ethics and privacy concerns, and emphasized the need for collaboration among educators, researchers, and AI technologists to fully leverage AI's educational benefits. They also suggest that AI technologies, such as intelligent tutoring systems and expert systems, can enhance learning outcomes but are often underutilized due to insufficient educational theory integration in AI applications. Finally, Zamri and Mohamad (2024) proposed that AI integration should not be viewed merely as a technological upgrade but as a transformation that must be aligned with pedagogical goals. Likewise, Muslimin et al. (2023) stressed the need for targeted interventions, such as digital literacy workshops and AI-specific teacher training programs, to mitigate technostress and improve teaching outcomes.

TPACK MODEL IN AI INTEGRATION

The TPACK model developed by Mishra and Koehler (2006) provides a comprehensive framework for integrating technology into teaching. The TPACK model identifies three primary knowledge areas: technological knowledge, pedagogical knowledge, and content knowledge, all of which must interact to support effective teaching. The model is especially relevant to AI integration in classrooms, as it helps educators balance their understanding of AI technologies with pedagogical strategies and content-specific knowledge.

In this context, the TPACK framework emphasizes the importance of teachers having a thorough understanding of technology and how it can be used to enhance teaching. For AI to be effectively integrated into EFL instruction, educators must develop their technical skills alongside their pedagogical expertise to create interactive and student-centered learning environments. As a guiding structure, this framework helps guide the research by framing the evaluation of teachers' technological and pedagogical capabilities when incorporating AI into language instruction. In his comprehensive analysis, Graham (2011) explored the increasing use of the model within the field of educational technology, highlighting both its strengths and critical areas needing further theoretical development.

Overall, the TPACK framework is widely recognized for its potential in conceptualizing how teachers integrate technology with pedagogical and content knowledge to improve instructional practices. Graham (2011) acknowledged the enthusiasm surrounding TPACK, as evidenced by its widespread adoption in both research and practice. However, a key issue Graham emphasized is the framework's balance between parsimony and complexity. While the TPACK model is praised for its simplicity in linking three major domains (i.e., technology, pedagogy, and content), it also conceals significant complexity beneath this surface. For instance, each of the domains is broad and often ill-defined, which complicates the task of delineating clear boundaries between them. For example, defining what constitutes "technological knowledge" has been problematic, with some researchers including basic tools like pencils and chalkboards, while others focus solely on modern digital technologies. Graham argued that without greater precision in defining TK, the framework risks becoming too vague to be meaningful.

Additionally, another area of concern is the integration versus transformation debate. The TPACK model is often depicted using a Venn diagram, suggesting that it represents the integration of distinct knowledge domains. Nevertheless, some researchers, including Angeli and Valanides (2009), argue that TPACK should be viewed as a transformative form of knowledge that is more than the sum of its parts. This debate has significant implications for how researchers conceptualize and measure TPACK (Figure 1).

Figure 1. TPACK Model representing the integration of distinct knowledge domains

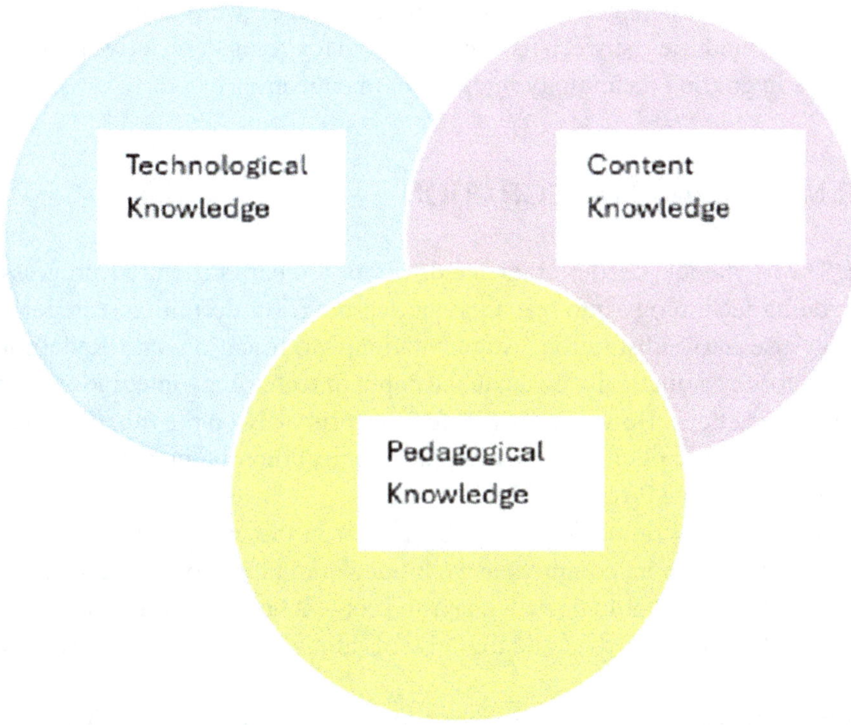

Furthermore, Graham also critiqued the boundaries between TPACK's constructs, noting that researchers often struggle to distinguish between overlapping areas such as Technological Pedagogical Knowledge (TPK) and Technological Content Knowledge (TCK). He argued that without clearer boundaries, studies on TPACK may fail to contribute to a cohesive body of knowledge, as they risk conflating different aspects of teacher knowledge without sufficiently distinguishing their unique contributions. Moreover, Graham addressed the framework's prescriptive value, or lack thereof. While TPACK has been useful in describing the complex interactions between technology, pedagogy, and content, it has been less effective in guiding instructional interventions or predicting outcomes. As a result, Graham suggested that more work is needed to understand how educators can develop TPACK and how the framework can be used to improve teaching practices.

For this reason, integrating the Substitution, Augmentation, Modification, and Redefinition (SAMR) model with the Technological Pedagogical Content Knowledge (TPACK) framework in this study could be highly beneficial, particularly in addressing some of the limitations identified by Graham (2011). While complementary in purpose, TPACK provides a theoretical lens to understand the interplay between technology, pedagogy, and content knowledge; it has been critiqued for lacking clear boundaries between its constructs and for being descriptive rather than prescriptive in guiding technology integration in education.

SAMR MODEL IN AI INTEGRATION

The SAMR model, on the other hand, offers a clear, structured progression for integrating technology into teaching and learning. By definition, categorizing technology use into Substitution, Augmentation, Modification, and Redefinition helps educators systematically evaluate the depth of technology integration in their instructional practices. However, SAMR focuses primarily on the functional use of technology without explicitly addressing pedagogical or content-related considerations, an area where TPACK excels.

Therefore, by integrating SAMR with TPACK in the current study, educators could benefit from a more comprehensive framework that not only explains the relationships between technology, pedagogy, and content but also guides instructional interventions by positioning AI and digital tools along a progressive continuum of integration.

Moreover, this integration could help address Graham's concern that TPACK lacks predictive power for guiding instructional improvements. Specifically, by using SAMR's hierarchical structure alongside TPACK's multidimensional knowledge framework, educators can be better supported in progressing toward deeper, transformative AI integration rather than remaining at surface-level technology adoption. Thus, combining SAMR with TPACK would not only clarify the instructional role of AI and digital tools but also ensure that technology is meaningfully aligned with pedagogical objectives, creating a structured yet flexible approach for AI integration in English language teaching.

Exploring the theoretical underpinnings, Zamri and Mohamad (2024) analyzed the role of the SAMR model in education, arguing that as technology becomes more prevalent in classrooms, structured models like SAMR provide a valuable guide for educators, helping them transition from merely replacing traditional tools with digital alternatives to fundamentally transforming the learning process. Their study emphasized that while substitution and augmentation represent the initial phases of technology integration, true pedagogical transformation occurs at the modification and redefinition stages, where technology enables new ways of learning that were previously impossible. Nonetheless, this study also highlighted criticisms of the model, particularly its rigid hierarchical structure, which may not always align with the varying technological competencies of educators. The authors advocated for a more adaptable approach, ensuring that technology is implemented with clear pedagogical intent rather than for the sake of innovation alone.

Complementing this theoretical exploration, Muslimin et al. (2023) found that while EFL lecturers in Indonesia were confident in their pedagogical and content knowledge, many lacked technological skills, hindering effective AI integration. Lower digital literacy was linked to higher technostress, and most lecturers used AI at basic substitution or augmentation levels, with few achieving deeper pedagogical transformation.

The findings from Zamri and Mohamad (2024) and Muslimin et al. (2023) underscore the challenges of AI integration in ELT. While the SAMR model offers a structured lens for evaluating technology use, its linear classification may not reflect the diverse digital competencies among educators. Zamri and Mohamad (2024) noted that the model assumes a progressive trajectory that doesn't align with real-world variations in digital literacy. Similarly, Muslimin et al. (2023) found that many educators remain at the augmentation stage due to limited training and elevated technostress. Their study highlights the critical need for institutional support and targeted professional development to enable teachers to adopt AI meaningfully. Without such support, rapid technological change may heighten stress and hinder teaching performance.

The role of SAMR as a framework for AI integration in ELT is further examined in these studies, revealing both its potential benefits and inherent limitations. At the lower levels of integration, substitution and augmentation, AI tools such as speech recognition software, chatbots, and automated grading systems serve as enhancements to existing teaching methods. However, the transition to modification and redefinition requires a shift in pedagogical approach, where AI is not just an aid but a fundamental component of the learning experience. This shift is particularly challenging for educators who lack digital literacy, as shown in the study by Muslimin et al. (2023), which highlighted the difficulties faced by EFL lecturers in navigating AI-driven learning environments. Their findings suggest that while AI holds great promise for personalizing instruction and enhancing student engagement, its successful implementation depends on bridging the gap between digital competence and pedagogical application.

Ultimately, combining SAMR with TPACK allows this study to not only identify whether teachers have the necessary technological and pedagogical competencies to integrate AI but also to evaluate the effectiveness and depth of AI application in language instruction. In doing so, this dual-framework approach ensures a holistic analysis of AI integration, highlighting both educators' technological readiness and the extent to which AI is enhancing or transforming EFL teaching and learning.

RECENT STUDIES ON AI IN EFL EDUCATION

As AI technologies continue to gain ground in educational settings, the demand for practical, context-sensitive strategies to integrate AI into EFL instruction has become increasingly urgent. In response to this need, Bykonia (2025) addressed this need through a case study conducted at the Penitentiary Academy of Ukraine, where she explored AI's role in professional English learning. Her study demonstrated how tools like intelligent tutoring systems and speech technologies can foster individualized learning pathways in highly specialized contexts. At the same time, she also highlighted critical constraints such as limited teacher training and the ethical use of learner data, laying the foundation for broader discussions on preparedness and institutional support.

Building on these concerns, Chan and Tang (2024) applied the TPACK model to assess English teachers' readiness and training needs for AI integration in Hong Kong. Their findings showed that while teachers are aware of AI's potential, they often lack the pedagogical and information literacy required for effective classroom application. These insights reinforce Bykonia's (2025) argument that successful AI use demands more than access to technology; it requires strategic training focused on aligning pedagogical goals with technological capabilities.

This need for deeper professional development is echoed in Kohnke, Moorhouse, and Zou's (2023) case study on university language instructors' preparedness to adopt generative AI. Their results indicate variable levels of teacher confidence and competence, with many expressing a need for more support in understanding how tools like ChatGPT can meaningfully enhance teaching and learning. Notably, these findings expand the TPACK discourse by emphasizing not only the technical and pedagogical aspects but also emotional readiness and digital confidence, especially as roles shift from knowledge delivery to facilitation.

Further contextualizing this shift, Kohnke and Ulla (2024) examined the perspectives of English instructors in Thai higher education. Their study showed that while instructors value generative AI for enhancing academic writing and reducing workload, they were also concerned about student over-reliance and ethical implications. The authors advocated for redefining teacher roles and strengthening ethical and pedagogical frameworks to ensure that AI use supports, not supplants, critical thinking and creativity. This aligns with Chan and Tang's (2024) call for evolving pedagogical models and positions teachers as central agents in managing AI's impact.

Expanding the discussion to include institutional and curricular transformation, Krisbiantoro and Ashari (2024) reviewed how the SAMR model can guide deeper ICT and AI integration in tertiary EFL settings. Their analysis revealed that most implementations remain in the lower stages of substitution and augmentation, largely due to resistance to change and inadequate support systems. Consequently, this reinforces the earlier studies' shared conclusion: that for AI to be transformative, institutions must go beyond tool adoption and invest in long-term pedagogical innovation and teacher empowerment.

Together, these interrelated studies suggest that AI's potential in EFL education can only be fully realized through a strategic blend of targeted professional development, pedagogical redefinition, ethical awareness, and supportive infrastructure. From highly specific contexts like penitentiary education (Bykonia, 2025) to broader regional perspectives in Asia (Kohnke & Ulla, 2024; Chan & Tang, 2024), the consensus is clear: AI integration must be grounded in thoughtful, adaptive, and teacher-centered practices to genuinely enhance language learning outcomes.

PRACTICAL STRATEGIES FOR AI INTEGRATION, CHALLENGES, AND ETHICAL CONSIDERATIONS

As AI technologies continue to influence educational paradigms, practical strategies for integrating these tools into EFL instruction are essential for educators seeking to align with modern pedagogical demands. Georgieva (2025) offered a comprehensive set of task-based strategies for incorporating free or low-cost AI tools, such as ChatGPT, Speechace, and Newsela, in both EFL and ESP (English for Specific Purposes) contexts. Her study emphasized how AI enhanced learner autonomy and engagement, especially in adult education, through immediate feedback mechanisms and multimedia interaction. The use of AI in this context supported personalized learning and reflection, demonstrating practical ways to bridge theory and classroom application through adaptive learning technologies.

Extending this perspective into teacher training, Pitura et al. (2024) investigated the use of AI-integrated Virtual Reality (VR) simulations in preparing pre-service EFL teachers to apply content knowledge. Drawing on Cognitive Flexibility Theory, the study illustrated how immersive VR-AI environments enhanced pedagogical competence, allowing teacher candidates to practice and reflect on real-world scenarios. This hands-on strategy not only improved instructional readiness but also showcased AI's potential to simulate complex teaching dynamics in a low-risk setting, providing a replicable model for teacher education programs globally.

Focusing more specifically on teacher beliefs and preparedness, Babanoğlu et al. (2025) adopted a reflexive thematic analysis approach to explore the conceptualizations of prospective EFL teachers regarding AI's role in language instruction. The participants advocated for a "human-centered" AI model that emphasized teacher-AI collaboration rather than replacement. Their findings stressed the need for ethical awareness and professional development, underscoring that effective AI strategies had to be rooted in human agency and pedagogical context, not merely technological novelty.

Complementing these insights, Metwally and Bin-Hady (2025) explored the necessity of structured AI integration training for Saudi EFL educators. Their mixed-methods study identified a strong demand for AI-related professional development, revealing that such training significantly enhanced teachers' capabilities in maintaining student engagement, ensuring data ethics, and aligning instruction with 21st-century educational goals. The study advocated for national-level policies and institutional programs to equip educators with AI competencies essential for practical classroom application.

These findings converged with strategies identified by Resyadi (2025), who focused on novice teachers navigating the AI landscape. He highlighted a gap between AI's potential and its application due to low digital literacy and lack of scaffolding. However, when supported with targeted training and tool-specific guidance, novice teachers reported higher engagement and more efficient lesson planning, reinforcing the practicality of structured onboarding in AI for EFL teaching.

Together, these studies presented a cohesive narrative: practical AI integration in EFL education hinged not only on tool availability but also on pedagogical alignment, professional development, and ethical literacy. Whether enhancing learner autonomy (Georgieva, 2025), simulating real teaching experiences (Pitura et al., 2024), or reshaping teacher beliefs and competencies (Babanoğlu et al., 2025; Metwally & Bin-Hady, 2025), these strategies collectively suggested that sustainable AI adoption required a multifaceted, human-centered approach tailored to real classroom needs.

The integration of AI into EFL education introduced both transformative opportunities and substantial challenges. Benek (2025) conducted a comprehensive study exploring the perceptions of EFL learners and teachers regarding AI-powered language learning technologies. The findings highlighted that while learners generally perceived AI tools as highly personalized and beneficial for language acquisition, teachers expressed significant concerns about compatibility with existing curricular standards, ethical implications, and the dehumanization of the educational experience. Notably, issues such as data privacy, lack of alignment with national education standards, and insufficient teacher training created systemic barriers that hindered the effective use of AI in classroom settings. This research underscored the pressing need for professional development, ethical guidelines, and more adaptable technological infrastructures to support EFL educators in AI implementation.

In a related study, Resyadi (2025) delved specifically into the experiences of novice EFL teachers, revealing that while they recognized AI's potential to enhance lesson planning and student engagement, they struggled with limited digital literacy, inadequate infrastructure, and contextual mismatches between AI-generated content and local classroom realities. The study pointed to a lack of structured training as a major impediment, with many teachers expressing uncertainty about prompt engineering and concerns about students' over-reliance on AI tools. These findings complement Benek's (2025) work by focusing on early-career educators, who often face compounded challenges due to inexperience. Taken together, the studies provided a nuanced understanding of the barriers to AI integration in EFL education, emphasizing the importance of institutional support, ethical AI literacy, and context-sensitive training initiatives to bridge the gap between AI's potential and its practical use in diverse EFL environments.

As AI became increasingly embedded in educational practices, particularly in EFL contexts, critical ethical considerations emerged concerning data privacy, algorithmic bias, and the evolving role of educators and learners within AI-mediated environments. Kayyali (2025) presented a foundational critique of the ethical implications of generative AI in education, particularly emphasizing how data privacy, algorithmic bias, and academic integrity were jeopardized when AI systems were deployed without proper oversight. His work underlined the urgency of designing responsible policies and frameworks that involve educators, developers, and policymakers alike. The chapter highlighted how ethical breaches could lead to systemic marginalization of students, especially in language-rich domains like EFL, where nuanced human judgment was crucial.

Building on this, Kehinde-Awoyele and Adeowu (2024) explored Nigerian students' perceptions of AI in Social Studies education, drawing parallels to the EFL context through similar concerns about algorithmic transparency, data usage, and the potential dehumanization of learning. Their findings revealed that while AI enhanced academic outcomes, unresolved ethical issues, especially surrounding privacy and trust, diminished students' confidence in these systems. They advocated for integrating ethical AI discourse within the curriculum itself to foster a critically informed student body.

From a practical standpoint, Mishara (2024) examined how AI systems in education could inadvertently amplify societal inequalities through biased algorithms and insufficient accountability. In the context of EFL, these biases might have affected language assessment systems, privileging dominant dialects or cultural references. Mishara emphasized the need for explainable AI and enforceable ethical governance to protect student rights and foster equitable learning environments.

Adding a philosophical dimension, Nurhasanah and Nugraha (2024) contrasted AI's benefits, such as personalized learning and automation, with its ethical drawbacks, including diminished human interaction and algorithmic discrimination. Their literature-based inquiry suggested that AI's alignment with constructivist pedagogies could have supported EFL instruction, yet without humanist safeguards, it risked eroding essential interpersonal elements of language learning.

Finally, Chris, Kate, and Frank (2024) emphasized the dual nature of generative AI, acknowledging its capacity to personalize education while cautioning against deepened inequities and dependence on opaque systems. They proposed ethical frameworks that balanced innovation with accountability, especially pertinent in EFL contexts where access to AI tools might have been unevenly distributed. Their work advocated for transparent AI deployment to ensure that language learners were not further disadvantaged by digital divides or hidden algorithmic decisions.

Most existing studies examined TPACK and SAMR separately, often in relation to general ICT tools rather than artificial intelligence. This chapter addressed this gap by integrating TPACK's knowledge-based structure with SAMR's implementation-oriented stages, offering a dual-layered lens to better understand and support AI integration in EFL contexts. Unlike prior work, which often focused on general ICT tools, this study was situated specifically in the context of AI technologies, including generative tools like ChatGPT and AI-assisted writing platforms, which posed new pedagogical and ethical challenges. The combined model allowed for both diagnosing teacher preparedness and guiding instructional transformation, making it especially relevant for AI, where teachers had to navigate complex intersections of content, pedagogy, and evolving technologies. This integrative approach offered both theoretical depth and practical relevance, contributing a novel perspective to the existing literature.

As such, this study contributes to language education by offering a dual-framework approach, combining TPACK and SAMR, that enables educators to navigate AI integration with both theoretical depth and practical relevance, ultimately supporting informed pedagogical decision-making and ethical classroom implementation.

METHODOLOGY

This study employed a descriptive quantitative research design to investigate the integration of AI tools in EFL instruction, with a particular focus on the Substitution, Augmentation, Modification, and Redefinition (SAMR) model as a framework for AI adoption. By structuring the inquiry around a well-established model, the objective was to examine educators' experiences with AI, evaluate the pedagogical benefits and challenges of AI integration, and assess the extent to which AI enhances teaching effectiveness and student engagement. Through this approach, the study provided a comprehensive understanding of AI's role in EFL classrooms from the perspective of experienced educators.

Participants

The study included 32 EFL educators who are staff members at the College of Languages and Translation, King Khalid University in Saudi Arabia. These participants represented a diverse range of teaching backgrounds and experiences, offering valuable insights into AI integration in language instruction. Among them, 15 educators had over 15 years of teaching experience, 10 educators had between 10 and 15 years of experience, and 7 educators had between 5 and 10 years of experience.

This distribution allowed for comparative insights across various stages of professional development. As faculty members, these educators brought perspectives from higher education settings, allowing the study to examine how AI technologies are incorporated into university-level language instruction. Moreover, the variation in teaching experience facilitated an exploration of how educators at different career stages perceive and implement AI-driven tools in their teaching, as well as the challenges they encounter in adopting AI-enhanced methodologies. This diverse sample ensured that the study captured a comprehensive understanding of AI integration across various levels of expertise and instructional approaches within the College of Languages and Translation.

Ethical approval and informed consent was collected from all participants. To uphold ethical integrity and enhance the trustworthiness of findings, member checking was conducted by sharing preliminary findings with participants to confirm interpretations.

Data Collection

Data were collected using a structured questionnaire, designed to gather quantitative data from participants regarding their familiarity with AI tools, teaching strategies, and perceived challenges. The questionnaire was divided into three key sections, each addressing specific aspects of AI integration in EFL instruction. This division allowed for a targeted and systematic exploration of key research dimensions.

The first section, Technological Understanding and Experience, examined educators' digital literacy skills and their familiarity with AI applications in language teaching. Participants were asked about their experience with AI-powered tools such as chatbots, automated grading systems, speech recognition software, and adaptive learning platforms. These questions were aimed at uncovering the technological baseline of participants. This section further helped assess whether AI use among EFL educators was aligned with the TPACK-SAMR frameworks and whether technology integration varied based on teaching experience.

The second section, Pedagogical Impact of AI Tools, focused on how AI technologies influenced teaching strategies and student engagement. Participants evaluated the extent to which AI improved lesson delivery, provided personalized instruction, facilitated interactive learning, and enhanced assessment methods. In addition to technical implementation, the section also explored how AI integration altered classroom dynamics, particularly in relation to learner autonomy and real-time feedback.

The third section, Challenges in AI Integration, sought to identify the barriers educators face when incorporating AI into their teaching. These challenges included limited access to AI tools, insufficient training, and the impact of technostress on teaching performance. A Likert scale was used to measure participants' agreement with various statements regarding AI's impact on teaching effectiveness, student engagement, and professional development. By capturing perceived obstacles, this section offered crucial insights into the support systems required for successful AI implementation.

The research instrument, a structured questionnaire, was developed using established constructs from previous TPACK and SAMR studies and tailored to address the specific context of AI integration in EFL instruction. To ensure content validity and clarity, the questionnaire was reviewed by two experts in educational technology and one experienced EFL teacher educator. Their feedback informed revisions to enhance the alignment of the items with the study's objectives and to improve the overall clarity and relevance. A small-scale pilot test with two participants was conducted to assess the comprehensibility and appropriateness of the items, thereby contributing to the reliability of the instrument.

Data Analysis

The data were analyzed using SPSS software, employing descriptive statistical methods such as frequency distributions, standard deviations, percentages, and mean scores to summarize participants' responses. This analysis provided insights into the trends of AI adoption, variations in digital literacy, and educators' perceptions of AI as an enhancement or transformation of their teaching methods. The frequency distribution helped in understanding the overall agreement or disagreement levels regarding AI integration, while the mean scores and standard deviations indicated the extent of consensus or variability among respondents.

Higher standard deviations in some responses suggested diverse levels of AI proficiency, whereas consistent mean scores reflected a general consensus on AI's potential in education. These statistical patterns helped pinpoint specific areas of strength and concern. The analysis also highlighted areas where faculty members require more training and support to effectively utilize AI tools in digital language teaching. Thus, the findings not only reflect current practices but also inform future directions for professional development and institutional support.

RESULTS

The distribution of responses regarding educators' technical skills for AI technology reveals that 40.6% of respondents agree that they possess the necessary technical skills, while 18.8% strongly agree, indicating that a majority (59.4%) feel confident in their AI proficiency. However, a significant portion (37.5%) disagrees, suggesting that over a third of the participants feel they lack adequate technical expertise. Additionally, 3.1% strongly disagree, highlighting a small yet notable group that may require substantial training and support.

These findings indicate that while a majority of educators perceive themselves as technically competent, a considerable percentage still experience challenges in AI integration, emphasizing the need for targeted digital literacy programs and professional development initiatives to bridge this gap (Fig 2).

Figure 2. Educators' technical skills for AI technology integration

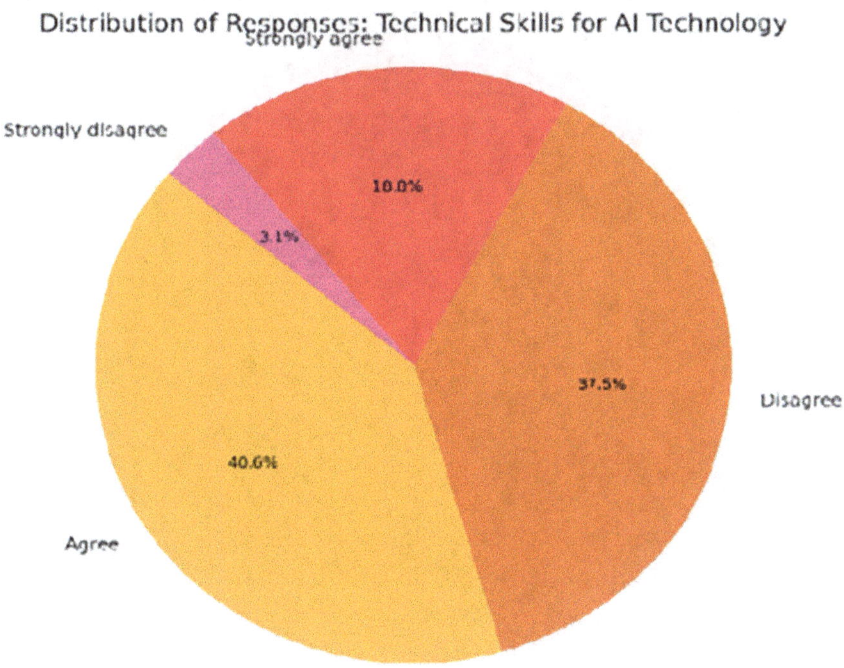

Expanding the analysis to perceptions of AI's educational value, the analysis of responses to the question "AI Applications in Smart Educational Systems" reveals a predominantly positive perception of AI's role in modernizing education. A significant majority (71.9%) agreed, while an additional 12.5% strongly agreed, bringing the total positive responses to 84.4%. This suggests that most participants recognize the benefits of AI-driven educational systems, which enhance adaptive learning, automation, and data-driven instruction in classroom settings. However, 15.6% of respondents remained neutral, indicating that some educators may be uncertain about AI's impact or have limited experience with AI applications in educational environments. Importantly, the absence of disagreement in the responses highlights a consensus on AI's positive influence in enhancing smart learning systems.

Taken together, these findings suggest that while AI is widely regarded as an essential component of smart education, additional efforts may be required to increase awareness, accessibility, and training to ensure that all educators feel confident in leveraging AI-driven tools for improved teaching and learning outcomes (Figure 3).

Figure 3. AI application in Smart Education system

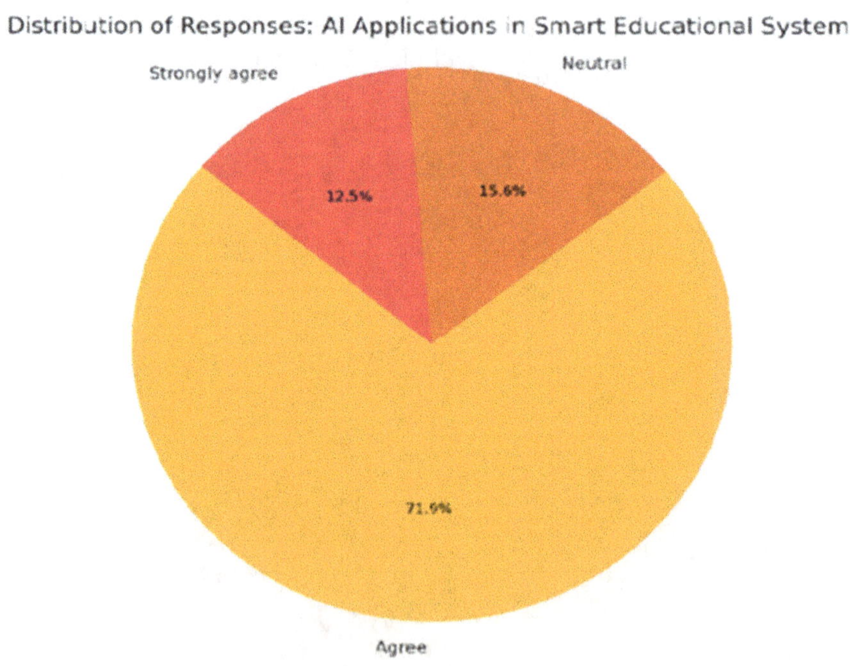

Turning to student engagement, the analysis of responses to the question "Impact of AI Tools on Student Motivation in Language Learning" indicates a predominantly positive perception of AI's role in fostering student engagement. A majority of respondents (53.1%) agreed, while an additional 3.1% strongly agreed, bringing the total positive responses to 56.2%. This suggests that AI-driven tools, such as gamified learning platforms, interactive feedback systems, and adaptive learning technologies, contribute to enhancing student motivation by making learning more engaging, interactive, and personalized.

Despite this optimism, 34.4% of respondents remained neutral, indicating that a significant proportion of educators were uncertain about the extent to which AI enhances student motivation. This could suggest limited exposure to AI tools, uncertainty about their long-term effectiveness, or a lack of direct evidence in classroom settings. Additionally, 9.4% disagreed, and 3.1% strongly disagreed, suggesting that a small percentage of educators did not perceive AI as a motivational factor in language learning, possibly due to concerns about over-reliance on technology, lack of human interaction, or ineffective AI implementation.

As a result, these findings indicate that while AI is widely recognized as a beneficial tool for increasing motivation in language learning, further training, research, and targeted implementation may be needed to help educators fully understand and utilize AI's motivational potential in EFL instruction (Figure 4).

Figure 4. The impact of AI tools on students' motivation

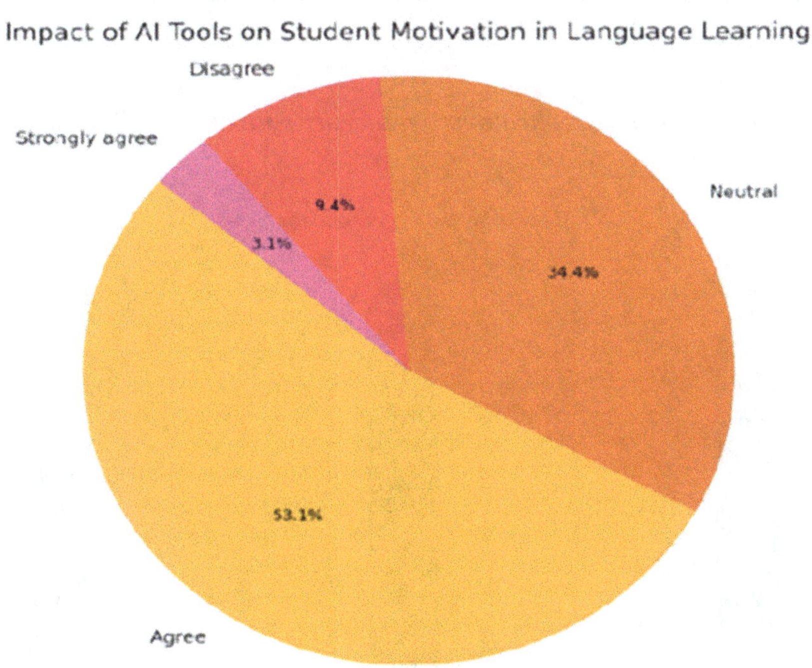

When examining skill-specific outcomes, the analysis of responses to questions regarding the impact of AI applications on students' speaking, reading, and writing skills in English indicates a predominantly positive perception among participants. A majority of respondents either “Agree” or “Strongly agree” that AI enhances students’ abilities in these areas, with a higher agreement observed for reading and writing skills compared to speaking. This suggests that AI-powered tools such as grammar checkers, automated essay scoring systems, and reading comprehension platforms are perceived as particularly effective in supporting written and reading-based language learning.

Nevertheless, while a strong consensus exists for speaking skills, the slightly lower agreement rate implies that AI's effectiveness in improving spoken English may not be as widely recognized or utilized as in reading and writing. A small percentage of respondents remain neutral or disagree, indicating that some educators or students may have limited exposure to AI tools for language learning or perceive them as less effective in enhancing fluency and pronunciation.

Therefore, these findings suggest that while AI plays a significant role in developing students' reading and writing abilities, further research and development may be needed to enhance AI-driven speaking tools, such as conversational AI, speech recognition, and real-time pronunciation feedback, to maximize its impact on spoken English proficiency (Figure 5).

Figure 5. The impact of AI applications on students' speaking, reading, and writing skills

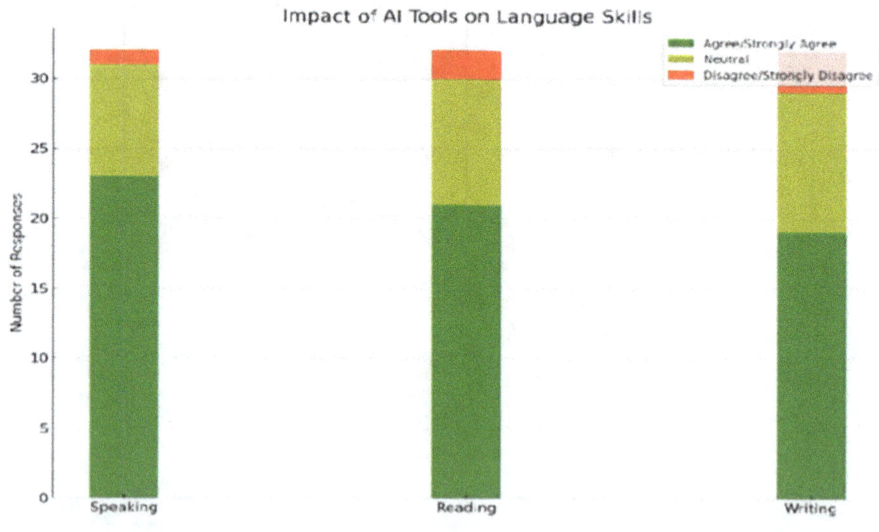

The analysis of responses to the question "AI applications enhance students' skill of listening to English" indicates a strong positive perception of AI's role in improving listening skills. A majority of respondents either "Agree" or "Strongly agree" that AI tools effectively support students in developing their listening comprehension abilities. This suggests that AI-powered platforms, such as speech recognition software, automated transcription tools, and interactive listening exercises, are recognized as valuable resources for improving auditory processing and comprehension in English learning.

At the same time, a smaller proportion of respondents remain neutral or disagree, indicating that some educators or learners may either have limited exposure to AI-driven listening tools or perceive their effectiveness as inconsistent. The presence of neutral and disagreeing responses suggests that while AI is generally accepted as beneficial for listening skill development, further efforts may be needed to increase awareness and adoption of AI-driven listening technologies, ensuring that students can maximize their learning outcomes through these digital tools (figure 6).

Figure 6.AI applications enhance students' skill of listening to English

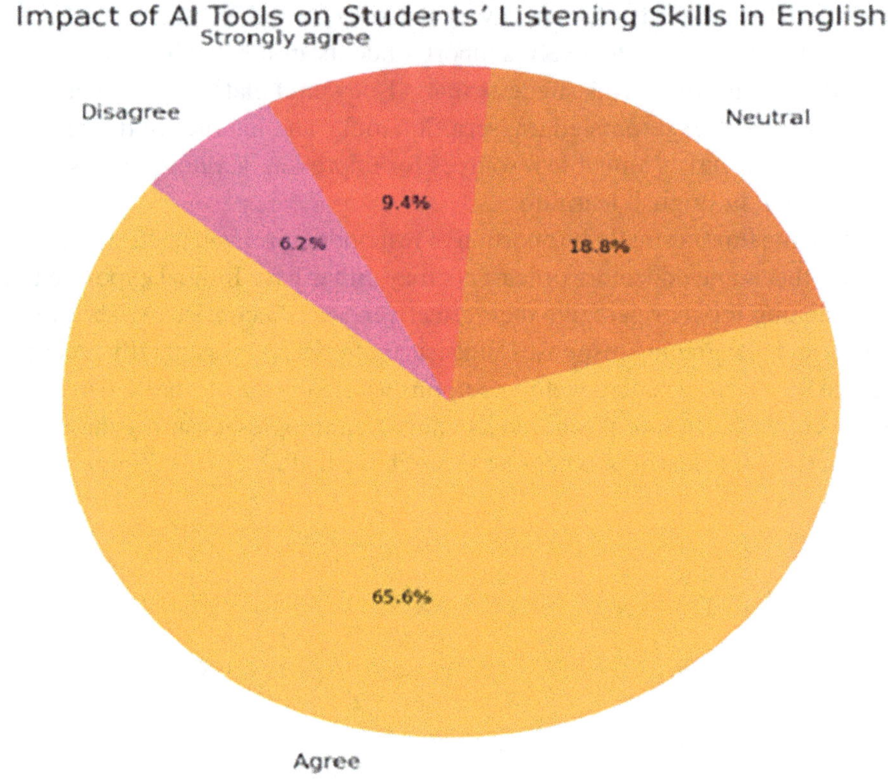

Further reinforcing these patterns, the analysis of responses to the question "AI applications enhance students' ability to write in English" reveals a strong positive perception of AI's impact on writing skills. A significant majority (65.6%) agree, while an additional 9.4% strongly agree, bringing the total positive responses to 75%. This indicates that AI-powered tools, such as automated grammar checkers, plagiarism detectors, and AI-based writing assistants, are widely perceived as effective in enhancing students' writing abilities by providing real-time feedback and structural improvements.

Extending this discussion, the analysis of faculty perceptions regarding AI's role in English language learning reveals an overall positive outlook, with notable variations across different language skills. AI applications are widely acknowledged for their effectiveness in enhancing students' writing skills, with 59.3% of respondents expressing agreement. This suggests that AI-powered tools such as grammar checkers and writing assistants are seen as valuable resources for improving written communication. However, the relatively high percentage of neutral responses (31.2%) highlights the need for greater familiarity and training in utilizing these technologies effectively.

Similarly, AI's impact on reading skills is perceived positively, with 65.6% of respondents agreeing that AI tools aid in reading development. The effectiveness of text-to-speech software and adaptive learning applications is well recognized, yet 28.1% of participants remain neutral, indicating some uncertainty about AI's role in improving reading comprehension. This neutrality may stem from a lack of exposure to AI-driven reading tools or limited evidence of their effectiveness in fostering deeper comprehension and critical reading abilities.

In terms of speaking skills, AI-driven tools such as pronunciation assessment software and conversational AI chatbots receive strong support, with 65.6% of respondents acknowledging their benefits. However, a quarter of participants (25.0%) remain neutral, suggesting some hesitation regarding AI's ability to replace traditional speaking practice. The presence of skeptics (9.4% disagree, 3.1% strongly disagree) highlights concerns about AI's ability to provide effective feedback comparable to human interaction, reinforcing the need for improvements in AI-based pronunciation and conversation tools.

Beyond skill development, the overall impact of AI on the learning experience in classrooms also garners positive feedback, with 56.2% of respondents agreeing that AI enhances engagement and individualized instruction. However, uncertainty remains, as 21.9% express neutrality, possibly due to inconsistent AI integration in different teaching environments. Additionally, 18.8% of respondents disagree, and 3.1% strongly disagree, signaling concerns about AI's effectiveness, potential technical limitations, and the need for more structured implementation.

Collectively, these findings suggest that while AI is generally viewed as a valuable tool in language education, there is still room for improvement in terms of awareness, accessibility, and training. Addressing skepticism through teacher development programs, refining AI-driven feedback mechanisms, and ensuring reliable AI implementation can help maximize its potential. Future research should focus on optimizing AI tools to provide more personalized, interactive, and effective support across various language learning domains.

In addition, the analysis of responses to the question "AI tools impact students' attention levels in the classroom" reveals a predominantly positive perception of AI's role in maintaining student focus during lessons. A significant majority (71.9%) agree that AI technologies contribute to sustaining students' attention, suggesting that AI-driven interactive learning platforms, gamification techniques, and adaptive learning systems are effective in engaging students and keeping them focused.

However, 21.9% of respondents remain neutral, indicating that some educators or learners are uncertain about the extent of AI's influence on attention levels. This could be due to variability in AI implementation, differences in students' adaptability to AI-driven instruction, or the balance between AI-enhanced engagement and potential distractions. Meanwhile, 6.2% of respondents disagree, reflecting a small percentage of skepticism regarding AI's ability to improve students' attention span effectively.

Thus, these findings suggest that while AI is generally viewed as a valuable tool for enhancing classroom engagement and attention levels, further research and practical applications may be needed to optimize AI-driven teaching methods for different learning styles. Increasing educator awareness and providing targeted training on how to effectively integrate AI into classroom management strategies could help maximize its potential in fostering sustained student attention (Figure 7).

Figure 7. AI tools impact students' attention levels in the classroom

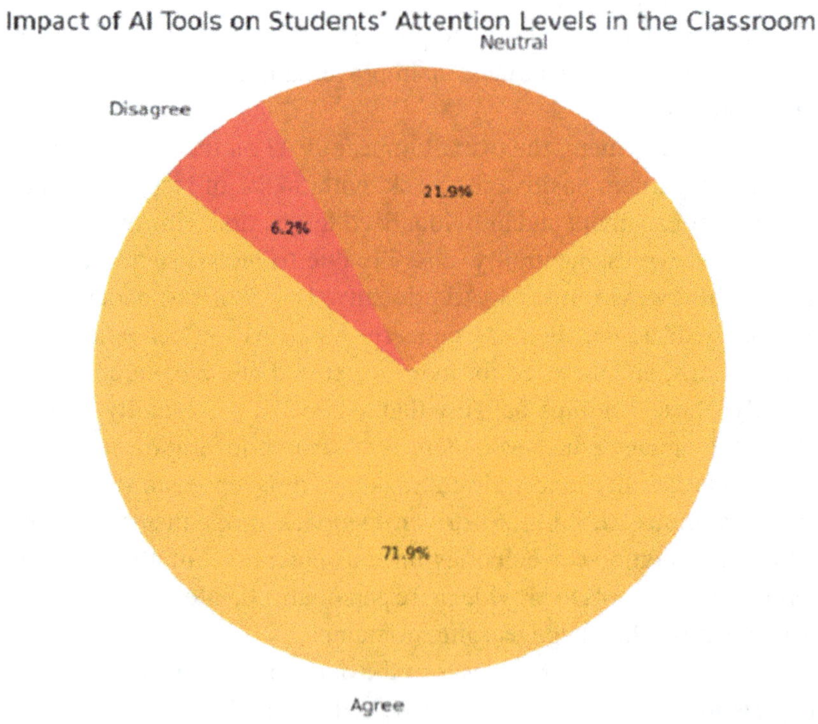

The analysis of responses to the question "Impact of AI Tools on Interactive Activities in EFL Teaching" reveals a strong positive perception of AI's role in fostering interactive learning. A majority of respondents (62.5%) agree, while an additional

9.4% strongly agree, bringing the total positive responses to 71.9%. This indicates a clear trend in favor of AI's contribution to engagement, suggesting that AI-powered tools, such as chatbots, virtual reality simulations, gamified learning platforms, and adaptive learning technologies, are perceived as effective in enhancing interactive engagement in English as a Foreign Language (EFL) classrooms. However, 25.0% of respondents remain neutral, indicating that a significant portion of educators or learners may be uncertain about AI's effectiveness in promoting interactive activities. This could stem from limited experience with AI-driven engagement strategies, lack of access to interactive AI tools, or variations in classroom integration methods. Meanwhile, 3.1% strongly disagree, and 9.4% disagree, suggesting a small percentage of skepticism, possibly due to concerns about AI replacing traditional interactive methods or challenges in effectively implementing AI-driven activities.

Taken together, these findings suggest that while AI is widely recognized for enhancing interactivity in EFL teaching, further research, training, and practical demonstrations may be needed to bridge the gap for those who remain neutral or skeptical. Increasing access to AI-driven interactive tools and providing targeted training for educators could help maximize AI's potential in fostering engaging and immersive language learning experiences (Figure 8).

Figure 8. Impact of AI Tools on Interactive Activities in EFL Teaching

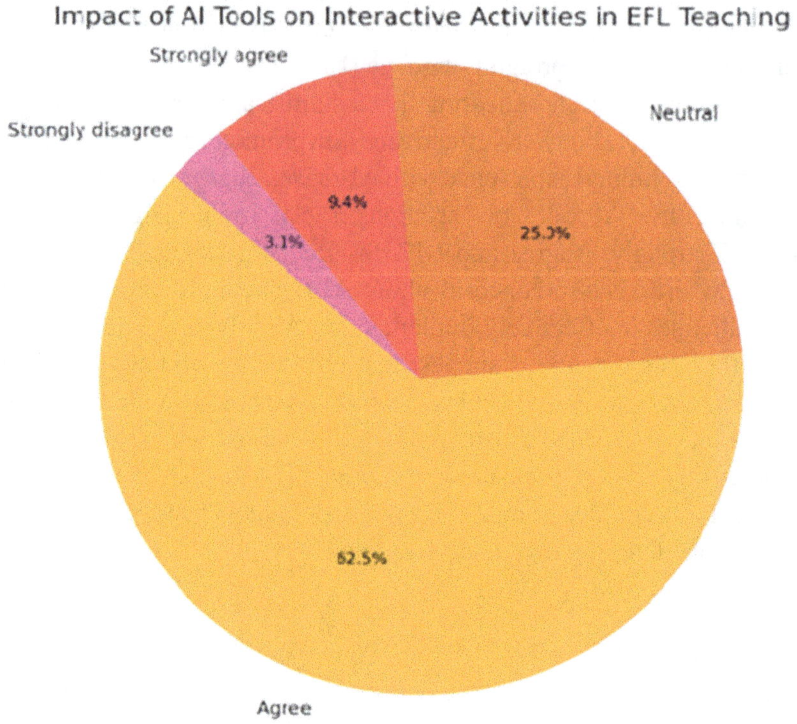

Building on the previous finding, the analysis of responses to the question "Impact of AI Tools on Teaching Strategies in EFL" reveals a strong positive perception of AI's role in shaping teaching methodologies for English as a Foreign Language (EFL). A majority of respondents (68.8%) agree, while an additional 9.4% strongly agree, bringing the total positive responses to 78.2%. This indicates substantial confidence among educators that AI-powered tools enhance instructional strategies by helping personalize lessons, automate assessments, and provide adaptive learning experiences for students.

However, 12.5% of respondents remain neutral, suggesting that a portion of educators may not yet be fully convinced of AI's effectiveness in improving teaching methods. This could be due to limited hands-on experience with AI tools, lack of institutional support for AI integration, or concerns about AI replacing traditional pedagogical approaches. Meanwhile, 6.2% disagree, and 3.1% strongly disagree, indicating a small but relevant level of skepticism regarding AI's influence on teaching strategies, possibly due to technical challenges, resistance to change, or concerns about AI's impact on teacher autonomy.

Therefore, these findings suggest that while AI is generally seen as a valuable asset in modernizing EFL teaching strategies, further professional development and training programs may be needed to equip educators with the necessary skills and confidence to integrate AI effectively into their instructional practices. Addressing concerns related to pedagogical alignment, accessibility, and teacher support could further enhance AI's acceptance and utilization in EFL education (figure 9).

Figure 9. Impact of AI Tools on Teaching Strategies in EFL

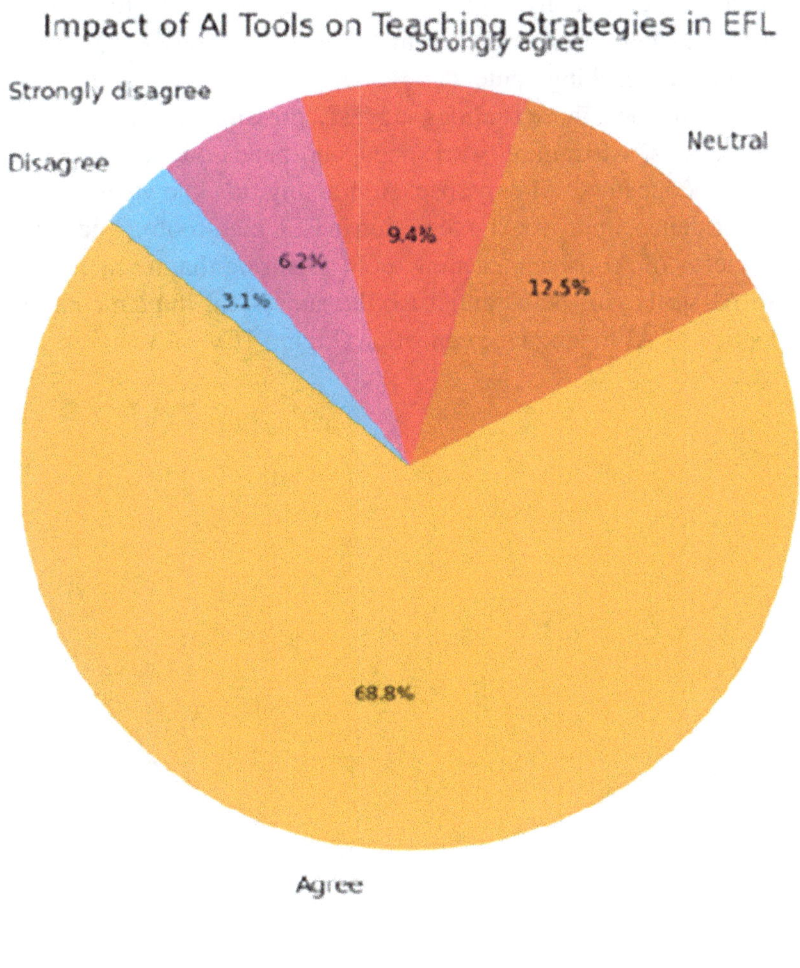

Shifting the focus to educator competence, the analysis of responses to the question "Expertise in AI Tools for EFL Teaching" reveals a diverse range of opinions regarding educators' proficiency in using AI for English as a Foreign Language (EFL) instruction. A total of 40.6% of respondents agree or strongly agree that they possess the necessary expertise, with 34.4% agreeing and 6.2% strongly agreeing.

Despite this, this suggests that while some educators feel confident in their ability to use AI tools in teaching, this percentage is relatively low compared to other areas of AI integration in education. However, 25.0% of respondents disagree and 15.6% strongly disagree, meaning that 40.6% of educators feel they lack the necessary expertise in AI tools for EFL teaching. This highlights a significant gap in AI literacy and proficiency among teachers, which could hinder effective AI implementation in language instruction. Additionally, 18.8% of respondents remain neutral, indicating that a portion of educators may be uncertain about their AI skills or have limited exposure to AI tools in teaching contexts.

In light of these insights, these findings suggest a pressing need for professional development programs, AI training workshops, and hands-on experience opportunities to enhance educators' AI expertise. Addressing this knowledge gap could help increase confidence, improve AI integration in EFL classrooms, and maximize the potential benefits of AI-driven teaching tools. Ensuring that teachers are well-equipped with AI skills will be essential for the successful implementation and long-term adoption of AI in language education (Figure 10).

Figure 10. Expertise in AI Tools for EFL Teaching

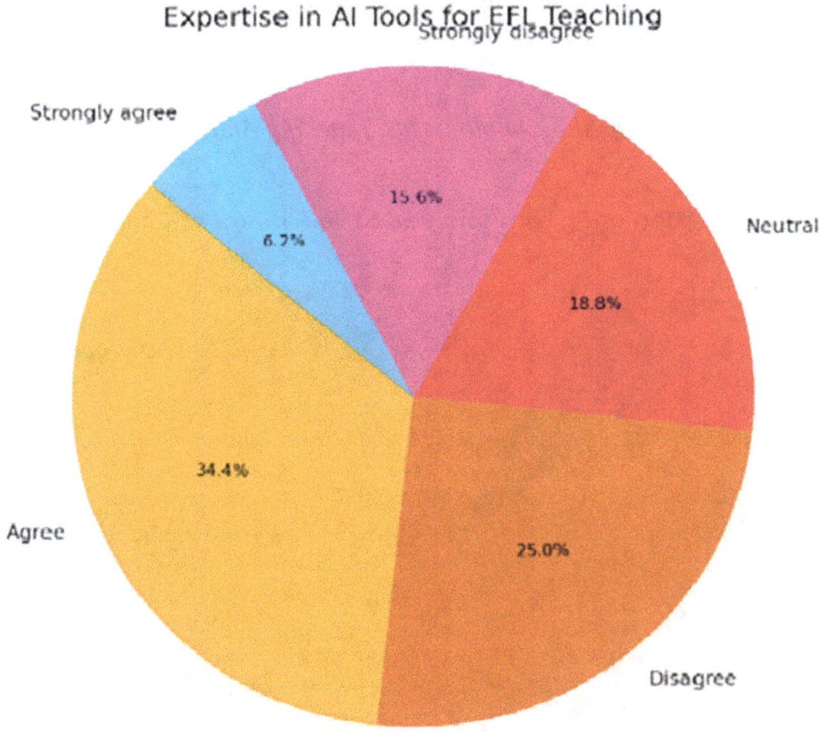

Further exploring instructional integration, the analysis of responses to the question “Adaptation of AI Technologies to Teaching Activities” reveals a mixed perception of AI's integration into educational practices. A majority of respondents (43.8%) agree, while an additional 12.5% strongly agree, bringing the total positive responses to 56.3%. This suggests that more than half of the participants recognize AI as a useful tool in adapting teaching activities, enabling personalized learning experiences, automated assessments, and interactive classroom engagement. However, 18.8% of respondents remain neutral, indicating a level of uncertainty regarding AI's role in effectively enhancing teaching methodologies. Additionally, 18.8% disagree, and 6.2% strongly disagree, meaning that a quarter (25%) of the respondents express skepticism about AI's adaptability to teaching activities. This may stem from concerns related to technical challenges, resistance to AI-based pedagogical shifts, or a lack of training in AI integration.

Consequently, these findings highlight the ongoing need for teacher training, institutional support, and practical demonstrations of AI-driven teaching strategies.

While there is a growing acknowledgment of AI's potential in enhancing instructional methods, addressing educators' concerns through professional development and AI-focused curriculum design could help maximize AI's effectiveness in adapting to diverse teaching activities (Figure 11).

Figure 11. Adaptation of AI Technologies to Teaching Activities

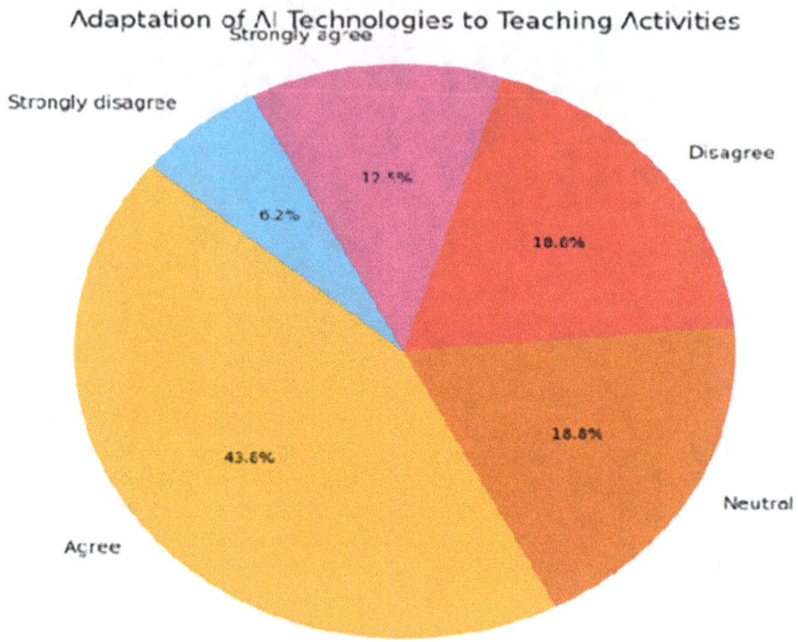

To better understand these findings, the questionnaire includes Likert Scale statements which were designed following the TPACK model, which emphasizes the integration of technology, pedagogy, and content knowledge. The questions focus on faculty's AI knowledge, teaching strategies, and expertise in AI tools (Table 1).

Table 1. Statements in the questionnaire designed according to TPACK model (2006)

1.I have the technical skills I need to use AI technology.
8. I have sufficient knowledge about incorporating AI tools in my EFL classroom.
13. I know how to use AI technologies to help me teach my courses.
18. I can select AI technologies to use in my classroom that enhance what I teach, how I teach, and what students learn.
24. I can use strategies that combine content, technologies, and teaching approaches.
25. I have the required expertise in AI tools for EFL teaching

Table 2. SPSS analysis of TPACK Model question statements

Question statement	**1. I have the technical skills I need to use AI technology.**	**8. I have sufficient knowledge about incorporating AI tools in my EFL classroom.**	**13. I know how to use AI technologies to help me teach my courses.**	**18. I can select AI technologies to use in my classroom that enhance what I teach, how I teach, and what students learn.**	**24. I can use strategies that combine content, technologies, and teaching approaches.**	**25. I have the required expertise in AI tools for EFL teaching.**
mean	3.34375	3.21875	3.0625	3.34375	3.71875	2.90625
Std deviation	1.26004	1.099395	1.134147	0.937029	0.92403	1.227622

Complementing this model, there were questions designed according to the SAMR model, which categorizes technology integration into Substitution, Augmentation, Modification, and Redefinition. These questions focus on AI's impact on teaching, student learning, and instructional methods (Table 3).

Table 3. Statements in the questionnaire designed according to SAMR model (2006)

6. AI tools help solve problems of language teaching (i.e. classroom density, time and place flexibility, availability of teaching material).
10. AI applications augment self-paced autonomous learning through various cognitive tracks.
11. AI technologies augment student-centered learning and boost students' motivation, interaction, and self-efficacy.
15. I can choose AI technologies that enhance the teaching approaches for a lesson.
21. AI applications enhance students' ability to master the skill of reading in English.
26. I can adapt the use of AI technologies to different teaching activities.

Table 4. Table 2. SPSS analysis of SAMR Model question statements

Question statement	mean	std
6. AI tools help solve problems of language teaching (i.e. classroom density, time and place flexibility, availability of teaching material).	3.875	0.659912
10. AI applications augment self-paced autonomous learning through various cognitive tracks.	3.5	0.672022
11. AI technologies augment student-centered learning and boosts students' motivation, interaction, and self-efficacy.	3.5	0.718421
15. I can choose AI technologies that enhance the teaching approaches for a lesson.	3.46875	0.949851
21. AI applications enhance students' ability to master the skill of reading in English.	3.625	0.793116
26. I can adapt the use of AI technologies to different teaching activities.	3.375	1.128802

Drawing on both models, the analysis of faculty perceptions regarding AI integration in EFL teaching, based on the TPACK and SAMR models, presents significant insights into their technical competence, pedagogical adaptation, and overall engagement with AI-driven instruction. The SPSS analysis of TPACK-related statements (Table 2) highlights a moderate level of confidence in technical skills (M = 3.34, SD = 1.26) and knowledge about AI integration in EFL teaching (M = 3.22, SD = 1.10). However, a notable gap exists in faculty members' perceived expertise in AI tools (M = 2.91, SD = 1.23), indicating a need for further training and hands-on experience with AI applications in educational settings. The relatively higher mean score for the ability to use strategies combining content, pedagogy, and technology (M = 3.72, SD = 0.92) suggests that educators recognize the importance of integrating AI within their teaching methodologies, even if their practical expertise remains limited.

Similarly, the analysis of the SAMR model-related questions (Table 4) sheds light on how faculty members perceive AI's role in transforming language teaching. The highest mean score (M = 3.88, SD = 0.66) was observed in AI's ability to address language teaching challenges, such as classroom density and access to learning materials. This finding implies that faculty acknowledge AI's utility in overcoming logistical barriers in education. Additionally, AI's impact on enhancing students' reading skills received a relatively high score (M = 3.63, SD = 0.79), reflecting a positive outlook on AI's capacity to support fundamental language skills.

On the other hand, the responses indicate more moderate confidence in AI's ability to augment self-paced autonomous learning (M = 3.5, SD = 0.67) and student-centered motivation (M = 3.5, SD = 0.71), suggesting that while faculty see AI as a beneficial tool, they may still be uncertain about its effectiveness in fostering engagement and independent learning.

Comparing both models, it becomes evident that faculty members are more confident in AI's functional applications (as highlighted in the SAMR analysis) than in their own ability to effectively integrate AI within their teaching strategies (as observed in the TPACK analysis). The relatively higher variability in responses (e.g., SD = 1.26 for technical skills in TPACK and SD = 1.12 for AI adaptation in SAMR) further emphasizes inconsistencies in AI adoption across educators, which may be due to differences in training, experience, or institutional support. In summary, the data suggest that while AI is perceived as a promising tool for language teaching, faculty members require structured training programs to bridge the gap between AI's potential and its practical implementation in pedagogy.

In conclusion, the results highlight the importance of professional development initiatives aimed at equipping educators with both the technical expertise and pedagogical strategies necessary for AI integration. As faculty members acknowledge AI's role in enhancing teaching methods and language learning, targeted interventions, such as workshops, hands-on training, and AI-driven curriculum development, are essential to ensure effective adoption.

DISCUSSION

The study's findings align with previous research, confirming AI's role in enhancing EFL instruction, student engagement, and language skill development while also highlighting implementation challenges. Responses from 32 participants reflect both opportunities and barriers in AI adoption, reinforcing the need for strategic integration and teacher training to maximize its potential.

Educators' capabilities to integrate AI tools into their teaching practices

To begin with, the study found that 78% of participants agreed or strongly agreed that they possessed the necessary technical skills to integrate AI tools effectively into their teaching. This suggests that a majority of educators feel technologically competent and comfortable utilizing AI-driven platforms for instructional purposes. These findings are consistent with the study by Drugova et al. (2021), which emphasized that educators with sufficient technological pedagogical content knowledge (TPACK) are more likely to integrate AI seamlessly into their teaching practices.

Furthermore, 75% of respondents indicated that AI tools helped them automate repetitive tasks such as grading and assessment, allowing them to allocate more time to higher-order instructional activities. AI-powered grading tools and adaptive learning platforms have been cited in prior research as effective means of reducing teacher workload and enabling more personalized instruction (Sumakul et al., 2022). However, 32% of participants expressed concerns regarding limited access to diverse AI tools, reflecting a gap in hands-on experience with advanced AI technologies. This aligns with Kukulska-Hulme and Lee (2020), who emphasized the importance of professional development programs in equipping educators with AI literacy and practical skills. The lack of direct experience with AI tools could hinder teachers from exploring AI's full potential, limiting the scope of pedagogical innovation.

Enhanced Student Engagement and Learning

In addition to teacher proficiency, AI technologies also demonstrated a significant impact on student engagement. The study found that 68% of educators observed an increase in student motivation when using AI-enhanced learning tools such as gamification platforms, real-time feedback systems, and interactive AI-driven exercises. These tools introduced elements of competition, rewards, and interactivity, making language learning more dynamic and engaging. These results align with Pikhart (2020), who found that AI-driven gamification improves learner motivation and participation by fostering a more student-centered learning environment.

Moreover, 60% of participants reported that AI tools facilitated self-paced learning, enabling students to work independently and refine their skills. Applications such as Grammarly and AI-powered writing assistants provided real-time feedback and corrections, allowing students to enhance their writing accuracy. Similar findings were reported by Al Mukhallafi (2020), who noted that AI-driven writing support systems improve student autonomy and self-regulated learning behaviors. The ability of AI to adjust to individual learning needs and provide personalized feedback makes it a valuable tool in developing independent learners.

Language Skills Development

Equally important, the study further confirmed that AI tools play a crucial role in developing students' language proficiency. 72% of educators reported that AI-powered speech recognition software and pronunciation tools significantly improved listening and speaking skills by offering real-time corrective feedback and interactive speaking practice. This supports the findings of Jing (2024), who highlighted the effectiveness of AI-driven pronunciation assessment tools in refining students' speaking accuracy and fluency. Jing (2024) examined the use of speech recognition and synthesis technologies in an automated English oral correction system designed to improve pronunciation accuracy among Chinese college students.

In a similar vein, 65% of participants observed that AI-supported activities enhanced reading and writing skills. AI-assisted grammar correction tools and vocabulary-building exercises contributed to students' writing accuracy and lexical expansion. These findings are in line with prior research by Muslimin et al. (2023), who noted that AI-enhanced learning environments promote reading comprehension, vocabulary acquisition, and writing fluency. The accessibility of AI-driven support tools allows students to refine their language skills independently, reinforcing self-directed learning strategies.

Challenges in AI Integration

Despite the numerous advantages of AI in EFL instruction, several challenges remain. 35% of participants reported that existing AI tools were not fully tailored to EFL instruction, as many AI applications are designed for general education rather than language-specific learning. This concern aligns with the findings of Bahri et al. (2022), who noted that EFL teachers often struggle to find AI tools that address the nuanced aspects of language learning, such as grammar instruction, idiomatic expressions, and contextualized feedback.

Additionally, 40% of respondents highlighted insufficient training and professional development opportunities as a significant barrier to effective AI integration. Educators expressed the need for structured training programs to enhance AI literacy and classroom implementation strategies. These findings resonate with Kukulska-Hulme and Lee (2020), who emphasized that teacher training is essential for maximizing AI's impact in education. Without adequate training and institutional support, teachers may struggle to integrate AI beyond basic functionalities, limiting its transformative potential in language education.

The findings confirm AI's effectiveness in enhancing EFL instruction, empowering teachers, and improving student engagement and language skills. However, challenges such as limited AI access, insufficient training, and a lack of EFL-specific tools highlight the need for further educator training and AI refinement. Moving forward, ensuring targeted training, better AI resources, and effective integration strategies will be crucial for maximizing AI's long-term impact in language education.

Alignment with and Contribution to Previous Research

The results of this study align with and expand upon recent empirical and theoretical research on AI integration in EFL education. The high levels of educator agreement regarding the benefits of AI tools in enhancing writing, motivation, and personalized learning echo findings from Georgieva (2025), who demonstrated how low-cost AI applications increased learner autonomy and engagement. Similarly, participants' recognition of AI's role in reducing workload and facilitating self-paced instruction supports the conclusions of Kohnke and Ulla (2024) and Metwally and Bin-Hady (2025), who observed that AI tools can streamline instruction and support teacher efficiency when paired with ethical awareness. Additionally, positive responses about AI's contribution to reading and writing proficiency correspond with the observations of Al Mukhallafi (2020), Muslimin et al. (2023), and Bykonia

(2025), who emphasized the role of AI-powered platforms in improving academic writing and vocabulary acquisition.

At the same time, neutral or skeptical views about AI's effectiveness in speaking skills and interactive activities reflect concerns raised by Benek (2025) and Babanoğlu et al. (2025), who reported that instructors often face uncertainty regarding AI's ability to support communicative competence and pedagogical nuance. Similarly, findings related to inconsistent teacher expertise and limited training mirror the conclusions of Chan and Tang (2024) and Resyadi (2025), who highlighted the ongoing gap between AI's potential and teachers' readiness to implement it effectively. Moreover, the moderate levels of AI adaptation and strategic integration resonate with Krisbiantoro and Ashari's (2024) SAMR-based analysis, which found that most AI use in EFL classrooms remains at the substitution or augmentation levels due to institutional and infrastructural barriers.

This study's use of both the TPACK and SAMR frameworks further reinforces earlier calls, particularly from Pitura et al. (2024) and Chris, Kate, and Frank (2024), to move beyond surface-level adoption and instead pursue ethically grounded, pedagogically aligned, and teacher-driven approaches to AI integration. Overall, these results contribute to a growing consensus: while AI offers promising tools to support language learning, its success ultimately depends on sustained professional development, human-centered design, and institutional strategies that empower educators to navigate both the technological and ethical complexities of 21st-century classrooms.

RECOMMENDATIONS

The findings from this study highlight both the benefits and challenges of AI integration in EFL instruction, aligning with previous research on AI-driven pedagogy.

Structured Professional Development Programs for Teachers

Given the training concerns identified, with 40% of participants reporting insufficient training in AI tools, structured professional development programs are essential for equipping educators with the necessary skills and confidence to integrate AI effectively. Previous studies, such as those by Kukulska-Hulme and Lee (2020), emphasized that teacher training plays a crucial role in facilitating AI adoption and ensuring that educators can utilize AI to personalize instruction and enhance student engagement.

Educational institutions should implement regular AI-focused training programs that provide hands-on experience with AI tools, covering areas such as adaptive learning, automated assessment, speech recognition, and AI-driven writing support systems. Furthermore, these training initiatives should be interactive and continuous, incorporating real classroom applications to ensure that educators can seamlessly incorporate AI beyond basic functionalities.

Development of AI Tools Tailored for EFL Instruction

Another significant recommendation arises from tool relevance. A major challenge identified by 35% of participants was the lack of AI tools specifically designed for language education. While AI technologies have proven beneficial in general education, many current tools lack customization for EFL learning, particularly in areas such as pronunciation training, real-time grammar correction, and contextual vocabulary development. This finding aligns with the concerns raised by Bahri et al. (2022), who emphasized that AI tools should be tailored to the linguistic and cultural complexities of language learners to maximize their effectiveness.

To address this gap, AI developers and educational technology companies should prioritize the creation of EFL-specific AI applications that integrate features such as context-aware grammar correction, interactive pronunciation coaching, and multilingual learning support. In this context, collaboration between linguists, AI developers, and language educators will be crucial in ensuring that these tools cater to the unique challenges faced by non-native English learners.

Investment in Technical Infrastructure for AI Integration

In parallel with teacher training and tool development, the successful integration of AI into EFL instruction requires adequate technological infrastructure to support AI-powered platforms, cloud-based learning environments, and real-time interactive applications. Without reliable access to AI-supported systems, the benefits of AI in education remain inaccessible to many teachers and students. For example, Drugova et al. (2021) highlighted the critical role of infrastructure in determining the effectiveness of technology-enhanced learning. Therefore, educational institutions should prioritize investments in digital infrastructure, ensuring that classrooms are equipped with high-speed internet, AI-compatible devices, and advanced language-learning software.

Collaborative AI Tool Development and Feedback Mechanisms

Finally, for AI technologies to remain relevant and effective in language education, it is essential to establish continuous feedback loops between educators, AI developers, and educational institutions. The study findings indicate that educators often have limited input in the design of AI tools, resulting in technology that does not always align with pedagogical needs. This aligns with Pikhart (2020), who emphasized the importance of teacher involvement in AI development to ensure that AI applications remain user-friendly and pedagogically effective.

There should be a facilitated collaboration between AI developers and language educators, ensuring that teachers' insights and classroom experiences inform AI tool improvements. Educators should be actively involved in pilot programs and iterative AI refinement processes, ensuring that AI applications evolve in ways that directly support student learning outcomes.

These recommendations align with prior research on AI in education, reinforcing the need for teacher training, tailored AI tools, infrastructure development, and collaborative feedback mechanisms to ensure sustainable and effective AI integration in EFL teaching. By addressing the challenges identified in this study, educators and institutions can fully leverage AI's potential to create engaging, personalized, and interactive language-learning experiences.

CONCLUSION

This case study highlights the transformative potential of integrating AI into EFL instruction by employing the TPACK framework and aligning AI integration with the SAMR model. The findings confirm that AI-driven tools significantly enhance personalized learning, improve student engagement, and support educators by automating repetitive tasks and providing real-time feedback. However, the effectiveness of AI integration is contingent upon addressing key challenges, including the need for comprehensive teacher training, equitable access to digital resources, and the development of AI tools specifically designed for EFL instruction.

Through this lens, the study demonstrates that teachers who possess technological, pedagogical, and content knowledge are more likely to integrate AI effectively into their instructional practices. However, a lack of structured professional development was identified as a major barrier, aligning with prior research that emphasizes the importance of AI literacy among educators.

Additionally, the application of the SAMR model reveals that most teachers primarily use AI at the Substitution and Augmentation levels, where AI serves as a tool for content delivery and minor enhancements rather than a means of fundamentally transforming pedagogical approaches. Only a limited number of educators reached the Modification and Redefinition stages, where AI enables interactive, student-driven learning experiences that go beyond traditional classroom capabilities.

Importantly, the study underscores that while AI can augment and transform traditional teaching methods, it should complement rather than replace the role of teachers. Educators remain central to facilitating meaningful language learning experiences, and AI should be leveraged as a tool to enhance human instruction, not diminish it.

Looking ahead, professional development programs should focus on enabling teachers to progress beyond basic AI integration, ensuring that AI is strategically used to create innovative and student-centered learning environments.

This study reinforces the idea that AI holds immense potential to reshape EFL education, making it more dynamic, interactive, and student-centered when thoughtfully integrated within established pedagogical frameworks such as TPACK and SAMR. By addressing existing challenges and implementing strategic AI adoption, educational institutions can harness AI's capabilities to foster engaging, personalized, and effective English language instruction for learners worldwide.

Pedagogical Contribution and Implication

This study contributes to the field of language education by offering a practical and theoretically grounded framework that helps teachers navigate the integration of AI tools in EFL classrooms. By combining the TPACK and SAMR models, the study provides educators with a dual lens to assess their technological-pedagogical knowledge and to implement AI tools in a structured, pedagogically meaningful way. The findings have important implications for teacher education and professional development, suggesting that AI integration should not be approached as a purely technical skill but as a process that requires informed pedagogical decision-making, ethical awareness, and curriculum alignment.

REFERENCES

Al Mukhallafi, T. R. (2020). Using Artificial Intelligence for Developing English Language Teaching/Learning: An Analytical Study from University Students' Perspective. *International Journal of English Linguistics*, *10*(6), 40–45. DOI: 10.5539/ijel.v10n6p40

Altınay, F., Altınay, Z., Dagli, G., & Yavuz, G. (2016). Information technology in learning organizations. *The Journal of Social Sciences Research*, *2*(4), 78–86. https://www.sciencedirect.com/science/article/pii/S2405844021021563

Angeli, C., & Valanides, N. (2009). Epistemological and methodological issues for the conceptualization, development, and assessment of ICT–TPCK: Advances in technological pedagogical content knowledge (TPCK). *Computers & Education*, *52*(1), 154–168. DOI: 10.1016/j.compedu.2008.07.006

Bahri, A., Jamaluddin, A. B., Arifin, A. N., & Saparuddin, S. (2022). Students' and teachers' digital literacy skill: A comparative study between schools, classes, and genders in urban and rural areas. [IJSR]. *International Journal of Science and Research (Raipur, India)*, *11*(2), 184–200. DOI: 10.21275/SR22130101519

Benek, K. (2025). EFL learners' and teachers' perceptions of AI-powered language learning technologies: Benefits and challenges. *International Journal of Instruction*, *18*(2), 103–120. DOI: 10.29333/iji.2025.1827a

Bykonia, O. (2025). Using artificial intelligence in the process of teaching English. *Scientific Herald of Sivershchyna: Series Education. Social and Behavioural Sciences*, *1*(14), 183–185. DOI: 10.32755/sjeducation.2025.01.183

Chan, K. K.-W., & Tang, W. K.-W. (2024). Evaluating English teachers' artificial intelligence readiness and training needs with a TPACK-based model. *World Journal of English Language*, *15*(1), 129–141. DOI: 10.5430/wjel.v15n1p129

Chris, E., Kate, J., & Frank, E. (2024). *The ethical implications of integrating generative AI in education: Opportunities and challenges.* https://www.researchgate.net/publication/387326280

Dewi, D., Sudirman, S., & Darmawan, D. (2021). The Use of Artificial Intelligence in Learning English: Enhancing University Students' Skills. *Journal of Educational Technology*, *12*(3), 24–37.

Drugova, E., Zhuravleva, I., Aiusheeva, M., & Grits, D. (2021). Toward a model of learning innovation integration: TPACK-SAMR based analysis of the introduction of a digital learning environment in three Russian universities. *Education and Information Technologies*, *26*(4), 4925–4942. DOI: 10.1007/s10639-021-10514-2 PMID: 33814955

Falloon, G. (2020). From digital literacy to digital competence: The teacher digital competency (TDC) framework. *Educational Technology Research and Development*, *68*(5), 2449–2472. DOI: 10.1007/s11423-020-09767-4

Farahani, M. S., & Ghasemi, G. (2024). Artificial Intelligence in education: A comprehensive study. *Forum for Education Studies*, *2*(3), 1379. DOI: 10.59400/fes.v2i3.1379

Georgieva, V. (2025). Embracing the inevitable: Tips for EFL and ESP learning with AI. *E-Learning Innovations Journal*, *3*(1), 89–115. DOI: 10.57125/ELIJ.2025.03.25.05

Graham, C. R. (2011). Theoretical considerations for understanding technological pedagogical content knowledge (TPACK). *Computers & Education*, *57*(3), 1953–1969. DOI: 10.1016/j.compedu.2011.04.010

Hassan, M. M., & Mirza, T. (2021). The digital literacy in teachers of the schools of Rajouri (J&K)-India: Teachers' perspective. *International Journal of Education and Management Engineering*, *11*(1), 28–40. DOI: 10.5815/ijeme.2021.01.04

Jing, W. (2024). Speech recognition sensors and artificial intelligence automatic evaluation application in English oral correction system. *Measurement. Sensors*, *32*, 101070. DOI: 10.1016/j.measen.2024.101070

Kayyali, M. (2025). Ethical implications of generative AI in education: Privacy, bias, and integrity. In *Ethical AI in Education* (pp. 185–202). IGI Global. DOI: 10.4018/979-8-3693-8744-3.ch008

Kehinde-Awoyele, A. A., & Adeowu, A. W. (2024). Exploring students' perceptions, academic outcomes, and ethical implications of AI in Social Studies education. *Social Science and Humanities Journal*, *8*(12), 6003–6013. DOI: 10.18535/sshj.v8i12.1490

Kohnke, L., Moorhouse, B. L., & Zou, D. (2023). Exploring generative artificial intelligence preparedness among university language instructors: A case study. *Computers and Education: Artificial Intelligence*, *5*, 100156. DOI: 10.1016/j.caeai.2023.100156

Kohnke, L., & Ulla, M. B. (2024). Embracing generative artificial intelligence: The perspectives of English instructors in Thai higher education institutions. *Knowledge Management & E-Learning*, *16*(4), 653–670. DOI: 10.34105/j.kmel.2024.16.030

Krisbiantoro, B., & Ashari, I. A. (2024). Evaluating the SAMR model for enhancing ICT integration in English language teaching at the tertiary level: A systematic literature review. *Frasa: English Education and Literature Journal*, *5*(2), 108–115. DOI: 10.47701/frasa.v5i2.4027

Kukulska-Hulme, A., & Lee, H. (2020). Intelligent assistants in language learning: An analysis of features and limitations. *Research-publishing.net*.

Metwally, A. A., & Bin-Hady, W. R. A. (2025). Probing the necessity and advantages of AI integration training for EFL educators in Saudi Arabia. *Cogent Education*, *12*(1), 2472462. DOI: 10.1080/2331186X.2025.2472462

Mishara, P. (2024). The ethical implications of AI in education: Privacy, bias, and accountability. *Journal of Informatics Education and Research*, *4*(2), 1–14.

Mishra, P., & Koehler, M. (2006). Technological pedagogical content knowledge: A framework for teacher knowledge. *Teachers College Record*, *108*(6), 1017–1054. DOI: 10.1111/j.1467-9620.2006.00684.x

Muslimin, A. I., Mukminatien, N., & Ivone, F. M. (2023). TPACK-SAMR digital literacy competence, technostress, and teaching performance: Correlational study among EFL lecturers. *Contemporary Educational Technology*, *15*(2), ep409. DOI: 10.30935/cedtech/12921

Niess, M. L., Sadri, P., & Lee, K. (2013). Technology-based instruction (TbI) model: A structured approach to integrating AI in EFL classrooms. *World Journal of English Language*, *12*(6), 304–320. DOI: 10.5430/wjel.v12n6p304

Nurhasanah, S., & Nugraha, M. S. (2024). The future of learning: Ethical and philosophical implications of AI integration in education. *Indonesian Journal of Multidisciplinary Research*, *4*(2), 341–352. DOI: 10.17509/ijomr.v4i2.78038

Ouyang, F., & Jiao, P. (2021). Artificial intelligence in education: The three paradigms. *Computers and Education: Artificial Intelligence*, *2*, 100020. DOI: 10.1016/j.caeai.2021.100020

Pikhart, M. (2020). Intelligent information processing for language education: The use of artificial intelligence in language learning apps. *Procedia Computer Science*, *176*, 1412–1419. DOI: 10.1016/j.procs.2020.09.151 PMID: 33042299

Pitura, J., Kaplan-Rakowski, R., & Asotska-Wierzba, Y. (2024). The VR-AI-assisted simulation for content knowledge application in pre-service EFL teacher training. *TechTrends*, *68*(6), 734–749. DOI: 10.1007/s11528-024-01022-4

Puentedura, R. R. (2006). Transformation, technology, and education in the state of Maine [Web log post]. https://www.hippasus.com/rrpweblog/archives/2006_11.html

Ramadhan, S., Sukma, E., & Indriyani, V. (2019). Teacher competence in utilizing digital media literacy in education. *Journal of Physics: Conference Series*, *1339*(1), 012111. DOI: 10.1088/1742-6596/1339/1/012111

Resyadi, H. (2025). Integrating AI in language teaching: Challenges and opportunities for novice EFL teachers. *Edukasi: Jurnal Pendidikan dan Pengajaran, 12*(1), 124–134. http://jurnal.radenfatah.ac.id/index.php/edukasi

Sadeghi, K., & Richards, J. C. (2021). Professional development among English language teachers: Challenges and recommendations for practice. *Heliyon*, *7*(9), e08053. DOI: 10.1016/j.heliyon.2021.e08053 PMID: 34622060

Shengquan, Y., & Yu, L. (2021). *An Introduction to Artificial Intelligence in Education*. Springer.

Sumakul, D. T., Hamied, F. A., & Sukyadi, D. (2022). Artificial intelligence in EFL classrooms: Friend or foe? *LEARN Journal: Language Education and Acquisition Research Network*, *15*(1), 232–256.

Tang, C. M., & Chaw, L. Y. (2016). Digital literacy: A prerequisite for effective learning in a blended learning environment? *Electronic Journal of e-Learning*, *14*(1), 54–65. https://www.ejel.org/

Woolf, B. P., Lane, H. C., Chaudhri, V. K., & Kolodner, J. L. (2013). AI Grand Challenges for Education. *AI Magazine*, *34*(4), 66–84. DOI: 10.1609/aimag.v34i4.2490

Zamri, M. T., & Mohamad, S. N. A. (2024). Technology integration in education: A review and analysis of SAMR model. *International Journal of Research and Innovation in Social Science*, *8*(3), 6195–6200. DOI: 10.47772/IJRISS.2024.803463S

Zhang, K., & Aslan, A. B. (2021). AI technologies for education: Recent research & future directions. *Computers and Education: Artificial Intelligence*, *2*, 100025. DOI: 10.1016/j.caeai.2021.100025

Chapter 4
Enhancing Second Language Acquisition Through Artificial Intelligence:
Current Insights and Future Directions

Mohamadreza Jafary
https://orcid.org/0009-0003-7816-1330
McGill University, Canada

Sedigheh Toshkent Shakib
https://orcid.org/0000-0001-6249-0293
Central Asian University, Uzbekistan

ABSTRACT

Abstract This chapter examines the role of Artificial Intelligence (AI) in Second Language Acquisition (SLA), exploring the opportunities and challenges associated with its integration into language education. Drawing on foundational SLA theories, the chapter analyzes how AI technologies, such as transformer-based NLP models, speech recognition tools, intelligent tutoring systems, and gamified applications, can enhance learner engagement, provide personalized feedback, support multilingual learners, and improve language instruction across different contexts. Ethical issues, such as algorithmic bias, lack of cultural awareness, threats to data privacy, and diminished human interaction, underscore the importance of developing AI systems that are inclusive, transparent, and culturally sensitive. The chapter also addresses

DOI: 10.4018/979-8-3373-0275-1.ch004

global implementation challenges, particularly in low-resource settings, as well as the lack of standardized assessment frameworks aligned with the CEFR and other global standards.

INTRODUCTION

In an increasingly interconnected world, multilingual competence plays a crucial role in enabling individuals to access diverse knowledge, foster intercultural understanding, and participate in international mobility and collaboration. Apart from facilitating communication, multilingualism significantly contributes to the formation of personal and social identities, as language is deeply linked to cultural beliefs, values, and modes of expression (Ortega, 2019; Uysal, 2023). Therefore, schools worldwide aim to cultivate multilingual abilities in learners, making language learning a central focus of 21st-century education.

However, Second Language Acquisition (SLA) remains a complex and time-consuming process, often hindered by cognitive, affective, sociocultural, and institutional barriers. Critics argue that traditional approaches to second language acquisition rely too heavily on standardized methods, which fail to fully address the importance of personalization and the unique needs of learners in plurilingual and multicultural contexts (Almelhes, 2023; Andreevich, 2023; Muñoz-Basols, 2019). Anxiety, lack of motivation, limited authentic input, and insufficient feedback are common obstacles that hinder language learning and fluency development (Kaiss et al., 2023; Piduru, 2023).

To address these shortcomings, language learners can integrate innovative advancements in computational and Artificial Intelligence (AI) to transform the second language acquisition. Piduru, 2023; Rebolledo Font de la Vall & González Araya, 2023; Yeh, 2024). AI creates interesting, learner-centered settings that are personalized, interactive, and have a profound impact, which aligns with sociocultural and constructivist notions (Andreevich, 2023; Ingley & Pack, 2023). Intelligent tutoring systems have proven efficient in assessing learners' progress and tailoring lessons to their language competency and learning pace, while simultaneously enhancing engagement and language skills (Alsadoon, 2021; Mageira et al., 2022; Song & Song, 2023). AI-powered programs that utilize speech recognition and automated assessments provide learners with instantaneous feedback on pronunciation, grammar, and vocabulary in real-time, facilitating autonomous learning and enhancing fluency (Cardon et al., 2023; Fitria, 2021; Harunasari, 2023). AI-driven chatbots can simulate real-world conversational practice in a secure and low-stress setting, facilitating social engagement for language learning, particularly in developing speaking and listening abilities (Madhavi et al., 2023; Xing, 2023). Affective computing, immersive systems that utilize virtual and augmented reality, and artificial intelligence present interesting new avenues for engagement. Such technologies facilitate the development of emotionally intelligent interfaces, offering engaging experiences that enhance motivation and language competency (Majid & Salam, 2021; Min & Yu, 2023). The use of AI in SLA has considerable potential, as it can help address the challenges of language learning by employing adaptive, learner-centered approaches and addressing ethical and cultural issues.

This chapter will examine the integration of AI and SLA by grounding AI applications in SLA theories, reviewing the current AI tools used in second language acquisition. The opportunities and real-world implementation of AI tools across different contexts will be discussed. It is followed by challenges, ethical, practical, and pedagogical challenges of integrating these tools. The chapter concludes with future directions and practical recommendations for designing an inclusive, effective, and ethical AI-enhanced language learning context.

THEORETICAL FOUNDATIONS OF AI-ENHANCED SLA

To understand how AI can meaningfully support language learning, it is essential to integrate its applications into SLA theories and principles of learning science. Theoretical models, such as Krashen's Input Hypothesis, Vygotsky's Sociocultural Theory, and Gardner's Theory of Multiple Intelligences, propose initial insights into how learners acquire a second language. These theories highlight the roles of meaningful input, social interaction, motivation, and affective factors; all of which AI technologies can currently support and strengthen through personalized, adaptive, and interactive learning experiences. The development of intelligent language learning systems. Intelligent tutoring systems, natural language processing (NLP), speech recognition, and AI technologies are all closely aligned with SLA theories. They provide scalable, data-driven solutions to improve learning (Son et al., 2025).

Monitor Model

Stephen Krashen's Monitor Model was developed as a significant theoretical paradigm shift in second language acquisition (SLA) during the late 1970s and early 1980s. The most significant distinction Krashen made was between subconscious language acquisition and conscious language learning. Based on this, he suggested five interrelated hypotheses: the Acquisition-Learning Hypothesis, the Monitor Hypothesis, the Natural Order Hypothesis, the Input Hypothesis, and the Affective

Filter Hypothesis. Krashen's hypotheses have shaped SLA cognitive and affective factors with AI-enhanced learning environments.

Krashen proposed that adults learn a second language through two fundamentally different processes: implicit, intuitive, and subconscious acquisition, and explicit and conscious learning. Krashen admits that the knowledge a student consciously learns or understands (for example, a grammar rule) will not become acquired linguistic competence. Therefore, there is no interface between the two systems. Today, fully-fledged AI-enabled platforms can be selectively developed to engage both dimensions, with immersive AI applications (conversational chatbots, VR language simulations, narrative-based interfaces) integrating many immersive elements that can support gut-level exposure to the target language, thus providing conditions for acquisition. At the same time, other formal knowledge, such as rule-based grammar modules, quizzes, and feedback tools, allows students to learn even on their own devices. AI can help both systems grow simultaneously, making learning experiences more coordinated and personalized to each person's profile. This is in line with Krashen's Input Hypothesis, which says that learners should get "i+1" content (Krahnke et al., 1985).

The Natural Order Hypothesis suggests that learners acquire grammatical structures in a natural order, and they acquire those structures in the same sequential order, regardless of the order in which they are formally taught the structure. While the concept is somewhat controversial and has methodological issues, it has generated a new research avenue using AI-based learning systems to analyze the same data longitudinally. Emerging intelligent tutoring systems can analyze real-world learning data to identify classes of learners acquiring structures in the same sequence. They can also identify cases where there are deviations from usual patterns. Furthermore, this data can enable AI to dynamically modify the subject matter, potentially shaping learner engagement with learning forms that are cognitively ready for acquisition. Unlike the same experience in traditional instruction, AI interventions may prematurely mitigate the intentions of teaching complex structures (Li et al., 2024; Mohamed et al., 2024). Instead, AI may change the difficulty and complexity not by each learner's perceived acquired/competencies but rather by learner performance and typical acquired patterns, thus allowing for operationalization in a natural order that is uniquely for each learner in potentially scalable ways (Meyer et al., 2024; Son et al., 2025).

Input Hypothesis

Krashen argued that meaningful, comprehensible input, not explicit grammar instruction, drives acquisition. AI technologies are ideally suited to assess learners' proficiencies and provide "i+1" content based on those assessments. In addition to recommendation systems for texts, such as adaptive video subtitles, and dialog systems that engage in real-time by adjusting lexical and syntactical complexity levels, the customizability provided by AI systems is unprecedented in language programs. AI can create rich, contextualized input opportunities where learners are equally engaged in meaningful, goal-oriented interactions with the language. Still, Krashen's hypothesis has been criticized because there was no clear path to define "i" and "+1". However, AI can help organize such concepts by using data analytics and learner modeling to measure "i+1" in adaptive learning systems (Kamal, 2022).

Affective Filter Hypothesis

Krashen developed the Affective Filter Hypothesis to explain the emotional factors that either aid or detract from language acquisition, including anxiety, motivation, and confidence. When the affective filter is "up", input may be understood but not absorbed; when the affective filter is "down", learners are in a state of acquisition. Incorporating affective computing into a language learning platform directly correlates to the Affective Filter Hypothesis. AI technology, embedded with emotion detection capabilities through facial expressions, vocal tonality, or behavioral analytics, can determine a learner's emotional state (e.g., anxiety) and adapt their instructional plan accordingly. If the learner expresses frustration or boredom, the AI system may simplify content, offer encouragement, or switch to another skill or activity type. Studies have shown that AI can lower the affective filter, which can lower learner anxiety by up to 20%, which can improve emotional well-being and language learning (Mao et al., 2025; Monika & Suganthan, 2024).

Despite inspiring a generation of SLA theory and practice, Krashen's model does not come without critique. For example, McLaughlin (1990) criticized the supplemental characterization of the fuzzy border areas between learning and acquisition, that the model privileged input and ignored output, and that there were slight problems with the i+1 figure. Still, AI gives us a way to respond to these criticisms by measuring and calibrating input, output, and emotional stimuli. This provides an empirical basis for refining Krashen's ideas (Son et al., 2023).

Howard Gardner's Multiple Intelligences

There is an emerging consensus that intelligence, commonly measured through linguistics and logical-mathematical standards (i.e., IQ), may not represent all the cognitive abilities that are relevant to learning a language, especially as science has proven on an operational level through Klitgaard & Gardner's (1984) work on multiple intelligences. Learners could have intelligences based on spatial, musical, bodily-kinesthetic, interpersonal, intrapersonal, or naturalist preferences, which may all impact their second language growth. AI-enhanced technologies could utilize these realities by transforming instructional means to cater to the learners' cognitive strengths. For example, a learner with musical intelligence would excel with pronunciation activities tied to rhythm, as an example of usage for "rhythm" in the social interactive they are showing. Conversely, a learner with interpersonal intelligence would excel with dialogue practices utilizing a chatbot. Systems could log interaction patterns and performance as a course of dynamic, continual practice so that they could ultimately make inferences about their engagement preferences and subsequently customize content delivery in ways aligned with constructivist ideals about respecting learner variability. This corresponds with Gardner's theory, which says that AI can work with a wide range of cognitive aspects (Bornstein & Gardner, 1986).

Language aptitude often seen as a collection of inborn or sometimes-stable traits that predict success in SLA is made up of subskills such as phonetic coding ability, grammatical sensitivity, working memory, and inductive reasoning. With the advent of AI, we can now diagnose and respond dynamically to aptitude patterns. Through real-time analytics, AI can measure a learner's performance on tasks that map onto these cognitive subskills (Ulla et al., 2023). For example, learners with a high propensity for inductive reasoning could be directed to pattern recognition. In contrast, a learner with a higher capacity for phonetic coding ability would be given tasks with advanced pronunciation. The shift becomes one where aptitude is not a static predictor of future success, but an evolution of the formation of learner profiles in SLA, and provides a more equitable approach to learning languages that is more responsive to their learner profiles (Savela et al., 2025).

More skilled second language learners tend to have a larger repertoire of strategies, including cognitive (e.g., summarization), metacognitive (e.g., self-monitoring), and social strategies (e.g., requesting clarification). While it cannot be determined whether strategy use produces better learning or improved learning leads to strategy use, one trait of successful learners is their strategic flexibility (Moulieswaran & Kumar, 2023; Zhai & Wibowo, 2022). AI can support strategic awareness through intelligent prompts, hints, and feedback that lead learners toward certain, more desirable behaviors. For example, suppose a learner has difficulty understanding the material. In that case, they may receive a prompt that tells them to reread, while another learner could receive a prompt to summarize or visualize the information. Through such strategy modeling, AI serves as a metacognitive partner that develops the self-regulated learning tendencies valued by constructivist learning theories (Bhatt & Muduli, 2023; Kasneci et al., 2023).

The affective domain, which includes aspects like anxiety, confidence, and emotional readiness, is an important part of SLA. For example, foreign language anxiety can take different forms, including: communication anxiety, test anxiety, and fear of negative evaluation. Recent advancements in affective computing have enabled computers and AI to respond to real-time emotional situations. Based on the analysis of facial expressions, tone of voice, pattern of typing, and pace of interaction, the computer can detect learner discomfort and adjust the learning experience accordingly (Savela et al., 2025). An anxious student, for example, might be prompted by the computer to get encouragement, simplify tasks, or practice privately, thus lowering their affective filter and having a more supportive experience.

In an SLA context, in addition to understanding the linguistic content, learners must interpret social and affective signals of their interlocutors communicating in a language in which they may feel uncertain or insecure. AI can still provide empathetic behavior, primarily through sentiment-aware conversational agents that aim to respond to the learner's responses. While the system will not respond with genuine empathy per se, it can respond to or simulate empathic behavior (Meyer et al., 2024). These systems should be able to recognize confusion, frustration, or excitement in the learners' written language and create opportunities for context-sensitive responses that maintain engagement and emotional neutrality. These responses can allow the learner to practice empathy themselves, particularly if they can include role-play and scenario-based learning, which require a degree of cultural nuance and emotional (Sargazi Moghadam et al., 2024; Savela et al., 2025).

Motivation is widely acknowledged as a foundational driver of second language acquisition. Scholars have identified several types of motivation, including Instrumental, Integrative, Resultative, Intrinsic, and Extrinsic. AI systems can predict student motivation using metrics that describe process completion, whether that means task completion, allocation of time to tasks, or clicking patterns (Meyer et al., 2024; Song & Song, 2023). Suppose the students appear to be losing motivation. In that case, the system can modify the challenges of the tasks, introduce a different format (such as games or interactive challenges), or integrate cooperative tasks (constructive activities where students work together) to rekindle their interest. AI can also assist in developing intrinsic motivation by allowing students to select the path they would like to follow in learning, choose topics of interest, and track their progress through visual dashboarding. These activities are closely associated with feelings of autonomy and competence, two key constructs in motivational theory.

Collectively, these theories align with constructivist principles, positioning learners as active participants in the construction of knowledge. AI-powered learning environments can represent this approach by enabling exploratory learning, immediate feedback, and dynamic progression tailored to each learner's needs. The interaction between these foundational theories and AI capabilities underlines the pedagogical validity of integrating intelligent technologies into SLA. AI can create personalized, adaptable, and learner-centered educational models by using constructivist and cognitive concepts. Instead of replacing human interaction, AI can work alongside individuals to create language learning experiences that change lives (Tangsakul & Poonpon, 2024; Wu, 2024).

AI TOOLS AND TECHNOLOGIES IN SLA

Transformer-Based NLP Models

Transformer-based models, such as BERT, GPT-3, GPT-4, and T5, have significantly advanced the quality of natural language understanding and generation. These models utilize self-attention mechanisms to capture context more effectively, yielding more coherent, accurate, and contextually appropriate outputs (Acheampong et al., 2021; Rahali & Akhloufi, 2023). In SLA, transformer-based models support grammar correction, paraphrasing, summarizing, and question generation, allowing learners to interact with more sophisticated and accurate language models (Chowdhury & Nath, 2021).

Natural Language Processing (NLP) and Chatbots

NLP is one of the branches of AI that enables machines to understand, interpret, and generate human language. NLP is integrated in several AI-driven chatbots that simulate human conversations, providing real-time interaction for language learning. Popular chatbots are ChatGPT (OpenAI), Google Bard, Bing Copilot, and Replika, which use NLP to support vocabulary building, grammar correction, and conversation practice (Bakdash et al., 2024; Lee & Hudson, 2024; Panagiotidis, 2024). These tools can help imitate real communicative environments, scaffold learners' interaction, and provide prompt corrective feedback, facilitating language learning. A few examples of such systems are Mitsuku, and Replika. Chatbots can provide learners with incorrect information about other cultures; therefore, it's essential to use culturally sensitive training data to ensure they function effectively in plurilingual environments. (Chinnaiyan et al., 2025).

Speech Recognition Tools

Speech recognition tools process spoken language and transform it into text or meaningful feedback. These technologies are used in SLA to help learners practice pronunciation, intonation, and speaking fluency (Mohamed et al., 2024; Sholekhah & Fakhrurriana, 2023). ELSA Speak provides individualized feedback on pronunciation and accent training. In addition, other tools such as Google's Speech-to-Text and Microsoft Azure provide strong speech applications for real-time oral assessment and feedback. Tools like iFlytek and CMU Sphinx even support multilingual speech processing, allowing more inclusive and localized learning experiences. These tools reduce learner anxiety, promote self-correction, and support oral language development in authentic contexts (Li et al., 2023).

AI-powered intelligent tutoring systems (ITS)

These ITS systems provide personalized and responsive language instruction by continuously analyzing learner input and offering targeted feedback. These systems diagnose learner strengths and weaknesses in real-time, identify knowledge gaps, and recommend customized strategies for improvement. For example, platforms like WeWrite and Yixue integrate NLP and learner analytics to guide students through writing tasks or grammar exercises with adaptive scaffolding (Chopade et al., 2023; Létourneau et al., 2025).

Gamified Language Apps

These apps incorporate game-based design elements, such as points, levels, rewards, and interactive challenges, to enhance learners' engagement and motivation. For instance, Duolingo offers structured lessons using a visually engaging and competitive format that encourages noticing and regular practice (Kazu & Kuvvetli, 2024; Smith et al., 2024). Other apps, such as Memrise and Drops, incorporate spaced repetition and multimedia content to support vocabulary retention and pronunciation. Another tool called Mondly combines gamification with augmented reality (AR) to create immersive learning experiences. These tools align with motivational theories in SLA, as they foster learner autonomy and sustain long-term commitment through goal-setting and an instant feedback mechanism.

Corpora and learner analytics

They offer powerful AI-driven tools for developing language acquisition through data-informed instruction. Corpora are large and structured databases of authentic language use that can be used to identify patterns in grammar, vocabulary, collocations, and discourse. Language learners and instructors can consult well-known corpora such as the British National Corpus (BNC), Corpus of Contemporary American English (COCA), and the Sketch Engine to identify correct examples and the frequency of the target language. AI tools can incorporate corpus data into real-time writing feedback, paraphrasing, and vocabulary suggestions (Boulton et al., 2017).

On the other hand, learner analytics collect and analyze data about learners' behavior, performance, and engagement. These systems track progress, identify learning gaps, and suggest personalized interventions (Paulsen & Lindsay, 2024; Susnjak et al., 2022). Platforms such as WeWrite or Knewton, use dashboards to inform both learners and instructors, enhancing reflective practice and targeted instruction. The combination of corpora and analytics enables evidence-based, adaptive, and self-regulated learning environments in SLA.

Machine Translation Tools and Language Generation Systems

AI language translation processes are an excellent instrument for acquainting learners with foreign texts, websites, or documents by reading or viewing them in the same way as a learner would in their native language. AI expedites the translation and processing of information for passages that enhance a learner's comprehension and promote the development of vocabulary and sentence structure. For low-resource languages, transformer-based models like T5 have made translations 10% more accurate.

These tools are widely used in SLA to provide real-time translations, paraphrasing support, and assistance with multilingual communication. Tools like Google Translate, DeepL, and Microsoft Translator help learners comprehend foreign language texts, generate target language output, and expand vocabulary (Mohamed et al., 2024; Shahmerdanova, 2025). While early versions of MT struggled with grammatical accuracy, current AI-enhanced models have significantly improved through neural machine translation (NMT), offering more context-aware and fluent translations (Tariq, 2024; Yuxiu, 2024).

Language generation systems such as ChatGPT and Jasper AI allow learners to generate coherent paragraphs, practice writing prompts, or simulate dialogues in different registers and tones. These tools help learners produce extended written output, support idea generation, and reinforce their understanding of syntactic structures. When used critically and with instructional guidance, these systems can enhance fluency, coherence, and stylistic awareness in writing (Bakdash et al., 2024).

OPPORTUNITIES OF AI IN SECOND LANGUAGE ACQUISITION

Personalized and Adaptive Learning Systems

These systems utilize learner data, including proficiency levels, performance metrics, and interaction patterns, to tailor content, pace, and support in real-time. These systems often deliver instruction that is aligned with learners' unique goals, needs, and strengths. Tools like Century Tech, Knewton, and Carnegie Learning dynamically adjust difficulty, suggest targeted resources, and provide differentiated pathways. This approach ensures that learners receive the right type of input at the right time, aligning with Krashen's notion of "i+1" and Vygotsky's concept of scaffolding within the Zone of Proximal Development (ZPD). These systems can also be aligned with the Common European Framework of Reference for Languages (CEFR), ensuring that learners meet standardized language proficiency benchmarks (Li et al., 2024).

Immersive Learning through VR/AR and Virtual Agents

Virtual Reality (VR) and Augmented Reality (AR), along with virtual agents, offer interactive, context-rich experiences that mimic real-world communication. Learners often engage with virtual characters, manipulate objects, and explore culturally authentic scenarios in a fully immersive environment (Azar & Tan, 2020; Schorr et al., 2024). For example, Mondly VR offers language lessons with virtual tutors in realistic environments, enhancing speaking and listening skills through contextual interaction. Similarly, platforms like ImmerseMe and ENGAGE use VR to place learners in simulated settings such as restaurants, airports, or classrooms, where they can practice language in situational contexts (Arnau-González et al., 2023; Kochmar et al., 2022; Sharma & Harkishan, 2022).

Virtual agents such as AI-powered avatars or chatbots provide responsive conversational practice, modeling authentic language use and enabling role-play scenarios (Létourneau et al., 2025). Such environments support experiential learning, boost learner confidence, and reduce anxiety associated with real-life communication. These technologies align with experiential and sociocultural learning theories and have been shown to increase learner engagement, language retention, and intercultural competence (Gu et al., 2023; Katsarou et al., 2023).

Support for Multilingual and Plurilingual Learners

AI-driven language tools facilitate translanguaging by enabling learners to use their whole linguistic repertoire (L1, L2, L3, etc.) to enhance comprehension and production (Danilina & Pichon, 2023; Jafary & Shakib Kotamjani, 2025). Recent developments, such as plug-ins allowing concurrent L1 and L2 support in writing platforms (Lawrance et al., 2024). Moreover, multilingual chatbots and code-switching-friendly interfaces facilitate students' connections between languages when encountering challenging concepts (Bawa et al., 2020; Bhimanwar et al., 2024). These innovations promote learners' linguistic resources and support metalinguistic awareness and cognitive flexibility (Haoming & Wei, 2024).

Gamified Language Learning Environments

Numerous AI-powered language learning environments incorporate gamified elements, including badges, leader boards, and rewards, to enhance the enjoyment and engagement of the learning experience. Gamified environments can facilitate the retention and motivation of language knowledge (Bachiri et al., 2023; Kherazi & Bourray, 2024; Tsvilodub et al., 2023).

Intelligent Tutoring Systems

Carnegie Learning and ALEKS are examples of intelligent tutoring systems. Virtual assistants such as Siri and Alexa from Apple and Amazon can help learners improve their speaking and listening abilities in the target language. However, these systems may struggle with languages that lack extensive resources, as they often lack sufficient training data. To improve performance, they need synthetic datasets (Dizon, 2023; Dizon et al., 2022; Dizon & Tang, 2020).

AI for Real-Time Feedback and Assessment

AI-based language learning tools can provide learners with real-time feedback on their pronunciation, assignments, and exercises. This feedback enables learners to identify and rectify errors in the moment, thereby facilitating more efficient language acquisition (Cherner et al., 2023; Escalante et al., 2023; Qiao & Zhao, 2023b; Yang et al., 2024; Zou et al., 2023).

Data-Driven Instructional Design and Decision-Making

AI-powered analytics has the potential to enable instructors to make informed and evidence-based decisions in language teaching (Paulsen & Lindsay, 2024; Susnjak et al., 2022).By collecting and analyzing data on learner behaviors, proficiency trends, and engagement patterns, instructors can tailor content delivery, identify struggling students, and adjust pacing to optimize learning outcomes. Tools like Knewton, Century Tech, and Smart Sparrow provide real-time dashboards and predictive analytics that support differentiated instruction and formative assessment (Ho, 2024). Moreover, data-driven design helps institutions align instruction with curricular standards such as the Common European Framework of Reference for Languages (CEFR), ensuring consistency in proficiency measurement and goal-setting. These systems empower teachers to improve learner tracking and support reflective practice (Li et al., 2024).

ILLUSTRATIVE CASE STUDIES OF AI INTEGRATION IN SLA

While theories and technological advancements highlight AI's potential in SLA, real-world implementation of AI offers critical insights on practical effectiveness in classroom settings. By focusing on case studies, we gain insight into how AI is applied in language learning, what works well, what does not, and how different settings impact its success. This section presents a series of case studies from different educational contexts, ranging from K-12 classrooms to higher education and adult learning programs. The best practices, learner outcomes, and pedagogical strategies related to AI-supported language instruction are highlighted. These real-world examples can raise awareness among educators, researchers, and policymakers by illustrating how AI tools can be tailored to meet specific learner needs, support inclusive practices, and foster effective language development.

The Effect of Voice Recognition on Pronunciation

ELSA Speak is an AI-powered mobile app that has been designed to improve learners' English pronunciation and speaking skills through voice recognition and personalized coaching. Nguyen et al. (2025) examined the effect of the ELSA Speak app on the pronunciation skills of Vietnamese EFL university students. Thirty-seven English majors were engaged in guided classroom use and self-paced learning with this app for 4.5 months. The app provided individualized feedback on pronunciation through speech recognition technology. Results of the post-test and pre-test showed that learners' pronunciation accuracy significantly improved in the post-test. Learners showed positive attitudes toward the ELSA app's real-time feedback. Despite its strengths in phonetic awareness and accent training, the tool's pedagogical efficacy is constrained by its focus on decontextualized pronunciation practice. It does not address suprasegmental features, such as rhythm and stress, in connected speech, nor does it engage learners in extended conversational turns. Moreover, dependence on standardized native-speaker models may disadvantage learners with diverse accents or speech patterns, reinforcing a narrow view of intelligibility.

In another study, Dubey et al. (2025) In a quasi-experimental study, the effect of an AI-powered speech recognition system based on Natural Language Processing (NLP) on improving EFL learners' speaking was examined. The comparison of pre- and post-tests showed that learners in the experimental group showed improvement in pronunciation accuracy and oral fluency compared to those using traditional methods. Real-time feedback enables learners to identify and self-correct errors, boosting their confidence, motivation, and autonomy as learners. They emphasized the importance of integrating such NLP-based tools within blended learning environments where teacher support can complement AI-driven practice. Moreover, several studies used AI-powered speech recognition tools, such as ELSA Speak, Duolingo, and Speechling in their studies and consistently reported improvements in learners' speaking fluency and pronunciation accuracy, emphasizing the effectiveness of real-time feedback and individualized oral practice in different EFL context (Dennis, 2024; Nguyen & Nguyen, 2020; Qiao & Zhao, 2023). However, accent bias, limited support for less common L1s, and inaccurate recognition in noisy or multilingual environments can compromise the quality of feedback. Additionally, the absence of scaffolding for pragmatic or sociolinguistic use of language limits their value for holistic language learning.

Improving Speaking Fluency and Autonomy via Duolingo

Duolingo is a well-known language learning app that is free to use and available on both mobile devices and online. It offers short, easy-to-follow lessons in more than 40 languages, utilizing fun, game-like features such as points, streaks, badges, and leaderboards to keep users motivated and engaged. Several studies have investigated its effectiveness in developing the speaking proficiency of EFL learners. For instance, Qiao & Zhao (2023) conducted a study to examine the effectiveness of Duolingo's AI-supported gamified learning on EFL students' speaking proficiency and self-regulated learning skills. Ninety-three Chinese university students were randomly assigned to a controlled traditional instruction group and a Duolingo experimental group. After several weeks, the results revealed that the AI group showed statistically significant improvements in speaking fluency and self-regulation, such as goal setting, planning, and persistence.

Similarly, Nursuhaniah (2025) found significant post-test improvements in Indonesian high school students' speaking proficiency and speaking interest when Duolingo was employed as a gamification tool. Similarly, Kazu & Kuvvetli (2024), in a mixed-method study with Turkish high school learners, reported that Duolingo's game-based interaction and pronunciation exercises significantly enhanced oral fluency and learner motivation. These results were supported in studies conducted by Sakkir & Syamsuddin (2023) and Smith et al. (2024) confirmed Duolingo's effectiveness in enhancing pronunciation accuracy, vocabulary recall, and learner autonomy, particularly when used in blended learning environments. In the Saudi Arabian context, Alfuhaid, (2021) found that Saudi secondary school students who used Duolingo for four months showed statistically significant improvements in speaking proficiency and an anxiety reduction. However, while post-test performance improved in the experimental group, the study's short duration and lack of qualitative follow-up limit its ability to assess long-term transfer to real-world speaking contexts. Moreover, the learning remained app-centered, raising questions about how effectively such tools promote interactional competence. The study also did not explore how learner differences (e.g., prior proficiency or motivation levels) shaped outcomes, which is crucial for assessing the generalizability of gamified AI tools in diverse educational settings.

AI-Powered Intelligent Tutoring Systems in K–12

Recent studies have examined the integration of Intelligent Tutoring Systems (ITS) in K–12 classrooms, revealing varying levels of effectiveness depending on the learning context, subject area, and the duration of implementation. For example, Wijekumar et al., (2022) implemented the WeWrite ITS to improve 5th-grade students' planning and writing skills. The results revealed that integration of WeWrite has a medium effect size on planning improvement, and they emphasized that this app should supplement rather than replace teacher instruction. Another case by Cui et al. (2018) compared two English language learning ITS platforms, namely Yixue and BOXFiSH. The results revealed that EFL learners found greater learning improvements in the Yixue group, which is characterized by its finer adaptivity in content delivery.

In another study, Holstein et al. (2025) demonstrated that the combination of the Lynnette ITS with Lumilo augmented reality glasses, which enabled teachers to monitor students in real-time, yielded better student outcomes than using the ITS alone. The results highlight the importance of blended models that maintain active teacher involvement. However, certain gaps still exist, such as the temporary impact caused by the novelty of new tools and the limited number of longitudinal studies with diverse learners needed to validate the results more widely.

Azzam & Charles (2025), in a qualitative study, researchers explored how K–12 English teachers in the United Arab Emirates are integrating AI tools into English language classrooms. They conducted semi-structured interviews with teachers from both public and private schools to examine their perceptions, current practices, and the pedagogical implications of AI integration. Most teachers reported familiarity with language learning applications, such as Duolingo and ELSA Speak, as well as grammar checkers, writing assistants, and voice recognition tools for pronunciation and speaking practice. They emphasized that these tools enhanced student engagement and supported individualized learning experiences. Teachers noted that integrating AI tools into K–12 classrooms enabled them to provide real-time feedback and error correction, which in turn boosted learners' confidence. Additionally, they highlighted the usefulness of these tools in managing large classes with mixed-ability learners. However, the study also revealed several challenges, including limited training and professional development opportunities for teachers, technological barriers, inadequate infrastructure in some schools, and concerns regarding data privacy and excessive reliance on automated feedback.

CHALLENGES AND ETHICAL CONSIDERATIONS OF INTEGRATING AI

Equity, Access, and Contextual Implementation Challenges

Despite the benefits of AI in SLA, significant obstacles remain, mainly in under-resourced and linguistically diverse contexts. Many AI tools need high-bandwidth internet, advanced devices, and consistent access, which may not be available in all educational settings. This raises concerns about equity and inclusivity in AI-driven language support. Another critical issue is teacher preparedness. Many educators, especially in low- and middle-income countries, lack the training and confidence to integrate AI into their teaching practices meaningfully (Bakdash et al., 2024). If professional development and supportive policies are lacking, integrating AI could deepen the digital gap instead of closing it. For AI to serve as a transformative tool rather than one that excludes, it must be implemented in ways that are sensitive to context, culturally appropriate, and supported by initiatives that strengthen teacher expertise.

Algorithmic Bias and Fairness

AI tools developed for SLA can still reflect biases that exist in their algorithms. Speech recognition tools often exhibit accent bias, demonstrating higher accuracy with native or standard accents, while struggling to transcribe non-native or regional speakers (Pessach & Shmueli, 2022; Tilmes, 2022). This might result in learner frustration, misrecognition, and unfair outcomes in automated feedback. Moreover, the data used to train AI systems may reflect cultural, racial, or gender biases, leading to harmful stereotypes or the exclusion of minority language perspectives (Liang et al., 2023; Min, 2023). For instance, chatbot replies suggest culturally unfamiliar scenarios such as 'Thanksgiving dinner' or 'Black Friday sales' in vocabulary practice for learners in Central Asia or Africa, resulting in confusion or disengagement.

To achieve fairness, AI developers and educators should emphasize transparent algorithm development, systematic checks for bias, and the use of representative training corpora. Ethical use of AI also involves consistent monitoring and adaptation to minimize negative effects and support fair access to effective language education for all learners with different backgrounds (González & Rampino, 2024).

Privacy, Data Sovereignty, and Learner Trust

AI tools collect massive amounts of learners' data, comprising voice recordings, writing samples, and measures of learner engagement. For instance, learners using free AI-powered mobile applications may mistakenly agree to have their speech or writing data stored and processed in regions with weaker privacy laws, often without a clear option to refuse (Pessach & Shmueli, 2022; Sebastian, 2023). Although such tools enable personalized learning and progress monitoring, they also raise concerns about privacy, informed consent, and data ownership. A lack of transparency about data usage, storage, and sharing can lead learners to lose confidence and raise ethical concerns. To overcome this shortcoming, the AI tool developers must prioritize transparency, clearly communicate data practices, and offer users control over their data (Huang, 2023).

Human Interaction and Emotional Connection

While AI-powered tools can mimic conversation and provide personalized learning pathways, they often fail to capture the nuanced human interaction needed to support the emotional and social components of acquiring a language (Gkinko & Elbanna, 2022; Meyer et al., 2024). Research in SLA emphasizes the importance of emotional connection, teacher presence, and peer collaboration in promoting motivation, persistence, and intercultural awareness. AI chatbots and virtual agents may provide efficient feedback, but they cannot yet replicate the nuanced emotional support or adaptive scaffolding that human teachers offer. For instance, a frustrated learner might get responses from an AI that are grammatically accurate but lack emotional sensitivity, which could lead to reduced motivation to continue practicing.

Cultural Sensitivity in AI Training

AI systems used in SLA often reflect the linguistic and cultural biases of the datasets on which they are trained. When these datasets mainly include Western-centric idioms, values, or communication styles, the resulting outputs may be culturally irrelevant or even misleading for learners from different backgrounds (Colas et al., 2022). For example, learners from Southeast Asia or Africa may encounter vocabulary examples or scenarios that assume familiarity with Western holidays, foods, or social norms, thereby limiting cultural inclusivity. To address this challenge, AI developers must incorporate diverse linguistic inputs to accommodate varied sociolinguistic realities and foster intercultural competence, by this means promoting rather than marginalizing linguistic diversity and cultural understanding.

Lack of Standardized Assessment Frameworks

While AI tools can provide real-time and personalized assessments, a significant gap remains in validated, standardized frameworks for evaluating AI-mediated learning. Questions of fairness, reliability, and alignment with language proficiency standards, such as the CEFR, endure. Without transparent assessment criteria, educators may struggle to interpret AI-generated scores and feedback. Future research and collaboration between educators, technologists, and policymakers are needed to design frameworks that integrate formative, summative, and self-regulated assessment practices.

Critical Reflection on Pedagogical Integration of AI in SLA

While AI tools like Duolingo, ELSA Speak, and NLP-based tutors offer support for language learners, their integration into language classrooms raises important educational considerations. Traditional SLA theories. Such as interactionism, sociocultural theory, and task-based language teaching, emphasize the importance of interaction, scaffolding, and authentic communicative tasks. Many current AI tools, however, focus narrowly on form-based practice and pronunciation drills, often in decontextualized settings. This may reinforce a behaviorist model of learning that prioritizes accuracy over communicative competence. For instance, tools that provide instant corrective feedback on pronunciation may help learners self-correct, but do not necessarily foster negotiation of meaning or pragmatic competence. Moreover, these platforms rarely provide opportunities for collaborative learning or dialogic interaction, which are central to constructivist SLA pedagogies. As such, educators must critically assess whether the AI tool supports deeper language processing and transferable communicative skills or merely surface-level engagement.

FUTURE DIRECTIONS AND RECOMMENDATIONS

Integration into Formal Curricula

Although AI tools are widely used in informal learning, their systematic incorporation into formal SLA curricula is still developing. Educational institutions should develop policies and frameworks that integrate AI into lesson planning, learning outcomes, teacher training, and assessment practices. Curricular integration should emphasize pedagogical alignment, the ethical use of AI, and support for teacher agency.

Development of Standardized, Transparent Assessment Frameworks

AI-mediated assessments require robust and transparent evaluation frameworks that align with global standards such as the Common European Framework of Reference for Languages (CEFR) (Li et al., 2024). Future directions should focus on designing AI tools that integrate formative, summative, and self-regulated assessment practices while ensuring fairness, interpretability, and cross-contextual applicability.

Toward Deep Personalization and Intelligent Adaptivity

AI's future in education lies in deep personalization and smart adaptability, utilizing advanced analytics to make learning experiences more personalized (Piduru, 2023). AI is currently at a very exciting and important period, much like other technologies that have come before it. As AI improves and becomes more widespread, it could transform the way we teach, learn, evaluate, and regulate schools. However, it is essential to recognize that the technology itself will not drive the current and future revolutions in AI for education, but rather by the ethical, pedagogical, and sociocultural contexts and frameworks in which AI is developed and implemented in schools.

Use of AI in Low-Resource Language Contexts

In many underserved regions, AI can provide scalable and cost-effective language learning solutions. Future work should prioritize designing lightweight, offline-compatible tools that cater to local languages, low-connectivity environments, and minimal digital literacy. Collaboration with local educators and communities is essential for relevance and sustainability (Dere et al., 2023; Getman et al., 2023).

Support for Multilingual and Plurilingual Education

AI systems should increasingly reflect the needs of multilingual learners through translanguaging tools, cross-lingual NLP, and culturally inclusive content (Danilina & Pichon, 2023). Future tools should allow learners to move fluidly across languages while leveraging their full linguistic repertoires, particularly in bilingual and heritage language contexts.

Ethical Algorithm Design and Cultural Sensitivity

Developers and educators must co-create AI systems that reflect linguistic diversity and cultural contexts. Future research should investigate bias mitigation strategies, equitable algorithm training, and explainable AI models (Khasawneh, 2023; Xia et al., 2024). Incorporating global perspectives will help ensure that AI systems support, not hinder, educational equity.

Human-AI Partnerships in Pedagogy

The future of AI in SLA should center on collaboration, not replacement. AI should support teachers with planning, feedback, and diagnostics, while educators retain the role of facilitators, cultural mediators, and emotional guides. Research on effective human-AI co-teaching models is a critical area for exploration.

AI as an Instructional Co-Designer

In the future of education, AI may well evolve into more than a reactive tutor and will develop alongside learners as a co-designer in the creation of learning experiences. Intelligent systems may be able to design individualized lesson plans autonomously, create formative assessments that reflect the individual student's goals, and make recommendations to human teachers about teaching interventions based on predictive analytics. In hybrid classrooms, teachers may collaborate with AI systems to design instruction, manage cognitive load, and regulate participation from a variety of learners (Alasadi & Baiz, 2023; Singh & Ram, 2024). In this scenario, the teacher's role is upgraded from a passive user of technology to an active one, making decisions and facilitating learning in an AI-mediated learning environment. In this way, AI in education might not replace the teacher's role, but instead become a data-driven, analytical partner that helps instructors make value-based decisions, share cultural knowledge, and demonstrate empathy.

Interdisciplinary and Global Collaboration

The growth of artificial intelligence within education will also create new opportunities for interdisciplinary collaboration, in which educators will work alongside data scientists, linguists, psychologists, and ethicists to co-design pedagogically informed and culturally responsive systems. Significantly, in global education contexts, AI can assist in bridging linguistic and curricular divides with features such as real-time translation and insights for cross-linguistic transfer, enabling the localization of content that is responsive to the needs of diverse learners. Still, this global reach needs to be aware of the need to be sensitive to local instances, especially in places with few resources, through community-driven development (Pfeiffer et al., 2023).

Anticipating Future Challenges

There are obstacles to overcome, while there is hope, the road ahead of us will still require focus on algorithmic accountability, data privacy, and equitable access to technology in the future of AI in education. As systems become more autonomous or automated, questions of agency, authorship, and transparency will become increasingly urgent. As AI technologies play a bigger role in making crucial decisions about things like placement in courses or programs or performance evaluations, it is important to follow ethical guidelines to make sure that all learners are treated fairly and with respect (Cheong, 2024).

While existing studies provide valuable insights into the short-term effects of AI in SLA, there remains a pressing need for more rigorous, longitudinal research that investigates the long-term effects on language development, learner autonomy, and the transferability of skills to real-world contexts. Most current studies focus on immediate gains in accuracy or fluency, but few explore how sustained use of AI tools affects motivation, identity, or pragmatic competence. Future research should adopt mixed-method approaches that combine quantitative performance data with qualitative insights into learner experience. Additionally, emerging technologies such as affective computing, intelligent feedback systems, and AI-integrated virtual reality (VR) platforms offer exciting possibilities for immersive, personalized, and emotionally responsive language learning. These innovations, if aligned with sound pedagogical principles, can extend the capabilities of AI beyond drill-based learning and toward a more holistic, communicative model of language acquisition. Furthermore, collaboration between AI developers, educators, and policymakers is essential to create frameworks that prioritize ethical use, learner agency, and educational equity.

CONCLUSION

The integration of artificial intelligence in second language acquisition (SLA) is transforming the way languages are taught and learned. From personalized learning and real-time feedback to immersive VR experiences and intelligent tutoring, AI presents vast opportunities to enhance engagement, accessibility, and linguistic competence. These developments are deeply grounded in SLA theories, aligning with pedagogical goals and addressing learner diversity across contexts. Yet, this transformation is not without its challenges. Issues such as algorithmic bias, cultural insensitivity, data privacy concerns, emotional disconnection, and the lack of standardized assessment frameworks underscore the need for ethically guided and human-centered design.

Moving forward, inclusive, adaptive, and culturally responsive AI systems must be developed in collaboration with educators, linguists, technologists, and learners themselves. Co-design practices, interdisciplinary research, and alignment with global standards, such as the CEFR and the SDGs, will be critical in ensuring that AI enhances rather than hinders equitable language learning. In summary, AI presents promising avenues for reimagining SLA in ways that are scalable, flexible, and learner-driven. With thoughtful design, ethical oversight, and policy support, AI can empower educators and learners alike to navigate the multilingual realities of our global society.

REFERENCES

Acheampong, F. A., Nunoo-Mensah, H., & Chen, W. (2021). Transformer models for text-based emotion detection: A review of BERT-based approaches. *Artificial Intelligence Review*, *54*(8), 5789–5829. Advance online publication. DOI: 10.1007/s10462-021-09958-2

Alasadi, E. A., & Baiz, C. R. (2023). Generative AI in Education and Research: Opportunities, Concerns, and Solutions. *Journal of Chemical Education*, *100*(8), 2965–2971. Advance online publication. DOI: 10.1021/acs.jchemed.3c00323

Alfuhaid, S. R. (2021). The Utilisation of Duolingo to Enhance the Speaking Proficiency of EFL Secondary School Students in Saudi Arabia. *English Language Teaching*, *14*(11), 9. DOI: 10.5539/elt.v14n11p9

Almelhes, S. A. (2023). A Review of Artificial Intelligence Adoption in Second-Language Learning. *Theory and Practice in Language Studies*, *13*(5), 1259–1269. Advance online publication. DOI: 10.17507/tpls.1305.21

Andreevich, K. E. (2023). Language Learning 2.0: the Role of Artificial Intelligence in Facilitating Second Language Acquisition. *Актуальные Проблемы Педагогики И Психологии*, *4*(1).

Azar, A. S., & Tan, N. H. I. (2020). The application of ICT techs (mobile-assisted language learning, gamification, and virtual reality) in teaching english for secondary school students in malaysia during covid-19 pandemic. *Universal Journal of Educational Research*, *8*(11 C). DOI: 10.13189/ujer.2020.082307

Azzam, A., & Charles, T. (2025). K-12 STEM Teachers' Experiences with Artificial Intelligence. *TEM Journal*, *14*(1), 463–468. https://doi.org/DOI: 10.18421/TEM141-41

Bachiri, Y. A., Mouncif, H., & Bouikhalene, B. (2023). Artificial Intelligence Empowers Gamification: Optimizing Student Engagement and Learning Outcomes in E-learning and MOOCs. *International Journal of Engineering Pedagogy*, *13*(8), 4–19. Advance online publication. DOI: 10.3991/ijep.v13i8.40853

Bakdash, L., Abid, A., Gourisankar, A., & Henry, T. L. (2024). Chatting Beyond ChatGPT: Advancing Equity Through AI-Driven Language Interpretation. *Journal of General Internal Medicine*, *39*(3), 492–495. Advance online publication. DOI: 10.1007/s11606-023-08497-6

Bawa, A., Khadpe, P., Joshi, P., Bali, K., & Choudhury, M. (2020). Do Multilingual Users Prefer Chat-bots that Code-mix? Let's Nudge and Find Out! *Proceedings of the ACM on Human-Computer Interaction, 4*(CSCW1). DOI: 10.1145/3392846

Bhatt, P., & Muduli, A. (2023). Artificial intelligence in learning and development: a systematic literature review. In *European Journal of Training and Development* (Vol. 47, pp. 7–8). Issues., DOI: 10.1108/EJTD-09-2021-0143

Bhimanwar, S., Viralekar, O., Anturkar, K., & Kulkarni, A. (2024). Deep Learning Approaches for English-Marathi Code-Switched Detection. *EAI Endorsed Transactions on Scalable Information Systems, 11*(3). Advance online publication. DOI: 10.4108/eetsis.3972

Bornstein, M. H., & Gardner, H. (1986). Frames of Mind: The Theory of Multiple Intelligences. *Journal of Aesthetic Education, 20*(2), 120. Advance online publication. DOI: 10.2307/3332707

Boulton, A., Thorne, S., & York, N. (2017). *Alex Boulton. (2017). Data-driven learning and language pedagogy. In S. Thorne & S. May (eds.), 1.* DOI: 10.1007/978-3-319-02328-1

Cheong, B. C. (2024). Transparency and accountability in AI systems: Safeguarding wellbeing in the age of algorithmic decision-making. *Frontiers in Human Dynamics, 6*, 1421273. Advance online publication. DOI: 10.3389/fhumd.2024.1421273

Cherner, T., Fegely, A., Hou, C., & Halpin, P. (2023). AI-Powered Presentation Platforms for Improving Public Speaking Skills: Takeaways and Suggestions for Improvement. *Journal of Interactive Learning Research, 34*(2), 339–367. Advance online publication. DOI: 10.70725/147215vyyrwx

Chinnaiyan, B., Balasubaramanian, S., Jeyabalu, M., & Warrier, G. S. (2025). AI Applications – Computer Vision and Natural Language Processing," in Model Optimization Methods for Efficient and Edge AI: Federated Learning Architectures. *Frameworks and Applications, IEEE*, 25–41.

Chopade, P., Pu, S., LaMar, M., & Kurzum, C. (2023). Task-Based Workplace English: An Adaptive Multimodal Tutoring System. *Communications in Computer and Information Science, 1831 CCIS*. DOI: 10.1007/978-3-031-36336-8_59

Chowdhury, S., & Nath, A. (2021). Trends In Natural Language Processing: Scope And Challenges. *International Journal of Scientific Research in Computer Science, Engineering and Information Technology*. DOI: 10.32628/CSEIT217698

Colas, C., Karch, T., Moulin-Frier, C., & Oudeyer, P.-Y. (2022). Vygotskian Autotelic Artificial Intelligence: Language and Culture Internalization for Human-Like AI. *Nature Machine Intelligence*, *4*(December).

Cui, W., Xue, Z., & Thai, K. P. (2018). Performance Comparison of an AI-Based Adaptive Learning System in China. *Proceedings 2018 Chinese Automation Congress, CAC 2018*. DOI: 10.1109/CAC.2018.8623327

Danilina, E., & Le Pichon, E. (2023). Embracing advances in AI-based language tools in EAP programs: Towards a plurilingual shift. In *Reconceptualizing Language Norms in Multilingual Contexts* (pp. 88–107). IGI Global., DOI: 10.4018/978-1-6684-8761-7.ch005

Dere, M. D., Dere, R. O., Adesina, A., & Yauri, A. R. (2023). An end-to-end framework for translation of American sign language to low-resource languages in Nigeria. *Scientific African*, *21*, e01809. Advance online publication. DOI: 10.1016/j.sciaf.2023.e01809

Dubey, P., Dubey, P., Raja, R., & Kshatri, S. S. (2025). Bridging language gaps: The role of NLP and speech recognition in oral english instruction. *MethodsX*, *14*, 103359. Advance online publication. DOI: 10.1016/j.mex.2025.103359

Escalante, J., Pack, A., & Barrett, A. (2023). AI-generated feedback on writing: Insights into efficacy and ENL student preference. *International Journal of Educational Technology in Higher Education*, *20*(1), 57. Advance online publication. DOI: 10.1186/s41239-023-00425-2

Getman, Y., Phan, N., Al-Ghezi, R., Voskoboinik, E., Singh, M., Grosz, T., Kurimo, M., Salvi, G., Svendsen, T., Strombergsson, S., Smolander, A., & Ylinen, S. (2023). Developing an AI-Assisted Low-Resource Spoken Language Learning App for Children. *IEEE Access : Practical Innovations, Open Solutions*, *11*, 86025–86037. Advance online publication. DOI: 10.1109/ACCESS.2023.3304274

Gkinko, L., & Elbanna, A. (2022). Hope, tolerance and empathy: Employees' emotions when using an AI-enabled chatbot in a digitalised workplace. *Information Technology & People*, *35*(6), 1714–1743. Advance online publication. DOI: 10.1108/ITP-04-2021-0328

González, A. S., & Rampino, L. (2024). A design perspective on how to tackle gender biases when developing AI-driven systems. *AI and Ethics*. Advance online publication. DOI: 10.1007/s43681-023-00386-2

Gu, X., Yu, T., Huang, J., Wang, F., Zheng, X., Sun, M., Ye, Z., & Li, Q. (2023). Virtual-Agent-Based Language Learning: A Scoping Review of Journal Publications from 2012 to 2022. *Sustainability (Basel), 15*(18), 13479. Advance online publication. DOI: 10.3390/su151813479

Haoming, L., & Wei, W. (2024). A systematic review on vocabulary learning in AR and VR gamification context. *Computers and Education: X Reality, 4*. DOI: 10.1016/j.cexr.2024.100057

Ho, C. C. (2024). Using AI-Generative Tools in Tertiary Education: Reflections on Their Effectiveness in Improving Tertiary Students' English Writing Abilities. *Online Learning : the Official Journal of the Online Learning Consortium, 28*(3), 33–54. DOI: 10.24059/olj.v28i3.4632

Huang, L. (2023). Ethics of Artificial Intelligence in Education: Student Privacy and Data Protection. *Science Insights Education Frontiers, 16*(2), 2577–2587. Advance online publication. DOI: 10.15354/sief.23.re202

Jafary, M., & Shakib Kotamjani, S. (2025). *Enhancing Linguistic Accessibility and Academic Inclusion through AI Tools: A Pilot Study on Plurilingual Graduate Students at McGill University*.

Kaiss, W., Mansouri, K., & Poirier, F. (2023). Effectiveness of an Adaptive Learning Chatbot on Students' Learning Outcomes Based on Learning Styles. *International Journal of Emerging Technologies in Learning, 18*(13), 250–261. Advance online publication. DOI: 10.3991/ijet.v18i13.39329

Kamal, A. (2022). Critical appraisement of Monitor Model. *Research Journal in Advanced Humanities, 3*(1). Advance online publication. DOI: 10.58256/rjah.v3i1.766

Kasneci, E., Sessler, K., Küchemann, S., Bannert, M., Dementieva, D., Fischer, F., Gasser, U., Groh, G., Günnemann, S., Hüllermeier, E., Krusche, S., Kutyniok, G., Michaeli, T., Nerdel, C., Pfeffer, J., Poquet, O., Sailer, M., Schmidt, A., Seidel, T., . . . Kasneci, G. (2023). ChatGPT for good? On opportunities and challenges of large language models for education. In *Learning and Individual Differences* (Vol. 103). DOI: 10.1016/j.lindif.2023.102274

Katsarou, E., Wild, F., Sougari, A. M., & Chatzipanagiotou, P. (2023). A Systematic Review of Voice-based Intelligent Virtual Agents in EFL Education. *International Journal of Emerging Technologies in Learning, 18*(10), 65–85. Advance online publication. DOI: 10.3991/ijet.v18i10.37723

Kazu, I. Y., & Kuvvetli, M. (2024). Improve speaking skills with Duolingo's mobile game-based language learning. *Asian Journal of Education and Training, 10*(1), 62–75. DOI: 10.20448/edu.v10i1.5488

Khasawneh, M. A. S. (2023). The potential of AI in facilitating cross-cultural communication through translation. *Journal of Namibian Studies, 37.*

Kherazi, A., & Bourray, M. (2024). Gamification and m-learning: An innovative approach to sustainable language learning. *E3S Web of Conferences, 477.* DOI: 10.1051/e3sconf/202447700066

Klitgaard, R., & Gardner, H. (1984). Frames of Mind: The Theory of Multiple Intelligences. *Journal of Policy Analysis and Management, 3*(4), 627. Advance online publication. DOI: 10.2307/3324560

Krahnke, K. J., Krashen, S. D., & Terrell, T. D. (1985). The Natural Approach: Language Acquisition in the Classroom. *TESOL Quarterly, 19*(3), 591. Advance online publication. DOI: 10.2307/3586280

Lawrance, J. C., Sambath, P., Shiny, C., Vazhangal, M., & Bala, K. (2024). Developing an AI-Assisted Multilingual Adaptive Learning System for Personalized English Language Teaching," 2024 10th International Conference on Advanced Computing and Communication Systems (ICACCS). *Coimbatore*, 428–434.

Lee, J. S., & Hudson, J. (2024). Digital education in teaching English as an international language. In *The Routledge Handbook of Teaching English as an International Language*. Routledge. DOI: 10.4324/9781003203261-21

Létourneau, A., Deslandes Martineau, M., Charland, P., Karran, J. A., Boasen, J., & Léger, P. M. (2025). A systematic review of AI-driven intelligent tutoring systems (ITS) in K-12 education. *NPJ Science of Learning, 10*(1), 29. Advance online publication. DOI: 10.1038/s41539-025-00320-7

Li, Z., Li, J. Z., Zhang, X., & Reynolds, B. L. (2024). Mastery of Listening and Reading Vocabulary Levels in Relation to CEFR: Insights into Student Admissions and English as a Medium of Instruction. *Languages (Basel, Switzerland), 9*(7), 239. Advance online publication. DOI: 10.3390/languages9070239

Liang, W., Yuksekgonul, M., Mao, Y., Wu, E., & Zou, J. (2023). GPT detectors are biased against non-native English writers. In *Patterns* (Vol. 4, Issue 7). Cell Press. DOI: 10.1016/j.patter.2023.100779

Mao, Y., Tao, D., Zhang, S., Qi, T., & Li, K. (2025). *Research and Design on Intelligent Recognition of Unordered Targets for Robots Based on Reinforcement Learning*. https://arxiv.org/abs/2503.07340 DOI: 10.1109/ICETCI64844.2025.11084189

McLaughlin, B. (1990). Restructuring. *Applied Linguistics, 11*(2), 113–128. DOI: 10.1093/applin/11.2.113

Meyer, J., Jansen, T., Schiller, R., Liebenow, L. W., Steinbach, M., Horbach, A., & Fleckenstein, J. (2024). Using LLMs to bring evidence-based feedback into the classroom: AI-generated feedback increases secondary students' text revision, motivation, and positive emotions. *Computers and Education: Artificial Intelligence, 6*, 100199. Advance online publication. DOI: 10.1016/j.caeai.2023.100199

Min, A. (2023). Artifical Intelligence and Bias: Challenges, Implications, and Remedies. *Journal of Social Research, 2*(11), 3808–3817. Advance online publication. DOI: 10.55324/josr.v2i11.1477

Mohamed, Y. A., Khanan, A., Bashir, M., Mohamed, A. H. H. M., Adiel, M. A. E., & Elsadig, M. A. (2024). The Impact of Artificial Intelligence on Language Translation: A Review. *IEEE Access : Practical Innovations, Open Solutions, 12*, 25553–25579. Advance online publication. DOI: 10.1109/ACCESS.2024.3366802

Monika, M., & Suganthan, C. (2024). A Study on analyzing the role of Chatgpt in English acquisition among ESL learners during English language classroom. *Bodhi International Journal of Research in Humanities, Arts and Science, 8*(2).

Moulieswaran, N., & Kumar, P. N. S. (2023). Investigating ESL Learners' Perception and Problem towards Artificial Intelligence (AI) -Assisted English Language Learning and Teaching. *World Journal of English Language, 13*(5), 290. Advance online publication. DOI: 10.5430/wjel.v13n5p290

Muñoz-Basols, J. (2019). Going beyond the comfort zone: Multilingualism, translation and mediation to foster plurilingual competence. *Language, Culture and Curriculum, 32*(3), 299–321. Advance online publication. DOI: 10.1080/07908318.2019.1661687

Nguyen, T. S., Nguyen, T. D. T., Hoang, N. Q. N., & Do, T. K. H. (2025). How AI-Powered Voice Recognition Has Supported Pronunciation Competence among EFL University Learners. *CALL-EJ, 26*(3), 64–83. DOI: 10.54855/callej.252634

Nursuhaniah, N. (2025). Improving Students' Speaking Skill And Interest Through Duolingo As Gamification Application. *Indonesian Journal Learning and Instruction, 8*(1), 23–32. DOI: 10.25134/ijli.v8i1.11625

Ortega, L. (2019). SLA and the Study of Equitable Multilingualism. *Modern Language Journal, 103*(S1), 23–38. Advance online publication. DOI: 10.1111/modl.12525

Panagiotidis, P. (2024). *LLM-Based Chatbots in Language Learning. 7*(1).

Paulsen, L., & Lindsay, E. (2024). Learning analytics dashboards are increasingly becoming about learning and not just analytics - A systematic review. *Education and Information Technologies*, *29*(11), 14279–14308. DOI: 10.1007/s10639-023-12401-4

Pessach, D., & Shmueli, E. (2022). A Review on Fairness in Machine Learning. *ACM Computing Surveys*, *55*(3), 1–44. Advance online publication. DOI: 10.1145/3494672

Pfeiffer, J., Gutschow, J., Haas, C., Möslein, F., Maspfuhl, O., Borgers, F., & Alpsancar, S. (2023). Algorithmic Fairness in AI: An Interdisciplinary View. In *Business and Information Systems Engineering* (Vol. 65, Issue 2). DOI: 10.1007/s12599-023-00787-x

Piduru, B. R. (2023). The Role of Artificial Intelligence in Content Personalization: Transforming User Experience in the Digital Age. *Journal of Artificial Intelligence & Cloud Computing*. DOI: 10.47363/JAICC/2023(2)193

Qiao, H., & Zhao, A. (2023a). Artificial intelligence-based language learning: Illuminating the impact on speaking skills and self-regulation in Chinese EFL context. *Frontiers in Psychology*, *14*, 1255594. Advance online publication. DOI: 10.3389/fpsyg.2023.1255594

Qiao, H., & Zhao, A. (2023b). Artificial intelligence-based language learning: Illuminating the impact on speaking skills and self-regulation in Chinese EFL context. *Frontiers in Psychology*, *14*, 1255594. Advance online publication. DOI: 10.3389/fpsyg.2023.1255594

Rahali, A., & Akhloufi, M. A. (2023). End-to-End Transformer-Based Models in Textual-Based NLP. In *AI (Switzerland)* (Vol. 4, Issue 1). DOI: 10.3390/ai4010004

Sakkir, G., & Syamsuddin, N. A. (2023). Students' Perceptions of Duolingo Mobile Assisted Language Learning (MALL) in Learning English Vocabulary. *EduLine: Journal of Education and Learning Innovation*, *3*(3), 381–388. Advance online publication. DOI: 10.35877/454RI.eduline1970

Sargazi Moghadam, T., Darejeh, A., Delaramifar, M., & Mashayekh, S. (2024). Toward an artificial intelligence-based decision framework for developing adaptive e-learning systems to impact learners' emotions. *Interactive Learning Environments*, *32*(7), 1–21. Advance online publication. DOI: 10.1080/10494820.2023.2188398

Savela, N., Pellert, M., Latikka, R., Bergdahl, J., Garcia, D., & Oksanen, A. (2025). Affective, cognitive, and contextual cues in Reddit posts on artificial intelligence. *Journal of Computational Social Science*, *8*(1), 6. Advance online publication. DOI: 10.1007/s42001-024-00335-x

Schorr, I., Plecher, D. A., Eichhorn, C., & Klinker, G. (2024). Foreign language learning using augmented reality environments: a systematic review. In *Frontiers in Virtual Reality* (Vol. 5). Frontiers Media SA. DOI: 10.3389/frvir.2024.1288824

Sebastian, G. (2023). Privacy and Data Protection in ChatGPT and Other AI Chatbots. *International Journal of Security and Privacy in Pervasive Computing*, *15*(1), 1–14. Advance online publication. DOI: 10.4018/IJSPPC.325475

Shahmerdanova, R. (2025). Artificial Intelligence in Translation: Challenges and Opportunities. *Acta Globalis Humanitatis et Linguarum*, *2*(1), 62–70. DOI: 10.69760/aghel.02500108

Sholekhah, M. F., & Fakhrurriana, R. (2023). The Use of ELSA Speak as a Mobile-Assisted Language Learning (MALL) towards EFL Students Pronunciation. *JELITA: Journal of Education, Language Innovation, and Applied Linguistics*, *2*(2), 93–100. Advance online publication. DOI: 10.37058/jelita.v2i2.7596

Singh, V., & Ram, S. (2024). Impact of Artificial Intelligence on Teacher Education. *Shodh Sari-An International Multidisciplinary Journal*, *03*(01), 243–266. Advance online publication. DOI: 10.59231/SARI7669

Smith, B., Jiang, X., & Peters, R. (2024). The effectiveness of Duolingo in developing receptive and productive language knowledge and proficiency. *Language Learning & Technology*, *2024*(1), 1–26. https://hdl.handle.net/10125/73595. DOI: 10.64152/10125/73595

Son, J.-B., Ružić, N. K., & Philpott, A. (2025). Artificial intelligence technologies and applications for language learning and teaching. *Journal of China Computer-Assisted Language Learning*, *5*(1), 94–112. Advance online publication. DOI: 10.1515/jccall-2023-0015

Song, C., & Song, Y. (2023). Enhancing academic writing skills and motivation: Assessing the efficacy of ChatGPT in AI-assisted language learning for EFL students. *Frontiers in Psychology*, *14*, 1260843. Advance online publication. DOI: 10.3389/fpsyg.2023.1260843

Susnjak, T., Ramaswami, G. S., & Mathrani, A. (2022). Learning analytics dashboard: A tool for providing actionable insights to learners. *International Journal of Educational Technology in Higher Education*, *19*(1), 12. Advance online publication. DOI: 10.1186/s41239-021-00313-7

Tangsakul, S., & Poonpon, K. (2024). Aligning Academic Reading Tests to the Common European Framework of Reference for Languages (CEFR). *Reflections: The SoL Journal*, *31*(2), 614–638. DOI: 10.61508/refl.v31i2.275057

Tariq, M. U. (2024). AI-powered language translation for multilingual classrooms. In *Integrating Generative AI in Education to Achieve Sustainable Development Goals* (pp. 29–46). IGI Global., DOI: 10.4018/979-8-3693-2440-0.ch002

Tilmes, N. (2022). Disability, fairness, and algorithmic bias in AI recruitment. *Ethics and Information Technology*, *24*(2), 21. Advance online publication. DOI: 10.1007/s10676-022-09633-2

Tsvilodub, P., Chevalier, E., Klütz, V., Oberbeck, T., Sigetova, K., & Wollatz, F. (2023). Improving a Gamified Language Learning Chatbot Through AI and UX Boosting. *Lecture Notes in Networks and Systems, 581 LNNS*. DOI: 10.1007/978-3-031-21569-8_52

Ulla, M. B., Perales, W. F., & Busbus, S. O. (2023). ChatGPT in Language Education: How To Use It Ethically? *PASAA*, *67*(1), 361–377. Advance online publication. DOI: 10.58837/CHULA.PASAA.67.1.12

Uysal, H. (2023). Multilingualism and identity: Interdisciplinary perspectives. *Journal of Multilingual and Multicultural Development*, 1–2. Advance online publication. DOI: 10.1080/01434632.2023.2222973

Wijekumar, K. K., Harris, K. R., Graham, S., & Lei, P. (2022). A teacher technology tango shows strong results on 5th graders persuasive writing. *Educational Technology Research and Development*, *70*(4), 1415–1439. Advance online publication. DOI: 10.1007/s11423-022-10117-9

Wu, Y. (2024). Exploring the Influence of Large Language Models (LLMs) on English Learners and their Teachers. In *Journal of Education, Humanities and Social Sciences IEMB* (Vol. 2023).

Xia, Y., Shin, S. Y., & Kim, J. C. (2024). Cross-Cultural Intelligent Language Learning System (CILS): Leveraging AI to Facilitate Language Learning Strategies in Cross-Cultural Communication. *Applied Sciences (Basel, Switzerland)*, *14*(13), 5651. Advance online publication. DOI: 10.3390/app14135651

Yang, H., Gao, C., & Shen, H. Z. (2024). Learner interaction with, and response to, AI-programmed automated writing evaluation feedback in EFL writing: An exploratory study. *Education and Information Technologies*, *29*(4), 3837–3858. Advance online publication. DOI: 10.1007/s10639-023-11991-3

Yuxiu, Y. (2024). Application of translation technology based on AI in translation teaching. *Systems and Soft Computing*, *6*, 200072. Advance online publication. DOI: 10.1016/j.sasc.2024.200072

Zhai, C., & Wibowo, S. (2022). A systematic review on cross-culture, humor and empathy dimensions in conversational chatbots: The case of second language acquisition. *Heliyon*, *8*(12), e12056. Advance online publication. DOI: 10.1016/j.heliyon.2022.e12056

Zou, B., Du, Y., Wang, Z., Chen, J., & Zhang, W. (2023). An Investigation Into Artificial Intelligence Speech Evaluation Programs With Automatic Feedback for Developing EFL Learners' Speaking Skills. *SAGE Open*, *13*(3), 21582440231193818. Advance online publication. DOI: 10.1177/21582440231193818

Chapter 5
AI in Enhancing Bilingual Proficiency

Rahul Kumar Ghosh
https://orcid.org/0000-0002-1814-2133
Brainware University, India

Sandip Chakraborty
https://orcid.org/0009-0000-1166-0846
Brainware University, India

Gourab Dutta
https://orcid.org/0000-0003-4493-6508
Brainware University, India

ABSTRACT

The chapter follows the disruptive transformation of artificial intelligence in bilingual education, showcasing AR/VR, emotional AI and large language models (LLMs). While offering immersive experiences for the learner, AR/VR allows the learner to virtually interact with the target language in society. The learner's engagement and sentiment are monitored by the emotional AI and personalized feedback is provided. Adaptive AI improves real-time translation and lesson personalization with the LLMs, which include GPT series and PaLM, providing conversational practice and dynamic content creation. Further problems centring on issues of bias, privacy, and cultural representation require an ethical focus. There are some practical recommendations for educators, developers, and learners to employ AI to the maximum, upholding diversity in language. The future agenda of research will have to compare the efficacies of methodologies for AI governance: concerns related to AI in ethics and long-term retention studies to maximize the usage of AI in bilingual education and intercultural interaction

DOI: 10.4018/979-8-3373-0275-1.ch005

1 INTRODUCTION TO AI IN ENHANCING BILINGUAL PROFICIENCY

In an interconnected and global world, bilingual proficiency is not simply a useful skill but rather a requisite for individuals who wish to flourish across diverse cultural, academic, and professional environments. Where two or more languages can be spoken, communication creates synergy across the cultural and geographical divide, thus fostering collaboration, mutual understanding, and the free flow of ideas. Bilingualism opens the doors to worldwide opportunities, ensuring personal enrichment and solidifying chances for professional advancement. However, acquiring and maintaining this skill involves a formidable challenge that includes intensive specialized instruction, immersion, and continuous practice.

Artificial Intelligence (AI) is a game-changer able to meet and surmount these challenges to create a revolution in bilingual education. AI analyzes data, responds to individual needs, and gives real-time feedback, thus transforming more traditional approaches to language learning. With a growing number of tailored, scalable, and efficient solutions, AI allows learners to overcome hurdles in innovative and effective ways to realize their language goals. Even in tracing the high impact of AI on bilingual proficiency, the chapter begins by discussing the importance of language skills in a globally interdependent world before seamlessly leading into AI's role in facilitating language learning (Abdelmaboud et al., 2022).

1.1 The Importance of Language Proficiency in a Globalized World

The capacity for language is a fundamental form of communication among all interconnections of global cultures, commerce, and active people of a range of societies. Once a strictly academic achievement, it has evolved into the single major skill one must have to achieve any just dimension of personal work. Multilingual communication, at its core, is crucial in enhancing cooperation, understanding, and furthering progress as humans engage in various interactions, globally fostered by globalization. In this global context, language serves as the connecting force between different cultures and languages, allowing individuals to relate to each other, and creating mutual goals accomplished from their communicative exchanges.

In the professional arena, multilingual professionals can enjoy using these languages as competitive edges when working in fields that require crossed-border mutual collaboration such as international business, trade, diplomacy, etc. For example, in customers' or partners' native language, oral communication denotes trust. Multilingual individuals hence would find an upper advantage in negotiations and can build a good working relationship. Similarly, in academia, such capabilities allow for the extension of access to global research, nurturing international collaborations, and international exchange of ideas and research. In addition to the professional advantages, it is generally argued that multilingual or bilingual individuals are critically flexible in traversing ways that lead them through various cultural worlds in very effective ways. Here, one travels, walks in the street, or attends international events.

Undoubtedly, learning and maintaining language proficiency is an uphill struggle for many learners. Traditional teaching methods fail to reach diverse levels of students with varied needs. Students' grammar-based learning, rote memorizing, and standardized exercise routines may be the fundamental scaffolding constituting the courses of many of these methods, but conversational fluency and appropriate skills of speaking are hardly developed in the process. Learners may find it difficult to use the knowledge that they have acquired in the classroom, a setback to their confidence in speaking a second language. (Yudintseva, 2023).

Furthermore, the popular premise that immersion experiences are an essential factor in learning a foreign language is rendered null for many learners. Financial, political, or institutional constraints limit many from interacting with native speakers, travelling to countries where the target language is spoken, or taking part in cultural exchanges. Without consistent exposure to real-life linguistic and cultural environments, students continuously face problems in their pursuit of fluency and cultural identification.

Adaptation to personal feedback is something far more wanting in conventional teaching systems, in the case of mispronunciations, vocabulary errors, or grammatical errors, all escape notice and go uncorrected, hence retarding the learners' progress and destructively hurting their self-esteem, especially in large class sizes; indeed, this whole process acts against scholastic personalization. Satisfaction and motivation for the learning process might be difficult to sustain after this (Juan & Murai, 2022).

Apart from computer interpreters or translation tools, many innovative ways can contribute to the promotion or study of a language or languages via the Internet. The global importance of the Internet is highlighted by the significance of the educational potential and cultural growth it holds for advocates. It signifies that the effort of all related parties and sectors towards subsidiarity and sustainability of all efforts entailing cultural appreciation and linguistic insights for larger portions of society is prudent. For this vision to come true and spread as quickly as possible, the development of an algorithm that could detect the disposition to one's mother language might help in providing feedback or motivation to different followers (Alfaisal et al., 2024).

1.2 AI's Role in Facilitating Language Acquisition

Artificial Intelligence (AI) has brought revolutionary changes in language teaching by furnishing tailor-made, efficient scalable solutions to overcome weaknesses in traditional methods. Due to all the technology innovations it is endowed with: Natural Language Processing (NLP), Machine Learning, and Speech Recognition; the tools enabled by AI have excelled in imparting language learning to work more efficiently.

Personalized learning has resulted from AI being able to instruct in many areas. In language learning, AI systems can gather information from huge amounts of data on learners, interpreting various aspects including proficiency level, learning styles, and problem areas to suggest individualized pathways to best cater to their demands. Personalized learning is all about targeting learners' specific weak points. For instance, one might wish to tone one's pronunciation, enhance one's vocabulary, or consume oneself in grammar. With personalized learning, one can do these things, progressing at his or her speed. Instead of employing a one-size-fits-all approach, AI-driven platforms eagerly make use of each person's uniqueness to foster the highest level of efficacy and engagement (Strielkowski et al., 2024).

Authoritative examples of AI's transformative capacity in language education include feedback in real-time. AI tools can instantly evaluate learners' speech, text, or written input, providing corrections and suggestions that would then be implemented immediately. The instant feedback present gives learners a quick platform to identify and address their mistakes, which further reinforces their language use and boosts their progression. For instance, a speech training AI that helps with pronunciation could detect subtle errors and analyze sound patterns, aiding in the actualizing of native-like accuracy. Although various AI-driven tools may help in the process of identifying and correcting structural errors in sentences, the proper use of the target language will be improved (Alharbi, 2023).

AI gives an extra advantage towards implementing hardly believable situations in an immaculate setting, generating real-life scenarios. Vital augmented and virtual reality amalgams (AI-supported) furnish opportunities for learners to apply each language learned in genuine contexts, for instance, one can be in a foreign city trying to search for a place, or even you can be in a restaurant eating and ordering something; always, the scope is open. Such simulations aid learners in further developing their fluency and help increase their interpersonal confidence in actual presentations. The environment appears lively and exciting because AI allows for dynamic adaptation to students' responses as opposed to the rigid rigidity observable in the conventional classroom concerning learning options (Yadav, 2024).

AI systems also encompass translation and language tools like Google Translate and DeepL, enabling learners to translate and use the target language in everyday use cases. These enable translations that are attached to context, helping in the comprehension of complex texts and the effective use of a language. AI chatbots and conversational agents also add utility to ensure simulations of interaction with a native speaker who is available to provide learners with appropriate responses and practice with conversation in the safety of virtual compounds (Huang et al., 2021).

The following are the major contributions of AI to democratize language-learning resources. So many of these portals are available for language learners, and their resources include audiobooks, videos, interactive lessons, and quizzes. These portals can adapt the materials they offer according to the learner's performance and preferences to facilitate learning. AI can destroy the walls of geographical and financial constraints that impede access to quality educational resources for language learning by ensuring all learners whether they come from different classes and castes (Green, 2024).

1.3 The Transformative Potential of AI in Bilingual Education

The integration of AI into a bilingual teaching system signifies an unexampled avenue of breaking time-honoured barriers and redefining elements that affect how languages are taught. Solutions that combine AI can be versatile enough to be applied to a multiplicity of conservative groups with different abilities as well. Innumerable opportunities arise when using tailored learning strategies within an adaptive platform, which cater to individual learning differences and help learners claim back their power despite financial strains or lack of access to native speakers.

AI achieves better engagement through the use of gamified lessons while providing continuous motivation through challenges, rewards, and tracking of progress. When combined with human instruction, AI enhances language education by fully improving all forms of learning. Both educators and educational developers can employ AI-oriented findings to adjust their teaching style, exploit knowledge about human behaviour, and achieve better outcomes.

As AI technology evolves, so does its ability to reform our approach towards bilingual education, joining the linguistic elite into the communication fabric of the global society (Song et al., 2023).

2 AI-DRIVEN TOOLS FOR BILINGUAL LEARNING

The use of AI in the field of bilingual education has led to the advent of ever-sophisticated tools catering to different learning needs. These tools make possible the task of language learning, not only by enlivening it but also by making the lesson interesting and accessible for the students. Presented below are various AI-based applications and case studies associated with renowned language teaching tools.

To strengthen the pedagogical basis of AI-filled bilingual education, one needs to anchor the discussion in well-established learning theories. Vygotsky's ZPD emphasizes the use of scaffolding in language learning: learners perform better if they have some assistance rather than working alone. AI systems, in particular adaptive systems and emotional AI, can become digital scaffolds by modulating the level of scaffolding according to learner needs, which change over time. Krashen's Input Hypothesis calls for input that is just beyond the learner's current level (i+1); LLMs and NLP tools provide content delivery at different levels. UDL further supports this by calling for flexible learning environments that can cater to the different learner profiles-the same levels of personalized AI-based learning environments accommodate. Together, these models justify the use of AI not only as a technological upgrade but as a pedagogically cohesive development in bilingual education.

2.1 Exploration of Specific AI-Powered Applications

The advent of AI-based apps has brought a complete revolution to bilingual learning. These projects provide customization and adaptation catered to the unique requisites of the individual learner. Personalized learning applications such as Lingvist and Busuu set a new checkpoint in educational instruction by offering dynamic adjustments for convenience, taking into account the student's weaker and stronger areas based on the student's progress. The learning platforms use sophisticated algorithms to ascertain learning patterns that can be used to change for real-time curriculum adjustment. The individual learning style thus prevents the student from being stressed or frustrated while still making the language acquisition effort as effective as possible (Zhu et al., 2024). Vocabulary retention exercises are a great fit for learners languishing in word memory; grammar exercises in such types can be repositioned toward complex sentence formulations beauty of these exercises is freeing the most natural languages, helping any interlocutor to connect with sentences. This is the level of autonomy AI acknowledges with flattery, urging the learner to become an active participant. Through the ascendancy of self; both confidence-boosting and better encouragement keep the user up repeatedly for participative engagement, intimately known as "My needs are being addressed" (Beaudry & Pinsonneault, 2005).

Beyond personalized learning, AI tools like Elsa Speak and Speechling for speech recognition and pronunciation training have become indispensable in bilingual teaching. These systems depend upon algorithmic evaluation of the learner's pronunciation in comparison to that of a native speaker. Feedback is given instantly after evaluation: it is a detailed one linking those areas in need of improvement with tone, pitch, and articulation. The effect comes during pronunciation-making the learner sound more fluent and natural. These AI-guided curation mechanisms keep the learner engaged by furnishing one piece of enticing, tangible, and context-specific information at a time in an almost perpetual cycle. Such platforms gain an immersion effect and add an intense quality to learning by providing suggestions on articles, videos, and interactive quizzes matched with the learner's interests and goals. This type of managed content inflow can take care of learner motivation and ground them to cultivate great cultural awareness along with some important language skills (Xia et al., 2024).

Integration of AI technology has opened up some ways in which innovation may be harnessed to include specialized customization making it possible for real-time grants of feedback and the fine adjustment of the level of challenges on a per-need basis. To state the obvious, intelligent tutoring systems are simulations of one-on-one instruction, with tailored assistance, explanation, and practice. From time to time, the system has placed awareness of an anthology of different cognitive models to postulate how they differ from the complex matrix of systematic learning involving several basic techniques adopted within AI research. This important development shall enhance multicultural education for students who already suffer from mixed learning experiences when they step outside of traditional methods of education. Such a situation offers these learners dynamic experiences that are not limited to the use of extremely relevant multimedia support such as books, CDs, DVDs, and many other resources to make learning so stimulating, practical, and efficient (Haleem et al., 2022).

2.2 Case Studies of Popular Language Learning Tools

When you consider AI and its incorporation into linguistic education, Duolingo instantly recommends itself among the most outstanding implementations of AI in linguistic education. And the very reason it has become so popular is its unique ideas on user engagement; theirs are models that set standards. Its pedagogical strategies are based on gamification, adaptive learning, and spaced repetition, creating the perfect learning platform for a variety of audiences. The platform's adaptive learning algorithms monitor a user's progress, fine-tuning exercises' difficulty to keep learners challenged yet not frustrated. The software has the flexibility to adapt to learner styles and paces, which led to its success with beginner language learners. Its use of spaced repetition memory can help fix the learned vocabulary and rules of grammar by bringing it back at optimum times, which thus conveys a kind of extended memory. The gamified items like streaks, leaderboards, and rewards help to add competitiveness, which inspires users to keep up the rhythm of study (Jhon et al., 2020). And, everyone, young or old, will find it very appealing because it underscores the charm of learning with fun.

As much as the innovative features and accessibility of Duolingo are appreciated, there are also limits to address. It seems that the program is very successful when used to attempt to build vocabulary and basic grammar, but does not offer many opportunities for advanced conversational practice. A largely exercise-free focus on structured activities and brief lessons is obstructing exposure to real-life contexts and cultural aspects necessary for achieving fluency in the target language. On the other side, while Duolingo does very well in delivering bite-size content that is entertaining and engaging, the number of instances where the program provides for addressing idiomatic expressions and the subtler aspects of context within language certainly pose issues. Such limitations cast doubt on the aptness of Duolingo for casual learners or for those interested in some support at the side of their primary language advertising effort (Shadiev & Feng, 2023).

The Rosetta Stone prioritizes immersion and step-by-step learning methods for language instruction. Its Dynamic Immersion approach is an extensive use of AI software that delivers live lessons completely in the target language without translation. It pushes practitioners to think, listen, and respond in the language they're learning intending to enhance cognitive depth. Rosetta Stone is dem crowded to cater to pronunciation guides. With a strong emphasis on developing listening, speaking, and reading skills, Rosetta Stone provides a structured and holistic learning experience. Using AI, the software includes detailed feedback on phonetic accuracy that substantially strengthens the speaking abilities of the language learner. By providing many valuable tools to help refine a user's native accents more appropriately, Rosetta Stone offers a perfect translation tool for those seeking meticulous versions of instruction (Bai, 2024).

Yet, its lack of gamified features may fail to allure millennial students or adult learners who thrive in highly interactive, game-like learning environments. The program provided a more traditional learning structure accosted with extensive pedagogy, which can sometimes seem old-fashioned or monotonous to those who enjoy the dynamic and engaging interfaces of modern tools such as Duolingo. In addition, with an excellent foundation in language instruction, Rosetta Stone does not emphasize as much cultural integration or encourage conversational fluency, so there is a wide gap between the context of learning here and the applied environment preferred by most students.

Duolingo and Rosetta Stone represent the varied uses of AI in language-bilingual education, catering to various learner preferences and goals. The non-threatening, gamified nature of Duolingo suits casual learners, as well as novices, whereas the structured immersion provided by Rosetta Stone offers learners a strict and thorough learning experience. Awareness about these advantages and disadvantages helps attune AI-used experiences to the specific goals and objectives for educating any specific language (Owan et al., 2023).

3 PERSONALIZED LEARNING AND ADAPTIVE AI

Today, in the ever-changing educational landscape, personalized learning comes as a game-changer, meant to adapt to the unique needs of each learner. Artificial Intelligence (AI) is here providing a helping hand to the cause, mainly for bilingual education. Through using AI-powered systems analyzing learning patterns, preferences, and processes at the level of the individual, dynamic and adaptable learning environments are built for numerous learners. Personalized learning creates engagement, boosts retention, and expedites language acquisition while challenging the language proficiency status quo.

3.1 Personalized Learning: A Paradigm Shift in Language Education

A bigger institutional reorganization is happening. Instruction is turned right around, assuming personality as the epitome of what must be taken care of, not something that is responded to; not about the assumed superiority of teachers. An AI can solve these issues because it can provide a crafted adaptive environment that modifies astutely in real-time according to students' actual needs.

In some Duolingo exercises, users are given exercises according to their language level. The system dynamically changes the forthcoming lessons based on where the users have difficulties such as verb conjugation, and sentence formation, and stops and focuses on topics the user has trouble with so that they are ready to go from simple challenges to more navigational learning material (Shortt et al., 2021).

In addition, customized learning meets various objectives. For some, conversing fluently as a traveller might be of utmost importance while others focus on the written style needed for academic and professional proposals. AI-driven interfaces such as Babbel have the convenience to tailor modules (from specialized ones dedicated to business communication, while some might be for travel-learning phrases or etiquette cues designed for vacations) based on their goals do they want to shine as language learners? In consequence, students can now engage in becoming proficient at language, especially when their personalized set of expectations is being met.

3.2 How Adaptive AI Enhances Learning

The core of personalized learning is Adaptive AI, a system that assesses the learner's performance throughout to personalize instruction based on the dynamically updated content. Advanced technologies such as Machine Learning, NLP and Speech Recognition are deployed by Adaptive AI in catering to the Learning Hubs. Let's illustrate how adaptive AI works out in practice:

1. Data-Driven Insights: Intelligent systems collect detailed data on learner behaviours, such as accuracy, reaction time, and error analysis. For instance, with data accumulated on the varied quizzes, adaptive AI systems can hone in on future exposure to grammar. Focusing the attention of the learners on those areas in which insights/evaluation indicates may assist in improving deficits is an additional unexpected benefit of the data-driven approach (Liu et al., 2021).
2. Dynamic Content Adjustment: The adaptive AI algorithms analyze the collected data, and modify lessons according to individual needs. If the student shows proficiency in basic vocabulary, the system will introduce more complex grammar rules or idiomatic expressions. If a student has a particular difficulty, the system might give simpler explanations, additional practice, or alternative learning aids (Shohieb et al., 2022).
3. Interactive Feedback: Indeed, real-time feedback is perhaps one of the most interesting features of adaptive AI. Rosetta Stone and other such language learning tools use speech recognition to analyze pronunciation and flash errors or suggest corrections immediately. This instant feedback helps in experimenting in the learning, enhances self-confidence and maintains the morale of students into the journey by providing also encouragement with evidence of progress (Bozkurt & Sharma, 2020).
4. Continuous Assessment: Adaptive AI can effectively assess in a manner that is inconsistent when compared with the usual assessment which takes place typically at fixed intervals. As continuous assessment with adaptive AI could also allow us to track progress, identify trends, and make precise course corrections, students who are making rapid progress can be tasked with more challenging work while students requiring help are given such assistance through guided practice (Strielkowski et al., 2024).

3.3 Benefits of Real-Time Feedback and Continuous Assessment

Real-time feedback and continuous assessment are two important gifts of AI for bilingual education that give learners an instant insight into their progress and create a vibrant feeling and way of learning.

1. Pronunciation Improvement with Speech Recognition: Pronunciation is a keystone of spoken language acquisition, and the technology of speech recognition is dramatically changing the way people practice it. Rosetta Stone and Mondly have developed highly sophisticated recognition algorithms to parallel student inquiry pronunciation and exact native speaker model pronunciation highlighting tongue placement, vocabulary stress, and phonetic accuracy, thereby providing hard-won results in real time. In the case of a strongly mispronounced word, the system will identify the error and offer a more accurate pronunciation, all done with visual supports. Such easy correction opportunities enable students to work and improve their speaking skills without waiting to hear critical welcomes from somebody else (Wang et al., 2020). This feature is particularly beneficial for independent learners who don't have access to native speakers or language helpers. It bridges the gap for students who feel reluctant to communicate in the traditional classroom owing to embarrassment or judgments.
2. Grammar and Syntax Mastery: AI can help in detecting particular patterns of errors and providing situationally appropriate explanations for correction. When a sentence is an incorrect example of subject-verb agreement or the past tense, the AI-based platform Grammarly or Babbel would highlight the error and explain if clauses, when to use estar/ser, and so on. This is not only a correction but also a reinforcement of linguistic rules for long-term memory help (Koka, 2024). The concept of continuous grammar and syntax evaluation stands out especially regarding intermediate and advanced learners, as the issue of the always-improving use of accurate and polished language comes into focus, mainly at the time of language practice.
3. Personalized Vocabulary Building: Vocabulary acquisition is a core for language learning with real-time feedback focusing the learner on words suitable for their level and goals. Adaptive AI systems track the frequently missed words and include them in subsequent exercises. Once an individual continually grapples with words related to business, Memrise would put these words on the terms highlighted on that learner's flashcards and quizzes. With continued reinforcement, this targeted development will significantly contribute to improving the individual's vocabulary base (Essafi et al., 2024).

4. Increased Engagement Through Immediate Rewards: Real-time feedback is often integrated with gamification like rewards, badges for accomplishments, or progress tracking. Such instant reward reinforces the correct answers, which serves to increase motivation and encourages the formation of helpful skills through continued practice. For example, Duolingo celebrates small victories with "streaks" and "XP" rewards, making it a fun place to learn and reinforce positive behaviour (Thurairasu, 2022).
5. Support for Educators: Hence, continuous assessment offers educators detailed feedback on the learner's performance. Artificial intelligence-generated dashboards highlight areas of excellence and challenge so teachers can intervene earlier. These insights enable educators to adjust their instruction to address common problems, thus, creating a more supportive and powerful learning environment (Lissitz, 2025).

As AI technology grows to perfection and takes to the skies, ever higher and farther will be the heights. The progressive AI with pearls of excellence and valour crossing realms looks towards the day when personalized learning is anything but an accepted practice in language education and more so a pure actuality.

4 CHALLENGES AND ETHICAL CONSIDERATIONS

Challenges in Artificial Intelligence (AI) being merged into bilingual education will engender transformative goods, together with evils and a variety of challenges and ethical dilemmas, which requires addressing as lack of that impacts the potential of AI to create inclusive, equitable, and effective conditions in language learning. This section will discuss major issues like privacy concerns, algorithmic discrimination, access, and ethical dilemmas raised by AI-operated tools.

4.1 Data Privacy and Security Concerns

User data is crucial for the customization of learning aids that use AI systems for language study. It includes very sensitive data such as voice recordings and habits of learning that track a person's location and log how the device is being used. Such info-centric data may be vital for enhancing learner experiences, but the process of its capture and possible storage infringes massively on user privacy.

There is a possibility by which people could easily learn with Duolingo and Rosetta Stone via the collection of their activity data. But the very fact is that generally they are left in the dark about their stored, shared or used data from the learning site (Ess, 2020). This lack of transparency questions trust, bringing risks in store, especially in the situation of data breaches or illegal access.

Key Concerns:

- Privacy: Supplying platforms with false data may deceive platforms and advertising services by making it difficult to provide goods or services to targeted consumers.
- Termination: Some platforms have the authority to modify services or disengage users at their discretion.
- Protection from Abuse: Protection against information and privacy abuse can be one of the benefits of being disclosed.
- Indirect Service Suspension: Based on evidence, some platforms tend to modify the way data is being handled or even start by notifying users directly.
- Process Due to Failure: This refers to liabilities-whether a function constrains a user's broader rights or establishes legal obligations against the users
- Security: By offering open data, serious doubts are being raised about the security of platforms.

Building confidence in the user, the developer has several challenges to face, including first building trust by soliciting user consent, enhancing the security through anonymization of the data and strong security protocols.

4.2 Algorithmic Bias and Inclusivity

Algorithmic bias is arguably the greatest challenge faced in AI-driven educational practices. Since representations of life in our data collection vary depending on the majority population's perspective, the models trained on them are apt to perpetuate those biases. Towards bilingual education, this could well lead to outcomes that are disparate for learners from distinct backgrounds, including language, culture, or socio-economic status.

Examples of Bias:

- Language Representation: Human-like and less inelegant encouragement to eschew so much corporatize: Other languages, especially underserved languages or Dialects, are left with even less because AI is driven by so many major languages, like English, Spanish, and Chinese. Such genuinely affirmative action will diminish representation for speakers of less-used languages and get rid of linguistic inequality (Chassignol et al., 2018).
- Accent and Dialect Discrimination: Speech recognition systems tend to do well on standard accents but tend to perform worse as soon as regional di-

alects, let alone non-native pronunciations, are begun, thus putting students from the deprived language background at historical disadvantage (Raj & Renumol, 2021).

Addressing the Issue:

- Feed more data: One should devise models while incorporating cultural and linguistic data, allowing for being inclusive.
- Bias audit: Performing regular audits helps to review the systems for inherent biases along with their subsequent minimization.
- Localize the Tools: With local translation, tools are culturally true and accessible to a broad number of users.

4.3 Accessibility and the Digital Divide

AI can provide a democratizing influence on language learning as it brings equal opportunities in education through access while corresponding advanced technology lays the groundwork for new kinds of barriers for learners struggling with fewer resources. These stalemates exist whereby adaptive AI systems necessitate high-speed internet, modern devices, and excess processing capability usually beyond the reach of economically disadvantaged communities (Alshamsi et al., 2024).

Challenges in Accessibility:

- High cost of Entry: Many platforms provide particular premium features that are tremendously expensive for low-income consumers.
- Technological Limitation: Conceptually, learners based in rural or underserved regions would be lacking the infrastructure support needed for access to AI tools.
- Vernacular Language Support: Those with neither placeholder dollars nor finding in other languages might largely be dropped out of this advanced insinuation of this elucidation.

These concerns can be addressed by giving importance to affordability, lack of network connectivity, and minority language perspectives. Assistance from the outside could be important in such areas as infusing civil society life with information technology access.

4.4 Over-Reliance on AI

AI has been evolving to fit in the description of aiding rather than supplying the whole course content. However, the concerning part is when learners lose some time trying to go to the customary essence of understanding or having practical conversations with the help of these tools. On victoriously teaching grammar, vocabulary, and pronunciation, AI pulls the weakest string on cultural context, emotion, and real-world conversation skills (Doğan & Talan, 2024, Werdiningsih et al., 2024).

Potential Drawbacks:

- Superficial learning: In the face of critical wording and in-depth interpretation, AI gives major emphasis to the rapid and efficient. Concerning the march of critical thinking and language comprehension, the former can slacken tremendously.
- Interaction with human beings is limited: Human interference is steadily reduced by the predominance of AI to prevent the learner from practising with native speakers in everyday life, a vital component in the sphere of cultural immersion and advanced fluency.

Solutions:

- Hybrid models: These ensure a more comprehensive study of a language by integrating modern AI tools with traditional pedagogical methods.
- Cultural challenge: Promote the discussion of cultural sensitivities and real-world applications to ensure even more inner depth for language learning.

4.5 Ethical Implications of AI in Education

Developers, educators, and policymakers must navigate complex issues such as algorithmic accountability, data ownership, and the societal impact of AI technologies when considering the ethical implications in the bilingual education setting (Lee et al., 2024).

Ethical Questions:

- Who Owns the Data? Learners should have control over their data, but in most of the AI-based systems, this is not the case.
- Transparency of Algorithm: AI technologies must provide easily understandable explanations concerning recommendations and actions since transparency is the bedrock of trust and accountability.

- Impact on Jobs: Teachers' role in the face of increased AI adoption in education-related systems has raised some serious issues, including that of job displacement.

The adoption of AI systems in bilingual education could both fair use and discrimination. Instead, AI would make learning a language more personal, inclusive, and effective but also predictively risk claims from privacy, bias, accessibility, and ethical integrity. Tackling such challenges will call on the concerted efforts of developers, educators, and policymakers to ensure AI-powered interventions are not only innovative but also equitable and ethical.

Switching the spotlight, a little, transparency, inclusiveness, and cultural sensibility are required for setting the scene for an accessible and efficacious education framework through AI in bilingual education, simply boosting learners hailing from all walks of life to realize and succeed in their language goals.

5 FUTURE TRENDS IN AI FOR BILINGUAL PROFICIENCY

The most commonly employed traditional linguistic instructional practices are essentially turning out to be supplementary measures in the face of cutting-edge AI. One common traditional method usually applied in language learning is the relay of various fragmental lessons interspersed with less effective sustaining memorization through very monotonous, wearisome interpretations and explanations from stereotypic and antiquated teachers. Today, AI-driven ways are customizing learning techniques to include integrated, real-time feedback in actual immersive and adaptive learning environments. Bilingual proficiency training is driven toward further interactive, dynamic, and engaging methods, enhancing linguistic and cultural understanding, more responsively and proactively as interactive language tutoring with gender-appropriate sessions (Alzahrani, 2024).

These new AI powers are the cause of increased accessibility, efficiency, and interactions with the language so that learners will get a feel of the language through real-life immersion rather than passively learning through other means. The AI is now designed to detect emotions (Yu et al., 2024) and to adapt to the learners where they are (Kabudi et al., 2021), while learners can feel they are engaged in conversation with a real person, rendering bilingual education interesting.

The latter will explore future dynamics that will shape the AI role in bilingual education by focusing on how AR, VR, emotion AI, and adaptive models redefine the reaching and refining of a bilingual field.

5.1 Augmented Reality (AR) and Virtual Reality (VR) in Language Learning

One of the most exciting developments in multilingual education accomplished through machine learning and AI space has been the integration of AR and VR into language learning environments. The ideas are experimenting with elaborate experiences with feedback from the real world, thus enhancing the ease of learning and can maximize the chances of retention.

Immersive Learning Environments

Augmented Reality (AR) and Virtual Reality (VR), for instance, create a context where the learner will use the target language. Providing a real-time sort of interaction is realized through virtual marketplaces, restaurants, or international offices. The learner has to interact with AI avatars or interact with the other participants in a virtual language (Soliman et al., 2024). Such simulations place the learner in an experiential environment that supports natural language learning through situational interaction as opposed to imparting words and phrases by rote memorization alone. The research shows that context-based learning improves cognitive retention, whereby a learner associates vocabulary and phrases with actions, emotions, and contexts.

Interactive Role-Playing for Language Mastery

VR goes beyond merely structured lessons by making possible interactive role-playing where the learners engage in mock conversations with AI-driven avatars, which themselves mimic both native speakers and cultural sensibilities too. These avatars can adjust their verbal communication to fit in with different types of speech. This allows learners to practice formal and informal speech, and even try some dialectic-specific communication styles. Speech recognition developed by AI can provide analysis of learner responses and provide instant corrections with tone and enunciation. This guarantees that programmed learners can develop both proper fluency and accentuation in a structured yet interactive setting (Karakas, 2023).

Gamification and Engagement in Language Learning

Certainly, maintaining a student's motivation is another challenging aspect of bilingual education. A VR-based language education gamification aims to reward learning. The user receives points and other rewards, including opening a doorway into a new environment, as well as being given performance feedback (Dehganzadeh & Dehganzadeh, 2020). AI-driven VR language-instruction platforms like

ImmerseMe and Mondly VR offer real-time conversational practice while adopting a game-like atmosphere that can keep a loyal devoted language learner coming back to reinforce his or her language skills.

Though virtual and augmented realities are amazing tools, they face challenges such as heavy costs, limited access, and requirements for high-speed internet. Put simply, the effectiveness of these platforms will heavily depend on widespread adoption and integration.

5.2 Emotional AI and Sentiment Analysis in Language Learning

A further development toward AI-supported bilingual education involves incorporating emotional intelligence into the language learning models. Emotional AI, also referred to as affective computing, allows AI tutors and conversational agents to identify and respond to a learner's state of emotion, motivation, and degree of frustration.

Adaptive Learning Based on Emotional Cues

Language learning platforms that use AI to create inferences concerning the sentiment of the authorized emotional experience based on the tone of speech, facial expressions, voice modification and other non-verbal behaviours are increasingly employing these enhancements to judge whether a student is engaged or not (Imamguluyev et al., 2024). Since how this setup allows monitoring of all cues, the system may decide to ramp up or down the difficulty level, give words of encouragement, or pace lessons based on the engagement status of the learner; for example, if the AI tutor's virtual software detects increasing anxiety or frustration in a student, then all the hints are automatically reinforced and made affirmatively, shepherded toward simpler problems or exhorted to take a break until all recovered (Woodruff, 2024). In the case of a confident student, a speaker will revert to a more vocab-rich or complex-structure talk.

Conversational AI with Emotional Intelligence

AI chatbots and voice-based tutors are developing to embody human-like interaction by amounting to empathy in conversations (Belda-Medina & Kokošková, 54). Standard AI tutors, as contrasted with emotion-aware AI tutors, do not interpret pauses in speaking, inappropriately loud intonations, or any indication of lack of confidence in speech and adjust their responses to encourage or reinforce. This bears very high significance to people who suffer from speaking anxiety since this helps the AI to enable a low-pressure, non-judgmental environment for them.

Enhancing Pronunciation and Speech Confidence

Educational software, including IBM Watson, Learn to Speak, and Rosetta Stone, are primed to develop emotional artificial intelligence and thereby targetable emotions in refining the critical skills of pronunciation and fluency. They correct phonetics in real-time by analyzing the intonation, pitch, and speed, also positively measuring the confidence levels of the speech. This localized feedback loop cultivates language self-efficacy; it helps overcome pronunciation hurdles and significantly contributes to effective two-way communication (Evers & Chen, 2020). Despite some challenges, there are a lot of positive ideas about the ventures between technology and education in general and emotions in AI in particular.

Yet, some scepticism surrounds issues related to data privacy and emotional biases in AI. Nascent emotion-detection algorithms need to be sensitive to cultural boundaries in addition to being entirely impartial and free from bias, so as not to wrongly interpret feelings gloriously spanning and transcending the vast seas of diversification among humankind.

5.3 AI-Driven Personalized Learning for Bilingual Proficiency

Adapting to each pupil has revolutionized the role of language learning to some extent; however, AI developments will push its limits. As of now, AI-driven adaptive learning systems are in the process of being modified according to the needs of situations, approaching case needs in the form of real-time performance, engagement index, and cognitive load.

Though AI tools offer autonomy, scale abilities, and provide real-time feedback, they cannot replace the irreplaceable human values of empathy, contextual understanding, and pedagogical judgment. Working with AI in bilingual classrooms allows the development of a hybrid learning ecosystem in which AI systems carry out the routine functions of correcting pronunciations, adaptive pacing, and drills on vocabulary so that the teachers can charge themselves with activities requiring critical thinking, cultural immersion, and the fine nuances of language. For example, teachers can refer to AI analytics to single out students from worthy of intervention and lead the class in a discussion of idiomatic expressions and cultural connotations-linguistic subtleties AI might misinterpret. AI as a co-teacher rather than a replacement fosters the holistic language-acquisition process.

The need to discuss curricular alignment and assessment-design issues arises from the integration of AI into bilingual education beyond adaptive content delivery. Teachers come face-to-face with the practical issues raised by embedding AI tools within structured syllabi, especially with traditional classrooms or low-tech settings. Such AI platforms need to be evaluated concerning just how well they instruct and how well they link with the formats of standardized tests or their learning outcomes. However, hardly any current tools offer summative assessment assistance; most are for formative practice. If AI systems can be developed and then allowed to mark an essay or assess oral proficiency in a human-like manner, basing these on rubrics referencing CEFR or TOEFL standards, this could allow for a deeper alignment with institutional structures. The gap between informal use of AI and formal educational requirements needs bridging so that language development can be more comprehensive.

Smart Adaptive Learning Systems

AI-driven programs such as Lingvist, Duolingo, and Babbel develop sophisticated adaptive learning algorithms to gather information on error patterns, retention time, and response time, adjusting the lesson complexity when needed. AI tutors of the future must predict cognitive fatigue and concentration and finally adjust by modifying the complexity of lessons or exerting game elements to keep the students from becoming distracted (Chen et al., 2021).

Real-Time Language Translation in Bilingual Education

In real-time AI translation empowered with NLP and AI translation models, the coming era will bring further fluid translations in line with cultural and idiomatic awareness. AI translation models include Google Neural Machine Translation (GNMT) and AI translator by Meta, which aim at mapping cultural contexts and idiomatic nuances to translate with better accuracy translations following more natural, informal phrases that resonate in the heads of bilingual learners (Klimova et al., 2022).

AI Integration in Formal Education

AI tutors and personalized virtual assistants are expected to become the bread-and-butter for bilingual education. Schools may consider incorporating AI assessment models generating instant grading, pronunciation feedback, and personalized support, taking some work off human teachers and increasing immediate help for learners (Giri, 2024).

Dealing with translation, and incorporating more AI means less human intervention. Unlike computers, human teachers can enforce cultural aspects connected to language because AI's authenticity is questionable.

5.4 Ethical and Implementation Challenges

Artificial intelligence implementation for bilingual education gains from several challenges that should be overcome.

1. Language representation against bias: More comprehensive datasets for lesser-known languages and dialects would be required so that it can avoid learning bias.
2. AI-Human Interaction Balance: AI-based education will alone not be enough to be culturally robust and critical in the face of human-technology tensions.
3. Privacy and Data Security: AI-based language-learning environments should have stringent data protection policies in place as part of the tools themselves.

With the aforesaid challenges met, AI will transform bilingual education, inclusively ensuring effectiveness and ethical responsibility. More interactive language acquisition, immersion, and personalization are all considered as effects of AI, which will help learners not only with vocabulary and grammar but also to converse. As the technologies progress, AI-based bilingual education will be much more efficient, inclusive, and open to all, thus shaping the future landscape of language learning in the digital age.

Consider global accessibility and equity when weighing the promise of AI in bilingual education. Infrastructure, digital literacy, and affordability in many resource-deprived regions of the Global South impede the implementation of sophisticated AI systems. Tools that need high-bandwidth connections, costly devices, or frequent updates will worsen the existing divides in education. Hence, future implementations must favor lightweight, mobile-friendly AI tools, open-source tools, and training datasets in more than one language that include minority languages and dialects. For edtech and public institutions to make scalable AI that meets such ethical standards in diverse linguistic and socio-economic settings, a great deal of cooperation will be required.

5.5 Large Language Models (LLMs) and Conversational AI in Bilingual Education

An incredible change in bilingual education comes through the application of huge language models (LLMs)—state-of-the-art AI systems trained on high-order algorithms to comprehend and generate human-like text. Setting the bar are OpenAI's GPT series, Google's PaLM, and Meta's LLaMA among LLMs; these language models, as opposed to run-of-the-mill language tools, cater to comprehensive functionalities in terms of translation, content creation, and conversational tutoring. These have far-reaching application possibilities to adapt to learners' different grades, diverse cultural circumstances, and nuances in language, thereby reshaping the essence of bilingual education. However, leveraging language models for educational purposes necessitates intelligent experimental series oriented toward educational context to ensure pedagogical soundness, ethical use, and learner engagement sustainability. (Giannakos et al., 2024).

Enhanced Conversational Practice

1. Real-World Simulations: LLMs can role play as conversational partners, involving learners in verbose dialogues that closely mirror actual communication. Unlike they are rule-based chatbots, LLMs rely on contextual and semantic understanding to mimic detailed, rich-context conversation. This allows the practice of negotiations, debates, and casual conversations in multiple languages in the context of a much more dynamic and realistic language learning environment.
2. Combining with Further Individualized Feedback: Current research objectives could also entail customizing LLM-driven activities so they are better suited to individual learner profiles. Literature on adaptive language tutoring has shown that learners respond best to feedback aligned to their language proficiency, learning style, motivation factors, etc. LLMs can marry these ideas by in-built calibration of complexity in vocabulary, mannerisms peculiar to a given culture, and principles of linguistic form into the system. This will provide streamlined, comprehensive support to their learners getting them to the goal much faster.
3. Engagement Metrics and Learning Outcomes: The LLMs that can offer good conversation are backed by little empirical research to assess their impact on long-term learning outcomes. It would be a good idea to measure time-on-task, error correction rates, and vocab retention for much longer periods to back up the pedagogical value of LLM-mediated practice sessions. Controlled studies of the efficacy and limitations of ICT-LMA against traditional instruction will further assist in discovering the vast application potentials of these technologies (Daryanto et al., 2024)

Dynamic Content Generation

1. Curriculum customization and divergence: One special strength provided by large language models is the generation of content, ranging from reading texts to exercises or bits of vocabulary, directly corresponding to a student's preferences of a variety of ranges, like that of science, business, and literature. This provision not only renders personalized curricula to which learners can attach themselves, preventing learner burnout but also sketches out a less exclusive

learning domain from academic writing and out to workplace communication. Future research may experiment more with the blended use of LLM-created and teacher-developed materials to avoid damping the learning process.

2. Cross-cultural and multilingual settings: Culturally and contextually highly sensitive LLMs trained on multilingual corpora can guide students with the cultural aspects of various lingual systems. Theoretical as well as empirical investigations are needed to evaluate how well LLMs can cope with code-switching and dialectical variations, particularly where minority languages or regional dialects face the risk of being eradicated (Abudalfa et al., 2024). The topic of linguistic inclusivity is very central to the research so as not to marginalize less endowed languages.
3. Feedback loop for refinement: Large language models can keep working, updating, and extending their knowledge base; however, the continuously updating version remains a basic necessity. Considering further teacher feedback or student feedback paradigms in future research could guide the evolution of large language models based on actual feedback from the classroom for better accuracy, contextual appropriateness, and alignment with learning objectives.

Automated Feedback and Correction

1. Real-Time Assessment of Syntax and Semantics: They render AI to be a copious provider of feedback on evaluations for learner input from text, speech, and myriad other ways, taking on such intricate grammatical flaws in structure, and also underlined semantics. When this is applied alongside another speech recognizer, it shows the weak pronunciation at the right point, or it calls the wrong target. Research challenges here are: (1) the crystallisation of a standard rubric for error classification and (2) determining a level to which this feedback could be granulated without at the same time overwhelming the learner.
2. Scalability in Large-Class Settings: In educational contexts with high student-to-teacher ratios, providing timely and personalized feedback can be daunting. LLM-driven tools offer a scalable mechanism to address common errors and supply remedial material. However, research remains to provide insight into defining a threshold for further revision by human beings. This is particularly true in complexities of linguistic nuances and errors that extend beyond merely requiring culturally informed context (Weidinger et al., 2021).
3. Longitudinal Studies on Learner Autonomy: Although LLMs provide instant feedback, do these foster learner autonomy and critical thinking in the long run? Longitudinal studies tracking learner growth for an extended time, exemplifying premise-controlled and post-treatment or qualitative studies, may shed light

on how should automated feedback influence a learner's self-regulation and cognitive development.

Challenges and Considerations

In bilingual education, the conversation concerns how to manage the ethical dilemmas raised by the widespread use of LLMs.

Model Bias and Inclusivity: LLMs are biased by the datasets they are trained on, and thus they tend to greatly underrepresent minority languages and dialects, while simultaneously stereotyping some groups. Researchers must, therefore, ensure more inclusive training data, de-bias algorithms, and regularly audit output from the model to overcome these limitations. These measures introduce linguistic fairness and user empowerment to people of various languages and cultures (Liu 2024).

Accuracy vs. Creativity: Although LLMs are good at generating coherent, smooth text, incorrect content may lower their value. This is often referred to as hallucination. This raises questions of its reliability, especially in the academic domain where the learners might be making heavy use of LLM-generated information. One solution to this issue is mixed-initiative interfaces that allow verification or adjustment of the model outputs by the teacher. In this sense, the potential for creativity within the LLM remains intact, while the authenticity and pedagogical relevance of the educational resources that are generated are ensured.

Ethical and Privacy Concerns: As all AI-based systems aim to manage the care of data in a hassle-free environment, the LLM-based platforms need to comply rigorously with privacy regulations like the GDPR and FERPA. This includes creating data collection, storage, and usage policies that have minute details, especially about cases of processing sensitive information such as student records or spoken data. Future research may also look into avenues like explainable AI so that information on how exactly LLM performs is explained. Transparency per se fosters accountability and builds trust between stakeholders in binational ethics guiding the LLMs (Piñeiro-Martín et al., 2023).

A comparative visualization of big AI tools in bilingual education will further enable the reader to navigate the technological landscape with precision. A synthesized matrix measuring Duolingo, Rosetta Stone, GPT-based chatbots, and emotional AI against parameters like feedback quality, language support, cost, cultural sensitivity, and scalability could serve a dual purpose: as a reference and a decision guide. This aids teachers and developers to decide upon the correct AI solutions, ultimately making sure that pedagogical intent remains the focus with respect to technological adoption. This structural injection can lessen redundancy and give thematic cohesion to overlapping subsections.

Table 1. Comparative Overview of AI Tools in Bilingual Education

Tool / Platform	Core Function	Language Support	Feedback Type	Cultural Sensitivity	Cost & Accessibility	Scalability
Duolingo	Vocabulary, Grammar Practice	40+ languages	Immediate, Gamified	Moderate (limited localization)	Freemium; Mobile-Friendly	High (global user base)
Rosetta Stone	Immersive Audio-Visual Learning	25+ languages	Real-time pronunciation	High (contextual visuals)	Subscription-Based	Moderate
ImmerseMe / Mondly VR	Immersive VR-Based Scenarios	9–15 languages (varied)	Simulated Interaction	Low to Moderate	Requires VR hardware	Low to Moderate
iTalki AI / Elsa Speak	Pronunciation & Speaking Support	English, Spanish, etc.	Phonetic, Emotional AI	Low (generic tone assessment)	Free / Paid Tiers	Moderate
OpenAI GPT / PaLM / LLaMA	Conversational AI & Content Gen	Multilingual (varied accuracy)	Text-Based, Dynamic	Low to Moderate (bias risk)	API-based; cost varies	High (developer dependent)
Google Translate / Meta AI Translator	Real-Time Translation	100+ languages	Contextual, improving	Varies (better in dominant languages)	Free (web & mobile)	Very High

The comparative matrix in Table 1, summarizes the strengths and weaknesses of highly utilized AI tools in bilingual education. There lie differences in cultural adaptation, cost model, and scalability that ought to be considered by educators and policy-makers prior to adopting said tools. Also, from this matrix, one recognizes the necessities of equity-based design in underrepresented language contexts and teacher-supported integration to increase pedagogical impact.

5.6 Research Directions and Outlook

For bilingual educational purposes, substantial opportunities for scalable, personalized, and context-dependent language learning experiences are offered by the large language models (LLM). Harnessing all the benefits entails a very strong research agenda. In the following, key areas are outlined for the study. By taking methodological investigation and empirical evidence further, these may guide the deliberate and impactful advancement of LLM-powered solutions for bilingual education.

Comparative Efficacy Studies: Comparing instructional outcomes achieved with LLM-based language learning tools to those obtained with traditional teaching methods and existing AI-powered platforms is a critical step and the very first in validating these tools. Using experimental designs, such as randomized control trials or quasi-experimental setups, assessments can be made regarding whether learners using LLM-assisted platforms can score higher on the proficiency tests, applied with more engagement, or remember more over a longer term than those belonging to the control groups. Demographic variables, such as the age of the learner and the language background, should also be controlled in such studies to ensure that the findings are indicative of a variety of learner profiles (Halpin et al., 2021).

In-Depth Error Analysis: Although LLMs offer feedback with inertia and less precise proximity, they are highly unpractical generators of errors. So closely developed comprehensive and systematic error analysis can delineate common types of LLM inaccuracies, ranging from improper word choice to misplaced contextual meanings, shedding critical light upon the impact arising from such errors on learner comprehension. Thus, by merging quantitative error tracking with qualitative user feedback for gauging what perception matches actuality and thereby refining an LLM-driven feedback loop guaranteeing that corrective input strikes with precise timing and is adequate to a good pedagogical direction.

Contextual and Cultural Adaptation: To be truly effective, LLM-based resources have to take into consideration the cultural and language nuances that are an essential part of any bilingual educational milieu. What is yet to be researched is the LLM output's treatment of code-switching, regional dialects, and the presence of cultural connotations, especially when dealing with minority languages or those endangered. Ethnographic studies and focal groups of local educators and students will provide a way to recognize where LLM outputs may collide with cultural norms or reflect biases. Once known, these findings can be utilized to improve the models or develop culturally sensitive pre-training datasets so that there could be a much more inclusive and culturally suitable language-learning system in place (Pawar et al., 2024).

Long-Term Retention and Proficiency Gains: Yet, short-term gains in vocabulary and grammatical accuracy pale in comparison to longitudinal inquiry aimed at gauging how LLM-supported interventions affect long-term retention and fluent use of learned grammar. Scholars may evaluate this in multifaceted designs with delayed post-tests, follow-up interviews, or even repeatedly administered assessments, all carried out over an extended period to make sure that learners holding on to the language's productive aspects never discontinue their interest in or exposure to the language but maybe even improve them. Thus do different intervention impacts between two methods—be it spaced repetition or g-adaptation of scheduling techniques—in the hope of ascertaining how the continued interaction with a student-driven LLM could transform language skills into real-world actions.

Working in such a way will lead to large-scale investigation work via experimental and mixed-method approaches to kick-start putting this research agenda on its feet. When more and more LLMs start becoming customized, this will require the cooperation of computational woman artists, educators, language instructors, and policymakers in blending these systems into bilingual education. Systematic research into efficacy, faultless placement, cultural adaptability, and long-term impact could pave the way to advance the development of ethical, inequitable, and genuinely transformative AI-driven language learning solutions (Khan et al., 2025).

In synergy with ethical laws, human monitoring, and human support, large language models can bring about radical changes in bilingual education through in-depth conversational exchanges and context-rich communication, with current updates and resources. Bridging the gap between automated and human aids will be pivotal in attesting to the inclusiveness and reliability of LLM against the futuristic transformation of the bilingual education system (Raiaan et al., 2024).

A crucial yet often overlooked facet of the debate on AI and bilingual education is teacher training. The robustness of digital tools depends on how digitally competent the educators are and whether they choose to embrace the use of such tools in their methods. In this regard, adequate investment in the professional development of teachers will be critical through digital pedagogy workshops and certification programs so that the teachers are indeed prepared for AI-empowered teaching. At the same time, policy must be adapted to foster this change. Those responsible for education policy should then deliberate on data governance standards, does it aid in the preservation of local languages concerns, and equitable financing schemes for AI integration (Ghosh et al., 2025). In multilingual settings, the language policy must intervene to guarantee that AI mechanisms support linguistic diversity instead of working against it by favoring global languages. At both the national and superseding regional levels, AI literacy should be mainstreamed into the in-service teacher education curricula, accompanied by quality standards for edtech procurement.

6 CONCLUSION

We can see how a range of AI-driven solutions, including augmented and virtual reality to educational technology, culturally interactive platforms that empathetically communicate, and emotionally intelligent platforms point to adaptive learning systems, and hold large language models, could bring the much-desired transformation in bilingual education. AR and VR tools are instrumental in creating interactive and incredibly life-like contexts for the learners to meaningfully use their language skills in various situations in situational learning. Emotion-aware AI technology seeks to study and adapt content in a manner that aligns with learners' emotional indicators, and in turn, it probably encourages engagement and reduces communication anxiety. Complete adaptive learning systems offer learners a system that is instantaneous and individual-paced, which is conducive to real-time translation activities as well as tailor-made lessons. Large Models of language, such as those of the GPT series, PaLM, and LLaMA, present important moments for one-on-one practice compositions and burn a hole in the sky in real-time content generation. Questions have arisen around biases, correctness of content, and cultural sensitivity.

The chapter also covered broader ethical and implementation issues that are chanced to arise when introducing AI tools into bilingual education, stressing the value of representative training datasets, strong protection of data sources, and accountable decisions that AI possibly makes. Equally important to holding onto language nuances, context and direct human mentorship ensure that learners gain stronger intercultural competency in addition to vocabulary and grammar skills. Focused research directions include contrasting AI-based strategies with traditional instruction, perfecting the automatic error-checking and feedback within the learning tools, and decomposing some AR/VR simulations or AI language learning mentor-based dialogues in terms of fostering long-term retention. This whole exercise, again, calls for collaboration between educators, honing their AI-based language teaching best practices to where they provide an ethical bridge and position literature on inequitable representation and sustainable use of AI in different language learning contexts.

Practitioners, developers, and learners share critical scrutiny over how AI impels ethical bilingual education. Educators can teach AI in the context of larger subjects, not replacing human instruction but enriching learning in the target language by crossing the border between cognitive and communicative language-study dimensions. Teachers will not only control output by AI but also provide ambiguous details that allow students to use the feedback beneficially while grounding the students' projects in real-world language use and cultural awareness. To developers, the expectation is localizability, user-friendliness, interface transparency, fairness toward issues, and other responsibilities as well. Such duties would encapsulate the generation of checks and balances to cleanse prejudicial elements out of the algorithm, ensuring that development practices recognize minority languages and dialects, and an onus on privacy data protocols. However, learners must assume responsibility by trying to find a middle path for utilizing AI: practice AI for almost reliable and instant corrections and simulated immersion as opposed to genuine social interaction and community language learning experiences. Learners can increase their voice by stopping to analyze realistically, subjecting AI outputs to questioning, and indicating accurately the boundaries they can navigate within their bilingual journey.

To make sure that the potential of AI in bilingual education is realized sustainably and inclusively, such decisions should stay grounded in practical realities. Educational institutions and policymakers should consider the phases of implementation, budgets, infrastructure readiness, teacher retraining, etc. Managerial frameworks that classify

AI tools according to the level of the learner (beginner vs. advanced), modality of learning (speaking vs. writing), or even access model (freemium vs. institutional licenses) could be set at the level of adoption under real-world conditions. These strategies should enable governments to further encourage private-public partnerships to pilot AI-based programs and collect longitudinal evidence of efficacy. Aligning ethical guidelines and pedagogical frameworks with administrative priorities will help AI in bilingual education grow into something more real and impactful.

In the future, it would mainly be the interplay of human insight on one side, and AI-based development on the other that could bring in an era where language education is personal, interactive and responding to the varied needs and expressions of the learner community across the world. As AI is getting more popular, stakeholders can serve this great boon using their respectable advancement, doing strong, acceptable research that draws in an array of practitioners. This oversight would take full advantage of AI-based capabilities to uplift the level of bilingual proficiency and intercultural understanding, ultimately changing how languages are learned, taught, and applied globally.

REFERENCES

Abdelmaboud, A., Ahmed, A. I. A., Abaker, M., Eisa, T. E., Albasheer, H., Ghorashi, S. A., & Karim, F. K. (2022). Blockchain for IoT Applications: Taxonomy, platforms, recent advances, challenges and future research directions. *Electronics (Basel)*, *11*(4), 630. DOI: 10.3390/electronics11040630

Abudalfa, S. I., Abdu, F. J., & Alowaifeer, M. M. (2024). Arabic Text Formality Modification: A review and future research directions. *IEEE Access : Practical Innovations, Open Solutions*, *1*, 1. Advance online publication. DOI: 10.1109/ACCESS.2024.3511661

Alfaisal, R., Hashim, H., & Azizan, U. H. (2024). Empowering the Metaverse in Education: ChatGPT's role in Transforming Learning Experiences. In *Communications in computer and information science* (pp. 13–31). DOI: 10.1007/978-3-031-65996-6_2

Alharbi, W. (2023). AI in the Foreign Language Classroom: A Pedagogical Overview of Automated Writing Assistance Tools. *Education Research International*, *2023*, 1–15. DOI: 10.1155/2023/4253331

Alshamsi, I., Sadriwala, K. F., Alazzawi, F. J. I., & Shannaq, B. (2024). Exploring the impact of generative AI technologies on education: Academic expert perspectives, trends, and implications for sustainable development goals. *Journal of Infrastructure Policy and Development*, *8*(11), 8532. DOI: 10.24294/jipd.v8i11.8532

Alzahrani, S. A. (2024). The future of AI in language education. In *Advances in educational marketing, administration, and leadership book series* (pp. 309–332). DOI: 10.4018/979-8-3693-7016-2.ch015

Bai, Y. (2024). A mixed methods investigation of Mobile-Based Language learning on EFL students' listening, speaking, foreign language enjoyment, and anxiety. *SAGE Open*, *14*(2), 21582440241255554. Advance online publication. DOI: 10.1177/21582440241255554

Beaudry, N., & Pinsonneault, N. (2005). Understanding User Responses to Information Technology: A coping model of user adaptation. *Management Information Systems Quarterly*, *29*(3), 493. DOI: 10.2307/25148693

Belda-Medina, J., & Kokošková, V. (2023). Integrating chatbots in education: Insights from the Chatbot-Human Interaction Satisfaction Model (CHISM). *International Journal of Educational Technology in Higher Education*, *20*(1), 62. Advance online publication. DOI: 10.1186/s41239-023-00432-3

Bozkurt, A., & Sharma, R. C. (2020, April 30). *Emergency remote teaching in a time of global crisis due to CoronaVirus pandemic*. Retrieved January 26, 2025, from http://asianjde.com/ojs/index.php/AsianJDE/article/view/447

Chassignol, M., Khoroshavin, A., Klimova, A., & Bilyatdinova, A. (2018). Artificial Intelligence trends in education: A narrative overview. *Procedia Computer Science*, *136*, 16–24. DOI: 10.1016/j.procs.2018.08.233

Chen, S., Fang, Y., Shi, G., Sabatini, J., Greenberg, D., Frijters, J., & Graesser, A. C. (2021). Automated disengagement tracking within an intelligent tutoring system. *Frontiers in Artificial Intelligence*, *3*, 595627. Advance online publication. DOI: 10.3389/frai.2020.595627

Daryanto, T., Ding, X., Wilhelm, L. T., Stil, S., Knutsen, K. M., & Rho, E. H. (2024). *Conversate: supporting reflective learning in interview practice through interactive simulation and dialogic feedback. arXiv*. Cornell University., DOI: 10.1145/3701188

Dehganzadeh, H., & Dehganzadeh, H. (2020). Investigating effects of digital gamification-based language learning: A systematic review. *Journal of English Language Teaching and Learning*, *12*(25), 53–93. DOI: 10.22034/elt.2020.10676

. Doğan, Y., & Talan, T. (2024). Artificial intelligence in foreign language learning: A bibliometric analysis. *Journal of Pedagogical Research*. DOI: 10.33902/JPR.202427734

Ess, C. (2020). *Digital Media Ethics* (3rd ed.). Polity Press., https://www.politybooks.com/bookdetail?book_slug=digital-media-ethics-3rd-edition--9781509533428

Essafi, M., Belfakir, L., & Moubtassime, M. (2024). Investigating Mobile-Assisted Language Learning apps: Babbel, Memrise, and Duolingo as a case study. *Journal of Curriculum and Teaching*, *13*(2), 197. DOI: 10.5430/jct.v13n2p197

Evers, K., & Chen, S. (2020). Effects of an automatic speech recognition system with peer feedback on pronunciation instruction for adults. *Computer Assisted Language Learning*, *35*(8), 1869–1889. DOI: 10.1080/09588221.2020.1839504

Ghosh, R. K., Ghosh, M., Roy, D., Gupta, B., Chakraborty, S., Biswas, A., & Basu, M. (2025). Personalized Financial Services through NLP and AI-Driven Innovations in FinTech. In *IGI Global eBooks* (pp. 371–420). DOI: 10.4018/979-8-3693-9944-6.ch019

Giannakos, M., Azevedo, R., Brusilovsky, P., Cukurova, M., Dimitriadis, Y., Hernandez-Leo, D., Järvelä, S., Mavrikis, M., & Rienties, B. (2024). The promise and challenges of generative AI in education. *Behaviour & Information Technology*, •••, 1–27. DOI: 10.1080/0144929X.2024.2394886

Giri, A. (2024). Revolutionizing student evaluation. In *Advances in educational technologies and instructional design book series* (pp. 333–362). DOI: 10.4018/979-8-3693-6170-2.ch012

Green, K. J. (2024). AI-Driven programming education for Black, Latinx, and Afro-Caribbean communities. *Deep Blue (University of Michigan)*. DOI: 10.7302/23676

Haleem, A., Javaid, M., Qadri, M. A., & Suman, R. (2022). Understanding the role of digital technologies in education: A review. *Sustainable Operations and Computers*, *3*, 275–285. DOI: 10.1016/j.susoc.2022.05.004

Halpin, E., Prishker, N., & Melzi, G. (2021). The Bilingual Language Diversity of Latino Preschoolers: A Latent Profile analysis. *Language, Speech, and Hearing Services in Schools*, *52*(3), 877–888. DOI: 10.1044/2021_LSHSS-21-00015

Huang, W., Hew, K. F., & Fryer, L. K. (2021). Chatbots for language learning—Are they really useful? A systematic review of chatbot-supported language learning. *Journal of Computer Assisted Learning*, *38*(1), 237–257. DOI: 10.1111/jcal.12610

Imamguluyev, R., Hasanova, P., Imanova, T., Mammadova, A., Hajizada, S., & Samadova, Z. (2024). AI-POWERED EDUCATIONAL TOOLS: TRANSFORMING LEARNING IN THE DIGITAL ERA. *International Research Journal of Modernization in Engineering Technology and Science*, *6*(12). Advance online publication. DOI: 10.56726/IRJMETS65040

Juan, A. Y. S., & Murai, Y. (2022). Turning frustration into learning opportunities during maker activities: A review of literature. *International Journal of Child-Computer Interaction*, *33*, 100519. DOI: 10.1016/j.ijcci.2022.100519

Kabudi, T., Pappas, I., & Olsen, D. H. (2021). AI-enabled adaptive learning systems: A systematic mapping of the literature. *Computers and Education Artificial Intelligence*, *2*, 100017. DOI: 10.1016/j.caeai.2021.100017

Karakas, A. (2023). Breaking down barriers with artificial intelligence (AI). In *Advances in educational technologies and instructional design book series* (pp. 215–233). DOI: 10.4018/978-1-6684-9893-4.ch012

Khan, S., Mazhar, T., Shahzad, T., Khan, M. A., Rehman, A. U., Saeed, M. M., & Hamam, H. (2025). Harnessing AI for sustainable higher education: Ethical considerations, operational efficiency, and future directions. *Discover Sustainability*, *6*(1), 23. Advance online publication. DOI: 10.1007/s43621-025-00809-6

Klimova, B., Pikhart, M., Benites, A. D., Lehr, C., & Sanchez-Stockhammer, C. (2022). Neural machine translation in foreign language teaching and learning: A systematic review. *Education and Information Technologies*, *28*(1), 663–682. DOI: 10.1007/s10639-022-11194-2

Koka, N. A. (2024). Exploring Insights from Undergraduates on the Use of Artificial Intelligence (AI) Tools to Enhance Proficiency in Tense and Aspect in Foreign Language Instruction. [PJLSS]. *Pakistan Journal of Life and Social Sciences*, *22*(2). Advance online publication. DOI: 10.57239/PJLSS-2024-22.2.001440

Lee, J., Hicke, Y., Yu, R., Brooks, C., & Kizilcec, R. F. (2024). The life cycle of large language models in education: A framework for understanding sources of bias. *British Journal of Educational Technology*, *55*(5), 1982–2002. DOI: 10.1111/bjet.13505

Lissitz, A. (2025). Insights Unleashed: Harnessing AI for learning Analytics. In *WORLD SCIENTIFIC eBooks* (pp. 155–196). DOI: 10.1142/9789811296475_0009

Liu, X., Li, Y., & Huang, Y. (2021). A model of teachers' excellent teaching behaviors based on natural language processing. In *Lecture notes in computer science* (pp. 303–311). DOI: 10.1007/978-3-030-92836-0_26

. Liu, Z. (2024). Cultural Bias in Large Language Models: A Comprehensive analysis and Mitigation Strategies. *Journal of Transcultural Communication*. DOI: 10.1515/jtc-2023-0019

Owan, V. J., Abang, K. B., Idika, D. O., Etta, E. O., & Bassey, B. A. (2023). Exploring the potential of artificial intelligence tools in educational measurement and assessment. *Eurasia Journal of Mathematics, Science and Technology Education*, *19*(8), em2307. Advance online publication. DOI: 10.29333/ejmste/13428

Pawar, S., Park, J., Jin, J., Arora, A., Myung, J., Yadav, S., Haznitrama, F. G., Song, I., Oh, A., & Augenstein, I. (2024). Survey of Cultural Awareness in Language Models: Text and Beyond. *arXiv (Cornell University)*. https://doi.org//arxiv.2411.00860DOI: 10.48550

Piñeiro-Martín, A., García-Mateo, C., Docío-Fernández, L., & Del Carmen López-Pérez, M. (2023). Ethical challenges in the development of virtual assistants powered by large language models. *Electronics (Basel)*, *12*(14), 3170. DOI: 10.3390/electronics12143170

Raiaan, M. K., Mukta, M. S. H., Fatema, K., Fahad, N. M., Sakib, S., Mim, M. M. J., Ahmad, J., Ali, M. E., & Azam, S. (2024). A review on large language models: Architectures, applications, taxonomies, open issues and challenges. *IEEE Access : Practical Innovations, Open Solutions, 12*, 26839–26874. DOI: 10.1109/ACCESS.2024.3365742

Raj, N. S., & Renumol, V. G. (2021). A systematic literature review on adaptive content recommenders in personalized learning environments from 2015 to 2020. *Journal of Computers in Education, 9*(1), 113–148. DOI: 10.1007/s40692-021-00199-4

Shadiev, R., & Feng, Y. (2023). Using automated corrective feedback tools in language learning: A review study. *Interactive Learning Environments*, •••, 1–29. DOI: 10.1080/10494820.2022.2153145

Shohieb, S. M., Doenyas, C., & Elhady, A. M. (2022). Dynamic difficulty adjustment technique-based mobile vocabulary learning game for children with autism spectrum disorder. *Entertainment Computing, 42*, 100495. DOI: 10.1016/j.entcom.2022.100495

Shortt, M., Tilak, S., Kuznetcova, I., Martens, B., & Akinkuolie, B. (2021). Gamification in mobile-assisted language learning: A systematic review of Duolingo literature from public release of 2012 to early 2020. *Computer Assisted Language Learning, 36*(3), 517–554. DOI: 10.1080/09588221.2021.1933540

Soliman, M. M., Ahmed, E., Darwish, A., & Hassanien, A. E. (2024). Artificial intelligence powered Metaverse: Analysis, challenges and future perspectives. *Artificial Intelligence Review, 57*(2), 36. Advance online publication. DOI: 10.1007/s10462-023-10641-x

Song, C., Shin, S., & Shin, K. (2023). Optimizing Foreign Language learning in Virtual Reality: A comprehensive theoretical framework based on Constructivism and Cognitive Load Theory (VR-CCL). *Applied Sciences (Basel, Switzerland), 13*(23), 12557. DOI: 10.3390/app132312557

Strielkowski, W., Grebennikova, V., Lisovskiy, A., Rakhimova, G., & Vasileva, T. (2024). AI-driven adaptive learning for sustainable educational transformation. *Sustainable Development*. Advance online publication. DOI: 10.1002/sd.3221

Strielkowski, W., Grebennikova, V., Lisovskiy, A., Rakhimova, G., & Vasileva, T. (2024). AI-driven adaptive learning for sustainable educational transformation. *Sustainable Development*. Advance online publication. DOI: 10.1002/sd.3221

Thurairasu, V. (2022). Gamification-Based Learning as the Future of Language Learning: An Overview. *European Journal of Humanities and Social Sciences*, *2*(6), 62–69. DOI: 10.24018/ejsocial.2022.2.6.353

Wang, S., Christensen, C., Cui, W., Tong, R., Yarnall, L., Shear, L., & Feng, M. (2020). When adaptive learning is effective learning: Comparison of an adaptive learning system to teacher-led instruction. *Interactive Learning Environments*, *31*(2), 793–803. DOI: 10.1080/10494820.2020.1808794

Weidinger, L., Mellor, J., Rauh, M., Griffin, C., Uesato, J., Huang, P., Cheng, M., Glaese, M., Balle, B., Kasirzadeh, A., Kenton, Z., Brown, S., Hawkins, W., Stepleton, T., Biles, C., Birhane, A., Haas, J., Rimell, L., Hendricks, L. A., . . . Gabriel, I. (2021). Ethical and social risks of harm from Language Models. *arXiv (Cornell University)*. https://doi.org//arxiv.2112.04359DOI: 10.48550

Werdiningsih, I., Marzuki, N., & Rusdin, D. (2024). Balancing AI and authenticity: EFL students' experiences with ChatGPT in academic writing. *Cogent Arts & Humanities*, *11*(1), 2392388. Advance online publication. DOI: 10.1080/23311983.2024.2392388

Woodruff, E. (2024). AI Detection of Human Understanding in a Gen-AI Tutor. *AI*, *5*(2), 898–921. DOI: 10.3390/ai5020045

Xia, Y., Shin, S., & Kim, J. (2024). Cross-Cultural Intelligent Language Learning System (CILS): Leveraging AI to facilitate language learning strategies in Cross-Cultural communication. *Applied Sciences (Basel, Switzerland)*, *14*(13), 5651. DOI: 10.3390/app14135651

Yadav, S. (2024). Advancing education with AI-Driven education for diverse learners. In *Advances in educational technologies and instructional design book series* (pp. 49–80). DOI: 10.4018/979-8-3693-6130-6.ch003

Yu, S., Androsov, A., Yan, H., & Chen, Y. (2024). Bridging computer and education sciences: A systematic review of automated emotion recognition in online learning environments. *Computers & Education*, *220*, 105111. DOI: 10.1016/j.compedu.2024.105111

. Yudintseva, A. (2023). Virtual reality affordances for oral communication in English as a second language classroom: A literature review. *Computers & Education X Reality*, *2*, 100018. DOI: 10.1016/j.cexr.2023.100018

Zhu, B., Chau, K. T., & Mokmin, N. M. (2024). Optimizing cognitive load and learning adaptability with adaptive microlearning for in-service personnel. *Scientific Reports*, *14*(1), 25960. Advance online publication. DOI: 10.1038/s41598-024-77122-1

Chapter 6

AI for Bilingual Mastery: Personalized Learning and Intelligence Tutoring in Language Education

Andi Asrifan
https://orcid.org/0000-0002-9934-6129
Universitas Negeri Makassar, Indonesia

Like Raskova Octaberliana
https://orcid.org/0009-0001-8829-5266
UIN Maulana Malik Ibrahim, Indonesia

Ali Sorayyaei Azar
https://orcid.org/0000-0003-3539-8250
University of Malaya, Malaysia

ABSTRACT

The integration of Artificial Intelligence (AI) in language teaching has revolutionized conventional learning methods, facilitating tailored and adaptive solutions that cater to varied student requirements. This study analyzes significant AI-driven breakthroughs, including Intelligent Tutoring Systems (ITS), Natural Language Processing (NLP), and immersive technologies such as Virtual Reality (VR) and Augmented Reality (AR). These tools augment engagement, deliver real-time feedback, and facilitate bilingual competency via interactive and tailored learning pathways. Moreover, AI-driven data analytics provides instructors with actionable insights to enhance educational tactics. Although the advantages are clear, issues such as data privacy, algorithmic bias, and equal access must be resolved to guarantee ethical

DOI: 10.4018/979-8-3373-0275-1.ch006

implementation. This study emphasizes AI's revolutionary capacity to develop inclusive, efficient, and engaging language education systems, providing a paradigm for promoting multilingual proficiency in a progressively networked society.

INTRODUCTION TO AI IN LANGUAGE EDUCATION

1.1 Overview of AI Technologies

Language acquisition has experienced considerable changes throughout time, transitioning from conventional techniques to modern strategies that utilize technology (Alam & Mohanty, 2023; Chowdhury, 2024). Traditionally, language education depended significantly on rote memorization, grammatical exercises, and repetitious tasks. These conventional methods, often defined by a uniform approach, mainly concentrated on vocabulary development and grammatical precision. Although they established the foundation for language acquisition, they frequently neglected to engage pupils effectively or cultivate practical communication abilities.

A key shortcoming of conventional approaches is their deficiency in personalizing. In a conventional classroom environment, educators provide material to a cohort of students exhibiting diverse skill levels and distinct learning modalities (Chen et al., 2021; Vikas & Mathur, 2022; Sharma et al., 2022). This standard methodology may inundate certain students, while others can get disenchanted owing to insufficient challenge. Moreover, conventional approaches frequently emphasize textual communication at the expense of verbal interaction, thus impeding learners' acquisition of vital conversational abilities.

A notable disadvantage is the insufficient feedback offered to trainees. In conventional contexts, feedback is generally postponed, frequently provided just post-assignment evaluation (Morris et al., 2021). This delay might hinder the learning process, since students may not obtain prompt corrections or feedback regarding their errors. As a result, students may find it difficult to recognize and rectify their deficiencies, resulting in dissatisfaction and decreased desire.

Furthermore, conventional language acquisition frequently prioritizes passive learning, wherein pupils are anticipated to assimilate knowledge rather than actively interact with the language (Ouariach et al., 2023). This passive methodology may lead to insufficient practical application, hindering learners' ability to apply their information in real-world contexts.

The emergence of Artificial Intelligence (AI) has created new opportunities for language education, overcoming the constraints of conventional techniques. AI-driven solutions can deliver customized learning experiences, adjusting to the unique needs and preferences of each student (Sundari et al.). By assessing a student's advancement and performance in real-time, these systems can provide customized exercises and feedback, guaranteeing that learners have the necessary support for success.

Moreover, AI can enhance interactive and immersive learning settings, promoting active engagement and practical application of language skills (Chen et al., 2022; Rapaka et al., 2025). AI-driven systems, equipped with speech recognition and natural language processing, may replicate authentic conversations, enabling learners to practice speaking and listening in a secure and encouraging environment.

As we commence this examination of AI in language teaching, it is crucial to acknowledge the significant transition from conventional techniques to individualized, technology-augmented learning experiences. This development improves engagement and enables learners to attain multilingual proficiency in a progressively interconnected environment.

1.2 The Importance of Bilingualism

Bilingualism, the capacity to converse proficiently in two languages, provides numerous advantages that surpass basic communication (Sivakumar & Vanitha, 2024). The benefits can be classified into cognitive, cultural, and economic dimensions, each enhancing the significance of bilingual education in the contemporary worldwide society. Research repeatedly indicates that bilingual persons exhibit superior mental flexibility and problem-solving abilities from a cognitive standpoint. The act of alternating between languages necessitates considerable cognitive exertion, perhaps enhancing executive abilities including attentional control, task switching, and working memory (Paap et al., 2021). Research suggests that bilingualism may postpone the onset of age-related cognitive deterioration and diminish the likelihood of dementia, rendering it a significant advantage throughout a person's life. Bilingual learners often cultivate a heightened awareness of linguistic structures, which deepens their comprehension of their original language and improves overall language proficiency.

Bilingualism culturally facilitates access to other ideas and experiences. It enables individuals to engage with diverse groups, cultivating empathy and awareness for cultural subtleties (Hossain, 2024). Bilingual individuals can interact with literature, music, and art from diverse cultures, enhancing their lives and expanding their perspectives. Cultural competence is increasingly vital in a heterogeneous society, where comprehension and tolerance for diversity can foster more amicable interactions. Bilingualism is essential for maintaining endangered languages and developing cultural heritage, hence ensuring the celebration and maintenance of varied identities.

The economic benefits of bilingualism are significant. In a progressively interconnected global economy, businesses frequently want personnel capable of communicating proficiently across linguistic and cultural divides. Bilingual workers may experience improved employment prospects, increased remuneration, and enhanced opportunities for professional progression. Industries such as international business, diplomacy, healthcare, and education highly regard multilingual professionals for their ability to enhance communication with varied clients and improve collaboration among multinational teams (Augustin et al., 2024). Bilingualism can augment a company's competitiveness in the global market, enabling enterprises to broaden their reach and engage with a wider audience.

Bilingualism holds significance that beyond mere proficiency in two languages. The cognitive, cultural, and economic advantages highlight the imperative of integrating bilingual education into educational systems. The examination of AI's function in language education reveals that tailored learning and intelligent tutoring systems can greatly improve bilingual proficiency, providing learners with essential abilities for success in a diverse and dynamic environment.

1.3 Current Trends in Language Learning

The domain of language acquisition has undergone significant transformation in recent decades, shifting from conventional methodologies prevalent in educational settings to contemporary strategies that leverage technological advancements (Tseng et al., 2022). This transition signifies an increasing acknowledgment of the necessity for more efficient, captivating, and individualized educational experiences that address the varied requirements of learners.

Conventional language acquisition techniques frequently depended on explicit instruction, rote memorization, and repeating exercises (Han & Reber, 2022). These methodologies generally prioritized grammatical rules, vocabulary lists, and memorization exercises, which, although fundamental, frequently did not captivate pupils or promote practical language application. The teacher-centered approach positioned the educator as the principal knowledge transmitter, while students functioned as passive recipients. These strategies frequently frustrated learners, especially those who found the instructional speed challenging or lacking opportunities for substantive involvement.

Conversely, contemporary language acquisition methods utilize technology to establish dynamic and engaging settings. A notable improvement is using digital platforms and applications that provide tailored learning experiences (Alamri et al., 2021). These technologies employ data analytics and artificial intelligence to customize information and exercises according to individual learners' competence levels, interests, and learning styles. Language learning applications such as Duolingo and Babbel offer customized lessons that modify in complexity according to user performance, promoting proficiency at each level.

Furthermore, technology has enabled the emergence of immersive learning experiences. Virtual reality (VR) and augmented reality (AR) applications enable learners to refine language abilities in simulated real-world contexts, hence improving their communicative competence (Al-Ansi et al., 2023). These immersive experiences can markedly enhance learners' confidence and proficiency by offering contextualized practice that conventional techniques frequently lack.

Online language learning communities and platforms have revolutionized the interactions between learners and native speakers. Social media, language exchange platforms, and online tutoring services facilitate worldwide connections among students, promoting genuine communication and cultural exchange (Dong et al. 2023). This transition to collaborative learning underscores the significance of social interaction in language acquisition, enabling learners to hone their speaking and listening abilities through real-time dialogues.

Moreover, the incorporation of gamification in language acquisition has rendered the process more captivating and stimulating. Modern language learning platforms promote constant practice and cultivate a sense of achievement by integrating game-like aspects, including prizes, challenges, and leaderboards (Chan & Lo, 2024).

The shift from conventional methods to technology-enhanced strategies has transformed language acquisition. Upon further examination of AI's involvement in language education, it is evident that contemporary trends not only augment the learning experience but also enable learners to attain bilingual proficiency in an evolving global landscape.

THEORETICAL FOUNDATIONS OF LANGUAGE LEARNING

2.1 Second Language Acquisition Theories

Comprehending the theoretical underpinnings of second language acquisition (SLA) is crucial for formulating effective language education strategies, especially within AI-enhanced learning contexts (Goh & Vandergrift, 2021). Numerous significant ideas have developed, each offering important perspectives on second language acquisition.

Stephen Krashen's Input Hypothesis is one of the most significant theories. Krashen asserts that language learning transpires when learners encounter "comprehensible input," defined as language that slightly exceeds their existing skill level (often referred to as "i+1") (Vu & Peters, 2021). This idea posits that exposure to meaningful language in context is essential for acquisition, enabling learners to assimilate grammatical structures and vocabulary without explicit teaching naturally. Krashen underscores the significance of a low-anxiety atmosphere, contending that when learners are at ease, they are more inclined to interact with the language and assimilate it proficiently. This idea significantly impacts AI-driven language learning, as tailored systems can customize input to align with learners' proficiency and interests, thus improving comprehension and motivation.

Another important idea is Vygotsky's Social contact idea, which emphasizes the significance of social contact in language acquisition. Vygotsky posits that language acquisition is a socially mediated process in which learners develop knowledge through interactions with more knowledgeable others, such as educators or peers (Alshuraiaan, 2023). This theory presents the notion of the "Zone of Proximal Development" (ZPD), denoting the spectrum of tasks a learner may accomplish with assistance but not autonomously. This highlights the significance of collaborative learning and scaffolding in language education, wherein learners obtain support customized to their developmental requirements. AI technology can enhance social connection by linking learners with tutors or discussion partners, fostering significant interactions that advance language learning.

Michael Long's Interaction Hypothesis underscores the importance of interaction in language acquisition (Spada & Lightbown, 2022). Long contends that significant conversation, defined by the negotiation of meaning and feedback, facilitates language development. This idea posits that learners gain advantages from engaging in dialogues, elucidating misconceptions, and obtaining corrected feedback. AI-driven platforms can replicate these interactions via chatbots or virtual tutors, offering learners prompt feedback and chances for practice.

Merrill Swain's Output Hypothesis asserts that language production (speaking or writing) is as crucial for language acquisition as comprehension. Swain contends that when learners are required to generate language, they must actively process their linguistic information, resulting in enhanced learning. Artificial intelligence can facilitate this by providing platforms for learners to practice speaking and writing, thereby fostering self-expression and enhancing fluency (Tai, 2024).

In conclusion, the principal SLA theories—Krashen's Input Hypothesis, Vygotsky's Social Interaction Theory, Long's Interaction Hypothesis, and Swain's Output Hypothesis—offer a comprehensive framework for comprehending second language acquisition. These theories will inform the integration of AI in language education, creating individualized and effective learning experiences tailored to the varied demands of bilingual learners.

2.2 Cognitive Science and Language Learning

Cognitive science provides the essential understanding of the mechanisms involved in language acquisition and guides efficient language instruction techniques. By comprehending the mechanisms via which the human brain processes, stores, and retrieves information, educators can create strategies that improve language learning experiences (Vu et al., 2022). Numerous fundamental themes from cognitive psychology are especially pertinent in this scenario.

A key insight from cognitive research is the significance of working memory in language acquisition. Working memory denotes the system tasked with temporarily retaining and manipulating information. Studies demonstrate that language learners possess a restricted capacity for processing new information, which may hinder their acquisition of vocabulary and grammar. Methods like spaced repetition and chunking can enhance the efficiency of working memory utilization. Spaced repetition entails reviewing content at progressively longer intervals, hence improving retention and minimizing cognitive overload. Chunking entails organizing information into digestible parts, facilitating learners' processing and retention of linguistic structures. AI-driven language learning tools can employ these strategies by customizing review schedules and delivering knowledge in manageable segments (Alias & Razak, 2024).

A fundamental term is a cognitive load, denoting the mental effort necessary for acquiring new information. Cognitive load theory asserts that instructional design must reduce superfluous cognitive load to enhance learning (Müller & Wulf, 2024). In language instruction, this is delivering material in a coherent and structured fashion, eschewing superfluous complexity that may inundate learners. Utilizing visual aids, interactive exercises, and real-world situations can diminish cognitive burden and enhance comprehension. Artificial Intelligence can facilitate this by tailoring content to align with learners' competence levels, preventing them from being inundated with difficult material.

Metacognition, defined as the awareness of one's learning processes, is essential in language acquisition. Promoting learner reflection on tactics, strengths, and areas for enhancement can augment their capacity for self-regulation and foster ownership of their educational journey. AI-driven tutoring systems can enhance metacognitive skills by offering learners insights into their performance, identifying patterns, and recommending tailored tactics for improvement (Halkiopoulos & Gkintoni, 2024).

Cognitive research underscores the significance of relevant context in language acquisition. Studies indicate that individuals are more inclined to recall knowledge when delivered inside a pertinent and captivating setting. This highlights the necessity for genuine resources and real-world contexts in language instruction. Artificial intelligence can enhance this by providing immersive experiences via simulations or virtual environments, enabling learners to practice language skills in contextually enriched settings (Chen, 2024).

In conclusion, cognitive science findings encompassing working memory, cognitive load, metacognition, and meaningful context establish a robust basis for formulating effective language instruction methodologies. Integrating these principles into AI-driven language education can yield tailored and engaging learning experiences that enhance language acquisition and foster multilingual proficiency.

2.3 Role of Motivation in Language Learning

Motivation is essential in language acquisition, affecting learners' engagement, perseverance, and total achievement. Comprehending the interplay between intrinsic and extrinsic motivation might yield significant insights toward cultivating effective language learning settings, especially within AI-enhanced education (Bukhari et al., 2023).

Intrinsic motivation denotes the internal impetus to participate in an activity for its inherent value, arising from personal interest, enjoyment, or fulfillment (Shahid & Paul, 2021). When genuinely motivated learners engage in language acquisition driven by a sincere desire to communicate, discover new cultures, or attain personal objectives. This motivation is frequently associated with profound learning since intrinsically driven learners are more inclined to dedicate time and effort to language mastery, pursue difficulties, and participate in substantive practice. A learner enamored with foreign films may be incentivized to acquire a language to comprehend the dialogues and appreciate the cultural subtleties, resulting in a deeper relationship with the language

Conversely, extrinsic motivation encompasses external influences that compel learners to participate in language acquisition. These may encompass incentives, acknowledgment, or the aspiration to attain particular objectives, such as passing an examination or obtaining employment. Although extrinsic incentives might effectively prompt learners to commence language study, they may not consistently result in prolonged engagement or profound acquisition (Bailey et al., 2021). A student studying a language merely to meet a requirement may exhibit less excitement and devotion than one driven by personal interests. When extrinsic motivators align with learners' intrinsic objectives, they can augment motivation and yield improved results.

The interaction between intrinsic and extrinsic motivation is essential in language acquisition (Hennebry & Gao, 2021). Research indicates that extrinsic rewards may occasionally diminish intrinsic motivation, especially when learners view the rewards as controlling or experience pressure to excel. Consequently, it is imperative to establish a balance that cultivates both forms of drive. AI-driven language learning platforms can integrate gamification components, offering incentives for accomplishments while fostering intrinsic motivation through captivating material and tailored learning pathways.

Moreover, cultivating a helpful and encouraging educational atmosphere can substantially boost motivation. Educators and AI systems can offer constructive comments, acknowledge learners' progress, and facilitate social engagement, which can enhance both internal and extrinsic motivation. Motivating learners to establish personal objectives and evaluate their advancement can augment their sense of agency and dedication to the language acquisition process.

In conclusion, internal and extrinsic motivation significantly influences language acquisition. By comprehending and utilizing these motivating variables, educators and AI systems can develop tailored and engaging language learning experiences that motivate learners to attain bilingual proficiency and maintain their interest in lifelong language acquisition.

AI-POWERED PERSONALIZED LEARNING

3.1 Adaptive Learning Systems

Adaptive learning systems exemplify a revolutionary method in education, especially in language acquisition. They employ artificial intelligence (AI) to customize learning experiences based on individual requirements and preferences (Sajja et al., 2024). These systems evaluate learners' interactions, performance, and progress in real time, facilitating a tailored educational experience that improves engagement and efficacy.

Adaptive learning fundamentally involves evaluating a learner's existing skills and recognizing their strengths and weaknesses. AI algorithms evaluate data from several sources, including quizzes, exercises, and interaction patterns, to construct a comprehensive profile of each student (Sajja et al., 2024). This profile conveys the learner's preferred learning style, pace, and areas needing more attention. For instance, if a student has difficulty with verb conjugations yet demonstrates proficiency in vocabulary acquisition, the adaptive learning system can emphasize exercises that strengthen verb application while offering advanced vocabulary difficulties.

A primary benefit of adaptive learning systems is their ability to deliver instantaneous feedback. Conventional language acquisition techniques sometimes entail postponed feedback, which impedes learning. Conversely, AI-driven platforms provide immediate corrections and recommendations, enabling learners to comprehend their errors and modify their techniques in real-time. This prompt feedback mechanism augments learning and sustains motivation, as learners may observe their advancement and enhancement.

Furthermore, adaptive learning systems can modify task complexity dynamically according to the learner's performance. Should a learner repeatedly exhibit mastery of a specific idea, the system may present more intricate difficulties to facilitate ongoing development. If a learner has difficulties, the system can offer more assistance, including more straightforward explanations, practice tasks, or alternate resources.

This adaptability guarantees that learners are neither disinterested in excessively simple assignments nor daunted by very challenging assignments, thereby cultivating an ideal learning atmosphere.

Furthermore, adaptive learning systems can integrate diverse multimedia components to accommodate varied learning styles. For example, certain learners may find visual aids advantageous, whilst others may choose aural materials or interactive simulations. AI-powered systems can successfully engage learners and satisfy varied tastes by providing a variety of content formats (Sundari et al., 2024).

The data gathered by adaptive learning systems can be essential for educators. By analyzing trends and patterns in student performance, educators can gain insights into prevalent obstacles encountered by learners and modify their instructional tactics accordingly. This data-centric methodology facilitates better-informed decision-making, ultimately resulting in enhanced educational outcomes.

In summary, adaptive learning systems utilize AI to develop individualized language learning experiences tailored to individual requirements. These technologies signify a substantial progression in achieving bilingual proficiency and efficient language teaching by delivering real-time feedback, modifying difficulty levels, integrating varied material forms, and furnishing vital insights for educators.

3.2 Data-Driven Insights

Data-driven insights are revolutionizing language training methodology for educators and students. Through analytics, AI systems can track learners' progress, identify patterns, and adjust teaching methods to improve language learning (Sajja et al., 2024). This data-driven approach enhances the effectiveness of language training and empowers learners to take charge of their educational journeys.

A primary advantage of utilizing analytics in language learning is the ability to monitor individual progress in real-time. AI systems compile data on several aspects of a learner's performance, including quiz scores, time spent on activities, engagement patterns, and completion rates. This wealth of information allows educators to have a comprehensive understanding of each student's strengths and weaknesses. For instance, research suggests that a kid consistently struggles with listening comprehension despite exhibiting aptitude in reading. In that scenario, educators can tailor their support by providing targeted listening exercises and resources.

Furthermore, analytics can reveal patterns and trends among a larger cohort of learners. By aggregating data from multiple students, educators can identify common challenges and areas for improvement within the curriculum (Martin-Alguacil et al., 2024). Assume a significant proportion of pupils encounter difficulties with a specific grammatical structure. Consequently, educators can adjust their instructional strategies to concentrate on that domain, guaranteeing that all students have the requisite support for achievement.

AI-powered analytics enable the personalization of learning pathways (Strielkowski et al., 2024). By analyzing learner preferences and engagement data, these systems can provide tailored materials and activities that align with personal interests. For example, if a learner has a particular interest in travel, the system may suggest language exercises focused on travel-related vocabulary and scenarios. This customized approach enhances motivation while fostering a deeper connection to a learned language.

Moreover, data-driven insights can offer timely and constructive feedback. AI systems can generate detailed reports that outline learners' progress over time, pinpointing areas needing improvement. This feedback is crucial for aiding learners in understanding their performance and setting achievable goals. Learners can receive feedback on their vocabulary retention progress and suggestions for additional practice or resources to enhance their learning (He & Loewen, 2022).

The use of analytics promotes the continuous improvement of teaching strategies. Educators can evaluate the effectiveness of many instructional methods and resources through data collected from students (Hooda et al., 2022). By assessing which strategies yield optimal results, educators can refine their approaches, thus meeting the diverse needs of their students.

In conclusion, data-driven insights are crucial for enhancing language training through analytics. AI technologies augment the language acquisition process by tracking progress, identifying trends, personalizing learning trajectories, and providing immediate feedback to both educators and students. This data-driven approach fosters bilingual proficiency and cultivates a more engaging and effective teaching environment.

3.3 Case Studies of Successful Implementation

Incorporating artificial intelligence (AI) in language acquisition has created advanced tools and platforms that markedly improve educational results. Numerous case studies demonstrate the successful application of AI technology in language instruction, highlighting their efficacy in fostering bilingual proficiency.

A notable instance is Duolingo, a language acquisition application that employs artificial intelligence algorithms to generate customized learning experiences for its users. Duolingo's adaptive learning algorithm evaluates user interactions, monitors progress, and identifies areas of difficulty for learners. Duolingo utilizes gamification strategies, including points, levels, and prizes, to maintain user engagement and motivation. The application modifies the exercise difficulty according to individual performance, guaranteeing that learners are adequately challenged without experiencing overwhelm (Shortt et al., 2023). Research by the City University of New York revealed that Duolingo users exhibited substantial language improvements, with numerous individuals attaining skills akin to conventional classroom learners after only a few months of usage. This study illustrates the efficacy of AI in personalizing language acquisition, rendering it accessible and interesting for a varied audience.

Rosetta Stone's TruAccent feature exemplifies a successful application of AI in language instruction, employing speech recognition technology to deliver instantaneous feedback on pronunciation. This program evaluates learners' speech patterns against those of native speakers, providing corrective feedback and recommendations for enhancement. The capacity to engage in spoken practice and obtain prompt feedback is especially advantageous for language learners, given that pronunciation frequently poses a significant challenge in language acquisition. The efficacy of TruAccent has been evidenced in multiple trials when learners utilizing the feature exhibited significant enhancements in their speaking abilities (Rajak et al., 2024). This case highlights the significance of AI in enabling interactive and immersive language learning experiences.

The platform Lingvist shows the application of AI in generating tailored vocabulary acquisition experiences. Lingvist utilizes machine learning algorithms to tailor content according to the learner's advancement and retention metrics. The platform identifies terms that a learner finds challenging to recall and prioritizes them in subsequent exercises, so directing attention to regions requiring enhancement (Bengsch, 2024). This customized strategy has increased retention rates and expedited user vocabulary development. Research by the developers revealed that learners could substantially enhance their vocabulary within a short timeframe, demonstrating the efficacy of data-driven customization in language instruction.

Finally, implementing AI-driven chatbots, such as the Chatbot for Language Learning (CLL), has become increasingly popular for offering conversational practice to language learners. These chatbots replicate authentic conversations, enabling learners to practice speaking and writing in a stress-free setting. CLL modifies its responses according to the learner's input, delivering contextually pertinent feedback and corrections (Tai & Chen, 2024). Users have shown enhanced confidence in their conversational abilities, illustrating the capacity of AI to generate effective, interesting language practice chances.

In conclusion, these case studies demonstrate the revolutionary influence of AI tools in language instruction. By personalizing learning experiences, providing real-time feedback, and facilitating interactive practice, AI technologies have markedly enhanced language learning results, fostering successful bilingual proficiency. The discipline's ongoing evolution suggests that the use of AI in language instruction will probably produce increasingly novel ways to improve the learning experience.

INTELLIGENT TUTORING SYSTEMS IN LANGUAGE EDUCATION

4.1 What are Intelligent Tutoring Systems (ITS)?

Intelligent Tutoring Systems (ITS) are sophisticated educational technologies aimed at delivering individualized instruction to students, emulating the advantages of personal tutoring (El et al., 2023). These systems utilize artificial intelligence (AI) to tailor themselves to the specific needs, preferences, and performance levels of individual learners, rendering them very beneficial in language instruction. By providing customized feedback and coaching, ITS can improve the language acquisition process and assist learners in attaining multilingual proficiency.

Intelligent Tutoring Systems fundamentally comprise numerous essential components that collaboratively establish an effective learning environment (Bradáč et al., 2022; Yilmaz et al., 2022; D'Mello & Graesser, 2023; Fang et al., 2022). The initial element is the learner model, which functions as a dynamic depiction of the particular learner's knowledge, skills, and learning preferences. This model is perpetually refined according to the learner's interactions with the system, enabling the Intelligent Tutoring System to customize the educational experience. If a learner encounters difficulties with verb conjugations, the system can modify its material to offer more practice.

The second component is the domain model, which includes the content and organization of the subject matter being taught, specifically the target language. The domain model encompasses data regarding vocabulary, grammatical rules, pronunciation, and cultural contexts. It functions as a repository of knowledge from which the ITS can extract when delivering exercises and resources to the learner. Utilizing a clearly delineated domain model enables the system to guarantee that the material is pertinent and corresponds with the learner's existing competence level.

The third essential element is the pedagogical model, which delineates the educational procedures and techniques utilized by the ITS. This model delineates the system's interaction with learners, encompassing the forms of feedback, the order of information delivery, and the strategies employed to engage learners. The pedagogical paradigm is based on theories of language acquisition and cognitive science, ensuring that the instructional tactics are rooted in effective educational practices.

A crucial component of ITS is the intelligent feedback mechanism. In contrast to conventional language learning approaches that frequently offer generic feedback, Intelligent Tutoring Systems (ITS) can furnish precise, context-specific feedback tailored to the learner's responses. For example, if a student commits a grammatical error, the system can identify the mistake, elucidate the relevant rule, and provide supplementary practice assignments specifically designed to address that issue. This prompt and specific feedback is essential for promoting language acquisition and assisting learners in rectifying their misconceptions.

Many Intelligent Tutoring Systems integrate assessment and analytics functionalities to monitor learners' progress over time. By evaluating performance data, the system can discern trends, modify learning pathways, and offer insights to learners and educators. This data-driven methodology augments the overall efficacy of language training and facilitates ongoing enhancement in the learning process.

In conclusion, Intelligent Tutoring Systems are effective instruments in language teaching, distinguished by their capacity to customize learning experiences via advanced learner models, domain expertise, pedagogical approaches, insightful feedback, and comprehensive analytics. ITS can substantially improve language acquisition by utilizing these components, rendering them an invaluable resource in the quest for bilingual proficiency.

4.2 Natural Language Processing in Language Tutoring

Natural Language Processing (NLP) is a branch of artificial intelligence that concentrates on the interaction between computers and human language. NLP improves interaction and feedback in Intelligent Tutoring Systems (ITS) within language instruction. NLP enhances the language learning experience by allowing robots to comprehend, interpret, and respond to human language, resulting in a more dynamic, personalized, and effective process.

NLP significantly improves language acquisition via speech recognition (Fendji et al., 2022). This technology enables learners to enhance their speaking skills through voice interaction with the system. For example, when a learner vocalizes into a device, the NLP algorithms evaluate the spoken input, transcribing it into text while analyzing pronunciation, intonation, and fluency. This prompt analysis allows the system to deliver real-time feedback, assisting trainees in rectifying their pronunciation and enhancing their speaking skills. This interactive practice simulates real-life discussions, enhancing confidence and proficiency in spoken language.

NLP enables text-based interaction between learners and the tutoring system, in addition to speech recognition (Wu et al., 2025). Chatbots and conversational agents enable learners to participate in textual dialogues, facilitating the practice of their writing and comprehension abilities. These systems can analyze user input, identify grammatical inaccuracies, and offer helpful criticism. For example, if a student constructs a sentence with an erroneous verb tense, the NLP component can detect the mistake and propose the correct version while elucidating the grammatical norm. This specific feedback aids learners in recognizing their errors while simultaneously enhancing their understanding through elucidation and practice.

Natural Language Processing also improves the customization of language learning sessions. NLP algorithms can discern trends in language usage, including frequent errors or particular vocabulary deficiencies, by examining learners' written and spoken inputs (Thukroo et al., 2022). This analysis enables the ITS to tailor its content and exercises to meet the specific needs of individual learners. For instance, if a student consistently misapplies a specific phrase, the system might provide supplementary practice centered on that word, guaranteeing that learners obtain the assistance necessary to comprehend difficult ideas.

Furthermore, NLP can enhance cultural context in language acquisition. Comprehending idiomatic phrases, colloquialisms, and cultural references enables NLP systems to furnish learners with pertinent examples and elucidations that enhance their linguistic understanding (Ariely et al., 2023). This contextualization is crucial for cultivating practical language skills that transcend grammar and vocabulary, equipping learners for authentic communication.

The incorporation of NLP in Intelligent Tutoring Systems facilitates data-driven insights regarding learners' advancement and difficulties. The system can produce reports that identify areas for enhancement and recommend tailored learning pathways through interaction analysis (Alamri et al., 2021). This data assists learners in self-evaluation and offers educators critical insights to enhance teaching methodologies.

In summary, Natural Language Processing markedly improves language teaching systems' interaction and feedback processes. NLP significantly contributes to effective language acquisition by enabling speech recognition, facilitating text-based dialogues, personalizing learning experiences, offering cultural context, and creating data-driven insights. As technology progresses, the prospects for NLP in language instruction will broaden, facilitating more engaging and effective learning experiences.

4.3 Challenges and Limitations of ITS

Intelligent Tutoring Systems (ITS) possess the capacity to transform language teaching, yet they encounter numerous problems and limits that must be resolved to enhance their efficacy. Comprehending these limitations is crucial for educators, developers, and learners as they engage with the deployment of AI-driven language learning systems (Al-khresheh, 2024).

A major difficulty is the quality of natural language processing (NLP). Despite progress in NLP enhancing ITS's capacity to comprehend and react to human language, the technology remains flawed. Misinterpretations of user input may result in erroneous feedback or insufficient answers, potentially causing frustration for learners. If a system fails to identify a learner's pronunciation problems or misinterprets their textual input, it may offer erroneous instruction, obstructing the learning process.

The ongoing enhancement of NLP algorithms is essential for improving accuracy and ensuring that systems can adequately assist learners (Younis et al., 2023).

A further restriction pertains to the deficiency of emotional intelligence in Intelligent Tutoring Systems (ITS). Although these systems can deliver factual feedback and corrections, they frequently fail to identify and address learners' emotional states. Language acquisition may be a formidable and perhaps disheartening endeavor, and learners may gain from empathic feedback and motivation. The lack of ITS's capacity to provide emotional support or comprehend the learner's displeasure may reduce motivation and engagement (Novak et al., 2023). Incorporating emotional intelligence into AI systems presents a promising opportunity for advancement, potentially fostering a more helpful educational atmosphere.

Moreover, accessibility and equity are concerns. Not all learners possess equitable access to the technology necessary for Intelligent Tutoring Systems, like smartphones, tablets, or dependable internet connections. The digital divide can intensify preexisting disparities in language instruction, placing certain learners at a disadvantage. Facilitating access to ITS for a wider audience, particularly in low-resource environments, is crucial for fostering equitable language learning opportunities (Heo et al., 2024).

Furthermore, reliance on technology may present difficulties. Although ITS can improve educational experiences, overdependence on these systems may result in reduced human connection. Language acquisition is fundamentally social, and insufficient opportunities for direct interaction with peers and instructors might hinder learners' development of practical conversational abilities (Fathi et al., 2024). Integrating ITS with conventional educational techniques and social interactions is essential for promoting holistic language proficiency.

Ultimately, continuous assessment and enhancement of ITS is essential. As technology and educational methodologies advance, it is imperative to consistently evaluate the efficacy of these systems and implement requisite modifications (Michel-Villarreal et al. 2023). Educators and developers must collaborate to collect input from learners and analyze performance data to pinpoint areas for enhancement. This iterative method will ensure that ITS stays pertinent and efficient in addressing the demands of varied learners.

In conclusion, although Intelligent Tutoring Systems (ITS) present promising opportunities for language teaching, they encounter obstacles related to NLP quality, emotional intelligence, accessibility, technological dependence, and the necessity for continuous assessment. Overcoming these constraints is essential for optimizing ITS's efficacy in fostering bilingual proficiency and facilitating successful language acquisition.

THE FUTURE OF AI IN BILINGUAL MASTERY

5.1 Emerging Technologies and Trends

The domain of language instruction is experiencing a profound upheaval, propelled by the advent of modern technologies such Virtual Reality (VR), Augmented Reality (AR), and artificial intelligence (AI). These advances possess the capacity to transform language acquisition, rendering the process more immersive, engaging, and efficacious.

Virtual Reality (VR) represents one of the most promising technologies for language acquisition. By constructing fully immersive worlds, virtual reality enables learners to refine language skills within authentic contexts. (Ma, 2021). A student can be immersed in a virtual marketplace, where they can interact with avatars of native speakers, negotiate pricing, and participate in quotidian conversations. This interactive experience develops speaking and listening skills while fostering cultural competence through the simulation of real-life settings. Practicing language in context enhances confidence and fluency, since learners encounter the subtleties of conversation typically lacking in conventional classroom environments.

Augmented Reality (AR) enhances Virtual Reality (VR) by superimposing digital information onto the physical environment. Augmented reality can augment educational resources and activities in language instruction (Marrahí-Gómez and Belda-Medina, 2022). For example, learners can utilize AR applications to scan things in their surroundings and obtain information in the target language, including vocabulary labels or pronunciation aids. This participatory method enhances engagement and contextualizes learning, enabling learners to associate language concepts with their environment. enhanced reality can enhance collaborative learning experiences, enabling learners to address language-related issues within an enhanced environment collectively.

Artificial Intelligence (AI) remains integral to the customization of language teaching. With the advancement of AI technology, they can offer increasingly sophisticated adaptive learning experiences (Sajja et al., 2024). Future AI systems will analyze learners' emotional states and engagement levels, modifying content and feedback accordingly. This aptitude fosters a more responsive learning environment where learners feel supported and comprehended. Moreover, AI-powered analytics will provide educators with an enhanced understanding of students' progress and difficulties, facilitating more precise interventions.

A notable trend is the incorporation of gamification in language acquisition. Educational systems can stimulate learners and improve engagement by integrating gamification components, including points, badges, and leaderboards. Gamification exploits learners' competitive instincts, motivating them to practice regularly and attain language milestones (Alomair & Hammami, 2024). The integration of gamification with VR and AR technology can produce very engaging and immersive language learning experiences.

Moreover, the emergence of social learning platforms is transforming language instruction. These services link learners with native speakers for immediate conversational practice, promoting cultural exchange and genuine contact. By employing AI to pair learners with conversation partners according to their interests and competence levels, these platforms can improve the efficacy of language practice.

In summary, upcoming technologies like VR, AR, and AI are set to revolutionize language education by facilitating immersive, tailored, and captivating learning experiences. As these technologies advance, they will be crucial in fostering multilingual proficiency, allowing learners to manage the intricacies of language acquisition through novel and effective methods. The future of language instruction is promising, with developments poised to enhance accessibility and enjoyment for all learners.

5.2 Ethical Considerations in AI and Education

The swift incorporation of artificial intelligence (AI) in language education requires a comprehensive analysis of the ethical ramifications linked to its use. Key concerns include data privacy, algorithmic bias, and the evolving function of educators in an AI-driven environment (Bhutani et al., 2024). Confronting these problems is crucial to ensure that AI technologies enhance education while safeguarding the rights and well-being of learners.

Data privacy is a critical concern in the deployment of AI systems within educational contexts (Nguyen et al., 2023). These systems often collect comprehensive personal data, including learners' performance metrics, engagement patterns, and, in some cases, biometric data. Protecting this sensitive information is essential for maintaining learners' trust and complying with regulations such as the General Data Protection Regulation (GDPR) in Europe. Educational institutions must have rigorous data security protocols and explicit data utilization policies to safeguard students' privacy. Moreover, students must be informed about the data gathered, its purpose, and their rights to their personal information. Facilitating discussions on data privacy may empower learners to make informed choices regarding their engagement with AI technologies.

Algorithmic bias represents a substantial ethical issue. AI systems depend on the quality of their training data; if this data reflects existing biases, the algorithms may perpetuate and exacerbate disparities. In language education, biased algorithms may disadvantage particular groups of learners, leading to inequitable access to resources and opportunities (Marras et al., 2022). An AI system predominantly trained on data from native speakers of a particular dialect may struggle to assess or support learners from diverse linguistic backgrounds effectively. Developers must ensure that AI systems are trained on diverse, representative datasets and undergo thorough testing to identify and mitigate bias.

The role of educators is likewise evolving in an AI-driven environment. While AI can provide personalized learning experiences and immediate feedback, it cannot replace the human elements of education, such as empathy, motivation, and cultural sensitivity. Educators must adapt to this changing landscape by adopting the roles of facilitators and guides, employing AI technology to enhance their instruction rather than viewing them as replacements. Professional development and training in AI literacy will be essential for educators to integrate new technologies into their classrooms effectively and to critically evaluate the available tools (Yu, 2024).

In summary, as AI revolutionizes language instruction, it is essential to emphasize ethical concerns related to data privacy, algorithmic bias, and educator accountability. By proactively addressing these issues, stakeholders may create a more equitable and efficient learning environment that utilizes AI's potential while respecting the rights and needs of all learners. Ethical norms must regulate the development and implementation of AI technologies to foster trust and improve good educational outcomes in attaining multilingual competence.

5.3 Conclusion and Vision for the Future

Upon reflecting on the revolutionary potential of artificial intelligence (AI) in bilingual education, it is evident that we are at the front of a substantial change in language learning approaches. The incorporation of AI technologies, such as Intelligent Tutoring Systems (ITS), Natural Language Processing (NLP), and immersive experiences via Virtual Reality (VR) and Augmented Reality (AR), has the capacity to transform language acquisition, rendering it more personalized, engaging, and effective (Ayotunde et al., 2023).

This investigation emphasizes the significance of adaptive learning systems that customize educational experiences to meet individual requirements. AI may leverage data-driven insights to monitor learners' progress and dynamically adapt content, ensuring that each learner receives the requisite support to succeed (Vashishth et al. 2024). This tailored method increases motivation and cultivates a more profound comprehension of language as learners interact with content that aligns with their individual interests and skill levels.

Furthermore, the significance of technology in enhancing engagement and feedback has been emphasized. Natural Language Processing facilitates instantaneous interaction between learners and AI systems, offering prompt feedback on speech and grammar. This interactive participation is essential for cultivating practical language abilities since it reflects genuine conversational experiences necessary for fluency.

Nonetheless, as we adopt these breakthroughs, it is crucial to maintain awareness of the ethical implications associated with the incorporation of AI in education. Concerns around data privacy, algorithmic bias, and educators' changing responsibilities must be resolved to establish a just and equitable educational setting. Developing and implementing AI technologies responsibly will cultivate trust among learners and instructors, facilitating excellent educational results (Fu & Weng, 2024).

The future vision for AI-enhanced bilingual education emphasizes inclusivity, accessibility, and ongoing enhancement. Emerging technologies will persist in improving the learning experience, rendering language acquisition more interesting and successful for varied groups (Su & Zou, 2022). The future will likely witness enhanced collaboration between educators and AI, as teachers utilize technology to augment their instructional methodologies while preserving the fundamental human aspects of empathy and cultural awareness.

The future of bilingual proficiency via AI is promising and optimistic. By leveraging advanced technologies while emphasizing ethical considerations and the role of educators, we may provide a language learning environment that empowers all learners. Advancing requires a steadfast commitment to innovation, diversity, and ethical behaviors, which are essential for maximizing AI's promise in bilingual education and adequately preparing learners for an interconnected world.

CONCLUSION

The incorporation of artificial intelligence (AI) into language teaching signifies a significant advancement in the acquisition of multilingual competency. The integration of AI technologies, including adaptive learning systems, intelligent tutoring systems (ITS), and natural language processing (NLP), has transformed the educational environment, providing individualized, engaging, and efficient language learning experiences. These advances have closed gaps in conventional approaches, promoting immediate feedback, direct participation, and customized lesson plans that correspond with the specific requirements and capabilities of individual learners.

The function of AI in language instruction extends beyond only aiding skill gain. It empowers learners through immersive settings like virtual reality (VR) and augmented reality (AR), allowing them to practice language in authentic contexts that improve fluency and cultural competence. These technologies enhance confidence and proficiency by emulating real-world interactions, frequently challenging to reproduce in traditional classrooms.

Nonetheless, the implementation of AI presents certain challenges. Ethical problems, including data privacy, algorithmic prejudice, and the changing role of educators, must be addressed to guarantee equitable access and a balanced approach to education. Developers and educators must cooperate to create transparent, inclusive, and accountable AI systems while preserving the human qualities of empathy and cultural sensitivity vital for comprehensive language instruction.

The prospects of AI in achieving bilingual proficiency are extensive. Emerging trends indicate a growing dependence on gamification, social learning platforms, and sophisticated analytics to develop more dynamic and inclusive educational environments. By overcoming existing limits and using technology breakthroughs, AI-driven education can transform multilingual learning, providing learners with the essential abilities to succeed in a globalized world.

The concept of AI-enhanced bilingual education encompasses diversity, innovation, and ethical responsibility. By promoting collaboration between technology and human knowledge, we can realize the full potential of language education, ensuring it remains accessible, interesting, and effective for learners globally.

REFERENCES

Al-Ansi, A. M., Jaboob, M., Garad, A., & Al-Ansi, A. (2023). Analyzing augmented reality (AR) and virtual reality (VR) recent development in education. [sciencedirect.com]. *Social Sciences & Humanities Open*, *8*(1), 100532. DOI: 10.1016/j.ssaho.2023.100532

Al-khresheh, M. H. (2024). Bridging technology and pedagogy from a global lens: Teachers' perspectives on integrating ChatGPT in English language teaching. Computers and Education: Artificial Intelligence. sciencedirect.com

Alam, A., & Mohanty, A. (2023). Educational technology: Exploring the convergence of technology and pedagogy through mobility, interactivity, AI, and learning tools. Cogent Engineering. tandfonline.com

Alamri, H. A., Watson, S., & Watson, W. (2021). Learning technology models that support personalization within blended learning environments in higher education. [HTML]. *TechTrends*, *65*(1), 62–78. DOI: 10.1007/s11528-020-00530-3

Alias, N. F., & Razak, R. A. (2024). Revolutionizing learning in the digital age: A systematic literature review of microlearning strategies. [HTML]. *Interactive Learning Environments*.

Alomair, Y., & Hammami, S. (2024). Enhancing the Achievement of Learning Outcomes for Foreign Language Learners Based on Gamification and Card Games. [wiley.com]. *International Journal of Computer Games Technology*, *2024*(1), 8084687. DOI: 10.1155/2024/8084687

Alshuraiaan, A. (2023). Exploring the relationship between teacher-student interaction patterns and language learning outcomes in TESOL classrooms. [al-kindipublisher.com]. *Journal of English Language Teaching and Applied Linguistics*, *5*(3), 25–34. DOI: 10.32996/jeltal.2023.5.3.3

Ariely, M., Nazaretsky, T., & Alexandron, G. (2023). Machine learning and Hebrew NLP for automated assessment of open-ended questions in biology. [HTML]. *International Journal of Artificial Intelligence in Education*, *33*(1), 1–34. DOI: 10.1007/s40593-021-00283-x

Augustin, T. J., Pudelko, M., & Kirkman, B. (2024). Examining Multiculturals' and Multilinguals' Paradoxical Bridging Behaviors in Overcoming Cultural and Language Barriers in Organizations. [sagepub.com]. *Journal of Management*, •••, 01492063241281457. DOI: 10.1177/01492063241281457

Ayotunde, O. O., Jamil, D. I., & Cavus, N. (2023). The impact of artificial intelligence in foreign language learning using learning management systems: A systematic literature review. [HTML]. *Information Technologies and Learning Tools*, *95*(3), 215–228. DOI: 10.33407/itlt.v95i3.5233

Bailey, D., Almusharraf, N., & Hatcher, R. (2021). Finding satisfaction: Intrinsic motivation for synchronous and asynchronous communication in the online language learning context. [springer.com]. *Education and Information Technologies*, *26*(3), 2563–2583. DOI: 10.1007/s10639-020-10369-z PMID: 33169066

Bengsch, G. (2024). Redefining traditional pedagogy: The integration of machine learning in the contemporary language education classroom. AI in Language Teaching. [HTML]

Bhutani, V., Bahadur, P. S., Sansaniwal, S. K., & Bais, P. (2024). Youth Studes in the AI Era: Navigating Uncharted Territory. In Exploring Youth Studies in the Age of AI (pp. 393-413). IGI Global. [HTML]

Bradáč, V., Smolka, P., Kotyrba, M., & Průdek, T. (2022). Design of an intelligent tutoring system to create a personalized study plan using expert systems. Applied Sciences. mdpi.com

Bukhari, S. G. A. S., Jamali, S. G., Larik, A. R., & Chang, M. S. (2023). Fostering intrinsic motivation among teachers: Importance of work environment and individual differences. [HTML]. *International Journal of School & Educational Psychology*, *11*(1), 1–19. DOI: 10.1080/21683603.2021.1925182

Chan, S. & Lo, N. (2024). Enhancing EFL/ESL instruction through gamification: a comprehensive review of empirical evidence. Frontiers in Education. frontiersin.org

Chen, X., Dewaele, J. M., & Zhang, T. (2021). Sustainable development of EFL/ESL learners' willingness to communicate: the effects of teachers and teaching styles. Sustainability. mdpi.com

Chen, Y. (2024, May). Enhancing Language Acquisition: The Role of AI in Facilitating Effective Language Learning. In 2024 3rd International Conference on Humanities, Wisdom Education and Service Management (HWESM 2024) (pp. 593-600). Atlantis Press. atlantis-press.com

Chen, Y. L., Hsu, C. C., Lin, C. Y., & Hsu, H. H. (2022). Robot-assisted language learning: Integrating artificial intelligence and virtual reality into English tour guide practice. Education Sciences. mdpi.com

Chowdhury, R. H. (2024). The evolution of business operations: unleashing the potential of Artificial Intelligence, Machine Learning, and Blockchain. World Journal of Advanced Research and Reviews. wjarr.co.in

D'Mello, S. K., & Graesser, A. (2023). Intelligent tutoring systems: How computers achieve learning gains that rival human tutors. Handbook of educational psychology. [HTML]

Dong, J., Lee, S., Wang, C. H., & Shannon, D. M. (2023). Impact on social capital and learning engagement due to social media usage among the international students in the US. [springer.com]. *Education and Information Technologies*, *28*(7), 8027–8050. DOI: 10.1007/s10639-022-11520-8 PMID: 36532798

Fang, Y., Lippert, A., Cai, Z., Chen, S., Frijters, J. C., Greenberg, D., & Graesser, A. C. (2022). Patterns of adults with low literacy skills interacting with an intelligent tutoring system. [springer.com]. *International Journal of Artificial Intelligence in Education*, *32*(2), 1–26. DOI: 10.1007/s40593-021-00266-y

Fathi, J., Rahimi, M., & Derakhshan, A. (2024). Improving EFL learners' speaking skills and willingness to communicate via artificial intelligence-mediated interactions. [HTML]. *System*, *121*, 103254. DOI: 10.1016/j.system.2024.103254

Fendji, J. L. K. E., Tala, D. C., Yenke, B. O., & Atemkeng, M. (2022). Automatic speech recognition using limited vocabulary: A survey. [tandfonline.com]. *Applied Artificial Intelligence*, *36*(1), 2095039. DOI: 10.1080/08839514.2022.2095039

Fu, Y. & Weng, Z. (2024). Navigating the ethical terrain of AI in education: A systematic review on framing responsible human-centered AI practices. Computers and Education: Artificial Intelligence. sciencedirect.com

Goh, C. C. M. & Vandergrift, L. (2021). Teaching and learning second language listening: Metacognition in action. [HTML]

Halkiopoulos, C. & Gkintoni, E. (2024). Leveraging AI in e-learning: Personalized learning and adaptive assessment through cognitive neuropsychology—A systematic analysis. Electronics. mdpi.com

Han, Y. C. & Reber, P. J. (2022). Implicit sequence learning using auditory cues leads to modality-specific representations. Psychonomic bulletin & review. springer.com

He, X. S., & Loewen, S. (2022). Stimulating learner engagement in app-based L2 vocabulary self-study: Goals and feedback for effective L2 pedagogy. [HTML]. *System*, *105*, 102719. DOI: 10.1016/j.system.2021.102719

Hennebry, M., & Gao, X. (2021). Interactions between medium of instruction and language learning motivation. [HTML]. *International Journal of Bilingual Education and Bilingualism*, *24*(7), 976–989. DOI: 10.1080/13670050.2018.1530190

Heo, K., Cheng, S., Joos, E., & Joharifard, S. (2024). Use of innovative technology in surgical training in resource-limited settings: A scoping review. [HTML]. *Journal of Surgical Education*, *81*(2), 243–256. DOI: 10.1016/j.jsurg.2023.11.004 PMID: 38161100

Hooda, M., Rana, C., Dahiya, O., Rizwan, A., & Hossain, M. S. (2022). Artificial intelligence for assessment and feedback to enhance student success in higher education. [wiley.com]. *Mathematical Problems in Engineering*, *2022*(1), 5215722. DOI: 10.1155/2022/5215722

Hossain, K. I. (2024). Reviewing the role of culture in English language learning: Challenges and opportunities for educators. Social Sciences & Humanities Open. sciencedirect.com

Ma, L. (2021). An immersive context teaching method for college English based on artificial intelligence and machine learning in virtual reality technology. Mobile Information Systems. wiley.com

Marrahí-Gómez, V., & Belda-Medina, J. (2022). The application of augmented reality (AR) to language learning and its impact on student motivation. International Journal of Linguistics Studies, 2(2), 07-14. al-kindipublisher.com

Marras, M., Boratto, L., Ramos, G., & Fenu, G. (2022). Equality of learning opportunity via individual fairness in personalized recommendations. [springer.com]. *International Journal of Artificial Intelligence in Education*, *32*(3), 636–684. DOI: 10.1007/s40593-021-00271-1

Martin-Alguacil, N., Avedillo, L., Mota-Blanco, R., & Gallego-Agundez, M. (2024). Student-Centered Learning: Some Issues and Recommendations for Its Implementation in a Traditional Curriculum Setting in Health Sciences. [mdpi.com]. *Education Sciences*, *14*(11), 1179. DOI: 10.3390/educsci14111179

Michel-Villarreal, R., Vilalta-Perdomo, E., Salinas-Navarro, D. E., Thierry-Aguilera, R., & Gerardou, F. S. (2023). Challenges and opportunities of generative AI for higher education as explained by ChatGPT. [mdpi.com]. *Education Sciences*, *13*(9), 856. DOI: 10.3390/educsci13090856

Morris, R., Perry, T., & Wardle, L. (2021). Formative assessment and feedback for learning in higher education: A systematic review. Review of Education. wiley.com

Müller, F. A. & Wulf, T. (2024). Differences in learning effectiveness across management learning environments: A cognitive load theory perspective. Journal of Management Education. sagepub.com

Nguyen, A., Ngo, H. N., Hong, Y., Dang, B., & Nguyen, B. P. T. (2023). Ethical principles for artificial intelligence in education. [springer.com]. *Education and Information Technologies*, *28*(4), 4221–4241. DOI: 10.1007/s10639-022-11316-w PMID: 36254344

Novak, E., McDaniel, K., & Li, J. (2023). Factors that impact student frustration in digital learning environments. Computers and Education Open. sciencedirect.com

Ouariach, S., Khaldi, M., Mohamed, E., & Khaldi, M. (2023). The Flipped Classroom: From Passive Information Absorption to Active Learning. In Handbook of Research on Language Teacher Identity (pp. 269-293). IGI Global. [HTML]

Paap, K. R., Mason, L., & Anders-Jefferson, R. (2021). Predictions about the cognitive consequences of language switching on executive functioning inspired by the adaptive control hypothesis fail more often than not. Brain Sciences. mdpi.com

Rajak, L., Chauhan, S., & Bara, S. (2024). Transforming English Pedagogy with Artificial Intelligence: Enroute to Enhanced Language Learning. In Artificial Intelligence: A Multidisciplinary Approach towards Teaching and Learning (pp. 216-241). Bentham Science Publishers. [HTML]

Rapaka, A., Dharmadhikari, S. C., Kasat, K., Mohan, C. R., Chouhan, K., & Gupta, M. (2025). Revolutionizing learning– A journey into educational games with immersive and AI technologies. [HTML]. *Entertainment Computing*, *52*, 100809. DOI: 10.1016/j.entcom.2024.100809

Sajja, R., Sermet, Y., Cikmaz, M., Cwiertny, D., & Demir, I. (2024). Artificial intelligence-enabled intelligent assistant for personalized and adaptive learning in higher education. Information. mdpi.com

Shahid, S., & Paul, J. (2021). Intrinsic motivation of luxury consumers in an emerging market. [HTML]. *Journal of Retailing and Consumer Services*, *61*, 102531. DOI: 10.1016/j.jretconser.2021.102531

Sharma, D., Sood, A. K., Darius, P. S., Gundabattini, E., Darius Gnanaraj, S., & Joseph Jeyapaul, A. (2022). A study on the online-offline and blended learning methods. Journal of The Institution of Engineers (India): Series B, 103(4), 1373-1382. springer.com

Shortt, M., Tilak, S., Kuznetcova, I., Martens, B., & Akinkuolie, B. (2023). Gamification in mobile-assisted language learning: A systematic review of Duolingo literature from public release of 2012 to early 2020. [tandfonline.com]. *Computer Assisted Language Learning*, *36*(3), 517–554. DOI: 10.1080/09588221.2021.1933540

Sivakumar, A. & Vanitha, V. (2024). Multilingualism in Global Education and Language Learning. Digital Skill Development for Industry 4.0. [HTML]

Spada, N., & Lightbown, P. M. (2022). In it together: Teachers, researchers, and classroom SLA. [HTML]. *Modern Language Journal*, *106*(3), 635–650. DOI: 10.1111/modl.12792

Strielkowski, W., Grebennikova, V., Lisovskiy, A., Rakhimova, G., & Vasileva, T. (2024). AI-driven adaptive learning for sustainable educational transformation. Sustainable Development. wiley.com

Su, F., & Zou, D. (2022). Technology-enhanced collaborative language learning: Theoretical foundations, technologies, and implications. [HTML]. *Computer Assisted Language Learning*, *35*(8), 1754–1788. DOI: 10.1080/09588221.2020.1831545

Sundari, M. S., Penthala, H. R., & Nayyar, A. (2024). Transforming Education through AI-Enhanced Content Creation and Personalized Learning Experiences. In *Impact of Artificial Intelligence on Society* (pp. 98–118). Chapman and Hall/CRC. [HTML]

Tai, T. Y. (2024). Effects of intelligent personal assistants on EFL learners' oral proficiency outside the classroom. [HTML]. *Computer Assisted Language Learning*, *37*(5-6), 1281–1310. DOI: 10.1080/09588221.2022.2075013

Tai, T. Y., & Chen, H. H. J. (2024). Improving elementary EFL speaking skills with generative AI chatbots: Exploring individual and paired interactions. [HTML]. *Computers & Education*, *220*, 105112. DOI: 10.1016/j.compedu.2024.105112

Thukroo, I. A., Bashir, R., & Giri, K. J. (2022). A review into deep learning techniques for spoken language identification. [HTML]. *Multimedia Tools and Applications*, *81*(22), 32593–32624. DOI: 10.1007/s11042-022-13054-0

Tseng, J. J., Chai, C. S., Tan, L., & Park, M. (2022). A critical review of research on technological pedagogical and content knowledge (TPACK) in language teaching. [HTML]. *Computer Assisted Language Learning*, *35*(4), 948–971. DOI: 10.1080/09588221.2020.1868531

Vashishth, T. K., Sharma, V., Sharma, K. K., Kumar, B., Panwar, R., & Chaudhary, S. (2024). AI-driven learning analytics for personalized feedback and assessment in higher education. In *Using traditional design methods to enhance AI-driven decision making* (pp. 206–230). IGI Global. [HTML] DOI: 10.4018/979-8-3693-0639-0.ch009

Vikas, S. & Mathur, A. (2022). An empirical study of student perception towards pedagogy, teaching style and effectiveness of online classes. Education and Information Technologies. springer.com

Vu, D. V. & Peters, E. (2021). Vocabulary in English language learning, teaching, and testing in Vietnam: A review. Education Sciences. mdpi.com

Vu, N. N., Hung, B. P., Van, N. T. T., & Lien, N. T. H. (2022). Theoretical and instructional aspects of using multimedia resources in language education: A cognitive view. [HTML]. *Multimedia Technologies in the Internet of Things Environment, 2*, 165–194. DOI: 10.1007/978-981-16-3828-2_9

Wu, Y., Albornoz-De Luise, R. S., & Arevalillo-Herráez, M. (2025). On improving conversational interfaces in educational systems. [sciencedirect.com]. *Computer Speech & Language, 89*, 101693. DOI: 10.1016/j.csl.2024.101693

Yilmaz, R., Yurdugül, H., Yilmaz, F. G. K., Şahín, M., Sulak, S., Aydin, F., & Ömer, O. R. A. L. (2022). Smart MOOC integrated with intelligent tutoring: A system architecture and framework model proposal. [sciencedirect.com]. *Computers and Education: Artificial Intelligence, 3*, 100092. DOI: 10.1016/j.caeai.2022.100092

Younis, H. A., Ruhaiyem, N. I. R., Ghaban, W., Gazem, N. A., & Nasser, M. (2023). A systematic literature review on the applications of robots and natural language processing in education. [mdpi.com]. *Electronics (Basel), 12*(13), 2864. DOI: 10.3390/electronics12132864

Yu, H. (2024). The application and challenges of ChatGPT in educational transformation: New demands for teachers' roles. Heliyon. cell.com

ADDITIONAL READING

Luckin, R., Holmes, W., Griffiths, M., & Forcier, L. B. (2016). *Intelligence unleashed: An argument for AI in education*. Pearson Education.

KEY TERMS AND DEFINITIONS

AI-Supported Evaluation: A methodology that incorporates artificial intelligence technologies into assessment procedures to improve the validity, efficiency, and personalization of educational evaluation.

Artificial Intelligence (AI): A subdivision of computer science dedicated to the development of intelligent machines that can replicate human cognitive abilities, including learning, problem-solving, and decision-making.

Automated Feedback: AI-generated feedback or assessments delivered to learners depending on their input or performance, frequently utilized in digital learning platforms.

Educational Data Mining (EDM): The application of data mining techniques to educational datasets to reveal patterns that enhance learning results.

Ethical AI: The design and implementation of artificial intelligence systems that uphold human rights, guarantee fairness, and foster transparency and accountability.

Formative Assessment: A continuous assessment procedure throughout instruction designed to monitor student learning and deliver continuing feedback to enhance teaching and performance.

Intelligent Tutoring System (ITS): A computer system that delivers instant and tailored education or feedback to learners, usually without the involvement of a human instructor.

Learning Management System (LMS): A software application utilized for the delivery, tracking, and management of educational courses and training programs in digital formats.

Self-Regulated Learning (SRL): A learning method wherein students autonomously manage their education by establishing objectives, tracking advancement, and evaluating results.

Teacher Professional Judgment: The capacity of educators to make informed decisions grounded in pedagogical skill, experience, and contextual comprehension.

Chapter 7
Enhancing Bilingual Communication Skills With AI-Powered Solutions in Foreign Language Education

Muthmainnah Muthmainnah
https://orcid.org/0000-0003-3170-2374
Universitas Al Asyariah Mandar, Indonesia

Yasir Ahmed Mohammed Ridha Alsbbagh
https://orcid.org/0009-0001-1948-600X
Al-Iraqia University, Iraq

Ahmad Al Yakin
https://orcid.org/0000-0003-3170-2374
Universitas Al Asyariah Mandar, Indonesia

Ahmed J. Obaid
https://orcid.org/0000-0003-0376-5546
Kufa University, Iraq

Luis Cardoso
https://orcid.org/0000-0003-3748-5593
Polytechnic Institute of Portalegre, Portugal & Centre for Comparative Studies, University of Lisbon, Portugal

Eka Apriani
https://orcid.org/0000-0002-8427-2817
IAIN Curup, Indonesia

ABSTRACT

This chapter investigates how language practices and AI systems can change the way foreign language learners acquire communication skills. The chapter aims to improve bilingual education by combining artificial intelligence (AI) tools with the Trifecta model, including adaptive learning platforms to help students overcome language barriers and have equal access to language learning materials. The study contributes by presenting a new approach to education that leverages artificial in-

DOI: 10.4018/979-8-3373-0275-1.ch007

telligence (AI) technologies such as gamification, conversational AI, and translation systems to make classrooms more engaging and interactive. The study discusses the implications for bilingual education, emphasizing the revolutionary significance of AI in promoting language acquisition, cultural exchange, and real-time translation to help students become more proficient and confident in multilingual situations as well as ways to improve language teaching and address the linguistic gap.

INTRODUCTION

For a long time, people have recognized the integration of AI as a medium and educational technology to enhance language education. However, the emergence of ChatGPT has sparked a wide discourse on the potential impact of advances in Artificial Intelligence (AI), particularly Generative AI (GAI), on bilingual language learning and education. The interactive flexibility, immediacy, and precision of AI have created new opportunities for researchers, allowing both learners and educators to build personal language learning communities that address different learning needs and improve the efficiency of teaching foreign languages more practically. These communities can address different learning requirements and improve teaching efficacy, potentially initiating a modern educational reform movement. But most of the recent research in language education has looked at how AI affects the learning environment or how people feel about AI in schools. However, it hasn't explored the potential of generative AI as an effective teaching tool in foreign language classrooms (Babu and Akshara, 2024).

To address these shortcomings, our chapter explores the potential of AI in language education by presenting a new teaching approach that prioritizes communication, starting with the design of AI-assisted conversation concepts and communication practices. Elsa AI, an online spoken dialogue system that engages users in conversation and provides additional assessment and feedback on their English proficiency, is one such application. The study employs a training methodology that enhances language awareness to gather data on students' reactions to AI use, specifically focusing on changes in L2 performance and awareness. It examines students' reactions to AI-assisted training from a language awareness perspective, optimizes AI as a tutor, assistant, and translator, and examines the pedagogical implications for both instructors and language learners. We also explore the potential of AI in language education by reporting innovative teaching practices that integrate AI-powered educational platforms into the speaking assessment process in instructional contexts. AI is not only considered a teaching aid but also an assessment coordinator and research assistant, with the aim of easing teachers' burdens by providing assessments and increasing opportunities for efficient teaching and reflection in the language classroom.

The application of AI-based technologies has prompted much research on their impact on communication dynamics, cultural preservation, and equitable allocation of linguistic resources (Xia et al., 2024). This study aims to examine the various impacts of an AI-based bilingual language learning ecosystem (in English and Indonesian) on communication equity and inclusion. This paper seeks to clarify the role of AI in overcoming linguistic barriers and increasing equitable access to communication channels by leveraging interdisciplinary insights from linguistics, computer science, and social sciences (Davoodi, 2024). Al Yakin et al. (2024) explores the use of AI integration systems as AI-powered multilingual learning assistants and translators by analyzing operational issues and their implications for communication and social inclusion. We look at how AI translation technology has evolved over time, from rule-based systems to more sophisticated neural machine translation (NMT) models such as Google's Neural Machine Translation (GNMT) and OpenAI's Generative Pre-Trained Transformer (GPT). We also look at how AI-powered translation systems work and how they're improving. They create educational resources that incorporate AI, showcasing its influence on the quality, accuracy, and accessibility of bilingual translation services.

These services, such as AI-powered translation systems, AI assistants, or AI tutors, aim to assist linguistic minority groups, translate languages with limited resources, or establish bilingual translation systems in EFL classrooms; however, they encounter challenges. The study by Kumar & Nagar (2024) employs a comprehensive analytical framework to examine the impact of AI applications on communication fairness and inclusion. It does this by using interpretive theory and a pragmatic approach to translation. This study provides detailed insights into the prospects and challenges of AI-powered bilingual learning applied in EFL classrooms. We examine various ways to make AI more flexible, such as text-guided domain adaptation, human-AI collaboration, and cross-language speaker adaptation (Huang et al., 2019), and try to find the best ways to use AI as a learning assistant and as a machine translator so that developers, policymakers, and practitioners can provide suggestions that will help everyone communicate more effectively and fix any problems that may arise in AI-based translation systems.

Language serves as a fundamental element of human communication, allowing individuals to articulate ideas, disseminate knowledge, and engage with others (Malyuga, 2024). Linguistic diversity presents a barrier to successful communication, especially in a more interconnected world where interactions transcend geographical and cultural boundaries. According to Muthmainnah et al. (2024), with the rapid advancement of globalization, the need for inclusive communication has become paramount, requiring solutions to overcome linguistic barriers and ensure equitable access to information and resources for all individuals, regardless of their language proficiency or background. The emergence of AI-based language learning systems presents a viable solution to address linguistic diversity and enhance communication equity and inclusivity. The advent of artificial intelligence (AI) has transformed the foreign language learning sector and ushered in a period of unparalleled innovation and change. For example, AI-based translation systems and learning content design leverage advanced algorithms and neural networks to automate language translation, facilitating real-time communication across language gaps (Tian, 2024). This technology has enormous potential to improve communication equity by offering translation in multiple languages.

AI POWERED BILINGUAL PLATFORM

AI acquisition has made significant progress in machine translation (Gatsiou et al., 2024). Instruments such as Google Translate, Cici Bot, and DeepL are increasingly leveraging NMT techniques to produce more accurate translations, such as between Indonesian and English. Historically, translation between these two languages has been challenging due to significant differences in sentence structure, idiomatic expressions, and cultural references (Ssemugabi, 2025), which introduce linguistic complexities that AI is increasingly adept at handling with greater accuracy (Pawlicka et al., 2024). These advances in AI translation are improving everyday communication and removing barriers in professional contexts, from international business transactions to academic research. However, despite these advances, machine translation between Indonesian, English, and other languages still requires human supervision to ensure contextual accuracy, especially in specialized domains.

The impact of AI technology in language learning extends far beyond language acquisition and translation, encompassing further applications of natural language processing (Obaid et al., 2023).NLP facilitates robots' understanding, interpreting, and generating human language, making applications such as sentiment analysis, text summarization, and automated customer support in Indonesian and English more practical. AI-based sentiment analysis can analyze Indonesian and English customer/social media feedback, offering important insights for companies or policymakers. As AI advances, its capacity to bridge the language and cultural gap between Indonesian and English increases significantly. AI-based technologies are evolving beyond mere communication tools; they are emerging as facilitators of cultural exchange, enhancing understanding between language communities. In a world where language can unite or divide, AI presents a viable option to foster closer relationships, facilitate seamless communication, and enhance global or international collaboration. For instance, AI serves as a bridge between Indonesian and English, specifically in the areas of language acquisition, translation, and natural language processing.

An analysis of the status of AI in this domain, along with the associated difficulties and opportunities, allows for a deeper understanding of AI's revolutionary capacity to bridge different linguistic domains. The above-mentioned goals correspond to the cognitive, behavioral, emotional, and psychomotor learning areas that combine human–artificial intelligence collaboration in modern language learning without the limitations of space and time (Muthmainnah et al., 2024; Zhang et al., 2025).

Language transmits culture, and a country's language cannot be separated from its national culture. Understanding students' current level of intercultural communication is essential to improving their ability to communicate across cultures. To become fluent in a foreign language, one must not only learn the alphabet, pronunciation, and basic grammatical principles, but also practice producing and delivering many sentences that adhere to these norms (Kremer and Pinto, 2025). The social production sector sees the widespread use and important role of artificial intelligence technology as a result of continuous progress in science and technology. Artificial intelligence has many potential uses, some of which include healthcare, diagnostics, stock markets, robot regulation, new discoveries in science, and even toys (Feng, 2025). We need to focus on analysing the current state of cross-cultural communication and finding ways to integrate artificial intelligence technology into the education system (Yuan and Liu, 2025).

Due to the rise of internet technology, we live in an era of exponential data growth, which requires us to adapt learning methods and find ways to extract the necessary information from large data sets. Increased work efficiency, time savings, and cost reduction are the results of continuous technology optimization, which allows users to select the necessary information based on keywords. Gaining linguistic competence requires us to first familiarize ourselves with relevant cultural information. Students' ability to communicate across cultural boundaries and their English proficiency can benefit from culturally relevant lessons taught in English classes. Incorporating AI into the classroom can improve students' knowledge and communication skills (Muthmainnah et al., 2024) while offering more opportunities to apply foreign language learning theories. In an innovative effort to integrate cross-cultural communication with academic disciplines, we address the challenges in teaching and propose ways to implement them in the classroom.

Currently, teaching foreign language or English proficiency in Indonesia also includes teaching students about AI, which will play an important role in the IT curriculum in the future. In various forms, AI will be part of the student's educational experience (Hutahaean, et al., 2024). The current artificial environment uses educational materials. University-level intelligence programs often use traditional textbooks and more modern forms of learning media, such as videos and software applications. Accessing and utilizing smart websites, smart devices, and smart software are some examples of AI-specific learning media. This work uses component analysis to theoretically explain the dimensions of cross-cultural competence and existing assessment scales by comparing and selecting comprehensive assessment methodologies with the aim of modernizing language learning in the GenAI era (Al Yakin et al., 2025).

AI serves as a medium and embodiment of classroom learning materials, accelerating language learning and facilitating the transfer of knowledge from instructor to student (Bellas, et al., (2024). Courseware, multimedia, and software, as well as websites such as Meta AI, play a significant role in this process. AI tools are some of the more traditional forms of AI education today, while smart software, smart gadgets, and smart websites are examples of modern forms of AI-specific education (Selvam, et al. 2025). Initially, when selecting AI-intervened learning materials, it is essential to align the AI requirements with the educational content of the curriculum. The field of artificial intelligence uses multimedia presentations, software, and courseware examples in its learning materials. Educational settings use different types of AI as needed to achieve different pedagogical goals (Ghosh, 2025). Video instruction, for example, can arouse students' interest to counteract the monotony of teacher narration. We can teach content using YouTube applications. Second, learning outcomes should guide the selection of learning media.

Figure 1. Bilingual by using the Trifecta model

Language transmits culture, and a country's language cannot be separated from its national culture. Understanding students' current level of intercultural communication is essential to improving their ability to communicate across cultures. To become fluent in a foreign language, one must not only learn the alphabet, pronunciation, and basic grammatical principles, but also practice producing and delivering many sentences that adhere to these norms (Kremer and Pinto, 2025).

The social production sector sees the widespread use and important role of artificial intelligence technology as a result of continuous progress in science and technology. Artificial intelligence has many potential uses, some of which include healthcare, diagnostics, stock markets, robot regulation, new discoveries in science, and even toys (Feng, 2025). We need to focus on analysing the current state of cross-cultural communication and finding ways to integrate artificial intelligence technology into the education system (Yuan and Liu, 2025).

Due to the rise of internet technology, we live in an era of exponential data growth, which requires us to adapt learning methods and find ways to extract the necessary information from large data sets. Increased work efficiency, time savings, and cost reduction are the results of continuous technology optimization, which allows users to select the necessary information based on keywords. Gaining linguistic competence requires us to first familiarize ourselves with relevant cultural information. Students' ability to communicate across cultural boundaries and their English proficiency can benefit from culturally relevant lessons taught in English classes. Incorporating AI into the classroom can improve students' knowledge and communication skills (Muthmainnah et al., 2024) while offering more opportunities to apply foreign language learning theories. In an innovative effort to integrate cross-cultural communication with academic disciplines, we address the challenges in teaching and propose ways to implement them in the classroom. Currently, teaching foreign language or English proficiency in Indonesia also includes teaching students about AI, which will play an important role in the IT curriculum in the future. In various forms, AI will be part of the student's educational experience (Hutahaean, et al., 2024).

The current artificial environment uses educational materials. University-level intelligence programs often use traditional textbooks and more modern forms of learning media, such as videos and software applications. Accessing and utilizing smart websites, smart devices, and smart software are some examples of AI-specific learning media. This work uses component analysis to theoretically explain the dimensions of cross-cultural competence and existing assessment scales by comparing and selecting comprehensive assessment methodologies with the aim of modernizing language learning in the GenAI era (Al Yakin et al., 2025). AI serves as a medium and embodiment of classroom learning materials, accelerating language learning and facilitating the transfer of knowledge from instructor to student (Bellas, et al., (2024). Courseware, multimedia, and software, as well as websites such as Meta AI, play a significant role in this process. AI tools are some of the more traditional forms of AI education today, while smart software, smart gadgets, and smart websites are examples of modern forms of AI-specific education (Selvam, et al. 2025). Initially, when selecting AI-intervened learning materials, it is essential to align the AI requirements with the educational content of the curriculum. The field of artificial intelligence uses multimedia presentations, software, and courseware examples in its learning materials. Educational settings use different types of AI as needed to achieve different pedagogical goals (Ghosh, 2025). Video instruction, for example, can arouse students' interest to counteract the monotony of teacher narration. We can teach content using YouTube applications. Second, learning outcomes should guide the selection of learning media.

Table 1. Outlining AI-powered for bilingual through Trifecta Model

Aspect	AI-Powered Bilingual Platform	English Skills	Indonesian Language Skills
Core Functionality	Real-time translation, transcription, and language analysis	Grammar, vocabulary, and pronunciation assistance	Syntax, vocabulary, and pronunciation enhancement
Language Learning Tools	There are interactive exercises, quizzes, and adaptive learning paths.	Reading comprehension, writing, and speaking drills	Writing structure, reading comprehension, and idioms
Conversation Practice	AI chatbots for simulated bilingual interactions	Enhances conversational fluency and listening skills	Supports conversational tone and cultural nuances
Feedback Mechanism	AI generates real-time feedback on usage and errors.	Provided grammar and style corrections for written content.	Please provide feedback on the contextual word choice and phrasing.
Cultural Integration	Features to teach cultural contexts of both languages	Understanding English idioms and expressions	Learning Indonesian proverbs and cultural expressions
Professional Application	Tools for formal writing and presentations are available in both languages.	There are business email templates and formal writing tips available.	Professional document formatting and speech writing
Assessment Features	AI-powered tests to gauge language proficiency	Proficiency levels: beginner-to-advanced	The language levels range from pemula (beginner) to mahir (expert).
User Interface	The interface is intuitively bilingual and features a language toggle.	Designed for English-first learners	Supports native Indonesian speakers learning English

In Table 1, we showcase the features and capabilities of AI-powered multilingual platforms that facilitate bilingual learning, such as English and Indonesian, or vice versa, through the trifecta method, which combines a bilingual platform with AI. For university students, the platform adapts its features to meet the cultural and linguistic needs of both languages, providing a holistic and personalized learning experience. This review further explores the usefulness of the platform in language classes and its complex architecture. The trifecta model's primary functions include activities like language analysis, real-time translation, transcription, editing, and layout, all of which can aid bilingual users in their language acquisition process. Simultaneously, the implementation of the trifecta model in this class aids in the acquisition of the target language's syntax and vocabulary, while also facilitating the learning of English grammar, vocabulary, and pronunciation. Through the trifecta model, students can understand the common and unique grammatical features of both languages.

All levels of students can benefit from the adaptive learning route, quizzes, and exercises that are part of the interactive tool. Similarly, when learning English, students can benefit from organized activities that focus on reading, writing, and speaking; for example, Indonesian students can improve their writing skills and idiomatic comprehension. This trifecta method encourages participation and reinforces knowledge by practicing it regularly and systematically. Learners can practice their conversational fluency or communication skills in a safe environment with the help of an AI-powered chatbot that mimics real-world multilingual conversations (Soon et al., 2024; Casheekar et al., 2024; Wei, 2025).

Bilingual learners practice their tone of voice and cultural sensitivity and improve their English listening and speaking skills in a practical way. Learners are better prepared for situations involving real-world conversations with the help of a trifecta-based learning model. The platform's feedback mechanism allows users to quickly identify and correct errors in real time. This trifecta model provides learners with feedback on how to use context, express their ideas more effectively, and improve their grammar and style independently. This personalized method takes learners' progress into account, which encourages successful language refinement. One of the main syntaxes of this trifecta model is cultural integration, which helps learners understand different cultures and not just learn the language.

This trifecta model promotes genuine and meaningful conversations that transcend language barriers by teaching English idioms and Indonesian proverbs. The platform provides facilities for formal writing and presentations in both languages, equipping users for professional AI applications. English learners get tips on how to write well-structured sentences, paragraphs, texts, or papers and how to structure their speeches and documents professionally. When working in an environment that requires bilingualism, these AI features are very helpful. Using AI-based assessment tools, students can take individual tests to measure their competency. Indonesian learners progress from “beginner” to “proficient” through the CEFR (Tangsakul and Poonpon, 2024; Li et al., 2024). This systematic assessment ensures the ability of the trifecta model to meet the unique requirements of users.

Through the trifecta model, bilingual learning becomes easier; AI is easy to use, and the bilingual interface makes it more accessible to students from all backgrounds. This trifecta model is easy to use for both native Indonesian speakers (Figure 1) and users who prefer English because it is easy to use and ensures that people from all language backgrounds can access it. Finally, the AI-based bilingual platform provides a holistic approach to language acquisition by developing linguistic competence, cross-cultural awareness, practical proficiency, and individualized assessments. Such a platform can completely transform bilingual education by encouraging the development of global communication competence.

MACHINE TRANSLATION AND DEEP LEARNING WITH AI FOR BILINGUAL CLASS

There are several AI-based language translation methods, such as statistical and NMT. These developments have marked significant progress in the field of creativity and collaboration between humans and technological advancements (Lijie, 2024). Here we will discuss the distinctive features of this topic, real-world applications, and innovative methods used. Data, neural networks, and human linguistic experience are some of the components that AI systems use to understand the complexities of many languages. In addition, this section discusses hybrid techniques that aim to improve translation accuracy by combining rule-based and data-centric artificial intelligence systems. Thanks to these technological developments, we can now parse idiomatic sentences, read contextual clues, and recognize emotional states, among others. Furthermore, ML and DL are synonymous concepts in the field of artificial intelligence (AI), which involve teaching computers to perform tasks without human intervention. Several fields, including language translation, have benefited greatly from this recently emerging revolutionary technology (Almasri, 2024).

Table 2 illustrates the interplay between Machine Learning (ML) and Deep Learning (DL), demonstrating their complementary roles in building a robust AI system for bilingual communication. It also demonstrates how we can utilize both fields to interpret diverse texts through the mastery of computational skills, a crucial aspect for this purpose (Samala et al. 2024).

Table 2. The correlation between computational thinking, machine translation, deep learning, and AI for bilingual communication:

Aspect	Computational Thinking	Machine Translation	Deep Learning	AI for bilingual communication.
Definition	The approach to problem-solving involves decomposition, pattern recognition, abstraction, and algorithms.	Text can be automatically translated from one language to another.	Neural networks, a subset of AI, are used to learn patterns and make predictions.	Integrating AI tools to facilitate seamless communication in two languages.
Role	The framework enables the creation of algorithms for bilingual communication systems.	Text translation serves as the foundation for language conversion.	The system powers high-quality translation and natural language understanding.	Facilitates real-time, accurate, and context-aware communication.
Contribution to AI	It assists in dissecting intricate language systems into feasible elements.	Enhances bilingual accessibility by automating translation tasks.	Acquires knowledge of the contextual nuances, grammar, and semantics of various languages.	The system integrates computational models to establish a user-friendly interface suitable for bilingual use.
Relation	Creates structured algorithms for machine translation.	It relies on computational models and algorithms for its operation.	It employs neural networks to enhance the precision of translation.	The system integrates computational thinking, machine translation, and deep learning for end-user applications.
Key Technologies	Algorithm design, pattern recognition, and abstraction.	Statistical models, phrase-based translation, and neural MT.	Recurrent Neural Networks (RNNs), transformers, and GPT models.	AI chatbots, virtual assistants, and multilingual systems.
Challenges	Complexity in designing adaptable algorithms.	The task involves handling idioms, context, and cultural nuances in translation.	We are training deep models with limited or noisy bilingual data.	Combining multiple technologies for seamless interaction.
Example Applications	Designing multilingual chatbots or educational tools.	Google Translate, DeepL.	GPT-based language models such as ChatGPT or Bard are utilized.	Use AI tools for customer service, education, or diplomacy.

Computational learning teaches computers to recognize patterns and derive conclusions from data analysis. This method involves giving a dataset to the computer and allowing it to learn from it, thereby gradually improving the performance of the computer. The goal of developing machine learning algorithms is to enable them to predict outcomes or evaluate previously unseen data by finding patterns in large datasets. Machines primarily aim to simplify the process of identifying trends, patterns, and connections in data, eliminating the need for explicit coding. One of the many forms of machine learning is supervised learning. Supervised learning involves training a model using a labeled case dataset and an algorithm. The dataset contains a pair of labels for each input data point. The system learns to associate input and output values, allowing it to predict data it has never seen before. To find patterns, clusters, or structures inherent in a dataset, unsupervised learning involves observing unannotated data.

Clustering and dimensionality reduction are two commonly used data analysis methods (Velander et al., 2024). Reinforcement learning is a computer technique that allows autonomous agents to learn from their encounters with the environment how to make sequential judgments. In response to the agent's behavior, the system rewards or punishes them. It adapts and learns to maximize its actions and rewards (Bittencourt et al., 2024). Deep Learning Deep learning (DL) is an area of machine learning (ML) that emphasizes the application of neural networks to efficiently capture representations and patterns in datasets. Layers of interconnected nodes, also known as neurones, in a neural network perform data processing and modification (Su et al., 2024). DL models, also called deep neural networks, have multiple hidden layers that help learn hierarchical data representations (Su and Yang, 2024). In DL, "deep" means combining multiple hidden layers in a neural network architecture, as illustrated in the essential part of DL based on ANN. Input, hidden, and output layers form the three main components of a neural network. Weighted connections connect each neuron at these levels to its neighbours in the layers below. DL models appear to excel at tasks involving large datasets and complex patterns, such as image and audio recognition, language processing, and autonomous vehicle development (Suhail et al. 2024).

The term ML is an umbrella term for a number of different methods. Deep learning, on the other hand, is concerned only with solving problems that require complex feature extraction and representation learning using deep neural networks. The main selling point of DL is its capacity to automatically learn important features from raw data, thereby eliminating the need for human feature engineers (Lastrucci et al., 2024). Hence, the field of language translation has benefitted greatly from the work of ML and DL. Improvements in DL techniques, especially with the help of models such as transformers, have led to a major shift in the accuracy and consistency of translation systems. By enhancing their ability to understand contextual cues and complex language patterns, these models are able to produce more accurate and consistent translations.

Using a multilingual corpus for word alignment offers a unique approach to training a recurrent neural network (RNN) and constructed this dataset with 1,200,000 paired words in English and Hindi, each with feature values (Mohamed et al., 2024). This example structure enables inference of Hindi word meaning and production of attribute vector values from a large set of word attributes. In essence, vector alignment is matching English and Hindi word vectors and then aligning each word accordingly. An initial assignment of parent terms, such as "C-DAC WAS," serves as the basis for the entire procedure. To obtain parent entities, one takes the word vectors and multiplies them by a parameter matrix and an activation function, such as tanh. A binary tree is a useful visual representation of the many levels of this method. NVIDIA GeForce GTX TitanX and other graphics processing units (GPUs) have been lifesavers when it comes to complex DL applications when comparing performance, GPUs clearly outperform central processing units (CPUs) because of how well they handle parallel processing. Machine translation (MT) is a rapidly growing subfield of NLP, and deep learning could one day lead to human-level translation systems (Mohanta, 2024).

In this context, RAE models—used for text processing—perform admirably. The Word2vec approach generates word vectors that are useful for sentence reconstruction and related applications. Missing vector history, insufficient data, and limited vocabulary are some of the constraints that MT has to overcome. However, the huge corpus required for accurate MT poses a significant challenge. DL architectures enhance translation systems. Using multiple GPUs can greatly improve the training process. We may be able to build an optimal MT system by integrating and harmonising different methods. Review on Effects of AI with Functions on Language Translation (Mohamed et al., 2024). Extensively studied the complex technical components of an English-Urdu MT system. The architecture of the system relies on a feed-forward-backward neural network. The main goal is to develop a more comprehensive understanding of Urdu grammar and vocabulary, with an emphasis on verbs, nouns/pronouns, and linguistic intricacies. The classification of English and Urdu as Subject-Verb-Object (SOV) and Subject-Object-Verb (SVO), respectively, fundamentally distinguishes them as distinct languages. Therefore, it is crucial to preserve grammatical structures during translation (Safder et al. 2024).

To overcome linguistic barriers, we should emphasize the preservation of logical relationships between grammatical components (Basit et al., 2024). The system's capacity to translate sentences containing a wide variety of linguistic features demonstrates its unexpected flexibility. Grammatically nuanced words and phrases include gerunds, infinitives (up to two), prepositions (up to three), direct and indirect objects, and more. The neural network can store an extensive database that includes lexicons from multiple languages and a set of grammatical rules. Direct translation from English to Urdu is not the only thing that the system's bilingual lexicon can handle.

The study also delves into its semantic and stylistic implications. Users will find the system's output in Romanised Urdu more readable. When combined, these metrics prove that the system is effective in translating between English and Urdu and can also overcome linguistic barriers (Ul Hassan et al., 2024). According to a study by (Singh et al., 2021) a bilingual study conducted in Marathi and English, divergence is a major bottleneck in machine translation (MT), with the main focus of investigation and classification being on topic, category, and structural differences. Artificial neural networks (ANNs) support an architecture that includes modules for thematic divergence, categorical divergence, and structural divergence. The main objective is to tokenize English sentences into components and train ANNs to match them with corresponding Marathi words, thereby accelerating Marathi to English translation.

Applying this method to thoroughly investigated neural network-based phrases and words yielded encouraging English results. This method emphasizes the importance of instructors in driving innovation in translation education through their pedagogical practices, which are recognized throughout the concerning English fluently is becoming increasingly important, not only for academic success but also for practical benefits in a complex social environment. This underscores the power of AI in transforming pedagogical practices in college English classrooms. The rise of AI necessitates a rethinking of current English translation programs, a shift in teaching strategies, and evidence of the interaction between artificial intelligence (AI) and academic English translation courses (Davoodi, 2024).

Arabic-English bilingual studies demonstrate the preservation of similar attributes in Arabic translations of English input sentences with similar syntactic features. The study (Razem, 2024) showcases the effectiveness of an artificial neural network approach in identifying case-by-case examples that share syntactic properties with a novel English phrase. By analysing the structures and features of English sentences, it facilitates the recognition of syntactic aspects of Arabic using a feed-forward artificial neural network. The dynamic technique accurately reflects the structure of the original English sentence to produce a coherent and contextually correct Arabic translation. The extensive use of deep learning models, architectures, and approaches has greatly influenced natural language processing, demonstrating the state-of-the-art in language processing systems, providing critical comments, and suggesting directions for future research (Akande, 2024).

Researchers have used various ML and DL algorithms in NLP (Obaid et al. 2023). Beyond conventional methods, natural language processing is on the rise, but the subject still has a lot of untapped potential that requires further study and anticipate that continued experimentation with various learning approaches will enhance the efficiency and accuracy of natural language processing (NLP) with an emphasis on real-time collected speech data, (Zhang et al. 2024) research attempts to improve the MT quality assessment. The new method in Mandarin and English combines deep neural networks with linguistic feature extraction to measure the quality of MT in real-time spoken discourse using a structure called Double Recurrent Neural Network (double-RNN). This approach provides an accurate and fair translation quality evaluation, as empirical evaluations show that it is similar to traditional quality evaluation standards and lays the foundation for future developments in intelligent MT for real-time natural language processing. By combining intelligent identification with deep learning approaches, Pan, et al., (2024) research proposes a new model for English translation that overcomes the problems with existing models. The proposed NMT system combines traditional neural networks with deep learning frameworks and attention mechanisms to achieve phrase recognition that is very accurate, translation quality that is better, and translation time that is shorter.

SOCIOLINGUISTIC PERSPECTIVES: IDENTITY, CULTURE, AND EQUITY

The addition of artificial intelligence (AI) to language education has enabled new ways of teaching and learning, especially in bilingual and multilingual settings. However, educators need to view AI-based language training through the lens of educational theory and sociolinguistics to properly understand its teaching implications and ensure appropriate use. This review looks at recent advances in AI-based language learning and relates them to key teaching models and sociolinguistic ideas to provide a comprehensive analytical picture of how beneficial it can be for education. Several recent studies have shown that AI tools have transformed the way second language (L2) learners interact with language content by providing personalized, data-driven, and adaptive experiences. Filippetti and Sbardella (2024) show that AI technologies, such as speech recognition and grammar feedback systems, can help students perform better by tailoring lessons to their unique learning styles. Their research suggests that AI is not just a tool for technology but also an extension of constructivist and adaptive learning ideas.

4Wu et al. (2024) examine how well AI tools align with learning theory in K–12 education. They found that despite the widespread use of AI technology, curriculum design generally does not make clear connections to teaching theories such as behaviorism, constructivism, or connectivism. Their work emphasizes the importance of placing AI in a theoretical context that is clear to teachers so that they can better understand AI literacy and how to use it in the classroom. AbuSahyon et al. (2023) explore this gap further by looking at how AI-powered chatbots such as ChatGPT and Duolingo Bots facilitate interactive L2 learning. These chatbots are based on the idea of Communicative Language Teaching (CLT), which states that people should practice real-time discussions in a stress-free setting. This engagement is important because it aligns with Vygotsky's sociocultural theory, which states that interaction is the primary way to learn a language, with intelligent systems acting as scaffolding tools.

When looking at AI-based language training, we also need to think about identity, cultural inclusivity, and linguistic equity. Gaballo (2024) talks about how important it is for AI applications to be sociolinguistically appropriate. She argues that AI offers new potential for oral language practice but often fails to take into account regional dialects, idiomatic expressions, and culturally specific meanings. These limitations can push non-native speakers to the brink and reinforce language hierarchies. Using activity theory, Zainab Faez Jasim (2025) links AI language tools to the cognitive development and social and cultural environment of learners. The study argues that AI-based multilingual systems influence language input and the social and linguistic identities of learners. In this situation, learners are not just learning grammar and vocabulary; they are also negotiating meaning within the social structures created by the AI platform. This is a clear example of Halliday's systemic functional linguistics.

Samantray et al. (2024) emphasize that AI systems must be built with an understanding of the cultural and communicative behaviours they are trying to emulate. Their research, using computational linguistics and social semiotics, suggests that AI can erase linguistic diversity if it is not aware of it. Instead, they want AI tools that incorporate user-generated information so that language learners can co-produce knowledge, in line with critical pedagogy.Inclusion, bias, and ethics are some of the issues and opportunities. Algorithmic bias is one of the biggest issues with AI-mediated instruction. Wiesinger (2024) criticises the widespread use of generative AI in English as a Foreign Language (EFL) program for their tendency to promote Western-centric language standards. This critique is consistent with Pennycook's (2010) claim that language teaching is never neutral and must be viewed in the context of global power relations. Therefore, teachers need to be aware of the bias embedded in AI systems and work to make language learning spaces more welcoming to all.

Incelli (2025) adds to this discussion by using corpus linguistics to show how AI-driven corpora can reproduce systemic inequalities if not adequately controlled. Their research shows that AI tools generally do not cover enough minority languages or dialects, making bilingual education less inclusive. Thus, AI systems need to be modified to be able to understand more languages and ensure that everyone has equal access to language resources. Arif et al. (2025) provide an example of Mandarin learners who used AI technology and showed that, although their grammar was correct, they struggled to understand sociocultural cues. These results suggest that current AI models are unable to fully capture the practical and contextual components of communication, which are critical in bilingual education. To understand how AI works within the larger semiotic environment, it is important to be aware of sociocultural theory, specifically Lantolf and Thorne's (2006) notion of mediated action.

Adding artificial intelligence (AI) to bilingual education has a lot of potential, but it also raises many ethical and practical questions that need to be addressed. Algorithmic bias is one of the most important concerns. This bias is usually caused by training data that is imbalanced or does not represent cultures well. Wiesinger (2024) argues that this kind of bias in AI-generated language tests and feedback systems could exacerbate current disparities, pushing non-native English speakers or speakers of less common dialects to the margins. AI tools tend to mimic prevailing linguistic ideas, especially Western ones, which makes this problem even worse. This can lead to a standard of English that is too similar to what other people speak, which may not reflect the different realities of learners around the world (Pennycook, 2010; Gaballo, 2024). Data privacy is a very important issue that is closely related to algorithmic bias. When AI is used in schools or universities, it usually means collecting and analysing a lot of personal information about children, such as their language skills, how engaged they are, and how well they are doing in school. Often, this data is collected without the user's knowledge or explicit consent. Without strong security measures, the risk of data misuse and unauthorised access increases. Thus, it is imperative to include ethical guidelines when using AI tools in schools. AbuSahyon et al. (2023) state that internationally accepted norms such as IEEE's Ethically Aligned Design and UNESCO's AI Ethics Recommendations should be followed. These principles emphasize accountability, data minimization, and equitable access; these standards are the baseline for using AI responsibly in the classroom.

Another important issue is equitable access, especially in low-resource settings where infrastructure, connectivity, and technological know-how may be non-existent or where there may be a digital divide. The digital divide remains a problem that makes it difficult for more people and more places to use AI-powered educational products. Students living in rural or poor areas are unable to benefit from AI-enhanced bilingual education because they lack access to up-to-date technology, reliable or affordable internet, or trained teachers. These inequities make it increasingly difficult for technology to make education more democratic. Davoodi (2024) suggests the EQUAL-AI framework as a way to get developers and policymakers to focus on AI applications that are linguistically and culturally relevant and work well in specific situations. Tailoring solutions to specific educational settings can make AI systems much more inclusive and useful.

A global and comparative view helps us learn more about how AI works in bilingual education. Researchers can find transferrable methods and localised problems by looking at how things are done in different languages and cultural settings, including Arabic-English translation models (Razem, 2024) and English-Urdu machine translation systems (Mohamed et al., 2024). Such comparisons demonstrate the importance of respecting language patterns and cultural differences when using AI techniques. They also demonstrate that there is no one-size-fits-all approach to integrating AI into education; AI needs to be tailored to each situation.This updated chapter also strengthens its theoretical foundation by drawing on key theories from education and sociolinguistics. For example, constructivist learning theory and Vygotsky's sociocultural theory suggest that learning is a process that occurs in a particular social environment. This perspective is consistent with the idea that AI can be a scaffold for personalised, interactive language learning. Lantolf and

Thorne's (2006) notion of mediated action is similar in that it shows how AI can be used to help learners grow cognitively and linguistically through interactions that are culturally important. Systemic functional linguistics and critical pedagogy also help us think about how AI systems can change the way students view their own language and support or challenge language hierarchies.

However, even the best models, such as the Trifecta Model presented in this chapter, have real problems when it comes to implementation. Some of these include unprepared teachers, overly restrictive curricula, unclear policies and poor technological skills. Many teachers lack the training they need to use AI tools in their lessons in meaningful ways. At the same time, institutional resistance to new ways of teaching and the lack of clear policies on AI in education make it difficult to change the system. Wiesinger (2024) and Samantray et al. (2024) argue that to address these problems, we need to invest money in teaching people about AI, continue to learn about it ourselves, and create policies that engage teachers, students, and other stakeholders.Thus, while understanding that AI technology has the power to change things by improving language skills, helping educators and people from different cultures get along better, and enabling personalised learning experiences, there are moral, practical, and policy issues that need to be addressed to ensure that AI is used in a fair and responsible way. Ultimately, the successful use of AI in bilingual education depends on developers, teachers, policymakers, and researchers working together to create systems that are open, adaptive, and friendly to all types of learners.

This article is a bridge to a thematically structured model of teaching where researchers and educators should use a thematically structured model of AI integration to get the most out of AI in multilingual contexts. These include: (1) Cognitive-Theoretical alignment: Linking AI features to learning theories, such as behaviorist exercises to improve grammar and constructivist simulations to improve communication skills, as shown in Wu et al. (2024); (2) Sociocultural mediation: Creating AI tools that help bilingual learners communicate with each other while taking into account the sociolinguistic environment in which they live (AbuSahyon et al., 2023; Samantray et al., 2024); (3) using ethical frameworks to address AI bias, student data privacy, and linguistic justice (Gaballo, 2024; Wiesinger, 2024); (4) having teachers scrutinize AI systems to see if they support their teaching goals and use language that is friendly to all (Incelli, 2025).

AI-powered language training has much potential to make language learning more personalized and accessible to all. However, to ensure that new technologies do not exacerbate existing inequities or turn language into meaningless structures, such training must be grounded in solid educational theory and sociolinguistic knowledge. This article shows that combining constructivist, sociocultural, and critical frameworks provides the support needed for bilingual education to use AI meaningfully and validly.

ENHANCING BILINGUAL COMMUNICATION THROUGH AI POWER

The application of artificial intelligence technologies in foreign language teaching emphasizes the utilization of digital neuropedagogical advancements to foster communicative bilingual or multilingual competence. The specificity of the way the human brain works in the direction of developing general cognitive connections correlates with the quality of new types of pedagogical tools offered by digital technologies used today for teaching foreign languages. By using digital technologies for foreign language acquisition, the suggested metacognitive approach can help improve self-awareness and metacognitive processes.

AI can adapt to the pace and level of learning of students and can also identify problem areas and provide reinforcement when needed. To help memorize new vocabulary and grammatical structures, many AI-powered platforms use spaced repetition algorithms (Rajak, 2024; Alwan, 2024). To help students gradually internalize the material, this strategy ensures that they learn complex concepts more frequently. If an ESL student is struggling with irregular verbs, for example, the teacher may suggest that they practice them more often until they understand them.

Students may be required to practice verb conjugations more frequently in order to learn complex language structures. A further benefit of these platforms is their ability to track user performance, allowing them to anticipate when students are likely to forget certain material and then proactively implement review sessions to strengthen retention. This level of adaptability reduces the cognitive load often involved in learning a new language and enhances long-term memory retention. Bilingual learning aims to simplify the process of learning the target language (English) and avoid overwhelming users with excessive new knowledge at once, enabling them to progress steadily (Bengsch, 2024).

In languages where even small changes in sound can have a significant impact on meaning, knowing how to pronounce words correctly is crucial (Strasser, 2023). The complex vowel system and emphasis on consonants in Arabic, for example, can make language learning challenging for non-native speakers. At the same time, varying accents and inconsistent spelling-to-sound correspondences are common challenges for English learners. The use of AI-powered speech recognition technology provides a solution by offering immediate feedback on the correctness of one's pronunciation. Rosetta Stone, Lola speak and Learna AI, among others, use artificial intelligence (AI) to compare a learner's spoken input with natural pronunciation models. Vowel length, stress patterns, and intonation are just a few of the areas this technology can identify for improvement, in addition to word pronunciation. For instance, this technology could instruct an English learner to focus on the pronunciation of diphthongs or the unique distinction between the word's "ship" and "sheep." In addition to speech recognition, AI can also provide students with the opportunity to practice speaking in a virtual environment. Using natural language processing (NLP), conversational AI facilitates conversations guided by a user bot or virtual tutor, providing a risk-free environment to hone public speaking skills. One of the hardest things for language learners to do is become comfortable and proficient in speaking in a real-world setting. This immersive method helps overcome that (Chinnaiyan, et al., 2025; Wu et al., 2025).

The concept of using gamification to increase student motivation in language learning or language acquisition is another domain where AI-powered platforms shine (Kujundziski and Bojadjiev 2025). Consistent practice is essential for language learning, which can be a daunting task that leaves many feelings exhausted or frustrated. Artificial intelligence (AI) language apps address this by integrating game features such as badges, leaderboards, and point systems to engage and inspire learners (Ulutas et al., 2025). The AI tracks user progress and adjusts the difficulty of the exercises to maintain an appropriate level of effort; for example, Duolingo uses a reward and challenge system to encourage daily practice. By incorporating game elements, this method makes learning a new language more engaging and fun, which in turn motivates students to persist and eventually master the material. AI that can monitor and display progress gives students a real sense of accomplishment, which can be a powerful incentive to continue learning. Gamification has the potential to increase bilingual learners' retention and improve their communication in practical ways. For example, a gamification approach can benefit bilingual learners who struggle with the syntax and writing of a language that is complex. However, constant reinforcement of unfamiliar words and phrases enhances the success of foreign language acquisition.

One of the most significant impacts of AI-powered language learning systems is their capacity to make language education accessible to a wider audience. These platforms have greatly reduced the barriers to learning a new language, increased motivation to learn, and improved communication by making language learning available to anyone with an internet connection (Khan, et al., 2025). This is especially important for bilingual learners in regions where conventional language programs may be inaccessible due to political, economic, or geographic factors. Using AI-driven platforms, people can learn whenever and wherever they like. Learners in today's fast-paced world may not have the time or budget to attend formal sessions, which is why this accessibility is so important. Even in places where language instructors are scarce, language learners can benefit from the exposure that AI tools can provide. These platforms also provide high-quality language training to learners in underserved or remote areas. The advent of AI-powered language learning platforms has revolutionized the way we learn bilingual languages by providing users with dynamic, engaging, and personalized experiences (Costa et al., 2025). From adaptive learning and speech recognition to gamification, AI enhances language learning in a fun and engaging way. These platforms not only eliminate conventional barriers to language learning but also enhance it. On the other hand, these platforms connect students with different languages, which is great for improving communication in our increasingly interconnected world.

Table 3. AI plays a pivotal role in overcoming linguistic barriers and enhancing communication across diverse languages

Aspect	Enhancing Bilingual Communication Using AI Power
Real-Time Translation	AI-powered tools like Google Translate and DeepL enable instant translation of spoken and written text, facilitating real-time communication.
Speech Recognition	AI systems like ASR (Automatic Speech Recognition) convert spoken language into text, bridging verbal communication gaps.
Natural Language Understanding	AI interprets context, tone, and cultural nuances, ensuring more accurate and context-sensitive translations.
Chatbots and Virtual Assistants	AI-based chatbots (e.g., ChatGPT) provide multilingual support for customer service and learning.
Personalised Learning	AI tools help individuals learn and practice a second language with adaptive exercises tailored to their progress.
Context-Aware Translation	AI systems utilize deep learning models to understand the meaning of words in context rather than relying on literal translation.
Document Translation	AI automates document translations with high accuracy, helping organizations and individuals work in multilingual environments.
Cross-Cultural Communication	AI helps navigate cultural subtleties by incorporating idiomatic expressions and regional dialects into translations.
Accessibility for the Hearing/Speech Impaired	AI enables sign language recognition and generation, as well as text-to-speech systems, ensuring inclusive communication.
Collaborative Platforms	AI-powered platforms like Microsoft Teams and Zoom offer real-time multilingual transcription and captions during meetings.
Language Modelling	AI advances in models like GPT and transformer architectures provide powerful language generation and understanding capabilities.
Multimodal Communication	AI integrates text, speech, and image processing for comprehensive bilingual interaction in various formats.

AI can eliminate language barriers and enable interaction across different languages. AI has completely changed the way people communicate as well as language learning. AI interventions make us adapt to cross-machine communication. Theoretical foundations and advancements in computer science, linguistics, and artificial intelligence (AI) support this revolutionary function. Theoretical advancements in machine translation and interlanguage theory have enabled real-time translation and bilingual language acquisition, which rely on neural machine translation (NMT) to provide immediate and accurate translations. This is essential for international communication in fields such as education and business (Bhardwaj et al., 2024). AI-driven speech recognition systems can transcribe spoken words into text or facilitate direct translation using signal processing and pattern recognition, and this theory strengthens the language support.

According to Savela et al. (2025), it facilitates communication between individuals who speak different languages. Cognitive linguistics and semantic theory provide the basis for natural language understanding, which in turn ensures that AI systems understand cultural and contextual nuances and avoid literal translation errors (Bonn et al, 2024). Conversational AI and reinforcement learning enable chatbots and virtual assistants to support multiple languages, allowing users to easily switch between them and manage complex queries, making language interaction and acquisition practical and efficient (Muthmainnah et al., 2024). According to Pérez-Marín et al. (2012), personalized learning tools based on adaptive learning and constructivist theory enable learners of all levels to acquire a second language through tailored activities. Artificial intelligence (AI) uses neural context encoding and contextualism in linguistics to automate document translation for domains such as business and academia and to preserve meaning even in idiomatic or polysemous expressions (Wang, et al., 2025).

Furthermore, AI promotes intercultural communication by incorporating regional dialects and culturally appropriate translations, drawing on theories of intercultural communication and cultural intelligence (CQ) (Maher et al, 2024). By leveraging technologies such as sign language recognition, speech-to-text, and text-to-speech systems, AI enhances accessibility for those with hearing or speech impairments. Collaboration platforms, such as Zoom and Microsoft Teams, combine network theory with computer-assisted collaboration (CSCW), allowing for simultaneous translation and text generation in multiple languages. To ensure consistent bilingual communication, AI uses sophisticated language modeling based on generative and transformational grammar to generate sentences that are grammatically correct and relevant in context. In short, AI ensures accurate, inclusive, and culturally sensitive bilingual communication through the integration of deep learning, computational linguistics, and natural language processing (NLP). AI revolutionizes cross-cultural communication and fosters teamwork in an interconnected world by detecting language and context in everyday life (Huertas-Abril & Hà, 2025).

Research on the potential drawbacks and dangers of implementing AI technology into the classroom constitutes an important part of the literature. The literature largely agrees that chatbots have a number of negative aspects, the most prominent of which are the prevalence of fake content and the reliability of the information they generate (Almatrafi, 2024). More concerning is the fact that the majority of chatbots fail to provide citations for their data, leaving users unable to confirm the accuracy of the information and, in theory, unaware of where the responses they receive come from. There is a greater likelihood that students will not learn to think critically or search for and process information due to the prevalence of various forms of imitation and the fact that many contemporary students have low levels of scientific literacy. According to some Suriano et al. (2025) chatbots can make people less likely to think critically and independently. The negative impact of AI on education is a source of concern among scientists. Because AI has the potential to open a "Pandora's box" in education, some worry that this generation will grow up without critical thinking skills due to over-reliance on technology (Li et al., 2024).

AI-POWERED LANGUAGE MODELS FOR DIVERSE AND ADAPTIVE LINGUISTIC EDUCATION

In the field of foreign language acquisition (Indonesian English), the concept of students' speech individuality strongly influences the achievement of professional bilingualism. This has a close relationship with "linguistic personality" and "personal code" (Kushnina et al., 2024). Professional bilingualism is more than just mastering two languages; it is about the ability to communicate and engage effectively in both the mother tongue and the target language in different professional environments, considering cultural nuances. Professional bilinguals, sometimes known as "beginning bilinguals", are people whose competence in two languages allows them to work effectively and efficiently in roles traditionally held by native speakers. The distinct personal and linguistic traits that students bring to the process of second language acquisition certainly enhance and accelerate the path to professional bilingualism (Solsona-Puig et al., 2024). The unique speech patterns, tactics, and peculiarities that students exhibit as they master a foreign language contribute to their unique speech identity. The learner's cultural experiences, cognitive abilities, personality qualities, and language background are some of the components that shape this distinctiveness of mastery. The development of native, competent language use depends on recognizing and exploiting its uniqueness (Meadows, 2024).

The charismatic delivery of a translator or interpreter is a shining illustration of the benefits of professional bilingualism. A professional translator is fluent in two languages and has an awareness of cultural differences. They translate a message from one language into another so that the target audience can understand it, including all the implied meanings and contexts. "Harmonious translation" refers to the process of translating a source text in a way that allows readers whose language is different from the original to understand and enjoy it as much as native speakers of the original language. Translating or acquiring a language from one to another requires extensive familiarity with both cultures, a keen understanding of linguistic conventions, and a great deal of empathy on the part of the translator, who must anticipate and avoid any problems that non-native speakers might have in understanding the original text. What distinguishes a professional bilingual from a casual bilingual is his or her ability to read with the intention of interpreting the material for speakers of the other language, rather than simply reading for his or her own understanding (Bayraktar, 2024).

The connection between the translator's linguistic personality and his/her oral personality is clearly visible during this process. Based on Filippova, (2024) comprehensive view has contributed to the popularization of the term "language personality" or "linguistic personality" in scientific and pedagogical discourse, other nominations are beginning to attract academic attention. The author provides strong evidence that the term "speech personality" best describes the mental operations involved in communicating using language (Asratyan, 2024). The notion of a "speaking person" includes not only the speaker but also the listener in view, since the creation and perception of language are integral aspects of the communication process. What we call a person's "linguistic personality" is the sum of their linguistic expressions of their cultural background, educational experiences, and life experiences. In the context of real-life communication, a "communicative personality" also emerges. Consequently, a "speech personality" is "the sum of personal choices made in the communication process involving various strategic, linguistic, and extralinguistic means." and a system of individual phenomena that, as far as we know, have nothing to do with human translation. Translators' strategies, linguistic forms, and extralinguistic means form an integral part of their personality as they interpret messages for speakers of other languages. They also contribute their unique cross-cultural and intercultural skills to the process. It therefore seems reasonable to draw a comparison between translation and speech personality.

Hence, the phrase "translator's speech personality" came into use. To be a successful professional bilingual, one must possess the personal quality of cross-cultural awareness (Liang, 2024) which helps in the development of both soft and tough character skills. The unique speech abilities of students accelerate intercultural competence, which is defined as "the ability to navigate and understand cultural differences while communicating effectively in diverse contexts." Students develop greater fluency in navigating cultural differences and adapting their communication styles to suit different work environments as they come to understand their unique and distinctive language identities.

The advent of Gene AI has profound implications for many areas, including language teaching." Working in tandem with AI enables a more personalized, hands-on, and adaptive learning experience, tailored to each learner's unique needs and preferences; as a result, this technology has transformed and continues to transform language teaching and learning around the world. The most advanced AI-powered language learning programs assess each student's progress, identify problem areas, and provide personalized feedback and suggestions. Natural language processing (NLP) techniques and large language models (LLMs) such as GPT-4 and BARD have greatly advanced the understanding and application of AI in this area (Lewington et al., 2024).

If a student wants to improve their academic writing, business communication, or vocabulary for a specific job or field of study, they can create a personalized learning path to help them do so. In addition, AI removes geographical barriers, allowing students to practice language and cultural immersion. To help students improve their speaking and listening skills in a fun and engaging way, virtual language instructors and advanced AI chatbots mimic real-world conversational situations. Students gain the competence, confidence, and accuracy needed for professional bilingualism through continued engagement with these AI-driven language models (Casheekar, et al., 2024).

Additionally, AI has given foreign language students access to a wealth of real-world language resources, including books, movies, podcasts, and articles. AI-driven content recommendation systems curate personalized learning materials that expose students to diverse language contexts and cultural perspectives more effectively. These systems consider students' interests and proficiency levels. Students gain a deeper understanding of the cultural nuances of the target language through this exposure, which is essential for professional bilingualism and improving their language skills. Additionally, AI makes it easy to continuously evaluate and measure progress, giving students real-time insight into how their language skills are developing. AI-powered assessment tools analysed students' progress across multiple language areas, including vocabulary, pronunciation, and grammar. They provide extensive feedback and practical insights to help students improve (Lee et al., 2024; Mohanty et al., 2024).

Several generative AI tools are currently entering the edtech landscape for teachers. Teachers can assess the efficacy of their lesson plans by examining student-generated content in online conversations through large language models (LLMs) encoded based on learning outcomes, and they can explore the benefits and drawbacks of these methods (Feng et al., 2024). The accuracy of the data encoded by these models is critical if teachers rely on LLMs for evaluation. Students can accelerate their journey toward professional bilingualism with data-driven language assessment methods that allow them to systematically assess their progress and take proactive steps to improve areas of weakness (Wu, 2024).

Multilingual large language models (MLLMs), which are capable of handling and generating text in multiple languages, present exciting new possibilities for facilitating true multilingual communication and the performance of MLLMs in a single language is outstanding, however their limitations in translanguaging or code-switching (Syamkumar et al., 2024) lead to misrepresentations of how bilingual learners use the languages. Further factors that exacerbate these issues include the lack of safety standards and thorough evaluation, as well as homogeneity in MLLM training due to a lack of code-switching data. Examining the benefits and drawbacks of MLLMs is critical as language model-driven learning analytics finds its way into the classroom. The current study extends previous work in the areas of translanguaging, bi/multilingualism, and natural language processing by incorporating MLLMs into the training and evaluation process (Al-Dokhny et al., 2024).

Using Indonesian and English as case studies using student writing assessments, we explore the code-switching and multilingual capabilities of MLLMs in the context of learning analytics. In order to foster genuine social contact, translanguaging encourages speakers to draw on their full linguistic and cultural identities while navigating and challenging the socio-political boundaries of "appropriate" language use and discourse. Furthermore, the phrase "translanguaging space" is defined by (Ateek, 2024) as an environment where barriers between languages and cultures become less visible in the bilingual's everyday experience. The collaborative efforts of critical thinking and creative expression in this environment shape bilingual students' understanding of socio-cultural and linguistic issues, as well as standards of language use. The focus of much of the discussion about this approach today is on how to leverage students' language production as a resource in the classroom.

Designing teaching materials such as using ChatGPT, Meta AI or Bot by incorporating pedagogical practices that leverage bilingualism to enhance learning, reflects the growing globalization of educational resources. The educational community seeking to apply the theory has made extensive use of these guidelines over the past decade (Li et al., 2024). These guidelines highlight the need for collaboration and offer language resources for different ages and grade levels. Effective use of these materials can help students build on prior knowledge of language, culture and multimodal practices (such as gesture) to make sense of the world. We see translanguaging as an increasingly valuable framework that enables bilingual learners to articulate ideas and understandings using their entire linguistic repertoire, especially as the field of learning analytics continues to expose students to multiple perspectives.

The capacity of large language models (LLMs) to generate natural-sounding words from large datasets has pushed them to the forefront of learning analytics. Essay grading and feedback generation are two examples of work that leverage them. This highlights the growing role of LLMs in reducing teacher workload and providing insightful student feedback (Meyer et al. 2024). Automated essay scoring (AES) systems, for example, ease the burden on examiners on large-scale exams such as the GMAT and TOEFL. LLMs such as BERT go beyond previous AES approaches, setting new standards in the field (Zhui et al. 2024). Researchers in education can benefit from LLMs because, in addition to scoring, they can provide tailored feedback to intelligent tutoring systems (Lyanda, et al. 2024). Additionally, they demonstrate proficiency in domain-specific subject areas, such as mathematics, and can-do things like generate multiple-choice questions, plot images, and offer simulations for teacher training (Fuller, et al. 2024). It is becoming increasingly important to provide similar assistance to bilingual and multilingual classrooms because these improvements show that LLMs have enormous potential in the classroom.

LLMs typically perform better in English than in non-English languages because they are trained on English-centric data. However, newer MLLMs, such as GPT-4, show improved multilingual capabilities and outperform their predecessors on multilingual benchmarks (Zhou et al. 2024). Although MLLM research has developed rapidly in recent years, there are still problems: code switching is still a major difficulty for many MLLMs because the training data does not have enough different linguistic resources (Kooli and Yusuf 2024). Furthermore, comprehensive benchmarks have not supported or adequately analysed the recent progress in MLLMs (Hou et al. 2024).

This has resulted in the exclusion of many languages that have limited access to digital resources (Neumann, et al. 2024). Since large-scale annotation, which requires human raters fluent in multiple languages, is limited, code-switching resources are extremely difficult to find. Due to this lack of data, researchers have turned to manually generated datasets that use random substitution and noun phrase translation (Chen and Alias, 2024) or MLLMs that create unrealistic code-switched texts. Researchers have shown that newer MLLMs like GPT-4, in the synthetic generation realm, are more capable of code-switching and cross-language comprehension (Khlaif, et al., 2024) making them a viable option for situations that require code-switching capabilities. Developing fair and reliable datasets for MLLMs to capture the dynamic bilingual/multilingual process is critical, especially for bilingual learners engaged in classroom conversations in two or more languages. The automatic analysis, translation, and production of linguistic data across multiple languages constitutes bilingual information processing. This field is essential for AI systems that interact with people from different language backgrounds, as it teaches them how to understand and speak the user's native language (Gu, et al. 2024).

Building robust natural language processing (NLP) algorithms that can handle the complexities of cross-language communication is an essential part of the scientific principles of AI related to bilingual information processing (Hashmi et al., 2024). Machine translation, multilingual sentiment analysis, and cross-lingual information retrieval fall under this category. Integrating these techniques into AI systems enables the automation of document translation, multilingual customer support, and cross-cultural market research. The overarching domain of bilingual information processing encompasses the automated procedures of linguistic content generation, translation, and analysis in multiple languages (Peng and Zhou 2024). This entails either creating new linguistic content in the target language or automatically processing and understanding data from one language to another using sophisticated computational methods. The capacity to communicate and interact fluently across language barriers depends on this capability. Bilingual information processing is essential for AI systems that aim to communicate with people who speak different languages. This feature facilitates a more efficient and personalised user experience by allowing the AI system to understand and communicate in the user's native language, thereby eliminating language barriers. This feature allows AI applications to connect with more people, which is critical to success and widespread adoption in the GenAI era (Prieto Ramos, 2024).

Advances in complex Natural Language Processing (NLP) methods are creating a scientific basis for AI's capacity to manage multilingual information processing. When communicating across languages, these methods must be robust enough to handle the peculiarities of syntax, vocabulary, grammar, and culture that are unique to each language. For AI systems to engage in meaningful cross-lingual conversations, it is necessary to develop natural language processing models that are able to understand and translate meaning across languages accurately. Machine translation, cross-lingual information retrieval, and multilingual sentiment analysis are some of the most important natural language processing (NLP) methods used in bilingual information processing (Orosoo et al. 2024). Automatic machine translation (or MT) is the process of translating text from one language to another while preserving its original meaning and context. With cross-lingual information retrieval, users can perform searches in multiple languages and get relevant results from all of them (Radhika, et al., 2024). In contrast, multilingual sentiment analysis involves examining and parsing the emotional undercurrents or sentiments conveyed in written materials in multiple languages. This paves the way for AI systems to understand and respond to public opinion or consumer feedback in multiple language settings.

Automating various tasks that require cross-language communication and understanding becomes possible with the integration of these advanced NLP approaches into AI systems. One example is the ease with which businesses can collaborate and exchange information with partners and clients across geographies and languages through automatic document translation. With the help of multilingual customers, businesses can reach customers worldwide and provide them with the best service, regardless of the language they speak. Companies can now conduct cross-cultural market research more easily, which provides valuable insights from data collected in different cultural and linguistic situations, allowing them to make informed decisions. Overall, these methods substantially enhance the capabilities of AI systems and their usefulness in today's interconnected environment (Priya et al., 2024).

We believe that the linguistic personality of student translators can be better understood by reviewing various approaches and emphasizing that "the personality-activity approach establishes an orientation on the translator's personality as the subject of translation pedagogy" (translation pedagogy). The competence approach is a theoretical and practical methodological tool for contemporary pedagogy (Shelestova et al., 2024). In line with the translator's speech personality, the works therefore pay much attention to the translator's internal and external resources. A language learning environment that recognizes and values each student's unique speech can greatly increase motivation and engagement.

Students tend to be prouder of their language learning when they can use the target language in a natural way. A sense of ownership fosters qualities such as resilience and tenacity, which are essential for achieving professional bilingualism (Trinh, et al. 2024). Experts in the field of translation pedagogy and didactics affirm that the formation of translation competence determines the success of translation activities. In the context of translation competence, discuss several personal abilities that are essential for producing harmonious translations. These competencies include knowledge, intuition, creativity, cultural sensitivity, carefulness, and non-trivial translation judgment. Modern advances in foreign language teaching practices have made it easier for students to develop and maintain the high level of motivation necessary for successful language learning. In the process of cultivating one's linguistic personality, communicative technology can enhance educational motivation by intensifying thinking-speaking activities and thus supporting students' ongoing motivation to express their attitudes toward real-world phenomena in their communication practices.

CONCLUSION

In this paper, we show how AI can fill the gap in bilingual education with a flexible, context-aware, inclusive solution and highlight how AI-driven platforms offer comprehensive and easy-to-use language learning methods with capabilities such as real-time translation, feedback mechanisms, and cultural integration. It reinforces the idea that AI in the classroom can foster meaningful cross-cultural interactions, enhance language proficiency, and create customized learning paths. We address important issues such as culturally sensitive translation and language inclusion with fewer resources. To address the needs in bilingual education, the study offers a trifecta model and provides practical insights to educators, legislators, and software developers by connecting theoretical frameworks with real-world implementations.

Furthermore, it provides a solid foundation for improving bilingual communication skills in an increasingly interconnected society. We integrate linguistic theory, AI advancements, and educational approaches to achieve this, thereby adopting an interdisciplinary approach.

REFERENCES

AbuSahyon, A. S. A. E., Alzyoud, A., Alshorman, O., & Al-Absi, B. (2023). AI-driven technology and chatbots as tools for enhancing English language learning in the context of second language acquisition: A review study. *International Journal of Membrane Science and Technology*, *10*(1), 1209–1223. DOI: 10.15379/ijmst.v10i1.2829

Akande, A. O. A. (2024). *Language Attitudes Towards Arabic and English in the State of Qatar: A study of secondary schoolchildren, in two dual language private schools predominantly attended by Qatari and native Arabic-speaking children* (Master's thesis, University of Wales Trinity Saint David (United Kingdom)).

Al-Dokhny, A., Alismaiel, O., Youssif, S., Nasr, N., Drwish, A., & Samir, A. (2024). Can Multimodal Large Language Models Enhance Performance Benefits Among Higher Education Students? An Investigation Based on the Task–Technology Fit Theory and the Artificial Intelligence Device Use Acceptance Model. *Sustainability (Basel)*, *16*(23), 10780. DOI: 10.3390/su162310780

Al Yakin, A., Viddy, A., Warsah, I., Al Matari, A. S., Cardoso, L., Elngar, A. A., & Obaid, A. J. (2025). Enabling Federated Learning in the Classroom: Sociotechnical Ecosystem on Artificial Intelligence Integration in Educational Practices. In *Artificial Intelligence Using Federated Learning* (pp. 37-56). CRC Press.

Al Yakin, A. M., Rasyid, A. R., Massyat, M., Muthmainnah, M., Aquino, A. B., Noche, T. H., & Cardoso, L. (2024). The Importance of Collaboration Between Human Intelligence and GenAI in Digitalization of Education. In *Impact and Potential of Machine Learning in the Metaverse* (pp. 129–160). IGI Global. DOI: 10.4018/979-8-3693-5762-0.ch006

Almasri, F. (2024). Exploring the impact of artificial intelligence in teaching and learning of science: A systematic review of empirical research. *Research in Science Education*, *54*(5), 977–997. DOI: 10.1007/s11165-024-10176-3

Alwan, A. A. (2024). Innovative Approaches in English Learning: AI Smart Chatbots As A Model. *Journal of Education College Wasit University*, *57*(2), 511–530.

Arif, M., Ismail, A., Aqib, M., Shaoan, M. R., Ali, W., & Okafor, M. U. (2025). The impact of AI-driven tools on foreign students' Chinese language acquisition: A case study at Southwest University. *Language, Technology, and Social Media*, *3*(1), 150–168. DOI: 10.70211/ltsm.v3i1.165

Asratyan, Z. D. (2024). Text, Discourse, Dicteme, Language Personality as Basic Concepts of Text Linguistics. *RUDN Journal of Language Studies. Semiotics and Semantics, 15*(1), 138–151.

Ateek, M. (2024). PARTICIPATORY TRANSLANGUAGING AS A PEDAGOGY FOR LANGUAGE LEARNERS IN CHALLENGING CIRCUMSTANCES: A DRIVE TO SOCIAL JUSTICE. *European Journal of Applied Linguistics & TEFL, 13*(1).

Babu, C. S., & Akshara, P. M. (2024). Revolutionizing conversational AI: unleashing the power of ChatGPT-Based applications in generative AI and natural language processing. In *Advanced applications of generative AI and natural language processing models* (pp. 228–248). IGI Global.

Basit, A., Azeemi, A. H., & Raza, A. A. (2024, August). Challenges in Urdu Machine Translation. In *Proceedings of the The Seventh Workshop on Technologies for Machine Translation of Low-Resource Languages (LoResMT 2024)* (pp. 44-49). DOI: 10.18653/v1/2024.loresmt-1.4

Bayraktar-Özer, Ö. (2024). Child language brokering in Turkey: Non-professional interpreting experiences from Kurdish, Arab, and Pomak ethnic minorities. *Journal of Multilingual and Multicultural Development*, •••, 1–15. DOI: 10.1080/01434632.2024.2351090

Bellas, F., Naya-Varela, M., Mallo, A., & Paz-Lopez, A. (2024). Education in the AI era: A long-term classroom technology based on intelligent robotics. *Humanities & Social Sciences Communications, 11*(1), 1–20. DOI: 10.1057/s41599-024-03953-y

Bengsch, G. (2024). Redefining traditional pedagogy: The integration of machine learning in the contemporary language education classroom. In *AI in Language Teaching, Learning, and Assessment* (pp. 195-221). IGI Global.

Bhardwaj, A., Sharma, M., Kumar, S., Sharma, S., & Sharma, P. C. (2024). Transforming pediatric speech and language disorder diagnosis and therapy: The evolving role of artificial intelligence. *Health Sciences Review (Oxford, England), 12*, 100188. DOI: 10.1016/j.hsr.2024.100188

Bittencourt, I. I., Chalco, G., Santos, J., Fernandes, S., Silva, J., Batista, N., Hutz, C., & Isotani, S. (2024). Positive artificial intelligence in education (P-AIED): A roadmap. *International Journal of Artificial Intelligence in Education, 34*(3), 732–792. DOI: 10.1007/s40593-023-00357-y

Bonn, J., Flanigan, J., Hajic, J., Jindal, I., Li, Y., & Xue, N. (2024, May). Meaning Representations for Natural Languages: Design, Models and Applications. In *Proceedings of the 2024 Joint International Conference on Computational Linguistics, Language Resources and Evaluation (LREC-COLING 2024): Tutorial Summaries* (pp. 13-18).

Casheekar, A., Lahiri, A., Rath, K., Prabhakar, K. S., & Srinivasan, K. (2024). A contemporary review on chatbots, AI-powered virtual conversational agents, ChatGPT: Applications, open challenges and future research directions. *Computer Science Review*, *52*, 100632. DOI: 10.1016/j.cosrev.2024.100632

Casheekar, A., Lahiri, A., Rath, K., Prabhakar, K. S., & Srinivasan, K. (2024). A contemporary review on chatbots, AI-powered virtual conversational agents, ChatGPT: Applications, open challenges and future research directions. *Computer Science Review*, *52*, 100632. DOI: 10.1016/j.cosrev.2024.100632

Chen, P., & Alias, S. B. (2024, September). Opportunities and Challenges in the Cultivation of Software Development Professionals in the Context of Large Language Models. In *Proceedings of the 2024 International Symposium on Artificial Intelligence for Education* (pp. 259-267). DOI: 10.1145/3700297.3700342

Chinnaiyan, B., Balasubaramanian, S., Jeyabalu, M., & Warrier, G. S. (2025). AI Applications–Computer Vision and Natural Language Processing. *Model Optimization Methods for Efficient and Edge AI: Federated Learning Architectures, Frameworks and Applications*, 25-41.

Costa, A. R., Vasconcelos, S. V., & Balula, A. (2025). Artificial Intelligence and Language Learning: Methods, Tools, and Challenges. In *Integrating Artificial Intelligence in Education: Enhancing Teaching Practices for Future Learning* (pp. 267-286). IGI Global.

Davoodi, A. (2024). Crafting innovative paths in non-linear professional learning for bilingual education: The role of connectivism in the age of AI. *Professional Development in Education*, •••, 1–17.

Davoodi, A. (2024). EQUAL AI: A Framework for Enhancing Equity, Quality, Understanding and Accessibility in Liberal Arts through AI for Multilingual Learners. *Language, Technology, and Social Media*, *2*(2), 178–203. DOI: 10.70211/ltsm.v2i2.139

Feng, L. (2025). Investigating the Effects of Artificial Intelligence-Assisted Language Learning Strategies on Cognitive Load and Learning Outcomes: A Comparative Study. *Journal of Educational Computing Research*, *62*(8), 1961–1994. DOI: 10.1177/07356331241268349

Feng, R., Brennan, K. A., Azizi, Z., Goyal, J., Deb, B., Chang, H. J., & Narayan, S. M. (2024). Engineering of Generative Artificial Intelligence and Natural Language Processing Models to Accurately Identify Arrhythmia Recurrence. *Circulation: Arrhythmia and Electrophysiology*, •••, e013023.

Filippetti, S., Sbardella, T., & Montanucci, G. (2024, November). AI-Driven Approaches to L2 Learning: Technology Applications and Perspectives. In *Conference Proceedings. Innovation in Language Learning 2024.*

Filippova, O. V. (2024). The Development of a Secondary Linguistic Personality as a Factor in the Successful Education of Foreign Students at a Russian University. *Integra Educativa, 28*(4), 641–655. DOI: 10.15507/1991-9468.117.028.202404.641-655

Fuller, , K., Morbitzer, K. A., Zeeman, J. M., M. Persky, A., C. Savage, A., & McLaughlin, J. E. (. (2024). Exploring the use of ChatGPT to analyze student course evaluation comments. *BMC Medical Education, 24*(1), 423. DOI: 10.1186/s12909-024-05316-2

Gaballo, V. (2024, November). Revolutionizing language teaching: AI in oral language assessment. In *Conference Proceedings. Innovation in Language Learning 2024.*

Gatsiou, C., Fragkou, E., Hatzidaki, A., & Korda, D. (2024). Artificial Intelligence (AI) in Translation and Interpreting: Exploring AI's Potential in Translation and Interpreting Profession and Pedagogy in the Medical Context and its Ethical Implications

Ghosh, S. (2025). Developing artificial intelligence (AI) capabilities for data-driven business model innovation: Roles of organizational adaptability and leadership. *Journal of Engineering and Technology Management, 75*, 101851. DOI: 10.1016/j.jengtecman.2024.101851

Gu, X., Chen, S., Peng, Y., & Qin, Y. (2024). One mind, two languages: researching language and cognition in bilinguals The Study of Bilingual Language Processing: by Nan Jiang, Oxford, Oxford University Press, 2023, ix+ 273 pp.,£ 35.00 (paperback), ISBN 9780198852513.

Hashmi, E., Yayilgan, S. Y., Hameed, I. A., Yamin, M. M., Ullah, M., & Abomhara, M. (2024). Enhancing multilingual hate speech detection: From language-specific insights to cross-linguistic integration. *IEEE Access : Practical Innovations, Open Solutions, 12*, 121507–121537. DOI: 10.1109/ACCESS.2024.3452987

Hou, R., Fütterer, T., Bühler, B., Bozkir, E., Gerjets, P., Trautwein, U., & Kasneci, E. (2024, July). Automated assessment of encouragement and warmth in classrooms leveraging multimodal emotional features and ChatGPT. In *International Conference on Artificial Intelligence in Education* (pp. 60-74). Cham: Springer Nature Switzerland. DOI: 10.1007/978-3-031-64302-6_5

Huertas-Abril, C. A., & Hà, T. A. (2025). Opportunities and challenges of using artificial intelligence in language education: Perspectives from Vietnam. *Computer-Assisted Language Learning in the Global South*, 81-98.

Hutahaean, B., Telaumbanua, S., Tamba, L., Hutabarat, R. G. N., & Sumani, S. (2024). Analysis of Innovative and Adaptive Higher Education Curriculum Development to Education 5.0 Based Challenges in Indonesia. *International Journal of Learning. Teaching and Educational Research*, *23*(4), 76–98.

Incelli, E. (2025). Exploring the Future of Corpus LInguistics: Innovations in AI and Social Impact. *International Journal of Mass Communication*, *3*, 1–10. DOI: 10.6000/2818-3401.2025.03.01

Khan, N. D., Khan, J. A., Li, J., Ullah, T., & Zhao, Q. (2025). Leveraging Large Language Model ChatGPT for enhanced understanding of end-user emotions in social media feedbacks. *Expert Systems with Applications*, *261*, 125524. DOI: 10.1016/j.eswa.2024.125524

Khlaif, Z. N., Ayyoub, A., Hamamra, B., Bensalem, E., Mitwally, M. A., Ayyoub, A., Hattab, M. K., & Shadid, F. (2024). University teachers' views on the adoption and integration of generative AI tools for student assessment in higher education. *Education Sciences*, *14*(10), 1090. DOI: 10.3390/educsci14101090

Kooli, C., & Yusuf, N. (2024). Transforming educational assessment: Insights into the use of ChatGPT and large language models in grading. *International Journal of Human-Computer Interaction*, •••, 1–12. DOI: 10.1080/10447318.2024.2338330

Kremer, M., & Pinto, S. (2025). Exploring the interconnectedness between English-medium instruction and intercultural competence: A systematic literature review. *International Journal of Instruction*, *18*(1), 193–214. DOI: 10.29333/iji.2025.18111a

Kujundziski, A. P., & Bojadjiev, J. (2025). Artificial Intelligence in Education: Transforming Learning Landscapes. In *Reimagining Intelligent Computer-Assisted Language Education* (pp. 1-54). IGI Global.

Kumar, A., & Nagar, D. K. (2024). AI-Based Language Translation and Interpretation Services: Improving Accessibility for Visually Impaired Students. As the editors of Transforming Learning. *Power and Education*, •••, 178.

Kushnina, L. V., Kudritskaya, M. I., & Bermukhambetova, A. A. (2024). Foreign Language Student Linguistic Personality as a Vector for the Professional Bilingualism. *Вестник Нижневартовского государственного университета*, (3), 65-76.

Lastrucci, A., Wandael, Y., Ricci, R., Maccioni, G., & Giansanti, D. (2024). The Integration of Deep Learning in Radiotherapy: Exploring Challenges, Opportunities, and Future Directions through an Umbrella Review. *Diagnostics (Basel)*, *14*(9), 939. DOI: 10.3390/diagnostics14090939

Lee, J. S., & Hudson, J. (2024). Digital education in teaching English as an international language. In *The Routledge Handbook of Teaching English as an International Language* (pp. 247–264). Routledge. DOI: 10.4324/9781003203261-21

Lewington, A., Vittalam, A., Singh, A., Uppuluri, A., Ashok, A., Athmaram, A. M., . . . Liu, Y. (2024). Creating a Cooperative AI Policymaking Platform through Open Source Collaboration. *arXiv preprint arXiv:2412.06936*.

Li, B., Lowell, V. L., Wang, C., & Li, X. (2024). A systematic review of the first year of publications on ChatGPT and language education: Examining research on ChatGPT's use in language learning and teaching. *Computers and Education: Artificial Intelligence*, 100266.

Li, L., Ma, Z., Fan, L., Lee, S., Yu, H., & Hemphill, L. (2024). ChatGPT in education: A discourse analysis of worries and concerns on social media. *Education and Information Technologies*, *29*(9), 10729–10762. DOI: 10.1007/s10639-023-12256-9

Li, Z., Li, J. Z., Zhang, X., & Reynolds, B. L. (2024). Mastery of Listening and Reading Vocabulary Levels in Relation to CEFR: Insights into Student Admissions and English as a Medium of Instruction. *Languages (Basel, Switzerland)*, *9*(7), 239. DOI: 10.3390/languages9070239

Liang, M. Y. (2024). Transcreation on social media through translingual English. *Asian Englishes*, •••, 1–18.

Lijie, D. (2024). A Review of Research in Translation Technology Based on Citespace. *International Journal of Education and Humanities*, *4*(2), 137–146. DOI: 10.58557/(ijeh).v4i2.222

Lyanda, J. N., Owidi, S. O., & Simiyu, A. M. (2024). Rethinking Higher Education Teaching and Assessment In-Line with AI Innovations: A Systematic Review and Meta-Analysis. *African Journal of Empirical Research*, *5*(3), 325–335. DOI: 10.51867/ajernet.5.3.30

Maher, B., Polezzi, L., & Wilson, R. (2024). *The Routledge Handbook of Translation and Migration*. DOI: 10.4324/9781003287797

Malyuga, E. N. (2024). *The Language of Corporate Communication: Functional, Pragmatic and Cultural Dimensions*. Springer Nature. DOI: 10.1007/978-3-031-58905-8

Meadows, E. (2024). *Exploring Classroom Teachers' Experiences of PD About Emergent Bilinguals: An Interpretative Phenomenological Analysis* (Doctoral dissertation, George Mason University).

Meyer, J., Jansen, T., Schiller, R., Liebenow, L. W., Steinbach, M., Horbach, A., & Fleckenstein, J. (2024). Using LLMs to bring evidence-based feedback into the classroom: AI-generated feedback increases secondary students' text revision, motivation, and positive emotions. *Computers and Education: Artificial Intelligence*, *6*, 100199. DOI: 10.1016/j.caeai.2023.100199

Mohamed, Y. A., Khanan, A., Bashir, M., Mohamed, A. H. H., Adiel, M. A., & Elsadig, M. A. (2024). The impact of artificial intelligence on language translation: A review. *IEEE Access : Practical Innovations, Open Solutions*, *12*, 25553–25579. DOI: 10.1109/ACCESS.2024.3366802

Mohanta, S. K., Mohapatra, A. G., Mohanty, A., & Nayak, S. (2024). Deep Learning is a State-of-the-Art Approach to Artificial Intelligence. In *Deep Learning Concepts in Operations Research* (pp. 27–43). Auerbach Publications. DOI: 10.1201/9781003433309-3

Mohanty, R. N., Thomas, A., & Kori, A. (2024). Next-Generation Innovative Teaching Ecosystems for Futuristic Management Education. In *Global Higher Education Practices in Times of Crisis: Questions for Sustainability and Digitalization* (pp. 5-28). Emerald Publishing Limited. DOI: 10.1108/978-1-83797-052-020241002

Muthmainnah, M., Al Yakin, A., Seraj, P. M. I., Darmawati, B., Elngar, A. A., & Obaid, A. J. (2024, April). Integrating Robot-Based Resources to Foster Computational Thinking and Communication Skills in EFL Education: A Path Towards Sustainable Development. In *International Conference on Sustainable Development through Machine Learning, AI and IoT* (pp. 70-80). Cham: Springer Nature Switzerland.

Neumann, A. T., Yin, Y., Sowe, S., Decker, S., & Jarke, M. (2024). An LLM-Driven Chatbot in Higher Education for Databases and Information Systems. *IEEE Transactions on Education*.

Obaid, A. J., Bhushan, B., & Rajest, S. S. (Eds.). (2023). *Advanced applications of generative AI and natural language processing models*. IGI Global. DOI: 10.4018/979-8-3693-0502-7

Orosoo, M., Goswami, I., Alphonse, F. R., Fatma, G., Rengarajan, M., & Bala, B. K. (2024, March). Enhancing Natural Language Processing in Multilingual Chatbots for Cross-Cultural Communication. In *2024 5th International Conference on Intelligent Communication Technologies and Virtual Mobile Networks (ICICV)* (pp. 127-133). IEEE. DOI: 10.1109/ICICV62344.2024.00027

Pan, K., Zhang, X., & Chen, L. (2024). Research on the training and application methods of a lightweight agricultural domain-specific large language model supporting Mandarin Chinese and Uyghur. *Applied Sciences (Basel, Switzerland)*, *14*(13), 5764. DOI: 10.3390/app14135764

Pawlicka, A., Pawlicki, M., Kozik, R., Andrychowicz-Trojanowska, A., & Choraś, M. (2024). AI vs linguistic-based human judgement: Bridging the gap in pursuit of truth for fake news detection. *Information Sciences*, *679*, 121097. DOI: 10.1016/j.ins.2024.121097

Peng, H., & Zhou, P. (2024). Evolution and Development of Artificial Intelligence Interpretation Technology in the Age of Large-scale Language Models. *Journal of Electrical Systems*, *20*(2), 1988–1996. DOI: 10.52783/jes.1646

Pennycook, A. (2010). *Language as a local practice*. Routledge. DOI: 10.4324/9780203846223

Prieto Ramos, F. (2024). Revisiting translator competence in the age of artificial intelligence: The case of legal and institutional translation. *The Interpreter and Translator Trainer*, *18*(2), 148–173. DOI: 10.1080/1750399X.2024.2344942

Priya, S. S., Manivannan, D., Kujani, T., & Bharathi, S. (2024, August). Cross-Language Connect: A Chat App for Smooth Multilingual Communication. In *2024 Second International Conference on Intelligent Cyber Physical Systems and Internet of Things (ICoICI)* (pp. 159-164). IEEE. DOI: 10.1109/ICoICI62503.2024.10696715

Radhika, A., Bhasin, N. K., Sabareesh, R., Raju, Y. R., Satyanarayana, K. N. V., & Raj, I. I. (2024, March). Optimization of Natural Language Processing Models for Multilingual Legal Document Analysis. In *2024 Third International Conference on Intelligent Techniques in Control, Optimization and Signal Processing (INCOS)* (pp. 1-6). IEEE. DOI: 10.1109/INCOS59338.2024.10527598

Rajak, L., Chauhan, S., & Bara, S. (2024). Transforming English Pedagogy with Artificial Intelligence: Enroute to Enhanced Language Learning. In *Artificial Intelligence: A Multidisciplinary Approach towards Teaching and Learning* (pp. 216-241). Bentham Science Publishers.

Razem, R. J. (2024). Codeswitching Among Arabic-English Bilingual Children: An Autoethnographic Case Study in Dubai. *International Journal of Information Technology and Language Studies*, *8*(2).

Safder, I., Abu Bakar, M., Zaman, F., Waheed, H., Aljohani, N. R., Nawaz, R., & Hassan, S. U. (2024). Transforming language translation: A deep learning approach to Urdu–English translation. *Journal of Ambient Intelligence and Humanized Computing*, *15*(10), 3651–3662. DOI: 10.1007/s12652-024-04839-2

Samala, A. D., Rawas, S., Wang, T., Reed, J. M., Kim, J., Howard, N. J., & Ertz, M. (2024). Unveiling the landscape of generative artificial intelligence in education: A comprehensive taxonomy of applications, challenges, and future prospects. *Education and Information Technologies*, •••, 1–40.

Samantray, K., İZGİ, F. D., Ocampo, M. B., Dehghan, M., Mohammadpour, S., Siriphaprapagon, Y., ... & Babu, S. D. (2024). *The Power of Words in AI-Driven World: Exploring the Interplay of Language, Culture, and Communication*. SKET-SAMEDIA.

Savela, N., Pellert, M., Latikka, R., Bergdahl, J., Garcia, D., & Oksanen, A. (2025). Affective, cognitive, and contextual cues in Reddit posts on artificial intelligence. *Journal of Computational Social Science*, *8*(1), 6. DOI: 10.1007/s42001-024-00335-x

Selvam, D. C., Devarajan, Y., & Raja, T. (2025). Exploring the potential of artificial intelligence in nuclear waste management: Applications, challenges, and future directions. *Nuclear Engineering and Design*, *431*, 113719. DOI: 10.1016/j.nucengdes.2024.113719

Shelestova, T. Y., Kalizhanova, A. N., & Bedelbayeva, M. V. (2024). Personality-based intercultural awareness in undergraduate translation students via postcrossing. *Cogent Arts & Humanities*, *11*(1), 2313839. DOI: 10.1080/23311983.2024.2313839

Singh, M., Kumar, R., & Chana, I. (2021). Machine translation systems for Indian languages: Review of modelling techniques, challenges, open issues and future research directions. *Archives of Computational Methods in Engineering*, *28*(4), 2165–2193. DOI: 10.1007/s11831-020-09449-7

Solsona-Puig, J., Muñoz-Muñoz, E., & Rodriguez-Valls, F. (2024). Reimaging Bilingual Education in California: A Critical Analysis of Bilingual Teacher Performance Expectations (BTPE). *Journal of Latinos and Education*, •••, 1–13.

Soon, G. Y., Abdullah, N. A. C. B., Suyan, Z., & Yiming, C. (2024). Integrating AI Chatbots in ESL and CFL Instruction: Revolutionizing Language Learning with Artificial Intelligence. *LatIA*, *2*, 23–23. DOI: 10.62486/latia202423

Ssemugabi, S. (2025). The Role of AI in Modern Language Translation and Its Societal Applications: A Systematic Literature Review. In *Southern African Conference for Artificial Intelligence Research* (pp. 390-404). Springer, Cham. DOI: 10.1007/978-3-031-78255-8_23

Strasser, T. (2023). Narrow AI-powered visualization facilitation tools in foreign language learning: a visual approach promoting equal opportunities in foreign language grammar teaching. In *Facilitating Visual Socialities: Processes, Complications and Ethical Practices* (pp. 85–98). Springer International Publishing. DOI: 10.1007/978-3-031-25259-4_5

Su, J., Guo, K., Chen, X., & Chu, S. K. W. (2024). Teaching artificial intelligence in K–12 classrooms: A scoping review. *Interactive Learning Environments*, *32*(9), 5207–5226. DOI: 10.1080/10494820.2023.2212706

Su, J., & Yang, W. (2024). Artificial Intelligence (AI) literacy in early childhood education: An intervention study in Hong Kong. *Interactive Learning Environments*, *32*(9), 5494–5508. DOI: 10.1080/10494820.2023.2217864

Suhail, F., Adel, M., Al-Emran, M., & AlQudah, A. A. (2024). Are students ready for robots in higher education? Examining the adoption of robots by integrating UTAUT2 and TTF using a hybrid SEM-ANN approach. *Technology in Society*, *77*, 102524. DOI: 10.1016/j.techsoc.2024.102524

Suriano, R., Plebe, A., Acciai, A., & Fabio, R. A. (2025). Student interaction with ChatGPT can promote complex critical thinking skills. *Learning and Instruction*, *95*, 102011. DOI: 10.1016/j.learninstruc.2024.102011

Syamkumar, A., Tseng, N., Barron, K., Yang, S., Karumbaiah, S., Uppal, R., & Hu, J. (2024). Improving Bilingual Capabilities of Language Models to Support Diverse Linguistic Practices in Education. *arXiv preprint arXiv:2411.04308*.

Tangsakul, S., & Poonpon, K. (2024). Aligning Academic Reading Tests to the Common European Framework of Reference for Languages (CEFR). *Reflections: The SoL Journal*, *31*(2), 614–638. DOI: 10.61508/refl.v31i2.275057

Tian, X. (2024). Personalized translator training in the era of digital intelligence: Opportunities, challenges, and prospects. *Heliyon*, *10*(20), e39354. DOI: 10.1016/j.heliyon.2024.e39354

Trinh, E., de Oliveira, L. C., & Selvi, A. F. (Eds.). (2024). *Multilingual Leadership in TESOL*. Taylor & Francis. DOI: 10.4324/9781003396079

Ul Hassan, M. N., Yu, Z., Wang, J., Li, Y., Gao, S., Yang, S., & Mao, C. (2024). LKMT: Linguistics Knowledge-Driven Multi-Task Neural Machine Translation for Urdu and English. *Computers, Materials & Continua*, *81*(1), 951–969. DOI: 10.32604/cmc.2024.054673

Ulutaş, N. K., Durmaz, M. E., Elbuğa, N., Sezgin, S., Kaya, K., & İsmailoğulları, B. (2025). The Use of Augmented Reality (AR), Virtual Reality (VR), and Artificial Intelligence (AI) in Language Education: A Systematic Literature Review. *Reimagining Intelligent Computer-Assisted Language Education*, 401-430.

Velander, J., Taiye, M. A., Otero, N., & Milrad, M. (2024). Artificial Intelligence in K-12 Education: Eliciting and reflecting on Swedish teachers' understanding of AI and its implications for teaching & learning. *Education and Information Technologies*, *29*(4), 4085–4105. DOI: 10.1007/s10639-023-11990-4

Wang, Y., Deng, Y., Wang, G., Li, T., Xiao, H., & Zhang, Y. (2025). The fluency-based semantic network of LLMs differs from humans. *Computers in Human Behavior: Artificial Humans*, *3*, 100103. DOI: 10.1016/j.chbah.2024.100103

Wei, J. (2025). Philosophical Examination of Conflict and Integration: English Education Policies and Cultural Values in the Age of Globalization. *Cultura. International Journal of Philosophy of Culture and Axiology*, *22*(1).

Wiesinger, M. (2024). ChatGPT and its Implications for EFL Learning: Issues with AI-driven language systems in undergraduate language degree programmes. *New Pathways in Teaching English*, *4*, 187–210.

Wu, D., Chen, M., Chen, X., & Liu, X. (2024). Analyzing K-12 AI education: A large language model study of classroom instruction on learning theories, pedagogy, tools, and AI literacy. *Computers and Education: Artificial Intelligence*, *7*, 100295. DOI: 10.1016/j.caeai.2024.100295

Wu, Y. (2024). Exploring the Influence of Large Language Models (LLMs) on English Learners and their Teachers. *Journal of Education. Humanities and Social Sciences*, *27*, 530–535.

Wu, Y., Albornoz-De Luise, R. S., & Arevalillo-Herráez, M. (2025). On improving conversational interfaces in educational systems. *Computer Speech & Language*, *89*, 101693. DOI: 10.1016/j.csl.2024.101693

Xia, Y., Shin, S. Y., & Kim, J. C. (2024). Cross-cultural intelligent language learning system (cils): Leveraging ai to facilitate language learning strategies in cross-cultural communication. *Applied Sciences (Basel, Switzerland)*, *14*(13), 5651. DOI: 10.3390/app14135651

Yuan, L., & Liu, X. (2025). The effect of artificial intelligence tools on EFL learners' engagement, enjoyment, and motivation. *Computers in Human Behavior, 162*, 108474. DOI: 10.1016/j.chb.2024.108474

Zhang, R., Du, H., Liu, Y., Niyato, D., Kang, J., Sun, S., Shen, X., & Poor, H. V. (2024). Interactive AI with retrieval-augmented generation for next generation networking. *IEEE Network*, *38*(6), 414–424. DOI: 10.1109/MNET.2024.3401159

Zhang, Z., Zhou, Y., Li, C., Zhao, B., Liu, X., & Zhai, G. (2024). Quality assessment in the era of large models: A survey. *arXiv preprint arXiv:2409.00031.*

Zhou, Y., Zhang, M., Jiang, Y. H., Liu, N., & Jiang, B. (2024, June). A Study on Educational Data Analysis and Personalized Feedback Report Generation Based on Tags and ChatGPT. In *Conference Proceedings of the 28th Global Chinese Conference on Computers in Education (GCCCE 2024). Chongqing, China: Global Chinese Conference on Computers in Education* (pp. 108-115).

Zhui, L., Yhap, N., Liping, L., Zhengjie, W., Zhonghao, X., Xiaoshu, Y., Hong, C., Xuexiu, L., & Wei, R. (2024). Impact of large language models on medical education and teaching adaptations. *JMIR Medical Informatics*, *12*(1), e55933. DOI: 10.2196/55933

Chapter 8

The Impact of AI-Enhanced Gamification on Vocabulary Learning in a Foreign Language Context

Serdar Hoşer
https://orcid.org/0009-0003-7190-2861
Istanbul Medeniyet University, Turkey

Selami Aydin
https://orcid.org/0000-0003-1614-874X
Istanbul Medeniyet University, Turkey

ABSTRACT

Previous studies have shown that the lack of vocabulary is one of the primary challenges learners face in the four basic skills. One solution to this problem is the integration of AI-supported gamification, which has garnered attention in EFL teaching and learning. However, while EFL learners have utilized online platforms, no studies have been conducted on the effects of AI-enhanced gamification on vocabulary learning. This study aims to explore the impact of AI-enhanced gamification on vocabulary learning, examine the vocabulary retention levels of EFL learners, and compare traditional gamification of vocabulary with AI-enhanced gamification of vocabulary. In this quasi-experimental study, data were collected from 32 secondary school students through a background questionnaire and a vocabulary test. The findings revealed that AI had a significant impact on vocabulary learning, particularly in terms of vocabulary retention levels.

DOI: 10.4018/979-8-3373-0275-1.ch008

INTRODUCTION

For several reasons, vocabulary plays a significant role in the context of EFL learning. First, it has the fundamental function of transmitting meaningful messages between interlocutors. Wilkins (1972) states that ''*Without grammar, very little can be conveyed; without vocabulary, nothing can be conveyed.*'' (Wilkins, 1972, p.111). One-word utterances of babies referring to objects or people around them are enough for them to express themselves (Hutauruk, 2015). Second, vocabulary learning is paramount for improving reading skills development in the EFL context (Brooks et al., 2021). It is necessary for reading comprehension, interpreting, and contextualizing new information (Mauidloh et al., 2024). It is challenging to understand written materials without knowing the meanings of the glossary terms. The more vocabulary is learned, the easier, the faster, and more effectively reading skills can be improved. Third, vocabulary learning helps us improve our listening; thus, it plays a significant role in listening comprehension (Mecartty, 2000). Learning vocabulary is a crucial requirement for learners to decode the sounds of the language and understand its meaning. The powerful vocabulary capacity and retention supports and activates effective listening skills (Asrida et al., 2024). Finally, vocabulary is the crucial building block for EFL learners to develop productive modalities, including writing and speaking skills (Kılıç, 2019). From this perspective, gamification may play a significant role in vocabulary learning among EFL learners.

As mentioned above, gamification is of great importance in terms of learning vocabulary for several reasons. First, gamification captures learners' attention and boosts their active participation while learning new words (Ahmed et al., 2022). It helps students avoid negative thoughts and prejudices associated with foreign language learning, as well as difficulties with pronunciation and spelling. In contrast, gamification fosters positive attitudes towards learning vocabulary (Thurairasu, 2022). Second, gamification enables learners to review words they have learned at their convenience at home (Waluyo & Bucol, 2021). Thus, gamification contributes to long-term vocabulary retention and permanent learning, provides regular revision of words, and enhances learning opportunities (Quynh, 2022). Next, learners can utilize gamification to transform monotonous and traditional vocabulary learning into engaging and enjoyable learning strategies (Cizrelioğlu & Aydin, 2025; Waer, 2021). In addition, gamification enhances learners' vocabulary self-efficacy (Cancino & Viguera, 2024). Considering the abovementioned reasons why gamification is crucial for learning vocabulary in the EFL context, AI applications may support its efficiency.

AI-enhanced gamification may also be important for learning vocabulary for several reasons. First, AI-supported gamification may foster active and participatory learning opportunities that adapt to personal development, making the vocabulary learning process more enjoyable and effective (Sumakul et al., 2022). It addresses the needs of Generation Z learners while they learn vocabulary (Saptiany et al., 2024). The dynamic, motivating, and appealing features of gamification may match the adjustability of AI. Second, by using AI algorithms, AI systems may reveal students' hidden capabilities, suggesting specialized challenges and opportunities to make the most of vocabulary retention (Aydın & Zeinolabedini, 2024); Zhai & Wibowo, 2023). AI-enhanced gamification may transform vocabulary learning into an active, efficient, and educational experience for learners (Abbas et al., 2023). In other words, the feeling of success and improvement may encourage learners to maintain learning vocabulary. Third, applying AI may encourage learners to learn more words daily by considerably increasing their motivation levels (Li, 2021). The more they get ahead, the easier it may be for them to focus on learning new words, and their intrinsic motivation will likely increase. Finally, AI-enhanced gamification of vocabulary may address learners' personal needs and desires related to EFL learning (Abbas et al., 2023). It also addresses to different learning styles, which is indispensable for vocabulary learning in language education (Wei-Xun & Jia-Ying, 2024). In this way, everyone may show progress on their side. Individualized learning opportunities provided by AI may support learners' vocabulary acquisition (Tapalova & Zhiyenbayeva, 2022). To conclude, thanks to innovations in AI and technology, it is now possible for AI-supported gamification in vocabulary learning to flourish and transform the way people learn vocabulary in the EFL context.

Vocabulary has been identified as one of the biggest challenges for EFL learners (Meara, 1980). Unlike syntax and phonology, vocabulary does not have established norms that students can adhere to as they learn and expand their vocabulary. In other words, while learning L2 vocabulary, it is unclear what rules to follow or which words to master first (Alqahtani, 2015). More specifically, several reasons contribute to the challenges of vocabulary learning for learners in the EFL context. First, learning the meaning of new vocabulary items is a heavy burden on students. Students often encounter difficulties in understanding the meanings of new words, including terminological or technical terms, multiple-meaning words, compound words, homophones, false friends, and culture-specific words (Altyari, 2017). Oxford (1990)notes that vocabulary is probably the most substantial and uncontrollable component in language learning, whether in a native or foreign language context, due to its thousands of diverse definitions and uses. Second, some factors that make learning vocabulary more challenging for learners include pronunciation, spelling, length and complexity, grammar, range, connotation, and idiomaticity (Thornbury, 2002). Words with identical forms can cause confusion in both spelling and pronunciation among learners (Schmitt, 2000). In addition, the literal correspondents of idioms, their figurative meanings, and their elimination from the conversation may cause learners to abstain from using them (Ahmed et al., 2022). Third, learners struggle to practice the words they have learned, memorize them, and infer their meaning from context. Since vocabulary reflects the need to interact with others (Neuman & Dwyer, 2009), learners require sufficient opportunities to practice it accurately, fluently, and efficiently in productive modalities. Furthermore, difficulties in memorizing vocabulary may stem from not knowing enough mnemonics or memory strategies. Not being able to predict the meaning of words from contextual clues is another challenge for EFL learners while learning vocabulary (Afzal, 2019). Last but not least, in addition to the various factors affecting vocabulary learning, it is beneficial to mention gamified vocabulary learning and related issues in the EFL context.

AI-supported gamification may strengthen vocabulary learning in the EFL context for several reasons. First, chatbots equipped with vocabulary aids, such as dictionaries, visuals, translation tools, and concordances, can provide learners with synonym-rich input, long-term memory support, contextual clues, and practice opportunities (Alsadoon, 2021). The visual support may be useful for visual learners, making it easier to recall word meanings from memory (Sadeghi & Farzizadeh, 2013). Second, automatic evaluation systems in the EFL context may help learners' pronunciation difficulties related to vocabulary learning (Ahn & Lee, 2016). Pronunciation practice supported by AI may enable words to be stored in long-term memory (Kazu & Kuvvetli, 2023). Third, intelligent VR tools in the EFL context may improve vocabulary learning and retention for learners (Lai & Chen, 2023). Furthermore, they benefit from speech recognition in analyzing learners' speech input and output during conversations, which can provide support and feedback to correct errors and help them evaluate their own performance (Heift & Schulze, 2007). Next, AI-supported translation applications can enable learners to easily search definitions, spellings, and pronunciations of words, sentences, and texts. Text-to-speech tools may also be beneficial for pronunciation and intonation (Ghafar et al., 2023). AI tools can automatically identify language expressions to make morphological analyses and suggest recommendations for vocabulary improvement (Liu et al., 2019). Moreover, AI-fueled toys or robots may teach students vocabulary and enable them to participate enthusiastically in role-play, storytelling, and game-based activities (Binh & Chau, 2023). Utilizing gamification components, such as quizzes, marathons, and competitions, can enhance engagement and capture students' interest. A software application can help students learn sentence formation, collocations, and multi-word structures necessary to create accurate, error-free sentences (Ghafar et al., 2023). AI tools can effectively enhance students' vocabulary capacity by promptly addressing their learning needs. However, research on the relationship between vocabulary learning and AI-enhanced gamification is limited, making it difficult to draw conclusions, especially in the Turkish EFL context, as illustrated below. Before presenting the review of the literature, a theoretical framework is established.

THEORETICAL BACKGROUND

Ghazal (2007) defines *vocabulary* as the building block of a language because it labels things, guides human actions, and expresses opinions without which people cannot interact with others effectively and correctly. Several approaches, theories, hypotheses, and models may be related to EFL *vocabulary*. First, *the Lexical Approach* suggests the centrality of vocabulary to language structure and focuses chiefly on the role of multi-word units, in other words, chunks and collocations (Lewis, 1993). This approach mainly focuses on *lexical units* rather than grammar rules. Second, *The Comprehensible Output Hypothesis* (Swain, 1985) suggests that productive modalities, such as writing and speaking, can support vocabulary learning. When learned words are used in learners' output, it reinforces the understanding and retention of vocabulary. Third, Krashen's (1985) Input Hypothesis suggests that exposure to a wide variety of words in meaningful contexts, where comprehensible input is a crucial element for efficient vocabulary learning (Krashen, 1989). Next, Schmidt's (1990) *Noticing Hypothesis* suggests that learners should be consciously aware of new words in the input to learn them efficiently. When words are noticed in a language material, it becomes easier for learners to connect them to their existing schemata. After that, *Frequency-based theories* underline the significance of exposing language learners to the most commonly used vocabulary. Focusing on high-frequency words can be beneficial for *vocabulary* and other language skills. Lastly, the Incidental Learning Hypothesis (Nagy, Herman, & Anderson, 1985) suggests that vocabulary is learned through repeated exposure in different contexts as a by-product, without intending to learn while engaging in language activities (Xu, 2010).

The term *gamification* is defined by Sheldon (2020) as the application of game components to non-game activities. Several theories and hypotheses are related to *gamification of vocabulary learning* in the EFL context. First, Laufer and Hulstijn's (2001) *Involvement Load Hypothesis* states that the efficiency of a task in supporting *vocabulary* learning is influenced by the task-induced involvement load, which is the total of significance degrees of the features having motivational and cognitive qualities: *need* (a learner's desire to finish doing the activity), *search* (a learner's effort to look up a vocabulary's meaning, use), and *evaluation* (a learner's comparison of *vocabulary* with its meaning and use, or constructing new contexts). Second, Long's (1981) *Interaction Hypothesis* suggests designing interactive and communicative language experiences for learners. For example, games that encourage interaction and communication for the purpose of learning contribute to vocabulary acquisition. Swain's (2000) notion of *collaborative dialogue* can be applied in collaborative vocabulary games, such as role-plays, to reinforce and practice vocabulary. Furthermore, Verga & Kotz's (2017) *analysis of interactions* as an attentional devi, along with studies on competition, suggests that interaction, collaboration, and competition elements pave the way for successful learning. Next, in the *Zone of Proximal Development*, Vygotsky underlines the significance of challenging learners at a level just beyond their current capabilities (Vygotsky, 1980). *Gamification* can be organized to gradually enhance the difficulty levels, keeping learners in their *ZPD* to enhance their vocabulary capacities. Last, another theory related to the gamification of vocabulary is the *Flow Theory. Flow* refers to an average cognitive state that learners experience when they are completely concentrated on an activity and fully engaged in a task, leading to permanent learning and significant levels of pleasure, thereby fostering successful learning outcomes in terms of vocabulary acquisition (Csikszentmihalyi & Davis, 1975).

AI is a computer-oriented technology that imitates and utilizes aspects of the human mind, including its useful features and powerful capabilities (Sindermann et al., 2021). Several theories and hypotheses may be related to *AI.* First, AI-based chatbots or dialogue systems may benefit from the *Interactional Competence Theory of* Young (2011) (Roever & Kasper, 2018). The theory emphasizes the importance of communication skills that EFL learners are expected to practice and develop. The second one is the Adult Learning Theory by Knowles (1980); in other words, the *Andragogy Theory* defines andragogy as empowering and supporting adults' learning. In this theory, in contrast to young learners, adult learners are viewed as autonomous, self-directed, and goal-oriented. These individualized learning needs and learner-centeredness qualities support the use of AI in creating personalized learning opportunities for EFL learners. Next, *Social Constructivism*, led by Vygotsky (1980), may support the use of *AI* due to the similarity between *chatbots* and the social surroundings of the learner. After that, the *Activity Theory*, as put forward by Vygotsky and his colleague Leontiev (1978), suggests that there are basic steps to follow when learning a language (Wertsch, 1985). Combining *AI* tools with *Activity Theory* principles may support language learning by enhancing opportunities to engage in individualized, technology-integrated activities within a social and contextually rich environment. Lastly, Connectionism, as coined by Thorndike (1930), views language as a mechanism of reciprocal action between input and output with neural structure (Binh & Chau, 2023).

PREVIOUS RESEARCH

Research indicates that vocabulary learning is considerably affected by digital technologies, web 2.0 tools, and social media applications. As an example, given that studies have mainly focused on the relationship between the use of digital technologies and vocabulary learning, Castillo and Quinonez (2022) aimed to demonstrate the effect of using digital comics to enhance EFL vocabulary capacity through a quasi-experimental research design. The data for this study were collected through pre-tests, post-tests, and a perception survey administered to 262 public high school students. They concluded that digital comics significantly improved vocabulary learning in the experimental group. The group also showed a positive perception of using digital comics to enhance their EFL vocabulary capacity, as comics allowed them to create unique digital stories and adapt them according to their preferences. In another study, Yowaboot and Sukying (2022)investigated whether the use of digital flashcards could support primary school students' English vocabulary knowledge of the form-meaning relationship in the EFL context. They found that the students in the experimental group performed significantly better than those in the control group and that digital flashcards effectively supported vocabulary learning by leveraging the audio and visual components of digital platforms.

A considerable amount of research on the use of gamification in EFL vocabulary has demonstrated its effectiveness and positive impact on vocabulary learning. In their study, Ahmed et al. (2022) examined the impact of gamification on improving students' idiomatic knowledge, and their findings showed that the experimental group, which was taught new idioms using game-based instruction, performed better than the control group receiving traditional idiomatic instruction. Lam (2014) conducted a case study to examine the effect of Web 2.0 games on learners' vocabulary acquisition. The results indicated that gamification of vocabulary facilitated vocabulary retention, enhanced vocabulary learning, and improved learners' attitudes toward learning vocabulary. In their study, Thiagarajah et al. (2022) aimed to investigate learners' opinions on the efficacy of gamification tools in improving vocabulary skills. The results reported that Kahoot! is beneficial and influential for vocabulary learning. A quasi-experimental study by Saleh and Althaqafi (2022) aimed to investigate the impact of using educational games on the vocabulary learning of kindergarten students. The study showed that using games improved vocabulary retention. In another study, Panmei and Waluyo (2023) aimed to examine the impacts of gamified vocabulary learning utilizing an application, 'Quizizz'. The findings supported the integration of gamification into vocabulary learning.

Since research on AI-enhanced gamification has primarily focused on EFL language skills, including pronunciation, there is a lack of direct studies on AI-enhanced gamification in vocabulary learning. Current research on AI-enhanced gamification for vocabulary learning in the EFL context reveals a positive correlation between the use of AI-based and gamified platforms and vocabulary learning. For instance, Irzawati (2023) aimed to present an overview of the positive impacts of integrating Duolingo into EFL learning and found that integrating this application into EFL learning had favorable contributions to achieving higher mastery of vocabulary. In a similar study, Kusumadewi and Widyastuti (2018) aimed to discover the impacts of Duolingo on learners' vocabulary enhancement. The results indicated a positive effect on the mastery of English vocabulary between learners who benefited from the application. In another study, Esmaeili and Shahrokhi (2020) explored the impact of the Memrise application on Iranian EFL students' collocation learning and vocabulary retention. The researchers used a quasi-experimental design with 75 students studying at a private language institute. The findings revealed that the application had a significant impact on collocation learning. Moreover, there was a significant difference between the experimental group, which used the application, and the control group, which received traditional teaching. In a similar study, Nasution (2022 sought to investigate the effect of the Memrise application on vocabulary mastery among seventh-grade junior high school students. This quantitative study, employing a quasi-experimental design, concluded that the application has a significant impact on vocabulary enhancement and mastery. The study by Prasetyo et al. (2018) aimed to investigate the impact of the Rosetta Stone application on learners' vocabulary mastery and found that participants could memorize new words more easily, pronounce most of them accurately, and seldom make mistakes in their sentences.

OVERVIEW OF THE STUDY

The significance of vocabulary is central to basic language skills in the EFL context. Gamification of educational games, implemented both inside and outside the classroom, may enrich vocabulary knowledge and increase the size of EFL learners by making them more engaged and attracted to this method. From this perspective, integrating AI with gamification for vocabulary learning may enable researchers and instructors to investigate individualized or personalized learning phenomena, closely track learners' progress, and adjust content and word choice according to learners' needs, desires, learning pace, and current levels. In addition, when technology is integrated into vocabulary learning, the gamification method may replace traditional, rote-learning-based, and monotonous vocabulary learning methods that learners frequently use. However, while most previous studies focused on basic language skills and pronunciation, there has been a lack of exploration of the use of AI-enhanced gamification concerning vocabulary learning. Moreover, there is no direct study on the effect of AI-enhanced gamification on vocabulary learning. Furthermore, no study has focused on this issue within the scope of the Turkish EFL context. Therefore, this aims to explore the impacts of AI-enhanced gamification on EFL vocabulary learning. Considering the problems related to vocabulary learning, the support of AI may be beneficial in encouraging students to learn vocabulary in a motivating, high-quality, and enjoyable digital environment. Concerning these problems, the study aims to find answers to the following research questions:

- Does the use of gamification in traditional environments contribute to vocabulary learning among EFL learners?
- Does the use of AI-enhanced gamification contribute to vocabulary learning among EFL learners?
- Is there a difference between the use of gamification in traditional environments and AI-enhanced gamification regarding vocabulary learning among EFL learners?

METHOD

Research Context

The study, which aims to explore how AI-enhanced gamification impacts EFL vocabulary learning, employs an analytical approach, breaking down the data into smaller components and establishing connections to provide a cohesive understanding within the context of the existing vocabulary area. Moreover, the study adopts a deductive approach, examining whether AI-enhanced gamification effectively contributes to vocabulary learning, building on the recognized advantages of AI and gamification in the EFL context. The study, which employed a quasi-experimental research design, does not randomly assign participants to groups but instead selects pre-existing groups, such as classes, for both the experimental and control groups (Creswell, 2014). Both groups undergo pre-tests and post-tests, with the experimental group receiving special treatment while the control group serves as a baseline for comparison (Seliger & Shohamy, 1989).

Participants

Thirty-two students at a public secondary school in Turkey participated in the research. They were beginner-level EFL learners, corresponding to A1 based on The Common European Framework of Reference for Languages (CEFR). Fifteen participants were females (47%), while 17 were males (53%). The ages of the participants ranged from 11 to 12, with a mean score of 11. The participants were all non-native English speakers, and their L1 is Turkish. As for the participants' grades at the school, they were all in the 5th grade. They have 11 hours of English classes in one week. The students followed international coursebooks selected by their teachers, which covered all language skills, grammar, and vocabulary, in addition to the compulsory coursebook provided by the National Education Ministry. Furthermore, a focus group study was necessary to identify and investigate the potential causes of the results obtained from the analysis of the findings. Five participants from each group were randomly selected, and a 40-minute meeting was conducted separately for each group. The average age of the students was 10. Of the students, 5 (50%) were male, while 5 (50%) were female.

Tools

A background questionnaire and a vocabulary test were used in the study. A background questionnaire, which included demographic information such as age, gender, grade, and current English proficiency levels, was implemented. The vocabulary test developed by Tapia (2021) was implemented. The mentioned test was chosen because it was valid, reliable, and applicable for A1-level learners. Cronbach's alpha was 0.75, meaning the vocabulary test possessed an acceptable internal consistency. Regarding the validity of the tool, the technique adopted was highly effective in the data collection procedure. The content validity of this vocabulary test was supported by the critical evaluation and experience of three language instructors from distinct universities, who dedicated considerable time and effort to comprehensive work, review, and assistance in validating the test to confirm its validity. The tool was used as a pre-test to assess the present vocabulary level at A1 and as a post-test to assess the advancement after the experiment. The test included three parts: Parts A, B, and C. There were 30 questions in part A to test receptive vocabulary, and students marked the correct choice with a tick. Part B consisted of 10 questions to assess receptive vocabulary by selecting from multiple-choice options. Part C contained 20 open-ended questions to test productive vocabulary by benefiting from the given clues or definitions and writing the letters of missing words. The total score was 60 points (Tapia, 2021).

A focus group study was conducted with 10 participants to further understand the results and the reasons behind the differences in vocabulary retention, comprising five participants from the control group and five participants from the experimental group. Each group was interviewed separately to ensure that the opinions received were original and unbiased, and the interviews lasted nearly 20 minutes for each group.

Procedure

After obtaining approval from the ethical committee granted by the Faculty of Educational Sciences at a state university, the school administration of the public secondary school where the study was to be implemented was informed to obtain permission. Afterward, the participants were informed about the aim, benefits, and weekly procedures. It was also stated that the research was voluntary and anonymous. In addition, participants were assured that the research was confidential and that the data collected would be used solely for scientific and academic purposes.

An approval form was attached to the vocabulary test to obtain the consent of the participants.

The study was conducted in the Spring Semester of 2023-2024. First, two pre-existing classes were chosen for the research and randomly assigned as the control and experimental groups. After that, both groups took the vocabulary test as a pre-test. The control group used games to practice vocabulary, while the experimental group completed tasks with the aid of AI. ChatGPT was chosen as the AI tool. Finally, after a 5-week study, both groups took the post-test. Following the post-tests, a focus group interview was conducted with ten participants, comprising five participants from each group. The interview was conducted face-to-face and lasted a total of 40 minutes. The entire procedure is illustrated in Figure 1.

Figure 1. The flowchart of the randomized pre-test-post-test control and experimental design (Fraenkel et al., 2012)

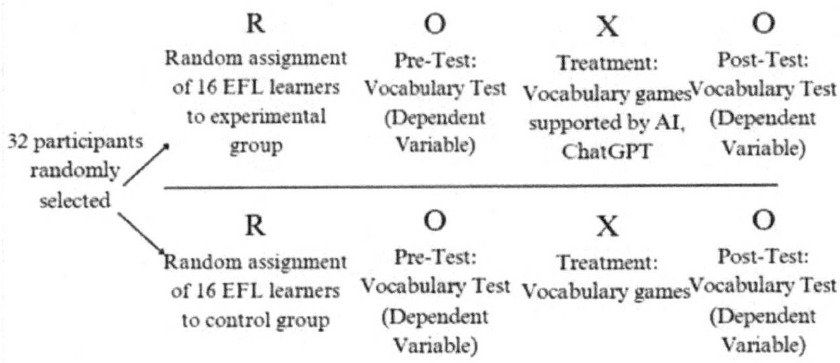

Pre-test Administration

Before the implementation, the participants were instructed to complete the vocabulary test. Then, the vocabulary test was administered, and participants were expected to respond to 60 items that examined their vocabulary knowledge. They were instructed to choose the best answer and fill in the blanks at their own pace, which took 40 minutes. As in the original study, the vocabulary test was administered in English, as the participants were competent enough to understand each explanation and answer appropriately. However, L1 translations were provided to the participants to prevent any misconceptions or hesitation where necessary.

The Practice Process

As shown in Table 1, the practice process lasted for five weeks, during which the participants received instructions and learned new vocabulary through flashcards, story cards or cubes, taboo game cards, digital or non-digital classroom games, and AI. The target words were chosen from the CEFR A1 level vocabulary test by Tapia (2021). The words were categorized under different themes, and each week, 12 target words were taught. During the process, the participants were encouraged to use the words they had learned in sentences and personalize their experiences. Both groups were exposed to the same instructions, activities, and educational materials during the practice sessions. Biased remarks and questions were avoided to prevent any potential effects.

Table 1. The practice process

Week	Tasks and Activities	Tools and resources used
Week 1	Introduction of twelve target words through flashcards. Learning the synonyms, antonyms, parts of speech, and collocations using ChatGPT. Playing a digital board game on Learn Hip.	Flashcards (Wordwall) Digital Board Game (Learn Hip) ChatGPT
Week 2	Teaching target words using contextual clues in a story created by ChatGPT. Conducting a game-based storytelling circle activity.	Smartboard ChatGPT Story cards
Week 3	Learning target words through taboo cards created on ChatGPT. Playing taboo game in groups.	Taboo cards prepared on ChatGPT Smartboard
Week 4	Learning vocabulary through a Heads-Up Game using associations and concepts related to target words on ChatGPT and Kahoot Quiz for assessment	Printable worksheet from the website themeasuredmom.com, Heads Up Game cards, Kahoot game
Week 5	Learning vocabulary by creating mnemonics on ChatGPT, revision of all weeks' words with a Jeopardy game	Flashcards (Wordwall) ChatGPT, Jeopardy Game (Playfactile)

Post-Test Implementation

During the final stage of the study, the vocabulary test was administered again. This test examined students' vocabulary knowledge. The aim was to detect any significant changes in students' vocabulary gains after the practice process.

Data Analysis

SPSS Statistics 21.0 software was used for data analysis. First, the participants' demographics were descriptively analyzed. First, the mean score for gender was computed. Additionally, numbers and frequencies were obtained for the grade levels, and the proficiency levels of the participants were calculated. Then, the reliability coefficients were calculated through Cronbach's alpha for the pre-tests and post-tests. The reliability coefficient for the pre-tests was 0.92 and 0.91 for the post-tests. Non-parametric methods were employed to further analyze and compare the data, as a normal distribution could not be assumed due to the small sample size of the participants in the study. First, descriptive analysis was conducted to reveal the mean scores of the pre-tests and post-tests, determining each group's vocabulary retention levels before and after implementation. Second, the Wilcoxon analysis was performed to determine if there were any significant differences concerning the vocabulary retention levels between the pre-tests and post-tests of the control and experimental groups due to the implementation. Finally, after implementation, the Mann-Whitney U analysis was performed to identify any differences in vocabulary retention levels between the groups.

RESULTS

Gamification Effect on Vocabulary Learning in Traditional Environments

Regarding the results gained from the vocabulary test, the score of 60 was evaluated as excellent, the score between 48-59 was evaluated as very satisfactory, the score between 43-47 was evaluated as satisfactory, the score between 36-42 was evaluated as little satisfactory, and the score under 35 was evaluated as not satisfactory (Tapia, 2021). Based on this scale, the score for the control group was not satisfactory before implementation but became satisfactory after implementation. Table 2 indicates the mean scores, standard error mean, and standard deviation of the pre and post-tests of the control group. According to the table, the vocabulary retention levels of the control group increased from 25.75 to 44.18 after they completed the vocabulary games.

Table 2. The mean scores for vocabulary retention levels in the control group (n=16)

Tests	Mean	Std. Error	Standard Deviation
Total scores for the pre-test	25.75	1.71	6.86
Total scores for the post-test	44.18	2.23	8.93

Table 3 shows the number of positive ranks, mean ranks, sum of ranks, and significance level of the comparison of pre-test and post-test scores of the control group. Based on the comparison, the significance level was .00, and the post-test scores with a mean rank of 8.50. In other words, there was a statistically significant change in the vocabulary retention levels of the control group.

Table 3. Comparison of pre-and post-test scores of the control group (Wilcoxon Test)

<table>
<tr><th colspan="2">Ranks</th><th>N</th><th>Mean Ranks</th><th>Sum of Ranks</th><th>Asymp. Sig. (2-tailed)</th></tr>
<tr><td rowspan="4">Post-test-Pre-test</td><td>Negative Ranks</td><td>16</td><td>8.50</td><td>136.00</td><td rowspan="4">.00</td></tr>
<tr><td>Positive Ranks</td><td>0</td><td>.00</td><td>.00</td></tr>
<tr><td>Ties</td><td>0</td><td rowspan="2" colspan="2"></td></tr>
<tr><td>Total</td><td>16</td></tr>
</table>

AI-Enhanced Gamification Effect on Vocabulary Learning

Based on the criterion, the score for the experimental group was not satisfactory before implementation but became very satisfactory afterward. Table 4 presents the mean scores, standard error of the mean, and standard deviation of the pre-tests and post-tests for the experimental group. As shown in the table, there was an increase in the mean scores for vocabulary learning from 31.50 to 49.06 after completing the games.

Table 4. The mean scores for vocabulary retention levels in the experimental group (n=16)

Tests	Mean	Std. Error	Standard Deviation
Total scores for the pre-test	31.50	3.45	13.81
Total scores for the post-test	49.06	2.31	9.24

Table 5 presents the number of positive and negative ranks, mean ranks, the sum of ranks, and the significance level of the comparison between the pre-test and post-test scores of the experimental group. Based on the comparison, the significance level was .00, and the post-test scores of 16 participants were higher than their pre-test scores, with a mean rank of 8.50. In other words, there was a change in the vocabulary retention levels of the experimental group, and a significant difference was observed between the tests.

Table 5. Comparison of pre-and post-test scores of the experimental group (Wilcoxon Test)

Ranks		**N**	**Mean Ranks**	**Sum of Ranks**	**Asymp. Sig. (2-tailed)**
Post-test-Pre-test	Negative Ranks	16	8.50	136.00	.00
	Positive Ranks	0	.00	.00	
	Ties	0			
	Total	16			

Comparison of Traditional Gamification and AI-Enhanced Gamification in Vocabulary Learning

The Mann-Whitney U test was conducted to reveal any differences between the control and experimental groups, as seen in Table 6. It was revealed that the mean rank was 15.13 for the control group, whereas it was 17.88 for the experimental group. Nevertheless, there was no significant difference between the two groups in terms of their pre-test scores, and the significance value was .40, which was above the specified significance level.

Table 6. Pre-test scores for the control and experimental groups (Mann Whitney U Test)

	Group	**Mean Rank**	**Sum of Ranks**	**Asymp. Sig. (2-tailed)**
Pre-test	Control Group	15.13	242.00	.40
	Experimental Group	17.88	286.00	

While there is no significant statistical difference in total scores, some items show differences in receptive and productive vocabulary retention, as shown in Table 7. The six items showed significant differences ($p < .05$) regarding the experimental group. In other words, the participants in the experimental group scored higher than those in the control group.

Table 7. Mann Whitney U Test results for the pre-tests of the control (n=16) and experimental groups (n=16)

Items	Group	Mean Rank	Sum of Ranks	Asymp. Sig. (2-tailed)
25. Not good	Control Group	14.50	232.00	.03
	Experimental Group	18.50	296.00	
33. UPSET: He is upset.	Control Group	14.00	224.00	.05
	Experimental Group	19.00	304.00	
42. They are the main ingredients for French fries.	Control Group	20.00	320.00	.01
	Experimental Group	13.00	208.00	
54. You can play soccer with this.	Control Group	13.50	216.00	.03
	Experimental Group	19.50	312.00	
58. If you want to buy food, you go to this place.	Control Group	13.00	208.00	.01
	Experimental Group	20.00	320.00	
60. You take this after learning a lot of subjects.	Control Group	13.50	216.00	.00
	Experimental Group	19.50	312.00	

Table 8 presents the mean rank, sum of ranks, and significance value of the post-test results for the control and experimental groups. It was revealed that the mean rank was 13.81 for the control group, whereas it was 19.19 for the experimental group, indicating a higher value. However, their post-test scores had no significant difference, as the significance value was .10.

Table 8. Post-test scores for the control and experimental groups (Mann Whitney U Test)

	Group	Mean Rank	Sum of Ranks	Asymp. Sig. (2-tailed)
Post-test	Control Group	13.81	221.00	.10
	Experimental Group	19.19	307.00	

While there is no significant statistical difference in total scores, some items show differences in receptive and productive vocabulary retention, as shown in Table 9. The six items showed significant differences ($p < .05$) regarding the experimental group. In other words, the participants in the experimental group had higher scores than those in the control group.

Table 9. The Mann-Whitney U Test results for the post-tests of the control (n=16) and experimental (n=16) groups

Items	Group	Mean Rank	Sum of Ranks	Asymp. Sig. (2-tailed)
15. Ingredient for the soup.	Control Group	14.00	224.00	.01
	Experimental Group	19.00	304.00	
29. Person who trains a team.	Control Group	13.00	208.00	.00
	Experimental Group	20.00	320.00	
32. STONE: She sat on a stone.	Control Group	13.50	216.00	.03
	Experimental Group	19.50	312.00	
39. POCKET: I keep it in my pocket.	Control Group	13.50	216.00	.00
	Experimental Group	19.50	312.00	
49. You use it to draw and write.	Control Group	13.00	208.00	.00
	Experimental Group	20.00	320.00	
51. It is played with small pieces on a large board.	Control Group	13.50	216.00	.02
	Experimental Group	19.50	312.00	

CONCLUSIONS AND DISCUSSION

Three key conclusions were drawn from the study. The first conclusion is that traditional gamification has a positive impact on vocabulary retention and overall learning outcomes by making the vocabulary learning process more engaging for learners. However, AI-enhanced gamification takes these benefits a step further by incorporating advanced technologies, such as ChatGPT, and its functions, including machine learning algorithms, adaptive or personalized learning systems, real-time feedback, and natural language processing. These enhancements lead to a more effective and fruitful learning process, resulting in improved vocabulary retention and learning outputs compared to the traditional gamification method. As a result, while the traditional gamification method has a positive impact on vocabulary retention and learning among EFL learners, AI-enhanced gamification appears to be more effective in promoting vocabulary retention and mastery. The second conclusion is that learners who benefit from the traditional gamification method achieve a satisfactory vocabulary capacity and retention level, effectively improving their vocabulary learning skills. However, AI-enhanced gamification leverages advanced technologies to further elevate the vocabulary learning experience. AI enhancement significantly boosts learners' vocabulary learning performance from a poor to a very satisfactory level, making them more competent in learning new vocabulary than traditional gamification. As a result, while the traditional gamification method improves vocabulary learning capacity among EFL learners, AI-enhanced gamification is markedly more effective. Thus, integrating AI into gamified learning environments significantly advances EFL vocabulary learning. The last conclusion is that learners achieve satisfactory improvements in receptive and productive vocabulary capacities after using the traditional gamification method. However, AI-enhanced gamification significantly enhances learners' receptive and productive vocabulary capacities and retention levels compared to traditional gamification methods, thanks to its advanced and contextually rich features and opportunities. The combination of AI with games enables learners to encounter new words, understand, remember, and use them efficiently in both virtual environments and real life, enhancing comprehension and communication. As a result, while traditional gamification improves EFL learners' receptive and productive vocabulary retention, AI-enhanced gamification seems significantly more effective in vocabulary learning.

The results of a focus group study suggest that the aforementioned conclusions may be related to several factors. Regarding vocabulary learning, participants who receive gamification state that games provide an opportunity for them to study, learn, practice, and revise new words in a fun way tailored to their proficiency levels. Additionally, they state that games are engaging and motivating sources for them to sustain their attention and participation in the lesson by boosting their desire to learn. Moreover, the participants believe that not only are games practical for vocabulary retention, but they can also help them overcome the problem of lack of concentration. They also believe that team games such as Taboo and Jeopardy positively contribute to their social identity development. Furthermore, some participants believe that games enhance their visual memory, enabling them to easily retrieve words from memory when needed for spoken and written production tasks, both inside and outside the classroom. Participants who receive AI-enhanced gamification from ChatGPT believe they are in a digital era and prefer modern and innovative learning strategies over conventional ones. Some participants believe that studying vocabulary from course books and printed dictionaries is a boring activity. They also believe that ChatGPT is a better assistant for creating authentic sentences and searching for specialized uses of vocabulary compared to non-digital or digital dictionaries. They state that when they do not have an opportunity to ask questions related to the problems encountered while using vocabulary from their teachers, ChatGPT assists them like a private tutor. They also state that AI-enhanced gamification addresses their individual needs through real-time feedback and personalization opportunities whenever and wherever they want. According to them, it is an easy and motivating way to address their vocabulary learning problems. Specifically, words in contextual stories created by ChatGPT attract the participants, and they state that they find this vocabulary learning strategy very beneficial for vocabulary revision and retention.

In conclusion, this study examines the impact of AI-enhanced gamification on EFL learners' vocabulary acquisition in comparison to traditional gamification. It finds that traditional gamification has a positive impact on vocabulary retention and learning outcomes by making the process more interactive and engaging. However, AI-enhanced gamification, incorporating technologies like ChatGPT, seems to be more effective. Learners using AI-enhanced gamification demonstrate improved vocabulary retention and learning outcomes, outperforming learners who use traditional gamification methods. In conclusion, EFL learners report that games, whether traditional or AI-enhanced, make learning fun, engaging, and practical for vocabulary retention. They find AI-enhanced gamification particularly beneficial due to its modern, innovative approach, real-time feedback, and personalization, which makes vocabulary learning more efficient and motivating. Therefore, integrating AI into gamified learning environments significantly advances EFL vocabulary learning and provides valuable insights for teachers, academicians, and application designers in creating and implementing vocabulary learning strategies.

Pedagogical Implications

Some pedagogical implications can be noted. First, the findings appear to align with previous research, indicating that gamification has a positive impact on receptive and productive vocabulary retention, as well as earning outcomes (Ahmed et al., 2022; Lam, 2014; Thiagarajah et al., 2022; Saleh & Althaqafi, 2022; Panmei & Waluyo, 2023). Moreover, the conclusions of the present study indicate that gamification offers an opportunity to study, learn, practice, and revise words in a fun and engaging manner(Waluyo & Bucol, 2021; Waer, 2021; Stephenson & Rumley, 2005). In addition, although this study does not find any negative effects of gamification on intrinsic motivation, Hanus and Fox (2015) note that for students who are already motivated to learn, gamified activities might harm their intrinsic motivation. On the contrary, the findings indicate that games' engaging and motivating features contribute to sustaining attention and participation by boosting learners' self-determination to learn new words (Ahmed et al., 2022; Genç Ersoy & Belet Boyacı, 2021). No findings are available regarding the negative effects caused by gamified competition, while Zhang and Hasim (2023) note that gamified competition has a negative impact on learning. The present study shows that gamification of vocabulary in the classroom, specifically the team-based ones including a gamified competition spirit, enhances learners' social interaction, collaboration, and mental lexicon through communicative tasks as previously concluded (Roebuck, 1998; Vygotsky, 1980; Verga & Kotz, 2017; Bakhsh, 2016; Gozcu & Caganaga, 2016). Next, the study has a correspondent finding to the prior ones showing that gamification aids visual memory and enables learners to retrieve words from their memory easily when needed to be used in spoken and written production (Sadeghi & Farzizadeh, 2013; Quynh, 2022; Hashemi, 2021; Razali & Ismail, 2017). In addition, the present findings suggest that gamification aids learners in overcoming their concentration difficulty in studying words (Ahmed et al., 2022; Csikszentmihalyi & Davis, 1975). On the other hand, while Zohrabi et al. (2018) conclude that gamification boosts rote learning and leads to isolated vocabulary learning, the current study concludes that using words in storytelling activities through gamification is beneficial for meaningful and contextualized learning, as also concluded in previous studies (Zhai & Wibowo, 2023; Chen, 2016). Since research on AI-enhanced gamification has primarily focused on EFL language skills and pronunciation, there is a lack of direct studies on AI-enhanced gamification in vocabulary learning. Considering these findings, it can be stated that the use of AI-enhanced gamification enhances EFL learners' receptive and productive vocabulary capacities and retention levels (Katemba, 2022; Wang & Petrina, 2013; Lai & Chen, 2023; Na-Young, 2020). Moreover, the AI-enhanced gamification method significantly boosts learners' vocabulary learning performances from a poor to a very satisfactory level, making them more competent in learning new vocabulary (Fryer et al., 2019; Irzawati, 2023; Kusumadewi & Widyastuti, 2018; Esmaeili & Shahrokhi, 2020; Nasution, 2022; Prasetyo et al., 2018). Additionally, the current findings suggest that learners prefer modern and innovative learning strategies, such as digital learning platforms, over conventional strategies or materials (Alshumaimeri, 2008; Arini et al., 2022). Interestingly, while Alsadoon (2021) concludes that the use of a printed dictionary is the most favored and effective tool when compared to AI chatbots, this study indicates that learners find studying vocabulary in printed dictionaries and course books boring, as concluded by Li (2021). Moreover, the conclusions of the current study indicate that AI chatbots are more effective assistants than private tutors in helping to create personalized, authentic, and semantically correct sentences from keywords and utilizing specialized and detaileduse of vocabulary (Alsadoon, 2021; Ghafar et al., 2023; Kasepalu et al., 2022). Furthermore, the study has a correspondent finding to the prior ones showing that AI chatbot addresses learners' individual needs through immediate feedback and personalization options while learning the special use of vocabulary (Şenel & Akman, 2016; Murtaza et al., 2022; Sumakul et al., 2022; Abbas et al., 2023; Tapalova & Zhiyenbayeva, 2022; Schmidt & Strasser, 2022). The results of the current study also show that AI-enhanced gamification is an effective and motivating way to address learners' problems that they encounter while learning vocabulary, as found by Li (2021). As a result, AI-enhanced gamification plays a crucial role in the vocabulary learning process by allowing students to enhance their receptive and productive vocabulary retention levels, optimize their vocabulary learning performances to better conditions, to be one step ahead of traditional methods by using innovative and trendy methods in the technology era, to receive support without limits of time and place, and to have differentiated and personalized vocabulary learning routes according to their own pace and levels.

Practical Recommendations

Based on the conclusions, several practical recommendations can be listed. Teachers should utilize games and AI chatbots, such as ChatGPT, to enhance learners' vocabulary retention levels and capacities and provide a fun, engaging, motivating, collaborative, competitive, research-oriented, and peaceful atmosphere in their classes. They should pay attention to matching the features of ChatGPT with their students' ages, levels, and interests while planning their vocabulary teaching lessons. In this way, students can be attracted to the game world and become open to learning new words. The chat feature of ChatGPT can improve students' vocabulary skills, and there may be incidental vocabulary learning opportunities for new words while searching the game characters' names, trying to understand the game's directions, and communicating with the chatbot. Students can easily access resources such as paraphrasing, creating fluent dialogues and plays, fun tongue-twisters, interesting individualized stories, brainstorming solutions, transcribing their audio materials, acting as role-play or discussion partners, and improving their vocabulary learning experiences. In terms of school administrations, they should integrate ChatGPT and vocabulary games into their agenda. For instance, there should be regular international or national seminars, in-service training, forums, conferences, and workshops for English teachers to help them teach vocabulary using ChatGPT and games and support their vocabulary teaching skills and strategies with the latest technology and trends in the AI sector. School administrations should invest in hardware and technical infrastructure such as AI-enhanced gamification platforms and internet connection protocols. Regarding curriculum designers, before integrating AI-based gamification procedures into vocabulary, they should begin with pilot programs and test the efficiency of AI and gamification tools for vocabulary in various parts of the country to get feedback and start attempts. Curriculum designers and material developers should plan by considering the opinions and innovative ideas of English teachers regarding vocabulary teaching. Finally, policymakers should invest in AI and gaming technologies by allocating funding to schools and universities to support their development. Policymakers should develop policies that facilitate the integration of AI and games into vocabulary instruction, taking into account the perspectives of English teachers and academicians. They should establish precise guidelines for utilizing AI and games to teach vocabulary in EFL classes. Although AI technology offers many services and pros to users, it is crucial to mention that there are also some ethical issues to be considered; there can be bias in produced works and their accuracy should be checked from reliable sources carefully. Aata safety and privacy issues should be also considered when using AI tools in language education.

Limitations and Recommendations for Further Research

This study has some limitations. First, this study is limited to 32 fifth-grade students from a public secondary school, comprising 16 students in the control group and 16 in the experimental group. Second, the implementation period is limited to five weeks. Third, this study benefits from a quasi-experimental design because it utilizes pre-existing groups instead of randomly sampling participants. Last, the current study used only ChatGPT as an AI tool.

The findings of the present study yield several recommendations for future studies. First, more research should be done on the effects of AI-enhanced gamification on EFL learners' vocabulary learning. The study sample diversity should be expanded by involving more learners from different secondary schools and from different social backgrounds. Furthermore, to further examine the quality and effect of AI-enhanced gamification, a content analysis should be implemented to compare the efficacy of both traditional and AI-enhanced gamification on learners' vocabulary learning. The impact of AI-enhanced gamification on vocabulary learning should be analyzed in detail across various aspects of vocabulary learning, including register, context, morphology, etymology, corpora, syntax, semantic relations, idiomatic expressions, and lexical relations. Thus, it can be analyzed in which areas of AI-enhanced gamification can be used more efficiently and efficaciously. In addition, implementing a similar study with learners with different language proficiency levels could indicate whether the efficiency of AI-enhanced gamification changes according to proficiency level. This can provide essential insight into customizing teaching methods and materials. Moreover, case studies highlighting how AI tools have been successfully integrated into the context of foreign language education should be carefully analyzed and implemented when creating new and modern educational systems in digital era. Furthermore, the correlation between vocabulary learning and reading comprehension skills, digital literacy, and academic success can be examined using AI-enhanced gamification.

REFERENCES

Abbas, N., Ali, I., Manzoor, R., Hussain, T., & Hussaini, A. L. (2023). Role of artificial intelligence tools in enhancing students' educational performance at higher levels. *Journal of Artificial Intelligence. Machine Learning and Neural Network*, *3*(5), 36–49. DOI: 10.55529/jaimlnn.35.36.49

Afzal, N. (2019). A study on vocabulary learning problems encountered by BA English majors at the university level of education. *Arab World English Journal*, *10*(3), 81–98. DOI: 10.24093/awej/vol10no3.6

Ahmed, A. A. A., Widodo, M., Komariah, A., Hassan, I., Abbas, A. K., & Rohi, A. (2022). Assessing the effects of gamification on developing EFL learners' idiomatic knowledge: Do attitudinal factors contribute to the learning of the idioms with the game? *Education Research International*, *2022*, 1–10. DOI: 10.1155/2022/2482570

Ahn, T., & Lee, S.-M. (2016). User experience of a mobile speaking application with automatic speech recognition for EFL learning. *British Journal of Educational Technology*, *47*(4), 778–786. DOI: 10.1111/bjet.12354

Alqahtani, M. (2015). The importance of vocabulary in language learning and how to be taught. *International Journal of Teaching and Education*, *3*(3), 21–34. DOI: 10.20472/TE.2015.3.3.002

Alsadoon, R. (2021). Chatting with AI Bot: Vocabulary learning assistant for Saudi EFL learners. *English Language Teaching*, *14*(6), 135–157. DOI: 10.5539/elt.v14n6p135

Alshumaimeri, Y. (2008). Perceptions and attitudes toward using CALL in English classrooms among Saudi secondary EFL teachers. *The JALT CALL Journal*, *44*(2), 29–66. DOI: 10.29140/jaltcall.v4n2.61

Altyari, A. W. (2017). English vocabulary uptake by Saudi Arabic speaking students at public schools. *British Journal of English Linguistics*, *5*(1), 10–16.

Arini, D. N., Hidayat, F., Winarti, A., & Rosalina, E. (2022). Artificial intelligence (AI)-based mobile learning in ELT for EFL learners: The implementation and learners' attitudes. *International Journal of Educational Studies in Social Sciences*, *2*(2), 88–95. DOI: 10.53402/ijesss.v2i2.40

Asrida, E., Syafitri, W., Sakti, G., & Dewi, M. P. (2024). The correlation between students' vocabulary mastery and their listening ability. *Journal of English Language Pedagogy*, *9*(1), 66–75. DOI: 10.36665/elp.v9i1.870

Aydın, S., & Zeinolabedini, M. (2024). Integrating artificial intelligence into foreign language learning: Learners' perspectives. EJER Congress: 2024 International Eurasian Educational Research Congress, Conference Proceedings, Ani Publishing, 2024, pp. 121-126. Kocaeli, Turkey.

Bakhsh, S. A. (2016). Using games as a tool in teaching vocabulary to young learners. *English Language Teaching*, *9*(7), 120–128. DOI: 10.5539/elt.v9n7p120

Binh, N. G., & Chau, V. N. B. (2023). The investigation on recent applications of artificial intelligence in second language acquisition. *AIJR Proceedings*, 200–209. DOI: 10.21467/proceedings.150.22

Brooks, G., Clenton, J., & Fraser, S. (2021). Exploring the importance of vocabulary for English as an additional language learners' reading comprehension. *Studies in Second Language Learning and Teaching*, *11*(3), 351–376. DOI: 10.14746/ssllt.2021.11.3.3

Cancino, M., & Viguera, C. (2024). The impact of a gamified approach on vocabulary learning and vocabulary self-efficacy: Evidence from a Chilean primary EFL school. *Revista de Lingüistica Y Lenguas Aplicadas, 19*, 33–43.

Castillo, L., & Quinonez, A. (2022). Using digital comics for enhancing EFL vocabulary learning during the covid-19 pandemic. *International Journal of Learning. Teaching and Educational Research*, *21*(5), 478–491. DOI: 10.26803/ijlter.21.5.24

Chen, Y. L. (2016). The effects of virtual reality learning environment on student cognitive and linguistic development. *The Asia-Pacific Education Researcher*, *25*(4), 637–646. DOI: 10.1007/s40299-016-0293-2

Cizrelioğlu, İ., & Aydin, S. (2025). Using artificial intelligence in EFL learning among multilingual young learners. In M. Sanmugam, B. Edwards, N. Mohd Barkhaya, & Z. Khlaif (Eds.), *Fostering inclusive education with AI and emerging technologies* (pp. 303-322). IGI Global. DOI: 10.4018/979-8-3693-7255-5.ch013

Creswell, J. W. (2014). *Research Design: Qualitative, Quantitative, and Mixed Methods Approaches* (4th ed.). SAGE Publication.

Csikszentmihalyi, M., & Davis, M. S. (1975). *Beyond boredom and anxiety* (1st ed.). Jossey-Bass.

Esmaeili, Z., & Shahrokhi, M. (2020). The impact of Memrise application on Iranian EFL learners' collocation learning and retention. *International Journal of Language Education*, *4*(2), 221–233. DOI: 10.26858/ijole.v4i2.10672

Fryer, L. K., Nakao, K., & Thompson, A. (2019). Chatbot learning partners: Connecting learning experiences, interests, and competence. *Computers in Human Behavior*, *93*, 279–289. DOI: 10.1016/j.chb.2018.12.023

Genç Ersoy, B., & Belet Boyacı, Ş. D. (2021). Devising gamification for vocabulary development and motivation: An experimental, mixed-model study. *International Technology and Education Journal*, *5*(1), 32–49.

Ghafar, Z. N., Salh, H. F., Abdulrahim, M. A., Farxha, S. S., Arf, S. F., & Rahim, R. İ. (2023). The role of artificial intelligence technology on English language learning: A literature review. *Canadian Journal of Language and Literature Studies*, *3*(2), 17–31.

Ghazal, L. (2007). Learning vocabulary in EFL contexts through vocabulary learning strategies. *NOVITAS-ROYAL*, *1*(2), 84–91.

Gozcu, E., & Caganaga, C. K. (2016). The importance of using games in EFL classrooms. *Cypriot Journal of Educational Sciences*, *11*(3), 126–135. DOI: 10.18844/cjes.v11i3.625

Hanus, M. D., & Fox, J. (2015). Assessing the effects of gamification in the classroom: A longitudinal study on intrinsic motivation, social comparison, satisfaction, effort, and academic performance. *Computers & Education*, *80*, 152–161. DOI: 10.1016/j.compedu.2014.08.019

Hashemi, A. (2021). The effects of using games on teaching vocabulary in reading comprehension: A case of gifted students. *Journal for the Education of Gifted Young Scientists*, *9*(2), 151–160. DOI: 10.17478/jegys.846480

Heift, T., & Schulze, M. (2007). Errors and intelligence in computer-assisted language learning: Parsers and pedagogues. *Computational Linguistics*, *34*(1), 1–283.

Hutauruk, B. S. (2015). Children first language acquisition at age 1-3 years old in Balata. *IOSR Journal of Humanities and Social Science*, *20*(8), 51–57. DOI: 10.14746/ssllt.2021.11.3.3

Irzawati, I. (2023). The integration of Duolingo into EFL learning. *ESTEEM: Journal of English Study Programme*, *6*(2), 328–337. DOI: 10.31851/esteem.v6i2.12317

Kasepalu, R., Prieto, L. P., Ley, T., & Chejara, P. (2022). Teacher artificial intelligence-supported pedagogical actions in collaborative learning coregulation: A wizard of Oz study. *Frontiers in Education*, *7*, 1–15. DOI: 10.3389/feduc.2022.736194

Katemba, C. V. (2022). Vocabulary enhancement through multimedia learning among grade 7th EFL students. *MEXTESOL Journal*, *46*(1), 1–13. DOI: 10.61871/mj.v46n1-8

Kazu, İ. Y., & Kuvvetli, M. (2023). The influence of pronunciation education via artificial intelligence technology on vocabulary acquisition in learning English. *International Journal of Psychology and Educational Studies*, *10*(2), 480–493. DOI: 10.52380/ijpes.2023.10.2.1044

Kılıç, M. (2019). Vocabulary knowledge as a predictor in writing and speaking: A case study of Turkish EFL Learners. *PASAA*, *57*, 133–164. DOI: 10.58837/CHULA.PASAA.57.1.6

Krashen, S. (1989). We acquire vocabulary and spelling by reading: Additional evidence for the Input Hypothesis. *Modern Language Journal*, *73*(4), 440–463. DOI: 10.1111/j.1540-4781.1989.tb05325.x

Kusumadewi, H., & Widyastuti, M. (2018). The effects of using Duolingo towards students' vocabulary mastery. [Indonesian Journal of English Teaching]. *IJET*, *7*(2), 172–186. DOI: 10.15642/ijet2.2018.7.2.172-186

Lai, K.-W. K., & Chen, H.-J. H. (2023). A comparative study on the effects of a VR and PC visual novel game on vocabulary learning. *Computer Assisted Language Learning*, *36*(3), 312–345. DOI: 10.1080/09588221.2021.1928226

Lam, S. L. (2014). Use of gamification in vocabulary learning: A case study in Macau. *Center for English Language Communication*, *13*, 90–97.

Laufer, B., & Hulstijn, J. (2001). Incidental vocabulary acquisition in a second language: The construct of task-induced involvement. *Applied Linguistics*, *22*(1), 1–26. DOI: 10.1093/applin/22.1.1

Li, R. (2021). Does game-based vocabulary learning APP influence Chinese EFL learners' vocabulary achievement, motivation, and self-confidence? *SAGE Open*, *11*(1), 1–12. DOI: 10.1177/21582440211003092

Liu, J., Shindo, H., & Matsumoto, Y. (2019). Development of a computer-assisted Japanese functional exression learning system for Chinese-speaking learners. *Educational Technology Research and Development*, *67*(5), 1307–1331. DOI: 10.1007/s11423-019-09669-0

Long, M. H. (1981). Input, interaction, and second language acquisition. *The New York Academy of Sciences, 379*(1), 259–278. DOI: 10.1111/j.1749-6632.1981.tb42014.x

Mauidloh, N. H., Anam, S., & Widyastuti. (2024). The correlation between students' engagement and reading comprehension while using Quizlet gamification for vocabulary learning. *JORER: International Journal of Recent Educational Research, 5*(4), 1013–1025.

Meara, P. (1980). Vocabulary acquisition: A neglected aspect of language learning. *Language Teaching, 13*(3-4), 221–246. DOI: 10.1017/S0261444800008879

Mecartty, F. (2000). Lexical and grammatical knowledge in reading and listening comprehension by foreign language speakers of Spanish. *Applied Language Learning, 11*(2), 323–348.

Murtaza, M., Ahmed, Y., Shamsi, J., Sherwani, F., & Usman, M. (2022). AI-based personalized e-learning systems: Issues, challenges, and solutions. *IEEE Access : Practical Innovations, Open Solutions, 10*, 81323–81342. DOI: 10.1109/ACCESS.2022.3193938

Na-Young, K. (2020). *Chatbots and language learning: Effects of the use of AI chatbots for EFL learning*. Eliva Press.

Nasution, A. (2022). The effect of Memrise application on students' vocabulary mastery at seventh grade of MTs PAB 1 Helvetia. *Bright Vision: Journal of Language and Education, 2*(1), 32–44.

Neuman, S. B., & Dwyer, J. (2009). Missing in action: Vocabulary instruction in Pre-K. *The Reading Teacher, 62*(5), 384–392. DOI: 10.1598/RT.62.5.2

Oxford, R. L. (1990). *Language learning strategies: What every teacher should know* (1st ed.). Heinle & Heinle.

Panmei, B., & Waluyo, B. (2023). The pedagogical use of gamification in English vocabulary training and learning in higher education. *Education Sciences, 13*(1), 1–22. DOI: 10.3390/educsci13010024

Prasetyo, G. A., Martono, & Suparno. (2018). The use of Rosetta Stone as teaching media to improve students' vocabulary mastery. *English Education Journal, 6*(3), 304–311.

Quynh, P. T. (2022). Maximizing vocabulary retention with gamification tools. *Scientific Journal of Tan Trao University, 8*(4), 5–15.

Razali, N. N. F. M., & Ismail, R. (2017). The use of simulation and role-play in enhancing speaking skills in learning English language. *Journal of Education and Social Sciences, 6*(2), 72–78.

Roebuck, R. (1998). *Reading and recall in L1 and L2: A sociocultural approach.* Ablex Publishing Co.

Roever, C., & Kasper, G. (2018). Speaking in turns and sequences: Interactional competence as a target construct in testing speaking. *Language Testing, 35*(3), 331–355. DOI: 10.1177/0265532218758128

Sadeghi, K., & Farzizadeh, B. (2013). The effect of visually supported vocabulary instruction on beginner EFL learners. *MEXTESOL Journal, 37*(1), 1–12. PMID: 24902323

Saleh, A. M., & Althaqafi, A. (2022). The effect of using educational games as a tool in teaching English vocabulary to Arab young children: A quasi-experimental study in a kindergarten school in Saudi Arabia. *SAGE Open, 12*(1), 1–10. DOI: 10.1177/21582440221079806

Saptiany, S. G., Hadi, S., Hardian, B. A. N., & Nashir, M. M. (2024). Artificial intelligence-moderated gamification apps: Elevating Gen-Z's English vocabulary mastery. *Al-Ishlah Jurnal Pendidikan, 16*(4), 4969–4983. DOI: 10.35445/alishlah.v16i4.5957

Schmidt, T., & Strasser, T. (2022). Artificial intelligence in foreign language learning and teaching. *Anglistic: International Journal of English Studies, 33*(1), 165–184. DOI: 10.33675/ANGL/2022/1/14

Schmitt, N. (2000). *Vocabulary in language teaching* (1st ed.). Cambridge University Press.

Seliger, H. W., & Shohamy, E. (1989). *Second language research methods.* Oxford University Press.

Şenel, M., & Akman, D. B. (2016). Fun teaching! Fun tech-ing! Interactive educational games for young learners. *Participatory Educational Research, 2016*(1), 12–21. DOI: 10.17275/per.16.spi.1.2

Sheldon, L. (2020). *The multiplayer classroom: Designing coursework as a game* (2nd ed.). CRC Press., DOI: 10.1201/9780429285035

Sindermann, C., Sha, P., Zhou, M., Wernicke, J., Schmitt, H. S., Li, M., Sariyska, R., Stavrou, M., Becker, B., & Montag, C. (2021). Assessing the attitude towards artificial intelligence: Introduction of a short measure in German, Chinese, and English language. *KI- Künstliche Intelligenz, 35*, 109–118. DOI: 10.1007/s13218-020-00689-0

Stephenson, P., & Rumley, G. (2005). Inclusive work at a European level: A case study. *Support for Learning*, *20*(3), 141–145. DOI: 10.1111/j.0268-2141.2005.00378.x

Sumakul, D. T. Y. G., Hamied, F. A., & Sukyadi, D. (2022). Artificial intelligence in EFL classrooms: Friend or foe? *LEARN Journal: Language Education and Acquisition Research Network*, *15*(1), 232–256.

Swain, M. (2000). *The output hypothesis and beyond: Mediating acquisition through collaborative dialogue* (Lantolf, J. P., Ed.). Oxford University Press.

Tapalova, O., & Zhiyenbayeva, N. (2022). Artificial intelligence in education: AIEd for personalized learning pathways. *Electronic Journal of e-Learning*, *20*(5), 639–653. DOI: 10.34190/ejel.20.5.2597

Tapia, J. (2021). *Puzzles to foster A1 vocabulary retention in teenagers (Master's Thesis)*. Pontificia Universidad Catolica del Ecuador.

Thiagarajah, K., Ng, M. M., Jeyaraja, S. S. B., Gunasehgaran, V., & Maniam, M. (2022). Effectiveness of gamification tool in teaching vocabulary. *International Journal of Academic Research in Business & Social Sciences*, *12*(9), 1046–1063. DOI: 10.6007/IJARBSS/v12-i9/14604

Thornbury, S. (2002). *How to teach vocabulary* (1st ed.). Pearson Education Limited.

Thurairasu, V. (2022). Gamification-based learning as the future of language learning: An overview. *European Journal of Humanities and Social Sciences*, *2*(6), 62–68. DOI: 10.24018/ejsocial.2022.2.6.353

Verga, L., & Kotz, S. A. (2017). Help me if I can't: Social interaction effects in adult contextual word learning. *Cognition*, *168*, 76–90. DOI: 10.1016/j.cognition.2017.06.018 PMID: 28658646

Vygotsky, L. S. (1980). *Mind in society: The development of higher psychological processes*. Harvard University Press. DOI: 10.2307/j.ctvjf9vz4

Waer, H. (2021). Using gamification in EFL vocabulary learning and learners' attitudes towards gamification use. *Journal of Scientific Research in Education*, *22*(2), 547–570.

Waluyo, B., & Bucol, J. L. (2021). The impact of gamified vocabulary learning using Quizlet on low-proficiency students. *Computer-Assisted Language Learning Electronic Journal*, *22*(1), 158–179.

Wang, Y. F., & Petrina, S. (2013). Using learning analytics to understand the design of an intelligent language tutor- Chatbot Lucy. [IJACSA]. *International Journal of Advanced Computer Science and Applications, 4*(11), 124–131. DOI: 10.14569/IJACSA.2013.041117

Wei-Xun, L., & Jia-Ying, Z. (2024). Impact of AI-driven language learning apps on vocabulary acquisition among English learners. *Journal of Research Studies in English Language Teaching and Learning, 2*(1), 2–10. DOI: 10.62583/rseltl.v2i1.32

Wertsch, J. V. (1985). *Vygotsky and the social formation of mind*. Harvard University Press.

Wilkins, D. A. (1972). *Linguistics in language teaching*. MIT Press.

Xu. (2010). The effects of glosses on incidental vocabulary acquisition in reading. *Journal of Language Teaching and Research, 1*(2), 117–120. DOI: 10.4304/jltr.1.2.117-120

Young, R. F. (2011). Interactional competence in language learning, teaching, and testing. In Hinkel, E. (Ed.), *Handbook of research in second language teaching and learning* (2nd ed., pp. 426–443). Routledge.

Yowaboot, C., & Sukying, A. (2022). Using digital flashcards to enhance Thai EFL primary school students' vocabulary knowledge. *English Language Teaching, 15*(7), 61–74. DOI: 10.5539/elt.v15n7p61

Zhai, C., & Wibowo, S. (2023). A systematic review on artificial intelligence dialogue systems for enhancing English as foreign language students' interactional competence in the university. *Computers and Education: Artificial Intelligence, 4*, 1–26. DOI: 10.1016/j.caeai.2023.100134

Zhang, & Hasim, Z. (2023). Gamification in EFL/ ESL instruction: A systematic review of empirical research. *Frontiers in Psychology, 13*, 1–12. DOI: 10.3389/fpsyg.2022.1030790

Zohrabi, M., Tadayyon, P., & Dobahkti, L. (2018). The effects of rote and contextualized memorization on Iranian immediate EFL learners' vocabulary development. *Iranian Journal of English for Academic Purposes, 7*(2), 16–31.

Chapter 9
The Role of Artificial Intelligence in Supporting Canadian Plurilingual Graduate Students:
Opportunities, Challenges, and Implications for inclusive Education

Mohamadreza Jafary
https://orcid.org/0009-0003-7816-1330
McGill University, Canada

Sadigheh Shakib Kotamjani
https://orcid.org/0000-0001-6249-0293
Central Asian University, Uzbekistan

ABSTRACT

The evolution of Artificial Intelligence (AI) in education offers new possibilities for supporting plurilingual students within Canada's varied linguistic landscape, where learners balance official and community languages while developing academic proficiency and negotiating identities. AI tools, such as adaptive learning platforms, natural language processing technologies, and real-time translation software, provide inclusive, personalized environments. Grounded in plurilingualism and inclusive education, this chapter outlines AI's potential to support language acquisition, foster cultural inclusivity, and promote identity negotiation. It also explores systemic barriers, presenting case studies from Canadian classrooms that

DOI: 10.4018/979-8-3373-0275-1.ch009

illustrate AI's impact on student engagement and learning. Although AI offers innovative opportunities, concerns regarding equitable access, algorithmic bias, and data privacy must be addressed. Strategies for ethical application are proposed, along with context-sensitive plurilingual practices to foster metalinguistic awareness and equitable learning spaces.

INTRODUCTION

Artificial Intelligence (AI) has revolutionized numerous industries, including education. Machine learning, adaptive learning, and natural language processing algorithms are increasingly being integrated into classrooms to enhance student engagement, learning experiences, and accommodate diverse learners (Harry, 2023; Gningue, Peach, Jarrah, and Wardat, 2022). As classrooms become increasingly multilingual and multicultural, the use of Artificial Intelligence (AI) in teaching and learning presents both exciting opportunities and significant challenges.

In Canada, a country renowned for its linguistic diversity, the role of artificial intelligence (AI) is particularly important for plurilingual students, who speak multiple languages, including the country's official languages (English and French) and their heritage languages from their cultural background. For these pupils, the task is not only to gain academic language proficiency in the language of instruction, but also to maintain and develop their native languages. AI tools provide an opportunity to bridge linguistic, cognitive, and accessibility gaps among learners. However, the effective integration of AI in education raises critical questions about ethics, inclusion, linguistic identity, and pedagogical design, particularly for plurilingual students and students with disabilities.

This chapter presents a critical examination of how AI can support inclusive and plurilingual education in Canadian higher education. Drawing on Universal Design for Learning (UDL), plurilingual pedagogy, and critical pedagogy, this study examines how AI can facilitate expanded access, personalized learning, and support the diverse linguistic and cultural identities of students, many of whom navigate between English, French, Indigenous, and heritage languages. The discussion highlights systemic and classroom challenges, underscores new opportunities, and examines the broader impact of AI on teaching practices and education policies within Canada's higher education system. The chapter aims to explore the major challenges involved in using AI in inclusive, linguistically diverse learning settings and identify ways in which AI can improve access, tailor learning experiences, and support students' linguistic identities; and third, to explore the pedagogical, policy, and equity implications of AI-enhanced education in Canadian higher education.

BACKGROUND

Plurilingualism refers to a person's ability to use multiple languages effectively and to switch fluidly between them, often depending on the social or cultural context of the interaction (Galante, 2022; Polyakova & Galstyan-Sargsyan, 2021).In contrast with multilingualism, which conceptualizes languages as separate entities held by individuals or societies, plurilingualism emphasizes how speakers draw from an integrated linguistic repertoire, often mixing languages flexibly across various social, cultural, and educational contexts (Piccardo, 2020). A plurilingual approach to language instruction aims to raise awareness of how languages interact with our society, while also highlighting the importance of language and culture.

In Canada's bilingual and multicultural educational setting, the plurilingual approach aligns well with lived realities. Most Canadian learners encounter multiple languages informally—on cereal boxes, product labels, and digital platforms—even before formal language instruction begins (Hebert et al., 2008; Kubota & Bale, 2020; Maatouk & Payant, 2022).Crucially, Canadian classrooms today are home to students who speak a wide range of languages—Indigenous languages, Punjabi, Mandarin, Arabic, Spanish, and more. These students navigate an education system that typically centers English or French as the primary language of instruction, posing challenges to linguistic equity and engagement. However, their plurilingualism is not a deficit but a powerful asset (Galante et al., 2019; Kubota & Bale, 2020; Maatouk & Payant, 2022). In this context, AI tools offer promising paths for speech recognition, AI-based translators, and adaptive learning applications can empower multilingual students by providing real-time support, making learning more accessible and dynamic. Studies in higher education have shown that recognizing and valuing students' plurilingual competence is essential for better learning.

Theoretical Framework: Plurilingualism and Inclusive Education

This theoretical framework integrates three dimensions of plurilingualism, inclusive education, and artificial intelligence (AI) to inform a Future-oriented perspective for multilingual education in Canadian higher education.

Inclusive education in this plurilingual context is not limited to physical access but extends to linguistic and cultural inclusion. It aims to validate students' identities and support learning pathways tailored to their diverse linguistic backgrounds (García & Otheguy, 2020). In Canadian settings, where linguistic heterogeneity is the norm, inclusive education guided by plurilingual principles fosters both equity and engagement (Marshall et al., 2021)

Tools such as adaptive learning platforms, natural language processing, and real-time translation can support 'plurilanguaging'—the intentional, context-responsive use of multiple languages. These technologies promote personalized instruction, metalinguistic awareness, and the formation of linguistic identity (Duarte & van der Ploeg, 2019; Galante, 2020; Hopp & Thoma, 2021). AI can scaffold differentiated learning paths, provide multilingual feedback, and enable multimodal expression, all of which align with the goals of plurilingual, inclusive education (Marshall et al., 2021).

Thus, educators should align AI applications with frameworks such as the CEFR's plurilingual and pluricultural competences to ensure an ethical and inclusive implementation (Council of Europe, 2020). This framework suggests that AI, when carefully designed and ethically applied, can serve as a pedagogical assistant in operationalizing plurilingualism and fostering inclusive, equity-driven education. It offers educators a pathway to engage learners' full linguistic repertoires in personalized and socially just learning environments.

Plurilingualism, Identity, and the Role of AI in Affirming Linguistic Belonging

Emphasizing the interdependence of language, identity, and belonging, a plurilingual approach to teaching and learning fundamentally challenges the concept of language as a bounded, individual skill, instead viewing it as a fluid, contextualized use of multiple linguistic resources that reflect students' multifaceted social realities. Students' educational success is not only a cognitive process but is also inherently tied to the assertion of their identity. When students correspond their linguistic and cultural identities as legitimate in and across pedagogy, they are positioned for increased engagement and academic success (Corsi, 2023).

To date, simplified models of language acquisition—often corroborated by high-stakes testing—stand to erode students' communicative repertoires, resulting in lowered self-esteem, reduced engagement, and compromised sense of belonging (D'warte, 2021) reiterates this sentiment, asserting that, "when educators ignore students' plurilingual knowledge in the classroom, they ignore students' social and cultural capital, inhibiting their abilities to create ties of significance in school, at home, and in the wider community." In Australia, the evolution of the curriculum supports reflective and inclusive practices that promote students' use of their experiences across subject areas (Dutton & Rushton, 2021; Tour et al., 2024). In the same vein, research emphasizes the need for students' cultural and linguistic identities to be a part of curricular content and teaching strategies (Fielding, 2016; Slaughter & Cross, 2021).

Artificial intelligence technologies are now being developed to support this pedagogical shift. AI can be a powerful ally in developing identity-promoting practices. With technologies in adaptive learning platforms, AI-generated language portfolios, and real-time multi-language feedback, teachers can more accurately represent their students' plurilingual realities. AI tools can also represent students' home languages in the teaching context without displacing the target language of instruction, which represents an inclusive practice while promoting equity of identity. For instance, intelligent language processing tools could analyze code-switching tendencies or translanguaging patterns in students, not only providing context scaffolds to support learning but also affirming students' language identity. AI technology affords thoughtful design options for user-driven language practices, such as a dual assessment language interface or the opportunity for student-created content annotation.

AI can also enable a student-generated portfolio that reflects content developed in their own identities across languages and modes (e.g., spoken word, digital storytelling, or poetic performance), thereby honoring students as language learners and knowledge producers. This concept is closely related to the idea of "identity texts," where students express themselves (Ntouvlis & Geenen, 2023; Sales et al., 2023). The potential of AI needs to be ethically considered at this stage. There is a possibility of affirming standard language ideologies if an AI system is developed with biases that utilize limited or monolingual datasets. In contrast, to enact a truly plurilingual and inclusive pedagogy, attention to AI design is imperative: AI should utilize multi-source corpora, allow design based on user linguistic input, and incorporate multilingual evaluation measures. Teachers will also need to be trained to view AI-constructed knowledge through a culturally responsive lens, thereby avoiding the homogenization of learners' diverse and complex identities when interpreting various data. Emerging research also substantiates applying students' lived narratives and language experiences in digital learning contexts to develop a relatedness between school knowledge and cultural identity (Dutton & Rushton, 2021). For example, AI multilingual writing platforms can assist students with reflective essays, family narratives, or community history texts that use a collection of their language inputs. This strategy will improve literacy development, metalinguistic awareness, and intergenerational knowledge transfer.

OPPORTUNITIES OF AI IN PLURILINGUAL AND INCLUSIVE PEDAGOGIES

Artificial Intelligence (AI) has the potential to reshape higher education in Canada significantly by supporting more inclusive and plurilingual teaching approaches. Particularly for students navigating multiple languages, including English and

French, Canada's official languages, as well as their heritage languages(Galante et al., 2019; Kubota & Bale, 2020; Maatouk & Payant, 2022). The integration of artificial intelligence (AI) into Canadian higher education offers transformative opportunities to promote pluralistic and inclusive education.(Gabriel, 2024; Garg & Sharma, 2020). These opportunities support the objectives of enhancing access, customization, and linguistic validation, while also meeting the diverse needs of plurilingual students. The following section highlights six key opportunities: adaptive learning platforms, AI-powered translation and speech recognition tools, enhanced learner autonomy, validation of heritage languages, expansion of Universal Design for Learning (UDL) principles, and metalinguistic awareness.

Adaptive Learning Platforms: Personalizing Instruction for Linguistic Diversity

Adaptive learning systems utilize AI to create educational content tailored to students' linguistic profiles and performance data, resulting in personalized learning paths that meet the diverse needs of multilingual students. These systems analyze student interactions using algorithms, then adjust the content, complexity, and pace of training to accommodate varying degrees of student ability across multiple languages. In Canadian higher education, where students sometimes combine English, French, and heritage languages such as Punjabi, Mandarin, or Indigenous languages like Cree, this customization is crucial.

Recent Research indicates that AI-mediated language instruction enhances grammar (Fitria, 2021), vocabulary (Agnes & Srinivasan, 2024; Alsadoon, 2021), pronunciation (Sun, 2023)reading comprehension(Dong et al., 2022; Kim & Cha, 2023), and writing ability (Harunasari, 2023; Marzuki et al., 2023; Rabbianty et al., 2023). With a 25% increase in test scores over ten weeks, Wei (2023) found in a mixed-methods study that university students who received AI-mediated training outperformed those who received traditional education. Qualitative results highlighted the interesting and immersive nature of AI-mediated learning, particularly among multilingual students, fostering intrinsic motivation and autonomy. In line with this, Maximova et al. (2023) reported that adaptive learning improved academic performance in 59% of 69 studies and student engagement in 36%, proving its potential to support various students, including plurilingual students. These results suggest that adaptive platforms are well-suited to meet the specific needs of children who speak multiple languages, thereby becoming a valuable tool for inclusive education.

For example, a French-speaking student studying sociology in English might benefit from English materials supplemented with French glossaries for added support. Moreover, AI provides real-time feedback, helping students identify correct grammar or vocabulary errors and encouraging more independent and self-regulated learning (Alsadoon, 2021) Many Indigenous languages, like Inuktitut, are underrepresented in the datasets that train these tools, making them far less inclusive. Moreover, privacy remains a major concern, especially with data tracking, which must comply with the Personal Information Protection and Electronic Documents Act (PIPEDA) in Canada.

AI-Powered Translation and Speech Recognition Tools

By removing language barriers, AI-powered translation and speech recognition tools allow plurilingual students to interact with academic materials in their preferred languages, therefore facilitating access to educational materials. These resources provide mentor texts, simplify complex materials, and adjust reading levels, thereby scaffolding learning for students with varying language competencies (Khasawneh, 2023; Yuxiu, 2024). In Canadian higher education, where students from diverse backgrounds, such as those who speak Arabic or Mandarin, may struggle with dense academic materials, these tools are invaluable for ensuring fair access to the curriculum.

Studies show that by offering individualized language support, artificial intelligence solutions help multilingual students (Ben, 2023). For example, Rabbianty et al. (2023) observed that AI systems can create language objectives and supports, including sentence frames and word banks, customized to students' competence degrees in under 30 seconds. These resources enable students to acquire challenging content while refining their language skills. AI can, for instance, simplify difficult academic material so that it is within reach for students who only speak the language of instruction. Pronunciation feedback provided by speech recognition software enables students to enhance their proficiency in the target language. For students navigating multiple languages, Wei (2023) found that those using AI-assisted speech recognition technologies demonstrated enhanced grammatical accuracy and vocabulary expansion, which are critical skills.

Speech recognition tools can help learners improve their pronunciation and build conversational fluency. For instance, a student who speaks Spanish might use artificial intelligence to translate English course notes into Spanish, thereby ensuring understanding without delaying their academic progress. During lectures, real-time translation platforms can provide transcripts and subtitles in dozens of languages, allowing students to follow along in their language. Large lecture halls, especially, benefit from this, as plurilingual students may struggle to follow English or French instruction. Speech recognition tools can support pronunciation practice, allowing a student studying French as a third language to receive instant feedback on conversational skills, thereby building confidence and competence.

While speech recognition tools promote English pronunciation practice and preserve fluency in heritage languages, a professor in a Canadian literature course could utilize artificial intelligence to translate important works into Hindi for Hindi-speaking students. Future developments in natural language processing (NLP) should prioritize less common languages. Working with linguists will help to improve tool efficacy and guarantee inclusiveness for every learner.

Validation of Heritage Languages: Multilingual AI Interfaces

By allowing students to speak their native languages in educational contexts, multilingual artificial intelligence interfaces authenticate them and help them to feel a sense of belonging and cultural affirmation. For plurilingual students, who may feel excluded if their languages are not acknowledged, AI interfaces foster linguistic identity and inclusiveness by allowing students to interact with academic materials in their native languages, thereby complementing Canada's commitment to linguistic diversity.

Studies emphasize the importance of achieving plurilingual competency for enhanced learning outcomes (Galante, 2020). (Akinsanya Atchrimi et al., 2023) highlighted that by allowing students to use their heritage languages in academic activities, AI systems can create multilingual support, including word banks and sentence frames, therefore reinforcing their linguistic identities. For instance, a student who speaks Spanish might utilize artificial intelligence to translate English course notes into Spanish, thereby enhancing their understanding while maintaining their proficiency in the original language. Celebrating linguistic diversity and encouraging students to view their languages as academic assets, educators can create inclusive materials, such as bilingual textbooks or multimedia tools, incorporating Arabic or Hindi.

These interfaces can be effectively integrated into educational settings to support students who speak multiple languages. In a course on Canadian history, for example, a lecturer may display slides in Spanish alongside English materials, allowing a Spanish-speaking student to submit homework that includes mixed languages with AI-generated comments. This method not only confirms the student's heritage language but also encourages involvement by simplifying academic content. However, two very important issues are accuracy and cultural sensitivity. Translations can overlook subtleties or cultural references; therefore, teacher confirmation is necessary to ensure accuracy and precision. Support for fewer widely spoken languages, including Indigenous languages like Cree or Inuktitut, is scant, running the risk of excluding minority language speakers. Inclusivity can be undermined by bias in AI datasets that favor dominant languages; therefore, different training data is needed to ensure fair representation.

Fostering Metalinguistic Awareness: Supporting Hybrid Language Practices

By facilitating hybrid language activities, such as translanguaging, in which students dynamically use multiple languages to construct meaning, artificial intelligence promotes metalinguistic awareness. For plurilingual students, this is natural and improves their grasp of language structures across their repertoire—a vital ability for academic and practical communication. AI fosters linguistic competency and cultural awareness by providing feedback on language use and supporting multilingual interactions, thereby helping students develop a deeper understanding of how their languages interact.

By assessing and providing feedback on students' use of multiple languages, research suggests that artificial intelligence systems can support translanguaging (Duarte, 2019; Vallejo & Dooly, 2020). AI can, for instance, deconstruct texts to examine figurative language, syntax, and punctuation, thereby guiding students toward linguistic structures that transcend languages. By comparing the structures of their native language with AI, a student examining a phrase from 'The Great Gatsby' book can learn idioms in English. AI also offers multilingual writing feedback, therefore enhancing grammar, vocabulary, and style in all languages. For example, a plurilingual student producing an article in English that incorporates Spanish words can receive AI recommendations for clarity, thereby improving their ability to navigate multiple languages.

Practically, educators can utilize artificial intelligence to provide multilingual resources, including texts that combine English and Hindi terminology, thereby enabling students to recognize linguistic connections. During conversations, real-time translating lets students participate in their preferred languages, therefore promoting translanguaging and inclusive communication. AI may, however, struggle to translate between languages, especially in less commonly spoken languages, such as Indigenous ones, necessitating ongoing improvements in accuracy. Improving AI's support of hybrid behaviors depends on cooperation between educators and linguists.

In a Canadian linguistics course, a student might employ artificial intelligence to practice conversational translanguaging—mixing English and Hindi—with feedback on grammar and vocabulary to improve metalinguistic awareness. To ensure inclusivity, future tools should provide enhanced support for sophisticated language mixing, particularly for Indigenous and minority languages, thereby promoting inclusiveness. Interactive language analysis tools should be investigated further through research to enhance metalinguistic awareness in plurilingual environments.

Enhanced Learner Autonomy: Real-Time Feedback and Differentiated Pathways

Through real-time feedback and tailored learning paths, artificial intelligence enhances learner autonomy, enabling plurilingual students to manage their education and development at their own pace. Students managing multiple languages rely on this autonomy, as it enables them to meet specific language requirements while working toward academic objectives. Studies reveal that artificial intelligence can support students' language competence, allowing access to challenging content and promoting language growth (Madhavi et al., 2023).

For example, a learner proficient in English but a novice in French could access differentiated modules in both languages. When a learner writes a grammatically incorrect French sentence, for example, AI can identify errors, explain them, and provide corrections, thereby supporting learning. Differentiated paths enable students to choose learning activities tailored to their interests and ability levels. A student who speaks advanced English but has a basic level of Spanish might receive advanced English assignments and basic Spanish exercises on the same platform, allowing them to improve their weaker language using their stronger one. This adaptability meets the needs of plurilingual students who manage courses across multiple languages.

To properly utilize these AI tools, however, students must be digitally literate, a skill that requires institutional support and training. A dependency on artificial intelligence that is too great runs the risk of diminishing human interaction, which is essential for emotional support and navigating complex language challenges. Teachers must strike a balance between the use of AI and group projects to maintain student interest. Future tools could include social-emotional learning (SEL) trackers to track affective engagement, therefore guaranteeing motivation among multilingual students. Studies on self-regulated learning techniques tailored for multilingual environments should help to improve the function of artificial intelligence in promoting autonomy.

Expansion of Universal Design for Learning (UDL) Principles: AI-Based Environments

Universal Design for Learning (UDL) is a revolutionary educational framework that proactively attends to the diversity of learning needs, experiences, and preferences of all students. Drawing its roots from architecture and disability studies, Universal Design for Learning (UDL) reshapes education in a way that is always inclusive, thereby celebrating flexibility, choice, and access (Almeqdad et al., 2023; Boothe et al., 2018. UDL signifies that variability is normal, not exceptional, and instructional design should be flexible from the outset, rather than providing support for students with exceptionalities through retrofitting. UDL is built around three core pillars: multiple means of representation, multiple means of engagement, and multiple means of expression (Black et al., 2015; Bray et al., 2024). These three dimensions should encourage educators to represent content in different formats (e.g., text, video, audio, infographics), participate through different means of engagement (e.g., projects based on the students' interests, collaborative inquiry), and allow for multiple means for learners to demonstrate their understanding (e.g., essays, multimedia projects, oral presentations).

To serve diverse students, Universal Design for Learning (UDL) proposes several approaches to representation, engagement, and expression. AI-based environments enhance accessibility and engagement by offering materials in multiple languages and formats, thereby aligning with the objectives of inclusive education in Canadian higher education.

Supporting students with different language and learning needs, artificial intelligence may create information in multiple formats, including text, audio, or video (Song et al., 2024). For video courses, for instance, artificial intelligence can offer subtitles or captions in many languages, therefore helping deaf or native language speakers. While interactive simulations serve those who study visually, text-to-speech alternatives in languages such as Mandarin or French allow students to listen to the materials. AI ensures students receive suitable challenges by adjusting content complexity based on their performance. For example, AI can explain English scientific vocabulary in a student's native language, therefore enabling knowledge and involvement even if the student struggles with English.

Real-time feedback and support provide quick help for language-related difficulties, therefore aligning with UDL principles. For students who speak multiple languages and require assistance with grammar or vocabulary, this is especially useful. A scoping study by Maximova et al. (2023) highlighted that adaptive learning platforms, which align with Universal Design for Learning (UDL), enhance academic achievement and engagement, making them a valuable tool for diverse learners. AI systems must, however, utilize diverse datasets to avoid biases that favor dominant languages or cultures, thereby excluding speakers of minority languages. Students with disabilities also have great access; hence, inclusive design is essential to guarantee that every student can benefit. To effectively integrate artificial intelligence into Universal Design for Learning (UDL) systems and ensure pedagogical alignment and optimal utilization of these technologies, educators must receive training.

Case Studies: Supporting Plurilingual Graduate Students in a Canadian University

This section highlights a pilot study on integrating AI into a plurilingual and inclusive environment at McGill University in Canada, where a diverse graduate student population, comprising both local and international students who speak English, French, and their native languages such as Farsi, Hindi, Igbo, and Mandarin, is present (Jafary & Shakib Kotamjani, 2025). The goal of this pilot study was to investigate how AI tools can be utilized to improve linguistic accessibility and academic inclusion within a multilingual context in Canada.

The university's learning management system was equipped with AI-powered translation tools, such as DeepL and Google Translate, to enable students to translate assignments, announcements, and reading sections into their preferred languages (Khasawneh, 2023; Muñoz-Basols et al., 2023). The university also provided writing support platforms, such as Grammarly and Writefull, to help students improve their coherence, grammar, and vocabulary in their multilingual academic writing (Harunasari, 2023; Marzuki et al., 2023; Rabbianty et al., 2023). Furthermore, speech-to-text and pronunciation feedback tools have been introduced to support non-native speakers in developing their spoken communication skills, primarily in English and French(Sun, 2023). To support AI integration, several workshops were held to help lecturers understand how to interpret AI-generated feedback and lead students in using these tools correctly. Students were also assigned to reflect on their language learning strategies through blending translanguaging practices and AI-assisted journaling (Heugh et al., 2022).

The results of the pilot study revealed that plurilingual students increased their academic literacy and confidence while using AI tools to support their writing and reading comprehension. For instance, one of the international French-speaking students from Algeria shared his experience with AI translation tools to understand complex academic texts better and used grammar checkers to proofread his assignments and thesis in English. Similarly, an Iranian student who was struggling with fluency used AI-driven speech recognition software to practice her presentations and improve her fluency and pronunciation. These students reported that AI tools supported them in their language learning journey and boosted their confidence. Moreover, many students became more active in class discussions through the linguistic support available to them. Some students who were disadvantaged due to their language backgrounds reported feeling less stressed while interacting with AI.

However, some students face some challenges with AI Translation tools when they fail to translate culturally nuanced language and idiomatic phrases, thereby leading to confusion rather than clarity. Some students also reported that AI systems showed bias toward standardized dialects by suggesting less accurate responses for non-standard varieties of languages. This result is supported by other research indicating that AI tools lack meaningful support for Indigenous languages, which raises serious concerns about equity in AI use (Kaur et al., 2023; Martin et al., 2020; Maximova et al., 2023). Moreover, Canada's PIPEDA legislation has raised valid ethical concerns about data privacy in the reliance on AI platforms (Office of the Privacy Commissioner of Canada, 2022). Regardless of these issues, the results of this pilot study revealed that AI tools have the potential to support plurilingual learners in tertiary education when they are implemented with ethical oversight and cultural sensitivity.

CHALLENGES IN IMPLEMENTING AI FOR INCLUSIVE PLURILINGUAL EDUCATION IN CANADA

Plurilingual education, which builds upon a learner's full linguistic and cultural repertoire – including Indigenous languages, official languages of English and French, and immigrant languages – is aligned with Canada's commitment to diversity and inclusion. While AI offers a range of potential for personalizing learning, providing feedback, and real-time translation, its implementation in inclusive plurilingual education in Canada poses major challenges.

Data Bias and Representativeness

The fairness and effectiveness of AI systems are related to the datasets from which they learn. The majority of AI systems are programmed on English language corpora, compiled from internet content, formal texts, and communication data that reflect Western discourse (Lin, 2023; Zhang & Zhu, 2023). Therefore, these systems might lack exposure to the lexical, grammatical, and cultural patterns of minority languages and dialects(Khasawneh, 2023; Liu, 2025). This leads to reduced accuracy in recognizing, translating, or generating language for speakers of Indigenous, heritage, and minority languages. When AI educational tools fail to recognize regional expressions, code-switching, or culturally embedded meanings (Kang et al., 2024). Language learners may receive incorrect feedback, which can impact their academic confidence and engagement. This will create significant challenges for Canada's diverse linguistic landscape.

Linguistic Bias

Most AI models are primarily trained on large English-language corpora, which often makes it challenging for them to effectively understand, generate, or process content in other languages spoken across Canada, such as French, Indigenous languages, and the numerous languages used by immigrant communities. This kind of bias often results in less effective personalized learning and inaccurate or culturally insensitive language assessments, where non-English languages are overlooked or misrepresented. For instance, an AI writing tool might offer grammatically accurate suggestions in English, but struggle to recognize and support the nuances of Canadian French or specific structures of Indigenous languages.

Cultural and Contextual Bias

Language and culture are deeply intertwined; therefore, understanding cultural content is vital for mastering a second language. Cultural and contextual bias occurs when AI systems reflect the values, assumptions, and norms of a dominant culture, often excluding those of other cultures (Galante, 2022).This bias becomes especially important in education, where AI tools are playing a key role in language learning and cross-cultural communication.

Obed Boateng & Bright Boateng (2025) conducted research to explore how AI-based language learning systems often overlook cultural nuances, which can alienate learners whose identities are shaped by diverse languages and cultural backgrounds. Similarly, Lewis (2025) found that biases in AI tools caused participation among minority students to drop by over 30%. This highlights the importance of developing AI systems that are trained on diverse and representative datasets to ensure fair and inclusive educational experiences for all learners. In the same vein, Font de la Vall & Araya (2023) explained that while AI language learning tools often remain "blind" to the cultural origins of learners. When cultural sensitivity is lacking, learning environments can become ineffective, leaving students feeling overlooked or marginalized. Stibel & Barrett (2023) highlight how the systemic biases present in society often make their way into AI technologies. They argue that language learning tools can inadvertently reinforce stereotypes and marginalize minority groups.

Plurilingual learners—those who move between multiple languages and cultural contexts—often find that AI tools fail to reflect the complexity of their linguistic identities. As Danilina & Pichon, (2023) points out that AI tools overlook or disregard such nuances, which leads to alienation. Recent studies by Ben (2023) and Lewis (2025) have highlighted that AI tools often overlook cultural contexts, which are crucial for effective learning. These studies underscore the importance of culturally responsive AI systems in education. This lack of recognition can reduce learners' engagement and work against the goals of inclusive education.

Moreover, errors in machine translation or speech recognition—especially when dialectal differences are overlooked—can intensify these challenges. To overcome this shortcoming, Lewis (2025) proposes the METAL (Multicultural Education through Technology-Assisted Learning) framework, which entrenches multicultural content and adaptive algorithms into AI tools to create more inclusive learning environments and improve language learning outcomes for students from diverse cultural backgrounds. Several studies emphasize the importance of adding multilingual capabilities to artificial intelligence in educational settings (Nguyen et al., 2023; de la Vall & Araya, 2023; Soylu & Şahin, 2024).

Underrepresentation of Indigenous Languages

Data bias is a serious challenge for Indigenous languages, which need to be preserved and revitalized. There is a lack of digital resources, transcribed texts, and spoken data in these languages, which makes it difficult to train AI models that could truly support their preservation, learning, and integration into educational settings(Martin Doherty, 2025). If such a foundational dataset cannot be created and curated ethically, AI endangers marginalizing these linguistic and cultural heritages, accelerating language loss rather than promoting revitalization (Soylu & Şahin, 2024).

Pedagogical Integration and Teacher Preparedness

The successful integration of AI into plurilingual education is not merely a technological feat but fundamentally a pedagogical challenge that necessitates significant shifts in teaching practices and robust teacher preparedness ;(Lotherington et al., 2022; Shakib Kotamjani et al., 2023).

Developing AI tools that authentically support and enhance complex plurilingual pedagogical approaches, such as translanguaging, code-switching, or fostering metalinguistic awareness across languages, requires a deep understanding of these practices (Galante et al., 2022). AI models initially designed for traditional, monolingual instruction may not be readily adaptable to the dynamic and fluid linguistic practices common in plurilingual classrooms. There is a need for AI solutions that can leverage, rather than tolerate, students' diverse linguistic repertoires (Dela Cruz, 2022).

Teacher Training and Digital Literacy

Many educators in Canada, while proficient in their subject areas, may lack the specialized training, digital literacy, and critical understanding required to effectively select, utilize, and adapt AI tools for diverse linguistic needs (Maatouk & Payant, 2022). There is a pressing need for comprehensive professional development programs that equip teachers not only with the technical skills to operate AI tools but also with a critical pedagogical lens to integrate AI ethically and effectively into plurilingual contexts (Chan, 2023; Kitcharoen et al., 2024). Such training should address how AI can support cross-linguistic connections and validate students' diverse linguistic identities.

Maintaining Human Connection and Pedagogical Judgment

While AI can provide personalized learning paths, automate feedback (Sharples, 2023) and assist with administrative tasks, there is a legitimate concern about the potential for dehumanizing the learning experience if AI is implemented without careful consideration (Michel-Villarreal et al., 2023). For plurilingual learners, the empathetic understanding, cultural responsiveness, and personal connection provided by human educators who can navigate complex linguistic and cultural identities are paramount. AI should be viewed as an assistive technology that augments, rather than replaces, the irreplaceable human element of teaching and mentorship (Chemnad & Othman, 2024; Gabriel, 2024; Kang et al., 2024).

Equity and Accessibility

One of the primary challenges of integrating AI in plurilingual education is the unequal access to AI tools and digital infrastructure. Ensuring equitable access to AI technologies is a foundational challenge, particularly given Canada's vast geography and socio-economic diversity (Attard-Frost et al., 2023; Martin Doherty, 2025). Particularly among students residing in rural schools, newcomer communities, and those from lower socioeconomic backgrounds who might not have access to the necessary devices, internet connectivity, or institutional support to benefit from AI-enhanced learning environments fully (Bakdash et al., 2024; Trust et al., 2023). This creates a significant barrier when attempting to utilize AI tools, such as speech-to-text applications or real-time translation software, which rely heavily on robust connectivity and compatible technology.

Not all schools, particularly those in rural, remote, and Indigenous communities across Canada, possess the reliable high-speed internet or the necessary technological infrastructure such as sufficient devices, robust Wi-Fi networks to support AI-powered learning tools effectively (Attard-Frost et al., 2023).These existing disparities in connectivity and device availability can significantly exacerbate the digital divide, limiting the potential benefits of AI for already underserved populations.

Financial Barriers to AI in Plurilingual Education

Cost is another significant barrier to the use of AI tools in education. While platforms like Grammarly, DeepL Pro, and ChatGPT Plus offer powerful features, such as multilingual support, instant feedback, and tools that enhance accessibility, these are often locked behind paywalls (Humble & Mozelius, 2022; Selwyn, 2024). For many students, especially those from low-income backgrounds or those who are immigrants or refugees, these costs are not affordable. As a result, students who might benefit most from these tools are often the ones left out. Even when universities provide institutional access, it does not always help—some students are excluded due to limited licenses or complicated login procedures that make the tools difficult to access (Harry, 2023a; Pisica et al., 2023).

Furthermore, students from lower socio-economic backgrounds may face additional barriers, such as a lack of personal devices or stable internet access at home. This can limit their ability to engage with and benefit from AI-enhanced learning outside of school hours, potentially widening existing achievement gaps rather than narrowing them (Amin, 2023; Androshchuk, 2023). Ensuring universal and equitable access to such specialized plurilingual AI tools across all school boards and provinces will require substantial and sustained financial investment from various levels of government, coupled with strategic partnerships (Harry, 2023b; Vallejo & Dooly, 2020).

Barriers for Students with Disabilities

AI must be designed to be accessible to all students, including those with disabilities. Research by Pierres et al. (2024), Garg & Sharma (2020) and Wald (2021) found that AI applications often fail to consider the specific needs of students with disabilities. A report by Garg & Sharma (2020) and Wise et al. (2020) emphasize that technology must be designed to meet the needs of all learners, particularly in diverse classrooms. In addition, adaptive learning systems can sometimes misinterpret the needs of students with learning differences or neurodiverse traits, placing them on unsuitable learning tracks or excluding them from more advanced material (Guo et al., 2020; Rajagopal et al., 2023). For example, AI-powered writing assessment tools may unfairly penalize students with dyslexia or ADHD, focusing deeply on issues like structure and coherence without considering alternative ways of expressing ideas or recognizing their unique strengths (Guo et al., 2020; Shiva Dalili & Bahman Zohuri, 2023).

Ethical Considerations and Data Privacy

Student Data Privacy

AI systems essentially collect and analyze massive amounts of sensitive students' data, such as learning patterns, academic performance, behavioral data, and linguistic data. Protecting this information from unauthorized access and misuse is paramount, particularly when dealing with minors (Huang et al., 2023; Morley et al., 2023; Siau & Wang, 2020).Morley et al. (2023) emphasize that clear, enforceable regulations, robust cybersecurity measures, and transparent data governance policies are crucial for sustaining trust and protecting student rights.

Algorithmic Transparency and Accountability

The “black box” nature of many complex AI algorithms makes it challenging to entirely understand how decisions, such as personalized learning recommendations, automated assessment results, or content generation, are made (Nitzberg & Zysman, 2022; Sandu et al., 2022).In plurilingual education, this lack of transparency can lead to concerns about fairness and accountability, particularly if an AI system unintentionally disadvantages speakers of certain languages, dialects, or those employing specific plurilingual strategies. Mechanisms for auditing and explaining AI decisions are crucial (Danilina & Pichon, 2023).

Fairness and Bias Mitigation

Beyond the biases in training data, inherent biases can also exist within the AI algorithms themselves, leading to unfair or discriminatory outcomes (Lewis, 2025b; Obed Boateng & Bright Boateng, 2025). Continuous monitoring, rigorous auditing, and iterative refinement of AI models are crucial for identifying and mitigating these biases, particularly those that may affect plurilingual learners who exhibit unique linguistic or cultural patterns that are not adequately captured or understood by current AI. This includes addressing biases that might impact non-native English writers or those using diverse accents (Min, 2023; Nitzberg & Zysman, 2022).

Policy, Governance, and Standardization

Canada's constitutionally decentralized education system, with primary jurisdiction residing with provincial and territorial governments, introduces another layer of complexity for AI integration (Gaon & Stedman, 2019; Lepage-Richer & McKelvey, 2022). There is currently no comprehensive, harmonized national framework or consistently clear provincial/territorial policies specifically addressing the ethical, equitable, and pedagogical implementation of AI in K-12 education, let alone for complex plurilingual contexts (Lepage-Richer & McKelvey, 2022).

This fragmented approach can lead to inconsistencies in AI adoption, quality assurance, data safeguards, and educational outcomes across different regions. While some provinces like British Columbia, New Brunswick, and Quebec have introduced guidelines, a broader, coordinated strategy is needed (Attard-Frost et al., 2023; Kubota & Bale, 2020; Lepage-Richer & McKelvey, 2022).

Procurement and Vetting Challenges

School boards and individual educators often face the daunting task of vetting a vast array of AI tools from various vendors. Without clear, comprehensive, and widely accepted guidelines for evaluating AI educational technologies, there is a significant risk of adopting tools that are not pedagogically sound for plurilingual education, lack robust privacy protections, perpetuate biases, or are not adaptable to the specific needs of diverse learners (Attard-Frost et al., 2023; Kubota & Bale, 2020).

Sustainability and Scalability

Developing and maintaining AI tools specifically tailored for the diverse linguistic needs of Canada, particularly for smaller Indigenous language communities or less commonly taught immigrant languages, requires significant and ongoing investment in research, development, and infrastructure. Ensuring the long-term sustainability and scalability of these specialized AI solutions is a considerable challenge that necessitates collaborative efforts between government, academia, industry, and linguistic communities (Gaon & Stedman, 2019; Hebert et al., 2008; Hervieux & Wheatley, 2021).

Implications for Practice, Policy, and Equity

The integration of AI into plurilingual and inclusive education in Canadian higher education offers exciting possibilities—but also comes with significant responsibilities. Building on the opportunities explored earlier, this section highlights key takeaways for educators, institutional leaders, and policymakers. The focus is on how to turn AI-supported strategies into meaningful, equitable, and linguistically responsive practices that truly benefit all learners.

Pedagogical Implications: Humanizing AI through Plurilingual Pedagogy

Teachers should be equipped to use AI not just for efficiency, but as a meaningful partner in creating more inclusive and engaging learning environments. This means:

- Designing multilingual learning experiences that reflect and respect students' language backgrounds and cultural identities.

- Integrating translanguaging into AI-supported activities to encourage metalinguistic awareness and support cross-language learning.
- Giving students flexible options in how they express themselves—through their choice of language, format, and medium—using AI tools, in line with Universal Design for Learning (UDL) principles.

To support this, teacher education programs need to include critical AI literacy. Educators should be prepared to interpret algorithmic feedback, recognize built-in biases, and adjust AI-generated content in culturally responsive ways.

Institutional Implications: Building Inclusive Digital Infrastructure

To truly support inclusive and plurilingual education, institutions need to invest in digital infrastructure that is multilingual, multimodal, and accessible to all learners. This means:

- Choosing or developing AI platforms that accommodate a broad range of languages, including Indigenous and heritage languages, not just dominant ones.
- Putting policies in place to provide free or low-cost access to essential AI tools for students from underrepresented or low-income backgrounds.
- Making sure AI tools work seamlessly with accessibility features like screen readers, closed captions, and adaptive input devices.

In addition, institutions should actively promote collaboration across disciplines, bringing together technologists, linguists, and educators to co-design AI tools that are culturally and linguistically responsive.

Policy Implications: Safeguarding Equity and Linguistic Rights

Policymakers have a crucial role to play in ensuring that the integration of AI in education promotes both innovation and fairness. To do this, they should:

- Require transparency in how educational AI systems are trained, with an emphasis on cultural and linguistic representation.
- Encourage institutions to track and report how AI is being used, breaking down outcomes by language, disability, and other key equity factors.
- Invest in research and development of AI tools that prioritize linguistic diversity and respond to the needs of specific communities.

Importantly, policy frameworks must also align with Canada's Official Languages Act and the Calls to Action from the Truth and Reconciliation Commission, especially in ensuring fair and meaningful access for both Francophone and Indigenous learners.

Ethical Implications: Centering Plurilingual Justice in AI Design

AI tools in plurilingual education should uplift and reflect linguistic and cultural diversity, rather than flattening or erasing it. Ethical design requires careful attention to:

- Challenging the built-in biases of language models that tend to favor standardized English or French, often at the expense of other languages and dialects.
- Protecting student data and ensuring full compliance with Canadian privacy laws like PIPEDA, especially when AI tracks how students use language or monitors their progress.
- Establishing clear and accessible channels for students and educators to report when AI tools misinterpret dialects, heritage languages, or culturally specific content.

Ultimately, ethical AI design in education means prioritizing linguistic justice, ensuring that all learners feel seen, respected, and supported.

Research Implications: Expanding Evidence and Co-Design Approaches

Looking ahead, research needs to play a central role in shaping how AI supports inclusive, plurilingual education. Key areas of focus should include:

- Studying the long-term effects of AI on plurilingual students' academic achievement, sense of identity, and personal agency.
- Exploring the potential of AI to aid in revitalizing Indigenous languages and supporting community-led language preservation efforts.
- Using participatory design approaches that involve plurilingual students, educators, and community members in co-creating AI tools that reflect their real needs and experiences.

By grounding future research in lived realities and inclusive practices, we can ensure that AI in education serves all learners, not just the dominant majority. Despite increasing discourse, empirical research on how AI tools perform across heritage languages in Canadian universities remains scarce.

CONCLUSION

This chapter has explored the role of Artificial Intelligence (AI) in supporting plurilingual graduate students in Canadian tertiary education. We have explored the opportunities that AI offers, including adaptive learning platforms, multilingual tools, and real-time feedback, as well as personalized learning, validating heritage languages, and promoting metalinguistic awareness. We also explored the challenges that AI presents in linguistically diverse classrooms, such as accessibility, language bias, cultural misrepresentation, and insufficient AI support for students with disabilities, that must be addressed to prevent the reinforcement of existing educational inequities. Future directions must include inclusive policy development, educator training, and equitable access to ensure AI becomes a transformative assistant in plurilingual and inclusive education. AI must be applied in plurilingual education in an ethical, critical, and creative manner to support all learners' linguistic and cultural identities.

REFERENCES

Agnes, D., & Srinivasan, R. (2024). Fostering Vocabulary Memorization: Exploring the Impact of AI-Generated Mnemonic Keywords on Vocabulary Learning Through Anki Flashcards. *World Journal of English Language*, *14*(2), 434. Advance online publication. DOI: 10.5430/wjel.v14n2p434

Akinsanya Atchrimi, A., Toyin Kareem, F., & Collins Asemota, E. (2023). Artificial Intelligence (AI) in Multilingual Education: Investigating Its Potential in Supporting the Preservation and Instruction of Indigenous Languages in Formal Education. *Journal of College of Languages and Communication Arts Education*, *2*(1), 2971–5067. DOI: 10.5281/zenodo.14635760

Almeqdad, Q. I., Alodat, A. M., Alquraan, M. F., Mohaidat, M. A., & Al-Makhzoomy, A. K. (2023). The effectiveness of universal design for learning: A systematic review of the literature and meta-analysis. In *Cogent Education* (Vol. 10, Issue 1). DOI: 10.1080/2331186X.2023.2218191

Alsadoon, R. (2021). Chatting with AI Bot: Vocabulary Learning Assistant for Saudi EFL Learners. *English Language Teaching*, *14*(6), 135. Advance online publication. DOI: 10.5539/elt.v14n6p135

Amin, M. Y. M. (2023). AI and Chat GPT in Language Teaching: Enhancing EFL Classroom Support and Transforming Assessment Techniques. *International Journal of Higher Education Pedagogies*, *4*(4), 1–15. Advance online publication. DOI: 10.33422/ijhep.v4i4.554

Androshchuk, H. O. (2023). Policies and strategies for the development of artificial intelligence in the countries of the world: Quo vadis? (part 2). *Science, Technologies. Innovation*, *2*(26), 40–47. Advance online publication. DOI: 10.35668/2520-6524-2023-2-05

Attard-Frost, B., Brandusescu, A., & Lyons, K. (2023). The Governance of Artificial Intelligence in Canada: Findings and Opportunities from a Review of 84 AI Governance Initiatives. SSRN *Electronic Journal*. DOI: 10.2139/ssrn.4414212

Bakdash, L., Abid, A., Gourisankar, A., & Henry, T. L. (2024). Chatting Beyond ChatGPT: Advancing Equity Through AI-Driven Language Interpretation. *Journal of General Internal Medicine*, *39*(3), 492–495. Advance online publication. DOI: 10.1007/s11606-023-08497-6

Ben, H. (2023). *Challenges and Opportunities of Multilingual Content Creation in the Age of AI*. www.locaria.com

Black, R. D., Weinberg, L. A., & Brodwin, M. G. (2015). Universal design for learning and instruction: Perspectives of students with disabilities in higher education. *Exceptionality Education International*, *25*(2). Advance online publication. DOI: 10.5206/eei.v25i2.7723

Boateng, O., & Boateng, B. (2025). Algorithmic bias in educational systems: Examining the impact of AI-driven decision making in modern education. *World Journal of Advanced Research and Reviews*, *25*(1), 2012–2017. DOI: 10.30574/wjarr.2025.25.1.0253

Boothe, K. A., Lohmann, M. J., Donnell, K. A., & Dean Hall, D. (2018). Applying the Principles of Universal Design for Learning (UDL) in the College Classroom. *The Journal of Special Education Apprenticeship*, *7*(3). Advance online publication. DOI: 10.58729/2167-3454.1076

Bray, A., Devitt, A., Banks, J., Sanchez Fuentes, S., Sandoval, M., Riviou, K., Byrne, D., Flood, M., Reale, J., & Terrenzio, S. (2024). What next for Universal Design for Learning? A systematic literature review of technology in UDL implementations at second level. *British Journal of Educational Technology*, *55*(1), 113–138. Advance online publication. DOI: 10.1111/bjet.13328

Chan, C. K. Y. (2023). A comprehensive AI policy education framework for university teaching and learning. *International Journal of Educational Technology in Higher Education*, *20*(1), 38. Advance online publication. DOI: 10.1186/s41239-023-00408-3

Chemnad, K., & Othman, A. (2024). Digital accessibility in the era of artificial intelligence—Bibliometric analysis and systematic review. In *Frontiers in Artificial Intelligence* (Vol. 7). DOI: 10.3389/frai.2024.1349668

Corsi, E. (2023). Insight into plurilingual and pluricultural identity in multigenerational homes: A case study of three young adults. *Journal of Multilingual and Multicultural Development*, *44*(4), 288–308. Advance online publication. DOI: 10.1080/01434632.2020.1817045

Council of Europe. (2020). *Common European Framework of Reference for Languages: Learning, teaching, assessment*. Strasbourg.

D'warte, J. (2021). Facilitating agency and engagement: Visual methodologies and pedagogical interventions for working with culturally and linguistically diverse young people. *Language Teaching Research*, *25*(1), 12–38. Advance online publication. DOI: 10.1177/1362168820938826

Dalili, S., & Zohuri, B. (2023). Revolutionizing Treatment: AI-Driven Noninvasive Approaches for ODD and ADHD. *Management Studies*, *11*(4). Advance online publication. DOI: 10.17265/2328-2185/2023.04.003

Danilina, E., & Le Pichon, E. (2023). Embracing advances in AI-based language tools in EAP programs: Towards a plurilingual shift. In *Reconceptualizing Language Norms in Multilingual Contexts*. DOI: 10.4018/978-1-6684-8761-7.ch005

Dela Cruz, J. W. (2022). "I Subtitle Myself": Affordances and Challenges of Canadian EAL Students' Plurilingual Learning Strategies in a Francophone College. *TESL Canada Journal*, *38*(2), 36–62. DOI: 10.18806/tesl.v38i2.1356

Martin Doherty. (2025, January 24). *Bridging the Gap: Democratizing Access to Quality Education with AI.*

Dong, Y., Yu, X., Alharbi, A., & Ahmad, S. (2022). AI-based production and application of English multimode online reading using multi-criteria decision support system. *Soft Computing*, *26*(20), 10927–10937. Advance online publication. DOI: 10.1007/s00500-022-07209-2

Duarte, J. (2019). Translanguaging in mainstream education: A sociocultural approach. *International Journal of Bilingual Education and Bilingualism*, *22*(2), 150–164. Advance online publication. DOI: 10.1080/13670050.2016.1231774

Duarte, J., & van der Ploeg, M. (2019). Plurilingual lecturers in English medium instruction in the Netherlands: The key to plurilingual approaches in higher education? *European Journal of Higher Education*, *9*(3), 268–284. Advance online publication. DOI: 10.1080/21568235.2019.1602476

Dutton, J., & Rushton, K. (2021). Using the translanguaging space to facilitate poetic representation of language and identity. *Language Teaching Research*, *25*(1), 105–133. Advance online publication. DOI: 10.1177/1362168820951215

Fielding, R. (2016). Students' use of their plurilingual resources in Australian schools. *Language and Education*, *30*(4), 361–377. Advance online publication. DOI: 10.1080/09500782.2015.1114631

Fitria, T. N. (2021). Grammarly as AI-powered English Writing Assistant: Students' Alternative for Writing English. *Metathesis: Journal of English Language, Literature, and Teaching*, *5*(1), 65. Advance online publication. DOI: 10.31002/metathesis.v5i1.3519

Gabriel, J. (2024). How Artificial Intelligence (AI) impacts inclusive education. *Educational Research Review*, *19*(6), 95–103. DOI: 10.5897/ERR2024.4404

Galante, A. (2020). The moment I realized I am plurilingual": Plurilingual tasks for creative representations in EAP at a Canadian university. *Applied Linguistics Review, 11*(4), 551–580. Advance online publication. DOI: 10.1515/applirev-2018-0116

Galante, A. (2022). Plurilingual and pluricultural competence (PPC) scale: The inseparability of language and culture. *International Journal of Multilingualism, 19*(4), 477–498. Advance online publication. DOI: 10.1080/14790718.2020.1753747

Galante, A., Chiras, M., Wayne, J., Dela Cruz, N., & Zeaiter, L. F. (2022). *Implementing Critical Plurilingual Pedagogy in Language Education Plurilingual Guide.* https://www.mcgill.ca/plurilinguallab/files/plurilinguallab/plurilingual

Galante, A., Okubo, K., Cole, C., Elkader, N. A., Carozza, N., Wilkinson, C., Wotton, C., & Vasic, J. (2019). Plurilingualism in Higher Education: A Collaborative Initiative for the Implementation of Plurilingual Pedagogy in an English for Academic Purposes Program at a Canadian University. *TESL Canada Journal, 36*(1), 121–133. Advance online publication. DOI: 10.18806/tesl.v36i1.1305

Gaon, A., & Stedman, I. (2019). A Call to Action: Moving Forward with the Governance of Artificial Intelligence in Canada. *Alberta Law Review*, 1137. Advance online publication. DOI: 10.29173/alr2547

García, O., & Otheguy, R. (2020). Plurilingualism and translanguaging: Commonalities and divergences. *International Journal of Bilingual Education and Bilingualism, 23*(1), 17–35. Advance online publication. DOI: 10.1080/13670050.2019.1598932

Garg, S., & Sharma, S. (2020). Impact of artificial intelligence in special need education to promote inclusive pedagogy. *International Journal of Information and Education Technology (IJIET), 10*(7), 523–527. Advance online publication. DOI: 10.18178/ijiet.2020.10.7.1418

Guo, A., Kamar, E., Vaughan, J. W., Wallach, H., & Morris, M. R. (2020). Toward fairness in AI for people with disabilities SBG@a research roadmap. *ACM SIGACCESS Accessibility and Computing, 125*(125), 1. Advance online publication. DOI: 10.1145/3386296.3386298

Harry, A., & Sayudin, S. (2023). Role of AI in Education. [INJURITY]. *Interdiciplinary Journal and Hummanity, 2*(3), 260–268. Advance online publication. DOI: 10.58631/injurity.v2i3.52

Harunasari, S. Y. (2023). Examining the Effectiveness of AI-integrated Approach in EFL Writing: A Case of ChatGPT. *International Journal of Progressive Sciences and Technologies, 39*(2), 357. Advance online publication. DOI: 10.52155/ijpsat.v39.2.5516

Hebert, Y., Guo, Y., & Pellerin, M. (2008). New Horizons for Research on Bilingualism and Plurilingualism: A Focus on Languages of Immigration in Canada. *Encounters in Theory and History of Education, 9*, 57–74. Advance online publication. DOI: 10.24908/eoe-ese-rse.v9i0.647

Hervieux, S., & Wheatley, A. (2021). Perceptions of artificial intelligence: A survey of academic librarians in Canada and the United States. *Journal of Academic Librarianship, 47*(1), 102270. Advance online publication. DOI: 10.1016/j.acalib.2020.102270

Heugh, K., French, M., Arya, V., Pham, M., Tudini, V., Billinghurst, N., Tippett, N., Chang, L.-C., Nichols, J., & Viljoen, J.-M. (2022). Multilingualism, translanguaging and transknowledging: Translation technology in EMI higher education. *AILA Review, 35*(1), 89–127. DOI: 10.1075/aila.22011.heu

Hopp, H., & Thoma, D. (2021). Effects of Plurilingual Teaching on Grammatical Development in Early Foreign-Language Learning. *Modern Language Journal, 105*(2), 464–483. Advance online publication. DOI: 10.1111/modl.12709

Huang, C., Zhang, Z., Mao, B., & Yao, X. (2023). An Overview of Artificial Intelligence Ethics. *IEEE Transactions on Artificial Intelligence, 4*(4), 799–819. Advance online publication. DOI: 10.1109/TAI.2022.3194503

Humble, N., & Mozelius, P. (2022). The threat, hype, and promise of artificial intelligence in education. *Discover Artificial Intelligence, 2*(1), 22. Advance online publication. DOI: 10.1007/s44163-022-00039-z

Jafary, M., & Shakib Kotamjani, S. (2025). *Enhancing Linguistic Accessibility and Academic Inclusion through AI Tools: A Pilot Study on Plurilingual Graduate Students at McGill University.*

Kang, B. O., Jeon, H. B., & Lee, Y. K. (2024). AI-based language tutoring systems with end-to-end automatic speech recognition and proficiency evaluation. *ETRI Journal, 46*(1), 48–58. Advance online publication. DOI: 10.4218/etrij.2023-0322

Kaur, P., Kumar, H., & Kaushal, S. (2023). Technology-Assisted Language Learning Adaptive Systems: A Comprehensive Review. In *International Journal of Cognitive Computing in Engineering* (Vol. 4). DOI: 10.1016/j.ijcce.2023.09.002

Khasawneh, M. A. S. (2023). The potential of AI in facilitating cross-cultural communication through translation. *Journal of Namibian Studies, 37.*

Kim, H. S., & Cha, Y. (2023). The Role of AI Translators on Reading Comprehension. *Korean Journal of English Language and Linguistics, 23*, 38–58. Advance online publication. DOI: 10.15738/kjell.23..202301.38

Kitcharoen, P., Howimanporn, S., & Chookaew, S. (2024). Enhancing Teachers' AI Competencies through Artificial Intelligence of Things Professional Development Training. *International Journal of Interactive Mobile Technologies, 18*(2), 4–15. Advance online publication. DOI: 10.3991/ijim.v18i02.46613

Kubota, R., & Bale, J. (2020). Bilingualism—But Not Plurilingualism—Promoted by Immersion Education in Canada: Questioning Equity for Students of English as an Additional Language. *TESOL Quarterly, 54*(3), 773–785. Advance online publication. DOI: 10.1002/tesq.575

Lepage-Richer, T., & McKelvey, F. (2022). States of computing: On government organization and artificial intelligence in Canada. *Big Data & Society, 9*(2), 20539517221123304. Advance online publication. DOI: 10.1177/20539517221123304

Lewis, A. A. (2025). Unpacking Cultural Bias in AI Language Learning Tools: An Analysis of Impacts and Strategies for Inclusion in Diverse Educational Settings. *International Journal of Research and Innovation in Social Science, IX*(I), 1878–1892. DOI: 10.47772/IJRISS.2025.9010151

Lin, P. (2023). ChatGPT: Friend or foe (to corpus linguists)? *Applied Corpus Linguistics, 3*(3), 100065. Advance online publication. DOI: 10.1016/j.acorp.2023.100065

Liu, Z. (2025). Cultural Bias in Large Language Models: A Comprehensive Analysis and Mitigation Strategies. *Journal of Transcultural Communication, 3*(2), 224–244. DOI: 10.1515/jtc-2023-0019

Lotherington, H., Thumlert, K., Boreland, T., & Tomin, B. (2022). Redesigning for mobile plurilingual futures. *OLBI Journal, 11*, 141–172. Advance online publication. DOI: 10.18192/olbij.v11i1.6179

Maatouk, Z., & Payant, C. (2022). The pertinence and feasibility of implementing a plurilingual approach in Quebec, Canada: The beliefs of pre-service ESL teachers. *International Journal of Bilingual Education and Bilingualism, 25*(10), 3685–3697. Advance online publication. DOI: 10.1080/13670050.2022.2072681

Madhavi, E., Sivapurapu, L., Koppula, V., Esther Rani, P. B., & Sreehari, V. (2023). Developing Learners' English Speaking Skills using ICT and AI Tools. *Journal of Advanced Research in Applied Sciences and Engineering Technology, 32*(2), 142–153. Advance online publication. DOI: 10.37934/araset.32.2.142153

Marshall, S., Moore, D., & Himeta, M. (2021). French-Medium Instruction in Anglophone Canadian Higher Education: The Plurilingual Complexity of Students and Their Instructors. *Canadian Journal of Applied Linguistics, 24*(1), 181–204. Advance online publication. DOI: 10.37213/cjal.2021.29345

Martin, F., Chen, Y., Moore, R. L., & Westine, C. D. (2020). Systematic review of adaptive learning research designs, context, strategies, and technologies from 2009 to 2018. *Educational Technology Research and Development, 68*(4), 1903–1929. Advance online publication. DOI: 10.1007/s11423-020-09793-2

Marzuki, W., Widiati, U., Rusdin, D., Darwin, , & Indrawati, I. (2023). The impact of AI writing tools on the content and organization of students' writing: EFL teachers' perspective. *Cogent Education, 10*(2), 2236469. Advance online publication. DOI: 10.1080/2331186X.2023.2236469

Maximova, M. V., Frolova, O. V., Etuev, Kh. Kh., & Aleksandrova, L. D. (2023). Adaptive personalized learning: Implementation of emerging technologies in higher education. *Informatics and Education, 38*(4), 14–27. Advance online publication. DOI: 10.32517/0234-0453-2023-38-4-14-27

Michel-Villarreal, R., Vilalta-Perdomo, E., Salinas-Navarro, D. E., Thierry-Aguilera, R., & Gerardou, F. S. (2023). Challenges and Opportunities of Generative AI for Higher Education as Explained by ChatGPT. *Education Sciences, 13*(9), 856. Advance online publication. DOI: 10.3390/educsci13090856

Min, A. (2023). Artifical Intelligence and Bias: Challenges, Implications, and Remedies. *Journal of Social Research, 2*(11), 3808–3817. Advance online publication. DOI: 10.55324/josr.v2i11.1477

Morley, J., Kinsey, L., Elhalal, A., Garcia, F., Ziosi, M., & Floridi, L. (2023). Operationalising AI ethics: Barriers, enablers and next steps. *AI & Society, 38*(1), 411–423. Advance online publication. DOI: 10.1007/s00146-021-01308-8

Muñoz-Basols, J., Craig, N., Lafford, B. A., & Godev, C. (2023). Potentialities of Applied Translation for Language Learning in the Era of Artificial Intelligence. *Hispania, 106*(2), 171–194. Advance online publication. DOI: 10.1353/hpn.2023.a899427

Nguyen, A., Ngo, H. N., Hong, Y., Dang, B., & Nguyen, B. P. T. (2023). Ethical principles for artificial intelligence in education. *Education and Information Technologies, 28*(4), 4221–4241. Advance online publication. DOI: 10.1007/s10639-022-11316-w

Nitzberg, M., & Zysman, J. (2022). Algorithms, data, and platforms: The diverse challenges of governing AI. *Journal of European Public Policy, 29*(11), 1753–1778. Advance online publication. DOI: 10.1080/13501763.2022.2096668

Ntouvlis, V., & Geenen, J. (2023). "Ironic memes" and digital literacies: Exploring identity through multimodal texts. *New Media & Society*. Advance online publication. DOI: 10.1177/14614448231189801

Office of the Privacy Commissioner of Canada. (2022). *PIPEDA and AI: Principles for the ethical use of artificial intelligence in education.*

Piccardo, E. (2020). "We are all (potential) plurilinguals": Plurilingualism as an Overarching, Holistic Concept. *OLBI Working Papers, 10*. DOI: 10.18192/olbiwp.v10i0.3825

Pierres, O., Christen, M., Schmitt-Koopmann, F. M., & Darvishy, A. (2024). Could the Use of AI in Higher Education Hinder Students With Disabilities? A Scoping Review. *IEEE Access : Practical Innovations, Open Solutions*, *12*, 27810–27828. Advance online publication. DOI: 10.1109/ACCESS.2024.3365368

Pisica, A. I., Edu, T., Zaharia, R. M., & Zaharia, R. (2023). Implementing Artificial Intelligence in Higher Education: Pros and Cons from the Perspectives of Academics. *Societies (Basel, Switzerland)*, *13*(5), 118. Advance online publication. DOI: 10.3390/soc13050118

Polyakova, O., & Galstyan-Sargsyan, R. (2021). Sustainable Higher Education via Telecollaboration: Improving Plurilingual and Pluricultural Competence. *Integra Educativa*, *25*(4), 544–561. Advance online publication. DOI: 10.15507/1991-9468.105.025.202104.544-561

Rabbianty, E. N., Azizah, S., & Virdyna, N. K. (2023). AI in academic writing: Assessing current usage and future implications. *INSANIA : Jurnal Pemikiran Alternatif Kependidikan*, *28*(1a), 14–35. Advance online publication. DOI: 10.24090/insania.v28i1a.9278

Rajagopal, A., Nirmala, V., Jebadurai, I. J., Vedamanickam, A. M., & Kumar, P. U. (2023). Design of Generative Multimodal AI Agents to Enable Persons with Learning Disability. *ACM International Conference Proceeding Series*. DOI: 10.1145/3610661.3617514

Rebolledo Font de la Vall, R., & González Araya, F. (2023). Exploring the Benefits and Challenges of AI-Language Learning Tools. *International Journal of Social Sciences and Humanities Invention*, *10*(01), 7569–7576. Advance online publication. DOI: 10.18535/ijsshi/v10i01.02

Sales, A., Marzà, A., & Torralba, G. (2023). "Daddy, Can You Speak Our Language?" Multilingual and Intercultural Awareness through Identity Texts. *Journal of Language, Identity, and Education*, *22*(6), 510–526. Advance online publication. DOI: 10.1080/15348458.2021.1901586

Sandu, I., Wiersma, M., & Manichand, D. (2022). Time to audit your AI algorithms. *Maandblad Voor Accountancy en Bedrijfseconomie*, *96*(7/8), 253–265. Advance online publication. DOI: 10.5117/mab.96.90108

Selwyn, N. (2024). On the Limits of Artificial Intelligence (AI) in Education. *Nordisk Tidsskrift for Pedagogikk Og Kritikk*, *10*(1). Advance online publication. DOI: 10.23865/ntpk.v10.6062

Shakib Kotamjani, S., Shirinova, S., & Fahimirad, M. (2023). Lecturers' perceptions of using Artificial Intelligence in Tertiary Education in Uzbekistan. *Proceedings of the 7th International Conference on Future Networks and Distributed Systems*, 570–578. DOI: 10.1145/3644713.3644797

Sharples, M. (2023). Towards social generative AI for education: Theory, practices and ethics. *Learning: Research and Practice*, *9*(2), 159–167. Advance online publication. DOI: 10.1080/23735082.2023.2261131

Siau, K., & Wang, W. (2020). Artificial intelligence (AI) Ethics: Ethics of AI and ethical AI. In *Journal of Database Management* (Vol. 31, Issue 2). DOI: 10.4018/JDM.2020040105

Slaughter, Y., & Cross, R. (2021). Challenging the monolingual mindset: Understanding plurilingual pedagogies in English as an Additional Language (EAL) classrooms. *Language Teaching Research*, *25*(1), 39–60. Advance online publication. DOI: 10.1177/1362168820938819

Song, Y., Weisberg, L. R., Zhang, S., Tian, X., Boyer, K. E., & Israel, M. (2024). A framework for inclusive AI learning design for diverse learners. In *Computers and Education* (Vol. 6). Artificial Intelligence., DOI: 10.1016/j.caeai.2024.100212

Soylu, D., & Şahin, A. (2024). The Role of AI in Supporting Indigenous Languages. *AI and Tech in Behavioral and Social Sciences*, *2*(4), 11–18. DOI: 10.61838/kman.aitech.2.4.2

Stibel, J. M., & Barrett, H. C. (2023). How cultural framing can bias our beliefs about robots and artificial intelligence. In *Behavioral and Brain Sciences* (Vol. 46). DOI: 10.1017/S0140525X22001686

Sun, W. (2023). The impact of automatic speech recognition technology on second language pronunciation and speaking skills of EFL learners: A mixed methods investigation. *Frontiers in Psychology, 14*, 1210187. Advance online publication. DOI: 10.3389/fpsyg.2023.1210187

Tour, E., Turner, M., Keary, A., & Tran-Dang, K. L. (2024). Bringing plurilingual strategies into linguistically diverse classrooms: Affordances of digital multimodal composing. *Language and Education, 38*(3), 465–481. Advance online publication. DOI: 10.1080/09500782.2023.2203124

Trust, T., Whalen, J., & Mouza, C. (2023). Editorial: ChatGPT: Challenges, Opportunities, and Implications for Teacher Education. *Contemporary Issues in Technology & Teacher Education, 23*(1).

Vallejo, C., & Dooly, M. (2020). Plurilingualism and translanguaging: Emergent approaches and shared concerns. Introduction to the special issue. *International Journal of Bilingual Education and Bilingualism, 23*(1), 1–16. Advance online publication. DOI: 10.1080/13670050.2019.1600469

Wald, M. (2021). AI Data-Driven Personalisation and Disability Inclusion. *Frontiers in Artificial Intelligence, 3*, 571955. Advance online publication. DOI: 10.3389/frai.2020.571955

Wei, L. (2023). Artificial intelligence in language instruction: Impact on English learning achievement, L2 motivation, and self-regulated learning. *Frontiers in Psychology, 14*, 1261955. Advance online publication. DOI: 10.3389/fpsyg.2023.1261955

Wise, G., Dickinson, C., Katan, T., & Gallegos, M. C. (2020). Inclusive higher education governance: Managing stakeholders, strategy, structure and function. *Studies in Higher Education, 45*(2), 339–352. Advance online publication. DOI: 10.1080/03075079.2018.1525698

Yuxiu, Y. (2024). Application of translation technology based on AI in translation teaching. *Systems and Soft Computing, 6*, 200072. Advance online publication. DOI: 10.1016/j.sasc.2024.200072

Zhang, A., & Zhu, X. (2023). Analysis of english translation of corpus based on blockchain. *International Journal of Web-Based Learning and Teaching Technologies, 18*(2), 1–14. Advance online publication. DOI: 10.4018/IJWLTT.332767

Chapter 10
Revolutionizing Language Learning and Proficiency With Adaptive Assessments and AI-Driven System

Elvira Nurfadhilah
https://orcid.org/0000-0003-2227-331X
National Research and Innovation Agency, Indonesia

Radhiyatul Fajri
https://orcid.org/0000-0003-2812-1077
National Research and Innovation Agency, Indonesia

Dian Isnaeni Nurul Afra
https://orcid.org/0000-0001-5128-9682
National Research and Innovation Agency, Indonesia

Siska Pebiana
https://orcid.org/0009-0006-7473-7541
National Research and Innovation Agency, Indonesia

Prabu Kresna Putra
https://orcid.org/0000-0001-9246-8863
National Research and Innovation Agency, Indonesia

Hammam Riza
https://orcid.org/0000-0002-5449-6828
National Research and Innovation Agency, Indonesia

Nimas Ayu Untariyati
https://orcid.org/0009-0001-6466-9534
National Research and Innovation Agency, Indonesia

DOI: 10.4018/979-8-3373-0275-1.ch010

ABSTRACT

Bilingual and multilingual education integrated with artificial intelligence (AI) has fundamentally altered conventional education paradigms, increasing the engagement of learning, individualized, and adaptive. This chapter examines AI technologies for instance Intelligent Tutoring Systems (ITS), adaptive learning algorithms, and Natural Language Processing (NLP) aid language acquisition by personalizing material delivery, offering real-time feedback, gamification, and promoting cultural competence. AI-driven curriculum caters to a variety of learning styles and boost understanding, motivation, and retention while addressing cognitive problems. However, issues such as algorithmic prejudice, data privacy, and the digital divide need fair technological access and ethical considerations. The balance of AI and human supervision is critical to developing effective learning experiences. Future breakthroughs in agentic AI will provide adaptive, context-aware interactions that improve language learning, but they must be carefully implemented to ensure inclusivity and ethical integrity.

INTRODUCTION

Background and Motivation

Language proficiency has become a critical skill in today's interconnected and globalized world, necessitating the development of innovative educational strategies that address the diverse learning needs of individuals. Traditional language learning methods often follow a rigid curriculum and provide limited personalized feedback, which can result in disengagement and inefficient learning. In contrast, the advent of Artificial Intelligence (AI) in language education offers new possibilities by tailoring learning experiences to individual needs and providing real-time, adaptive feedback. This evolution in language learning systems is particularly transformative in multilingual and bilingual contexts, where learners may be at different stages of fluency across various languages.

The integration of AI-driven adaptive assessments in language learning presents a paradigm shift that enhances the personalization and efficiency of language acquisition. AI systems such as those detailed in the studies of Lawrance et al. (2024) and Qin & Zhong (2024) emphasize adaptive learning technologies that adjust the content based on the learner's progress, proficiency levels, and linguistic backgrounds. These systems leverage Natural Language Processing (NLP) to analyze and respond to learners' interactions, offering real-time corrections and feedback on pronunciation, fluency, and grammar. Such personalized feedback systems allow learners to progress at their own pace, which is crucial in multilingual environments where students might be at varying stages of proficiency in each language (Lawrance et al., 2024; Qin & Zhong, 2024).

Moreover, AI-based platforms like those described by Li and Wang (2024) employ recommendation algorithms powered by NLP to adjust learning materials based on students' interests and needs, further promoting engagement and improving learning outcomes (Li & Wang, 2024). These adaptive systems not only cater to individual learning styles but also foster an inclusive learning environment by providing personalized resources that meet the diverse linguistic needs of learners (Gyonyoru & Katona, 2024). AI's ability to optimize learning pathways, as explored by Chicherina et al. (2024), has the potential to revolutionize language education by improving retention, motivation, and learner satisfaction (Chicherina et al., 2024).

The motivation behind incorporating AI in language learning is multifaceted. One key motivation is to enhance learner autonomy. AI systems enable students to track their progress, receive instant feedback, and engage in self-paced learning. This approach is particularly beneficial in fostering independent learning, where students can practice continuously and receive feedback without the constraints of traditional classroom environments. Additionally, the adaptability of AI systems ensures that learners receive targeted guidance that aligns with their current skill level, which is crucial for both novice and advanced language learners (Bhandare, 2024; Demianenko & Moroz, 2024).

Despite the numerous advantages, challenges remain in the widespread adoption of AI in language education. The potential for algorithmic bias, ethical concerns surrounding data privacy, and the need for continued research into the cultural and contextual nuances in language use are important considerations that must be addressed (Jane et al., 2024). However, the evidence suggests that AI's potential to transform language learning through personalized, adaptive systems is vast, making it a compelling area for further exploration and development in educational contexts.

Scope and Objectives

Scope

In this book chapter, the scope of discussion includes an in-depth exploration of the application of AI in supporting bilingual learning, such as various implemented features to enhance the learning experience. The focus mainly includes an analysis of AI technologies used in adaptive learning systems, such as NLP, machine learning, and ITS that enable personalization of learning based on individual needs. In addition, various forms of feedback provided by AI systems, including real-time feedback in evaluating speaking and writing skills, as well as learning recommendations tailored to the user's level of understanding are also discussed in this book chapter. Not only about those aspects, but also it discusses how AI can solve challenges in bilingual learning, such as language interference and difficulties in understanding cultural contexts, and how advanced features are. For instance, gamification and automated evaluation systems can improve learner motivation and retention. Overall, this book chapter aims to provide a comprehensive understanding of how AI contributes to the development of bilingual proficiency and its implications in the world of education.

Objective

This chapter explores AI's development, techniques, challenges, and impacts on bilingual learning to understand its transformative role in language education.

1. Trace the evolution and application of AI in bilingual learning

Examines how AI technologies such as NLP and adaptive platforms which have evolved and been applied to enhance bilingual and multilingual education.

2. Explore techniques and frameworks used in AI-based bilingual learning

Investigates technical methods include machine learning and reinforcement learning alongside frameworks which are intelligent tutoring systems and personalized learning models.

3. Identify key challenges in implementing AI for bilingual learners

Analyses technical and ethical challenges—e.g. algorithmic bias and privacy—and cognitive issues such as language interference in bilingual contexts.

4. Evaluate the impact and implications of AI on bilingual education

Assesses AI's effectiveness in enhancing learning outcomes, motivation, and accessibility and considers its long-term role in shaping inclusive education systems.

Structure of the Chapter

This chapter is divided into seven sub-chapters.

- Sub-chapter 1: the Introduction, lays out the fundamental concepts of AI in language learning. It clarifies the rationale for integrating AI technologies and underscores the importance of personalized, adaptive learning in contemporary education. The chapter also depicts the scope and objectives and provides an overview of its structure.

- Sub-chapter 2: Personalized and Adaptive Learning through AI delves into adaptive learning principles and explains how AI enables personalized learning experiences. It explores key aspects including the adaptive learning lifecycle, the role of datasets in tailoring learning paths, and the algorithms powering these systems. In addition, it involves the role of Intelligent Tutoring Systems (ITS) and examines the impact of AI on learner engagement and performance.
- Sub-chapter 3: AI-Driven Language Proficiency Evaluation, focuses on how language proficiency is assessed by AI systems. This sub-chapter explores the methods used to evaluate speaking, writing, and reading comprehension, emphasizing the importance of real-time feedback mechanisms for enhancing learning.
- Sub-chapter 4: Motivation, Self-Regulation, and Gamification in AI Learning Systems explains how AI-driven systems are designed to cultivate learners' motivation, autonomy, and self-regulation. It includes strategies for enhancing learner engagement through adaptive features, goal setting, and the integration of gamification elements such as personalized learning pathways, immersive learning scenarios, and reward systems. The sub-chapter also discusses how leaderboards and competitive elements can enhance motivation and behavioral insights based on empirical evidence.
- Sub-chapter 5: Integrating AI Tools into Language Learning Frameworks, offers an overview of effectively integrating AI tools into existing language learning frameworks. Furthermore, the pedagogical strategies and approaches supporting AI-based instruction, highlights AI's strengths in language education, and addresses limitations and ethical considerations is being discussed. The sub-chapter also covers challenges related to multilingual and cross-cultural language learning and the design of AI-integrated curricula.
- Sub-chapter 6: The Role of NLP in Creating Interactive and Engaging Learning Environments discusses the applications of NLP in education, focusing on how NLP can enhance language learning. It explores how AI-powered interventions can solve problems in language interference, addresses challenges, and provides empirical evidence and case studies. Additionally, this sub-chapter examines the role of AI in building cultural competence and its broader societal and educational impacts, along with real-world applications in language learning.
- Sub-chapter 7: Challenges and Future Directions concludes the chapter by discussing the current challenges in implementing and adopting AI in lan-

guage learning. It also examines emerging trends and opportunities, and the work needed to leverage agentic AI to ensure the continued evolution of language education in the future.

PERSONALIZED AND ADAPTIVE LEARNING THROUGH AI

Bilingual Education is a teaching and studying process that in its implementation uses more than one language (García, 2011). In bilingual education, students are taught academic subjects in both languages alternately or simultaneously, the hope is that students are capable of enhancing their academic capacity in the subjects being taught and improve their language skills according to the language used in the process of teaching and learning (Mcgovern et al., 2017).

Personalized learning is a method in the process of teaching and studying where each person can obtain a personalized education plan based on their instructional preferences, speed of education, learning materials, etc. (Raj & Renumol, 2022). Personalized learning is a method of the teaching-learning process where each person can get a personalized learning program based on their preferred method of instruction, learning materials, learning pace, etc. How can AI provide feedback according to each student's preferences? Simply explained, an AI Model will be developed using an adaptive learning algorithm. The model is trained using a dataset obtained from the teacher. Then based on the user profile it will be used as a feature in determining the content provided for each student. This section will also discuss in more detail the general algorithm/framework used in Personalized Learning, the feedback given to students and how the benefits are felt by students.

Adaptive Learning: Concepts and Applications

The teaching strategy known as "adaptive learning" modifies instruction to learning through innovative involvement to the person needs of understudies. The main idea behind adaptive learning is that the system can continuously assess the progress and performance of students and after that, alter the subject matter, degree of difficulty, and learning speed based on the information collected. This permits the framework to supply challenges that are suitable to the capacities of understudies and back them in overcoming troubles they confront, with the point of expanding the viability and proficiency of the learning handle. The technology utilized in adaptive learning regularly includes calculations that are able to choose and show significant substance based on students' intuitive with the fabric. These calculations work by gathering and examining information from different sorts of sources, such as test coming about, intelligence with learning materials, and advance in understanding the concepts being instructed. In this way, versatile learning can give convenient and focused feedback, and alter the level of trouble or sort of substance to be learned. This section will describe how the workflow of adaptive learning works, when the algorithm is used, how AI can provide appropriate feedback to students, what data is used, etc.

Adaptive Learning Life Cycle

The Adaptive Learning Lifecycle is an iterative workflow that allows AI systems to personalize learning to students' needs. By continually collecting data, analyzing patterns, adjusting content, and providing feedback, this workflow ensures that the learning experience evolves in response to student progress. Figure 1 below explains the stages that are implemented or the processes that run behind how the system provides feedback to students according to their respective needs.

Figure 1. AI Learning Cycle: Adapting multilingual education through data, analysis, personalized content, feedback, and evaluation

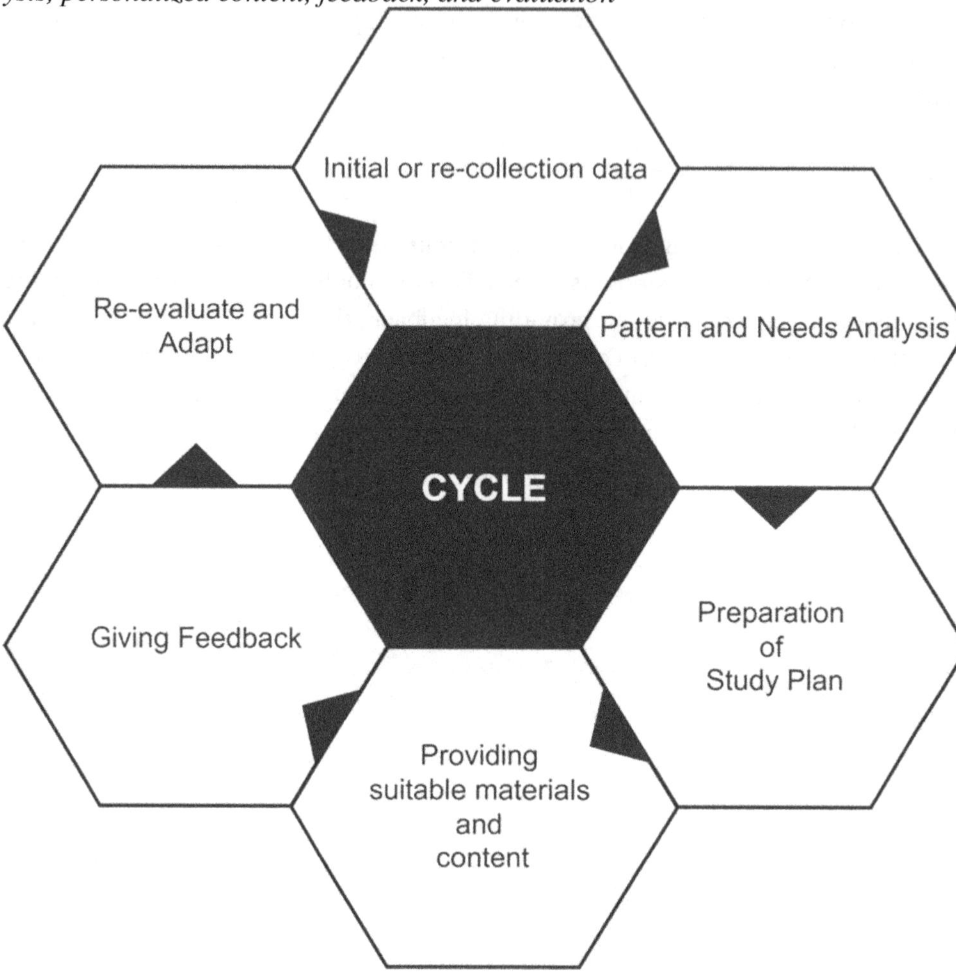

Here are the details of the life cycle of the Adaptive learning process:

1. The process starts with the initial data collection; in this process the system will collect the first data related to students. In some applications, for example, Duolingo, upon initially signing up for the system, the user will be directed to fill in the Profile, User preferences or even take a placement test. The data collected will be used as initial information related to students who will be learning using the system. The data collection process will be implemented regularly in addition to the process of teaching and learning. For example, for old users, the data collection process carried out is not only limited to initial

data but also extends to data regarding interactions with the system, evaluation or test outcomes, and other relevant information.

2. At this stage, the initial data that has been collected is then analyzed to identify information that can be used for student needs. For example, according to the placement test results, student preferences and demographics can be classified into a particular group. The analysis process can use several approaches, such as rule based, machine learning and deep learning. Each approach will use different algorithms or techniques.
3. Based on the analysis that has been done, the study plan/learning curriculum will be prepared to adjust to the level of student ability. Things that may be discussed in the study plan are teaching methods, teaching time, content or what is given, etc. Here is an example: Student "A" has a placement test result with a lower writing score than other sections, then the test results also show that the student has a lower score in a certain foreign language than from the preference data, it is known that students tend to prefer studying at night and prefer direct trials. Based on the data above, the model may assume and make conclusions in the form of an appropriate study plan such as additional materials will be given to the section where the student gets a low score, then the learning time will also be arranged, in addition, the question-and-answer method and quizzes may also be increased compared to one-way learning based on student preference data.
4. Based on the study plan details, the system will search the content database to identify which content is suitable to be given to students. The process will use data from the study plan and content metadata in the database.
5. During the learning process, the system will routinely provide feedback that is expected to increase motivation, help students understand the material, etc. The following is an example of feedback, if the user chooses the wrong form of a word in English, the system will provide the correct answer, correct the error complete with an explanation. There are several types of feedback that may be provided by the system, including Formative Feedback, Summative Feedback, Positive Feeback, Negative Feedback, Immediate Feedback, Constructive Feedback, etc (Bimba et al., 2017; Gligorea et al., 2023).
6. At this stage, the system will consistently evaluate the user's performance on exercises or quizzes. If the user is having difficulty in one area, the system will adjust the algorithm to provide more practice in the part where the student is having difficulty. For example, when a student experiences low writing results during a quiz, it is likely that the next or current study plan will be adjusted so that it can focus more on improving the writing section that still gets low scores (Awais et al., 2019).

Dataset

Bilingual adaptive learning systems rely on various types of data to be used according to the needs of each student. The data collected is in various aspects, starting from the demographic background of the students to their interactions with the learning materials. The data that has been collected can be used by the system to adjust the material, difficulty level, and teaching methods that are suitable for the pupils' characteristics and stage of development in the lessons being studied. Table 1 below shows several types of data that are often used in bilingual adaptive learning systems.

Table 1. Data Types in Bilingual Adaptive Learning Systems

Data Type	Description	Reference
Demographic	Information about the linguistic pairs or general bilingual information such as primary and secondary languages, domains of use, etc.	(Chen et al., 2016; Jiang et al., 2009)
Interaction	Records of alignment and engagement metrics, such as token-level mutual information (BMI, CBMI), frequency distribution, and interaction between bilingual pairs.	(Xu et al., 2021; Zhang et al., 2022)
Content	Information related to bilingual data extracted from the web, including consistent patterns in sentences, terms, and translation alignment.	(Jiang et al., 2009)
Score	Evaluation metrics, including BLEU scores and translation quality assessments derived from machine translation tasks.	(Chen et al., 2016; Zhang et al., 2022)
Speech Data	Data related to speech emotion recognition, including features from audio datasets and classification results.	(Shahin et al., 2023)

In building a bilingual adaptive learning system, various types of data are used to support the performance and effectiveness of the model. One important data type is demographic data, which includes information about linguistic pairs or general characteristics of bilinguals, such as their primary and secondary languages and domains of use. This data can be obtained from sources such as bilingual web pages that contain consistent patterns, which are identified and utilized to mine bilingual sentence pairs and terms. An example of its application is seen in the study of adaptive bilingual data mining methods from the web by Jiang et al., who found that bilingual data often appear collectively following certain patterns (Jiang et al., 2009). In addition, interaction data plays a significant role in recording engagement metrics, such as the level of bilingual mutual information at the token level, either through BMI or CBMI. This data is used to assess target tokens' learning complexity based on associations with the source context. This approach was further developed by Xu et al. by introducing CBMI, which considers the target context for more efficient training adaptation (Xu et al., 2021). By balancing the varying distribution of tokens in the dataset, this data provides deeper insights to improve translation quality. Meanwhile, content data includes information about patterns and structures in bilingual datasets, such as term pairs or sentences extracted based on format uniformity from web pages. Research by Jiang et al. on adaptive pattern-based data extraction highlights the potential of this data in supporting adaptive learning (Jiang et al., 2009). On the other hand, score data such as BLEU scores are used to assess the quality of translation models. Research by Chen et al. describes that the use of data selection methods such as Bi-SSCNN significantly improves BLEU scores on English-to-French translation tasks (Chen et al., 2016). In addition, in more specific domains, such as bilingual voice emotion recognition, speech data that includes multidimensional voice features is also used to improve the accuracy of emotion classification through transfer learning, as explained by Shahin et al. in their research (Shahin et al., 2023).

Methods and Algorithms for Adaptive Learning

Algorithms are an important element in adaptive learning systems. Algorithms are used to personalize the learning process by modifying the pace, material, and degree of difficulty based on the system's collected data. Examples of the application of various methods and algorithms used in several bilingual adaptive learning systems.

1. Statistical and Mathematical Modeling
    - Item Response Theory (IRT)

The complexity of a language task is assessed by IRT (e.g., comprehension or grammar exercises) considering the student's past performance in an adaptive language learning system. For instance, if a pupil regularly answers comprehension questions correctly, the system will increase the difficulty of subsequent questions but keep them at the same level. The hope is that this will make the student who is working on the problem more challenged in answering the problem. Some existing IRT models are the Graded Response Model, Rasch Model (1PL, 2PL, 3PL - Parameter Logistic Model), and Nominal Response Model.

- Regression

Regression is a statistical method that simulates the connection between independent and dependent variables. The goal of regression is to forecast the dependent variable's value using the independent components. In a bilingual context, regression algorithms can be used to predict several cases, such as how long it will take a student to achieve fluency based on their previous engagement, time spent on tasks, and success rate in exercises. For instance, suppose that a student is struggling with English word structure exercises, the system might predict a longer period of time it will take to master English word structures. This would have an impact on adjusting the pace of lessons on that topic. Some examples of simple regression algorithms that are commonly used are Linear Regression and Polynomial Regression.

2. Machine Learning for Personalized Content
    - Collaborative Filtering

Collaborative filtering is a mechanism for making recommendations based on system users' behavior patterns and then comparing them to those of other users. Based on these similarities, recommendations will be given. For example, if many beginner students with certain preferences often interact or access content that is called “A”, then it is possible that the system will suggest content “A” to other beginner users who have never accessed content “A”.

- Classification and Clustering

Classification and clustering are two main techniques used in machine learning. These methods are used to categorize and group data based on features or characteristics of an element. The difference is that data classification requires class labels that are used for model training, while Clustering does not. Some examples in the context of Adaptive Learning are when you want to categorize students based on their proficiency level (e.g. beginner, intermediate, advanced). If the student is having difficulty in solving the problem, the system might categorize the student at the beginner stage. Besides that, clustering algorithms can group students based on student attributes, for example, several students who have high scores, are located close to each other, or have the same study time might be grouped together for study group purposes.

3. Advanced Learning and Predictive Models
    - Reinforcement Learning (RL)

In an adaptive language learning system, RL algorithms reward learners for completing exercises correctly and penalize them for incorrect responses, adjusting the difficulty of subsequent tasks accordingly. For instance, if a student answers a set of grammar exercises correctly, the system will reward them with higher-level exercises that challenge their proficiency. If they make repeated mistakes, the system will present easier exercises to reinforce foundational knowledge.

- Deep Learning

A deep learning model in the system can examine massive amounts of data, such as patterns of student interaction, types of errors made, and responses to speaking exercises, to predict future learning needs. For example, if a student frequently mispronounces certain words, the system can use deep learning to identify patterns in these errors and provide tailored pronunciation exercises, as well as recommend targeted lessons that focus on specific language sounds.

4. NLP

NLP in the adaptive system is used to assess and provide feedback on written responses from the student. For example, when a student submits a short essay or answers an open-ended question, the system uses NLP algorithms to check for grammatical errors, sentence structure, and vocabulary usage. It then provides immediate feedback, such as highlighting mistakes and offering suggestions for improvement. NLP can also analyze the sentiment of student responses to gauge their confidence levels, enabling the system to appropriately modify the tasks' level of complexity. For example, if a pupil's responses indicate frustration, the system might slow down and introduce simpler content to rebuild their confidence.

By integrating these methods and algorithms, adaptive learning systems can produce a dynamic, responsive, and personalized environment for learning, helping pupils to study at their own speed and reach their goals more effectively. Each of these approaches ensures that the educational process is customized to meet each student's needs, continuously adjusting to maximize student engagement and success.

Intelligent Tutoring Systems (ITS)

Bilingual ITS, particularly in circumstances involving multiple languages, have appeared as a game-changing tool in tailored learning. These systems use cutting-edge AI technology to dynamically adapt material in order to supply learners with a tailored experience of learning in the languages they choose. Bilingual ITS promotes inclusion and makes high-quality education accessible to students from diverse linguistic backgrounds by overcoming language obstacles. This strategy, with its emphasis on individualized teaching and tailored strategies, produces better learning outcomes and is consistent with modern pedagogical techniques (Akyuz, 2020; Bhutoria, 2022).

The ability of bilingual ITS to deliver personalized, real-time feedback is one of its unique features. The system analyzes student responses using generative AI to spot misconceptions and offer ideas for corrections in the language that the user chooses. To guarantee that students receive the right amount of support at every stage, this feedback is regularly enhanced by dynamic modifications based on student success. For instance, bilingual ITS can provide alternative answers or detailed explanations for mathematics problems based on the needs of the student (Maity & Deroy, 2024; Marouf & Abu-Naser, 2019).

Bilingual ITS's utility is enhanced by dynamic lesson adjustments, which allow the system to modify delivery and content based on learner performance. Continuous observation of students' interactions acts as the foundation for these changes, ensuring that the learning path remains consistent with their comprehension and pace. The system may alter lessons to ensure clarity and engagement by providing more examples, clearer explanations, or even a language shift as needed. Bilingual ITS is an invaluable teaching tool due to its versatility, which is comparable to that of human teachers (Alkhatlan & Kalita, 2018; Marouf & Abu-Naser, 2019).

Key benefits of bilingual ITS include:

1) Real-time translation capabilities are necessary for engagement in multilingual courses (Akyuz, 2020).
2) Mechanisms for adaptive feedback that effectively address individual misconceptions (Alkhatlan & Kalita, 2018; Maity & Deroy, 2024).
3) Lessons are dynamically changed to match students' developmental and comprehension levels (Marouf & Abu-Naser, 2019).
4) The ability to adapt to varied language and cultural contexts (Bhutoria, 2022).
5) Improved participation through personalized and interactive learning routes (Bhutoria, 2022; Maity & Deroy, 2024).

While multilingual ITS has enormous potential, there are still obstacles to overcome, particularly in terms of assuring pedagogical accuracy and reducing bias in AI models. To address these difficulties, developers must use a variety of datasets, strong validation processes, and continual system upgrades. Adding capabilities like speech recognition and interactive conversations can also improve the usability and effect of these systems. By addressing these obstacles, bilingual ITS can become a pillar of the future of inclusive and individualized education (Akyuz, 2020; Bhutoria, 2022; Maity & Deroy, 2024).

Impact on Learner Engagement

Personalized learning has become popular as a transformative educational method that increases student motivation and retention by customizing the educational process to individual needs, preferences, and abilities. By leveraging big data and advanced analytics, education systems are able to offer real-time information about how well students are performing, allowing teachers to tailor learning strategies and provide timely interventions. This method not only assists prevent students from falling behind but also makes a better and more engaging environment for learning, thereby increasing students' motivation to succeed (Papadopoulos & Hossain, 2023).

A significant advantage of personalized learning is its transition from a conventional method to a curriculum that is more focused on the needs of the students. Digital tools like adaptive platforms help students manage their own learning, set goals, monitor progress, and receive feedback, leading to increased engagement and retention (Alamri et al., 2021; du Plooy et al., 2024). Personalization learning enhances retention using data-driven methods that fit content to students' learning styles and pace. Adaptive systems identify students' struggles and modify content accordingly. Pre-tests and activity logs guide effective information presentation, leading to better long-term knowledge retention (du Plooy et al., 2024). Additionally, the integration of gamification strategies in personalized learning environments has been found to boost motivation and engagement. By including elements, for example, rewards, leaderboards, and challenges, gamification systems make learning interactive and fun. For example, using platforms such as Kahoot! and Badgeville encourages participation and develops a sense of accomplishment and collaboration among students. This gamified personalization has been linked to increased student performance of up to 30% and a strong relationship between knowledge retention and engagement levels (Smirani & Yamani, 2024).

Another important aspect of personalized learning is its capability to give immediate and actionable feedback, which is essential for motivation and retention. Real-time data collection through learning management systems enables educators to address students' learning gaps promptly and reinforce their strengths. This feedback mechanism helps students track their progress and builds their confidence, preparing them for curriculum challenges (du Plooy et al., 2024; Papadopoulos & Hossain, 2023). The scalability of personalized learning is enhanced by technology and advanced analytics. Platforms designed for personalized learning often include predictive models and AIto project student performance and recommend tailored interventions. Consequently, institutions using personalized learning strategies report improved academic outcomes and higher student satisfaction and retention rates (Alamri et al., 2021; du Plooy et al., 2024). Additionally, personalized learning addresses broader educational challenges like inclusivity and accessibility. By adapting content delivery to cater to diverse learning preferences, cognitive abilities, and socio-cultural backgrounds, this approach fosters a fair learning environment. For instance, underrepresented groups or students with learning disabilities benefit significantly from customized content, enabling them to achieve success comparable to their peers (Alamri et al., 2021; du Plooy et al., 2024).

Considering the prior discussion, we may deduce that there are several points of personalization in bilingual learning to increase motivation and retention:

1) Adaptation of Materials According to Language Ability Level
2) Real-Time Feedback
3) Gamification for Motivation
4) Adjustment of Learning Styles Based on Culture
5) Enrichment with Local and Global Contexts

The evidence shows that personalized learning boosts motivation and retention. Focusing on individual needs and using technology makes education more engaging and effective for students, helping them reach their full potential (Alamri et al., 2021; du Plooy et al., 2024; Papadopoulos & Hossain, 2023; Smirani & Yamani, 2024).

AI-DRIVEN LANGUAGE PROFICIENCY EVALUATION

Assessing language proficiency has long been a complex task, often relying on methods that are time-consuming, subjective, and difficult to scale (Zou et al., 2023). For instance, evaluating speaking skills may require manual transcription and detailed analysis of pronunciation, fluency, and intonation. Similarly, writing assessments often depend on human evaluators, whose judgments can vary due to personal biases, while comprehension tests typically use standardized questions that may fail to fully capture a learner's understanding. While these traditional approaches can be effective in controlled environments, they are often limited by the resources available and their inability to offer immediate feedback (Bouziane & Bouziane, 2024; Chiang & Lee, 2023).

Recent technological breakthroughs, particularly in AI, have introduced innovative solutions to these challenges. AI tools leverage capabilities like speech recognition, NLP, and machine learning to provide objective, consistent, and scalable assessments across various language domains, including speaking, writing, and comprehension. These systems go beyond identifying surface-level errors, analyzing deeper linguistic patterns, context, and meaning, resulting in a more comprehensive evaluation of a learner's language skills (Yakkala, 2024).

AI-powered assessments also make high-quality evaluations more accessible, especially in settings with limited resources or large-scale needs. By reducing dependence on skilled human evaluators, these tools allow for practical solutions such as simultaneous speaking proficiency assessments for thousands of learners or instant feedback on written work. This enables educators to dedicate more time to personalized teaching rather than repetitive grading tasks (Ng et al., 2023).

However, while AI has great potential, it also presents challenges. Issues like accounting for cultural and linguistic nuances, avoiding biases in algorithmic assessments, and preventing over-reliance on automated systems need careful attention to ensure fairness and inclusivity. Even so, the adoption of AI in language assessment represents a significant advancement, offering a more efficient and equitable method to measure language proficiency.

Speaking Skills Evaluation

Assessing speaking skills in language learning has traditionally been a challenging and subjective process. Trained evaluators are often needed to analyze elements such as pronunciation, intonation, fluency, and clarity (Kan & Ito, 2020; Zou et al., 2023). While effective in smaller, controlled settings, this manual approach is time-consuming, prone to inconsistencies, and difficult to scale for larger groups of learners. The advent of AI has transformed this area by incorporating speech recognition technologies and advanced acoustic analysis to automate and improve speaking assessments (Stošić & Malyuga, 2024; Zou et al., 2023).

AI-driven tools utilize a combination of speech recognition algorithms and acoustic models to evaluate spoken language. These systems focus on key parameters, including (Bahi & Necibi, 2020; Ding et al., 2019; Kan & Ito, 2020; Zou et al., 2023):

- Pronunciation accuracy: Comparing the learner's speech to native-like phonetic patterns.
- Intonation and stress: Examining pitch variation and word emphasis to assess natural speech quality.
- Fluency: Measuring factors such as speech rate, pause length, and hesitation frequency.

AI brings several key advantages to speaking assessments. One of the most important is its scalability. AI systems can assess the speaking abilities of hundreds or even thousands of learners at the same time, making them particularly useful for large educational programs. AI also provides more objectivity compared to human evaluators, offering consistent scoring that isn't influenced by personal biases or evaluator fatigue (Bouziane & Bouziane, 2024; Chiang & Lee, 2023). Another benefit is the ability to provide quick feedback allows learners to obtain real-time adjustments and suggestions that facilitate continuous improvement without having to wait for delayed responses (Yakkala, 2024).

Despite the numerous advantages of AI, it poses certain challenges. A significant concern is accent bias; speech recognition systems frequently struggle to accurately assess non-standard or regional accents due to insufficient training data that fails to encompass these variations. Another challenge is the ability of AI to recognize cultural nuances. AI tools may miss culturally specific pronunciation differences or idiomatic expressions, leading to inaccurate assessments (Feng et al., 2024; Nacimiento-García et al., 2024). Additionally, another crucial risk lies in over-correction, especially for beginners, where excessive feedback can discourage learners and hinder their confidence and progress.(Dikli & Bleyle, 2014; Guo et al., 2022; MacFarlane & Spring, 2024; Shi & Aryadoust, 2024).

For example, AI tools like ELSA Speak offer detailed feedback on pronunciation, pinpointing specific phonemes that need improvement. Similarly, applications using Google Speech-to-Text provide transcription and basic pronunciation analysis, making these technologies a valuable asset in modern language learning.

Writing Skills Evaluation

Assessing writing has traditionally been a time-consuming process, requiring teachers or evaluators to carefully review grammar, sentence structure, coherence, and overall organization (Plakans & Gebril, 2017). While thorough, this approach is often influenced by subjective biases and can vary in consistency, especially when evaluating creative or complex work (Ahmadi Shirazi, 2019; Poe & Elliot, 2019). The introduction of AI-based writing tools has brought significant changes to this field, enabling learners to receive feedback that is not only faster and more consistent but also easily scalable.

AI uses technologies like NLP and machine learning to assess written text in several ways. These systems focus on key parameters, including (Tran, 2024; Wulandari et al., 2024; Zhao, 2023):

- Grammar and Syntax: Identifying and correcting sentence structure, punctuation, and word usage errors.
- Semantic Coherence: Ensuring logical flow and alignment of ideas.
- Vocabulary Enrichment: Suggesting alternatives to improve lexical diversity.
- Tone Analysis: Evaluating formality, politeness, or appropriateness of tone based on the context.

AI offers numerous advantages in writing assessments by providing quick feedback that allows learners to detect and rectify faults as they write, alongside scalability that allows for the review of thousands of written submissions simultaneously, particularly beneficial for large educational programs. AI ensures consistency by delivering objective scores, avoiding the variability often seen in human grading. Moreover, it offers personalized feedback, helping learners address specific areas of improvement, such as minimizing the use of passive voice or avoiding repetitive phrases (L. Wu, 2024).

While AI tools have made significant progress, they also face limitations. One challenge is in evaluating creative writing, where qualities like originality and emotional depth are subjective and hard for AI to measure. Cultural context is another problem since AI might not comprehend region-specific language, idiomatic expressions, or cultural nuances, leading to inaccuracies (Agarwal et al., 2024; Jose & Jayaron Jose, 2024). Additionally, relying too much on AI can prevent learners from developing critical skills like self-editing and independent problem-solving, which are essential for improving their writing over time.

Tools like Grammarly, for example, provide instant corrections for grammar, suggestions for improving tone, and recommendations for better writing style. Similarly, ProWritingAid offers detailed insights into overused words, sentence variety, and readability.

Comprehension Skills Evaluation

Evaluating comprehension, encompassing both reading and listening skills, serves as a fundamental aspect of language proficiency assessment. Traditional approaches, such as multiple-choice questions or written summaries, often fall short in reflecting the full extent of a learner's understanding. These methods tend to be rigid and lack the flexibility to adapt to individual learning needs. With advancements in technology, AI has brought significant changes to comprehension assessments by offering tools that are dynamic, personalized, and context-sensitive, allowing for a deeper and more accurate evaluation of a learner's skills (Murtaza et al., 2022).

AI tools for assessing comprehension use technologies such as adaptive learning algorithms, NLP, and machine learning. These tools evaluate learners' responses to measure their ability to perform tasks like (Wang et al., 2024):

- Identifying Key Information: Recognizing main ideas and important details in written or spoken material.
- Drawing Inferences: Interpreting implied meanings and making logical conclusions.
- Understanding Context: Evaluating how well learners grasp cultural or situational nuances.

AI offers several key advantages in assessing comprehension skills. One major benefit is personalized assessment, as AI adapts questions to match each learner's proficiency level, ensuring that the challenges are not too simple nor too complex (Murtaza et al., 2022). Another advantage is real-time insights, where learners receive immediate feedback to help them identify areas of weakness and adjust their learning strategies accordingly (A Rahman & Nor, 2024). Additionally, AI enables holistic evaluation by integrating multiple inputs, such as text, audio, and even visual elements, allowing it to assess comprehension across different contexts.

While AI has significant potential in this area, it also comes with notable challenges. One limitation is in evaluating higher-order cognitive skills, including critical analysis or the synthesis of complex ideas, where AI may struggle to provide accurate assessments. Another challenge is cultural sensitivity; AI tools can misinterpret culturally specific references, which can undermine the accuracy of the evaluation. Finally, the quality and diversity of the training data have a significant impact on how effective AI-based products are, making it essential to have robust datasets for reliable assessments (Zheng & Fan, 2024).

Real-time Feedback Systems

Systems for Real-time Feedback are tools designed to provide immediate and context-specific responses to users' inputs, helping them recognize and correct mistakes as they occur. In language learning, these systems rely on modern technologies such as NLP and machine learning to analyze speech or writing as it is being produced. By offering instant feedback, they enable learners to refine their language skills in real time, creating a more lively and participatory learning experience (Owan et al., 2023).

Unlike traditional feedback methods, which often involve delays while waiting for an instructor or evaluator's input, real-time systems prioritize immediacy. For instance, as a learner speaks or writes, the system detects errors in areas such as pronunciation, grammar, syntax, or vocabulary and provides immediate recommendations for enhancement. This approach not only speeds up the learning process but also reinforces correct language use by addressing mistakes when they happen, making corrections more impactful (Evenddy, 2024).

These systems have become increasingly popular in educational technology, especially in language learning tools, because of their ability to deliver personalized instruction at scale. They are integrated into applications such as ELSA Speak, which focuses on speech recognition and pronunciation training (Kholis, 2021). Another notable example is Duolingo, which uses adaptive exercises and gamified elements to provide instant feedback on vocabulary, grammar, and sentence structure, making language practice engaging and effective (Rachels & Rockinson-Szapkiw, 2018). The consistent, unbiased evaluations and adaptability of these tools to individual learner needs make them indispensable for fostering language proficiency.

By incorporating real-time feedback into learning, these systems offer learners continuous, actionable guidance. This not only helps improve language skills but also enhances confidence and motivation, as learners can immediately see progress and the results of their efforts. As a result, real-time feedback systems mark a significant step forward in education, bridging traditional teaching methods with the demand for modern, adaptive learning technologies (Lee & Moore, 2024).

MOTIVATION, SELF-REGULATION, AND GAMIFICATION IN AI LEARNING SYSTEMS

Enhancing Learner Autonomy and Goal Setting

AI has transformed the study process of language, making it easier and more accessible for learners to take control of their own progress. By providing individualized experiences and immediate feedback, and adaptable content, AI helps learners set and achieve goals adapted to their particular strengths and weaknesses. This individualized approach not only encourages independence but also creates a more engaging and enjoyable learning journey. Learners can develop the strategies they need to tackle complex language skills like grammar, vocabulary, and communication.

One of the key ways AI fosters autonomies is by creating individualized educational pathways. These paths accommodate each learner's requirements, inclinations, and goals, ensuring an efficient and focused approach. For example, platforms like Busuu offer customized study plans based on the learner's proficiency level, helping them target specific areas for improvement (Katiyar et al., 2024). Similarly, Rosetta Stone allows learners to study at their own speed, providing them with the freedom to fit language learning into their schedules. This approach builds confidence and keeps learners engaged by showing them steady progress over time (Bai, 2024).

Another way AI supports autonomy is by giving learners the freedom to choose from a broad range of interactive activities. From role-playing exercises to vocabulary games and simulated conversations, platforms like Memrise offer gamified and diverse content that aligns with individual preferences, keeping learners motivated and in control (Wang et al., 2024). Rosetta Stone also stands out with immersive features like speech recognition and context-specific exercises, which not only make learning more enjoyable but also reduce anxiety, creating a positive and supportive environment (Bai, 2024).

Another key feature fostering learner autonomy is the variety of activities that AI platforms offer. Providing learners with the freedom to select from interactive tasks, such as role-playing exercises, vocabulary games, or simulated conversations, enhances their sense of agency. Platforms like Memrise, known for its gamified and diverse content, enable learners to engage in a learning experience that aligns with their preferences, keeping them motivated and in control (Wang et al., 2024).

Additionally, Rosetta Stone's immersive features, including speech recognition and contextual exercises, enhance learners' foreign language enjoyment (FLE) while reducing anxiety, creating a supportive and engaging environment (Bai, 2024).

AI also enhances autonomy by allowing learners to control how and when they receive feedback. Tools like ELSA Speak let users customize feedback frequency and level of detail, tailoring the learning process to their comfort and goals. For instance, learners focusing on pronunciation can use ELSA Speak's adjustable settings to target specific language challenges while receiving immediate and actionable feedback, which reinforces their progress and confidence (Rusmiyanto et al., 2023).

By integrating these features, AI platforms encourage students to take charge of their educational journey, promoting a deeper sensation of possession and responsibility. The ability to set personalized goals, choose engaging activities, and control feedback mechanisms ensures that learners remain motivated and focused on achieving their language learning objectives. This autonomy not only enhances their immediate learning outcomes but also provides them with the skills and strategies needed for lifelong learning.

AI-driven tools not only foster autonomy but also play a pivotal role in enhancing student' ability to set reasonable objectives, prioritize essential topics, and manage their time effectively. By leveraging automated reminders and personalized schedules, platforms like Busuu guide learners in creating achievable learning objectives while maintaining focus on their priorities (Rusmiyanto et al., 2023). This structured method allows students to optimize their study routines and achieve consistent progress.

Immediate feedback further enhances goal setting by allowing learners to identify mistakes promptly and refine their skills. For example, Duolingo provides real-time corrections during exercises, which helps maintain momentum and builds learner confidence (Khasawneh et al., 2024). Progress tracking and visualization features, such as visual dashboards and milestones, are equally crucial in motivating learners. Platforms like Memrise incorporate gamified elements like badges and performance analytics, offering clear indicators of progress that inspire sustained engagement (Wang et al., 2024).

Adaptive practices ensure learners face appropriately challenging tasks that align with their proficiency. AI dynamically adjusts the complexity of exercises that are determined by student achievement, offering a well-rounded educational experience that prevents frustration while ensuring continuous skill development (Wei, 2023). Moreover, gamified and adaptive learning environments enhance engagement by making the process enjoyable and rewarding, further driving motivation and commitment (Wang et al., 2024). These features collectively improve learning efficiency by enabling learners to concentrate on areas that require the most attention, supported by tailored content and immediate feedback (Katiyar et al., 2024).

By integrating goal-setting features, such as progress tracking and learning strategy adjustments, AI platforms enable learners to take charge of their educational path. This not only enhances motivation but also makes learners active participants in their education, fostering a sense of responsibility and engagement (Rusmiyanto et al., 2023).

Self-regulation depends heavily on motivation, and AI-powered solutions are especially good at meeting the psychological requirements for relatedness, competence, and autonomy that are listed in Self-Determination Theory (SDT). By cultivating self-motivation, AI tools help learners feel more engaged and empowered to regulate their learning processes. According to research by Noels (2023), fulfilling these psychological needs significantly enhances motivation, driving learners toward sustained engagement and improved learning outcomes (Noels, 2023).

AI platforms match closely with the ideas of SDT offering features that cater to these needs. For instance, autonomy is supported by tools like Duolingo and Busuu, which allow learners to take control of their progress through goal setting and tracking. Competence is reinforced through immediate feedback and adaptive difficulty, ensuring learners feel confident in mastering complex language skills (Katiyar et al., 2024). Relatedness, on the other hand, is fostered by conversational agents and collaborative features, such as those in Busuu, which encourage social interaction and a feeling of community among students (Rusmiyanto et al., 2023).

Adaptive Features of AI in Language Learning

The integration of adaptive AI technologies is revolutionizing language learning by offering innovative solutions that significantly enhance learner motivation, self-regulation, and overall progress. These advanced AI systems dynamically adjust the difficulty level and content of learning materials in real-time, tailoring the learning experience to individual performance and ensuring a balanced, personalized educational journey (Katiyar et al., 2024). A key feature of this adaptive approach is the sophisticated use of speech recognition technology, exemplified by systems such as ELSA Speak. This technology provides immediate and accurate feedback on pronunciation, enabling learners to refine their speaking skills in real-time, thereby building fluency and confidence (Rusmiyanto et al., 2023). Such real-time corrective guidance is transforming how learners practice and improve their spoken language abilities, offering an unprecedented level of support for mastering pronunciation.

In addition to speech recognition, contextual understanding represents another breakthrough in adaptive AI. AI systems are now capable of analyzing learner responses within conversational exercises, delivering feedback that is not only relevant but deeply personalized. This feature tailors guidance to each learner's unique communication patterns and context, enriching the learning experience by making it more responsive to individual needs (Wei, 2023). Furthermore, AI-enabled assessment tools, such as those for evaluating K-12 students' speaking skills through automated speech scoring engines, provide valuable insights into progress, contributing to a more nuanced understanding of a learner's capabilities (Chen et al., 2025).

Intelligent Tutoring Systems (ITSs) are another example of AI's adaptability. By leveraging machine learning algorithms, ITSs can detect errors and provide targeted feedback on pronunciation, vocabulary, grammar, and contextual usage, creating a more personalized approach to language acquisition. These systems offer a significant advantage in reducing learner anxiety and fostering a willingness to communicate, as they provide timely corrections in a supportive environment (Son et al., 2025). As such, AI is not only changing the mechanics of language learning but also profoundly influencing the learner's emotional engagement with the process.

The continuous integration of AI in language education, as suggested by (Son et al., 2025), promises to transform both learning and teaching methodologies. Educators are encouraged to harness AI's capabilities to create effective, AI-powered learning environments that not only enhance language acquisition but also ensure that pedagogical and technical considerations are carefully integrated into the learning process (Jose, 2025). This ongoing evolution is positioning AI as an indispensable tool in fostering more engaging, effective, and personalized language education experiences.

Case Studies and Empirical Evidence

Practical applications of AI in language learning further validate its effectiveness. Platforms like Duolingo enhance time management by using reminders and daily goals, ensuring learners maintain consistent schedules (Khasawneh et al., 2024). Self-assessment tools in Busuu enable learners to evaluate their performance and determine what needs to be improved, reinforcing self-regulation skills (Rusmiyanto et al., 2023). Research highlights that gamified elements in Duolingo increase engagement and retention rates by over 30%, showcasing its ability to sustain learner motivation (Wang et al., 2023). Similarly, ELSA Speak's real-time pronunciation feedback has been shown to enhance fluency and confidence, making it an effective tool for learners focusing on speaking skills (Rusmiyanto et al., 2023).

AI platforms give students the means to successfully accomplish their learning goals by fusing goal-setting techniques with interactive and adaptive elements. Features like progress visualization, instant feedback, and personalized learning paths encourage self-regulation and autonomy by encouraging pupils to take charge of their education. Additionally, AI's compatibility with psychological concepts such as SDT guarantees a comprehensive method of language acquisition that takes into account both technical and motivational requirements. Platforms like ELSA Speak,

Memrise, Busuu, and Duolingo are prime examples of how AI may revolutionize education by making it more efficient, effective, and learner-centered.

Gamification Strategies in AI Platforms

Gamification AI is an innovative approach that integrates game-like components such as leaderboards, levels, badges, and points into language learning platforms (Abbes et al., 2024; Al-Dosakee & Ozdamli, 2021). By leveraging AI, these platforms create an engaging and motivating experience, helping learners acquire a language more effectively by tapping into their intrinsic desire to play and compete (Hamari, 2017; Koivisto & Hamari, 2019). Below are the ways in which AI-driven gamification transforms the learning process.

Personalized Learning Pathways

AI enables platforms to analyze individual learner progress, tailoring lessons to their specific strengths, weaknesses, and goals. This dynamic adaptation ensures that the content evolves alongside the learner's abilities, providing a more meaningful and effective learning experience. For instance:

- Duolingo adjusts lesson difficulty in real-time based on user performance, helping learners focus on challenging areas.
- Memrise uses spaced repetition algorithms to optimize vocabulary retention.
- Busuu integrates AI with collaborative learning, offering personalized exercises and peer-reviewed assignments to enhance interactivity (Abbes et al., 2024; Katiyar et al., 2024).

This adaptive personalization fosters learner autonomy, allowing individuals to progress at their own speed and achieve specific language goals with increased engagement and long-term retention (Yeşilçınar, 2023).

Immersive Learning Scenarios

AI-created immersive scenarios simulate real-world scenarios that allow pupils to hone their language abilities in meaningful and contextually relevant ways. These scenarios allow learners to engage in practical language use, such as participating in mock interviews, ordering food at a restaurant, or navigating travel-related conversations, fostering fluency and confidence.

Generative AI systems can create dynamic, branching narratives that adapt to user responses, allowing learners to explore various conversational paths based on their choices (Abbes et al., 2024). For example, tools like Babbel offer interactive dialogues tailored to real-life scenarios, providing cultural and situational relevance to the learning process.

The authenticity of these scenarios encourages deeper engagement and enhances retention by making language practice enjoyable and relatable. This alignment with real-world applications fills the void between academic understanding and real-world communication, promoting better learner outcomes (Vlachopoulos & Makri, 2017).

Adaptive Feedback and Progress Tracking

AI ensures that learners can recognize and fix mistakes in real-time by providing instant, individualized feedback on vocabulary usage, grammar, and pronunciation. Accuracy and fluency are two essential elements of language competency that are supported by this adaptive feedback process.

Tools like ELSA Speak leverage AI-powered speech recognition to evaluate pronunciation and provide actionable feedback, boosting learner confidence in speaking. Similarly, platforms like Duolingo and Busuu offer grammar corrections and vocabulary suggestions based on user responses, helping learners refine their skills progressively (Al-Dosakee & Ozdamli, 2021).

Adaptive feedback not only improves individual performance but also enhances motivation by allowing learners to see tangible progress in their skills. This feedback loop, powered by AI, caters to the unique challenges faced by each learner, fostering consistent improvement and engagement over time (Sailer et al., 2017).

Reward Systems and Incentives

Reward systems within gamified platforms—such as points, badges, and virtual currency—act as powerful motivators, providing students who feel accomplished and who are consistently engaged (L. Liu, 2024). For instance:

- Duolingo uses experience points (XP) and streaks to reward daily participation, fostering habit formation.
- Memrise offers virtual rewards to reinforce vocabulary mastery.
- Busuu acknowledges learner progress with badges and certificates, emphasizing milestone achievements.

These systems reinforce intrinsic and extrinsic motivation, transforming learning into a rewarding and goal-oriented process (Hamari, 2017; L. Liu, 2024; Z. Wu et al., 2024).

Leaderboards and Competitive Elements

Leaderboards introduce a healthy competitive dynamic by enabling learners to compare their progress with peers. By fostering a sense of competition in a supportive learning environment, leaderboards motivate learners to improve their performance and maintain active participation (Hamari, 2017). For example, Duolingo ranks learners weekly on leaderboards, creating friendly competition that encourages consistent learning. This mechanism balances the drive for competition with collaboration, as users strive for higher rankings while remaining part of a community (Shortt et al., 2023). Research also suggests that gamified competitive elements improve cognitive engagement and participation, leading to better learning outcomes (L. Liu, 2024). Here are some examples of gamification AI in Language Learning.

1) Duolingo

Duolingo incorporates a wide range of gamification elements, including streaks, levels, and leaderboards, to keep learners motivated. Streaks encourage daily learning habits by rewarding consistent participation, while leaderboards foster friendly competition by ranking users based on their performance. Additionally, learners earn experience points (XP) for completing lessons and can unlock virtual rewards for achieving milestones. Duolingo's adaptive AI adjusts the difficulty of exercises based on user performance, ensuring personalized and engaging experiences (Shortt et al., 2023).

2) Babbel

Babbel integrates gamification through interactive dialogues and scenario-based challenges that mimic real-world situations. These features allow learners to engage in contextualized conversation practice, helping them build confidence and fluency. Babbel also offers completion badges for reaching milestones in their learning journey, providing a sense of achievement and motivation (Kessler et al., 2023).

3) Memrise

Memrise gamifies the learning process with spaced repetition algorithms and memory games, which optimize vocabulary retention. The platform also includes progress bars, badges, and rewards that visually track learners' achievements. The use of native speaker videos in exercises creates an immersive experience, helping learners practice pronunciation and contextually relevant language skills (Wang et al., 2024).

4) Busuu

Busuu combines gamified progress tracking with a social learning component. Learners earn completion badges and certifications as they advance through lessons, and AI adapts exercises to their skill levels. Busuu's unique peer review system allows users to receive feedback on their writing and speaking exercises from other learners, adding a collaborative and rewarding element to the platform (Rusmiyanto et al., 2023).

5) Rosetta Stone

Rosetta Stone utilizes gamification through speech recognition exercises and achievement tracking. The platform provides learners with visual progress dashboards and adaptive challenges to measure their improvement in real time. Its immersive features, such as simulated conversations and contextual exercises, gamify language practice by creating real-life scenarios for learners to navigate (Bai, 2024).

6) ELSA Speak

ELSA Speak gamifies pronunciation practice with instant feedback and goal-setting features. Users can set personal pronunciation targets and track their improvement through detailed analytics. The platform rewards learners with badges and streak achievements for consistent use, while its real-time feedback ensures learners feel a sense of accomplishment as they master new sounds and words (Rusmiyanto et al., 2023).

Behavioral Insights in Learning Patterns

AI-powered language learning resources foster learner ownership and persistence by providing customized and flexible experiences that enable learners to take control of their progress. By tailoring content to individual needs and offering real-time feedback, AI platforms enable learners to actively participate in the learning process, enhancing their sense of responsibility and commitment to achieving their goals.

One key mechanism for fostering ownership is the ability of AI tools to personalize learning paths. By modifying classes according on user performance, platforms such as Busuu and Memrise enable students to concentrate on their areas of improvement. This customization makes the learning process more relevant and engaging, which reinforces a learner's responsibility for their own progress (Katiyar et al., 2024). Platforms like Rosetta Stone provide individualized learning paths that adapt to individual schedules and needs, ensuring learners feel in control of their progress.

This customization fosters a sense of ownership, as learners can align their learning experience with personal goals and preferences (Bai, 2024). By aligning content with personal goals and preferences, learners are encouraged to persist even when challenges arise.

Immediate and adaptive feedback is another critical feature that supports persistence. Tools like Duolingo and ELSA Speak provide instant corrections and suggestions during exercises, helping learners identify and address mistakes in real time. This timely intervention builds competence and confidence, which motivates learners to continue engaging with the platform (Rusmiyanto et al., 2023). Research indicates that learners who receive regular feedback are more likely to continue their education and get better outcomes. (Khasawneh et al., 2024).

Progress tracking and visualization also play a significant role in fostering ownership. Platforms like Memrise incorporate features such as performance dashboards, badges, and milestones, giving learners tangible indicators of their achievements. These visual tools not only boost motivation but also allow learners to take pride in their progress, which encourages continued effort (Wang et al., 2024). Gamification elements like streaks and leaderboards, as seen in Duolingo, introduce a competitive yet supportive dynamic that motivates learners to stay consistent and strive for improvement (Shortt et al., 2023).

AI platforms further enhance persistence by addressing requirements of the mind as described by SDT, including autonomy, competency, and relatedness. By allowing students to determine goals, track progress, and adjust their learning strategies, tools like Busuu promote autonomy. Similarly, the adaptive difficulty and real-time feedback in Duolingo and ELSA Speak help learners build competence, while features like community-based interactions foster relatedness, creating a sense of belonging and mutual support (Noels, 2023; Rusmiyanto et al., 2023).

Ultimately, AI tools significantly enhance learner ownership and persistence through personalized content, real-time feedback, and effective progress visualization, all of which empower students to take control of their educational experience. By addressing both cognitive and motivational aspects, these tools establish a friendly and engaging workplace that helps learners stay committed to their goals, ensuring sustained success in learning a language.

Additional Empirical Evidence

Empirical research underscores the efficiency of language learning powered by AI platforms in enhancing learner motivation and improving success rates. These studies demonstrate that AI technologies offer tailored, flexible educational opportunities and foster sustained engagement through gamification and immediate feedback, leading to significant improvements in language acquisition outcomes.

Research by Shortt et al. (2023) focused on Duolingo, one of the most popular AI-powered language learning platforms, revealed that its gamified features, such as streaks, levels, and leaderboards, significantly increased learner motivation. The study found that learners who maintained daily streaks for more than seven days demonstrated a 25% higher retention rate compared to those who did not. Additionally, the adaptive lesson difficulty ensured that learners remained appropriately challenged, which was linked to increased confidence and better vocabulary retention (Shortt et al., 2023).

Similarly, research by Wang et al., (2024) highlighted the success of Memrise in enhancing language learning motivation through its use of spaced repetition algorithms and gamified elements. The study reported a 30% improvement in retention of vocabulary and learner engagement compared to conventional learning methods. Participants noted that the interactive nature of Memrise's exercises made the process more enjoyable and encouraged consistent practice (Wang et al., 2024).

Bai (2024) provided further evidence by examining the impact of Rosetta Stone on learner motivation and success rates. The study found that Rosetta Stone's personalized study plans and immersive features significantly reduced learners' foreign language anxiety (FLA) while increasing their foreign language enjoyment (FLE). Learners in the study group's findings substantial improvements in listening and speaking skills compared to those using traditional methods alone (Bai, 2024). This success was attributed to the platform's real-time feedback, progress-tracking tools, and adaptive learning pathways, which allowed learners to engage at their own pace and customize the experience to their requirements.

The effectiveness of AI in fostering motivation is further supported by a study on ELSA Speak conducted by Rusmiyanto et al. (2023). The platform's real-time pronunciation feedback was shown to significantly enhance learner confidence and fluency. Learners demonstrated a 40% improvement in their pronunciation scores, with many attributing their success to the platform's ability to identify specific challenges and provide actionable feedback. This personalized approach encouraged learners to persist in their language studies (Rusmiyanto et al., 2023).

Another study by Khasawneh et al. (2024) examined how AI tools like Busuu facilitate learner motivation through community-based learning and personalized study plans. The research found that the combination of AI-driven feedback and peer interaction led to higher levels of engagement and persistence. Learners who actively participated in Busuu's community features reported greater satisfaction and demonstrated better overall language proficiency (Khasawneh et al., 2024).

In addition to these findings, empirical evidence suggests that AI-driven platforms align well with psychological frameworks such as SDT. By addressing learners' requirements for relatedness, competence, and autonomy, AI tools like Duolingo, Memrise, and ELSA Speak establish a nurturing educational atmosphere that encourages intrinsic motivation. For example, personalized feedback and adaptive content enhance competence, while goal-setting and progress tracking foster autonomy.

In conclusion, the empirical evidence strongly supports the role of AI in increasing learner motivation and success rates. By integrating personalized learning paths, gamification, and real-time feedback, platforms like Duolingo, Memrise, Busuu, and ELSA Speak not only increase the interest level of language learning but also enable learners to achieve tangible results in their educational journey. These results demonstrate the revolutionary possibilities of AI in producing efficient and learner-centered approaches to language education.

INTEGRATING AI TOOLS INTO LANGUAGE LEARNING FRAMEWORKS

Integrating AI in language education has revolutionized traditional methods of teaching and learning languages. When comparing popular language learning tools/platforms, it is essential to evaluate their pedagogical strategies, strengths, limitations, language coverage, and curriculum. Each platform employs unique approaches and caters to specific aspects of language acquisition, making them suitable for different learner preferences and goals. The following table provides a side-by-side comparison of Duolingo, Babbel, Memrise, ELSA Speak, and Rosetta Stone based on these criteria, highlighting their distinctive features and areas of focus.

Table 2. Comparison of Duolingo, Babbel, Memrise, ELSA Speak, and Rosetta Stone

Criteria	Duolingo	Babbel	Memrise	ELSA Speak	Rosetta Stone
Pedagogical Strategies	Translation-based, gamified learning with adaptive tests.	Structured, conversation-based learning with speech recognition.	Vocabulary-focused with mnemonic techniques and spaced repetition.	AI-driven ASR technology with real-time feedback for pronunciation.	Immersive "Dynamic Immersion" method using images and sounds without translations.
Strengths	Free access, gamification, wide language variety (40+).	Focus on conversational skills and speech recognition.	Rich multimedia integration, engaging mnemonic methods.	Immediate pronunciation feedback, personalized learning paths.	Immersive learning, user-friendly interface, speech recognition.
Limitations	Heavy reliance on translation, limited offline functionality.	Limited free content, smaller language selection (14 languages).	Lack of structured progression, no placement tests.	Limited to English, ASR struggles in noisy environments.	Lacks explicit grammar instruction, repetitive exercises, limited cultural context.
Language Coverage	40+ languages, including popular and niche ones.	14 major languages focused on real-world application.	16 languages with user-generated content.	English pronunciation only.	25 languages, including less commonly taught ones like Swahili.
Curriculum	Vocabulary and grammar-focused, less structured.	Beginner-to-advanced progression with practical themes like travel.	Flexible vocabulary-centric learning with spaced repetition.	Structured exercises targeting sounds, intonation, and stress.	Multi-level, cumulative themes such as travel, health, and shopping.

The table above outlines the key features and characteristics of Duolingo, Babbel, Memrise, ELSA Speak, and Rosetta Stone, offering a comprehensive overview of their approaches to language learning. While each platform has its unique strengths, they also come with specific limitations that cater to different learner profiles. The following sections provide a detailed explanation of each criterion—pedagogical strategies, strengths, limitations, language coverage, and curriculum—enabling a deeper understanding of how these tools compare and what makes them suitable for different learning objectives.

Pedagogical Strategies and Approaches

Language learning platforms adopt diverse pedagogical strategies to cater to varying learner needs and goals. Duolingo utilizes a gamified approach, incorporating translation exercises and adaptive testing to create a highly engaging and motivational environment. While its game-like features encourage consistent practice, it falls short in fostering cultural immersion and conversational fluency (Essafi et al., 2024). In contrast, Babbel focuses on structured and practical lessons aimed at building conversational skills and improving pronunciation. This real-world emphasis makes it a strong choice for learners seeking functional language proficiency in everyday situations (Essafi et al., 2024). Similarly, Memrise leverages mnemonic techniques and spaced repetition to enhance vocabulary retention through a gamified learning journey. However, its focus on memorization often comes at the expense of conversational and grammatical skill development, which limits its comprehensiveness for well-rounded language acquisition (Essafi et al., 2024).

ELSA Speak offers a specialized approach by prioritizing pronunciation improvement with the use of AI-driven Automatic Speech Recognition (ASR) technology. By providing real-time feedback, it serves as a useful resource for non-native English speakers aiming to enhance their speaking accuracy and confidence (AI Review, 2023; Kholis, 2021). Meanwhile, Rosetta Stone employs its "Dynamic Immersion" method, which mimics natural language acquisition by exposing learners to images, text, and sounds without direct translations. This strategy fosters intuitive learning and strengthens vocabulary and pronunciation skills. However, its lack of explicit grammar instruction and cultural context can hinder learners who prefer more structured and rule-based learning. Despite these limitations, Rosetta Stone offers an immersive and user-friendly experience, encouraging learners to build their language skills organically, much like first-language acquisition (Jasmine, 2024).

Strengths of AI in Language Instruction

Each language learning platform boasts unique strengths tailored to various learner needs and goals. ELSA Speak excels in pronunciation improvement through its AI-driven Automatic Speech Recognition (ASR) technology, offering instant feedback that helps learners quickly identify and correct errors (Kholis, 2021). Its personalized learning paths, designed based on individual assessments, allow users to target areas of weakness, making their practice sessions more efficient and focused (AI Review, 2023). Additionally, studies highlight the app's engaging and motivating features, with learners reporting improved pronunciation and vocabulary skills while finding the platform enjoyable to use (Darsih et al., 2021).

Rosetta Stone stands out for its immersive learning experience, which eliminates direct translations and instead fosters an intuitive understanding of language by linking words with images and sounds. This method promotes deeper comprehension and mirrors first-language acquisition processes (Jasmine, 2024). Its advanced speech recognition technology further enhances learners' pronunciation by providing immediate and precise feedback, while its user-friendly and interactive interface ensures accessibility for a wide range of learners (Jasmine, 2024).

Duolingo offers unparalleled accessibility with its free model and a vast selection of over 40 languages, including niche ones like Klingon and High Valyrian. Its gamified environment, featuring streaks, badges, and daily challenges, keeps learners motivated and engaged, making it an ideal tool for casual learners (Essafi et al., 2024). Meanwhile, Babbel is lauded for its well-structured lessons that integrate speech recognition and explicit grammar instruction, helping users gain confidence in conversational and grammatical proficiency (Essafi et al., 2024). Memrise leverages its innovative mnemonic tools and multimedia-rich lessons, including videos with native speakers, to create a highly immersive learning experience. These features, combined with a gamified approach, make Memrise particularly effective for vocabulary retention and engaging for learners (Essafi et al., 2024).

Limitations and Ethical Considerations

Each language learning platform has its limitations that can impact user experience and learning outcomes. Rosetta Stone is critiqued for its lack of explicit grammar instruction, which can be a disadvantage for learners who prefer a structured approach to understanding language rules (Christiano, 2025). Additionally, its use of standardized images across all language courses often lacks cultural relevance, which may impede learners' ability to grasp the contextual nuances of language usage (Wikipedia, 2024). Another drawback is its reliance on repetitive exercises, which some users find monotonous over time, reducing engagement and motivation (Christiano, 2025).

Although ELSA Speak is highly effective for pronunciation practice, it does have certain limitations. The app's advanced features or higher-level content often require payment, which can restrict access for some learners (Darsih et al., 2021). Moreover, its speech recognition technology sometimes struggles to accurately assess pronunciation in noisy environments, necessitating a quiet setting for optimal performance (Darsih et al., 2021).

Duolingo, despite its popularity, faces criticism for its heavy reliance on translation-based tasks, which may hinder the development of conversational fluency. Its offline mode is also limited, which can reduce its utility for learners in areas with poor internet connectivity (Essafi et al., 2024). Babbel, on the other hand, provides high-quality content but restricts most features to premium subscribers, making it less accessible for learners on a budget (Essafi et al., 2024). Similarly, Memrise has its own shortcomings, including unstructured lesson progression and the lack of placement tests, which may leave learners uncertain about where to start or how to advance systematically. These issues can create challenges for those seeking a guided and comprehensive learning path (Essafi et al., 2024).

The research acknowledges a number of issues and worries despite the obvious promise of personalized learning with AI. The possibility of algorithmic prejudice, ethical issues, and data privacy issues remain important subjects that demand ongoing discussion and debate (Williamson, 2017) . To ensure that the application of AI in education places a high priority on equity, transparency, and the welfare of students, researchers and educators must address these issues.

Language Coverage

Language coverage varies significantly across platforms, with offerings ranging from broad selections to specialized focuses. Duolingo leads the way, offering an extensive range of over 40 languages, including less commonly taught options such as Klingon and High Valyrian. This broad selection caters to a diverse audience, making Duolingo a top choice for learners with varied language interests (Essafi et al., 2024). The most widely used language on the Duolingo platform is English, particularly in regions like South America, Asia, Europe, and Africa, as shown in Figure 2. Meanwhile, the second most widely studied language varies by region. For instance, in Southeast Asia and China, Japanese is the most popular, whereas in Asia and Northern Europe, German dominates, as illustrated in Figure 3.

Figure 2. Most popular language studied on Dualingo in each country in 2024 (Blanco, 2024)

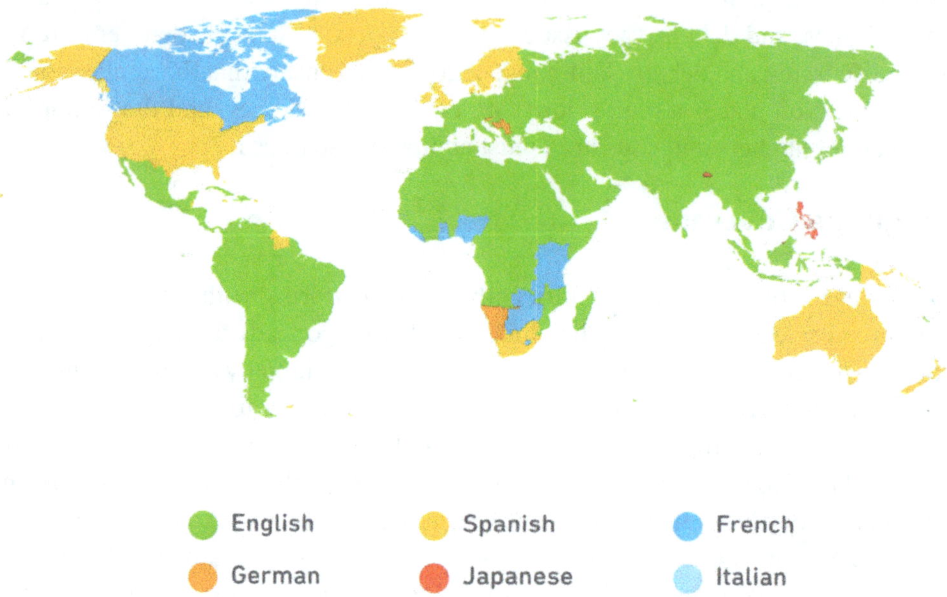

Figure 3. Second most popular language studied on Duolingo in each country in 2024 (Blanco, 2024)

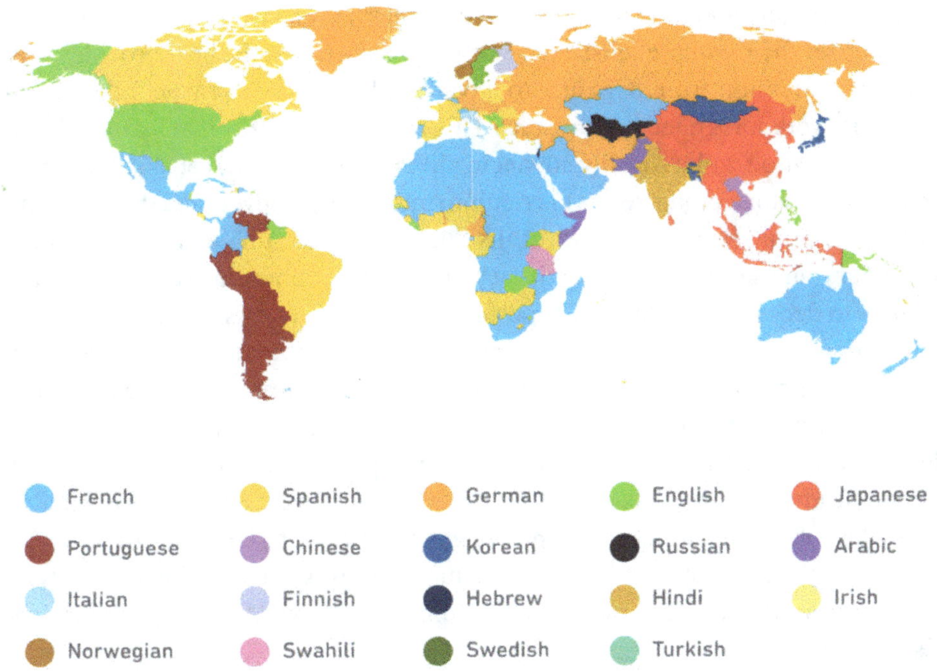

Following Duolingo, Rosetta Stone offers 25 languages, striking a balance between widely spoken languages such as Spanish, French, German, and Mandarin, as well as less commonly studied ones like Swahili and Tagalog. This diverse selection is well-suited for learners looking to explore both major and niche languages (Christiano, 2025).

Memrise offers courses in 16 languages, with the added flexibility of user-generated content. This unique feature allows for greater diversity in topics and language resources, though the quality of user-generated courses may vary (Essafi et al., 2024). Babbel narrows its focus to 14 widely spoken languages, emphasizing depth and quality in its curriculum. By concentrating on languages with high practical use, Babbel provides learners with robust and comprehensive resources tailored for real-world applications (Essafi et al., 2024). At the other end of the spectrum, ELSA Speak specializes exclusively in English pronunciation and speaking skills, targeting non-native English speakers aiming to refine their spoken English proficiency. While its scope is limited to a single language, its specialization makes it highly effective for this particular aspect of language learning (Kholis, 2021).

Curriculum Integration and Design

Language learning platforms vary in their curriculum design, offering different levels of structure and focus to suit diverse learner needs. Babbel and Rosetta Stone stand out for their comprehensive and structured curricula. Babbel provides a systematic progression from beginner to advanced levels, with practical themes like travel and work integrated into lessons. This approach ensures that learners build a strong foundation while steadily advancing in their skills (Essafi et al., 2024). Similarly, Rosetta Stone organizes its curriculum into multiple levels and thematic units, such as shopping, health, and travel. Its cumulative learning approach reinforces vocabulary and grammar, though it lacks explicit grammar instruction, requiring learners to deduce rules through exposure and practice (Christiano, 2025).

Duolingo and Memrise take a more flexible, less structured approach to curriculum design. Duolingo focuses on vocabulary and grammar but does not follow a clear progression, often resulting in disjointed learning experiences. While this flexibility appeals to casual learners, it may not provide the coherence needed for consistent advancement (Essafi et al., 2024). Memrise, on the other hand, emphasizes vocabulary-building through a self-paced, gamified learning environment. However, it lacks the thematic integration and structured progression seen in Babbel, which can limit its effectiveness for learners aiming for broader language proficiency (Essafi et al., 2024).

ELSA Speak offers a highly specialized curriculum, targeting pronunciation improvement through structured exercises. These exercises address aspects such as vowel and consonant sounds, intonation, stress patterns, and word connections, designed to mirror real-life scenarios. This makes ELSA Speak particularly effective for practical speaking skills and oral proficiency (Kholis, 2021).

Language learning platforms differ significantly in their pedagogical strategies, strengths, limitations, language coverage, and curriculum, catering to various learner needs and goals. Duolingo adopts a gamified approach, emphasizing motivation and accessibility with over 40 languages, but it often lacks depth in conversational fluency and cultural immersion. Babbel and Rosetta Stone stand out for their structured curricula, with Babbel focusing on real-world conversational skills and Rosetta Stone leveraging its immersive "Dynamic Immersion" method, though both have limitations like restricted free content or a lack of explicit grammar instruction. Memrise prioritizes vocabulary retention through mnemonics and spaced repetition but offers less structured progression. ELSA Speak specializes in pronunciation improvement with AI-driven feedback, making it ideal for non-native English speakers despite its narrower language focus. Each platform offers unique advantages and challenges, enabling learners to choose based on their specific objectives and preferences.

THE ROLE OF NLP IN CREATING ENVIRONMENTS THAT INTERACTIVE AND ENGAGING LEARNING

NLP for Education

The implementation of NLP in language acquisition has greatly modified feedback systems, enabling skill enhancement and personalized learning journeys. NLP technologies analyze learners' written and spoken outputs, identifying grammatical, phonetic, and cultural inaccuracies with high precision (Jia et al., 2022). This granular feedback empowers learners to target specific weaknesses, accelerating their journey to language proficiency through actionable, data-driven insights.

Beyond surface-level corrections, NLP systems address deeper challenges faced by multilingual learners, such as language interference. Cognitive interference, wherein structures from a native language disrupt the acquisition of a target language, is a frequent obstacle in multilingual contexts (M. Liu, 2023). AI-powered NLP tools mitigate these challenges by dynamically analyzing learner outputs, diagnosing patterns of interference, and providing tailored feedback. By adapting instructional pathways to the unique needs of learners, these systems enhance comprehension and retention, ultimately fostering proficiency across multiple languages.

The role of NLP extends beyond linguistic accuracy to the cultivation of cultural competence, a vital component of language mastery. Effective communication requires understanding idiomatic expressions, colloquialisms, and cultural norms. NLP-based systems integrate cultural context into language analysis, offering corrective feedback and resources to address gaps in cultural understanding. This holistic approach ensures that learners are more prepared to navigate the complexities of linguistic and cultural interactions.

Moreover, AI technologies have demonstrated remarkable efficacy in practical applications. For instance, AI-driven chatbots serve as conversational partners, providing learners with flexible, contextualized language practice. Similarly, automated writing evaluation tools deliver detailed corrective feedback, helping learners refine their writing skills (Jia et al., 2022). These innovations emphasize the capacity for transformation of NLP in overcoming cognitive and cultural barriers, allowing for a more customized and efficient language learning experience.

The theoretical foundations of collaborative learning and feedback, as outlined by Vygotsky and further explored by contemporary scholars, highlight the pivotal role of AI in addressing the cognitive and cultural characteristics of language acquisition (Song & Song, 2023). By seamlessly integrating linguistic analysis, cultural competence, and adaptive learning, NLP-powered systems are reshaping language education, empowering learners to achieve fluency and confidence in an increasingly globalized world.

Overcoming Language Interference

Language acquisition is a dynamic and complex process shaped by cognitive, social, and cultural factors, each contributing to diverse learning outcomes. AI's incorporation into schooling has transformed how learners develop subject knowledge and critical skills across disciplines (Woo & Choi, 2021). Within language education, AI-powered NLP offers transformative potential, particularly in addressing the cognitive issues involved with multilingual learning.

Understanding the Challenges

Multilingual learners often experience language interference, where structures, rules, or vocabulary from their native language intrude upon their target language acquisition. This phenomenon can manifest as errors in grammar, syntax, or pronunciation, complicating the learning process (M. Liu, 2023). Language interference arises from the cognitive load involved in managing multiple linguistic systems and is further exacerbated by limited exposure to the target language's nuances. For example, native speakers of tonal languages may struggle with stress-based pronunciation patterns in non-tonal languages, leading to confusion and errors.

AI-Powered Interventions Strategies

AI-powered NLP tools address these challenges by leveraging advanced computational techniques to analyze learners' linguistic output. These systems use machine learning methods for detecting and categorize errors stemming from language interference. For instance, AI models can compare learners' spoken or written inputs against native speaker benchmarks to identify specific points of deviation. Once identified, these tools provide actionable, personalized feedback, enabling learners to understand and rectify their errors.

Moreover, AI utilizes adaptive learning pathways to tailor instructional content based on individual progress, significantly empowering students to concentrate on problems that need to be fixed. For example, if a learner consistently confuses sentence structures due to native language interference, the system can prioritize grammar-focused exercises tailored to address this specific weakness. These adaptive mechanisms ensure a more effective and personalized learning experience, empowering students to overcome linguistic barriers with greater confidence (Shao et al., 2022).

Empirical Evidence and Case Studies

The incorporation of AI-based learning technologies has demonstrated significant success in real-world applications. Instruments like ITS and automated writing evaluation platforms have been widely used to address the needs of multilingual learners. Case studies reveal how these tools enhance learning outcomes. For instance, AI-powered chatbots function as conversational partners, enabling students to work on their linguistic abilities in a stress-free environment while receiving instant corrective feedback. Similarly, automated writing evaluation tools analyze textual inputs to identify patterns of interference, offering detailed feedback on grammar, syntax, and style.

Implications for Language Education

The role of AI in language learning extends beyond correcting interference to fostering cognitive and cultural competence. By integrating linguistic analysis with cultural insights, AI systems enable learners to grasp idiomatic expressions, colloquialisms, and context-dependent language use. This comprehensive approach not only improves linguistic accuracy but also equips learners to navigate cross-cultural communication effectively.

As multilingualism becomes increasingly valuable in a globalized world, AI-powered NLP tools represent a critical innovation in language education. By addressing the cognitive challenges of language interference, these technologies empower learners to achieve fluency and confidence, transforming their language acquisition journeys.

Building Cultural Competence

Cultural competence is an essential component of language learning, enabling learners to navigate the complexities of linguistic and cultural interactions effectively. AI's incorporation into language instruction has brought about creative approaches to simultaneously addressing linguistic and cultural dimensions, fostering a more holistic understanding of the target language. By going beyond vocabulary and grammar, AI-powered systems help learners appreciate idioms, colloquialisms, and cultural references, enriching their ability to communicate meaningfully in diverse contexts (Prabhakaran et al., 2022).

AI-based learning environments achieve this by embedding cultural nuances within language instruction, providing insights into historical, social, and pragmatic factors shaping the language's use. Through advanced NLP techniques, these systems analyze learners' language outputs to identify gaps in cultural competence.

Targeted feedback and personalized resources are then delivered to address these deficiencies, giving students the tools to participate confidently and appropriately in intercultural communication.

AI-Driven Approaches to Cultural Learning

AI-powered systems enhance cultural learning through diverse methods, such as interactive simulations and role-playing exercises that allow learners to adeptly navigate cultural differences in realistic scenarios. These systems provide immediate feedback on their use of culturally appropriate expressions and behaviors, reinforcing effective communication strategies (Godwin-Jones, 2018). Additionally, AI-based platforms offer access to multimedia resources, such as videos and articles, that explore the cultural contexts and social norms of the target language.

By integrating these cultural elements with linguistic instruction, AI technologies promote a comprehensive understanding of the target language. Learners not only gain proficiency in grammar and syntax but also develop the cultural awareness necessary for authentic and meaningful interactions. This dual focus enables students to thrive in multilingual and multicultural settings, fostering both linguistic and cultural adaptability.

Applications and Broader Impacts

AI's revolutionary potential in language learning is evident in its practical applications. AI-powered chatbots, for instance, serve as conversational partners, providing learners with personalized and flexible language practice across diverse scenarios. These chatbots simulate real-world discussions to help learners acquire confidence and fluency. Similarly, automated writing evaluation tools analyze learners' written outputs, offering corrective feedback on grammar, syntax, and style while incorporating cultural insights into their assessments (Jia et al., 2022).

Empirical evidence highlights how well these technologies work to improve learning output. For instance, AI-driven systems identify and address gaps in learners' cultural understanding by analyzing their interactions and adapting instructional content accordingly. This adaptability ensures that learners receive context-specific guidance, further solidifying their cultural competence.

Societal and Educational Implications

AI's incorporation into language instruction extends beyond individual learner benefits to addressing broader challenges in multilingual and multicultural communication. As global interactions become more frequent, the ability to navigate cultural differences is increasingly critical. AI-powered systems close this gap by providing students with the linguistic and cultural tools needed for effective collaboration across diverse environments.

The combination of linguistic precision and cultural sensitivity inherent to AI-based systems is redefining the language learning experience. Learners can engage in nuanced and contextually appropriate communication with these technologies, fostering a stronger bond with the language and culture being studied. The holistic approach ensures that students possess the ability to speak the target language and culturally competent, enhancing their ability to succeed in an interconnected world.

Real-World Applications of AI in Language Learning

In the evolving area of language education, AI has emerged as a transformative technological advancement, fundamentally changing the manner in which multilingual learners engage in language acquisition. For many years, language learners have struggled with traditional methods, often unable to access the personalized support required for effective learning, particularly in a multilingual context. However, the introduction of AI-powered language learning tools has fundamentally altered this landscape, offering a wealth of new opportunities for learners to refine the skills necessary for effective communication and build confidence in their language talents.

One of the most significant innovations in AI-driven language learning is the development of AI-powered chatbots. These intelligent systems serve as virtual conversation partners, providing learners with a flexible and personalized way to practice their target language. For a multilingual learner, who may be juggling several languages at once, AI chatbots become invaluable. These resources let students to practice speaking, writing, and listening by simulating real-world discussions in various scenarios. The beauty of these chatbots lies in their ability to provide instant feedback—if a learner makes a grammatical error or misuses a word, the system can correct them immediately, suggesting better alternatives. This real-time correction fosters learning in a way that feels immediate and interactive, similar to the experience of speaking with a tutor (Kim et al., 2022).

For example, an individual engaged in the process of learning multiple languages, whether as a second or third language, may experience difficulties in engaging in spoken language practice outside the confines of the classroom. An AI chatbot provides learners with the chance to participate in simulated conversations whenever they wish, allowing them to practice a range of linguistic skills, from basic greetings to complex sentence structures. The chatbot offers immediate corrections and suggestions, enabling learners to enhance their pronunciation, grammar, and overall fluency. The constant interaction fosters confidence in learners' abilities and motivates them to persist in practicing, which is a critical aspect of language acquisition.

The application of automated writing assessment tools has led to another breakthrough in the field of linguistic analysis. These AI-powered tools are tailored to analyze written language submissions, identifying areas where learners can improve, such as grammar, syntax, and style. For those engaged in multilingual learning, these tools are particularly efficacious in addressing issues such as language interference (Li, 2014).

Individuals who are multilingual often encounter difficulties when attempting to transfer grammatical rules or vocabulary from their first language to their second or third language. As a result, errors and misunderstandings may occur. Automated writing evaluation systems facilitate the identification of errors and offer suggestions for improvement. Furthermore, these systems assess the cultural appropriateness of language use, which is of paramount importance for multilingual learners. Frequently, learners may utilize a correct word or phrase in an inappropriate cultural context, which potentially leading to miscommunication. By integrating cultural insights into writing feedback, learners not only enhance their linguistic abilities but also become more attuned to the cultural nuances of the language under study (Kato, 2024).

A great example of this approach is the development of an AI-powered tutor for Arabic language and speech. This system, designed to assist learners of the Moroccan Arabic dialect, uses NLP and chatbots to provide adaptive and individualized learning experiences. Learners can practice speaking and writing in Moroccan Arabic while receiving personalized feedback based on their proficiency level. In addition to grammatical corrections, the system offers insights into cultural contexts and regional dialects, helping learners understand the subtleties of the language that go beyond its grammar and syntax. This strategy is especially beneficial for multilingual learners, as it enables them to gain a deeper appreciation for the language's cultural underpinnings while also improving their technical language skills (Shao et al., 2022).

Beyond the individual learning experience, AI-driven tools have led to broader shifts in language education. One of the most significant benefits is the flexibility these tools offer. Traditionally, language learners had to attend in-person classes or adhere to rigid schedules, which may not suit their personal or professional obligations. AI-powered systems, however, allow learners to access resources and receive feedback at any time, from anywhere. This flexibility has made language learning more accessible, especially for multilingual individuals who may not have the time or resources to attend traditional language classes. By providing on-demand learning experiences, AI technologies empower students to be in control of their language development, tailoring their learning journeys to their unique schedules and needs (Ayotunde et al., 2023).

Additionally, incorporating AI into language instruction helps minimize the cognitive challenges associated with language interference. Multilingual learners often face challenges when switching between languages, especially when grammatical structures or vocabulary overlap. AI systems can detect these cognitive hurdles and offer learners targeted practice to address them. For instance, a multilingual learner might struggle with word order when speaking in English after learning Spanish, where word order is more flexible. An AI-powered language learning tool can identify such issues and provide exercises to help the learner strengthen their understanding of English grammar (M. Liu, 2023).

Equally important is the role AI plays in fostering cultural competence. Language is deeply intertwined with culture, and to communicate effectively in a new language, learners must also understand the social norms, values, and historical context that shape the language's use. AI-based systems could help close this gap by integrating cultural learning with language acquisition. Learners are exposed to cultural scenarios and social contexts, learning not just the "what" of language but also the "why" behind its usage. This dual approach to linguistic and cultural learning prepares multilingual learners for real-world communication, where understanding cultural nuances is often just as important as mastering grammar and vocabulary (Prabhakaran et al., 2022).

AI's application to language acquisition isn't just about improving language skills; it's about fostering a more immersive and personalized learning journey. Research has demonstrated that AI-powered language tools considerably increase learner motivation and engagement. By providing customized feedback and resources tailored to each learner's needs, these tools help students remain motivated and involved in their learning path. Additionally, AI systems offer learners a safe space to practice without fear of judgment, enabling them to experiment with language and build their confidence (Song & Song, 2023).

In the classroom or through remote learning, AI-powered tools have made language learning more interactive and accessible. The examples of multilingual learners benefiting from these tools are numerous, and the positive impact is undeniable. Whether it's an AI chatbot offering a low-pressure way to practice speaking or an automated writing evaluation system giving targeted feedback, AI is transforming the way learners engage with language. AI technology continue to progress., their role in multilingual education will only grow, further enhancing the effectiveness of language acquisition for learners worldwide (Hasumi & Chiu, 2024).

By integrating these powerful AI tools into the learning process, multilingual learners are not only improving their linguistic skills but also becoming more culturally competent, more confident, and more prepared to negotiate the challenges of communication in a more international society.

CONCLUSION, CHALLENGES AND FUTURE DIRECTIONS

Conclusion

AI has advanced rapidly in bilingual education, significantly transforming traditional teaching methodologies. AI facilitates personalized and adaptive learning, provides real-time feedback mechanisms, and demonstrably boosts learner motivation and retention rates. Technologies such as NLP, adaptive learning, and AI-based learning systems have proven effective in improving language proficiency. Through automated feedback and data-driven insights, AI not only aids in evaluating language skills but also significantly accelerates the acquisition of new languages.

However, implementing AI in bilingual education still faces complex challenges. Despite its sophistication, NLP often struggles to capture cultural nuances and language context, which can affect the accuracy of the feedback provided. Additionally, algorithmic biases, data security concerns, and difficulties in addressing language interference remain significant obstacles. Therefore, balancing automation with human oversight remains crucial to ensuring the effectiveness of AI-driven learning systems. Furthermore, various techniques and frameworks have been developed to support adaptive learning, including reinforcement learning, deep learning, and machine learning-based recommendation systems. These technologies enable AI to tailor learning materials to each user's proficiency level. Consequently, this ensures a more efficient and personalized learning experience. Additionally, gamification in AI-powered language learning platforms has been proven to enhance user engagement and motivation through reward systems, interactive challenges, and game-like elements.

With continuous technological advancements, AI holds great potential to revolutionize bilingual education. Implementing more inclusive, accurate, and learner-oriented AI can further improve language learning effectiveness. Therefore, the development of AI for language education must continue to be refined, considering linguistic, pedagogical, and ethical aspects to maximize its benefits for learners from diverse backgrounds and proficiency levels.

Challenges

In recent years, there have been substantial changes in education as a result of technology advancements, especially in the area of AI. However, educators are having difficulty implementing the generally applicable strategy of traditional education techniques; as a result, researchers are realizing the potential of personalized learning paths to solve these challenges. The concept of AI-enabled personalized learning envisions a classroom environment in which each student's unique learning preferences, abilities, and deficiencies are meticulously studied to build a customized curriculum. This concept change is especially relevant when discussing AI-powered curriculum building, where the combination of advanced algorithms and instructional materials promises to adapt educational activities to each student's unique requirements.

The research examined the degree to which the AI-powered curriculum accommodates various learning preferences. The outcomes demonstrated how well a range of learning preferences were catered for by the AI system's personalized learning routes. The curriculum enabled students to engage with educational content in ways that were customized to meet their individual learning needs by utilizing visual, aural, kinesthetic, and other learning modes. Concepts from neuro-education, gamification, social and emotional learning, cognitive science, and teacher preparation are becoming more and more significant in expanding our understanding of individualized learning as AI-driven curriculum development advances. Developing comprehensive and successful learning experiences that satisfy the various needs of students and actively involve teachers requires the integration of various points of view. AI implementation will be improved by more studies in these fields.

The study meticulously investigated the efficacy of an AI-powered curriculum in learning environments. A detailed analysis of student performance indicators revealed that, when compared to traditional teaching techniques, students using the AI-based curriculum consistently displayed greater levels of comprehension and retention. The curriculum's versatility allowed for tailored information delivery, which improved learning outcomes in a variety of disciplines. According to scholars like (Anderson & Dron, 2011), personalization is critical for increasing student participation and enhancing learning results. Personalized training, they argue, can boost motivation and foster a deeper comprehension of the subject matter.

In order to make sure that technology helps instead of hindering the learning process, factors like equity and access, an excessive dependence on digital technologies, privacy issues, and the caliber of instructional materials need to be thoroughly taken into account. The integration of technology in education is still hampered by the digital divide. Inequalities may worsen if some kids do not have equitable access to high-speed internet and technology (Warschauer, 2003). It's possible that underfunded schools lack the technology infrastructure necessary to successfully adopt individualized learning. The lack of technology might cause pupils to lag behind their peers, which can result in unequal learning opportunities and outcomes. In order to resolve these problems, educators and legislators must prioritize granting all children fair access to technology and making sure that they all gain from individualized learning materials (Van Dijk, 2020). According to studies, closing the digital divide is essential to guaranteeing fair educational results (Eynon & Geniets, 2016).

Despite the many advantages of technology, there is a chance that it will be overused, which could diminish in-person interactions that are essential for language acquisition. Technology cannot completely replace human connection in the development of conversational skills and cultural awareness (Turkle, 2016). Furthermore, kids could grow unduly reliant on technology, thereby disregarding the improvement of their capacity for critical thought and problem-solving. In order to reduce these hazards, teachers should strike a balance between using technology and conventional teaching techniques, making sure that technology complements human connection rather than takes its place (Eynon & Geniets, 2016). Excessive screen usage has been shown to have detrimental effects on social skills and cognitive development (Reinhardt, 2019).

The AI-driven curriculum's capacity to adjust to individual pacing preferences allowed students to proceed through the course at their own speed. This adaptability created a more pleasant learning environment, reduced academic stress, and gave students a sense of competence and mastery. The system's adaptability promotes equitable learning by eliminating achievement inequalities between students from various backgrounds.

The ability of the AI-driven curriculum to adapt to different learning styles and facilitate group projects signifies a shift in educational philosophy toward one that is more centered on each student's unique needs. In addition to having practical applications, this transformative approach enhances teacher-student interactions by empowering teachers to take on the roles of mentor and facilitator and develop closer relationships with students.

Furthermore, the essay emphasizes how children can develop lifelong learning abilities by promoting curiosity, self-directed learning, and adaptability in the face of new information. Furthermore, educational policymakers can profit from the data-driven decision-making process, which optimizes educational policies and resource allocation by gathering and examining of data generated by the AI-driven curriculum.

Learning can be hampered by technical challenges such hardware failures, software bugs, and problems with internet connectivity. For instructional technologies to function properly, regular maintenance, upgrades, and technical support are necessary (Haßler et al., 2016). Low-resource schools could find it difficult to satisfy these criteria because they might be expensive and need ongoing dedication. Schools should make investments in dependable technology and give staff and students the necessary training and assistance to handle these problems. Furthermore, the impact of technical disruptions on learning can be reduced by having a backup plan in place (Haßler et al., 2016). To maximize the advantages of educational technology, research emphasizes the significance of continuing technical assistance and professional development (Tondeur et al., 2017). They discovered that teachers' proficiency and self-assurance with technology are essential for its effective integration.

The quality and clarity of educational platforms and apps' material may vary greatly. For learning to be effective, materials must be both culturally relevant and pedagogically sound. A less hands-on learning experience may come from one-size-fits-all solutions that fail to satisfy each student's specific needs (Scherer et al., 2019). To ensure high-quality knowledge, teachers should carefully select and evaluate the resources they use in the classrooms. Collaboration with content providers, as well as regular feedback, can improve the quality and usefulness of instructional materials (Hodges et al., 2020).

Reinhardt (2019) emphasizes how crucial culturally appropriate teaching resources are to language learning (Reinhardt, 2019). Educational policymakers can learn a great deal from the data collection and analysis of the AI-driven curriculum. In order to optimize curriculum creation, resource allocation, and instructional strategies at a broader institutional level, the study emphasized the necessity of data-driven decision-making.

Interactive tools have numerous advantages, but they can have drawbacks. For example, how well they are implemented and incorporated into the curriculum determines how effective they are. To properly use these technologies and make sure they enhance rather than replace conventional teaching techniques, educators must receive sufficient training (Turkle, 2016). Concerns over screen time and the possibility of fewer in-person connections are also raised by the dependence on digital technologies (Eynon & Malmberg, 2021). All things considered, interactive and captivating resources have a great deal of promise to improve ESL instruction by making learning more pleasurable and customized for each student. Teachers can build more dynamic and effective learning environments that meet the different requirements of their students by implementing these tools into their teaching techniques. The AI-powered curriculum additionally facilitated cooperative learning opportunities. Students engaged in cooperative problem-solving through interactive elements and group-based exercises, improving their communication and cooperation abilities. In addition to emphasizing individualized instruction, the curriculum encouraged peer-to-peer information exchange and social contact.

NLP algorithms still face difficulties in accurately capturing cultural nuances and interpreting contextual language use, as AI models are often biased toward dominant languages and cultures. As highlighted by Tao et al. (2024), the cultural values embedded in AI models can skew AI outputs, especially in bilingual contexts where language and culture are deeply intertwined. For instance, AI systems, including large language models like GPT, have been shown to exhibit cultural biases, often reflecting values from English-speaking and Protestant European cultures, which can impact the inclusivity and relevance of AI tools in bilingual education and communication. The integration of cultural prompts is suggested as a strategy to improve AI's cultural alignment, but ongoing evaluation is crucial to ensure its effectiveness (Tao et al., 2024).

Furthermore, ensuring an appropriate balance between automation and human oversight is essential to maintaining empathy and cultural sensitivity in AI-driven applications. As Mirek-Rogowska et al. (2024) discuss, while AI enhances efficiency, it also presents significant ethical challenges, particularly related to privacy, data security, and algorithmic bias. These challenges are particularly pronounced in bilingual settings, where cultural sensitivities and language proficiency must be managed effectively to prevent the marginalization of certain linguistic or cultural groups (Mirek-Rogowska et al., 2024).

Moreover, ethical concerns about data privacy and algorithmic biases pose risks to inclusivity and security in AI applications. In the context of bilingual education, these concerns highlight the need for transparent AI systems that ensure data privacy while avoiding the reinforcement of harmful stereotypes or inequities. As highlighted by Zhumatayeva et al. (2024), AI-driven tools used in foreign language teaching must be carefully evaluated for their potential biases and inclusivity issues. The paper stresses the importance of integrating AI in a way that promotes cultural competence without compromising ethical standards (Zhumatayeva et al., 2024).

Additionally, issues like language interference—where one language impacts the acquisition of another—require further optimization in AI algorithms to effectively support multilingual learners. In this regard, Yu et al. (2019) show how bilinguals exhibit attentional biases towards cultural cues, with fluency levels influencing how effectively bilingual learners engage with both languages. Fluent bilinguals tend to show different responses to cultural cues than limited bilinguals, which could inform how AI systems should be tailored to support different levels of bilingual proficiency (Yu et al., 2019).

Effectively addressing these issues is critical for AI to provide responsible and impactful solutions in bilingual education. By developing AI systems that are not only linguistically adept but also culturally competent and ethically sound, we can help ensure that AI serves as a tool for inclusive, effective learning for multilingual and multicultural learners.

An examination of the ideal ratio between human instruction and AI integration in the educational process is still required, as is research on the long-term impacts of AI-driven curriculum development and personalized learning pathways. These studies can offer crucial insights for successful implementation. According to survey results and feedback, student engagement and motivation significantly increased when the study examined student context-specific motivation and contentment of an AI-driven curriculum. Because they felt more empowered and in charge of their education, students' satisfaction levels increased as a result of learning pathways' flexibility and customization. Students were happier and felt more in control of their education when learning pathways were flexible and customized. The positive benefits on motivation were most noticeable when students engaged with the program on a consistent basis.

The results showed improved long-term information retention among students exposed to an AI-driven curriculum. Furthermore, evidence of improved cross-subject transferability of acquired concepts and abilities was found, indicating a more comprehensive and integrated comprehension of the course content.

The involvement of educators in supporting personalized learning through AI is a critical factor that warrants further consideration. The study emphasizes the value of professional growth in the context of AI-driven education (Darling-Hammond et al., 2017). To enable the successful deployment and achievement of individualized learning objectives, it is crucial to make sure that educators have the necessary abilities to navigate and supplement AI technologies.

The assessment of content customization highlighted the AI-driven curriculum's ability to modify learning resources to meet the needs of specific students. According to the results, students with different backgrounds, learning styles, learning speeds, and degrees of prior knowledge all had different competence levels, and tailored content was crucial in addressing these differences. By accommodating different academic talents and problems, this customization not only enhanced students' comprehension but also fostered a more inclusive learning environment.

The potential of the AI-driven curriculum to customize content to meet the unique needs of each student was highlighted during the test. Personalized learning paths successfully integrated continuous assessment systems with adaptive feedback loops, which provide students with accurate suggestions on areas for improvement and provide instructors and students with real-time feedback. In addition to encouraging personal growth, this iterative feedback system gave teachers the ability to modify and enhance the curriculum by integrating real-time data on student performance and comprehension. Rapid interventions and changes to teaching methods were made possible by this ongoing evaluation approach, which helped teachers identify and address any emerging problems while also ensuring that students continued to meet their learning goals.

In essence, the research findings make a strong argument in favor of adoption of AI-driven curricula in the classroom by emphasizing how they can enhance learning outcomes, promote better adaptability, and establish a more inclusive and fair learning environment. Future research, policy creation, and the expansion of instructional strategies can all be based on the findings of this study.

In essence, the research findings strongly advocate adopting AI-driven curricula in classrooms, highlighting their potential to enhance learning outcomes, improve adaptability, and create a more inclusive and equitable learning environment. Educators, researchers, and policymakers can use these findings to guide future studies, shape policies, and expand instructional strategies.

Future Work: Leveraging Agentic AI for Language Learning

As the field of AI evolves, the emergence of agentic AI introduces a transformative opportunity for personalized language learning. Agentic AI frameworks consist of multiple AI agents, each specializing in distinct tasks or data types, working collaboratively to address complex challenges. By integrating multimodal Generative AI (GenAI), these frameworks enable the processing of diverse data modalities, fostering a deeper understanding of learner needs and preferences.

Agentic AI has the ability to completely change language instruction by providing incredibly immersive and adaptive learning environments. Learners can practice communication skills in dynamic, context-aware environments by using intelligent systems driven by agentic AI that can mimic real-world interactions. Chatbots and virtual assistants powered by AI, for example, may do conversational practice, offer real-time feedback, and customize learning materials according to each user's skill level. By guaranteeing that students receive tailored assistance, this improves engagement and language learning.

Moreover, agentic AI can facilitate multilingual mastery by addressing language interference and promoting cross-linguistic understanding. Advanced algorithms within these systems analyze user responses, identify areas for improvement, and adapt content to evolving learning patterns. This adaptability is crucial in multilingual settings, where learners must navigate complex linguistic landscapes.

Nevertheless, the application of agentic AI to language learning presents several ethical challenges that must be addressed to ensure the responsible operation of these systems. One of the primary concerns is algorithmic bias, which can arise when AI models are trained on unrepresentative or biased data, potentially leading to discriminatory outcomes. This issue is compounded by the lack of transparency in how these algorithms make decisions, which can further undermine trust and fairness. Data privacy is another critical consideration, as the collection and processing of personal data for AI-driven educational tools must be conducted in a way that protects user information and complies with privacy regulations. To mitigate these risks, it is essential for developers to prioritize ethical design practices, such as ensuring the diversity and fairness of training datasets and implementing transparency mechanisms to allow users to understand how decisions are made.

Additionally, cultural inclusivity and relevance are vital when developing AI tools for language learning. These systems should respect and accommodate the diverse linguistic and cultural contexts of users, ensuring that AI models do not inadvertently favor one language or cultural perspective over another. This requires using datasets that reflect a wide range of languages, dialects, and cultural backgrounds, as well as employing development teams that are culturally diverse. Moreover, while AI can greatly enhance the efficiency and personalization of learning experiences, human oversight remains crucial. Educators must continue to play an active role in guiding students, providing empathy, and fostering meaningful interactions, which are essential components of a successful learning environment. Striking the right balance between automation and human involvement will help ensure that AI supports education in a way that is both effective and humane. Looking forward, future work should focus on advancing the capabilities of agentic AI to support personalized language learning while addressing these challenges. Investments in research and development are necessary to refine algorithms, enhance cultural sensitivity, and improve real-time adaptation. Working together, educators, technologists, and legislators are essential to create a robust ecosystem for agentic AI in education.

By embracing the potential of agentic AI, we can unlock new possibilities for language learning, empowering learners to achieve fluency and cross-cultural competence. This transformative technology offers a pathway to more inclusive, effective, and engaging education, paving the way for a future where linguistic barriers no longer hinder communication and understanding.

REFERENCES

Abbes, F., Bennani, S., & Maalel, A. (2024). Generative AI and Gamification for Personalized Learning: Literature Review and Future Challenges. *SN Computer Science*, *5*(8), 1154. DOI: 10.1007/s42979-024-03491-z

Agarwal, D., Naaman, M., & Vashistha, A. (2024). AI Suggestions Homogenize Writing Toward Western Styles and Diminish Cultural Nuances. *ArXiv*. https://doi.org/https://doi.org/10.48550/arXiv.2409.11360

Ahmadi Shirazi, M. (2019). For a Greater Good: Bias Analysis in Writing Assessment. *SAGE Open*, *9*(1), 2158244018822377. Advance online publication. DOI: 10.1177/2158244018822377

Akyuz, Y. (2020). Effects of Intelligent Tutoring Systems (ITS) on Personalized Learning (PL). *Creative Education*, *11*(06), 953–978. DOI: 10.4236/ce.2020.116069

Al-Dosakee, K., & Ozdamli, F. (2021). Gamification in Teaching and Learning Languages: A Systematic Literature Review. *Revista Romaneasca Pentru Educatie Multidimensionala*, *13*(2), 559–577. DOI: 10.18662/rrem/13.2/436

Alamri, H. A., Watson, S., & Watson, W. (2021). Learning Technology Models that Support Personalization within Blended Learning Environments in Higher Education. *TechTrends*, *65*(1), 62–78. DOI: 10.1007/s11528-020-00530-3

Alkhatlan, A., & Kalita, J. (2018). *Intelligent Tutoring Systems: A Comprehensive Historical Survey with Recent Developments*. https://arxiv.org/abs/1812.09628

Anderson, T., & Dron, J. (2011). Three generations of distance education pedagogy. *International Review of Research in Open and Distance Learning*, *12*(3), 80. DOI: 10.19173/irrodl.v12i3.890

Awais, M., Habiba, U., Khalid, H., Shoaib, M., & Arshad, S. (2019). An Adaptive Feedback System to Improve Student Performance Based on Collaborative Behavior. *IEEE Access : Practical Innovations, Open Solutions*, *7*, 107171–107178. DOI: 10.1109/ACCESS.2019.2931565

Ayotunde, O. O., Jamil, D. I., & Cavus, N. (2023). The Impact of Artificial Intelligence in Foreign Language Learning using Learning Management Systems: A Systematic Literature Review. *Information Technologies and Learning Tools*, *95*(3), 215–228. DOI: 10.33407/itlt.v95i3.5233

Bahi, H., & Necibi, K. (2020). Fuzzy Logic Applied for Pronunciation Assessment. *International Journal of Computer-Assisted Language Learning and Teaching, 10*(1), 60–72. DOI: 10.4018/IJCALLT.2020010105

Bai, Y. (2024). A Mixed Methods Investigation of Mobile-Based Language Learning on EFL Students' Listening, Speaking, Foreign Language Enjoyment, and Anxiety. *SAGE Open, 14*(2), 21582440241255550. DOI: 10.1177/21582440241255554

Bhandare, V. (2024). The Role of Artificial Intelligence in Learning and Development. *INTERNATIONAL JOURNAL OF SCIENTIFIC RESEARCH IN ENGINEERING AND MANAGEMENT, 08*(05), 1–5. DOI: 10.55041/IJSREM34968

Bhutoria, A. (2022). Personalized education and Artificial Intelligence in the United States, China, and India: A systematic review using a Human-In-The-Loop model. *Computers and Education: Artificial Intelligence, 3*, 100068. Advance online publication. DOI: 10.1016/j.caeai.2022.100068

Bimba, A. T., Idris, N., Al-Hunaiyyan, A., Mahmud, R. B., & Shuib, N. L. B. M. (2017). Adaptive feedback in computer-based learning environments: A review. *Adaptive Behavior, 25*(5), 217–234. DOI: 10.1177/1059712317727590

Blanco, C. (2024, December). *2024 Duolingo Language Report*. https://blog.duolingo.com/2024-duolingo-language-report/

Bouziane, K., & Bouziane, A. (2024). AI versus human effectiveness in essay evaluation. *Discover Education, 3*(1), 201. DOI: 10.1007/s44217-024-00320-6

Chen, A., Zhang, Y., Jia, J., Liang, M., Cha, Y., & Lim, C. P. (2025). A systematic review and meta-analysis of AI -enabled assessment in language learning: Design, implementation, and effectiveness. *Journal of Computer Assisted Learning, 41*(1), e13064. Advance online publication. DOI: 10.1111/jcal.13064

Chen, B., Kuhn, R., Foster, G., Cherry, C., & Huang, F. (2016). Bilingual Methods for Adaptive Training Data Selection for Machine Translation. In Green, S., & Schwartz, L. (Eds.), *Conferences of the Association for Machine Translation in the Americas: MT Researchers' Track* (pp. 93–106). The Association for Machine Translation in the Americas., https://aclanthology.org/2016.amta-researchers.8/

Chiang, C.-H., & Lee, H. (2023). Can Large Language Models Be an Alternative to Human Evaluations? *Proceedings of the 61st Annual Meeting of the Association for Computational Linguistics (*Volume 1*: Long Papers)*, 15607–15631. DOI: 10.18653/v1/2023.acl-long.870

Chicherina, N., Zharkynbekova, S., Azamatova, A., & Akhmetbekova, A. (2024). OPTIMIZATION OF ADAPTIVE LANGUAGE LEARNING USING ARTIFICIAL IN LIGENCE. *Bulletin of Shokan Ualikhanov Kokshetau University Philological Series*, *3*(3), 279–290. DOI: 10.59102/kufil/2024/iss3pp279-290

Christiano, M. (2025, January 19). *Full Rosetta Stone Review: Effective Legacy Program but Lacks Interactive Features*. FluentU. https://www.fluentu.com/blog/reviews/rosetta-stone/

Darling-Hammond, L., Burns, D., Campbell, C., Goodwin, A. L., Hammerness, K., Low, E. L., & Zeichner, K. (2017). *Empowered Educators: How High-Performing Systems Shape Teaching Quality Around the World*. John Wiley & Sons.

Darsih, E., Wihadi, M., & Hanggara, A. (2021, March 2). Using ELSA App in Speaking Classes: Students' Voices. *Proceedings of the 1st Universitas Kuningan International Conference on Social Science, Environment and Technology*. https://eudl.eu/doi/10.4108/eai.12-12-2020.2304993

Demianenko, O., & Moroz, T. (2024). LINGUISTIC AND DIDACTIC POTENTIAL OF ARTIFICIAL IN LIGENCE TECHNOLOGIES IN TEACHING FOREIGN LANGUAGES. *Scientific Journal of Polonia University*, *66*(5), 9–16. DOI: 10.23856/6601

Dikli, S., & Bleyle, S. (2014). Automated Essay Scoring feedback for second language writers: How does it compare to instructor feedback? *Assessing Writing*, *22*, 1–17. DOI: 10.1016/j.asw.2014.03.006

Ding, S., Liberatore, C., Sonsaat, S., Lučić, I., Silpachai, A., Zhao, G., Chukharev-Hudilainen, E., Levis, J., & Gutierrez-Osuna, R. (2019). Golden speaker builder – An interactive tool for pronunciation training. *Speech Communication*, *115*, 51–66. DOI: 10.1016/j.specom.2019.10.005

du Plooy, E., Casteleijn, D., & Franzsen, D. (2024). Personalized adaptive learning in higher education: A scoping review of key characteristics and impact on academic performance and engagement. *Heliyon*, *10*(21), e39630. DOI: 10.1016/j.heliyon.2024.e39630

Essafi, M., Belfakir, L., & Moubtassime, M. (2024). Investigating mobile-assisted language learning apps: Babbel, Memrise, and Duolingo as a case study. *Journal of Curriculum and Teaching*, *13*(2), 197–212. DOI: 10.5430/jct.v13n2p197

Evenddy, S. S. (2024). Investigating AI's Automated Feedback in English Language Learning. *FLIP Foreign Language Instruction Probe*, *3*(1), 76–87. DOI: 10.54213/flip.v3i1.401

Eynon, R., & Geniets, A. (2016). The digital skills paradox: How do digitally excluded youth develop skills to use the internet? *Learning, Media and Technology*, *41*(3), 463–479. DOI: 10.1080/17439884.2014.1002845

Eynon, R., & Malmberg, L. (2021). Lifelong learning and the Internet: Who benefits most from learning online? *British Journal of Educational Technology*, *52*(2), 569–583. DOI: 10.1111/bjet.13041

Feng, S., Halpern, B. M., Kudina, O., & Scharenborg, O. (2024). Towards inclusive automatic speech recognition. *Computer Speech & Language*, *84*, 101567. DOI: 10.1016/j.csl.2023.101567

García, O. (2011). *Bilingual education in the 21st century: A global perspective*. John Wiley & Sons.

Gligorea, I., Cioca, M., Oancea, R., Gorski, A. T., Gorski, H., & Tudorache, P. (2023). Adaptive Learning Using Artificial Intelligence in e-Learning: A Literature Review. In *Education Sciences* (Vol. 13, Issue 12). Multidisciplinary Digital Publishing Institute (MDPI). DOI: 10.3390/educsci13121216

Godwin-Jones, R. (2018). Contextualized vocabulary learning. *Language Learning & Technology ISSN*, *22*(3), 1–19. https://scholarspace.manoa.hawaii.edu/server/api/core/bitstreams/fe8e9343-3e0c-4bfb-858f-c47c4f36ff41/content

Guo, Q., Feng, R., & Hua, Y. (2022). How effectively can EFL students use automated written corrective feedback (AWCF) in research writing? *Computer Assisted Language Learning*, *35*(9), 2312–2331. DOI: 10.1080/09588221.2021.1879161

Gyonyoru, K. I. K., & Katona, J. (2024). Student Perceptions of AI-Enhanced Adaptive Learning Systems: A Pilot Survey. *2024 IEEE 7th International Conference and Workshop Óbuda on Electrical and Power Engineering (CANDO-EPE)*, 93–98. DOI: 10.1109/CANDO-EPE65072.2024.10772884

Hamari, J. (2017). Do badges increase user activity? A field experiment on the effects of gamification. *Computers in Human Behavior*, *71*, 469–478. DOI: 10.1016/j.chb.2015.03.036

Haßler, B., Major, L., & Hennessy, S. (2016). Tablet use in schools: A critical review of the evidence for learning outcomes. *Journal of Computer Assisted Learning*, *32*(2), 139–156. DOI: 10.1111/jcal.12123

Hasumi, T., & Chiu, M. S. (2024). Technology-enhanced language learning in English language education: Performance analysis, core publications, and emerging trends. *Cogent Education*, *11*(1), 2346044. Advance online publication. DOI: 10.1080/2331186X.2024.2346044

Jane, O. C., Ezeonwumelu, C. G., Barah, C. I., & Jovita, U. N. (2024). Personalized Language Education in the Age of AI: Opportunities and Challenges. *NEWPORT INTERNATIONAL JOURNAL OF RESEARCH IN EDUCATION*, *4*(1), 39–44. DOI: 10.59298/NIJRE/2024/41139448

Jasmine. (2024, November 15). *Rosetta Stone Review: Learning Made Easier*. Language Throne. https://www.languagethrone.com/rosetta-stone-review/

Jia, F., Sun, D., Ma, Q., & Looi, C. K. (2022). Developing an AI-Based Learning System for L2 Learners' Authentic and Ubiquitous Learning in English Language. *Sustainability (Basel)*, *14*(23), 15527. Advance online publication. DOI: 10.3390/su142315527

Jiang, L., Yang, S., Zhou, M., Liu, X., & Zhu, Q. (2009). Mining Bilingual Data from the Web with Adaptively Learnt Patterns. In *ACL and AFNLP*. http://cul.beelink.com/20060205/2021119.shtml

Jose, J., & Jayaron Jose, B. (2024). Educators' Academic Insights on Artificial Intelligence: Challenges and Opportunities. *Electronic Journal of E-Learning*, 00–00. DOI: 10.34190/ejel.21.5.3272

Jose, L. (2025, January). *Harnessing Artificial Intelligence for Language Learning: A Mixed-Methods Study on ChatGPT Integration in Secondary Education*. DOI: 10.21203/rs.3.rs-5703952/v1

Kan, M. S., & Ito, A. (2020). Language Cognition and Pronunciation Training Using Applications. *Future Internet*, *12*(3), 42. DOI: 10.3390/fi12030042

Katiyar, P. D. N., Awasthi, M. V. K., Pratap, D. R., Mishra, M. K., Shukla, M. N., Singh, M. R., & Tiwari, D. M. (2024). *Ai-Driven Personalized Learning Systems: Enhancing Educational Effectiveness*. Educational Administration Theory and Practices., DOI: 10.53555/kuey.v30i5.4961

Kato, M. (2024). Scoring Difficulty in Summary Writing Assessment: Toward the Reconstruction of Analytic Rubric. *Journal of Education and Learning*, *14*(2), 74. DOI: 10.5539/jel.v14n2p74

Kessler, M., Loewen, S., & Gönülal, T. (2023). Mobile-assisted language learning with Babbel and Duolingo: Comparing L2 learning gains and user experience. *Computer Assisted Language Learning*, •••, 1–25. DOI: 10.1080/09588221.2023.2215294

Khasawneh, M. A. S., Ismail, S. M., & Hussen, N. (2024). The blue sky of AI-assisted language assessment: Autonomy, academic buoyancy, psychological well-being, and academic success are involved. *Language Testing in Asia*, *14*(1), 47. DOI: 10.1186/s40468-024-00318-9

Kholis, A. (2021). Elsa Speak App: Automatic Speech Recognition (ASR) for Supplementing English Pronunciation Skills. *Pedagogy: Journal of English Language Teaching*, *9*(1), 1–14. DOI: 10.32332/joelt.v9i1.2723

Kim, H., Yang, H., & Ho Lee, J. (2022). Design principles and architecture of a second language learning chatbot. *Language Learning & Technology*, *26*(1), 1–18. http://hdl.handle.net/10125/73463. DOI: 10.64152/10125/73463

Koivisto, J., & Hamari, J. (2019). The rise of motivational information systems: A review of gamification research. *International Journal of Information Management*, *45*, 191–210. DOI: 10.1016/j.ijinfomgt.2018.10.013

Lawrance, J. C., Sambath, P., Shiny, C., Vazhangal, M. S. P., & Bala, B. K. (2024). Developing an AI-Assisted Multilingual Adaptive Learning System for Personalized English Language Teaching. *2024 10th International Conference on Advanced Computing and Communication Systems (ICACCS)*, 428–434. DOI: 10.1109/ICACCS60874.2024.10716887

Lee, S. S., & Moore, R. L. (2024). Harnessing Generative AI (GenAI) for Automated Feedback in Higher Education: A Systematic Review. *Online Learning : the Official Journal of the Online Learning Consortium*, *28*(3). Advance online publication. DOI: 10.24059/olj.v28i3.4593

Li, D., & Wang, H. (2024). Natural language processing in language learning: Personalized and adaptive English language teaching using artificial intelligence. *Applied Mathematics and Nonlinear Sciences*, *9*(1), 20243290. Advance online publication. DOI: 10.2478/amns-2024-3290

Li, J. (2014). Examining genre effects on test takers' summary writing performance. *Assessing Writing*, *22*, 75–90. DOI: 10.1016/j.asw.2014.08.003

Liu, L. (2024). Impact of AI gamification on EFL learning outcomes and nonlinear dynamic motivation: Comparing adaptive learning paths, conversational agents, and storytelling. *Education and Information Technologies*. Advance online publication. DOI: 10.1007/s10639-024-13296-5

Liu, M. (2023). Exploring the Application of Artificial Intelligence in Foreign Language Teaching: Challenges and Future Development. *SHS Web of Conferences*, *168*, 03025. DOI: 10.1051/shsconf/202316803025

MacFarlane, E., & Spring, R. (2024). Automated feedback on fluency and complexity measures for L2 academic paragraphs: Student perspectives and impacts on human-rater scores. *Technology in Language Teaching & Learning*, *6*(3), 1536. DOI: 10.29140/tltl.v6n3.1536

Maity, S., & Deroy, A. (2024). *Generative AI and Its Impact on Personalized Intelligent Tutoring Systems*. DOI: 10.36227/techrxiv.172954174.48041095/v1

Marouf, A. M., & Abu-Naser, S. S. (2019). Intelligent Tutoring System for Teaching Computer Science I in Al-Azhar University, Gaza. [IJAAR]. *International Journal of Academic and Applied Research, 3*(3), 31–53. http://ijeais.org/wp-content/uploads/2019/03/IJAAR190306.pdf

Mcgovern, R. J., Garcia, O., Lin, A. M. Y., May, S., & Hornberger, N. (2017). *Encyclopedia of Language and Education Series Editor: Bilingual and Multilingual Education Third Edition*. https://www.springer.com/series/15111

Mirek-Rogowska, A., Kucza, W., & Gajdka, K. (2024). AI in Communication: Theoretical Perspectives, Ethical Implications, and Emerging Competencies. *Communication Today*, 16–29. DOI: 10.34135/communicationtoday.2024.Vol.15.No.2.2

Murtaza, M., Ahmed, Y., Shamsi, J. A., Sherwani, F., & Usman, M. (2022). AI-Based Personalized E-Learning Systems: Issues, Challenges, and Solutions. *IEEE Access : Practical Innovations, Open Solutions, 10*, 81323–81342. DOI: 10.1109/ACCESS.2022.3193938

Nacimiento-García, E., Díaz-Kaas-Nielsen, H. S., & González-González, C. S. (2024). Gender and Accent Biases in AI-Based Tools for Spanish: A Comparative Study between Alexa and Whisper. *Applied Sciences (Basel, Switzerland), 14*(11), 4734. DOI: 10.3390/app14114734

Ng, D. T. K., Leung, J. K. L., Su, J., Ng, R. C. W., & Chu, S. K. W. (2023). Teachers' AI digital competencies and twenty-first century skills in the post-pandemic world. *Educational Technology Research and Development, 71*(1), 137–161. DOI: 10.1007/s11423-023-10203-6

Noels, K. A. (2023). Self-Determination Theory and Language Learning. In Ryan, R. M. (Ed.), *The Oxford Handbook of Self-Determination Theory* (1st ed., pp. 619–637). Oxford University Press., DOI: 10.1093/oxfordhb/9780197600047.013.31

Owan, V. J., Abang, K. B., Idika, D. O., Etta, E. O., & Bassey, B. A. (2023). Exploring the potential of artificial intelligence tools in educational measurement and assessment. *Eurasia Journal of Mathematics, Science and Technology Education, 19*(8), em2307. Advance online publication. DOI: 10.29333/ejmste/13428

Papadopoulos, D., & Hossain, M. M. (2023). Education in the Age of Analytics: Maximizing Student Success Through Big Data-Driven Personalized Learning. *Emerging Trends in Machine Intelligence and Big Data, 15*(9), 20–36. https://orientreview.com/index.php/etmibd-journal/article/view/19

Plakans, L., & Gebril, A. (2017). Exploring the relationship of organization and connection with scores in integrated writing assessment. *Assessing Writing*, *31*, 98–112. DOI: 10.1016/j.asw.2016.08.005

Poe, M., & Elliot, N. (2019). Evidence of fairness: Twenty-five years of research in Assessing Writing. *Assessing Writing*, *42*, 100418. DOI: 10.1016/j.asw.2019.100418

Prabhakaran, V., Qadri, R., & Hutchinson, B. (2022). *Cultural Incongruencies in Artificial Intelligence*. https://arxiv.org/abs/2211.13069

Qin, L., & Zhong, W. (2024). Adaptive System of English-Speaking Learning Based on Artificial Intelligence. *Journal of Electrical Systems*, *20*(6s), 267–275. DOI: 10.52783/jes.2637

Rachels, J. R., & Rockinson-Szapkiw, A. J. (2018). The effects of a mobile gamification app on elementary students' Spanish achievement and self-efficacy. *Computer Assisted Language Learning*, *31*(1–2), 72–89. DOI: 10.1080/09588221.2017.1382536

Rahman, M. H., & Nor, H. (2024). Unveiling The Role of Artificial Intelligence on Reading Processes. *PRIMACY Journal of English Education and Literacy*, *3*(1), 18–27. DOI: 10.33592/primacy.v3i1.4877

Raj, N. S., & Renumol, V. G. (2022). A systematic literature review on adaptive content recommenders in personalized learning environments from 2015 to 2020. *Journal of Computers in Education*, *9*(1), 113–148. DOI: 10.1007/s40692-021-00199-4

Reinhardt, J. (2019). *Gameful Second and Foreign Language Teaching and Learning*. Springer International Publishing., DOI: 10.1007/978-3-030-04729-0

Review, A. I. (2023). *ELSA: Price, Pros & Cons, Alternatives, App Reviews*. https://www.ai-review.com/

Rusmiyanto, R., Huriati, N., Fitriani, N., Tyas, N. K., Rofi'i, A., & Sari, M. N. (2023). The Role Of Artificial Intelligence (AI) In Developing English Language Learner's Communication Skills. *Journal of Education*, *6*(1), 750–757. DOI: 10.31004/joe.v6i1.2990

Sailer, M., Hense, J. U., Mayr, S. K., & Mandl, H. (2017). How gamification motivates: An experimental study of the effects of specific game design elements on psychological need satisfaction. *Computers in Human Behavior*, *69*, 371–380. DOI: 10.1016/j.chb.2016.12.033

Scherer, R., Siddiq, F., & Tondeur, J. (2019). The technology acceptance model (TAM): A meta-analytic structural equation modeling approach to explaining teachers' adoption of digital technology in education. *Computers & Education, 128*, 13–35. DOI: 10.1016/j.compedu.2018.09.009

Shahin, I., Nassif, A. B., Thomas, R., & Hamsa, S. (2023). Novel Task-Based Unification and Adaptation (TUA) Transfer Learning Approach for Bilingual Emotional Speech Data. *Information (Basel), 14*(4), 236. Advance online publication. DOI: 10.3390/info14040236

Shao, S., Alharir, S., Hariri, S., Satam, P., Shiri, S., & Mbarki, A. (2022). AI-based Arabic Language and Speech Tutor. *2022 IEEE/ACS 19th International Conference on Computer Systems and Applications (AICCSA)*, 1–8. DOI: 10.1109/AICCSA56895.2022.10017924

Shi, H., & Aryadoust, V. (2024). A systematic review of AI-based automated written feedback research. *ReCALL, 36*(2), 187–209. DOI: 10.1017/S0958344023000265

Shortt, M., Tilak, S., Kuznetcova, I., Martens, B., & Akinkuolie, B. (2023). Gamification in mobile-assisted language learning: A systematic review of Duolingo literature from public release of 2012 to early 2020. *Computer Assisted Language Learning, 36*(3), 517–554. DOI: 10.1080/09588221.2021.1933540

Smirani, L., & Yamani, H. (2024). Analysing the Impact of Gamification Techniques on Enhancing Learner Engagement, Motivation, and Knowledge Retention: A Structural Equation Modelling Approach. *Electronic Journal of e-Learning, 22*(9), 111–124. DOI: 10.34190/ejel.22.9.3563

Son, J.-B., Ružić, N. K., & Philpott, A. (2025). Artificial intelligence technologies and applications for language learning and teaching. *Journal of China Computer-Assisted Language Learning, 5*(1), 94–112. DOI: 10.1515/jccall-2023-0015

Song, C., & Song, Y. (2023). Enhancing academic writing skills and motivation: Assessing the efficacy of ChatGPT in AI-assisted language learning for EFL students. *Frontiers in Psychology, 14*, 1260843. Advance online publication. DOI: 10.3389/fpsyg.2023.1260843

Tao, Y., Viberg, O., Baker, R. S., & Kizilcec, R. F. (2024). Cultural bias and cultural alignment of large language models. *PNAS Nexus, 3*(9), pgae346. Advance online publication. DOI: 10.1093/pnasnexus/pgae346

Tondeur, J., van Braak, J., Ertmer, P. A., & Ottenbreit-Leftwich, A. (2017). Understanding the relationship between teachers' pedagogical beliefs and technology use in education: A systematic review of qualitative evidence. *Educational Technology Research and Development*, *65*(3), 555–575. DOI: 10.1007/s11423-016-9481-2

Tran, T. T. H. (2024). AI Tools in Teaching and Learning English Academic Writing Skills. *Proceedings of the AsiaCALL International Conference, 4*, 170–187. DOI: 10.54855/paic.23413

Turkle, S. (2016). *Reclaiming Conversation: The Power of Talk in a Digital Age*. Penguin Press.

Van Dijk, J. (2020). *The Digital Divide*. John Wiley & Sons.

Vlachopoulos, D., & Makri, A. (2017). The effect of games and simulations on higher education: A systematic literature review. *International Journal of Educational Technology in Higher Education*, *14*(1), 22. DOI: 10.1186/s41239-017-0062-1

Wang, Y., Zhou, J., Li, Z., Zhang, S., & Han, X. (2024). Automatically Difficulty Grading Method for English Reading Corpus With Multifeature Embedding Based on a Pretrained Language Model. *IEEE Transactions on Learning Technologies*, *17*, 474–484. DOI: 10.1109/TLT.2023.3319582

Warschauer, M. (2003). *Technology and Social Inclusion*. The MIT Press., DOI: 10.7551/mitpress/6699.001.0001

Wei, L. (2023). Artificial intelligence in language instruction: Impact on English learning achievement, L2 motivation, and self-regulated learning. *Frontiers in Psychology*, *14*, 1261955. Advance online publication. DOI: 10.3389/fpsyg.2023.1261955

Wikipedia. (2024). *Rosetta Stone (software)*. Wikipedia. https://en.wikipedia.org/wiki/Rosetta_Stone_(software)

Williamson, B. (2017). *Big Data in Education: The digital future of learning, policy and practice*. SAGE Publications Ltd., DOI: 10.4135/9781529714920

Woo, J. H., & Choi, H. (2021). Systematic Review for AI-based Language Learning Tools. *Journal of Digital Contents Society*, *22*(11), 1783–1792. DOI: 10.9728/dcs.2021.22.11.1783

Wu, L. (2024). AI-based Writing Tools: Empowering Students to Achieve Writing Success. *Advances in Educational Technology and Psychology*, *8*(2). Advance online publication. DOI: 10.23977/aetp.2024.080206

Wu, Z., Abdul Halim, H., & Mohd Saad, M. R. (2024). Artificial Intelligence (AI) and Gamification in Blended Learning: Enhancing Language and Literacy in Shanxi, China. [MJSSH]. *Malaysian Journal of Social Sciences and Humanities, 9*(12), e003159. DOI: 10.47405/mjssh.v9i12.3159

Wulandari, F., Astuti, M. T., & Marhamah, M. (2024). Enhancing Writing Literacy Teachers' through AI Development. *Jurnal Onoma: Pendidikan, Bahasa. Dan Sastra, 10*(1), 246–256. DOI: 10.30605/onoma.v10i1.3175

Xu, Y., Liu, Y., Meng, F., Zhang, J., Xu, J., & Zhou, J. (2021). *Bilingual Mutual Information Based Adaptive Training for Neural Machine Translation*. https://arxiv.org/abs/2105.12523 DOI: 10.18653/v1/2021.acl-short.65

Yakkala, K. K.Krishna Kashyap Yakkala. (2024). AI-powered assessment tools for E-learning: Enhancing feedback and grading systems. *World Journal of Advanced Engineering Technology and Sciences, 13*(1), 792–802. DOI: 10.30574/wjaets.2024.13.1.0497

Yeşilçınar, S. (2023). Personalized Learning Through Gamification: A ChatGPT Approach to English Language Learning. In Kartal, G. (Ed.), (pp. 44–64). Advances in Educational Technologies and Instructional Design. IGI Global., DOI: 10.4018/978-1-6684-9893-4.ch003

Yu, H., Yao, N., Zhang, J., & Gao, B. (2019). Time-course of attentional bias for culture-related cues in Mongolian-Chinese bilingual children. *The International Journal of Bilingualism, 23*(6), 1483–1501. DOI: 10.1177/1367006918808047

Zhang, S., Liu, Y., Meng, F., Chen, Y., Xu, J., Liu, J., & Zhou, J. (2022). *Conditional Bilingual Mutual Information Based Adaptive Training for Neural Machine Translation*. https://arxiv.org/abs/2203.02951 DOI: 10.18653/v1/2022.acl-long.169

Zhao, X. (2023). Leveraging Artificial Intelligence (AI) Technology for English Writing: Introducing Wordtune as a Digital Writing Assistant for EFL Writers. *RELC Journal, 54*(3), 890–894. DOI: 10.1177/00336882221094089

Zheng, X., & Fan, H. (2024). Exploration of the Effectiveness and Experience of AI-Assisted Academic Reading. *Proceedings of the Association for Information Science and Technology, 61*(1), 447–456. DOI: 10.1002/pra2.1041

Zhumatayeva, Z. N., Mametkarim, Z. M., & Dosanova, A. M. (2024). THE ROLE OF ARTIFICIAL IN LIGENCE IN THE FORMATION OF COMMUNICATIVE COMPETENCE IN FOREIGN LANGUAGE LESSONS. *THE BULLETIN, 412*(6). Advance online publication. DOI: 10.32014/2024.2518-1467.858

Zou, B., Du, Y., Wang, Z., Chen, J., & Zhang, W. (2023). An Investigation Into Artificial Intelligence Speech Evaluation Programs With Automatic Feedback for Developing EFL Learners' Speaking Skills. *SAGE Open*, *13*(3), 21582440231193818. Advance online publication. DOI: 10.1177/21582440231193818

ADDITIONAL READING

AbuSahyon, A. S. E., Alzyoud, A., Alshorman, O., & Al-Absi, B. (2023). AI-driven Technology and Chatbots as Tools for Enhancing English Language Learning in the Context of Second Language Acquisition: A Review Study. *International Journal of Membrane Science and Technology*, *10*(1), 1209–1223. DOI: 10.15379/ijmst.v10i1.2829

Billingsley, F., & Gardner, S. (2024). *Utilizing Generative AI With Second-Language Users and Bilingual Students*., DOI: 10.4018/979-8-3693-0487-7.ch005

Bui, H. P. (Ed.). (2024). *Applied Linguistics and Language Education Research Methods*. IGI Global., DOI: 10.4018/979-8-3693-2603-9

Keengwe, J. (Ed.). (2023). *Creative AI Tools and Ethical Implications in Teaching and Learning*. IGI Global., DOI: 10.4018/979-8-3693-0205-7

Keengwe, J., Mbae, J. G., & Onchwari, G. (Eds.). (2016). *Handbook of Research on Global Issues in Next-Generation Teacher Education*. IGI Global., DOI: 10.4018/978-1-4666-9948-9

Naseer, F., Khalid, M. U., Ayub, N., Rasool, A., Abbas, T., & Afzal, M. W. (2024). *Automated Assessment and Feedback in Higher Education Using Generative AI*., DOI: 10.4018/979-8-3693-1351-0.ch021

Pan, F. (Ed.). (2024). *AI in Language Teaching, Learning, and Assessment*. IGI Global., DOI: 10.4018/979-8-3693-0872-1

KEY TERMS AND DEFINITIONS

Adaptive Learning: A teaching technique that uses cutting-edge technology to tailor learning experiences to each student's requirements by adjusting the pace, material, and level of difficulty based on information gleaned from student interactions and performance.

Gamification in Learning: The incorporation of game-like elements such as points, badges, leaderboards, and challenges into educational systems to boost learner motivation and engagement.

Intelligent Tutoring Systems (ITS): AI-powered systems that dynamically adjust educational materials, feedback, and teaching methods in bilingual and multilingual contexts to match the needs of individual learners, resulting in personalized learning experiences.

Natural Language Processing (NLP): A branch of AI that enables machines to comprehend, analyze, and synthesize human language. It is commonly used in language learning systems to provide grammar correction, pronunciation analysis, and cultural context recommendations.

Personalized Learning: A: strategy that uses AI-driven tools to improve teaching techniques, learning plans, and educational content to fit each student's preferences, learning objectives, and pace.

Real-Time Feedback: Instant responses provided by AI systems to learners during educational activities, such as corrections in pronunciation, grammar, or syntax, enabling immediate improvements.

Speech Recognition Technology: AI-powered instruments that evaluate spoken language for fluency, intonation, and pronunciation while giving students useful feedback to help them become better speakers.

Chapter 11
The Role of AI in Language Preservation:
Revitalizing Endangered Languages Through Technology

Mohammad Teduh Uliniansyah
https://orcid.org/0000-0002-5224-3704
National Research and Innovation Agency, Indonesia

Kokoy Siti Komariah
https://orcid.org/0000-0003-2618-3039
National Research and Innovation Agency, Indonesia

Ambar Yoganingrum
https://orcid.org/0000-0003-3618-7594
National Research and Innovation Agency, Indonesia

Nimas Ayu Untariyati
https://orcid.org/0009-0001-6466-9534
National Research and Innovation Agency, Indonesia

Agung Santosa
https://orcid.org/0000-0002-9827-4397
National Research and Innovation Agency, Indonesia

Siska P. S. Pebiana
https://orcid.org/0009-0006-7473-7541
National Research and Innovation Agency, Indonesia

Andi Djalal Latief
https://orcid.org/0000-0001-9511-8797
National Research and Innovation Agency, Indonesia

Yuyun Wabula
https://orcid.org/0000-0003-4936-1862
National Research and Innovation Agency, Indonesia

Dian Isnaeni Nurul Afra
https://orcid.org/0000-0001-5128-9682
National Research and Innovation Agency, Indonesia

DOI: 10.4018/979-8-3373-0275-1.ch011

ABSTRACT

This chapter discusses the role of artificial intelligence (AI) in preserving and revitalizing endangered languages. Amidst language decline caused by globalization, urbanization, and the dominance of international languages, AI is developing technologies with documentation approaches (e.g., creation of machine translation, audio recordings, written texts, and linguistic analyses) and collaboration (applications for joint activities). Despite challenges such as data scarcity and ethical issues related to indigenous knowledge, successful cases, such as the revitalization of Hawaiian and Maori, highlight the potential of AI to combat language extinction. This chapter provides valuable insights for linguists, researchers, and policymakers who advocate for interdisciplinary collaboration and the development of ethical AI that respects and preserves the rights of indigenous peoples.

I. INTRODUCTION

AI is making a practical contribution to the preservation of linguistic diversity through approaches to language documentation and collaboration. Projects such as Google's Neural Machine Translation (NMT) (Wu et al., 2016), Mozilla's Common Voice (Ardila et al., 2020), and the Endangered Languages Documentation Program (Kondic, 2021) illustrate the ability of AI to support language preservation. AI relies on interdisciplinary collaboration that requires the expertise of linguists, technologists, anthropologists and cultural practitioners (Bisconti et al., 2023; Dai & Hua, 2024; Gedeon et al., 2024). For example, linguists and AI researchers are working together to develop algorithms that can accurately transcribe, analyze and document languages. At the same time, cultural representatives are ensuring that traditional practices and values are respected in language preservation efforts.

While the application of AI to language preservation is promising, it also presents ethical and logistical challenges that must be carefully considered. Respecting the rights of indigenous peoples and ensuring that they retain control over their linguistic data is crucial to the responsible use of AI. Building trusting partnerships with these communities and transparent and mutually beneficial data sharing practices will help ensure that AI tools support, rather than exploit vulnerable languages.

Ultimately, the combination of technological innovation and cultural respect offers a path to sustainable language preservation. This chapter provides an overview of the role of AI in language preservation, focusing on the use of technology to revitalize extinct languages. The preservation of linguistic diversity depends not only on technological innovation, but also on aligning these advances with the values and aspirations of the language communities themselves. The convergence of

AI, cultural respect and community-based initiatives has the potential to revitalize endangered languages and ensure they thrive for future generations.

II. BACKGROUND

According to UNESCO, the world's languages are threatened with extinction at an alarming rate, with one language disappearing approximately every two weeks (Barrios, 2022). Factors driving language extinction include globalization, urbanization and the dominance of global languages (Amano et al., 2014; Linguistics News, 2023; Wood, 2022). Globalization has led young people in many developing countries to prefer international languages such as English or Spanish for education and employment at the expense of their mother tongue. In India, English and Hindi dominate in many regions, marginalizing many local languages. Meanwhile, urbanization also plays an important role. For example, Mandarin often displaces languages such as Manchu among younger speakers in China's major cities. The dominance of global languages is also evident in the digital world. The widespread use of English on social media and the internet encourages young people to adopt this language in their daily interactions. In Scandinavia, for example, while Swedish and Danish are still spoken by many adults, children are increasingly using English, especially in digital and entertainment contexts.

The effects of language extinction are manifold, as each language brings with it a unique worldview, knowledge and cultural identity. Language serves as a vessel for a community's worldview and contains concepts, idioms and expressions that are unique to its culture (Kramsch, 2014). Recent cases such as the extinction of the Ubykh and Amurdag languages (Joyner, 2007; Pereltsvaig, 2012) make it clear that the loss of the last speakers means the end of an entire cultural epoch, further emphasizing the urgent need for action. The loss of a language has an impact on the preservation of biodiversity. Many indigenous languages contain complex systems for naming plants, animals and natural phenomena that reflect a deep understanding of the environment (Wilder et al., 2016). At the same time, traditional healing practices, such as those found in the indigenous languages of South America and Africa, are rooted in linguistic knowledge that transmits wisdom from generation to generation. The loss of language would mean the end of traditional healing practices and unique knowledge systems that are passed orally from generation to generation (Wilder et al., 2016).

In response to these challenges, artificial intelligence (AI) has emerged as a transformative tool for language preservation and revitalization. AI is providing diverse communities with unprecedented access to language resources, especially in low-resource settings where formal language education is limited. AI-based tools democratize access to language learning and enable youth and diaspora communities to reconnect with their cultural roots (Kavitha et al., 2023; Nanduri & Bonsignore, 2023). This democratization is critical to reversing language shift and fostering cultural pride. AI chatbots and mobile apps, for example, provide real-time feedback on pronunciation, grammar and vocabulary in simulated conversational environments, making learning a heritage language engaging and meaningful. Initiatives such as Duolingo's Hawaii and Māori courses demonstrate the effectiveness of AI-driven language apps as they facilitate language learning and foster cultural pride and interest among younger speakers (Strang, 2020; Wu, 2018). The future of AI in language preservation holds exciting possibilities, especially as new technologies such as synthetic data generation (Li et al., 2023), metaverses such as augmented and virtual reality (AR/VR) (Parmaxi & Demetriou, 2020) and personalized language tutors gain traction (Nanduri & Bonsignore, 2023).

In summary, the background illustrates how language extinction, driven by globalization, urbanization, and the dominance of global languages in digital spaces, poses a serious threat to humanity's cultural diversity and ecological knowledge systems. The decline of indigenous and minority languages leads to the irreversible loss of worldviews, traditional healing practices, and ecological wisdom passed through generations. Against this backdrop, artificial intelligence (AI) emerges as a powerful and inclusive tool for language preservation and revitalization. By providing interactive, culturally relevant, and accessible language learning experiences, AI enables younger and diaspora generations to reconnect with their linguistic heritage. The integration of technologies such as chatbots, speech recognition, and immersive AR/VR environments not only facilitates learning but also fosters a renewed sense of pride and identity in endangered language communities.

III. THE IMPORTANCE OF LANGUAGE PRESERVATION

The preservation of endangered languages is a linguistic and worldview issue, since every language contains the core of human diversity. This subchapter addresses the role of language in the preservation of cultural identity and knowledge, social and global challenges, cultural and intellectual costs, language and innovation, and collaborative and ethical endeavors.

1. Cultural Identity and Knowledge Preservation

Language encodes the values and beliefs of a society and serves as a repository of cultural heritage (Jafarzade, 2020). The extinction of a language means the loss of a culture's uniqueness and leads to a homogenization of cultural diversity (Chui,

2023; Hale, 1992). In Asia, especially in Southeast Asia, the linguistic landscape is one of the richest in the world. In countries such as Indonesia, the Philippines and Malaysia, hundreds of languages are spoken, and each of them is associated with a particular ecological and cultural knowledge. As shown in Table 1, Indonesia is the country with the highest number of endangered languages in the world, with 506 languages classified as endangered (Eberhard et al., 2024). This shows how rich Indonesia's linguistic heritage is and how important efforts to preserve these languages are.

Table 1. Global Endangered Languages

Continent	Country	Number of Endangered Languages
Asia	Indonesia	506
Pacific	Papua New Guinea	314
Americas	United States	193
Pacific	Australia	190
Africa	Nigeria	163
Asia	China	153
Asia	India	132
Americas	Mexico	131
Americas	Brazil	127
Africa	Cameroon	96

Source: (Eberhard et al., 2024)

The loss of indigenous languages leads to the loss of knowledge about natural features, medicine and plants, which can have an impact on global sustainability. In Indonesia, for example, the rugged geography and isolated communities encourage linguistic diversity in Papua (Sawaki, 2019). Balinese reflects cultural practices that are closely linked to Hindu rituals (Erawati et al., 2023). The Bugis and Makassarese languages are an integral part of maritime traditions and oral literature (Rahman et al., 2024). The Kayapó people in Brazil also use their language to classify over 300 plant species (Ribeiro et al., 2017). Indigenous peoples in Papua New Guinea and the Amazon rely on linguistic knowledge to maintain sustainable relationships with ecosystems (Epps, 2020; Facundes et al., 2019; Kik et al., 2021). The Sami language of northern Europe contains over 300 terms for snow, reflecting the nuances of life in the Arctic (Skille et al., 2023). The Navajo language in the United States also reveals complex knowledge about local ecosystems (McCarty et al., 2006).

2. Cultural and Intellectual Costs

The extinction of a language means the loss of a community's historical narrative and intellectual traditions. Each language represents a particular way of understanding the world and offers insights into human cognition, culture and philosophy. In Indonesia, oral traditions such as the Pantun Melayu or the epic poetry of the Bugis (La Galigo) are closely linked to the languages in which they are performed. These traditions serve as repositories of historical knowledge, ethics and community values. The decline of these languages threatens the survival of such narratives and underlines the urgency of preserving language as a means of cultural continuity. Historical examples such as the extinction of the Ubykh language in the 1990s (Arkadiev & Lander, 2021) and the recent Juma language in Brazil (Eberhard et al., 2024) illustrate the severity of this loss. When these languages disappeared, they took their oral traditions, ecological knowledge and unique linguistic structures with them.

In addition, the loss of language leads to a generational gap that makes it difficult for younger members of a community to access and pass on traditional knowledge. Traditional songs, myths and rituals, which are often encoded in a language, are lost, leading to a weakening of cultural continuity. Language documentation and revitalization efforts can help bridge this gap, as demonstrated by the Maori language revitalization program in New Zealand (Berardi-Wiltshire et al., 2020). Such programs show how technology and community collaboration can play a crucial role in preserving not only words, but also the cultural essence they represent.

3. Social and Global Challenges

Globalization and urbanization have accelerated the decline in linguistic diversity. This trend is particularly pronounced in urban areas, where migration and integration into dominant cultures have led to a decline in the use of local languages (Ugwu, 2020; Zhang, 2024). In India, the dominance of Hindi and English in educational and professional settings has marginalized many regional languages, including Khasi and Garo (Singh, 2021). Similarly, in Scandinavia, the increasing use of English among children in digital and entertainment contexts threatens the intergenerational transmission of indigenous languages. Digital platforms and social media, which are mainly dominated by global languages, make this problem even worse. As a result, minority languages face a double challenge: they are often seen as less practical in modern contexts and at the same time lose their traditional meaning within communities (Aikhenvald, 2020).

4. Collaborative and Ethical Efforts

Language preservation requires a collaborative approach involving linguists, technologists, policy makers and community leaders. The challenges of preserving languages through technology can be overcome through interdisciplinary collaboration. For example, community-driven documentation initiatives ensure that linguistic resources are developed in accordance with the needs and values of native speakers. By combining linguistic expertise with community participation, these initiatives create extensive archives that serve as valuable resources for education and research (Wiltshire et al., 2024). Furthermore, by respecting the rights and knowledge of indigenous communities, the application of ethical technologies can further strengthen efforts to preserve endangered languages (Pinhanez et al., 2024).

In conclusion, the preservation of endangered languages is important because it helps to protect the culture, knowledge and identity of different communities. Each language holds unique stories, traditions and ways of thinking that are valuable both locally and globally. The disappearance of a language means the loss of history, traditional knowledge and a part of human diversity. With the support of technology and the collaboration of communities, researchers and policy makers, many efforts can be made to document and revitalize these languages. Language preservation is not only about honoring the past, but also about supporting a more inclusive and connected future.

5. Language and Innovation

Technological innovations such as Artificial Intelligence (AI) have influenced language preservation efforts. AI-powered tools such as automatic transcription, speech recognition and machine translation offer efficient solutions to document and revitalize endangered languages (Nanduri & Bonsignore, 2023). Google's Neural Machine Translation (NMT), for example, has recorded Hawaiian and Maori and makes them digitally accessible. Similarly, Mozilla's Common Voice project collects voice data from minority languages and gives developers the opportunity to create customized tools (Ardila et al., 2020).

Digital platforms enable diaspora communities to reconnect with their heritage languages. Mobile applications and online courses provide accessible resources for language learning and ensure that younger generations can engage with their linguistic heritage, even if they are in non-native settings. Innovations such as augmented reality (AR) or virtual reality (VR) allow users to practice their language skills in simulated environments that reflect authentic contexts (Nanduri & Bonsignore, 2023).

IV. CHALLENGES IN LANGUAGE DOCUMENTATION AND REVITALIZATION

Efforts to revitalize endangered languages and ensure their continued existence are referred to as documentation and revitalization. Documentation focuses on efforts to preserve languages by collecting, organizing and storing information manually and digitally. These activities include compiling dictionaries and grammars, recording audio-visual material, transcribing and annotating conversations, collecting folktales and documenting other forms of local knowledge. In the meantime, the revival focuses on using the results of the documentation. These activities include language teaching in formal and informal programs, the development of modern media such as digital applications and social media content, and the use of languages in daily life in various settings, including schools, families, and communities. The challenges facing these efforts are as follows:

1. Language Documentation

a. Ethical

When personal data becomes the raw material for various analyzes, a fundamental question arises: to what extent does the collection and use of data respect the rights of the individual and the community to which the language belongs? This challenge requires a balance between the advancement of knowledge and the protection of the dignity and privacy of those whose data is used. When documenting data, researchers must ensure that participants fully understand how their recordings will be used. For example, the resulting records may contain personal data, traditional stories, historical accounts or cultural practices that are considered sacred and only accessible to members of a particular community (Seyfeddinipur et al., 2019). In data collection, the information collected can enrich the narrative of the research, especially aspects that may be underrepresented in general data sets. For example, audio or video interviews can be conducted with individuals or members of indigenous communities that involve the performance of traditional rituals. These include traditional marriage customs, religious rituals, customary laws, or the use of certain symbols that are considered controversial in some modern societies. Consequently, their participation in this cultural activity led to social stigmatization. They may be ostracized by society because they support practices that contradict modern values or common norms. Such stereotypes may further reinforce prejudice and discrimination against their group.

In addition, participants may not have the expertise or authority to tell their cultural-historical stories, which may cause them to be lost. Another scenario is that modern technology has the potential to be biased through the unintentional learning of stereotypes or inaccurate perceptions. Another aspect is that caution is needed when documenting traditional knowledge due to a lack of information about the target audience (Austin, 2021; Chigwada & Ngulube, 2024). Researchers need to consider the ethics of using documents after permission has been granted, as a community's beliefs may no longer be relevant for public performance. There is also a risk that these valuable cultural assets will be exploited for commercial purposes (Deacon, 2020).

b. Data scarcity

Data scarcity refers to the limited availability of data needed for research, analysis and technology development. For minority and endangered languages, the available materials need to be further processed (Uliniansyah et al., 2024). Furthermore, in the linguistic context, differences in vocabulary, grammar and pronunciation complicate data processing and analysis (Kanoksilapatham, 2020). Another challenge is the limited number of native speakers and the geographical isolation of the speaker communities. For example, native speakers of Bugis, Makassar and Mamuju languages are rare in Indonesia (Afra et al., 2024; Latief et al., 2024; Yuyun et al., 2024).

c. Financial support

Another challenge is financial support for the collection of text, audio or video data. This process requires resources ranging from funding technological equipment such as recording devices and data processing software to the storage and management of data on digital platforms. In addition, a budget is required to remunerate annotators, pay language experts, train the teams and cover travel costs to access communities in remote areas. Therefore, financial support is crucial for the success of data documentation.

In conclusion, caution is required when using data as analysis material. The documentation process must be conducted transparently by ensuring that participants fully understand how their data will be used, especially if the data includes cultural practices that are susceptible to negative community judgment. Furthermore, this ethical discussion is made even more complex by the potential exploitation of knowledge by outsiders for commercial purposes. Furthermore, the scarcity of data is a significant obstacle to the development of linguistic resources, especially for undocumented languages. The limited number of speakers, geographical restrictions and the low availability of experts also slow down the ongoing documentation process. Finally, without sufficient financial support, there is a risk that efforts to document and revitalize languages will stop halfway, resulting in incomplete data.

This condition also weakens the long-term commitment to preserving the language and cultural heritage of the community.

2. Language Revitalization

a. Pragmatic

Pragmatic aspects include resource scarcity and standardization issues. These include logistical constraints, scarcity of resources and standardization issues. One of the most pressing pragmatic issues is the lack of teaching and learning materials. For example, the lack of Kazakh language teaching at universities is hindered by the lack of Kazakh-speaking teaching staff (Kucherbayeva & Smagulova, 2023). Another problem is the lack of extensive data sets for training machine learning models, which hinders the development of language technologies (Liu et al., 2022; Ngoc Le & Sadat, 2020). Standardization issues also include the lack of standardized variants in efforts to revitalize the Tongan language in Zimbabwe (Mumpande & Barnes, 2022). Similarly, debates around language norms and the need for standardization in language revitalization are also prevalent in Australia (Couzens et al., 2020).

b. Ideological and Emotional

These challenges arise from cultural identities, historical narratives and emotional investments in language. They often reflect deeply held beliefs and ontological assumptions about what constitutes a language. This challenge arises in the revitalization of the Sámi language in Northern Norway, where emotional aspects and the effects of colonialism create tensions that complicate the process (Lane, 2023). Then there is the failure to revitalize the Occitan language due to the complex ontological differences between the traditional speakers and the proponents of the language (Costa, 2024).

c. Social Politics

Socio-political challenges relate to governance structures, policy frameworks, social attitudes and power relations. These factors can significantly affect the outcome of revitalization efforts. These challenges include insufficient government support and weak inter-agency coordination that hinder the revitalization of regional languages in Lampung, Indonesia (Andina, 2023). Furthermore, political opposition and discriminatory language policies are hindering Tongan language revitalization efforts in Zimbabwe (Mumpande & Barnes, 2022). Furthermore, competition within the Tongan community is hindering language revitalization efforts (Mumpande & Barnes, 2022).

d. Education and Pedagogy

This category addresses the difficulties in developing and implementing effective teaching and learning strategies for endangered languages. The revitalization of Ladino, a Hebrew-Spanish language, in educational institutions is hindered by different linguistic backgrounds and students' confidence in using the language (Fredholm, 2023). This challenge can be addressed through the use of media and technology to increase awareness and familiarity with the language (Nagy & Hortobagyi, 2023) and through collaboration between researchers and communities with a focus on ethical aspects (Guerrettaz & Engman, 2023).

V. ARTIFICIAL INTELLIGENCE AND LANGUAGE PRESERVATION

The world is currently experiencing a profound language crisis. A significant number of languages are in danger of disappearing within the next few generations. This loss goes beyond the mere loss of words; it also includes the erosion of cultural heritage, traditional knowledge systems and unique worldviews. In response to this critical situation, the United Nations has declared the period from 2022 to 2032 as the International Decade of Indigenous Languages, emphasizing the global urgency to support the revitalization and preservation of these invaluable linguistic resources (UNESCO, 2023). In this context, innovative strategies are crucial. While technology, including Artificial Intelligence (AI), is not a panacea for the complex socio-political and economic factors that contribute to language endangerment (Bender, 2024; UNESCO, 2023), recent advances in AI offer unprecedented opportunities when coupled strategically and ethically with community-led revitalization efforts.

The narrative around the role of AI in language preservation has evolved significantly. Initial applications focused on the potential of AI for documentation and analysis, often pointing to limitations such as questionable accuracy for languages with complex grammatical structures. However, the landscape is shifting. The emergence and rapid development of Generative AI (GenAI) and Large Language Models (LLMs) signal a significant leap in the capabilities of AI that goes beyond basic documentation to include generative features and the co-development of tools with linguistic communities (Morales et al., 2025). The NüshuRescue project, for example, has shown how LLMs can adapt to translate an extremely low-resource language from minimal data, demonstrating transformative potential that was previously considered unattainable (Lisagor, 2025).

1. Natural Language Processing and its Applications

Natural Language Processing (NLP) systems can document the vocabulary, grammar and phonology of a language (Bird, 2020; Chomsky, 1957). AI-based models can be used to build language corpora, i.e. extensive, structured collections of texts. Corpora help in the development of technologies such as machine translation systems (Wu et al., 2016). The creation of treebanks - syntactically annotated corpora - is invaluable for less studied languages (Tseng et al., 2005). However, NLP tools often struggle with the nuances of regional dialects and accents, leading to inaccuracies in transcription and linguistic analysis (Eisenstein, 2013).

2. Machine Learning and Language Revitalization

Machine learning, a subset of AI, plays an important role in language preservation. Google Neural Machine Translation (GNMT) is an example of this technology, which can document the vocabulary, grammar and even phonology of a language (Wu et al., 2016). Machine learning models can be trained to recognize patterns in endangered languages (Snyder, 2010). Another example is Mozilla's Common Voice project, an AI application to develop speech recognition for underserved languages (Ardila et al., 2020). Machine learning models have developed text prediction tools for multiple languages (Krashen, 1982). In addition, AI has been developed to digitize handwritten documents (Arnold, 2022).

The emergence of Generative AI (GenAI) and Large Language Models (LLMs) represents a paradigm shift. These technologies, exemplified by models such as GPT-3 and its successors, can generate coherent and contextually relevant text and speech in multiple languages. This capability enables the production of large amounts of language material — written or spoken — almost instantly, which can be invaluable for educational initiatives, cultural revitalization projects and the creation of digital archives (Morales et al., 2025). In addition, LLMs can be trained on diverse and often sparse data sources specific to endangered languages, such as oral traditions, folktales, interviews and existing audio recordings, capturing richer linguistic and cultural nuances than previously possible.

Recent advances in AI speech technology (2023-2024) have also been particularly impressive. There have been notable breakthroughs in the accuracy of AI speech translation as well as a significant reduction in latency and an expansion of language coverage by major providers (Zabetian, 2024). For example, in June 2024, Google added 110 new languages to its language offering in Google Translate, including

31 African languages such as Tamazight, Afar, Wolof, Dyula and Baoulé, which together represent 200 million speakers. Similarly, in 2024, Meta AI developed the NLLB-200 model, which can translate 200 different languages with state-of-the-art quality. At the same time, improvements in speech-to-text Application Programming Interfaces (APIs) have increased the accuracy of real-time transcription, a crucial function for the documentation of spoken languages and the creation of text data from oral sources. A practical example is the development of Automatic Speech Recognition (ASR) models for certain endangered languages such as Cook Islands Māori, which significantly speed up the transcription of extensive audio archives, a traditionally labor-intensive process (Lisagor, 2025).

A crucial development for endangered languages, which often suffer from extreme data scarcity, is the emergence of specialized models and techniques for low-resource and previously unseen languages. One such innovative approach is LingoLLM, a training-free method introduced in 2024. LingoLLM enables existing LLMs such as GPT-4 and Mixtral to process and translate unseen languages by utilizing available linguistic descriptions such as dictionaries and grammar books included in the model's input prompt (Wu et al., 2024). This method has shown remarkable results by increasing translation ability from near zero to significant BLEU scores for multiple language directions (Wu et al., 2024). Complementing this, research on adapting pre-trained English language models such as Llama-2 for extremely low-resource languages (XLRs), including the Finno-Ugric languages Võro, Livonian and Komi, has shown promising results (Novák et al., 2024). These adaptations employ techniques such as continued pre-training in related languages with higher resources and cross-lingual transfer to teach capabilities in the XLR target language (Novák et al., 2024). In addition, there is an increasing focus on developing foundation models that specifically target low-resource language education and emphasize multilingual capabilities and the integration of cultural context into the learning process (Chen et al., 2024).

These advances represent a shift from AI models that were predominantly data-hungry and required large corpora for effective training to more data-intelligent approaches. The historical reliance on extensive, structured text collections has been a significant obstacle for many endangered languages for which such resources are simply not available. The observation that AI does not provide accurate information about poorly documented languages and that "many endangered languages do not [have extensive digital corpora]" (Morales et al., 2025) has long been a key challenge. However, recent methods such as LingoLLM, which explicitly utilize an existing "grammar book or dictionary" in the absence of large corpora (Wu et al., 2024), and projects such as NüshuRescue, which demonstrated the ability of an LLM to learn translation from as few as 35 sentence pairs (Lisagor, 2025), point towards a move towards AI that can learn more efficiently from limited or different types of data. Research focusing on "extremely low-resource (XLR) languages"," such as the Finno-Ugric LLM project, further emphasizes this trend by exploring techniques such as transfer learning (Novák et al., 2024). This evolution is crucial because it democratizes the potential of AI and makes sophisticated tools applicable to a much wider range of languages in the world, especially those most in need of technological support for their revitalization.

3. Challenges and Opportunities in AI-Driven Language Preservation

The use of AI in language revitalization is promising, but it faces several significant and persistent challenges that must be overcome for it to be effective and ethical.

- **Data Scarcity and Quality:** This remains a fundamental hurdle. For many endangered languages, the extensive digital corpora required to train robust AI models do not exist (Morales et al., 2025). The quality and representativeness of the available data is also crucial, as biases or gaps can lead to erroneous AI models.
- **Technological Limitations:** Current AI models still struggle with the subtleties of languages that have highly complex grammatical structures, or the subtle nuances of regional dialects and accents. AI often struggles to capture the deep cultural context and implicit knowledge that is essential for language use. Therefore, AI is considered a powerful tool, but not a substitute for human expertise, and it still has a long way to go to reach the quality of qualified human interpreters (Zabetian, 2024).
- **Biases in AI Models:** AI models trained predominantly on languages with large resources are often biased and do not adequately capture the unique linguistic structures of endangered languages (Bender, 2024). There is also a risk that AI tools may focus on more dominant or standardized dialects, which could inadvertently marginalize less common forms and their speakers.
- **Cost, Accessibility, and Sustainability**: Sophisticated AI tools can be expensive to develop and maintain, potentially putting them out of reach for under-resourced communities. The digital divide, including inequalities in access to technology and internet connectivity, may further limit the accessibility of AI-powered solutions. In addition, ensuring long-term success requires sustainable funding and capacity building, which can be difficult to achieve (UNESCO, 2023).
- **Risk of Cultural Dilution**: Over-reliance on AI, especially when it is not driven by the language community, risks unintentionally flattening linguistic diversity or imposing the structures of dominant languages on vulnerable

languages. Even the processing of language by AI can sometimes remove contextual elements if not done with care and cultural sensitivity (Kramsch, 1995).

Despite the challenges, recent advances in AI have created unprecedented opportunities to support language preservation efforts, especially when strategically and ethically coupled with community-led revitalization efforts (Morales et al., 2025; UNESCO, 2023).

- **Advanced AI for Richer Resources:** Continued exploration of Generative AI and LLMs can lead to the creation of more diverse and engaging educational materials, highly interactive learning tools, and more sophisticated documentation systems that capture cultural context (Morales et al., 2025).
- **Automated transcription and digitization:** AI-powered tools for automated transcription, speech recognition and digitization of handwritten documents can drastically reduce the manual labor involved in creating textual corpora (Historica Canada, 2023). This is crucial for languages with a rich oral tradition, as it removes the historical bottleneck in documentation efforts (Lisagor, 2025).
- **Support for Low-Resource Languages:** Recent AI methods show a move towards AI that can learn more efficiently from limited data (Lisagor, 2025; Wu et al., 2024). Innovative approaches such as LingoLLM enable existing LLMs to process and translate unseen languages by using available linguistic descriptions such as dictionaries and grammar books (Wu et al., 2024). This evolution is crucial because it makes sophisticated tools applicable to a much wider range of languages in the world.
- **Community-Driven Initiatives and Empowerment:** AI-powered platforms are increasingly enabling community-driven documentation. The Living Dictionaries project, for example, creates online repositories where community members can collaboratively document their endangered languages (Historica Canada, 2023). Such initiatives ensure the accuracy and cultural relevance of the data and instill a sense of ownership that is essential for sustainable revitalization efforts (Historica Canada, 2023).
- **Enhanced Learning and Accessibility:** Broader technological initiatives are improving the accessibility of language resources. Google's Woolaroo app is an open-source tool that uses image recognition to provide words in Indigenous languages, promoting interactive learning (Historica Canada, 2023). In addition, the development of digital keyboards for endangered languages promotes digital inclusion and helps preserve linguistic identity in daily online interactions (Historica Canada, 2023).

- **Bridging Communication Gaps:** AI-powered translation systems hold significant potential to improve communication for minority language speakers. They can help bridge linguistic gaps and enable speakers of endangered languages to communicate with a wider audience and gain access to information. Such tools are particularly valuable for communities that are geographically dispersed or have limited access to formal language education resources (Morales et al., 2025).

Ultimately, while the use of AI in language preservation is not a complete solution to the complicated socio-political and economic factors that lead to language endangerment, it offers significant and evolving opportunities (Bender, 2024; UNESCO, 2023). The journey from basic documentation and analysis to the advanced capabilities of Generative AI and LLMs marks a crucial shift, enabling the creation of rich educational resources and the digitization of oral traditions (Historica Canada, 2023; Morales et al., 2025). Recent breakthroughs show the growing ability of AI to work with scarce data, a crucial development for low-resource languages (Lisagor, 2025; Wu et al., 2024). However, persistent challenges such as data scarcity (Morales et al., 2025), technological limitations, model bias (Bender, 2024) and the risk of cultural dilution require a cautious and ethical approach. The most effective way forward lies in the strategic and ethical integration of these powerful AI tools with community-led revitalization efforts to ensure that the technology empowers and amplifies the voices of the language communities themselves (Morales et al., 2025; UNESCO, 2023).

VI. AI-POWERED LANGUAGE LEARNING AND COMMUNITY ENGAGEMENT

In the face of increasing language extinction, one of the most promising solutions is the integration of artificial intelligence (AI) into language learning systems. AI-powered tools are changing the way endangered languages can be learned, taught and revitalized. These tools also offer an accessible and sustainable way to preserve linguistic heritage. AI offers a different approach to overcoming challenges in language learning, such as limited resources, lack of teachers and geographical isolation. Furthermore, AI involves community engagement by enabling speakers, especially the younger generation, to reconnect with their linguistic heritage in innovative and interactive ways. Therefore, this subchapter explores the role of AI in language learning and community engagement. It highlights its potential in revitalizing endangered languages and creating a lasting impact on cultural preservation.

1. Machine Translation

Machine translation (MT) plays an important role in preserving linguistic heritage by facilitating the documentation of grammar, vocabulary and oral traditions (Robles et al., 2024). AI-powered MT systems enable the translation of text and audio into widely spoken languages and support research and documentation (Prieto et al., 2024). Meanwhile, neural model-based machine translation (NMT), which can be trained with parallel corpora, helps to preserve endangered languages and make them more accessible. For example, the Gex'ez-English Bidirectional Neural Machine Translation (Getachew & Yayeh, 2023) focused on translating the ancient Ge'ez script and used the Transformer model to improve translation quality. Similarly, in the development of Amharic-Kistanigna MT (Negia et al., 2022), a Transformer and an LSTM were used to create a machine translation system between Amharic and Kistanigna. In addition, the NLLB-200 machine translation model has proven to be effective in low-resource languages, e.g. the translation of Toba Batak into Indonesian (Samuel & Ali, 2024). In the context of language revitalization, this technology enables the translation of folktales and academic papers so that the important cultural knowledge embedded in the language is not lost. The potential of AI-powered machine translation ensures that the language remains relevant and accessible for future generations (Nanduri & Bonsignore, 2023).

2. Speech Recognition

Speech recognition systems are used to document and preserve endangered languages by improving pronunciation training. Speech recognition systems also provide real-time feedback features that help learners recognize and correct pronunciation errors (Dai & Wu, 2021). These features are particularly valuable in remote or underserved communities where there are few native speakers. For example, the study by Meelen et al. (2024) examined end-to-end speech recognition systems for Dzardzongke and Newar, two endangered languages in Nepal. The study showed the effectiveness of transfer learning and modifications such as normalization of amplitude and pitch to improve recognition accuracy in low-resource settings (Meelen et al., 2024). Similarly, Chizzoni & Vietti (2024) overcame the challenges of developing speech recognition systems for Campidanese, an endangered language spoken in Sardinia. The systems were developed using multilingual ASR models (Chizzoni & Vietti, 2024). Chen & Yang (2020) also applied deep learning methods for speech recognition in the Yi language, a branch of the Tibetan-Burmese language family recognized as an endangered minority language. These studies highlight the potential of speech recognition systems to aid in the documentation and preservation of endangered languages by improving pronunciation training. These studies have also proven that speech recognition systems can enable language learners to practice even in low-resource conditions.

3. Interactive and Personalized Learning Experience

Large Language Models (LLMs) and generative AI are advances in the ability of AI to understand and produce text that is similar to human text. LLMs such as Generative Pre-trained Transformers (GPT) are trained on very large amounts of data and can therefore be used for a variety of activities, including question answering, translation, summarization and text synthesis (Brown et al., 2020). These methods can be applied to language learning to develop individualized learning programs that meet the needs of individual learners. LLMs can also facilitate the creation of dynamic, contextualized language learning materials. Through generative AI, these models can create dialogs, stories and real-world conversational scenarios that help learners practice the language in diverse and authentic contexts (Håkansson & Phillips-Wren, 2024). By simulating human-like conversations, learners can engage in interactive speaking practice with AI systems that mimic native speakers. These generative capabilities provide a more immersive experience that allows learners to engage with language in a way that is similar to natural language acquisition (Godwin-Jones, 2024).

AI-driven chatbots enhance interactive and personalized language learning by serving as virtual companions that immerse learners in natural conversations. Through the use of generative AI, these chatbots simulate realistic dialogs and adapt to the learner's language level to support the development of speaking and comprehension skills (Chiaráin & Chasaide, 2016). They can deal with language-specific features such as tonal distinctions or syntactic structures and provide real-time practice and feedback in a safe, accessible environment. By enabling learners to practice regularly and gain confidence in speaking, chatbots play an important role in language revitalization by providing a dynamic, engaging tool that supports learners.

An example of such a chatbot is @llegra, which was developed in 2023 to facilitate communication in Vallader, a Rhaeto-Romanic dialect (Bendel & Jabou, 2024). Powered by GPT-4, this chatbot is incredibly interactive and engaging as a teaching tool as it can process and output both text and voice. The effectiveness of AI-driven technology in supporting language revitalization initiatives is illustrated by this chatbot, which is an example of how conversational agents can be a creative tool for the promotion and preservation of endangered languages.

4. AI and Collaborative Language Projects

AI has the potential to promote community engagement in collaborative language projects. For example, Mozilla's Common Voice project (Ardila et al., 2020) provides a platform for community participation, such as a speech-to-text system, helping with documentation, transcription and language learning (Ardila et al., 2020). The project makes individuals active participants in the preservation process and emphasizes that language revitalization is a collective and continuous effort (Park et al., 2022). These projects help build networks between language speakers, linguists, technologists and educators, all working together to ensure the survival and development of the language.

5. Community Engagement and Empowerment

Revitalizing a language is not only the responsibility of language experts or teachers, but also the responsibility of the people who speak the language and maintain its culture. AI promotes an inclusive methodology that enables community members to actively participate in the revitalization of local languages. AI tools can be used by speakers of indigenous languages to create a range of digital resources, including educational materials, narrative videos, voice recordings, music and poetry, which they can then disseminate online (Jafari, 2023). This makes their languages accessible to a wider audience and provides valuable resources for language learners. By sharing their stories and cultural practices in their native language, they enrich the digital space with authentic content and help breathe new life into these languages. These efforts not only raise awareness, but also get younger generations to reconnect with their cultural heritage (Font de la Vall & Araya, 2023).

A crucial part of involving communities in language preservation is documenting languages to create well-organized corpora. These corpora, which contain both text and audio, are essential for the development of AI technologies such as transcription and speech recognition. By recording their languages in digital formats, communities contribute valuable data that helps AI systems capture linguistic details such as tonal variations and grammatical structures. Crowdsourced translation projects have also emerged as a powerful way to translate digital content into endangered languages (Agyei et al., 2024; Jaworski et al., 2023). Platforms such as Duolingo, Wikipedia and TED Talks have used crowdsourcing to make their content more linguistically inclusive (Hatipoğlu et al., 2022). Native speakers and language enthusiasts volunteer their time to translate materials and ensure that these languages are represented in global conversations. These initiatives not only help with translation, but also play an important role in documenting languages and their unique characteristics. Crowdsourced translations show how digital technology can bridge the gap between global content and endangered languages so that no language is left behind in the digital age.

6. Future Possibilities for AI and Language Learning

AI and language learning are becoming increasingly multimodal, combining several ways of conveying information at the same time. AI-based applications will be able to generate images or video clips based on text commands and provide multimodal output based on user-provided images or audio data. AI-powered metaverse approaches are likely to play an important role (Nanduri & Bonsignore, 2023). Such approaches simulate traditional ceremonies or historical events and allow users to learn a language while interacting with cultural practices and artifacts. In addition, AI can lead to more personalized learning experiences where systems track progress and anticipate future learning needs.

In conclusion, looking to the future, AI-powered language learning tools will undeniably become powerful and practical solutions to protect and revitalize endangered languages around the world. Using tools such as machine translation, speech recognition, generative AI and chatbots, learners can access interactive and personalized learning experiences, even in low-resource environments. These tools not only help individuals improve their language skills, but also encourage community members to participate in creating and sharing digital content in their native language. By combining modern technology with local knowledge and active community participation, AI is helping to keep endangered languages alive and meaningful in today's digital world. This advanced technology expands access to language education to a wider audience and particularly benefits people in underserved or remote regions. It achieves this by providing scalable, adaptable and highly interactive learning experiences that transcend geographical barriers.

In addition to individual learning, AI also actively promotes community engagement by empowering native speakers to directly contribute to the documentation and revitalization of the language. This ensures that the language not only survives, but remains vibrant and relevant for generations to come. As AI continues to develop at a rapid pace, its immense potential to bridge the gap between traditional language learning methods and modern technological possibilities is becoming increasingly clear. Through collaborative projects, community-developed content and truly personalized learning journeys, AI will play a crucial role in preserving our precious linguistic heritage and ensuring that endangered languages not only survive, but truly thrive in the digital age.

VII. CASE STUDIES OF AI-DRIVEN LANGUAGE REVITALIZATION

AI technologies are playing a growing role in efforts to revitalize endangered languages, especially when used in participatory and ethically informed approaches. The following six case studies illustrate how different methods from speech recognition to machine translation to immersive learning are shaped by community leadership and local cultural frameworks.

1. Initiatives for Revitalizing Endangered Languages

a. Te Hiku Media and the Māori Language (Aotearoa/New Zealand)

Te Hiku Media has developed an automatic speech recognition (ASR) system tailored to te reo Māori using over 300 hours of carefully tagged speech data provided by the community. The team utilized deep neural networks trained specifically for the phonological and grammatical structures of the Māori language. What makes this project unique is its strict adherence to the principle of data sovereignty: the organization rejected offers from large technology companies to commercialize the data and instead ensured that control of the linguistic corpus remained firmly in the hands of Māori communities. As a result, the ASR system achieved an accuracy rate of around 92%, a remarkable success that demonstrates the effectiveness of combining high-quality local data with AI-driven tools (Te Hiku Media, 2018; Te Hiku Media, 2024; Wired, 2021).

b. Mozilla Common Voice for Indigenous Languages

In the United States, the Indigenous Language Institute (ILI) has developed a chatbot for the Navajo language that uses a rule-based natural language processing (NLP) system. Unlike data-driven machine learning approaches, this chatbot was created through hand-crafted dialog trees and intent-based scripting. The content was developed in close collaboration with Navajo elders to ensure cultural authenticity and appropriate language use. Its primary function is educational, providing interactive language exercises that reflect Navajo worldviews and communicative norms. The methodology reflects a preference for interpretability, control, and alignment with community goals rather than optimization based solely on the availability of data (Ofosu-Asare, 2024).

c. Indigenous Language Institute's Navajo Chatbot (USA)

In the United States, the Indigenous Language Institute (ILI) has developed a chatbot for the Navajo language that uses a rule-based natural language processing (NLP) system. Unlike data-driven machine learning approaches, this chatbot was created through hand-crafted dialog trees and intent-based scripting. The content was developed in close collaboration with Navajo elders to ensure cultural authenticity and appropriate language use. Its primary function is educational, providing interactive language exercises that reflect Navajo worldviews and communicative norms. The methodology reflects a preference for interpretability, control, and alignment with community goals rather than optimization based solely on the availability of data (Ofosu-Asare, 2024).

d. Masakhane and African Languages

Masakhane is a pan-African research collective focused on machine translation for African languages. The group uses a participatory approach in which native speakers and researchers jointly create training datasets, annotate texts and evaluate the translation results. Technically, they employ transfer learning with pre-trained multilingual models such as mBART or NLLB and fine-tune them to local languages. Their workflow emphasizes transparency, community co-authorship and joint capacity building. The result is a growing number of machine translation systems for dozens of African languages that are challenging the dominance of English-centric AI development and empowering language communities across the continent (Nekoto et al., 2020).

e. AR/VR-Based Immersion for Sámi (Scandinavia)

In Northern Europe, educators and Sámi language activists have developed immersive learning environments for the North Sámi using augmented and virtual reality (AR/VR). These systems simulate traditional Sámi life such as reindeer herding or fishing in interactive digital environments created using platforms such as Unity and Unreal Engine. The design process was led by Sámi educators to ensure cultural relevance, and the systems integrate voice commands, gesture recognition and localized content. Methodologically, this approach combines pedagogical design with advanced multimodal technologies to increase learner engagement and support contextualized language acquisition (Virtanen et al., 2021).

f. Google Woolaroo: Image-Based Vocabulary Learning

Woolaroo, developed by Google Arts & Culture, is a mobile application that uses computer vision to teach vocabulary in endangered languages. By pointing a smartphone camera at everyday objects, users receive on-screen labels in indigenous languages such as Māori, Louisiana Creole and Yugambeh. The method combines AI-based object recognition with a community-contributed lexicon that allows users to submit new translations and pronunciation recordings. The system is dynamic and expandable, allowing vocabulary to be learned in the context of the real world. Its mobile design makes it accessible and participatory and promotes the documentation and dissemination of languages through everyday use (Google, 2021).

2. Reflections on Ethics, Sustainability, and Community Co-Design

Several key themes can be derived from these six case studies:

- Community control of data is critical —Te Hiku Media and Woolaroo show that language technology needs to empower communities, not take from them (Carroll et al., 2020; Google, 2021).
- Participatory design minimizes the risk of linguistic bias and promotes inclusivity, as practiced by Mozilla Common Voice and Masakhane (Bird, 2020).
- Sustainability requires more than just technology; it requires human skills, long-term investment and culturally informed pedagogy (Virtanen et al., 2021).
- Ethical AI must reflect principles such as CARE (Collective Benefit, Authority to Control, Responsibility, Ethics), especially in low-resource and indigenous contexts (Carroll et al., 2020; Ofosu-Asare, 2024)

In summary, the case studies presented in this chapter highlight that the success of AI-driven language revitalization efforts depends not only on technological innovation, but also on the deep integration of community agency, cultural knowledge and ethical design principles. Projects such as Te Hiku Media and Masakhane exemplify how indigenous data sovereignty and grassroots participation can shape more equitable and contextualized AI applications. Similarly, platforms such as Google Woolaroo and Mozilla Common Voice show that open, collaborative infrastructures — when led by local voices — can democratize access to language technologies and foster inclusive digital ecosystems.

However, these efforts also highlight critical challenges: ensuring long-term sustainability, preserving linguistic and cultural authenticity, avoiding extractive data practices, and addressing systemic imbalances in AI development. These challenges cannot be overcome by technical solutions alone. They require interdisciplinary collaboration, policy-level support, and the active inclusion of indigenous epistemologies and pedagogies in the AI research pipeline.

Ultimately, the revitalization of endangered languages through AI is not about whether machines can speak a language, but whether the communities that possess these languages can meaningfully shape, govern, and benefit from the technologies that represent them. The role of AI should be supportive rather than directive, so that communities can take control of their linguistic future.

VIII. ETHICAL CONSIDERATIONS IN AI FOR LANGUAGE PRESERVATION

Ethics is one of the challenges in using AI for language preservation. Below are some aspects that need to be considered:

1. Data Sovereignty and Informed Consent

The principle of data sovereignty is crucial in language preservation through AI. Language communities must have complete control over their linguistic data, from collection to use to dissemination. Informed consent must involve individuals, indigenous authorities and relevant cultural institutions and clearly explain the objectives, risks and benefits.

For example, Te Hiku Media in Aotearoa (New Zealand) developed a speech recognition system for Māori by involving communities in data collection and introducing a Kaitiakitanga license to ensure community control over their data (Time, 2024a). This approach is also iterative and allows for renegotiation as the context changes. Data sovereignty frameworks developed by Indigenous communities are becoming important tools to counter data colonization in today's AI ecosystems (Carroll et al., 2020).

2. Designing Culturally Sensitive Technologies

AI for language preservation must be highly culturally sensitive. NLP applications must reflect the values, norms and perspectives of the user community. Representations of indigenous vocabulary, social structures in the language and taboo norms must be respected so that the technology does not violate or undermine these value systems.

The NushuRescue project, for example, uses AI to revitalize the Nüshu language a writing system developed by Yao women in China while respecting its cultural and historical context (Yang et al., 2024).

3. Ethical Approaches to Linguistic Data Collection

Linguistic data collection should be conducted ethically and respect privacy and local values. Exploitative practices, such as data collection without consent or adequate compensation, should be avoided. AI researchers and developers should avoid extractive approaches and instead adopt collaborative documentation and annotation processes (Miceli et al., 2022).

In Indonesia, the Language Development and Fostering Agency has worked with universities and local communities to collect regional language data through a participatory approach. However, it still faces challenges in comprehensive documentation (Time, 2024b).

4. Addressing Linguistic and Dialectal Diversity

Many minority languages have a multitude of dialects and local variations. An ethical approach to language preservation through AI must include all variations (Corbett, 2023). This is important to prevent the dominance of one dialect over another.

For example, the Cree# project enables programming with concepts in Cree, a polysynthetic language that reflects its particular linguistic and cultural structure (AI & Society, 2024).

5. Ethical and Responsible Development Model

Model developers should commit to inclusivity and fairness in model design and testing, and ensure that the results of machine learning support the preservation of languages without harming communities that depend on those languages (Kimera et al., 2024). To maintain ethical integrity, model outputs must be transparent and scrutinized by both community stakeholders and regulators to avoid potential harm to marginalized groups and ensure adherence to established ethical frameworks. Continuous evaluation of model performance is critical to identify and correct errors or biases that arise over time. To maintain accountability, comprehensive documentation of the model's development cycle is required, including data provenance, rationale for design, and decision-making processes.

6. Building Local Capacity and Ownership

It is important to build local capacity through training, technology transfer and active community engagement. Communities should be viewed as equal partners. For example, *the Lakota AI Code Camp* trains indigenous youth in coding and AI development to preserve their language (TeenVogue, 2023).

7. Equitable Access and Benefit Sharing

Technologies developed using community data must bring tangible benefits to the community, such as access to the technology, participation in monetization or the development of local applications. The principle of *fair benefit sharing* prevents the exploitation of data (Viterbi Conversations in Ethics, 2025).

8. Ensuring Transparency and Explainability in AI

Transparency includes the documentation of processes, datasets and model design decisions. Local communities have a right to know how the system works and to understand its risks and limitations. Efforts to make the system explainable (*explainable AI*) are also an important part of development ethics (Baker et al., 2023).

9. Continuous Ethical Engagement and Impact Evaluation

Continuous assessment of social, cultural and political impact is essential. Sustained engagement with society is an ongoing ethical imperative to ensure that AI systems are in harmony with evolving cultural and social contexts (Liu et al., 2022).

In conclusion, language preservation through artificial intelligence opens up new opportunities to document, visualize and revitalize endangered languages. However, these initiatives must be undertaken with careful consideration of their ethical implications. This paper outlines nine key ethical issues that need to be considered when developing AI for language preservation: Data sovereignty and informed consent, ethical approaches to linguistic data collection, culturally sensitive technology design, inclusion of dialect diversity, equitable and responsible model development, transparency and explainability, local capacity building and ownership, equitable benefit-sharing, and ongoing ethical engagement.

The nine principles affirm that technology should not only focus on efficiency or accuracy, but also on social justice and community-based support. Ethically developed AI can be a tool that supports language empowerment and sustainability, rather than an instrument of exploitation or marginalization.

IX. FUTURE DIRECTIONS: AI AND THE FUTURE OF LANGUAGE PRESERVATION

Potential New Technology for Language Conservation

1. Synthetic Data Generation for Language Preservation: An Advanced Approach

In today's language technology landscape, synthetic data generation has emerged as a key tool for creating realistic and representative datasets especially for endangered languages. Synthetic data is artificially generated textual content designed to mimic the structural, syntactic and semantic features of authentic linguistic use. As many indigenous and minority languages are at risk of extinction due to sociocultural and demographic changes, the development of robust, faithful datasets is crucial for both documentation and revitalization.

One of the biggest challenges in language preservation is the lack of naturally occurring data. For endangered languages, there are often not enough written records or spoken corpora, which are essential for training machine learning models. In addition, privacy and ethical use concerns complicate the collection and sharing of data from native speakers. Synthetic data offers a compelling solution, as it enables the creation of linguistically plausible samples that circumvent these limitations while preserving the integrity and richness of the original language.

a. Human Digitization through Deep Learning Techniques

Recent advances in deep learning have significantly improved the ability to generate high quality synthetic linguistic data. Neural architectures such as Transformers and recurrent neural networks (RNNs) can be trained on limited corpora to produce texts that reflect the grammatical structures, phonetic patterns and stylistic idiosyncrasies of endangered languages (Shorten et al., 2021). These models learn latent representations of the language and produce output that is contextually coherent and stylistically consistent. By adapting these systems to specific linguistic features — such as morphological complexity or tonal variation — researchers can create datasets that are not only large in volume but also rich in linguistic authenticity. This capability is particularly valuable when dealing with low-resource languages where traditional methods of data collection are inadequate.

b. Ensuring Privacy in Synthetic Data

Another critical dimension of synthetic data generation lies in its ability to address privacy and ethical concerns related to the use of real-world data. In many cases, speakers of endangered languages are reluctant to share personal narratives or cultural expressions for fear of misrepresentation or exploitation. Synthetic data mitigates this problem by generating content that retains the linguistic essence of the source material without reproducing identifiable information (Kurakin et al., 2023). Through techniques such as differential privacy and fine-tuning of anonymized models, researchers can ensure that the synthetic output respects the rights and sensitivities of language communities while still serving as a useful resource for computational analysis and educational applications.

c. Integrating Domain Expertise into Synthetic Data Generation Processes

While algorithmic approaches provide powerful tools for generating synthetic data, they cannot function in isolation. The linguistic accuracy and cultural relevance of synthetic datasets is highly dependent on the integration of the expertise of linguists, anthropologists and native speakers. Collaborative frameworks that incorporate expert feedback into the generation pipeline improve the accuracy and contextual appropriateness of the resulting data (Goncalves et al., 2020). For example, rule-based constraints derived from phonological or syntactic theories can guide generative models so that they do not produce linguistically implausible results. However, the success of such integrations depends on the quality of the underlying models and the precision of the knowledge involved. Therefore, continuous refinement and validation by experts is essential for the long-term use of synthetic data in language preservation initiatives.

Despite their promising potential, synthetic data should not be seen as a substitute for real linguistic heritage. Rather, they serve as a complementary strategy that supports broader preservation efforts. Ongoing research must focus on improving the reliability, adaptability, and inclusivity of these methods to ensure that technological interventions are consistent with the goals of linguistic equity and cultural sustainability.

Several practical implementations illustrate the potential of synthetic data for language preservation. For example, the Endangered Languages Archive (ELAR) has experimented with the generation of synthetic speech to augment audio datasets for under-resourced languages and improve their usability in speech recognition systems. Similarly, projects such as Mozilla Common Voice have explored the cloning of synthetic voices to preserve oral traditions in languages spoken by only a few speakers. Another notable case is the use of GAN-based (Generative Adversarial Network) text generation to reconstruct lost texts in historical variants of Celtic languages. These examples show how synthetic data not only compensates for the scarcity of data, but also facilitates the development of digital tools that make the language more accessible.

2. Utilizing Augmented Reality (AR) and Virtual Reality (VR) for Enhanced Immersive Language Learning

The worldwide decline in linguistic diversity has become an urgent cultural and intellectual challenge. As globalization accelerates and dominant languages increasingly eclipse smaller linguistic communities, many endangered languages are threatened with extinction (Parmaxi & Demetriou, 2020). In response to this growing crisis, emerging technologies such as Augmented Reality (AR) and Virtual Reality (VR) have begun to play a transformative role in language revitalization efforts. These immersive digital tools offer innovative ways to engage learners in authentic, context-rich environments — particularly beneficial for preserving and teaching languages that are rarely heard outside their home communities.

Unlike traditional classroom instruction, which often lacks contextual depth and real-world application, AR and VR can simulate culturally grounded experiences that bring language learning to life. These technologies allow users to interact with virtual environments where language use is embedded in its natural sociocultural framework. This chapter explores how AR and VR contribute to immersive language learning, emphasizes the importance of community-driven development, and addresses the ethical and technical challenges associated with the use of these tools in language preservation initiatives.

a. Enhancing Language Learning Through Immersive Technologies

One of the most compelling benefits of AR and VR lies in their ability to create experiential learning environments that mirror real-life situations. By immersing learners in digitally constructed worlds, these technologies allow them to practice the target language in its cultural and communicative context, a particularly important feature for endangered languages, which often entail unique worldviews and modes of expression (Huang et al., 2021).

For example, AR applications can overlay digital content over physical spaces and allow learners to engage with the language through interactive signage, visual prompts or voice-activated conversations. Similarly, VR platforms can place users in fully simulated environments, such as virtual villages or historical settings, where they can interact with native speakers, complete everyday tasks and participate in culturally relevant dialogs. Research shows that such immersive experiences significantly improve learner engagement and retention (Tulgar et al., 2022). In addition, these tools provide the opportunity to practice conversational skills in realistic scenarios, which is often not possible in traditional language courses.

b. Community-Led Approaches in AR/VR Language Revitalization

Sustainable preservation of a language cannot be done in isolation from the communities that speak or once spoke the language. Effective revitalization efforts must be rooted in the values, traditions and experiences of native speakers and cultural custodians. Community-led initiatives that integrate indigenous perspectives into technology-enhanced language learning have shown particular promise (Heath et al., 2024). When local knowledge holders, elders, and educators are actively involved in the design and implementation of AR and VR content, the resulting materials are more likely to reflect authentic linguistic and cultural practices.

This participatory model not only ensures accuracy, but also fosters a sense of ownership and pride among community members. It empowers them to shape the history of their language and heritage while guiding developers towards respectful and meaningful representations. In addition, such collaborations support equitable multilingual education by focusing on the voices and needs of historically marginalized communities.

c. Ethical Considerations and Technological Challenges

Despite their potential, AR and VR solutions for language learning are not without limitations. One major problem is the issue of accessibility. Many endangered languages are spoken by communities that have limited access to high-speed internet, advanced hardware or training in digital literacy (Voinov, 2010). If these inequalities are not addressed, the use of immersive technologies risks exacerbating existing inequalities rather than bridging them.

Furthermore, the creation of culturally sensitive AR and VR content requires careful collaboration with native speakers and cultural experts. Misrepresentation—even unintentional—can perpetuate stereotypes or distort linguistic nuances. Therefore, ethical considerations must play a role at every stage of development, including informed consent, data sovereignty and intellectual property rights (Parmaxi & Demetriou, 2020). To build trust and foster long-term partnerships, it is important to ensure that communities retain control over their linguistic resources.

Several pilot projects have demonstrated the practical value of AR and VR for language preservation. The Māori Language in Virtual Worlds initiative in New Zealand, for example, uses VR to recreate traditional Māori environments and give learners the opportunity to learn the language in a culturally rich setting. Another project, FirstVoices VR, developed in collaboration with indigenous communities in Canada, allows users to interact with elders and learn the language through storytelling and ceremonial practices. Meanwhile, AR-based apps like SayIt! Hawaiian helps users practice pronunciation and vocabulary using augmented overlays on real objects. These examples illustrate how immersive technologies can serve as powerful tools for language acquisition and intergenerational transmission, especially when co-developed with the communities they are intended to serve.

3. AI Storytelling for Preserving Oral Tradition

Oral traditions have long been important carriers of cultural memory, transmitting values, history and collective wisdom across generations. However, in the face of rapid globalization and cultural homogenization, many of these traditions are in danger of being forgotten. In response to this growing concern, artificial intelligence — particularly AI-powered storytelling platforms — offers a promising way to preserve, revitalize and pass on oral narratives that define communities and identities. By combining advanced language models with deep cultural understanding, these systems can generate stories that not only preserve linguistic structures but also reflect the symbolic depth and moral framework of traditional tales (Han & Cai, 2023).

a. Using Knowledge Graphs for Cultural Immersion

At the heart of effective AI storytelling is the ability to understand and contextualize cultural meanings — a task enabled by the integration of knowledge graphs. These structured representations of information serve as digital encyclopedias that capture relationships between entities such as people, places, events and beliefs (Tiddi et al., 2020). When applied to oral traditions, knowledge graphs enable AI systems to capture the intricate web of meanings that shape the narrative world of a culture.

By encoding historical facts, mythological motifs and social norms, knowledge graphs help AI models generate stories that are consistent with a community's worldview. For example, they help the machines to recognize why certain characters appear repeatedly in different stories or how certain symbols have meaning across generations. This method not only improves the coherence of the generated narratives, but also ensures their cultural fidelity. Through such a semantic framework, AI goes beyond mere text generation and becomes a guardian of cultural memory.

b. Character-Centric Narratives and Cultural Continuity

In oral traditions, characters are often more than just individuals — they represent archetypes, moral teachings and communal values. Therefore, developing AI systems that emphasize character-driven storytelling is essential to preserving the essence of these traditions. By adhering to narratological frameworks, AI platforms can construct consistent, culturally appropriate personas whose actions and interactions reflect the norms and expectations of the source culture (Rameshkumar & Bailey, 2020).

Such an approach enables AI to generate narratives that are not only linguistically accurate but also emotionally engaging. The characters become vehicles of cultural transmission, embodying values and behaviors that the audience recognizes and can identify with. Whether you are retelling a well-known folktale or inventing a new story inspired by tradition, the integrity of character roles ensures that the cultural significance of oral narratives is preserved — even when adapted for digital formats.

c. Building Socio-Technical Solutions: The Role of Human-AI Collaboration

Integrating AI into cultural storytelling is not just a technical challenge, but a deeply social endeavor. Ensuring that AI-generated narratives remain respectful, accurate and meaningful requires close collaboration between technologists, anthropologists, linguists and members of the cultural communities being represented (Herrera-González et al., 2020).

A human-in-the-loop approach allows experts to steer AI systems, check the results for cultural sensitivity and correct misinterpretations before dissemination. Furthermore, it addresses one of the most pressing limitations of current AI storytelling: the risk of oversimplification or misrepresentation of complex cultural contexts (Jiang et al., 2023). By combining the computational power of AI with human interpretative skills and ethical judgment, we can create storytelling systems that are both innovative and responsible.

Several initiatives have begun to explore the intersection of AI storytelling and cultural preservation. One notable example is StoryWeaver, an open-source platform that uses AI to transform traditional Indian folktales into multilingual, interactive stories for children. Another example is AI Māori, which uses natural language processing to generate new stories based on Māori oral traditions, using input from native speakers to refine the output. The Living Archive of Aboriginal Stories project in Australia is also using knowledge graphs to ensure that AI-generated narratives remain true to the Indigenous worldview. These examples show how AI can be used responsibly and effectively to support — rather than supplant — the rich, living heritage of oral storytelling.

4. Limited Data Challenges and AI Solutions for More Accurate Models

Linguistic diversity is not just a reflection of cultural richness — it is an essential part of humanity's collective heritage. Yet many languages at risk of extinction are poorly documented, as there are often no standardized writing systems or extensive textual records. This lack of data poses a major challenge for computational approaches aimed at preserving and processing these languages. Fortunately, recent advances in artificial intelligence (AI) offer promising solutions by enabling effective learning from limited linguistic resources.

Two particularly powerful strategies have emerged: transfer learning, which allows knowledge from high-resource languages to be applied to low-resource ones, and synthetic data generation, which artificially augments training datasets to compensate for the lack of natural data (Guo & Chen, 2024). Together, these methods allow researchers to create robust language models even when real-world data is sparse, providing a lifeline for languages at risk of falling into obscurity.

a. Continuous Pre-Training and the Role of Synthetic Datasets

A cornerstone of developing effective language models for low-resource languages is continuous pre-training — a process in which large multilingual models are further trained on domain-specific or language-specific data to improve their performance. Recent developments, such as the creation of the Nemotron-Mini-Hindi model, show how this method can significantly improve capabilities for underrepresented languages (Joshi et al., 2024).

Crucially, synthetic datasets play a pivotal role in this process. These datasets, created using techniques such as back-translation and data augmentation, allow researchers to expand the pool of available training material beyond what is naturally available. By simulating realistic linguistic patterns, synthetic data helps to fill gaps created by historical underrepresentation and enables models to perform more reliably in downstream tasks such as translation, speech recognition and text generation.

b. Efficient Refinement Strategies for Low-Resource Adaptation

In addition to pre-training, refinement strategies offer a cost-effective way of adapting existing models to specific languages without having to completely retrain them. Methods such as prompt tuning and adapter fine-tuning have proven to be particularly promising in this respect (Liu, 2022). In these approaches, only a small fraction of the model's parameters are changed — either by introducing adaptive prompts or by inserting lightweight adapter modules — allowing for targeted adaptation with minimal computational effort.

In the case of Tibetan and other low-resource languages, for example, these techniques enable the integration of linguistic features unique to these languages into broader NLP applications. Whether for sentiment analysis, machine translation or learning programs, such strategies enable the development of functional, high-quality language models even when little native language data is available.

c. Cross-Linguistic Knowledge Transfer and Unsupervised Learning

Another innovative approach is to use cross-linguistic similarities to improve model performance in different languages. Techniques that extract translation pairs from monolingual corpora — without resorting to parallel texts — have opened up new ways to enrich representations of low-resource languages (Conneau et al., 2019). These unsupervised methods exploit semantic alignment between languages, allowing models to infer meaning and structure even when direct translations are not available.

By applying data augmentation techniques, researchers can generate consistent bilingual dictionaries or sentence alignments for languages for which no linguistic resources are available. This not only improves model accuracy, but also contributes to the overall goal of preserving and documenting under-resourced languages in a scalable and sustainable way.

d. Future Directions: Addressing Gaps and Strengthening Community Engagement

Despite significant progress, there are still some challenges in the area of low-resource language modeling. Chief among these is the issue of data quality and availability (Chiang & Lee, 2022). While synthetic data and cross-lingual transfer have expanded the toolkit for language preservation, there is still an urgent need for methods that ensure higher fidelity of generated content and more nuanced adaptation to specific linguistic structures.

Future research should focus on the following:

- Improving the quality of synthetic data through better evaluation metrics and validation mechanisms.
- Developing more sophisticated fine-tuning frameworks that balance efficiency and linguistic accuracy.
- Exploring complex cross-lingual transfers, especially between typologically distinct languages.
- Working directly with language communities and linguists to ensure that AI-driven efforts align with local needs, values and aspirations

Only through such collaborative, community-centered innovation can we hope to create truly inclusive and impactful language technologies.

Several initiatives illustrate how these techniques are being applied in practice. The Masakhane project, for example, focuses on NLP for African languages, using transfer learning and community collaboration to develop machine translation models for dozens of underserved languages. Similarly, Google's Indic Language Initiative has used synthetic data and multilingual pre-training to improve NLP support for Indian languages such as Tamil, Telugu and Bengali. These examples show how

AI can be used effectively to support, not just simulate, the linguistic heritage of marginalized communities.

5. Improved AI Tools and Apps for Language Preservation

Language is more than just a means of communication — it is the cornerstone of identity, culture and social cohesion. As Crystal (2002) notes, the vitality of a language is closely linked to its use in daily life. If a language is no longer spoken regularly, there is a risk that it will become obsolete and centuries of cultural memory and community heritage will be lost (Crystal, 2002). Yet for many speakers of minority, indigenous or endangered languages, access to effective language learning tools remains limited. Traditional education systems often fail to reach these communities due to geographic, economic or institutional barriers, leaving many without the resources they need to maintain their language skills or pass on their linguistic traditions.

Artificial intelligence (AI), particularly through natural language processing (NLP) and machine learning (ML), offers the opportunity to bridge this gap. By offering personalized, scalable and accessible solutions, AI can democratize language learning and empower marginalized communities to reclaim and preserve their linguistic identities (Bahroun et al., 2023). This chapter explores how AI-driven technologies can support inclusive language learning, particularly for underrepresented groups, and presents real-world applications that demonstrate the potential of these innovations.

a. Bridging the Access Gap in Language Education

Access to quality language education has long been unevenly distributed across socio-economic boundaries. Scarino (2008) highlights that traditional models of language instruction are often costly, location-dependent, and ill-suited to the diverse needs of learners from different backgrounds. These challenges are particularly acute for speakers of indigenous, minority or endangered languages who do not have access to native teachers, formal curricula or even written materials in their own language.

Without sufficient exposure and opportunities to practice, younger generations struggle to speak the language fluently, further jeopardizing the survival of these languages. Furthermore, the lack of culturally relevant teaching resources exacerbates disinterest, especially among young people who view their heritage languages as impractical or outdated. Innovative approaches that go beyond traditional teaching are needed to address these issues.

b. AI-Powered Tools for Inclusive and Adaptive Language Learning

AI-based platforms offer a compelling solution by enabling personalized, adaptive and accessible language learning experiences. These systems use NLP, ML algorithms and speech recognition technologies to tailor content to the needs, pace and proficiency of individual learners (Pedro, 2019). In contrast to blanket teaching methods, AI can dynamically adjust the level of difficulty, provide immediate feedback and create targeted exercises based on the learner's performance (Kohnke et al., 2023).

For example, AI-supported tutoring systems can simulate conversation exercises, correct pronunciation errors in real time and reinforce vocabulary through interactive quizzes. Gamification modules, virtual reality (VR) environments and chatbots further increase engagement by making learning more immersive and enjoyable — especially for younger target groups (Chiang & Lee, 2022). Not only do these tools make language learning more accessible, but they also foster a sense of ownership and pride among users, leading to consistent usage and deeper cultural engagement.

Crucially, AI can be deployed across mobile devices and low-bandwidth platforms, allowing communities with limited infrastructure to benefit from high-quality language education. This scalability ensures that even the most remote or underserved populations can participate in the preservation of their linguistic heritage.

Several initiatives have already demonstrated the power of AI in promoting equal access to languages. For example, Duolingo, one of the most widely used language learning platforms, uses AI to create customized learning paths, offer instant corrections and track user progress. This makes language learning attractive and accessible to millions of people worldwide (Munday, 2015). Similarly, the Endangered Languages Project uses digital technologies to document and revitalize endangered languages, often in collaboration with indigenous communities. Their efforts include AI-generated learning materials, voice recognition tools and online repositories to help preserve linguistic diversity.

c. Deployment of AI-based Language Learning in Remote Areas

Language is a fundamental pillar of cultural identity and an important channel for the transmission of knowledge across generations. Its preservation is not only a matter of cultural heritage, but also a key factor in promoting mutual understanding between cultures and supporting broader sustainable development goals (UNESCO, 2010). However, for many communities in remote or underserved regions, access to quality language education remains difficult. Factors such as physical isolation, inadequate educational infrastructure and the limited availability of qualified instructors often pose serious obstacles — especially when it comes to preserving indigenous and minority languages that are already at risk of extinction.

Artificial Intelligence (AI) offers the opportunity to close this gap. Through the use of natural language processing (NLP), machine learning (ML), and speech recognition technologies, AI-powered language tools can provide personalized, scalable, and accessible educational experiences for even the most underserved populations (Dolenc et al., 2021). This chapter explores how AI-based solutions are being used in remote areas to support inclusive language learning, improve engagement and empower local communities to preserve their linguistic heritage.

d. Educational Access Challenges in Remote Communities

In many remote and rural areas, access to formal education particularly in local or minority languages — remains a major barrier. Dueñas (2015) points out that geographical distance and poor transportation infrastructure often prevent learners from attending schools or participating in structured language courses. These challenges are exacerbated by a chronic shortage of qualified language teachers, particularly those fluent in indigenous or endangered languages.

As a result, children who grow up speaking these languages struggle to fully master them, limiting their ability to engage socially and economically in both local and broader national contexts. Over time, this inequality threatens not only individual opportunities, but also the survival of entire language traditions. Without meaningful intervention, such inequalities risk deepening the cycle of marginalization and accelerating language loss.

e. AI-Driven Solutions: Expanding Reach through AR/VR and Mobile Platforms

To address these limitations, AI-powered language learning platforms are increasingly being developed with flexibility and accessibility in mind. Many of these systems are delivered via mobile devices — such as smartphones and tablets — which are now widely available even in underdeveloped regions (Wan & Cumming, 2015). These tools use NLP and ML algorithms to dynamically adapt content to the learner's language level. They offer customized exercises, real-time feedback on grammar and pronunciation, and interactive exercises tailored to individual needs (Schmidt & Strassner, 2022).

In addition, new applications integrate Augmented Reality (AR) and Virtual Reality (VR) to create immersive language environments. These technologies allow users to experience realistic conversations, explore culturally rich environments and interact with virtual native speakers — all without leaving their homes. Such innovations not only make learning more engaging, but also provide a depth of experience that traditional classroom instruction often lacks.

By combining the adaptable capabilities of AI with low-cost delivery mechanisms, these platforms offer a promising solution for reaching learners in remote areas where physical schooling is impractical or inaccessible.

Several initiatives illustrate the growing importance of AI for language learning in remote and underserved areas. One notable example is the Mobile-Assisted Language Learning (MALL) programs, which use AI-driven apps to deliver lessons offline and synchronize data when internet access is available (Shadiev et al., 2020). These tools have proven to be effective in overcoming infrastructural limitations and enabling consistent learning even in areas with intermittent internet connectivity. In Africa, AI-powered tools are being used to promote literacy and language retention in local languages such as Yoruba and Zulu (Sambamurthy, 2024). Projects such as the Afaan Oromo Language App utilize voice recognition and adaptive learning to help users master their language regardless of location. Similarly, interactive VR-based language games developed for indigenous communities in Latin America immerse learners in simulated cultural environments and reinforce both linguistic and cultural knowledge.

In conclusion, Artificial Intelligence (AI) can preserve and revitalize potentially endangered languages. AI technologies such as NLP, machine learning, machine translation, speech recognition systems and chatbots can document language attributes such as vocabulary, grammar, phonology of a language and even oral traditions. AI also has the potential to support collaborative language projects, for example by engaging stakeholders, including indigenous communities, and integrating AI into storytelling platforms. Examples of the use of AI for language preservation and revitalization include Hawaiian and Maori revitalization projects. Mozilla Common Voice and platforms like Duolingo, which use crowdsourcing techniques, are sparking interest in endangered languages, especially among the younger generation. Finally, involving the public in data collection and decision making is a concept that should be adopted in AI development projects to overcome ethical challenges. In the future, synthetic data needs to be developed to create low-resource languages and AI-based metaverses to create significant opportunities for language preservation.

X. CONCLUSIONS

The preservation of endangered languages is much more than the preservation of mere means of communication; it is a valuable task to save cultural identity, traditional knowledge and the great wealth in human diversity. Each language contains unique perspectives on history, ecology and worldviews that are invaluable in preserving local and global heritage. The loss of a language means the loss of this cultural capital and the strengthening of social bonds between groups of people. Despite the immense pressures of globalization and modernization, new technologies — especially Artificial Intelligence (AI) — combined with ethical, community-centered approaches provide encouraging new opportunities to support the documentation and revitalization of languages.

However, the challenges of language documentation and revitalization remain complex. Limited resources, ethical considerations, political reluctance, AI bias and the risk of cultural dilution require respectful, thoughtful and inclusive practices. Therefore, AI must be developed and deployed on a solid ethical foundation that seeks to promote community agency, cultural sovereignty and fair benefit-sharing. Human-AI collaboration should be an empowerment, not a substitution, so that technology is a complementary, augmentative tool that extends the voice and agency of native speakers.

Speech recognition, machine translation, adaptive learning systems, and virtual and augmented reality-based simulated environments are all artificial intelligence-based language learning technologies with unprecedented potential to provide language education that is accessible, interactive, and culturally sensitive, particularly for remote and marginalized populations. Their success depends on participatory design processes that prioritize members of these communities in the development and control of language technologies, in a way that respects and takes into account their cultural beliefs and values.

Synthetic data creation and other such technologies address the age-old problem of data scarcity in endangered languages by generating linguistically rich and privacy-preserving content that supports computational modeling without compromising authenticity. AI-supported storytelling with culturally sensitive knowledge graphs and narrative frameworks facilitates the digital preservation and dissemination of oral traditions with moral and symbolic undertones that bridge intergenerational gaps in language use and cultural awareness.

Ultimately, the fate of endangered language preservation depends on a balance between technological progress and community empowerment. A sustained collaboration between linguists, technologists, policy makers and indigenous communities based on social justice and cultural sustainability is needed. With this collaboration, AI can be a wise and useful partner in language preservation so that the world's languages are preserved as living, dynamic repositories of human heritage for the enrichment of future generations.

REFERENCES

Afra, D. I. N., Uliniansyah, M. T., Latief, A. D. Yuyun, Nurfadhilah, E., Gunarso, & Sampurno, T. (2024). Neural Machine Translation for Low-Resource Languages: Experiments on Makassar-Indonesian. 2024 International Conference on Computer, Control, Informatics and Its Applications (IC3INA), 66–71. DOI: 10.1109/IC3INA64086.2024.10732202

Agyei, E., Zhang, X., Bannerman, S., Quaye, A. B., Yussi, S. B., & Agbesi, V. K. (2024). Low-resource Twi-English parallel corpus for machine translation in multiple domains (Twi-2-ENG). *Discover Computing*, *27*(1), 17. Advance online publication. DOI: 10.1007/s10791-024-09451-8

AI & Society. (2024). Cognitive imperialism in artificial intelligence: Counteracting bias with indigenous epistemologies. https://link.springer.com/article/10.1007/s00146-024-02065-0

Aikhenvald, A. Y. (2020). Language Contact and Endangered Languages. In Grant, A. P. (Ed.), *The Oxford Handbook of Language Contact* (pp. 240–260). Oxford University Press., DOI: 10.1093/oxfordhb/9780199945092.013.11

Amano, T., Sandel, B., Eager, H., Bulteau, E., Svenning, J. C., Dalsgaard, B., Rahbek, C., Davies, R. G., & Sutherland, W. J. (2014). Global distribution and drivers of language extinction risk. Proceedings of the Royal Society B: Biological Sciences, 281(1793). DOI: 10.1098/rspb.2014.1574

Andina, E. (2023). Implementasi dan Tantangan Revitalisasi Bahasa Daerah di Provinsi Lampung. Aspirasi. *Jurnal Masalah-Masalah Sosial*, *14*(1). Advance online publication. DOI: 10.46807/aspirasi.v14i1.3859

Ardila, R., Branson, M., Davis, K., Henretty, M., Kohler, M., Meyer, J., Morais, R., Saunders, L., Tyers, F. M., & Weber, G. (2020). Common voice: A massively-multilingual speech corpus. LREC 2020 - 12th International Conference on Language Resources and Evaluation, Conference Proceedings, 4218–4222. https://aclanthology.org/2020.lrec-1.520/

Arkadiev, P., & Lander, Y. (2021). The northwest caucasian languages. In The Oxford Handbook of Languages of the Caucasus. DOI: 10.1093/oxfordhb/9780190690694.013.3

Arnold, M. (2022). Multilingual Research Projects: Non-Latin Script Challenges for Making Use of Standards, Authority Files, and Character Recognition. Digital Studies / Le Champ Numérique, 12(1). DOI: 10.16995/dscn.8110

Austin, P. K. (2021). Language Documentation and Language Revitalization. In Revitalizing Endangered Languages (pp. 199–219). Cambridge University Press. DOI: 10.1017/9781108641142.014

Bahroun, Z., Anane, C., Ahmed, V., & Zacca, A. (2023). Transforming Education: A Comprehensive Review of Generative Artificial Intelligence in Educational Settings through Bibliometric and Content Analysis. In Sustainability (Switzerland) (Vol. 15, Issue 17). Multidisciplinary Digital Publishing Institute (MDPI). DOI: 10.3390/su151712983

Baker, S., & Xiang, W. (2023). Explainable AI is Responsible AI: How Explainability Creates Trustworthy and Socially Responsible Artificial Intelligence. arXiv. https://arxiv.org/abs/2312.01555

Barrios, C. D. (2022, February 21). A decade to prevent the disappearance of 3000 languages. UNESCO IESALC. https://www.iesalc.unesco.org/en/2022/02/21/a-decade-to-prevent-the-disappearance-of-3000-languages/

Bendel, O., & Jabou, D. (2024). @llegra: A chatbot for Vallader. *International Journal of Information Technology : an Official Journal of Bharati Vidyapeeth's Institute of Computer Applications and Management*, *16*(4), 2035–2045. DOI: 10.1007/s41870-024-01779-0

Bender, E. K. (2024, January 25). Can small language models revitalize Indigenous languages? Brookings. https://www.brookings.edu/articles/can-small-language-models-revitalize-indigenous-languages/

Berardi-Wiltshire, A., Whan, C., Maia, M., Nascimento, M. G., Petrucci, P., Te-Hei, B. M. R., & Warren, K. T. R. (2020). The Challenge of New Intercultural Maps: Indigenous Language Revitalization Between Brazil and Aotearoa/New Zealand. In Handbook of the Changing World Language Map (pp. 1547–1569). Springer International Publishing. DOI: 10.1007/978-3-030-02438-3_121

Bird, S. (2020). Decolonising Speech and Language Technology. *Proceedings of the 28th International Conference on Computational Linguistics*, 3504–3519. DOI: 10.18653/v1/2020.coling-main.313

Bisconti, P., Orsitto, D., Fedorczyk, F., Brau, F., Capasso, M., De Marinis, L., Eken, H., Merenda, F., Forti, M., Pacini, M., & Schettini, C. (2023). Maximizing team synergy in AI-related interdisciplinary groups: An interdisciplinary-by-design iterative methodology. *AI & Society*, *38*(4), 1443–1452. DOI: 10.1007/s00146-022-01518-8

Brown, T. B., Mann, B., Ryder, N., Subbiah, M., Kaplan, J., Dhariwal, P., Neelakantan, A., Shyam, P., Sastry, G., Askell, A., Agarwal, S., Herbert-Voss, A., Krueger, G., Henighan, T., Child, R., Ramesh, A., Ziegler, D. M., Wu, J., Winter, C., . . . Amodei, D. (2020, May 28). *Language Models are Few-Shot Learners*. arXiv.org. https://arxiv.org/abs/2005.14165

Carroll, S. R., Garba, I., Figueroa-Rodríguez, O. L., Holbrook, J., Lovett, R., Materechera, S., Parsons, M., Raseroka, K., Rodriguez-Lonebear, D., Rowe, R., Sara, R., Walker, J. D., Anderson, J., & Hudson, M. (2020). The CARE Principles for Indigenous Data Governance. *Data Science Journal*, *19*(1), 43. DOI: 10.5334/dsj-2020-043

Chen, C.-Y., Chen, W.-T., & Huang, H.-Y. (2024). Foundation models for low-resource language education (Vision Paper). arXiv. https://arxiv.org/abs/2412.04774

Chen, Z., & Yang, H. (2020). Yi Language Speech Recognition using Deep Learning Methods. Proceedings of 2020 IEEE 4th Information Technology, Networking, Electronic and Automation Control Conference, ITNEC 2020, 1064–1068. DOI: 10.1109/ITNEC48623.2020.9084771

Chiang, C.-H., & Lee, H.-Y. (2022). On the Transferability of Pre-trained Language Models: A Study from Artificial Datasets. *Proceedings of the 36th AAAI Conference on Artificial Intelligence, AAAI 2022*, 36, 10518–10525. DOI: 10.1609/aaai.v36i10.21295

Chiaráin, N. N., & Chasaide, A. N. (2016, May 1). *Chatbot Technology with Synthetic Voices in the Acquisition of an Endangered Language: Motivation, Development and Evaluation of a Platform for Irish*. ACL Anthology. https://aclanthology.org/L16-1547/?utm_source=chatgpt.com

Chigwada, J., & Ngulube, P. (2024). Librarians' role in the preservation and dissemination of indigenous knowledge. *IFLA Journal*, *50*(2), 242–256. DOI: 10.1177/03400352231217270

Chizzoni, I., & Vietti, A. (2024). Towards an ASR System for Documenting Endangered Languages: A Preliminary Study on Sardinian. *CEUR Workshop Proceedings*, *3878*, •••. https://ceur-ws.org/Vol-3878/25_main_long.pdf

Chomsky, N. (1957). *Syntactic Structures*. Mouton. DOI: 10.1515/9783112316009

Chui, J. (2023). The Effects of Cultural Assimilation on the Loss of the Tuvan and Seri Languages. *Journal of Student Research*, *11*(3). Advance online publication. DOI: 10.47611/jsr.v11i3.1714

Conneau, A., Khandelwal, K., Goyal, N., Chaudhary, V., Wenzek, G., Guzmán, F., Grave, E., Ott, M., Zettlemoyer, L., & Stoyanov, V. (2019). Unsupervised Cross-lingual Representation Learning at Scale. https://arxiv.org/abs/1911.02116

Corbett, J. (2023). Cree coding decolonizes computer programming. SFU. Cree coding decolonizes computer programming - Simon Fraser University.

Costa, J. (2024). Why language revitalization fails: Revivalist vs. traditional ontologies of language in Provence. *Language in Society*, •••, 1–21. DOI: 10.1017/S0047404524000204

Couzens, V., Gaby, A., & Stebbins, T. (2020). Standardise This! Prescriptivism and Resistance to Standardization in Language Revitalization. In Allan, K. (Ed.), *Dynamics of Language Changes* (pp. 37–55). Springer Singapore., DOI: 10.1007/978-981-15-6430-7_3

Crystal, D. (2002). *Language Death*. Cambridge University Press., DOI: 10.1017/CBO9781139871549

Dai, D. W., & Hua, Z. (2024). When AI meets intercultural communication: New frontiers, new agendas. In *Applied Linguistics Review*. De Gruyter Mouton., DOI: 10.1515/applirev-2024-0185

Dai, Y., & Wu, Z. (2021). Mobile-assisted pronunciation learning with feedback from peers and/or automatic speech recognition: A mixed-methods study. *Computer Assisted Language Learning*, *36*(5–6), 861–884. DOI: 10.1080/09588221.2021.1952272

Deacon, H. J. (2020). Ethics, intellectual property, and commercialization of cultural heritage. *Pravovedenie*, *64*(1), 93–111. DOI: 10.21638/spbu25.2020.108

Dolenc, K., Šorgo, A., & Ploj-Virtič, M. (2021). Perspectives on Lessons From the COVID-19 Outbreak for Post-pandemic Higher Education: Continuance Intention Model of Forced Online Distance Teaching. European Journal of Educational Research, volume-11-2022(volume-11-issue-1-january-2022), 163–177. DOI: 10.12973/eu-jer.11.1.163

Dueñas, F. K. (2015). Negotiating Ideological and Implementational Spaces for Indigenous Languages in Peru. Working Papers in Educational Linguistics, 30(1), 21–41. https://wpel.gse.upenn.edu/sites/default/files/WPEL30.1Kvietok_Duenas.pdf

Eberhard, D. M., Simons, G. F., & Fennig, C. D. (2024). Ethnologue: Languages of the World. Twenty-seventh edition. http://www.ethnologue.com

Eisenstein, J. (2013). What to do about bad language on the internet. Proceedings of the 2nd Workshop on Computational Linguistics for Literature, CLfL 2013 at the 2013 Conference of the North American Chapter of the Association for Computational Linguistics: Human Language Technologies, NAACL-HLT 2013, 359–369. https://aclanthology.org/N13-1037/

Epps, P. (2020). Amazonian linguistic diversity and its sociocultural correlates. In Language Dispersal, Diversification, and Contact (pp. 275–290). Oxford University Press. DOI: 10.1093/oso/9780198723813.003.0016

Erawati, N. K. R., Laksmi, N. K. P. A., & Suparwa, I. N. (2023). The Historical Dynamics of the Archaistic Lexicon in Modern Balinese Languages. *Journal of Language Teaching and Research*, *14*(1), 172–180. DOI: 10.17507/jltr.1401.18

Facundes, S. da S., Virtanen, P. K., de Freitas, M. F. P., Lima-Padovani, B. F. S., & do Nascimento Costa, P. (2019). Language Revitalization and Engagements in the Amazon: The Case of Apurinã. In Handbook of the Changing World Language Map (pp. 1–17). Springer International Publishing. DOI: 10.1007/978-3-319-73400-2_35-1

Font de la Vall, R. R., & Araya, F. G. (2023). Exploring the Benefits and Challenges of AI-Language Learning Tools. *International Journal of Social Sciences and Humanities Invention*, *10*(01), 7569–7576. DOI: 10.18535/ijsshi/v10i01.02

Fredholm, K. (2023). Challenges and needs in Ladino teaching among ten language revitalisation activists. Meldar. *Revista Internacional de Estudios Sefardíes*, *4*(4), 43–69. DOI: 10.46661/meldar.8525

Gedeon, M. M., Samantaray, S., & René, K. B. (2024). Changing the Trajectory: Preserving the Linguistic Diversity of Shi Language Using AI and NLP (pp. 57–69). DOI: 10.1007/978-981-97-1987-7_5

Getachew, S., & Yayeh, Y. (2023). Gex'ez-English Bi-Directional Neural Machine Translation Using Transformer. 2023 International Conference on Information and Communication Technology for Development for Africa (ICT4DA), 160–164. DOI: 10.1109/ICT4DA59526.2023.10302254

Godwin-Jones, R. (2024, March 29). Distributed agency in second language learning and teaching through generative AI. arXiv.org. https://arxiv.org/abs/2403.20216

Goncalves, A., Ray, P., Soper, B., Stevens, J., Coyle, L., & Sales, A. P. (2020). Generation and evaluation of synthetic patient data. *BMC Medical Research Methodology*, *20*(1), 108. Advance online publication. DOI: 10.1186/s12874-020-00977-1

Google. (2021, May 5). Woolaroo: A new tool for exploring indigenous languages. Google Arts & Culture Blog. https://blog.google/outreach-initiatives/arts-culture/woolaroo-new-tool-exploring-indigenous-languages/

Guerrettaz, A. M., & Engman, M. M. (2023). Indigenous Language Revitalization. In *Oxford Research Encyclopedia of Education*. Oxford University Press., DOI: 10.1093/acrefore/9780190264093.013.559

Guo, X., & Chen, Y. (2024). Generative AI for Synthetic Data Generation: Methods, Challenges and the Future. https://arxiv.org/abs/2403.04190

Håkansson, A., & Phillips-Wren, G. (2024). Generative AI and large language models - benefits, drawbacks, future and recommendations. *Procedia Computer Science*, *246*, 5458–5468. DOI: 10.1016/j.procs.2024.09.689

Hale, K. (1992). Endangered languages: On endangered languages and the safeguarding of diversity. *Language*, *68*(1), 1–42. DOI: 10.1353/lan.1992.0052

Han, A., & Cai, Z. (2023). Design implications of generative AI systems for visual storytelling for young learners. Proceedings of IDC 2023 - 22nd Annual ACM Interaction Design and Children Conference: Rediscovering Childhood, 470–474. DOI: 10.1145/3585088.3593867

Hatipoğlu, Ç., Delibegović Džanić, N., Gajek, E., & Miloshevska, L. (2022). Crowdsourcing and language learning habits and practices in Turkey, Bosnia and Herzegovina, the Republic of North Macedonia and Poland in the pre-pandemic and pandemic periods. Slovenščina 2.0: Empirical. *Applied and Interdisciplinary Research*, *10*(2), 132–183. DOI: 10.4312/slo2.0.2022.2.132-183

Heath, M. K., Gleason, B., Mehta, R., & Hall, T. (2024). More than knowing: Toward collective, critical, and ecological approaches in educational technology research. *Educational Technology Research and Development*, *72*(5), 2519–2541. DOI: 10.1007/s11423-023-10242-z

Herrera-González, B. D., Gelbukh, A., & Calvo, H. (2020). Automatic Story Generation: State of the Art and Recent Trends (pp. 81–91). DOI: 10.1007/978-3-030-60887-3_8

Historica Canada. (2023, November 28). AI-powered preservation of endangered languages. https://www.historica.org/blog/ai-powered-preservation-of-endangered-languages

Huang, X., Zou, D., Cheng, G., & Xie, H. (2021). A Systematic Review of AR and VR Enhanced Language Learning. *Sustainability (Basel)*, *13*(9), 4639. DOI: 10.3390/su13094639

Jafari, Z. (2023). The Role of AI in Supporting Indigenous Languages. *AI and Tech in Behavioral and Social Sciences*, *1*(2), 4–11. DOI: 10.61838/kman.aitech.1.2.2

Jafarzade, S. (2020). Culture has an impact on a language. *Science Bulletin*, *2*, 12–18. DOI: 10.54414/lbsc1457

Jaworski, R., Seljan, S., & Dunđer, I. (2023). Four Million Segments and Counting: Building an English-Croatian Parallel Corpus through Crowdsourcing Using a Novel Gamification-Based Platform. *Information (Basel)*, *14*(4), 226. Advance online publication. DOI: 10.3390/info14040226

Jiang, N., Liu, X., Liu, H., Lim, E. T. K., Tan, C. W., & Gu, J. (2023). Beyond AI-powered context-aware services: The role of human–AI collaboration. *Industrial Management & Data Systems*, *123*(11), 2771–2802. DOI: 10.1108/IMDS-03-2022-0152

Joshi, R., Singla, K., Kamath, A., Kalani, R., Paul, R., Vaidya, U., Chauhan, S. S., Wartikar, N., & Long, E. (2024). Adapting Multilingual LLMs to Low-Resource Languages using Continued Pre-training and Synthetic Corpus. https://arxiv.org/abs/2410.14815

Joyner, J. (2007, September 19). Dying Languages – Cause for Concern? Outside The Beltway. https://outsidethebeltway.com/dying_languages_-_cause_for_concern/

Kanoksilapatham, B. (2020). Local Culture Preservation through Southern Thainess-Based English Lessons. *KEMANUSIAAN The Asian Journal of Humanities*, *27*(2), 179–199. DOI: 10.21315/kajh2020.27.2.10

Kavitha, R., Fathma, S. S., & Vinitha, V. (2023). AI: a catalyst for language Preservation in the digital era. *Shanlax International Journal of English, 12*(S1-Dec), 102–106. DOI: 10.34293/rtdh.v12iS1-Dec.39

Kik, A., Adamec, M., Aikhenvald, A. Y., Bajzekova, J., Baro, N., Bowern, C., Colwell, R. K., Drozd, P., Duda, P., Ibalim, S., Jorge, L. R., Mogina, J., Ruli, B., Sam, K., Sarvasy, H., Saulei, S., Weiblen, G. D., Zrzavy, J., & Novotny, V. (2021). Language and ethnobiological skills decline precipitously in Papua New Guinea, the world's most linguistically diverse nation. *Proceedings of the National Academy of Sciences of the United States of America*, *118*(22), e2100096118. Advance online publication. DOI: 10.1073/pnas.2100096118

Kimera, R., Kim, Y.-S., & Choi, H. (2024). Advancing AI with Integrity: Ethical Challenges and Solutions in Neural Machine Translation. arXiv. https://doi.org//arXiv.2404.01070DOI: 10.48550

Kohnke, L., Moorhouse, B. L., & Zou, D. (2023). ChatGPT for Language Teaching and Learning. In Journal, R. E. L. C. (Ed.), *Issue 2* (Vol. 54, pp. 537–550). SAGE Publications Ltd., DOI: 10.1177/00336882231162868

Kondic, A. (2021). Data collection for a documentation project: South Eastern Huastec (Mayan, Mexico). In Strategies for Knowledge Elicitation: The Experience of the Russian School of Field Linguistics. DOI: 10.1007/978-3-030-79341-8_14

Kramsch, C. (1995). The cultural component of language teaching. *Language, Culture and Curriculum, 8*(2), 83–92. DOI: 10.1080/07908319509525192

Kramsch, C. (2014). Language and Culture. *AILA Review, 27*, 30–55. DOI: 10.1075/aila.27.02kra

Krashen, S. D. (1982). *Principles and practice in second language acquisition.* Pergamon Press.

Kucherbayeva, D., & Smagulova, J. (2023). Language Revitalization: Challenges for Kazakh in Higher Education. *Journal of Eurasian Studies, 14*(2), 166–178. DOI: 10.1177/18793665231189326

Kurakin, A., Ponomareva, N., Syed, U., MacDermed, L., & Terzis, A. (2023). Harnessing large-language models to generate private synthetic text. https://arxiv.org/abs/2306.01684

Lane, P. (2023). From Silence to Silencing? Contradictions and tensions in language revitalization. *Applied Linguistics, 44*(5), 833–847. DOI: 10.1093/applin/amac075

Latief, A. D. Yuyun, Uliniansyah, M. T., Nurfadhilah, E., Komariah, K. S., Isnaeni Nurul Afra, D., Gunarso, Sampurno, T., Jufri, N., Gusnawaty, Rosvita, I., Kaharuddin, M. N., Muis, A., & Hazriani. (2024). Enhancing Bugis Language POS Tagging Using Recurrent Neural Networks and Semi-Supervised Self-Training. 2024 International Conference on Computer, Control, Informatics and Its Applications (IC3INA), 219–224. DOI: 10.1109/IC3INA64086.2024.10732738

Li, Z., Zhu, H., Lu, Z., & Yin, M. (2023). Synthetic Data Generation with Large Language Models for Text Classification: Potential and Limitations. *Proceedings of the 2023 Conference on Empirical Methods in Natural Language Processing*, 10443–10461. DOI: 10.18653/v1/2023.emnlp-main.647

Linguistics News. (2023, December 19). How Globalization is Impacting Language Extinction Rates. Linguistics News. https://linguisticsnews.com/insight/how-globalization-is-impacting-language-extinction-rates/

Lisagor, M. (2025, April 10). Language preservation efforts get an AI boost. Dartmouth News. https://home.dartmouth.edu/news/2025/04/language-preservations-efforts-get-ai-boost

Liu, Z. (2022). Effective Transfer Learning for Low-Resource Natural Language Understanding. https://arxiv.org/abs/2208.09180 DOI: 10.14711/thesis-991013106358603412

Liu, Z., Richardson, C., Hatcher, R., Jr., & Prud'hommeaux, E. (2022). Not always about you: Prioritizing community needs when developing endangered language technology. arXiv preprint arXiv:2204.05541. https://arxiv.org/abs/2204.05541 DOI: 10.18653/v1/2022.acl-long.272

McCarty, T. L., Romero-Little, M. E., & Zepeda, O. (2006). Native American Youth Discourses on Language Shift and Retention: Ideological Crosscurrents and Their Implications for Language Planning. *International Journal of Bilingual Education and Bilingualism*, *9*(5), 659–677. DOI: 10.2167/beb386.0

Meelen, M., O'Neill, A., & Coto-Solano, R. (2024). End-to-End Speech Recognition for Endangered Languages of Nepal. Proceedings of the Seventh Workshop on the Use of Computational Methods in the Study of Endangered Languages, 83–93. https://aclanthology.org/2024.computel-1.12/

Miceli, M., Yang, T., Alvarado Garcia, A., Posada, J., Wang, S. M., Pohl, M., & Hanna, A. (2022). Documenting data production processes: A participatory approach for data work. arXiv: 2207.04958 Documenting Data Production Processes: A Participatory Approach for Data Work

Morales, A., Ono, K., & Kim, S. (2025). Generative AI and large language models in language preservation: Opportunities and challenges. arXiv. https://arxiv.org/abs/2501.11496v2

Mumpande, I., & Barnes, L. (2022). Obstacles and Challenges Confronting Tonga Revitalisation in Zimbabwe. *Language Matters (Pretoria)*, *53*(3), 25–46. DOI: 10.1080/10228195.2022.2125553

Munday, P. (2015). The Case for Using Duolingo as Part of the Language Classroom Experience. *RIED Revista Iberoamericana de Educación a Distancia*, *19*(1). Advance online publication. DOI: 10.5944/ried.19.1.14581

Nagy, L., & Hortobagyi, I. (2023). Novel approaches to contemporary minority language revitalization. Bulletin of the Transilvania University of Brasov. Series IV: Philology and Cultural Studies, 85–100. DOI: 10.31926/but.pcs.2023.65.16.1.6

Nanduri, D. K., & Bonsignore, E. M. (2023). Revitalizing Endangered Languages: AI-powered language learning as a catalyst for language appreciation. https://doi.org//arXiv.2304.09394DOI: 10.48550

Negia, M. K., Tamiru, R. M., & Meshesha, M. (2022). Amharic-Kistanigna Bi-directional Machine Translation using Deep Learning. 2022 International Conference on Information and Communication Technology for Development for Africa (ICT4DA), 61–65. DOI: 10.1109/ICT4DA56482.2022.9971194

Nekoto, W., Marivate, V., Matsila, T., Fasubaa, T., Fagbohungbe, T., Akinola, S. O., . . . Adelani, D. I. (2020). Participatory research for low-resourced machine translation: A case study in African languages. Findings of EMNLP 2020, 2144–2160. https://aclanthology.org/2020.findings-emnlp.195

Ngoc Le, T., & Sadat, F. (2020). Revitalization of Indigenous Languages through Pre-processing and Neural Machine Translation: The case of Inuktitut. *Proceedings of the 28th International Conference on Computational Linguistics*, 4661–4666. DOI: 10.18653/v1/2020.coling-main.410

Novák, A., Barcza, B., & Horváth, D. (2024). LLMs for extremely low-resource Finno-Ugric languages. arXiv. https://arxiv.org/abs/2410.18902

Ofosu-Asare, Y. (2024). Cognitive imperialism in artificial intelligence: Counteracting bias with indigenous epistemologies. *AI & Society*, *40*(4), 3045–3061. DOI: 10.1007/s00146-024-02065-0

Park, N., Regenbrecht, H., Duncan, S., Mills, S., Lindeman, R. W., Pantidi, N., & Whaanga, H. (2022). Mixed Reality Co-Design for Indigenous Culture Preservation Continuation. Proceedings - 2022 IEEE Conference on Virtual Reality and 3D User Interfaces, VR 2022, 149–157. DOI: 10.1109/VR51125.2022.00033

Parmaxi, A., & Demetriou, A. A. (2020). Augmented reality in language learning: A state-of-the-art review of 2014–2019. In Journal of Computer Assisted Learning (Vol. 36, Issue 6, pp. 861–875). Blackwell Publishing Ltd. DOI: 10.1111/jcal.12486

Pedro. (2019). Challenges and Opportunities for Sustainable Development Education Sector United Nations Educational, Scientific and Cultural Organization. https://en.unesco.org/themes/education-policy-

Pereltsvaig, A. (2012, January 25). Obituary: The Ubykh Language. Languages of The World. https://www.languagesoftheworld.info/geolinguistics/obituary-the-ubykh-language.html

Pinhanez, C., Cavalin, P., Storto, L., Finbow, T., Cobbinah, A., Nogima, J., Vasconcelos, M., Domingues, P., De Souza Mizukami, P., Grell, N., Gongora, M., & Gonçalves, I. (2024, July 17). Harnessing the power of artificial intelligence to vitalize endangered Indigenous languages: technologies and experiences. arXiv.org. https://arxiv.org/abs/2407.12620

Prieto, J., Martinez, C., Robles, M., Moreno, A., Palacios, S., & Manrique, R. (2024). Translation systems for low-resource Colombian Indigenous languages, a first step towards cultural preservation. *Proceedings of the 4th Workshop on Natural Language Processing for Indigenous Languages of the Americas (AmericasNLP 2024)*, 7–14. DOI: 10.18653/v1/2024.americasnlp-1.2

Rahman, N., Wahyuddin, W., & Fariza, M. N. (2024). La Galigo: Representation and Reference in Bugis Culture. *International Journal of Religion*, *5*(10), 3635–3644. DOI: 10.61707/xwc7fr98

Rameshkumar, R., & Bailey, P. (2020). Storytelling with Dialogue: A Critical Role Dungeons and Dragons Dataset. *Proceedings of the 58th Annual Meeting of the Association for Computational Linguistics*, 5121–5134. DOI: 10.18653/v1/2020.acl-main.459

Ribeiro, R. V., Bieski, I. G. C., Balogun, S. O., & Martins, D. T. de O. (2017). Ethnobotanical study of medicinal plants used by Ribeirinhos in the North Araguaia microregion, Mato Grosso, Brazil. *Journal of Ethnopharmacology*, *205*, 69–102. DOI: 10.1016/j.jep.2017.04.023

Robles, M., Martínez, C. A., Prieto, J. C., Palacios, S., & Manrique, R. (2024). Preserving Heritage: Developing a Translation Tool for Indigenous Dialects. *Proceedings of the 17th ACM International Conference on Web Search and Data Mining*, 1200–1203. DOI: 10.1145/3616855.3637828

Sambamurthy, P. (2024). The Intersection of AI and Human Intelligence. [IJCET]. *International Journal of Computer Engineering and Technology*, *15*(4), 251–264. https://iaeme.com/Home/article_id/IJCET_15_04_021

Samuel, C., & Ali, I. T. (2024). Batak Toba language-Indonesian machine translation with transfer learning using no language left behind. *International Journal of Advances in Applied Sciences*, *13*(4), 830. DOI: 10.11591/ijaas.v13.i4.pp830-839

Sawaki, Y. W. (2019). Meneropong Tipologi Bahasa-bahasa di Papua: Suatu Tinjauan Singkat. *Linguistik Indonesia*, *36*(2), 129–143. DOI: 10.26499/li.v36i2.79

Scarino, A. (2008). Community and culture in intercultural language learning. *Australian Review of Applied Linguistics, 31*(1), 5.1–5.15. Advance online publication. DOI: 10.2104/aral0805

Schmidt, T., & Strassner, T. (2022). Artificial Intelligence in Foreign Language Learning and Teaching. *Anglistik, 33*(1), 165–184. DOI: 10.33675/ANGL/2022/1/14

Seyfeddinipur, M., Krifka, M., Ameka, F., Kung, S., Bolton, L., Monroig, M., Blumtritt, J., Neba, A. N., Carpenter, B., Nordhoff, S., Cruz, H., Pakendorf, B., Drude, S., von Prince, K., Epps, P. L., Rau, F., Ferreira, V., Rice, K., Galucio, A. V., & Woodbury, T. (2019). Public access to research data in language documentation: Challenges and possible strategies. *Language Documentation and Conservation, 13*, 545–563. http://hdl.handle.net/10125/24901

Shadiev, R., Liu, T., & Hwang, W. (2020). Review of research on mobile-assisted language learning in familiar, authentic environments. *British Journal of Educational Technology, 51*(3), 709–720. DOI: 10.1111/bjet.12839

Shorten, C., Khoshgoftaar, T. M., & Furht, B. (2021). Text Data Augmentation for Deep Learning. *Journal of Big Data, 8*(1), 101. Advance online publication. DOI: 10.1186/s40537-021-00492-0

Singh, A. K. (2021). Legal Protection of Endangered Languages in India with Reference to Meghalaya. *IARS International Research Journal, 11*(1), 25–30. DOI: 10.51611/iars.irj.v11i1.2021.152

Skille, E. Å., Pedersen, S., & Skille, Ø. (2023). Friluftsliv and olggonastin – multiple and complex nature cultures. *Journal of Adventure Education and Outdoor Learning*, •••, 1–13. DOI: 10.1080/14729679.2023.2254862

Snyder, B. (2010). Unsupervised multilingual learning [Doctoral dissertation, Massachusetts Institute of Technology, Massachusetts Institute of Technology]. http://dspace.mit.edu/handle/1721.1/7582

Strang, B. (2020, January 15). Duolingo app to add te reo Māori course for beginners. RNZ (Radio New Zealand). https://www.rnz.co.nz/news/te-manu-korihi/407379/duolingo-app-to-add-te-reo-maori-course-for-beginners

Te Hiku Media. (2018). Papa Reo: Sovereign Māori data and the future of language technology. https://www.tehiku.nz/te-hiku-media/te-reo/27153/papa-reo-maori-data-and-language-tech

Te Hiku Media. (2024, September 5). Thousands of Indigenous languages face extinction, but AI provides hope. Time Magazine. https://time.com/6321970/ai-indigenous-languages-preservation/

TeenVogue. (2023). Indigenous youth are using coding and AI to save Native languages. https://www.teenvogue.com/story/these-coding-camps-are-teaching-indigenous-youth-to-save-native-language-through-ai

Tiddi, I., Lécué, F., & Hitzler, P. (2020). *Knowledge Graphs for eXplainable Artificial Intelligence: Foundations, Applications and Challenges* (Vol. 47). IOS Press.

Time. (2024a). Peter-Lucas Jones. https://time.com/7012841/peter-lucas-jones/

Time. (2024b). Endang Aminudin Aziz. https://time.com/7012839/endang-aminudin-aziz/

Tseng, H., Jurafsky, D., & Manning, C. (2005). Morphological features help POS tagging of unknown words across language varieties. SIGHAN@IJCNLP 2005 - 4th SIGHAN Workshop on Chinese Language Processing, Proceedings of the Workshop, 32–39. https://aclanthology.org/I05-3005.pdf

Tulgar, A. T., Yilmaz, R. M., & Topu, F. B. (2022). Research Trends on the Use of Augmented Reality Technology in Teaching English as a Foreign Language. *Participatory Educational Research*, *9*(5), 76–104. DOI: 10.17275/per.22.105.9.5

Ugwu, E. O. (2020). English Language, Globalisation and the Future of the Nigerian Indigenous Languages. *European Scientific Journal*, *16*(14), 38. Advance online publication. DOI: 10.19044/esj.2020.v16n14p38

Uliniansyah, M. T., Santosa, A., & Perdana, R. A. (2024). Enhancing OCR Accuracy for Bugis Language to Bahasa Indonesia Dictionary Conversion through Image Pre-processing and Scaling Techniques. 2024 International Conference on Computer, Control, Informatics and Its Applications (IC3INA), 452–457. DOI: 10.1109/IC3INA64086.2024.10732090

UNESCO. (2010). Reaching the marginalized | EFA Global Monitoring Report. UNESCO Publishing. https://www.unesco.org/gem-report/en/reaching-marginalized

UNESCO. (2023, November 28). National consultation on Indigenous languages: A call for preservation and technology integration. https://www.unesco.org/en/articles/national-consultation-indigenous-languages-call-preservation-and-technology-integration

Virtanen, T., Lindén, M., & Haaranen, A. (2021). AR/VR solutions for Sámi language learning. *Nordic Journal of Indigenous Studies*, *3*(2), 45–60. DOI: 10.7557/13.6461

Viterbi Conversations in Ethics. (2025). Preserving the past: AI in Indigenous language preservation. https://vce.usc.edu/weekly-news-profile/preserving-the-past-ai-in-indigenous-language-preservation/

Voinov, V. (2010). Words should be fun: Scrabble as a tool for language preservation in Tuvan and other local languages 1. 4, 213–230. https://scholarspace.manoa.hawaii.edu/items/2157ea03-e476-4f15-bd96-fe3422a46610

Wan, N., & Cumming, T. M. (Eds.). (2015). *Sustaining Mobile Learning*. Routledge., DOI: 10.4324/9781315766553

Wilder, B. T., O'Meara, C., Monti, L., & Nabhan, G. P. (2016). The Importance of Indigenous Knowledge in Curbing the Loss of Language and Biodiversity. In BioScience (Vol. 66, Issue 6, pp. 499–509). Oxford University Press. DOI: 10.1093/biosci/biw026

Wiltshire, B., Bird, S., & Hardwick, R. (2024). Understanding how language revitalisation works: A realist synthesis. *Journal of Multilingual and Multicultural Development*, *45*(9), 3946–3962. DOI: 10.1080/01434632.2022.2134877

Wired. (2021, June 24). Māori are trying to save their language from Big Tech. Wired. https://www.wired.com/story/maori-language-artificial-intelligence/

Wood, J. (2022, January 5). 1,500 endangered languages could disappear by the end of the century. World Economic Forum. https://www.weforum.org/stories/2022/01/languages-endangered-diversity-loss-spoken/

Wu, N. (2018, October 9). Hawaiian language course now available on Duolingo. Star Advertiser. https://www.staradvertiser.com/2018/10/09/breaking-news/hawaiian-language-course-now-available-on-duolingo/

Wu, Y., Schuster, M., Chen, Z., Le, Q. V., Norouzi, M., Macherey, W., Krikun, M., Cao, Y., Gao, Q., Macherey, K., Klingner, J., Shah, A., Johnson, M., Liu, X., Kaiser, Ł., Gouws, S., Kato, Y., Kudo, T., Kazawa, H., & Dean, J. (2016). Google's Neural Machine Translation System: Bridging the Gap between Human and Machine Translation. https://arxiv.org/abs/1609.08144

Wu, Z., Qi, S., & Zuo, L. (2024). Learning endangered languages in LLMs with in-context linguistic descriptions. arXiv. https://arxiv.org/abs/2402.18025v2

Yang, I., Ma, W., & Vosoughi, S. (2024). NüshuRescue: Revitalization of the endangered Nüshu language with AI. CoRR, abs/2412.00218.

Yuyun, Y., Prakasa, E., Uliniansyah, M. T., Latief, A. D., Karsanti, H. T., Jarin, A., Munawirah, M., Hazriani, H., Zahrani, Z., & Gunarso, G. (2024). Enhancing Neural Machine Translation Model for Low-Resource Languages: A Case Study of Indonesian to Mamuju. DOI: 10.2139/ssrn.4872856

Zabetian, F. (2024, April 1). 10 stats & breakthroughs in AI speech translation in 2024. KUDO. https://kudo.ai/blog/the-10-most-important-statistics-breakthroughs-in-ai-speech-translation-from-2024/

Zhang, F. (2024). Globalisation and Minority Languages: A Critical Analysis of the Impact of Globalisation on Minority Languages. *International Journal of Frontiers in Sociology*, *6*(4). Advance online publication. DOI: 10.25236/IJFS.2024.060404

ADDITIONAL READING

Apriliani, D. (2023). Penggunaan artificial intelligence dalam pembelajaran bahasa Indonesia. *DIKBASTRA: Jurnal Pendidikan Bahasa dan Sastra*. https://online-journal.unja.ac.id/dikbastra/article/download/33262/18921/110441

Badan Pengembangan dan Pembinaan Bahasa. (2024). *Revitalisasi bahasa daerah di Indonesia: Integrasi teknologi AI dan pendekatan berbasis komunitas*. https://badanbahasa.kemdikbud.go.id/resource/doc/files/risalah_nomor_7_rev.pdf

Dewantoro, R. (2024). Kecerdasan buatan untuk pelestarian bahasa lokal. *Kumparan*. https://kumparan.com/rizki-dewantoro/kecerdasan-buatan-untuk-pelestarian-bahasa-lokal-23hVmCF4LNI

Febrian, A. (2024). Mesin penerjemah bertenaga AI untuk selamatkan bahasa daerah yang terancam punah. *VOA Indonesia*. https://www.voaindonesia.com/a/mesin-penerjemah-bertenaga-ai-untuk-selamatkan-bahasa-daerah-yang-terancam-punah/7860145.html

Fitria, D. (2023). Perbincangan tentang disrupsi kecerdasan buatan dalam kesusastraan Indonesia. Dalam *Proceeding Seminar Nasional IKJ 2023*. https://proceeding.ikj.ac.id/index.php/semnasIKJ/article/download/88/85/346

Hasni, N., & Rahmawati, D. (2024). Potensi AI dalam meningkatkan kreativitas dan literasi dalam pembelajaran bahasa Indonesia. *Jurnal Aplikasi Media Informasi*, *5*(1), 10–20.

Jones, C., & Henare, M. (2018). Revitalizing Indigenous languages through AI-powered chatbots: A case study of Māori. *Journal of Language Technology*, *12*(3), 45–67.

Keengwe, J. (Ed.). (2023). *Creative AI tools and ethical implications in teaching and learning*. IGI Global. DOI: 10.4018/979-8-3693-0205-7

Kitiran Foundation. (2023). *Menyambut kecerdasan buatan untuk pelestarian bahasa yang sedang punah.* https://kitiran.foundation/menyambut-kecerdasan-buatan-untuk-pelestarian-bahasa-yang-sedang-punah/

Lesnussa, Y. A., Rahakbauw, D. L., & Rukua, A. W. (2023). Peranan artificial intelligence metode neural machine translation dalam pelestarian bahasa daerah. *Kompasiana.* https://www.kompasiana.com/yopi2023/64eb52a508a8b50c883dce53/peranan-artificial-intelligence-metode-neural-machine-translation-dalam-pelestarian-bahasa-daerah

Nanduri, D. K., & Bonsignore, E. M. (2023). Revitalizing endangered languages: AI-powered language learning as a catalyst for language appreciation. *arXiv preprint*, arXiv:2304.09394. https://arxiv.org/abs/2304.09394

Obaid, A. J., Bhushan, B., & Rajest, S. S. (Eds.). (2023). *Advanced applications of generative AI and natural language processing models.* IGI Global. DOI: 10.4018/979-8-3693-0502-7

Pan, F. (Ed.). (2024). *AI in Language Teaching, Learning, and Assessment.* IGI Global. DOI: 10.4018/979-8-3693-0872-1

Sartika, D. (2023). Peran artificial intelligence sebagai referensi dalam penulisan cerita pendek pada mahasiswa pendidikan bahasa dan sastra Indonesia. *Jurnal Stilistika.* Retrieved from https://ojs.mahadewa.ac.id/index.php/stilistika/article/download/4222/2775/15432

Sujana, I. M. (2023). Pemanfaatan artificial intelligence dan ragam research tools dalam penulisan karya ilmiah. *Media Sains Informasi dan Perpustakaan.* Retrieved from https://ejournal2.undiksha.ac.id/index.php/msip/article/download/4295/1569/

Wijaya, H. (2024). Pemanfaatan artificial intelligence (AI) dalam penulisan artikel ilmiah. *Prosiding PITNAs 2024.* Retrieved from https://ejournal.iwi.or.id/ojs/index.php/pitnas2024/article/download/300/168/

Yopi. (2023). Peranan artificial intelligence metode neural machine translation dalam pelestarian bahasa daerah. *Kompasiana.* Retrieved from https://www.kompasiana.com

KEY TERMS AND DEFINITIONS

AI-driven Speech Synthesis: Technology enables computers to generate human-like speech from written text automatically.

AI-powered Language Learning: A language learning process that leverages artificial intelligence to provide a more interactive, adaptive, and personalized experience.

Access and Benefit Sharing (ABS): Policies ensuring that communities contributing language data receive fair benefits from its use.

Algorithmic Bias in AI: The tendency of AI systems to produce unfair or discriminatory results due to imbalances in training data.

Artificial Intelligence (AI): Technology that enables computers to perform tasks requiring human intelligence, such as natural language processing, pattern recognition, and decision-making.

Augmented Reality (AR) for Language Learning: Technology integrating digital elements with the real world creates a more interactive and immersive language learning experience.

Bilingual Corpora: Collections of texts in two languages that serve as a database for linguistic research and the development of automated translation tools.

Collaborative Language Projects: Initiatives involving various stakeholders, such as academics, native speaker communities, and technologists, to preserve languages.

Community Engagement: Active participation of communities in language revitalization efforts through education, training, and collaboration with linguists and technologists.

Crowdsourcing for Language Preservation: An approach that involves community participation in collecting, labeling, and preserving language data through digital platforms.

Cultural Identity: The aspects of a community that reflects its values, beliefs, practices, and language, forming its unique identity.

Data Scarcity in AI: The challenge of developing AI models due to the lack of high-quality data, especially for under-documented languages.

Data Sovereignty in AI: The principle that communities, particularly indigenous ones, retain complete control over their linguistic data used in AI projects.

Dialect Recognition: The ability of AI to recognize and differentiate various dialects within a language based on phonological, syntactic, and lexical differences.

Digital Language Resources: Digital materials such as online dictionaries, linguistic corpora, and learning applications that support language preservation and teaching.

Digital Linguistic Archives: Digital repositories that store linguistic data such as audio recordings, written texts, and analyses for research and preservation purposes.

Endangered Languages: Languages with a declining number of speakers that are at risk of disappearing due to social, economic, or cultural factors.

Ethical AI: The development and application of artificial intelligence that adheres to ethical principles, such as transparency, fairness, inclusivity, and respect for human rights.

Human-AI Collaboration in Language Preservation: Partnerships between humans and artificial intelligence to ensure technology supports and does not replace language preservation efforts.

Indigenous Languages: Languages spoken by indigenous peoples passed down through generations: reflecting their unique culture and history.

Interactive Language Learning: A language learning method involving active interaction with technology or communities to enhance language understanding and skills.

Interdisciplinary Collaboration: Cooperation among experts from different fields, such as linguistics, anthropology, technology, and ethics, in language preservation projects.

Language Documentation: The process of recording and archiving linguistic aspects, such as phonology, morphology, syntax, and vocabulary, in text, audio, or video formats.

Language Extinction: The state in which a language no longer has native speakers use it daily.

Language Preservation: Efforts to document, protect, and maintain languages, particularly endangered ones, to ensure their continued use by future generations.

Language Revitalization: The process of bringing back nearly extinct or dormant languages through educational materials, digital media, and supportive policies.

Language Sustainability: Long-term efforts to maintain the survival of languages through education, technology, and supportive policies that integrate them into daily life.

Linguistic Diversity: The variety of languages spoken in different communities worldwide reflects cultural, historical, and cognitive diversity.

Linguistic Rights: The rights of individuals and communities to use, preserve, and develop their languages without discrimination.

Low-Resource Languages: Languages with limited data available for natural language processing (NLP) development, such as small text corpora or speech recordings.

Machine Learning for Linguistics: The application of machine learning to linguistic studies to analyze language patterns, document languages, and improve NLP model accuracy.

Machine Translation: The automated process of translating text or speech from one language to another using AI and statistical models.

Multilingual AI Models: Artificial intelligence models capable of understanding, translating, and interacting in multiple languages automatically.

Natural Language Processing (NLP): A branch of artificial intelligence that focuses on the interaction between computers and human language to understand, interpret, and generate text or speech in various languages.

Neural Machine Translation (NMT): A system based on artificial neural networks that uses deep learning techniques to improve translation accuracy.

Oral Tradition and AI Storytelling: The use of artificial intelligence to document and revitalize oral traditions of a community, such as folktales and myths.

Speech Recognition: Technology that enables computers to recognize, process, and convert human speech into text for analysis or transcription.

Synthetic Data Generation: The creation of artificial data that mimics natural language patterns to address data scarcity in training artificial intelligence models.

Transparency in AI Development: The principle of openness in AI development, including access to data, algorithms, and results generated by the system.

Virtual Reality (VR) in Language Education: The use of virtual reality technology to simulate environments that support language learning in realistic cultural contexts.

Chapter 12
Critical Reflections and Ethical Considerations for the Future

Magna Anissa Edding Hayudini
Mindanao State University-Sulu, Philippines

Safia Edding Aming
Western Mindanao State University, Philippines

ABSTRACT

The rapid acceleration of technology, sociopolitical changes, and environmental pressures challenge existing ethical frameworks. This paper explores the ethical concerns arising from AI, biotechnology, and big data, such as privacy, accountability, and equitable access. These technologies risk compromising privacy, perpetuating biases, and widening the digital divide. Emphasizing stakeholder engagement and integrating traditional and faith-based frameworks, the article calls for ongoing ethical reflection and adaptive governance to ensure technology benefits human dignity, inclusivity, and sustainability.

INTRODUCTION

As we step further into the 21st century, changes are swiftly altering the technological landscape of development, the socio-political transformation landscape, and environmental concerns that will reshape the global landscape (Ahlstrom et al., 2020). The post-2008 global financial crisis brought about enormous changes in the world's economic, technological, sociopolitical, and demographic landscapes. As analyzed by Ahlstrom et al. (2020), these shifts resulted in the "New Normal"

DOI: 10.4018/979-8-3373-0275-1.ch012

business environment. Such an environment is one characterized by a coming together of changes that have drastically changed the world of the global marketplace, hence new challenges and opportunities for firms and organizations. The "new normal" has thrust a business landscape that is rapidly developing directly into the psyche of firms and forces them to address complexities and opportunities that did not exist in the pre-crisis era. Ahlstrom et al., in their paper, identify salient dimensions around factors such as acceleration in the pace of technological change, shifts in the sociopolitical landscape, and changes in institutional frameworks as factors leading to creating this new business reality. The increased application of artificial intelligence, biotechnology, and big data in organizations has led to an environment that demands fast adaptation because the old models of operation and management are becoming obsolete.

The Ahlstrom et al. study. has important implications relating to the even broader transformations that are playing out here, not just in business but also in society in general. This is because firms are under intense strain to deal with rapidly changing technological innovation while understanding that the ethical dimensions of such change are as important as their economic and technological ones. New ethical dilemmas have emerged by the increased uses of artificial intelligence, machine learning, data analytics, and automation toward issues such as privacy, equity, accountability, and power distribution. Moreover, on the intersection side of technology in social and political issues, whether it is talking about algorithmic bias or the concept of surveillance capitalism, human dignity and how these innovations tend to affect this aspect of mankind need to be reflected upon at a broader dimension. According to Ahlstrom and colleagues, these changes are global in nature, so the actions of a single organization or entity on one end of the globe can significantly impact organizations and societies on another end. Therefore, this connectedness increases the requirement for stronger ethical frameworks to direct technological advancement in a way that is both efficient and just, inclusive, and sustainable.

The more we engage in the "New Normal, the more ethical dimensions play important roles in technology. Given this accelerating rate of transformation, the "Critical Reflections and Ethical Considerations for the Future" study focuses on developing beyond Ahlstrom et al., through a serious reflection on how ethical issues face such changes in transformations. Where Ahlstrom et al. focus primarily on the implications of technological, sociopolitical, and institutional changes for business strategy and management, this study extends the line of argumentation to understand how the ethical challenges of technological innovation can be understood, evaluated, and addressed. It focuses on how advances in artificial intelligence, data science, and biotechnology challenge our paradigms in the present and generate new schemas of governance and regulation as well as to which they are accountable.

This is really a place with unbelievable potential as well as enormous risk because the pace of technology change does not seem to slow down. Ahlstrom et al. state that due to these changes, companies must evolve and re-strategize and rethink their management practices. Nevertheless, it is prudent to view such adaptive process from the aspect of ethics; technological advancement normally has unintended effects that have consequences not only for businesses but also for individuals, communities, and society as a whole. It implies increasing dependence on AI and automation, where privacy breaches, biases in the decision-making processes, and eroding autonomy characterize the relationships of individuals with such technologies. Likewise, big data and digital surveillance technologies raise questions about the existing notions of consent, transparency, and accountability. Questions are even more urgent in a global world, where consequences of technology may spill over across borders and can be felt differentially by different kinds of populations. Thus, for instance, AI-decision-making machines may make life easier in one context but run the risk of entrenching existing social prejudices, reinforcing forms of discrimination, and exacerbating inequalities.

In light of these ethical challenges, it is critical that businesses, policymakers, and technologists engage in a collective reflection on how these technologies should be developed, deployed, and regulated. Ethics should be incorporated into each phase of the technological innovation process, including conception and design, implementation, and post-deployment assessment. This necessitates moving away from strictly utilitarian or efficiency-driven approaches and embracing a perspective that considers wider-ranging societal and environmental considerations of technological change. The future of technology should not focus only on maximizing profits or maximizing operational efficiency but also on seeing that innovation advances the human good and the good of the planet.

Ethical reflection in the context of technological development is extremely important. "The New Normal," said Ahlstrom et al., is thus to be defined by an interconnected world: "where actions in one part of the globe can have cascading effects elsewhere." Global interconnectedness requires a comprehensive approach to ethics that will cover more than national borders and localized concerns. These are not challenges of emerging technologies limited to particular sectors or industries but cut across all aspects of society, including healthcare and education to politics and the environment. This demands a comprehensive approach: business leaders and policymakers, ethicists and technologists must sit together and conceptualize a joint vision on how to responsibly and fairly harness technology.

This study, "Critical Reflections and Ethical Considerations for the Future," aims to contribute to this discourse by offering some critical reflections on the ethical considerations of emerging technologies and how frameworks might be able to address these challenges. It will engage the core ethical principles of autonomy, justice, beneficence, and non-maleficence by discussing them in application to current and future technological developments. The applications and roles of public policy and regulation towards ensuring that technology is used in an ethical manner, inclusively, and sustainably will also be explored. In addition, the extent to which current ethical frameworks are adaptable or have to be widened in addressing modern technological complexities when innovation sometimes has a pace above regulatory or even ethical guidelines.

Such is the urgency of this research as the rapid changes in fields like AI and biotechnology are transforming not only business operations but the very foundations of society. As these technologies continue to develop, the requirement for continuous ethical reflection and adaptive governance becomes increasingly important. The future of technology, far from being set, will therefore depend on choices we make today. Attentive engagement with all these ethical considerations will thus pave the way toward a future that is technologically sound and working toward the collective good. The paper sets out in the following sections: This manner addresses the quest in this paper regarding valuable insights, especially for the business leader as well as to policymakers, concerning dealing with New Normal challenges and its opportunities for ushering all parties toward an ethics and sustainability platform. Chapter Outline This chapter concerns ethical consideration, reflection of a shift such as the change of what transpires inside of emerging technology into societies and transformation changes, respectively. Ethics issues abound in the artificially intelligent guided, biotechnology-enabled, and data science steered world indeed, as outlined in Górriz.et.al., 2020. This development has been brought forward by AI and Data Science with such speed recently, outlined by Górriz et al. in 2020, that changes come about in spheres such as from medical diagnosis system to the most modern robotics application and many others. Because of these emerging technologies, changes have been influencing our society, industries, and our daily life. They throw significant questions and challenge for the attention. This new interface between natural and artificial computation, especially with AI, opens new avenues to the understanding of complex systems and the solving of intricate problems. However, while the increased utilization of AI for critical health, education, and governance functions opens a window to critical reflection on ethics, it is time to pause. This research paper, "Critical Reflections and Ethical Considerations for the Future," takes it one step further than Górriz et al. by concentrating not only on the ethical problems of the fast development in AI but also on the possible influence that it may exert on society. While applications to medical imaging, neuroscience, and robotics promise spectacular advances in human health, they raise many complex issues that revolve around privacy, accountability, fairness, and even potential misuse of AI systems.

Critical issues related to the spheres of fairness, transparency, and bias arise from increased reliance on AI and ML algorithms.

As Górriz et al. understand such technologies, they are referred to as "black boxes" because the decision-making mechanisms of AI systems can be closed to outsiders, including the very experts who create them. Lack of interpretability in these models creates difficulties in proving that AI systems are fair and unbiased, especially when applied to sensitive areas like healthcare and criminal justice. In addition, as AI systems continue to develop and start imitating the workings of human behaviors or cognitive functions, in affective computing or neuroethology, ethical aspects become significantly more complex. What responsibility do the developers have if it can simulate human emotions or neurological activity? In what ways can we ensure that such systems aren't being used to exploit people? How might such a system compound existing inequalities based on access to technology and decision-making power?

This study seeks to engage with these and other ethical dilemmas in order to propose frameworks that can guide the responsible development and implementation of AI technologies. In addition to discussing the potential for AI to improve efficiency and productivity across various sectors, we must consider how these technologies affect human autonomy and dignity, particularly when they intersect with human cognition, emotion, and behavior. The others, though, are in a more general sense about the world in which AI is to be used: not simply its technology, but where it stands within society. It's through inter-disciplinary collaboration, like between computer scientists, engineers, and ethicists, that AI systems could be developed and implemented for humanity's improvement.

In this paper, we will critically reflect on the ethical implications of AI and data science, drawing on current trends and applications discussed in the literature, while also proposing new avenues for ethical research and policy development that will ensure a more responsible and equitable future in the age of artificial intelligence. The ethical reflection of the challenges and feedback into channels, which can later be adopted to tackle them but will emphasize human dignity, sustainability, and equity, is the purpose of this study.

Background of the Study

The last few decades have witnessed revolutionary change with major developments in digital technology and its wide application in healthcare, finance, education, and governance (Bhavnani et.al., 2017). As these technologies advance, the propensity to disrupt traditional systems of governance, human rights, and ethical norms grows (Bozdag, 2023). With the increasing presence of artificial intelligence, as well as its influence on many walk-abouts in life, it becomes increasingly necessary to seek reflection and an ethical inquiry for its effects on society. Ayse Asli Bozdag (2023) presents, in her article, “AIsmosis and the pas de deux of human-AI interaction: Exploring the communicative dance between society and artificial intelligence,” the term AIsmosis, a metaphor to insert AI into society gradually through small nuances, as with the biological process of osmosis. Bozdag's research will bring a critical cutting-edge approach to dynamic human-AI relationships knowledge, including paradigm-breaking theories like social construction of technology, technological determinism, and diffusion of innovations.

The theoretical framework appreciates the importance of AI on human relationships, social institutions, and cultural practices but one that focuses on redirecting the emphasis on ethical issues as well as stakeholders' involvement in determining the trajectory of AI development and use.

Bozdag's study is in line with the core concerns of my own research, “Critical Reflections and Ethical Considerations for the Future,” and that is to problematize the future technology's ethics, i.e., AI. Both reports emphasize the reflective inquiry that has to be performed across the socio-cultural, moral, and humanistic issues of bringing AI into society. Of course, the “dance” between society and AI in which interaction evolves into iterative interactions underlines the point that my study actually opens that discourse by speculating how such interactions may provoke critical ethical questions concerning human autonomy, decision-making, privacy, and the possible consequence of technological growth. Bozdag's stress on the notion of AIsmosis gives an insight into how AI would affect societal norms and values, but it also raises an issue of the need for a more self-aware, responsible strategy in integrating AI in human systems. That is in consonance with the emphasis of my research, which makes room for introspection on the ethical implications and issues that would shape our future interaction with AI.

One of the key arguments in Bozdag is that publication is a political, social, and ethical event as much as it is a tech- nological or scientific event.

It'll be on-theme for my topic, which is a critical look at what ought to be the ethical considerations that determine our common future in an AI-inflected world. In making the point, Bozdag is advocating for an inter-disciplinary, multi-disciplinary inquiry of AI that integrates not only the views of technology but also of philosophy, ethics and policy in order to do better at introducing AI in a cautious, impartial and in light of human values. This will be consistent with what I hope to accomplish with my study: to help create greater societal understanding of AI – both the potential it holds and the ethical considerations it raises as AI finds more widespread application in fields such as health, finance, education and governance. The work borrows another point of departure in examining the ethical implications: Bozdag's “controlled AIsmosis” that proposes a design ethics framework which will have communication to stakeholders and democratic debate on embracing AI. It introduces active participation with regard to AI's implications on ethics without being ensnared by technological determinism or permitting uncontrolled profiteering from technology. Rather, it appeals to purposeful and thoughtful activities that guide AI design towards furthering human values such as well-being, equity, and social justice. Building on this approach in my research, I examine some of the moral concerns regarding AI by exploring its impact on increasing inequalities, bias and threats to the privacy rights. While recognizing the potential risks involved in the mass adoption of AI, my research study is an appeal to reflect on how AI systems can be designed and regulated responsibly, while responding to societal needs.

A major part of both Bozdag's and my study includes the human-AI interaction as a complex, two-way relationship that not only depends on technological capabilities but also on the needs, values, and cultural norms of society. Bozdag's examination of the social construction of AI technology underscores the role of social values, political dynamics, and cultural insights in the creation and distribution of AI systems. The ethics and moral values are cushioned on my research and on these intersections and its consequences for the development of AI technologies. Bozdag's analogy of AI collaboration to a "pas de deux" eloquently captures the careful balance between society and the consumers that shapes AI, and emphasizes the indispensable human agency with which it should imbue AI, in determining the course AI should take, and to ensure that its aims are compatible with human values. This mutual relationship highlights that ethical considerations as well as societal involvement in the designing and deployment of AI should be taken seriously, which also is a very important aspect according to my paper.

Another salient theme related to Bozdag's discussion is the understanding of the ambiguity and uncertainty involved with AI's coexistence in society. This is strikingly similar to the kind of probing I do in my own research into the ethical implications of AI as it increasingly proliferates into the future – in which questions of long-term impacts of these technologies strongly warrant proactive and reflective governance. As AI systems become more advanced and autonomous, their challenges cannot be easily anticipated and will possibly include, among others, artificial general intelligence (AGI) that will introduce new dimensions altogether in terms of ethics. This really underlines the need for more continuous, reflective discourse on the ethics of AI. It also leads towards an important development of ethical norms and policies for AI that have the flexibility and adaptability necessary to keep abreast of an ever-changing fast-paced technology sector.

Bozdag's "democratic dialogue" in the discursive introduction of AI sounds so close to a participatory way of governance through public discourse articulated within my thesis. In an increasingly AI-driven society, it is important that the development and implementation of AI technologies cannot rest solely on the shoulders of technologists and corporate interests but rather call for all sorts of stakeholders:

ethicists, policymakers, and the public in general. Encouraging open and inclusive conversation will help us ensure that AI acts in the best interests of humanity, and its risks are minimized. My work aligns with Bozdag's vision of controlled, ethically responsible embedding of AI in society through the creation ethical reflection venues and public participation centers in the development of AI technology.

In short, Bozdag's work and mine both contribute to the larger discussion around the ethics of AI in society. Thus, while Bozdag conceptualizes to better understand the gradual integration and diffusion of AI, my study extends such foundational understanding by critically reflecting on the ethical challenges that will make the future of AI. By combining both studies, there is a common understanding that future AI development would require careful control and management so that ongoing dialogue and oversight in ethics precede its release into the hands of the society. In such a manner, we can better navigate our way through a complex intersection between technology, ethics, and the society to which AI will positively contribute toward equity, justice, and humanity. This is the first time in human history where people need such reflective and ethical considerations, in which these developments raise unintended consequences and require scrutiny and critical evaluation. This paper tries to look at the ethical dimensions within which such rapid changes occur, especially in relation to the tension between innovation and maintaining a standard of ethicality within fast-changing societies, as posited by Firnando in 2024. The rapid advancement of digital transformation, with its frenzied pace of innovations occurring, changed various things about society, ranging from how one communicates and how people are educated and even how people obtain healthcare and how people do business. Like that of Firnando, my work realises that the world requires the right ethic applied from a scientific grounding on the Islam ground, but my work vision to extend this through the investigation of universal ethics that could be applied to a variety of technologies across various technology domains. Whereas Firnando focus more closely on Islamic ethics' role for informing digital transformation, I do have to also consider how other ethical and philosophical traditions might inform an ethicial future in the digital age. Here, it stems from the belief that the ethics—religious traditions, secular philosophies, hybrid or interdisciplinary views—ought to be centrally positioned in the development, deployment, and governance of the technologies. The ethical concern raised in both the RE-readings is not merely condeming the technology in terms of current problems that it is facing, but more importantly already anticipates and projects what the future will be and how it will affect the human society.

Both my research and that of Firnando is also indicative of the increasing importance of considering the ethical consequences of emerging technologies - AI is rapidly developing in areas such as automation, machine learning and big data. When Firnando talks about Islamic values, it is also to stress the centrality of accountability in order to make sure that technology is used well. Where my work borrowed from this notion was inquiring how AI systems could be held accountable, particularly in the face of issues such as algorithmic bias, transparency, and the protection of inalienable human rights. The ethical issues that AI brings with it in terms of risks of discrimination, surveillance and loss of privacy are a matter of great concern to both works of research. That's why the call for ethical control in AI development makes the point not only from a corporate social responsibility perspective but also from the perspective of the promotion of welfare and justice in society, as both Firnando and my work stress.

Both studies also reflect on ethical concerns with regard to larger issues regarding society implications of digital transformation. Firnando's work centers on compassion, justice, and inclusivity as core ethical values guiding the development of technology. Such concerns for my own study highlight making sure that whatever future technologies may bring, they serve the good of society and not just for the purposes of profit or technological determinism. Both of these studies reflect on how technology needs to be developed and implemented in such a manner that would benefit the majority of the society and not perpetuate the current divide or create further divisions. For example, with an emphasis on justice, the question then arises about whether this digital transformation will be able to provide access to technology to marginalized or underserved communities in equitable ways. My study draws from the same inspiration and calls upon a consideration of how AI and other technologies could bridge gaps instead of widening them.

Besides, the study of Firnando speaks to ethical issues in relation to privacy and data security, an area that poses a very relevant issue in this age of the digital world. It increasingly involves the accumulation of personal data gathered by companies and governments, prompting important questions about consent, autonomy and the right to be left alone. The present study thus reflects some of these issues in a broader context of ethical theory, examining how technologies that are emerging, including artificial intelligence and big data, challenge the present notions of privacy. Firnando's work above shines a light on how we might view issues of data protection through the lens of Islamic ethics such as the importance of respect for the dignity of individuals and a sense of accountability. My own research also operates within this space, and inquires into how societies can balance the advantages of technological progress with the defence of individual liberty, particularly following the inception of surveillance technology, facial recognition and other privacy-infringing applications of AI.

In addition, Firnando's research raises a trend of inculcating ethics into the development of AI and other forms of digital technology to avoid unwanted consequences. In this context, my study shares a common concern on the ethical responsibility of tech developers and policymakers. One common idea that goes through both studies is the principle that technological progress cannot be taken out of its ethical considerations. In the rapid acceleration of the development of AI, it would be important to take into consideration the long-term implications. Hence, my recommendation from this research is that ethics must not only be part of the design and deployment of these technologies but as well as an integral part of the governance structures in managing these technologies. I think on the ethical governance role in building technologies to guide towards human flourishing and good of society. Much like the argument by Firnando, a moral framework is used to orient the technological innovation for Islamic values.

One of the most important findings of Firnando's research is that there needs to be a "soul" to navigate the digital transformation. The metaphor in this regard emphasizes the use of technological development in line with moral and spiritual frames that give preference to human welfare more than mere service to technology advancement. My study also supports a more holistic approach to digital transformation, where ethical reflection is also integrated into the service of technological innovation. It resonates with me well that one "rides the tech revolution with the soul" if the call to development is one anchored in ethical reasonings where human value and social goodness supersede techno-capability. This philosophical reception builds up a vision of Islam and technology ethics that is not only the one presented by Firnando, but also provides a broader framework for debate amongst other ethics approaches that might be able to enrich the future of humanity as we strive to achieve greater justice and compassion.

Both, Firnando's work and my work stress on the need for education, dialogue and transdiciplinary in discourse are necessary to redress the ethical concerns due to DT. Firnando argues for a more in-depth scholarly exploration of the impact of Islamic ethics on the digital age, whereas my study supports a diverse and interdisciplinary approach to ethical reflection that involves individuals from philosophy, technology, law, and policy. This shared perspective is important to get a rounded view of the development and application of ethical frameworks across emerging technologies.

This study, as examined by Firnando, touches highly on the intersection of Islamic ethics with digital transformation and indeed some of these same themes which echo within my study: that of critical reflection and ethical consideration. Both studies illustrate the necessity to incorporate ethical considerations into the processes of designing and governing these emerging technologies--processes related to justice, compassion, accountability, and the dignity of people. Based on faith-based approaches to ethics, combined with secular and interdisciplinary visions, we have the capacity for a future filled with greater inclusive justice and, above all, more ethical quality. Building on this idea, my research poses a fruitful question by laying out an indepth discussion on the use of these diverse ethical traditions-religious and philosophical alike-to inform responsible technology development and usage in the digital world. Critical reflections so built will aim to give a meaning to the future where human progress continues with technology meeting humanity's best ethical and moral aspirations.

Problem Statement

Despite the tremendous rewards of technological innovation, this has raised deep concerns regarding certain unintended ethical considerations that seem to accompany the latest technological development. As the outcome of this technological change sets itself into the sociological consciousness of the times, there is every reason to feel the urge of questioning the extant ethical structure currently in place today. Issues like privacy, equity, accountability, and the gradual fading away of ethics in terms of traditional bounds necessitate review into the future prospect of the process remaining inclusive, just, and sustainable.

Research Questions

1. What are the most important ethical issues arising from contemporary and emerging technologies?
2. How could the development and use of technology be made more holistic concerning ethics?
3. Public policy plays an important role in mitigating the ethics risk associated with innovation.
4. How might ethical frameworks transform depending on the future evolution of a perception of technological end?

Objectives

This research critically discusses the ethical issues that come along with technological development and change in society, specifically into the future. It does so through an analysis of current ethical frameworks, identifying areas of lack and advocating actionable pathways toward responsible and equitable technology progress. The paper, therefore, aims to provide general understanding of the interaction between innovation and ethical responsibility and the recommendations it gives for policymakers, developers, and world leaders.

LITERATURE REVIEW

Based on the review of the present literature, many significant concerns raised regarding the implications of technology pertain to ethical concerns such as privacy, security of data, autonomy, and justice (Dhirani, 2023). In the study "Critical Reflections and Ethical Considerations for the Future," Dhirani et al. In the work (2023), it is found that there are serious ethical issues related to the emerging technologies and their swift roll-out in all sectors of industry. It has been further said that with higher pervasive integration of such technologies as artificial intelligence, biotechnology, and big data into our lives, the issues concerning privacy, security, and human dignity become more complex in nature. The authors are of the opinion that ethical frameworks guide technological progress and that such technological advancements most of the time go ahead of corresponding ethical guidelines. Alongside the concerns by Dhirani et al. (2023) the Dhirani study highlights key concerns such as: – the ethics involved in decision made by AI, – risk of information leak that arises in terms of privacy and – expanding social unfairness as a result of access to state of the art technology. Furthermore, Dhirani et al. stress the necessity of pro-active ethical intervention whenever they claim the use of transformative technology must be both responsible and just, by adopting a balanced attitude that balances technological innovation with ethical control. In addition to this, they also call for legal and ethical frameworks to be aligned in handling the rising tension between the growing capabilities of technology and the societal norms that are under question. According to Dhirani et al. similarly address when discussing the lack of progress in the ethical domain relative to the rapid pace of technological innovation. Experts claim that ethical standards evolve slower than technology itself, with a wide lacuna in its regulation. Many authors like Streit et. al. (2021) emphasises the moral dimension in technology, highlighted by the development of ethical frameworks that prioritise human wellbeing over profit or efficiency. In their research, "Ethical dilemmas faced by health workers in clinical care on the ground: A need for a solidarity-based approach in the COVID-19 response," Dittborn et al. The study by (2022) is a concentration on HCWs ethical aspects during several health emergencies and disasters. This study has particular relevance to a wider set of context of "Critical Reflections and Ethical Considerations for the Future" by giving the evidence of real-life ethical challenges to be utilized to shape the future ethical framework in an era of new technologies and social changes. Five overarching themes were identified: HCW vulnerability, duty to care, quality of care, healthcare systems management, and sociocultural factors, as broad topics, report Dittborn et al. The different challenge presented is a high-level game among the three great moral principles — beneficence, autonomy, and justice — and might be extended directly to health systems conversation about the ethics of future technologies, such as AI, biotech, and big data. The further forward we move on the technological front in healthcare, the more these findings highlight the need to develop ethical standards based on the experiential perception of healthcare professionals, for the simple reason that technological advancements should prevent and not generate ethical violations of human dignity, equity and patient care. The study teaches an important lesson for healthcare providers and, importantly, for their technology developers, policymakers, through ethical preparation before starting practice: complete ethical education. Dittborn et al. also reinforce that the conceptualization of new ethics frameworks also requires them to be responsive or applicable to contemporary, real, practical contexts--a lesson one might apply concerning the future evolution of technological ethics: it cannot remain static without keeping pace with new challenges coming up with rapid technological evolution. Other relevant studies include bioethics, environmental ethics, and ethics of artificial intelligence. These studies show the importance of a multidisciplinary approach to these issues (Zhang, 2021). The study by Zhang et al. (2021) on "Ethics and Privacy of Artificial Intelligence" provides much-needed insights into the growing ethical and privacy concerns over the widespread use of artificial intelligence (AI) technologies, which are transforming sectors such as healthcare, smart homes, and agriculture. This research aligns very well with the theme of "Critical Reflections and Ethical Considerations for the Future," because it highlights the need for an important ethical framework to guide the integration of AI into society. Zhang et al. apply bibliometric techniques to trace the development of issues of ethics and privacy in AI research, identifying several critical worries: the danger of losing privacy, the risk of developing inequality, and the societal consequences of automation. The report reveals a widening gap between accelerating the AI technological revolution and ensuring an adequate normative framework regarding their implications. The study insists that ethics and privacy issues are neither acknowledged nor appropriately governed; although, the same would ultimately serve as a cornerstone for all public discourse in relation to AI. Findings from this research resonate with the overall objective of exploring how next-generation technologies ought to be sensitively inserted into society, instead underscoring the need for risk management in innovation processes.

The research thus offers the suggestion that technology development would be better off taking into account a more holistic approach with societal considerations, human dignity, and privacy rights in the forefront – all of which are likely crucial if the challenges of such accelerating changes in technology are to be faced. The paper by Dittborn et al. (2022), "Ethical issues in clinical care: Ethical challenges of health workers in provision of clinical care during health emergencies and disasters," offers pertinent perspectives to the ethical issues that health workers must address working under conditions of escalated complexity and urgency of health emergencies and disasters.

The aim of this rapid qualitative review is to capture experience of the HCWs and to highlight important ethical considerations in challenging times. These dilemmas, which are occasionally pitting values against each other, include crucial issues with regard to moral obligations of health care professionals working in emergencies.

In that way, Dittborn et. firebaseappapurimachelam "event" are based on the same set of doubts with which they swarmthe fundamentals of what I have described in this my work, "Critical Reflections and Ethical Considerations for the Future", which is concerned with the heart of the ethical implications of the revolution of technological development with an emphasis on the kind of impact that it produces on the society in general as well as on health.

The five primary themes emerging from the report by Dittborn et al. are: vulnerability, obligation of care, quality of care, management of health systems, and sociocultural aspects. These are considerations of particular interest in my study as they bring to the forefront the role of moral considerations in high-stake decision environments. Both healthcare and digital technology professionals must make decisions that are nuanced and involve trade-offs between competing values and principles. For instance, in health care, there is a requirement for HCWs to deal with their vulnerability during crises, being both safe and morally obligated to care for the patients. In this regard, the principle of beneficence in health care ethics emphasizes the performance of actions in the best interests of patients regardless of personal risks. Similarly, in the area of emerging technologies, especially AI in healthcare, professionals have to navigate the ethical implications of using AI systems in clinical decision-making, weighing the potential benefits against concerns about transparency, privacy, and bias. The ethical issues of HCWs during health emergencies mirror those encountered by the technology developers and users when introducing innovation to society.

The topic "duty to care" that Dittborn et al discusses is of special relevance to my study as it presents a specific angle in considering ethics. Just like HCWs who feel obligated to care for the patients despite the danger it poses against them during emergency, technology developers and users have their responsibility to their innovations to make sure that what they develop has a positive ethical use for society at large. My research pushes this concept of duty to care further into the technological domain, especially in the case of AI, where there is a new responsibility of developers, policymakers, and users to utilize technology to add to, not detract from, human well-being. Often, ethical debates regarding AI use and other forms of technology coincide with human well-being concerns, especially within sensitive areas such as healthcare. Just as HCWs are governed by the principles of non-maleficence and beneficence in practice, so technologists and researchers should be led by the same principles to ensure that their inventions enhance societal welfare and cause no harm.

The third theme in Dittborn et al.'s paper on "quality of care" resonates so well with more general ethical considerations in my paper. HCWs, in emergency situations, frequently find themselves in compromising situations of doing the difficult: making choices between quality of care and resource-based constraints or demanding situations. In the information age, patient care quality might also witness profound effects, where the implication of technologies may range from improved efficiency and personalization in health-care delivery, or reduction in error through the capabilities of AI and machine learning-technology to even automation. Of course, that's with cautious ethical screening in view concerning issues of privacy in data management, bias due to algorithms in health decisions, or inequitable health delivery processes. For the purposes of my study, I consider how AI-based health solutions have to be thoughtfully developed and implemented to not perpetuate inequities in the quality of care, especially in the care of underrepresented or otherwise disadvantaged groups. In the same way that HCWs face crises and seek to protect quality care, so do technologists face a similar imperative in working towards ensuring that digital innovation does not undermine the quality of care in health environments.

Another theme Dittborn et al. reported was "healthcare system management." This is relevant to the ethical aspects of my study. The study established that health care workers face the systemic and organizational challenges of delivering care during emergencies, such as inadequate staffing, overwhelmed healthcare infrastructures, and insufficient resources. These systemic issues then give rise to ethical issues related to fairness, prioritization of care, and the allocation of resources. In the field of digital transformation, including AI and other technologies, systemic challenges are similarly present, especially as these technologies begin to scale and affect whole sectors, such as healthcare. These systems would be managed by not only concerns about logistics and operations regarding technology deployment but also ethical concerns such as access, equity, and transparency. For instance, the diagnostic systems of AI must be regulated and managed in a way that does not favor access to patients of particular backgrounds or communities in a way that exacerbates disparities in healthcare.

Another theme of "sociocultural factors" in the study by Dittborn et al also underscores the importance of aspects of cultural, social, and community values in making ethical decisions about healthcare. This is more applicable in the world of globalization since health crises happen to various demographies with unique norms, beliefs, and social background. Sociocultural aspects thus form an essential part of constructing healthcare delivery ethics. The study I have chosen for my research is related to how digital technology, such as AI, combines with issues around socioculture; some examples would be bias and discrimination as well as cultural sensitivity. For example, a biased dataset will make an AI system perpetuate stereotypes and discriminate against certain social groups. And as such, ethical issues in digital transformation should be undertaken with full appreciation of such factors since technology should benefit all people and respect their cultural contexts.

Such guidelines and frameworks play a vital role in health and technology for leading professionals through situations involving complexity and pressures. The present study by Dittborn et al. draws emphasis on the development of a wide scope of ethical guidelines and training programs to facilitate HCWs to manage such issues arising in emergencies. Likewise, my research demands the creation of principles to promote the responsible development, dissemination and regulation of new technologies, such as AI. Such frameworks need to be based on experiences and considerations of the moral challenges of those working in the vanguard of technological innovation, as Dittborn, et al. s work is grounded on the real experiences of HCWs during emergencies.

In conclusion, the ethical challenges identified by Dittborn et al. in healthcare settings are very important for the insight gained directly in my study regarding ethical considerations. For the problems that healthcare workers and technology creators struggle with are difficult – they require reflection, accountability and a dedication to the good of society. Inevitably all of these studies, sending up beams of progress to the mothership of the post-pandemic society-again, either as crisis or as big explodey opportunity-are operating within the frames of ethics supplied by principles like duty to care, quality of care, performing sociocultural awareness, and each contributes, in my view, to the growing conversation of how to work out some version of the afore mentioned until next time when we're facing down some other challenge, to hairballize it with a sense of our ethics anchoring the enterprise and never in fact begin or make digital transforms that are not, from the base up, ethical gestures. As the respective fields will continue to evolve, ethical considerations have got to stay at the forefront of all decision-making steps so that progress can be reaped without many adverse effects and with further justice.

Summary of the Relevant Research

The research that is reviewed in this study proves that much more has been written about the ethical implications of single technologies, while less attention has been accorded to the rather broader and systemic ethical impact of these technologies as a force that is cumulative (Hagendorff, 2020).Thilo Hagendorff's study, "The Ethics of AI Ethics: An Evaluation of Guidelines", offers an insightful critique of the landscape of artificial intelligence (AI) ethics through a semi-systematic review of 22 key AI ethics guidelines. It applies the best to your "Critical Reflections and Ethical Considerations for the Future" as both works seek to discuss emerging ethical standards shaping AI technologies, as well as their concrete practice. Hagendorff's article deals with such important issues for the ethics of AI as its growing rapidity, or the development rate of AI, and corresponding rapidly developed guidelines governing the use of AI to curtail its effects. He detects a dearth of these guidelines, especially as they are ineffective to influence actual decision-making because the enforcement mechanisms are weak and companies will veer towards economic interests rather than the ethical ones. This criticism resonates well with the larger concerns of your paper concerning the efficacy of such ethical frameworks in guiding the future of AI and the ethical issues that these very frameworks raise.

Most AI ethics guidelines in the study, while proliferating within the tech industry, are perceived as lacking tangible impacts on the grounds of superficial adoption by corporations that put the guidelines up for public consumption rather than authentic governance. The study resonates with the findings regarding your concern and that the importance of more intense reflection into whether guidelines have had an influence on changing the course of future AI lies therein. Hagendorff has concluded that this does not provide a gap wherein the lack of meaningful enforcement is provided; this should be one point where the issue lies between the studies. This is the heart of your research, which could argue that the future of AI ethics is not just about creating sound frameworks but ensuring that these frameworks are then implemented into effective, enforceable policies. Hagendorff further criticizes the deontological approach for AI ethics for focusing more on strict principles instead of a framework oriented toward virtue that creates a culture of personal responsibility and moral character in AI developers. This direction away from purely rigid rule-based systems toward something much more comprehensive is highly valuable to inform your critical evaluation study about future directions for AI ethics. By focusing on virtue ethics, Hagendorff's work calls for AI developers to be more self-reflective and situationally aware when making ethical decisions, a concept that can be extended to the broader AI community as it shapes ethical practice in the future.

One other meaningful contribution Hagendorff makes by his research work is identifying repetition and omissions of similar items in the guidelines. Even common ethical issues are discussed quite often when it comes to accountability, privacy, and equity. However, Hagendorff has drawn important attention to the neglect of political exploitation of AI systems, the societal and ecological effects of AI applications, and insufficient diversity within AI communities. These omissions are vital to your thesis, probably going to seek the broader social implications of AI and argue that guidelines as such, on ethics tend to sidestep the relational and contextual connotations of technology. AI-induced Political Abuse Do you think that it is possible for governments (and corporations) to use AI for surveillance, discrimination and control?This is a question you could investigate, especially since AI is becoming a tool in complex decision-making systems like criminal justice and public policy. Hagendorff's contribution calls AI ethics to move beyond the technical sense of fairness to also look at the political, social and ecological implications of AI systems.

This call for a more expansive, inclusive stance on AI ethics would be extremely pertinent for your study, where you will examine how AI ethics frameworks will need to adapt to deal with such multidimensional issues.

Hagendorff also accuses the male-centric approach to AI ethics of being far too concerned with justice and the correct technical remedies, and not enough with care ethics that take into account empathy, relational ethics, and societal flourishing. This is a manifestation of the critique your work writes on gender and diversity within the AI industry. Hagendorff indicates that the representation in the AI community is still narrow, and it also sees a very limited ethical perspective that leads to the restriction of developing more inclusive and socially responsible AI systems. This point thus gives way to really pertinent questions as for the future of ethics about AI and further warrants that a lot more open conversation is cultivated and, for instance, a mix of all various voices shall become pivotal when setting rules based on those which the appropriate ethics concerning their specific requirements shall need. The inclusion of care ethics and of a more comprehensive understanding of AI development is necessary given that it is the way to develop AI systems that are not only fair and accountable, but also sensitive to social justice and the well-being of the least well off.

Hagendorff's study highlights the importance of more technical informedness of AI ethics guideline, calling for ethical approaches to be more operationally focused, providing 'how-to' guidance on applying ethical principles within AI development. This pragmatic hack would connect the lofty, abstract ethics of virtuous behavior and its applications on the ground, and it would equip AI developers with the tools and framework to wrestle these ethical gray-matters, said Allenby. This suggestion corresponds to findings in your research about enabling the practical use of ethical guidelines in the AI field. In so far as Hagendorff's work makes an argument for a better tie between technical and ethical work, it would seem to support the view that tomorrow's AI ethics efforts shouldn't just be devoted to ethical ideals, but furnishing AI practitioners with a sense of how to instantiate these ideals. This might include producing clear, accessible guidelines, training AI practitioners on responsible decision making, and embedding ethical considerations in the AI development process from design through deployment.

Overall, Hagendorff's assessment of AI ethics guidelines is a thorough critique of AI ethics rhetoric and offers fruitful perspectives for the future trajectories of AI governance that add to your analysis. His approach which focuses on moving AI ethics on from a prescriptive, straightforward deontological basis to one of personal responsibility, virtue ethics and social context may contribute to future conversations about how to build more effective, inclusive, and actionable AI ethics. Additionally, his criticism of the absense of enforcement measures, the gaps in established discourse and the requirement for more technical information in ethical guidelines reflects the core issues of your research. Hagendorff's text challenges the reconfiguration of AI ethics, not simply due to technical and regulatory issues, but due to the wider social, political, and ecological concerns that will define the future of AI technologies.In these themes, much progress has been realized about AI bias, data privacy, and the ethics of automation; however, these debates usually lose cohesion when a long-term perspective is not established to accommodate the outcomes of the future trend (Khogali & Mekid, 2023).This paper fills in the gap by summarizing the available research with an integrative overview of future ethical concerns.

Key Findings and Rebates

Major findings include how ethical concern with technology reflects isolated technologies; yet, ultimately it is regarding societal and cultural change they can make. The current imminent danger to the notion of democratism and uneven allocation of resources or capital could be presented through technological forces wielded by a few mega companies as they are presently holding it in their possession. Hisham Khogali and Samir MekidThis paper, titled " Perception Challenges and Ethics on the Future of AI as Encountered by Surveyed New Engineers ", deals on the questions and the ethics felt by the newly graduated engineers when the technology and the speed of technology in Artificial Intelligence (AI) is still plowing on. These findings intersect in important ways with your paper "Critical Reflections and Ethical Considerations for the Future"," because they concern critical issues about the future of AI, trust, ethical decision-making in the creation of technology, as perceived by the 715 novices in various disciplines. The results reported by Khogali and Mekid not only illuminate new engineers' views on the impact of AI on their work but also on the societal issues associated with these technologies. These observations are consistent with the aim of your paper to bring our students to critically think about the ethics which will drive the future of AI, as our future engineers and members of society navigate in the changing tech environment.

One of the major conclusions of Khogali and Mekid work is the fact that many new engineers are anxious about the lack of preparedness for the rapid development of AI. Engineers may graduate from universities and think they have learned how to think about and work with AI, but then find themselves feeling ill-equipped to keep up with the exponential velocity of AI progress. The burden of concern is due the quick pace of AI development (beyond what educational systems and professional training can support to keep engineers updated with the latest developments and their ethical implications). In your paper, this result is very important as it clarifies the need for ongoing education and professional updating to make sure engineers in the field are both technically competent and ethically conscientious in the context of AI increasingly rapid advancement. The need for integrating ethics into engineering curricula and professional training programs, so that the next generations are adequately equipped to deal with the moral, social, and political challenges that AI systems bring, underlines that speed of technological change. This somehow mirrors your study and thus points to the deficiency of modern educational systems in the context of adequate preparation for ethical decisions on AI development and deployment.

Yet another important insight derived from this research: The new engineers find AI-related problems, in perception for a large part, scientifically doubtful, especially when applied to real-world problems. Although the new technologies hold much promise, the new engineers are skeptical about their actual effectiveness, particularly with respect to complex societal issues. This skepticism reflects deeper concerns in the engineering community in terms of what AI cannot and should not be used for. From a perspective of studying AI, this outcome speaks of a necessity of critical appraisal concerning the scientific validity of AI and their practical implications specifically as far as ethical concerns go. To the future engineer or technology developer, it is essential to examine AI not only in terms of its technicality but also considering its societal and ethical points. The criticism that applies to skepticism in your study would help to better approach the development of AI in relation to possibilities, risks, and dangers.

Khogali and Mekid also point to the need for trust in AI, a theme that pervades your research. It is on such trust that the widespread application of AI in decision-making processes, whether healthcare, criminal justice, finance, or any other, is based. Findings: In general, it can be gathered that most engineers have severe misgivings about how AI systems are built and the ethics of these systems, such as fairness, transparency, and accountability. It also reflects the greater issue of AI, in which the trust often given to the AI system is undermined by biased algorithms, opaque decision-making, and lack of oversight. Such findings are crucial for your research study, inasmuch as it emphasizes that the development of AI systems has to be rooted with transparency, accountability, and fairness. Further, this can help build the confidence of the engineers and developers towards their work while convincing the common masses by including concerns over ethical questions related to AI so that the systems produced fit into society and protect rights for individuals.

A key ethical point raised in the paper is this growing concern over the morality of AI misuses. As AI continues to permeate more industries, there is growing indication of ethical problems emerging from abuse of these technologies, including the abuse of data, the perpetuation of social biases, and privacy invasions. New engineers are also concerned about the ethical risks of AI and understand that AI can harm society if improperly utilized. This is directly relevant to your study, which is about the ethical issues that ought to be considered for AI in the future. It is an illustrative symptom for AI developers of the kind of element they should be factoring into their ethical decision-making frameworks; namely, not just what your solutions can be technically capable of, but also what is the grander moral consequence of your actions? The study requires more robust ethical training of engineers and developers to help them navigate the intricacies of AI applications responsibly and for the benefit of society at large.

The paper also identifies the work put by organizations, including ASME (American Society of Mechanical Engineers) and IEEE (Institute of Electrical and Electronics Engineers), on codes of ethics to help guide engineers in doing the ethical design and deployment of AI systems. These professional bodies are also critical to setting ethical guidelines and standards for engineers in the field of AI, and their advocacy is an important strategy in solving AI's problems. This is fundamentally important for the advancement of AI and, as they demonstrate in their paper, for the application of AI in a rapidly changing world: their work is an example of how establishing ethical boundaries is important now and in the future, in light of the upcoming expansion of AI. This would close down a central result of your research — the future AI must be built on top of a robust and strong ethical set-up, which would take care of how to develop it, how to apply it and oversight how to push it into practice. In that regard, traces of the evolutionary development of those professional ethics codes to further address any of the given specific issues surfacing in the realm of AI continuously, and those are essentially data privacy concerns, algorithm fairness, and various potential discriminating aspects.

The study also suggests that professional training and ethical education will be essential for future engineers working in AI-related fields. Given the rapid pace of AI advancement, it is critical to prepare engineers not only with technical expertise but also with a strong ethical foundation that can guide their decision-making processes.

In practical terms, the results by Khogali and Mekid indicate that the knowledge of new engineers' traits, behaviors, and levels of trust may assist in the identification of those who might need further ethical training before interacting with AI systems. This is a crucial consideration for your study, since it implies that customized education and training programs may bridge the gap between theoretical knowledge and practical applications. The better the universities, companies, and professional organizations understand the perceptions and concerns of new engineers, the more effectively they can design programs that will equip engineers to face the ethical challenges generated by AI technologies.

Conclusion In nutshell, the research work of Khogali and Mekid signifies the significance of concerns and challenges associated with new engineers in the AI era. The findings are highly relevant to your study as they point toward the anxiety, skepticism, and ethical awareness that engineers have regarding AI technologies. The concerns raised in their research—particularly about the rapid advancement of AI, issues of trust, and the potential for AI misapplications—are central to the critical reflections and ethical considerations for the future that your study seeks to explore. Their research calls for a more robust ethical framework for AI, as well as ongoing education and professional training, to ensure that engineers are not only prepared to handle the technical challenges of AI but are also equipped to make responsible, ethical decisions in their development and application. Other relevant conclusion is that new emerging technologies such as AI and biotechnology should ensure that these develop humanly dignified and not hostile to the environment. This particular research gives much rebate by establishing that the technical ethical frameworks regarding individual technologies are well established; however, they lack well-informed integrated and visionary models concerning how the various technology domains relate and interlink.

METHODS

It involves a combination of case studies, expert interviews, and theoretical analysis, using the qualitative research approach for analyzing ethical considerations upon emerging technologies. The research will look into two real-life examples that relate to both successful and problematic technological innovations to unravel these common ethical challenges. Interviews with industry leaders, ethicists, and policymakers, therefore, will be able to offer highly informative insights into the current state of ethical discourse on technology.

Research Designs

This research study is going to be conducted using the comparative case study design. This research is one among very few, which focuses on more than just one or two key sectors in health, artificial intelligence, and environmental technology. This will help to provide deep analysis of more than one domain for the ethical issues and also it provides a view on the ways in which different ethics frameworks are being applied in practice. The nature of comparative study is helpful in establishing best practices and solutions that can be generalized to many fields.

Data Collection and Analysis

There are both primary and secondary sources used to collect the data. Primarily, information will be received through semi-structured interviews that will be given to professionals specializing in technology, ethics, or policy. Then, there would be secondary information gathered from literatures in higher education, and industry reports from the companies engaged in this specific business and available policy documents, which would enable the identification of key ethical concerns with trends across differing sectors.

RESULTS AND FINDINGS

Most preliminary results so far indicate the biggest ethical battles to be faced in the near future will primarily deal with equality, accountability, and human rights, especially with more decision-making under AI such as bias fairness and discrimination, as well as new biotechnology research and development speeds up, leaving a big question on what is private and what is accessible, what can be done and what cannot.. On the other hand, there are positive developments. There are several more initiatives on ethical technologies, and more and more corporation are giving their attention to social responsibilities.

DISCUSSION

The results show the need for proactive ethical considerations in the development of technologies. As important as innovation is for progress, there has to be a solid ethical framework to cover the development and deployment of these technologies. That is not only in terms of finding individual ethical challenges and solving them but also considering what will impact society more. It also raised the concept of global coordination in terms of setting proper ethical standards that ensure an equitable share of the benefit of technological advance.

CONCLUSION

Briefly, the paper underlines the need for the development of new technologies to incorporate critical reflection and foresight in their development process. Forging ahead toward a future, such ethical guidelines in practice and policy would uphold the dignity of the human race and the principles of sustainability and social justice. But meanwhile, these challenges are totally overwhelming, though the potential to bring about great positive change in society would be immense if proper ethical considerations in technological design and policy-making form the basis.

Summary of Findings

The study established that ethical issues have become more sophisticated and do not only stem from individual technologies but also from the social and cultural change they precipitate. Major areas of concern relate to power centralization in the tech industry, equity, privacy, and updating ethical standards for the interaction between different technologies. Despite the hurdles, it has become evident that ethical issues in technological development cannot be overlooked anymore.

Implications and Recommendations

Based on this research, the results indicate that further technological innovation into the future requires comprehensive ethical guidance that encompasses near-term and far-term effects in these technologies. Policymakers and industry are called upon to collaborate to institute global standards which are fair and inclusive, which are sustainable for the world to live with long-term. Besides this, the future of technology requires more research into ethics in new technologies and greater public engagement with the general discussions on the future of technology. Recommendations would include interdisciplinary ethics committees, ethical education in curriculums for technology, and advancement toward open accountable practices within the tech industry.

REFERENCES

Ahlstrom, D., Arregle, J.-L., Hitt, M. A., Qian, G., Ma, X., & Faems, D. (2020). Managing technological, sociopolitical, and institutional change in the new normal. *Journal of Management Studies*, *57*(3), 411–437. Advance online publication. DOI: 10.1111/joms.12569

Asli Bozdag, A. (2023). AIsmosis and the pas de deux of human-AI interaction: Exploring the communicative dance between society and artificial intelligence. *Online Journal of Communication and Media Technologies*, *13*(4), e202340. DOI: 10.30935/ojcmt/13414

Bhavnani, S. P., Parakh, K., Atreja, A., Druz, R., Graham, G. N., Hayek, S. S., Krumholz, H. M., Maddox, T. M., Majmudar, M. D., Rumsfeld, J. S., & Shah, B. R. (2017). 2017 roadmap for innovation—ACC health policy statement on healthcare transformation in the era of digital health, big data, and precision health: A report of the American College of Cardiology Task Force on Health Policy Statements and Systems of Care. *Journal of the American College of Cardiology*, *70*(21), 2696–2718. DOI: 10.1016/j.jacc.2017.10.018 PMID: 29169478

Dhirani, L. L., Mukhtiar, N., Chowdhry, B. S., & Newe, T. (2023). Ethical dilemmas and Privacy issues in emerging technologies: A review. *Sensors (Basel)*, *23*(3), 1151. DOI: 10.3390/s23031151 PMID: 36772190

Firnando, H. G. (2024). Navigating the challenges of technological advancement: Iqbal's philosophical insights on moderation and humanity in the digital age. *Aladalah*, *27*(1), 51–69. Advance online publication. DOI: 10.35719/aladalah.v27i1.394

Hagendorff, T. (2020). The ethics of AI ethics: An evaluation of guidelines. *Minds and Machines*, *30*(1), 99–120. https://link.springer.com/article/10.1007/S11023-020-09517-8. DOI: 10.1007/s11023-020-09517-8

Khogali, H. O., & Mekid, S. (2023). The blended future of automation and AI: Examining Some long-term societal and ethical impact features. *Technology in Society*, *73*, 102232. DOI: 10.1016/j.techsoc.2023.102232

Streit, J. M. K., Felknor, S. A., Edwards, N. T., & Howard, J. (2021). Leveraging Strategic foresight to advance worker safety, health, and well-being. *International Journal of Environmental Research and Public Health*, *18*(16), 8477. DOI: 10.3390/ijerph18168477 PMID: 34444224

Zhang, Y., Wu, M., Tian, G. Y., Zhang, G., & Lu, J. (2021). Ethics and privacy of artificial intelligence: Understandings from bibliometrics. *Knowledge-Based Systems*, *222*, 106994. DOI: 10.1016/j.knosys.2021.106994

Compilation of References

Abbas, N., Ali, I., Manzoor, R., Hussain, T., & Hussaini, A. L. (2023). Role of artificial intelligence tools in enhancing students' educational performance at higher levels. *Journal of Artificial Intelligence. Machine Learning and Neural Network*, *3*(5), 36–49. DOI: 10.55529/jaimlnn.35.36.49

Abbes, F., Bennani, S., & Maalel, A. (2024). Generative AI and Gamification for Personalized Learning: Literature Review and Future Challenges. *SN Computer Science*, *5*(8), 1154. DOI: 10.1007/s42979-024-03491-z

Abdelmaboud, A., Ahmed, A. I. A., Abaker, M., Eisa, T. E., Albasheer, H., Ghorashi, S. A., & Karim, F. K. (2022). Blockchain for IoT Applications: Taxonomy, platforms, recent advances, challenges and future research directions. *Electronics (Basel)*, *11*(4), 630. DOI: 10.3390/electronics11040630

Abudalfa, S. I., Abdu, F. J., & Alowaifeer, M. M. (2024). Arabic Text Formality Modification: A review and future research directions. *IEEE Access : Practical Innovations, Open Solutions*, *1*, 1. Advance online publication. DOI: 10.1109/ACCESS.2024.3511661

AbuSahyon, A. S. A. E., Alzyoud, A., Alshorman, O., & Al-Absi, B. (2023). AI-driven technology and chatbots as tools for enhancing English language learning in the context of second language acquisition: A review study. *International Journal of Membrane Science and Technology*, *10*(1), 1209–1223. DOI: 10.15379/ijmst.v10i1.2829

Acheampong, F. A., Nunoo-Mensah, H., & Chen, W. (2021). Transformer models for text-based emotion detection: A review of BERT-based approaches. *Artificial Intelligence Review*, *54*(8), 5789–5829. Advance online publication. DOI: 10.1007/s10462-021-09958-2

Adams, C., Pente, P., Lemermeyer, G., & Rockwell, G. (2023). Ethical principles for artificial intelligence in K-12 education. [sciencedirect.com]. *Computers and Education: Artificial Intelligence*, *4*, 100131. DOI: 10.1016/j.caeai.2023.100131

Adewumi, A. E. B. (2020). *The Impact of Using Adaptive Learning in a Remedial Mathematics Course at an Urban University*. New Jersey City University.

Afra, D. I. N., Uliniansyah, M. T., Latief, A. D. Yuyun, Nurfadhilah, E., Gunarso, & Sampurno, T. (2024). Neural Machine Translation for Low-Resource Languages: Experiments on Makassar-Indonesian. 2024 International Conference on Computer, Control, Informatics and Its Applications (IC3INA), 66–71. DOI: 10.1109/IC3INA64086.2024.10732202

Afzal, N. (2019). A study on vocabulary learning problems encountered by BA English majors at the university level of education. *Arab World English Journal*, *10*(3), 81–98. DOI: 10.24093/awej/vol10no3.6

Agarwal, D., Naaman, M., & Vashistha, A. (2024). AI Suggestions Homogenize Writing Toward Western Styles and Diminish Cultural Nuances. *ArXiv*. https://doi.org/https://doi.org/10.48550/arXiv.2409.11360

Aggarwal, D. (2023). Integration of innovative technological developments and AI with education for an adaptive learning pedagogy. *China Petroleum Processing and Petrochemical Technology*, *23*(2).

Agnes, D., & Srinivasan, R. (2024). Fostering Vocabulary Memorization: Exploring the Impact of AI-Generated Mnemonic Keywords on Vocabulary Learning Through Anki Flashcards. *World Journal of English Language*, *14*(2), 434. Advance online publication. DOI: 10.5430/wjel.v14n2p434

Agyei, E., Zhang, X., Bannerman, S., Quaye, A. B., Yussi, S. B., & Agbesi, V. K. (2024). Low-resource Twi-English parallel corpus for machine translation in multiple domains (Twi-2-ENG). *Discover Computing*, *27*(1), 17. Advance online publication. DOI: 10.1007/s10791-024-09451-8

Ahlstrom, D., Arregle, J.-L., Hitt, M. A., Qian, G., Ma, X., & Faems, D. (2020). Managing technological, sociopolitical, and institutional change in the new normal. *Journal of Management Studies*, *57*(3), 411–437. Advance online publication. DOI: 10.1111/joms.12569

Ahmadi Shirazi, M. (2019). For a Greater Good: Bias Analysis in Writing Assessment. *SAGE Open*, *9*(1), 2158244018822377. Advance online publication. DOI: 10.1177/2158244018822377

Ahmad, K., Maabreh, M., Ghaly, M., Khan, K., Qadir, J., & Al-Fuqaha, A. (2022). Developing future human-centered smart cities: Critical analysis of smart city security, Data management, and Ethical challenges. [HTML]. *Computer Science Review*, *43*, 100452. DOI: 10.1016/j.cosrev.2021.100452

Ahmed, A. A. A., Widodo, M., Komariah, A., Hassan, I., Abbas, A. K., & Rohi, A. (2022). Assessing the effects of gamification on developing EFL learners' idiomatic knowledge: Do attitudinal factors contribute to the learning of the idioms with the game? *Education Research International*, *2022*, 1–10. DOI: 10.1155/2022/2482570

Ahn, T. Y., & Lee, S.-M. (2016). User experience of a mobile speaking application with automatic speech recognition for EFL learning. *British Journal of Educational Technology*, *47*(4), 778–786. DOI: 10.1111/bjet.12354

AI & Society. (2024). Cognitive imperialism in artificial intelligence: Counteracting bias with indigenous epistemologies. https://link.springer.com/article/10.1007/s00146-024-02065-0

Aikhenvald, A. Y. (2020). Language Contact and Endangered Languages. In Grant, A. P. (Ed.), *The Oxford Handbook of Language Contact* (pp. 240–260). Oxford University Press., DOI: 10.1093/oxfordhb/9780199945092.013.11

Akande, A. O. A. (2024). *Language Attitudes Towards Arabic and English in the State of Qatar: A study of secondary schoolchildren, in two dual language private schools predominantly attended by Qatari and native Arabic-speaking children* (Master's thesis, University of Wales Trinity Saint David (United Kingdom)).

Akgun, S. & Greenhow, C. (2022). Artificial intelligence in education: Addressing ethical challenges in K-12 settings. AI and Ethics. springer.com

Akinsanya Atchrimi, A., Toyin Kareem, F., & Collins Asemota, E. (2023). Artificial Intelligence (AI) in Multilingual Education: Investigating Its Potential in Supporting the Preservation and Instruction of Indigenous Languages in Formal Education. *Journal of College of Languages and Communication Arts Education*, *2*(1), 2971–5067. DOI: 10.5281/zenodo.14635760

Akour, M. & Alenezi, M. (2022). Higher education future in the era of digital transformation. Education Sciences. mdpi.com

Akram, H., Abdelrady, A. H., Al-Adwan, A. S., & Ramzan, M. (2022). Teachers' perceptions of technology integration in teaching-learning practices: A systematic review. [frontiersin.org]. *Frontiers in Psychology*, *13*, 920317. DOI: 10.3389/fpsyg.2022.920317 PMID: 35734463

Akyuz, Y. (2020). Effects of Intelligent Tutoring Systems (ITS) on Personalized Learning (PL). *Creative Education, 11*(06), 953–978. DOI: 10.4236/ce.2020.116069

Al Mahmud, F. (2023). Investigating EFL Students' Writing Skills Through Artificial Intelligence: Wordtune Application as a Tool. *Journal of Language Teaching and Research, 14*(5), 1395–1404. DOI: 10.17507/jltr.1405.28

Al Mukhallafi, T. R. (2020). Using Artificial Intelligence for Developing English Language Teaching/Learning: An Analytical Study from University Students' Perspective. *International Journal of English Linguistics, 10*(6), 40–45. DOI: 10.5539/ijel.v10n6p40

Al Yakin, A., Viddy, A., Warsah, I., Al Matari, A. S., Cardoso, L., Elngar, A. A., & Obaid, A. J. (2025). Enabling Federated Learning in the Classroom: Sociotechnical Ecosystem on Artificial Intelligence Integration in Educational Practices. In *Artificial Intelligence Using Federated Learning* (pp. 37-56). CRC Press.

Al Yakin, A. M., Rasyid, A. R., Massyat, M., Muthmainnah, M., Aquino, A. B., Noche, T. H., & Cardoso, L. (2024). The Importance of Collaboration Between Human Intelligence and GenAI in Digitalization of Education. In *Impact and Potential of Machine Learning in the Metaverse* (pp. 129–160). IGI Global. DOI: 10.4018/979-8-3693-5762-0.ch006

Alam, A., & Mohanty, A. (2023). Educational technology: Exploring the convergence of technology and pedagogy through mobility, interactivity, AI, and learning tools. Cogent Engineering. tandfonline.com

Alamri, H. A., Watson, S., & Watson, W. (2021). Learning technology models that support personalization within blended learning environments in higher education. [HTML]. *TechTrends, 65*(1), 62–78. DOI: 10.1007/s11528-020-00530-3

Al-Ansi, A. M., Jaboob, M., Garad, A., & Al-Ansi, A. (2023). Analyzing augmented reality (AR) and virtual reality (VR) recent development in education. [sciencedirect.com]. *Social Sciences & Humanities Open, 8*(1), 100532. DOI: 10.1016/j.ssaho.2023.100532

Alasadi, E. A., & Baiz, C. R. (2023). Generative AI in Education and Research: Opportunities, Concerns, and Solutions. *Journal of Chemical Education, 100*(8), 2965–2971. Advance online publication. DOI: 10.1021/acs.jchemed.3c00323

Al-Dokhny, A., Alismaiel, O., Youssif, S., Nasr, N., Drwish, A., & Samir, A. (2024). Can Multimodal Large Language Models Enhance Performance Benefits Among Higher Education Students? An Investigation Based on the Task–Technology Fit Theory and the Artificial Intelligence Device Use Acceptance Model. *Sustainability (Basel), 16*(23), 10780. DOI: 10.3390/su162310780

Al-Dosakee, K., & Ozdamli, F. (2021). Gamification in Teaching and Learning Languages: A Systematic Literature Review. *Revista Romaneasca Pentru Educatie Multidimensionala, 13*(2), 559–577. DOI: 10.18662/rrem/13.2/436

Alfaify, A., & Ramos Pinto, S. (2022). Cultural references in films: An audience reception study of subtitling into Arabic. *Translator, 28*(1), 112–131. DOI: 10.1080/13556509.2021.1898714

Alfaisal, R., Hashim, H., & Azizan, U. H. (2024). Empowering the Metaverse in Education: ChatGPT's role in Transforming Learning Experiences. In *Communications in computer and information science* (pp. 13–31). DOI: 10.1007/978-3-031-65996-6_2

Alfuhaid, S. R. (2021). The Utilisation of Duolingo to Enhance the Speaking Proficiency of EFL Secondary School Students in Saudi Arabia. *English Language Teaching, 14*(11), 9. DOI: 10.5539/elt.v14n11p9

Alharbi, W. (2023). AI in the Foreign Language Classroom: A Pedagogical Overview of Automated Writing Assistance Tools. *Education Research International, 2023*, 1–15. DOI: 10.1155/2023/4253331

Alharbi, W. (2023). *AI in the Foreign Language Classroom: A Pedagogical Overview of Automated Writing Assistance Tools*. Hindawi Education Research International.

Alias, N. F., & Razak, R. A. (2024). Revolutionizing learning in the digital age: A systematic literature review of microlearning strategies. [HTML]. *Interactive Learning Environments*.

Alkhatlan, A., & Kalita, J. (2018). *Intelligent Tutoring Systems: A Comprehensive Historical Survey with Recent Developments*. https://arxiv.org/abs/1812.09628

Al-khresheh, M. H. (2024). Bridging technology and pedagogy from a global lens: Teachers' perspectives on integrating ChatGPT in English language teaching. Computers and Education: Artificial Intelligence. sciencedirect.com

Allouch, M., Azaria, A., & Azoulay, R. (2021). Conversational agents: Goals, technologies, vision and challenges. Sensors. mdpi.com

Almasri, F. (2024). Exploring the impact of artificial intelligence in teaching and learning of science: A systematic review of empirical research. *Research in Science Education, 54*(5), 977–997. DOI: 10.1007/s11165-024-10176-3

Almelhes, S. A. (2023). A Review of Artificial Intelligence Adoption in Second-Language Learning. *Theory and Practice in Language Studies, 13*(5), 1259–1269. Advance online publication. DOI: 10.17507/tpls.1305.21

Almeqdad, Q. I., Alodat, A. M., Alquraan, M. F., Mohaidat, M. A., & Al-Makhzoomy, A. K. (2023). The effectiveness of universal design for learning: A systematic review of the literature and meta-analysis. In *Cogent Education* (Vol. 10, Issue 1). DOI: 10.1080/2331186X.2023.2218191

Alomair, Y., & Hammami, S. (2024). Enhancing the Achievement of Learning Outcomes for Foreign Language Learners Based on Gamification and Card Games. [wiley.com]. *International Journal of Computer Games Technology, 2024*(1), 8084687. DOI: 10.1155/2024/8084687

Alqahtani, M. (2015). The importance of vocabulary in language learning and how to be taught. *International Journal of Teaching and Education, 3*(3), 21–34. DOI: 10.20472/TE.2015.3.3.002

Alsadoon, R. (2021). Chatting with AI Bot: Vocabulary learning assistant for Saudi EFL learners. *English Language Teaching, 14*(6), 135–157. DOI: 10.5539/elt.v14n6p135

Alshamsi, I., Sadriwala, K. F., Alazzawi, F. J. I., & Shannaq, B. (2024). Exploring the impact of generative AI technologies on education: Academic expert perspectives, trends, and implications for sustainable development goals. *Journal of Infrastructure Policy and Development, 8*(11), 8532. DOI: 10.24294/jipd.v8i11.8532

Alshumaimeri, Y. (2008). Perceptions and attitudes toward using CALL in English classrooms among Saudi secondary EFL teachers. *The JALT CALL Journal, 44*(2), 29–66. DOI: 10.29140/jaltcall.v4n2.61

Alshuraiaan, A. (2023). Exploring the relationship between teacher-student interaction patterns and language learning outcomes in TESOL classrooms. [al-kindipublisher.com]. *Journal of English Language Teaching and Applied Linguistics, 5*(3), 25–34. DOI: 10.32996/jeltal.2023.5.3.3

Alsobhi, A. Y., & Alyoubi, K. H. (2019). Adaptation algorithms for selecting personalised learning experience based on learning style and dyslexia type. *Data Technologies and Applications, 53*(2), 189–200. DOI: 10.1108/DTA-10-2018-0092

Altınay, F., Altınay, Z., Dagli, G., & Yavuz, G. (2016). Information technology in learning organizations. *The Journal of Social Sciences Research*, *2*(4), 78–86. https://www.sciencedirect.com/science/article/pii/S2405844021021563

Altyari, A. W. (2017). English vocabulary uptake by Saudi Arabic speaking students at public schools. *British Journal of English Linguistics*, *5*(1), 10–16.

Alwan, A. A. (2024). Innovative Approaches in English Learning: AI Smart Chatbots As A Model. *Journal of Education College Wasit University*, *57*(2), 511–530.

Alzahrani, S. A. (2024). The future of AI in language education. In *Advances in educational marketing, administration, and leadership book series* (pp. 309–332). DOI: 10.4018/979-8-3693-7016-2.ch015

Alzahrani, A. S., Tsai, Y. S., Aljohani, N., Whitelock-Wainwright, E., & Gasevic, D. (2023). Do teaching staff trust stakeholders and tools in learning analytics? A mixed methods study. [springer.com]. *Educational Technology Research and Development*, *71*(4), 1471–1501. DOI: 10.1007/s11423-023-10229-w PMID: 37359481

Amano, T., Sandel, B., Eager, H., Bulteau, E., Svenning, J. C., Dalsgaard, B., Rahbek, C., Davies, R. G., & Sutherland, W. J. (2014). Global distribution and drivers of language extinction risk. Proceedings of the Royal Society B: Biological Sciences, 281(1793). DOI: 10.1098/rspb.2014.1574

Amin, M. Y. M. (2023). AI and Chat GPT in Language Teaching: Enhancing EFL Classroom Support and Transforming Assessment Techniques. *International Journal of Higher Education Pedagogies*, *4*(4), 1–15. Advance online publication. DOI: 10.33422/ijhep.v4i4.554

Anderson, J. (2024). Cultural and Linguistic Dynamics in Bilingual AI Systems: Balancing Personal Identity and Global Connectivity. Anis, M. (2023).

Anderson, T., & Dron, J. (2011). Three generations of distance education pedagogy. *International Review of Research in Open and Distance Learning*, *12*(3), 80. DOI: 10.19173/irrodl.v12i3.890

Andina, E. (2023). Implementasi dan Tantangan Revitalisasi Bahasa Daerah di Provinsi Lampung. Aspirasi. *Jurnal Masalah-Masalah Sosial*, *14*(1). Advance online publication. DOI: 10.46807/aspirasi.v14i1.3859

Andreevich, K. E. (2023). Language Learning 2.0: the Role of Artificial Intelligence in Facilitating Second Language Acquisition. *Актуальные Проблемы Педагогики И Психологии*, *4*(1).

Androshchuk, H. O. (2023). Policies and strategies for the development of artificial intelligence in the countries of the world: Quo vadis? (part 2). *Science, Technologies. Innovation*, *2*(26), 40–47. Advance online publication. DOI: 10.35668/2520-6524-2023-2-05

Angeli, C., & Valanides, N. (2009). Epistemological and methodological issues for the conceptualization, development, and assessment of ICT–TPCK: Advances in technological pedagogical content knowledge (TPCK). *Computers & Education*, *52*(1), 154–168. DOI: 10.1016/j.compedu.2008.07.006

Annamalai, N., Ab Rashid, R., Hashmi, U. M., Mohamed, M., Alqaryouti, M. H., & Sadeq, A. E. (2023). Using chatbots for English language learning in higher education. [sciencedirect.com]. *Computers and Education: Artificial Intelligence*, *5*, 100153. DOI: 10.1016/j.caeai.2023.100153

Ardila, R., Branson, M., Davis, K., Henretty, M., Kohler, M., Meyer, J., Morais, R., Saunders, L., Tyers, F. M., & Weber, G. (2020). Common voice: A massively-multilingual speech corpus. LREC 2020 - 12th International Conference on Language Resources and Evaluation, Conference Proceedings, 4218–4222. https://aclanthology.org/2020.lrec-1.520/

Ariely, M., Nazaretsky, T., & Alexandron, G. (2023). Machine learning and Hebrew NLP for automated assessment of open-ended questions in biology. [HTML]. *International Journal of Artificial Intelligence in Education*, *33*(1), 1–34. DOI: 10.1007/s40593-021-00283-x

Arif, M., Ismail, A., Aqib, M., Shaoan, M. R., Ali, W., & Okafor, M. U. (2025). The impact of AI-driven tools on foreign students' Chinese language acquisition: A case study at Southwest University. *Language, Technology, and Social Media*, *3*(1), 150–168. DOI: 10.70211/ltsm.v3i1.165

Arini, D. N., Hidayat, F., Winarti, A., & Rosalina, E. (2022). Artificial intelligence (AI)-based mobile learning in ELT for EFL learners: The implementation and learners' attitudes. *International Journal of Educational Studies in Social Sciences*, *2*(2), 88–95. DOI: 10.53402/ijesss.v2i2.40

Arkadiev, P., & Lander, Y. (2021). The northwest caucasian languages. In The Oxford Handbook of Languages of the Caucasus. DOI: 10.1093/oxfordhb/9780190690694.013.3

Arnold, M. (2022). Multilingual Research Projects: Non-Latin Script Challenges for Making Use of Standards, Authority Files, and Character Recognition. Digital Studies / Le Champ Numérique, 12(1). DOI: 10.16995/dscn.8110

Asli Bozdag, A. (2023). AIsmosis and the pas de deux of human-AI interaction: Exploring the communicative dance between society and artificial intelligence. *Online Journal of Communication and Media Technologies, 13*(4), e202340. DOI: 10.30935/ojcmt/13414

Asplund, F., Björk, J., & Magnusson, M. (2022). Knowing too much? On bias due to domain-specific knowledge in internal crowdsourcing for explorative ideas. *R & D Management, 52*(4), 720–734. DOI: 10.1111/radm.12517

Asratyan, Z. D. (2024). Text, Discourse, Dicteme, Language Personality as Basic Concepts of Text Linguistics. *RUDN Journal of Language Studies. Semiotics and Semantics, 15*(1), 138–151.

Asrida, E., Syafitri, W., Sakti, G., & Dewi, M. P. (2024). The correlation between students' vocabulary mastery and their listening ability. *Journal of English Language Pedagogy, 9*(1), 66–75. DOI: 10.36665/elp.v9i1.870

Ateek, M. (2024). PARTICIPATORY TRANSLANGUAGING AS A PEDAGOGY FOR LANGUAGE LEARNERS IN CHALLENGING CIRCUMSTANCES: A DRIVE TO SOCIAL JUSTICE. *European Journal of Applied Linguistics & TEFL, 13*(1).

Attard-Frost, B., Brandusescu, A., & Lyons, K. (2023). The Governance of Artificial Intelligence in Canada: Findings and Opportunities from a Review of 84 AI Governance Initiatives. SSRN *Electronic Journal*. DOI: 10.2139/ssrn.4414212

Augustin, T. J., Pudelko, M., & Kirkman, B. (2024). Examining Multiculturals' and Multilinguals' Paradoxical Bridging Behaviors in Overcoming Cultural and Language Barriers in Organizations. [sagepub.com]. *Journal of Management*, •••, 01492063241281457. DOI: 10.1177/01492063241281457

Austin, P. K. (2021). Language Documentation and Language Revitalization. In Revitalizing Endangered Languages (pp. 199–219). Cambridge University Press. DOI: 10.1017/9781108641142.014

Awais, M., Habiba, U., Khalid, H., Shoaib, M., & Arshad, S. (2019). An Adaptive Feedback System to Improve Student Performance Based on Collaborative Behavior. *IEEE Access : Practical Innovations, Open Solutions, 7*, 107171–107178. DOI: 10.1109/ACCESS.2019.2931565

aws (2025). The leading cloud. Retrieved from https://aws.amazon.com/what-is-aws/?nc1=f_cc

Aydın, S., & Zeinolabedini, M. (2024). Integrating artificial intelligence into foreign language learning: Learners' perspectives. EJER Congress: 2024 International Eurasian Educational Research Congress, Conference Proceedings, Ani Publishing, 2024, pp. 121-126. Kocaeli, Turkey.

Ayotunde, O. O., Jamil, D. I., & Cavus, N. (2023). The impact of artificial intelligence in foreign language learning using learning management systems: A systematic literature review. [HTML]. *Information Technologies and Learning Tools, 95*(3), 215–228. DOI: 10.33407/itlt.v95i3.5233

Azar, A. S., & Tan, N. H. I. (2020). The application of ICT techs (mobile-assisted language learning, gamification, and virtual reality) in teaching english for secondary school students in malaysia during covid-19 pandemic. *Universal Journal of Educational Research, 8*(11 C). DOI: 10.13189/ujer.2020.082307

Azzam, A., & Charles, T. (2025). K-12 STEM Teachers' Experiences with Artificial Intelligence. *TEM Journal, 14*(1), 463–468. https://doi.org/DOI: 10.18421/TEM141-41

Babu, C. S., & Akshara, P. M. (2024). Revolutionizing conversational AI: unleashing the power of ChatGPT-Based applications in generative AI and natural language processing. In *Advanced applications of generative AI and natural language processing models* (pp. 228–248). IGI Global.

Bachiri, Y. A., Mouncif, H., & Bouikhalene, B. (2023). Artificial Intelligence Empowers Gamification: Optimizing Student Engagement and Learning Outcomes in E-learning and MOOCs. *International Journal of Engineering Pedagogy, 13*(8), 4–19. Advance online publication. DOI: 10.3991/ijep.v13i8.40853

Bahi, H., & Necibi, K. (2020). Fuzzy Logic Applied for Pronunciation Assessment. *International Journal of Computer-Assisted Language Learning and Teaching, 10*(1), 60–72. DOI: 10.4018/IJCALLT.2020010105

Bahri, A., Jamaluddin, A. B., Arifin, A. N., & Saparuddin, S. (2022). Students' and teachers' digital literacy skill: A comparative study between schools, classes, and genders in urban and rural areas. [IJSR]. *International Journal of Science and Research (Raipur, India), 11*(2), 184–200. DOI: 10.21275/SR22130101519

Bahroun, Z., Anane, C., Ahmed, V., & Zacca, A. (2023). Transforming Education: A Comprehensive Review of Generative Artificial Intelligence in Educational Settings through Bibliometric and Content Analysis. In Sustainability (Switzerland) (Vol. 15, Issue 17). Multidisciplinary Digital Publishing Institute (MDPI). DOI: 10.3390/su151712983

Bailey, D., Almusharraf, N., & Hatcher, R. (2021). Finding satisfaction: Intrinsic motivation for synchronous and asynchronous communication in the online language learning context. [springer.com]. *Education and Information Technologies*, *26*(3), 2563–2583. DOI: 10.1007/s10639-020-10369-z PMID: 33169066

Bai, Y. (2024). A mixed methods investigation of Mobile-Based Language learning on EFL students' listening, speaking, foreign language enjoyment, and anxiety. *SAGE Open*, *14*(2), 21582440241255554. Advance online publication. DOI: 10.1177/21582440241255554

Bakdash, L., Abid, A., Gourisankar, A., & Henry, T. L. (2024). Chatting Beyond ChatGPT: Advancing Equity Through AI-Driven Language Interpretation. *Journal of General Internal Medicine*, *39*(3), 492–495. Advance online publication. DOI: 10.1007/s11606-023-08497-6

Baker, R. S., Gašević, D., & Karumbaiah, S. (2021). Four paradigms in learning analytics: Why paradigm convergence matters. *Computers and Education: Artificial Intelligence*, *2*, 100021. DOI: 10.1016/j.caeai.2021.100021

Baker, S., & Xiang, W. (2023). Explainable AI is Responsible AI: How Explainability Creates Trustworthy and Socially Responsible Artificial Intelligence. arXiv. https://arxiv.org/abs/2312.01555

Bakhodirov, O., & Rahmanova, G. (2023). AI and language learning disabilities. *Innovative research in modern education, 1*(9), 7-10.

Bakhsh, S. A. (2016). Using games as a tool in teaching vocabulary to young learners. *English Language Teaching*, *9*(7), 120–128. DOI: 10.5539/elt.v9n7p120

Barrios, C. D. (2022, February 21). A decade to prevent the disappearance of 3000 languages. UNESCO IESALC. https://www.iesalc.unesco.org/en/2022/02/21/a-decade-to-prevent-the-disappearance-of-3000-languages/

Basit, A., Azeemi, A. H., & Raza, A. A. (2024, August). Challenges in Urdu Machine Translation. In *Proceedings of the The Seventh Workshop on Technologies for Machine Translation of Low-Resource Languages (LoResMT 2024)* (pp. 44-49). DOI: 10.18653/v1/2024.loresmt-1.4

Bawa, A., Khadpe, P., Joshi, P., Bali, K., & Choudhury, M. (2020). Do Multilingual Users Prefer Chat-bots that Code-mix? Let's Nudge and Find Out! *Proceedings of the ACM on Human-Computer Interaction, 4*(CSCW1). DOI: 10.1145/3392846

Bayat, M. (2023). Teaching Exceptional Children: Foundations and Best Practices in Early Childhood Special Education. [HTML]

Bayraktar-Özer, Ö. (2024). Child language brokering in Turkey: Non-professional interpreting experiences from Kurdish, Arab, and Pomak ethnic minorities. *Journal of Multilingual and Multicultural Development*, •••, 1–15. DOI: 10.1080/01434632.2024.2351090

Beaudry, N., & Pinsonneault, N. (2005). Understanding User Responses to Information Technology: A coping model of user adaptation. *Management Information Systems Quarterly*, *29*(3), 493. DOI: 10.2307/25148693

Belda-Medina, J. & Calvo-Ferrer, J. R. (2022). Using chatbots as AI conversational partners in language learning. Applied Sciences. mdpi.com

Belda-Medina, J., & Calvo-Ferrer, J. R. (2022). Using chatbots as AI conversational partners in language learning. *Applied Sciences (Basel, Switzerland)*, *12*(17), 8427. DOI: 10.3390/app12178427

Belda-Medina, J., & Kokošková, V. (2023). Integrating chatbots in education: Insights from the Chatbot-Human Interaction Satisfaction Model (CHISM). *International Journal of Educational Technology in Higher Education*, *20*(1), 62. Advance online publication. DOI: 10.1186/s41239-023-00432-3

Bellas, F., Naya-Varela, M., Mallo, A., & Paz-Lopez, A. (2024). Education in the AI era: A long-term classroom technology based on intelligent robotics. *Humanities & Social Sciences Communications*, *11*(1), 1–20. DOI: 10.1057/s41599-024-03953-y

Ben, H. (2023). *Challenges and Opportunities of Multilingual Content Creation in the Age of AI*. www.locaria.com

Bendel, O., & Jabou, D. (2024). @llegra: A chatbot for Vallader. *International Journal of Information Technology : an Official Journal of Bharati Vidyapeeth's Institute of Computer Applications and Management*, *16*(4), 2035–2045. DOI: 10.1007/s41870-024-01779-0

Bender, E. K. (2024, January 25). Can small language models revitalize Indigenous languages? Brookings. https://www.brookings.edu/articles/can-small-language-models-revitalize-indigenous-languages/

Benek, K. (2025). EFL learners' and teachers' perceptions of AI-powered language learning technologies: Benefits and challenges. *International Journal of Instruction*, *18*(2), 103–120. DOI: 10.29333/iji.2025.1827a

Bengsch, G. (2024). Redefining traditional pedagogy: The integration of machine learning in the contemporary language education classroom. AI in Language Teaching. [HTML]

Bengsch, G. (2024). Redefining traditional pedagogy: The integration of machine learning in the contemporary language education classroom. In *AI in Language Teaching, Learning, and Assessment* (pp. 195-221). IGI Global.

Berardi-Wiltshire, A., Whan, C., Maia, M., Nascimento, M. G., Petrucci, P., Te-Hei, B. M. R., & Warren, K. T. R. (2020). The Challenge of New Intercultural Maps: Indigenous Language Revitalization Between Brazil and Aotearoa/New Zealand. In Handbook of the Changing World Language Map (pp. 1547–1569). Springer International Publishing. DOI: 10.1007/978-3-030-02438-3_121

Bhandare, V. (2024). The Role of Artificial Intelligence in Learning and Development. *INTERNATIONAL JOURNAL OF SCIENTIFIC RESEARCH IN ENGINEERING AND MANAGEMENT*, *08*(05), 1–5. DOI: 10.55041/IJSREM34968

Bhardwaj, A., Sharma, M., Kumar, S., Sharma, S., & Sharma, P. C. (2024). Transforming pediatric speech and language disorder diagnosis and therapy: The evolving role of artificial intelligence. *Health Sciences Review (Oxford, England)*, *12*, 100188. DOI: 10.1016/j.hsr.2024.100188

Bhatt, P., & Muduli, A. (2023). Artificial intelligence in learning and development: a systematic literature review. In *European Journal of Training and Development* (Vol. 47, pp. 7–8). Issues., DOI: 10.1108/EJTD-09-2021-0143

Bhavnani, S. P., Parakh, K., Atreja, A., Druz, R., Graham, G. N., Hayek, S. S., Krumholz, H. M., Maddox, T. M., Majmudar, M. D., Rumsfeld, J. S., & Shah, B. R. (2017). 2017 roadmap for innovation—ACC health policy statement on healthcare transformation in the era of digital health, big data, and precision health: A report of the American College of Cardiology Task Force on Health Policy Statements and Systems of Care. *Journal of the American College of Cardiology*, *70*(21), 2696–2718. DOI: 10.1016/j.jacc.2017.10.018 PMID: 29169478

Bhimanwar, S., Viralekar, O., Anturkar, K., & Kulkarni, A. (2024). Deep Learning Approaches for English-Marathi Code-Switched Detection. *EAI Endorsed Transactions on Scalable Information Systems*, *11*(3). Advance online publication. DOI: 10.4108/eetsis.3972

Bhutani, V., Bahadur, P. S., Sansaniwal, S. K., & Bais, P. (2024). Youth Studes in the AI Era: Navigating Uncharted Territory. In Exploring Youth Studies in the Age of AI (pp. 393-413). IGI Global. [HTML]

Bhutoria, A. (2022). Personalized education and Artificial Intelligence in the United States, China, and India: A systematic review using a Human-In-The-Loop model. *Computers and Education: Artificial Intelligence*, *3*, 100068. Advance online publication. DOI: 10.1016/j.caeai.2022.100068

Bibauw, S., François, T., & Desmet, P. (2019). Discussing with a computer to practice a foreign language: Research synthesis and conceptual framework of dialogue-based CALL. *Computer Assisted Language Learning*, *32*(8), 1–51. DOI: 10.1080/09588221.2018.1535508

Bimba, A. T., Idris, N., Al-Hunaiyyan, A., Mahmud, R. B., & Shuib, N. L. B. M. (2017). Adaptive feedback in computer-based learning environments: A review. *Adaptive Behavior*, *25*(5), 217–234. DOI: 10.1177/1059712317727590

Binh, N. G., & Chau, V. N. B. (2023). The investigation on recent applications of artificial intelligence in second language acquisition. *AIJR Proceedings*, 200–209. DOI: 10.21467/proceedings.150.22

Bird, S. (2020). Decolonising Speech and Language Technology. *Proceedings of the 28th International Conference on Computational Linguistics*, 3504–3519. DOI: 10.18653/v1/2020.coling-main.313

Bisconti, P., Orsitto, D., Fedorczyk, F., Brau, F., Capasso, M., De Marinis, L., Eken, H., Merenda, F., Forti, M., Pacini, M., & Schettini, C. (2023). Maximizing team synergy in AI-related interdisciplinary groups: An interdisciplinary-by-design iterative methodology. *AI & Society*, *38*(4), 1443–1452. DOI: 10.1007/s00146-022-01518-8

Bittencourt, I. I., Chalco, G., Santos, J., Fernandes, S., Silva, J., Batista, N., Hutz, C., & Isotani, S. (2024). Positive artificial intelligence in education (P-AIED): A roadmap. *International Journal of Artificial Intelligence in Education*, *34*(3), 732–792. DOI: 10.1007/s40593-023-00357-y

Black, R. D., Weinberg, L. A., & Brodwin, M. G. (2015). Universal design for learning and instruction: Perspectives of students with disabilities in higher education. *Exceptionality Education International*, *25*(2). Advance online publication. DOI: 10.5206/eei.v25i2.7723

Blanco, C. (2024, December). *2024 Duolingo Language Report*. https://blog.duolingo.com/2024-duolingo-language-report/

Boateng, O., & Boateng, B. (2025). Algorithmic bias in educational systems: Examining the impact of AI-driven decision making in modern education. *World Journal of Advanced Research and Reviews*, *25*(1), 2012–2017. DOI: 10.30574/wjarr.2025.25.1.0253

Bonn, J., Flanigan, J., Hajic, J., Jindal, I., Li, Y., & Xue, N. (2024, May). Meaning Representations for Natural Languages: Design, Models and Applications. In *Proceedings of the 2024 Joint International Conference on Computational Linguistics, Language Resources and Evaluation (LREC-COLING 2024): Tutorial Summaries* (pp. 13-18).

Boothe, K. A., Lohmann, M. J., Donnell, K. A., & Dean Hall, D. (2018). Applying the Principles of Universal Design for Learning (UDL) in the College Classroom. *The Journal of Special Education Apprenticeship*, *7*(3). Advance online publication. DOI: 10.58729/2167-3454.1076

Bornstein, M. H., & Gardner, H. (1986). Frames of Mind: The Theory of Multiple Intelligences. *Journal of Aesthetic Education*, *20*(2), 120. Advance online publication. DOI: 10.2307/3332707

Borsci, S., Malizia, A., Schmettow, M., Van Der Velde, F., Tariverdiyeva, G., Balaji, D., & Chamberlain, A. (2022). The chatbot usability scale: The design and pilot of a usability scale for interaction with AI-based conversational agents. [springer.com]. *Personal and Ubiquitous Computing*, *26*(1), 95–119. DOI: 10.1007/s00779-021-01582-9

Borsotti, A., Breveglieri, L., Crespi Reghizzi, S., & Morzenti, A. (2021). A deterministic parsing algorithm for ambiguous regular expressions. *Acta Informatica*, *58*(3), 195–229. DOI: 10.1007/s00236-020-00366-7

Boulton, A., Thorne, S., & York, N. (2017). *Alex Boulton. (2017). Data-driven learning and language pedagogy. In S. Thorne & S. May (eds.), 1*. DOI: 10.1007/978-3-319-02328-1

Bouziane, K., & Bouziane, A. (2024). AI versus human effectiveness in essay evaluation. *Discover Education*, *3*(1), 201. DOI: 10.1007/s44217-024-00320-6

Bozkurt, A., & Sharma, R. C. (2020, April 30). *Emergency remote teaching in a time of global crisis due to CoronaVirus pandemic*. Retrieved January 26, 2025, from http://asianjde.com/ojs/index.php/AsianJDE/article/view/447

Boztemir, Y., & Calıskan, N. (2024). Analyzing and mitigating cultural hallucinations of commercial language models in Turkish. *Authorea Preprints*. DOI: 10.36227/techrxiv.171504678.80895811/v1

Bradáč, V., Smolka, P., Kotyrba, M., & Průdek, T. (2022). Design of an intelligent tutoring system to create a personalized study plan using expert systems. Applied Sciences. mdpi.com

Bray, A., Devitt, A., Banks, J., Sanchez Fuentes, S., Sandoval, M., Riviou, K., Byrne, D., Flood, M., Reale, J., & Terrenzio, S. (2024). What next for Universal Design for Learning? A systematic literature review of technology in UDL implementations at second level. *British Journal of Educational Technology, 55*(1), 113–138. Advance online publication. DOI: 10.1111/bjet.13328

Brooks, G., Clenton, J., & Fraser, S. (2021). Exploring the importance of vocabulary for English as an additional language learners' reading comprehension. *Studies in Second Language Learning and Teaching, 11*(3), 351–376. DOI: 10.14746/ssllt.2021.11.3.3

Brown, T. B., Mann, B., Ryder, N., Subbiah, M., Kaplan, J., Dhariwal, P., Neelakantan, A., Shyam, P., Sastry, G., Askell, A., Agarwal, S., Herbert-Voss, A., Krueger, G., Henighan, T., Child, R., Ramesh, A., Ziegler, D. M., Wu, J., Winter, C., . . . Amodei, D. (2020, May 28). *Language Models are Few-Shot Learners*. arXiv.org. https://arxiv.org/abs/2005.14165

Bukhari, S. G. A. S., Jamali, S. G., Larik, A. R., & Chang, M. S. (2023). Fostering intrinsic motivation among teachers: Importance of work environment and individual differences. [HTML]. *International Journal of School & Educational Psychology, 11*(1), 1–19. DOI: 10.1080/21683603.2021.1925182

Bykonia, O. (2025). Using artificial intelligence in the process of teaching English. *Scientific Herald of Sivershchyna: Series Education. Social and Behavioural Sciences, 1*(14), 183–185. DOI: 10.32755/sjeducation.2025.01.183

Caldarini, G., Jaf, S., & McGarry, K. (2022). A literature survey of recent advances in chatbots. *Information (Basel), 13*(1), 41. DOI: 10.3390/info13010041

Cancino, M., & Viguera, C. (2024). The impact of a gamified approach on vocabulary learning and vocabulary self-efficacy: Evidence from a Chilean primary EFL school. *Revista de Lingüistica Y Lenguas Aplicadas, 19*, 33–43.

Carroll, S. R., Garba, I., Figueroa-Rodríguez, O. L., Holbrook, J., Lovett, R., Materechera, S., Parsons, M., Raseroka, K., Rodriguez-Lonebear, D., Rowe, R., Sara, R., Walker, J. D., Anderson, J., & Hudson, M. (2020). The CARE Principles for Indigenous Data Governance. *Data Science Journal, 19*(1), 43. DOI: 10.5334/dsj-2020-043

Casheekar, A., Lahiri, A., Rath, K., Prabhakar, K. S., & Srinivasan, K. (2024). A contemporary review on chatbots, AI-powered virtual conversational agents, ChatGPT: Applications, open challenges and future research directions. *Computer Science Review, 52*, 100632. DOI: 10.1016/j.cosrev.2024.100632

Castillo, L., & Quinonez, A. (2022). Using digital comics for enhancing EFL vocabulary learning during the covid-19 pandemic. *International Journal of Learning. Teaching and Educational Research, 21*(5), 478–491. DOI: 10.26803/ijlter.21.5.24

Chakraborty, S., Misra, B., & Dey, N. (2024). AI-Empowered Knowledge [HTML]. *Management in Education.*

Chan, S. & Lo, N. (2024). Enhancing EFL/ESL instruction through gamification: a comprehensive review of empirical evidence. Frontiers in Education. frontiersin.org

Chan, C. K. Y. (2023). A comprehensive AI policy education framework for university teaching and learning. *International Journal of Educational Technology in Higher Education, 20*(1), 38. Advance online publication. DOI: 10.1186/s41239-023-00408-3

Chang, C. H., & Krulee, G. K. (1991). Resolution of ambiguity in Chinese and its application to machine translation. *Machine Translation, 6*(4), 279–315. DOI: 10.1007/BF00417653

Chang, W., Yuan, Y., & Lee, C. Y. (2021). Natural Language Processing in AI: Rethinking its role in language learning. *AI & Society, 36*(3), 709–721.

Chan, K. K.-W., & Tang, W. K.-W. (2024). Evaluating English teachers' artificial intelligence readiness and training needs with a TPACK-based model. *World Journal of English Language, 15*(1), 129–141. DOI: 10.5430/wjel.v15n1p129

Chassignol, M., Khoroshavin, A., Klimova, A., & Bilyatdinova, A. (2018). Artificial Intelligence trends in education: A narrative overview. *Procedia Computer Science, 136*, 16–24. DOI: 10.1016/j.procs.2018.08.233

Chemnad, K., & Othman, A. (2024). Digital accessibility in the era of artificial intelligence—Bibliometric analysis and systematic review. In *Frontiers in Artificial Intelligence* (Vol. 7). DOI: 10.3389/frai.2024.1349668

Chen, X., Dewaele, J. M., & Zhang, T. (2021). Sustainable development of EFL/ESL learners' willingness to communicate: the effects of teachers and teaching styles. Sustainability. mdpi.com

Chen, Y. (2024, May). Enhancing Language Acquisition: The Role of AI in Facilitating Effective Language Learning. In 2024 3rd International Conference on Humanities, Wisdom Education and Service Management (HWESM 2024) (pp. 593-600). Atlantis Press. atlantis-press.com

Chen, Y. L., Hsu, C. C., Lin, C. Y., & Hsu, H. H. (2022). Robot-assisted language learning: Integrating artificial intelligence and virtual reality into English tour guide practice. Education Sciences. mdpi.com

Chen, Z., & Yang, H. (2020). Yi Language Speech Recognition using Deep Learning Methods. Proceedings of 2020 IEEE 4th Information Technology, Networking, Electronic and Automation Control Conference, ITNEC 2020, 1064–1068. DOI: 10.1109/ITNEC48623.2020.9084771

Chen, A., Zhang, Y., Jia, J., Liang, M., Cha, Y., & Lim, C. P. (2025). A systematic review and meta-analysis of AI -enabled assessment in language learning: Design, implementation, and effectiveness. *Journal of Computer Assisted Learning*, *41*(1), e13064. Advance online publication. DOI: 10.1111/jcal.13064

Chen, B., Kuhn, R., Foster, G., Cherry, C., & Huang, F. (2016). Bilingual Methods for Adaptive Training Data Selection for Machine Translation. In Green, S., & Schwartz, L. (Eds.), *Conferences of the Association for Machine Translation in the Americas: MT Researchers' Track* (pp. 93–106). The Association for Machine Translation in the Americas., https://aclanthology.org/2016.amta-researchers.8/

Chen, C.-Y., Chen, W.-T., & Huang, H.-Y. (2024). Foundation models for low-resource language education (Vision Paper). arXiv. https://arxiv.org/abs/2412.04774

Cheng, L., Varshney, K. R., & Liu, H. (2021). Socially responsible ai algorithms: Issues, purposes, and challenges. *Journal of Artificial Intelligence Research*, *71*, 1137–1181. DOI: 10.1613/jair.1.12814

Chen, H. H.-J. (2011). Developing and evaluating an oral skills training website supported by automatic speech recognition technology. *ReCALL*, *23*(1), 59–78. DOI: 10.1017/S0958344010000285

Chen, H. H.-J., Yang, C. T. Y., & Lai, K. K. W. (2023). Investigating college EFL learners' perceptions toward the use of Google Assistant for foreign language learning. *Interactive Learning Environments*, *31*(3), 1335–1350. DOI: 10.1080/10494820.2020.1833043

Chen, P., & Alias, S. B. (2024, September). Opportunities and Challenges in the Cultivation of Software Development Professionals in the Context of Large Language Models. In *Proceedings of the 2024 International Symposium on Artificial Intelligence for Education* (pp. 259-267). DOI: 10.1145/3700297.3700342

Chen, S., Fang, Y., Shi, G., Sabatini, J., Greenberg, D., Frijters, J., & Graesser, A. C. (2021). Automated disengagement tracking within an intelligent tutoring system. *Frontiers in Artificial Intelligence*, *3*, 595627. Advance online publication. DOI: 10.3389/frai.2020.595627

Chen, X., Zou, D., Xie, H., Cheng, G., & Liu, C. (2022). Two decades of artificial intelligence in education. *Journal of Educational Technology & Society*, *25*(1), 28–47.

Chen, Y. L. (2016). The effects of virtual reality learning environment on student cognitive and linguistic development. *The Asia-Pacific Education Researcher*, *25*(4), 637–646. DOI: 10.1007/s40299-016-0293-2

Cheong, B. C. (2024). Transparency and accountability in AI systems: Safeguarding wellbeing in the age of algorithmic decision-making. *Frontiers in Human Dynamics*, *6*, 1421273. Advance online publication. DOI: 10.3389/fhumd.2024.1421273

Cherner, T., Fegely, A., Hou, C., & Halpin, P. (2023). AI-Powered Presentation Platforms for Improving Public Speaking Skills: Takeaways and Suggestions for Improvement. *Journal of Interactive Learning Research*, *34*(2), 339–367. Advance online publication. DOI: 10.70725/147215vyyrwx

Chiang, C.-H., & Lee, H. (2023). Can Large Language Models Be an Alternative to Human Evaluations? *Proceedings of the 61st Annual Meeting of the Association for Computational Linguistics (*Volume 1*: Long Papers)*, 15607–15631. DOI: 10.18653/v1/2023.acl-long.870

Chiang, C.-H., & Lee, H.-Y. (2022). On the Transferability of Pre-trained Language Models: A Study from Artificial Datasets. *Proceedings of the 36th AAAI Conference on Artificial Intelligence, AAAI 2022*, 36, 10518–10525. DOI: 10.1609/aaai.v36i10.21295

Chiaráin, N. N., & Chasaide, A. N. (2016, May 1). *Chatbot Technology with Synthetic Voices in the Acquisition of an Endangered Language: Motivation, Development and Evaluation of a Platform for Irish*. ACL Anthology. https://aclanthology.org/L16-1547/?utm_source=chatgpt.com

Chicherina, N., Zharkynbekova, S., Azamatova, A., & Akhmetbekova, A. (2024). OPTIMIZATION OF ADAPTIVE LANGUAGE LEARNING USING ARTIFICIAL IN LIGENCE. *Bulletin of Shokan Ualikhanov Kokshetau University Philological Series*, *3*(3), 279–290. DOI: 10.59102/kufil/2024/iss3pp279-290

Chigwada, J., & Ngulube, P. (2024). Librarians' role in the preservation and dissemination of indigenous knowledge. *IFLA Journal*, *50*(2), 242–256. DOI: 10.1177/03400352231217270

Chinnaiyan, B., Balasubaramanian, S., Jeyabalu, M., & Warrier, G. S. (2025). AI Applications – Computer Vision and Natural Language Processing," in Model Optimization Methods for Efficient and Edge AI: Federated Learning Architectures. *Frameworks and Applications, IEEE*, 25–41.

Chinnaiyan, B., Balasubaramanian, S., Jeyabalu, M., & Warrier, G. S. (2025). AI Applications–Computer Vision and Natural Language Processing. *Model Optimization Methods for Efficient and Edge AI: Federated Learning Architectures, Frameworks and Applications*, 25-41.

Chizzoni, I., & Vietti, A. (2024). Towards an ASR System for Documenting Endangered Languages: A Preliminary Study on Sardinian. *CEUR Workshop Proceedings, 3878*, •••. https://ceur-ws.org/Vol-3878/25_main_long.pdf

Chomsky, N. (1957). *Syntactic Structures*. Mouton. DOI: 10.1515/9783112316009

Chopade, P., Pu, S., LaMar, M., & Kurzum, C. (2023). Task-Based Workplace English: An Adaptive Multimodal Tutoring System. *Communications in Computer and Information Science, 1831 CCIS*. DOI: 10.1007/978-3-031-36336-8_59

Choukaier, D. (2024). Integrating AI In English Language Pedagogy: Innovations and Outcomes In Teaching English As Second/Foreign Language. *Educational Administration: Theory and Practice, 30*(5), 3311–3822.

Chowdhury, R. H. (2024). The evolution of business operations: unleashing the potential of Artificial Intelligence, Machine Learning, and Blockchain. World Journal of Advanced Research and Reviews. wjarr.co.in

Chowdhury, S., & Nath, A. (2021). Trends In Natural Language Processing: Scope And Challenges. *International Journal of Scientific Research in Computer Science, Engineering and Information Technology*. DOI: 10.32628/CSEIT217698

Chris, E., Kate, J., & Frank, E. (2024). *The ethical implications of integrating generative AI in education: Opportunities and challenges*. https://www.researchgate.net/publication/387326280

Christiano, M. (2025, January 19). *Full Rosetta Stone Review: Effective Legacy Program but Lacks Interactive Features*. FluentU. https://www.fluentu.com/blog/reviews/rosetta-stone/

Chui, J. (2023). The Effects of Cultural Assimilation on the Loss of the Tuvan and Seri Languages. *Journal of Student Research, 11*(3). Advance online publication. DOI: 10.47611/jsr.v11i3.1714

Cizrelioğlu, İ., & Aydin, S. (2025). Using artificial intelligence in EFL learning among multilingual young learners. In M. Sanmugam, B. Edwards, N. Mohd Barkhaya, & Z. Khlaif (Eds.), *Fostering inclusive education with AI and emerging technologies* (pp. 303-322). IGI Global. DOI: 10.4018/979-8-3693-7255-5.ch013

Colas, C., Karch, T., Moulin-Frier, C., & Oudeyer, P.-Y. (2022). Vygotskian Autotelic Artificial Intelligence: Language and Culture Internalization for Human-Like AI. *Nature Machine Intelligence*, *4*(December).

Conneau, A., Khandelwal, K., Goyal, N., Chaudhary, V., Wenzek, G., Guzmán, F., Grave, E., Ott, M., Zettlemoyer, L., & Stoyanov, V. (2019). Unsupervised Cross-lingual Representation Learning at Scale. https://arxiv.org/abs/1911.02116

Corbett, J. (2023). Cree coding decolonizes computer programming. SFU. Cree coding decolonizes computer programming - Simon Fraser University.

Corsi, E. (2023). Insight into plurilingual and pluricultural identity in multigenerational homes: A case study of three young adults. *Journal of Multilingual and Multicultural Development*, *44*(4), 288–308. Advance online publication. DOI: 10.1080/01434632.2020.1817045

Costa, A. R., Vasconcelos, S. V., & Balula, A. (2025). Artificial Intelligence and Language Learning: Methods, Tools, and Challenges. In *Integrating Artificial Intelligence in Education: Enhancing Teaching Practices for Future Learning* (pp. 267-286). IGI Global.

Costa, J. (2024). Why language revitalization fails: Revivalist vs. traditional ontologies of language in Provence. *Language in Society*, •••, 1–21. DOI: 10.1017/S0047404524000204

Council of Europe. (2020). *Common European Framework of Reference for Languages: Learning, teaching, assessment.* Strasbourg.

Couzens, V., Gaby, A., & Stebbins, T. (2020). Standardise This! Prescriptivism and Resistance to Standardization in Language Revitalization. In Allan, K. (Ed.), *Dynamics of Language Changes* (pp. 37–55). Springer Singapore., DOI: 10.1007/978-981-15-6430-7_3

Creswell, J. W. (2014). *Research Design: Qualitative, Quantitative, and Mixed Methods Approaches* (4th ed.). SAGE Publication.

Crowder, J. (2024). *AI chatbots: The good, the bad, and the ugly*. Springer Nature. DOI: 10.1007/978-3-031-45509-4

Crystal, D. (2002). *Language Death*. Cambridge University Press., DOI: 10.1017/CBO9781139871549

Csikszentmihalyi, M., & Davis, M. S. (1975). *Beyond boredom and anxiety* (1st ed.). Jossey-Bass.

Cui, W., Xue, Z., & Thai, K. P. (2018). Performance Comparison of an AI-Based Adaptive Learning System in China. *Proceedings 2018 Chinese Automation Congress, CAC 2018*. DOI: 10.1109/CAC.2018.8623327

D'Mello, S. K., & Graesser, A. (2023). Intelligent tutoring systems: How computers achieve learning gains that rival human tutors. Handbook of educational psychology. [HTML]

D'warte, J. (2021). Facilitating agency and engagement: Visual methodologies and pedagogical interventions for working with culturally and linguistically diverse young people. *Language Teaching Research*, *25*(1), 12–38. Advance online publication. DOI: 10.1177/1362168820938826

Dai, D. W., & Hua, Z. (2024). When AI meets intercultural communication: New frontiers, new agendas. In *Applied Linguistics Review*. De Gruyter Mouton., DOI: 10.1515/applirev-2024-0185

Dai, Y., & Wu, Z. (2023). Mobile-assisted pronunciation learning with feedback from peers and/or automatic speech recognition: A mixed-methods study. *Computer Assisted Language Learning*, *36*(5–6), 861–884. DOI: 10.1080/09588221.2021.1952272

Dale, R., & Viethen, J. (2021). The automated writing assistance landscape in 2021. *Natural Language Engineering*, *27*(4), 511–518. DOI: 10.1017/S1351324921000164

Dalili, S., & Zohuri, B. (2023). Revolutionizing Treatment: AI-Driven Noninvasive Approaches for ODD and ADHD. *Management Studies*, *11*(4). Advance online publication. DOI: 10.17265/2328-2185/2023.04.003

Daniels, P., & Iwago, K. (2017). The suitability of cloud-based speech recognition engines for language learning. *The JALT CALL Journal*, *13*(3), 229–239. DOI: 10.29140/jaltcall.v13n3.j220

Danilina, E., & Le Pichon, E. (2023). Embracing advances in AI-based language tools in EAP programs: Towards a plurilingual shift. In *Reconceptualizing Language Norms in Multilingual Contexts* (pp. 88–107). IGI Global., DOI: 10.4018/978-1-6684-8761-7.ch005

Darder, A., Hernandez, K., Lam, K. D., & Baltodano, M. (2023). Critical pedagogy: An introduction. In *The critical pedagogy reader* (pp. 1–30). Routledge. [HTML] DOI: 10.4324/9781003286080-1

Darling-Hammond, L., Burns, D., Campbell, C., Goodwin, A. L., Hammerness, K., Low, E. L., & Zeichner, K. (2017). *Empowered Educators: How High-Performing Systems Shape Teaching Quality Around the World*. John Wiley & Sons.

Darsih, E., Wihadi, M., & Hanggara, A. (2021, March 2). Using ELSA App in Speaking Classes: Students' Voices. *Proceedings of the 1st Universitas Kuningan International Conference on Social Science, Environment and Technology*. https://eudl.eu/doi/10.4108/eai.12-12-2020.2304993

Darwin, R., Rusdin, D., Mukminatien, N., Suryati, N., Laksmi, E. D., & Marzuki, . (2024). Critical thinking in the AI era: An exploration of EFL students' perceptions, benefits, and limitations. [tandfonline.com]. *Cogent Education, 11*(1), 2290342. DOI: 10.1080/2331186X.2023.2290342

Daryanto, T., Ding, X., Wilhelm, L. T., Stil, S., Knutsen, K. M., & Rho, E. H. (2024). *Conversate: supporting reflective learning in interview practice through interactive simulation and dialogic feedback. arXiv*. Cornell University., DOI: 10.1145/3701188

Davoodi, A. (2024). Crafting innovative paths in non-linear professional learning for bilingual education: The role of connectivism in the age of AI. *Professional Development in Education*, •••, 1–17.

Davoodi, A. (2024). EQUAL AI: A Framework for Enhancing Equity, Quality, Understanding and Accessibility in Liberal Arts through AI for Multilingual Learners. *Language, Technology, and Social Media*, *2*(2), 178–203. DOI: 10.70211/ltsm.v2i2.139

de Barcelos Silva, A., Gomes, M. M., da Costa, C. A., da Rosa Righi, R., Barbosa, J. L. V., Pessin, G., De Doncker, G., & Federizzi, G. (2020). Intelligent personal assistants: A systematic literature review. *Expert Systems with Applications*, *147*, 113193. DOI: 10.1016/j.eswa.2020.113193

de Vries, B. P., Cucchiarini, C., Bodnar, S., Strik, H., & van Hout, R. (2015). Spoken grammar practice and feedback in an ASR-based CALL system. *Computer Assisted Language Learning*, *28*(6), 550–576. DOI: 10.1080/09588221.2014.889713

Deacon, H. J. (2020). Ethics, intellectual property, and commercialization of cultural heritage. *Pravovedenie*, *64*(1), 93–111. DOI: 10.21638/spbu25.2020.108

Deep, L. (2025). DeepL Blog. Retrieved from https://www.deepl.com/en/blog

Dehganzadeh, H., & Dehganzadeh, H. (2020). Investigating effects of digital gamification-based language learning: A systematic review. *Journal of English Language Teaching and Learning*, *12*(25), 53–93. DOI: 10.22034/elt.2020.10676

Dela Cruz, J. W. (2022). "I Subtitle Myself": Affordances and Challenges of Canadian EAL Students' Plurilingual Learning Strategies in a Francophone College. *TESL Canada Journal*, *38*(2), 36–62. DOI: 10.18806/tesl.v38i2.1356

Demianenko, O., & Moroz, T. (2024). LINGUISTIC AND DIDACTIC POTENTIAL OF ARTIFICIAL IN LIGENCE TECHNOLOGIES IN TEACHING FOREIGN LANGUAGES. *Scientific Journal of Polonia University*, *66*(5), 9–16. DOI: 10.23856/6601

Dere, M. D., Dere, R. O., Adesina, A., & Yauri, A. R. (2023). An end-to-end framework for translation of American sign language to low-resource languages in Nigeria. *Scientific African*, *21*, e01809. Advance online publication. DOI: 10.1016/j.sciaf.2023.e01809

Dewi, D., Sudirman, S., & Darmawan, D. (2021). The Use of Artificial Intelligence in Learning English: Enhancing University Students' Skills. *Journal of Educational Technology*, *12*(3), 24–37.

Dhanapal, C., Asharudeen, N., & Alfaruque, S. Y. (2024). Impact of Artificial Intelligence Versus Traditional Instruction for Language Learning: A Survey. *World Journal of English Language*, *14*(2), 182–182. DOI: 10.5430/wjel.v14n2p182

Dhirani, L. L., Mukhtiar, N., Chowdhry, B. S., & Newe, T. (2023). Ethical dilemmas and Privacy issues in emerging technologies: A review. *Sensors (Basel)*, *23*(3), 1151. DOI: 10.3390/s23031151 PMID: 36772190

Dikli, S., & Bleyle, S. (2014). Automated Essay Scoring feedback for second language writers: How does it compare to instructor feedback? *Assessing Writing*, *22*, 1–17. DOI: 10.1016/j.asw.2014.03.006

Ding, S., Liberatore, C., Sonsaat, S., Lučić, I., Silpachai, A., Zhao, G., Chukharev-Hudilainen, E., Levis, J., & Gutierrez-Osuna, R. (2019). Golden speaker builder – An interactive tool for pronunciation training. *Speech Communication*, *115*, 51–66. DOI: 10.1016/j.specom.2019.10.005

Dizon, G. (2017). Using intelligent personal assistants for second language learning: A case study of Alexa. *TESOL Journal*, *8*(4), 811–830. DOI: 10.1002/tesj.353

Dizon, G. (2020). Evaluating intelligent personal assistants for L2 listening and speaking development. *Language Learning & Technology*, *24*(1), 16–26. DOI: 10.64152/10125/44705

Dizon, G., Tang, D., & Yamamoto, Y. (2022). A case study of using Alexa for out-of-class, self-directed Japanese language learning. *Computers and Education: Artificial Intelligence*, *3*, 100088. DOI: 10.1016/j.caeai.2022.100088

Dodigovic, M., & Tovmasyan, A. (2021). Automated writing evaluation: The accuracy of Grammarly's feedback on form. *International Journal of TESOL Studies*, *3*(2), 71–87.

Dolenc, K., Šorgo, A., & Ploj-Virtič, M. (2021). Perspectives on Lessons From the COVID-19 Outbreak for Post-pandemic Higher Education: Continuance Intention Model of Forced Online Distance Teaching. European Journal of Educational Research, volume-11-2022(volume-11-issue-1-january-2022), 163–177. DOI: 10.12973/eu-jer.11.1.163

Dong, C. (2024). Educational concepts and methodologies in the AI era: Challenges and responses. Frontiers of Digital Education. [HTML]

Dong, J., Lee, S., Wang, C. H., & Shannon, D. M. (2023). Impact on social capital and learning engagement due to social media usage among the international students in the US. [springer.com]. *Education and Information Technologies*, *28*(7), 8027–8050. DOI: 10.1007/s10639-022-11520-8 PMID: 36532798

Dong, Y., Yu, X., Alharbi, A., & Ahmad, S. (2022). AI-based production and application of English multimode online reading using multi-criteria decision support system. *Soft Computing*, *26*(20), 10927–10937. Advance online publication. DOI: 10.1007/s00500-022-07209-2

Drugova, E., Zhuravleva, I., Aiusheeva, M., & Grits, D. (2021). Toward a model of learning innovation integration: TPACK-SAMR based analysis of the introduction of a digital learning environment in three Russian universities. *Education and Information Technologies*, *26*(4), 4925–4942. DOI: 10.1007/s10639-021-10514-2 PMID: 33814955

du Plooy, E., Casteleijn, D., & Franzsen, D. (2024). Personalized adaptive learning in higher education: A scoping review of key characteristics and impact on academic performance and engagement. *Heliyon*, *10*(21), e39630. DOI: 10.1016/j.heliyon.2024.e39630

Duarte, J. (2019). Translanguaging in mainstream education: A sociocultural approach. *International Journal of Bilingual Education and Bilingualism*, *22*(2), 150–164. Advance online publication. DOI: 10.1080/13670050.2016.1231774

Duarte, J., & van der Ploeg, M. (2019). Plurilingual lecturers in English medium instruction in the Netherlands: The key to plurilingual approaches in higher education? *European Journal of Higher Education*, *9*(3), 268–284. Advance online publication. DOI: 10.1080/21568235.2019.1602476

Dubey, P., Dubey, P., Raja, R., & Kshatri, S. S. (2025). Bridging language gaps: The role of NLP and speech recognition in oral english instruction. *MethodsX*, *14*, 103359. Advance online publication. DOI: 10.1016/j.mex.2025.103359

Dueñas, F. K. (2015). Negotiating Ideological and Implementational Spaces for Indigenous Languages in Peru. Working Papers in Educational Linguistics, 30(1), 21–41. https://wpel.gse.upenn.edu/sites/default/files/WPEL30.1Kvietok_Duenas.pdf

Dutton, J., & Rushton, K. (2021). Using the translanguaging space to facilitate poetic representation of language and identity. *Language Teaching Research*, *25*(1), 105–133. Advance online publication. DOI: 10.1177/1362168820951215

Dwivedi, D. N., Mahanty, G., & nath Dwivedi, V. (2024). The Role of Predictive Analytics in Personalizing Education: Tailoring Learning Paths for Individual Student Success. In Enhancing Education With Intelligent Systems and Data-Driven Instruction (pp. 44-59). IGI Global. [HTML]

Eberhard, D. M., Simons, G. F., & Fennig, C. D. (2024). Ethnologue: Languages of the World. Twenty-seventh edition. http://www.ethnologue.com

Eisenstein, J. (2013). What to do about bad language on the internet. Proceedings of the 2nd Workshop on Computational Linguistics for Literature, CLfL 2013 at the 2013 Conference of the North American Chapter of the Association for Computational Linguistics: Human Language Technologies, NAACL-HLT 2013, 359–369. https://aclanthology.org/N13-1037/

Epps, P. (2020). Amazonian linguistic diversity and its sociocultural correlates. In Language Dispersal, Diversification, and Contact (pp. 275–290). Oxford University Press. DOI: 10.1093/oso/9780198723813.003.0016

Erawati, N. K. R., Laksmi, N. K. P. A., & Suparwa, I. N. (2023). The Historical Dynamics of the Archaistic Lexicon in Modern Balinese Languages. *Journal of Language Teaching and Research*, *14*(1), 172–180. DOI: 10.17507/jltr.1401.18

Escalante, J., Pack, A., & Barrett, A. (2023). AI-generated feedback on writing: Insights into efficacy and ENL student preference. *International Journal of Educational Technology in Higher Education*, *20*(1), 57. Advance online publication. DOI: 10.1186/s41239-023-00425-2

Esmaeili, Z., & Shahrokhi, M. (2020). The impact of Memrise application on Iranian EFL learners' collocation learning and retention. *International Journal of Language Education*, *4*(2), 221–233. DOI: 10.26858/ijole.v4i2.10672

Essafi, M., Belfakir, L., & Moubtassime, M. (2024). Investigating Mobile-Assisted Language Learning apps: Babbel, Memrise, and Duolingo as a case study. *Journal of Curriculum and Teaching*, *13*(2), 197. DOI: 10.5430/jct.v13n2p197

Ess, C. (2020). *Digital Media Ethics* (3rd ed.). Polity Press., https://www.politybooks.com/bookdetail?book_slug=digital-media-ethics-3rd-edition--9781509533428

Eswaran, U., Eswaran, V., Murali, K., & Eswaran, V. (2025). AI-Powered Language Teaching and Learning: Innovations and Challenges. In Reimagining Intelligent Computer-Assisted Language Education (pp. 55-92). IGI Global. [HTML]

Etaat, F. (2024). The Effect of AI-Based Applications on EFL Writing Skill Development: An Inquiry into Integration of AI into Language Learning. Master's thesis, UiT Norges arktiske universitet.

Evenddy, S. S. (2024). Investigating AI's Automated Feedback in English Language Learning. *FLIP Foreign Language Instruction Probe*, *3*(1), 76–87. DOI: 10.54213/flip.v3i1.401

Evers, K., & Chen, S. (2022). Effects of an automatic speech recognition system with peer feedback on pronunciation instruction for adults. *Computer Assisted Language Learning*, *35*(8), 1869–1889. DOI: 10.1080/09588221.2020.1839504

Eynon, R., & Geniets, A. (2016). The digital skills paradox: How do digitally excluded youth develop skills to use the internet? *Learning, Media and Technology*, *41*(3), 463–479. DOI: 10.1080/17439884.2014.1002845

Eynon, R., & Malmberg, L. (2021). Lifelong learning and the Internet: Who benefits most from learning online? *British Journal of Educational Technology*, *52*(2), 569–583. DOI: 10.1111/bjet.13041

Facundes, S. da S., Virtanen, P. K., de Freitas, M. F. P., Lima-Padovani, B. F. S., & do Nascimento Costa, P. (2019). Language Revitalization and Engagements in the Amazon: The Case of Apurinã. In Handbook of the Changing World Language Map (pp. 1–17). Springer International Publishing. DOI: 10.1007/978-3-319-73400-2_35-1

Falloon, G. (2020). From digital literacy to digital competence: The teacher digital competency (TDC) framework. *Educational Technology Research and Development*, *68*(5), 2449–2472. DOI: 10.1007/s11423-020-09767-4

Fang, Y., Lippert, A., Cai, Z., Chen, S., Frijters, J. C., Greenberg, D., & Graesser, A. C. (2022). Patterns of adults with low literacy skills interacting with an intelligent tutoring system. [springer.com]. *International Journal of Artificial Intelligence in Education, 32*(2), 1–26. DOI: 10.1007/s40593-021-00266-y

Farahani, M. S., & Ghasemi, G. (2024). Artificial Intelligence in education: A comprehensive study. *Forum for Education Studies, 2*(3), 1379. DOI: 10.59400/fes.v2i3.1379

Fathi, J., Rahimi, M., & Derakhshan, A. (2024). Improving EFL learners' speaking skills and willingness to communicate via artificial intelligence-mediated interactions. [HTML]. *System, 121*, 103254. DOI: 10.1016/j.system.2024.103254

Fazal, N., Tahir, M. S., Chaudhary, M., & Abbasi, M. (2024). Effectiveness of AI Integration into Computer-Assisted Language Learning (CALL) on Student Writing Skills Based on Gender. *Pakistan Journal of Humanities and Social Sciences, 12*(1), 224–230. DOI: 10.52131/pjhss.2024.v12i1.1974

Fendji, J. L. K. E., Tala, D. C., Yenke, B. O., & Atemkeng, M. (2022). Automatic speech recognition using limited vocabulary: A survey. [tandfonline.com]. *Applied Artificial Intelligence, 36*(1), 2095039. DOI: 10.1080/08839514.2022.2095039

Feng, L. (2025). Investigating the Effects of Artificial Intelligence-Assisted Language Learning Strategies on Cognitive Load and Learning Outcomes: A Comparative Study. *Journal of Educational Computing Research, 62*(8), 1961–1994. DOI: 10.1177/07356331241268349

Feng, R., Brennan, K. A., Azizi, Z., Goyal, J., Deb, B., Chang, H. J., & Narayan, S. M. (2024). Engineering of Generative Artificial Intelligence and Natural Language Processing Models to Accurately Identify Arrhythmia Recurrence. *Circulation: Arrhythmia and Electrophysiology*, •••, e013023.

Feng, S., Halpern, B. M., Kudina, O., & Scharenborg, O. (2024). Towards inclusive automatic speech recognition. *Computer Speech & Language, 84*, 101567. DOI: 10.1016/j.csl.2023.101567

Fielding, R. (2016). Students' use of their plurilingual resources in Australian schools. *Language and Education, 30*(4), 361–377. Advance online publication. DOI: 10.1080/09500782.2015.1114631

Filippetti, S., Sbardella, T., & Montanucci, G. (2024, November). AI-Driven Approaches to L2 Learning: Technology Applications and Perspectives. In *Conference Proceedings. Innovation in Language Learning 2024.*

Filippova, O. V. (2024). The Development of a Secondary Linguistic Personality as a Factor in the Successful Education of Foreign Students at a Russian University. *Integra Educativa*, *28*(4), 641–655. DOI: 10.15507/1991-9468.117.028.202404.641-655

Firnando, H. G. (2024). Navigating the challenges of technological advancement: Iqbal's philosophical insights on moderation and humanity in the digital age. *Aladalah*, *27*(1), 51–69. Advance online publication. DOI: 10.35719/aladalah.v27i1.394

Fitria, T. N. (2021). Grammarly as AI-powered English Writing Assistant: Students' Alternative for Writing English. *Metathesis: Journal of English Language, Literature, and Teaching*, *5*(1), 65. Advance online publication. DOI: 10.31002/metathesis.v5i1.3519

Floridi, L., & Chiriatti, M. (2020). GPT-3: Its nature, scope, limits, and consequences. *Minds and Machines*, *30*(4), 681–694. DOI: 10.1007/s11023-020-09548-1

Fredholm, K. (2023). Challenges and needs in Ladino teaching among ten language revitalisation activists. Meldar. *Revista Internacional de Estudios Sefardíes*, *4*(4), 43–69. DOI: 10.46661/meldar.8525

Frith, K. H. (2019). Artificial Intelligence. *Nursing Education Perspectives*, *40*(4), 261. DOI: 10.1097/01.NEP.0000000000000543 PMID: 31232902

Fryer, L. K., Coniam, D., Carpenter, R., & Lăpu neanu, D. (2020). Bots for language learning now: Current and future directions. *Language Learning & Technology*, *24*(2), 8–22. DOI: 10.64152/10125/44719

Fryer, L. K., Nakao, K., & Thompson, A. (2019). Chatbot learning partners: Connecting learning experiences, interests, and competence. *Computers in Human Behavior*, *93*, 279–289. DOI: 10.1016/j.chb.2018.12.023

Fu, Y. & Weng, Z. (2024). Navigating the ethical terrain of AI in education: A systematic review on framing responsible human-centered AI practices. Computers and Education: Artificial Intelligence. sciencedirect.com

Fuller, , K., Morbitzer, K. A., Zeeman, J. M., M. Persky, A., C. Savage, A., & McLaughlin, J. E. (. (2024). Exploring the use of ChatGPT to analyze student course evaluation comments. *BMC Medical Education*, *24*(1), 423. DOI: 10.1186/s12909-024-05316-2

Gaballo, V. (2024, November). Revolutionizing language teaching: AI in oral language assessment. In *Conference Proceedings. Innovation in Language Learning 2024.*

Gabriel, J. (2024). How Artificial Intelligence (AI) impacts inclusive education. *Educational Research Review*, *19*(6), 95–103. DOI: 10.5897/ERR2024.4404

Galante, A., Chiras, M., Wayne, J., Dela Cruz, N., & Zeaiter, L. F. (2022). *Implementing Critical Plurilingual Pedagogy in Language Education Plurilingual Guide*. https://www.mcgill.ca/plurilinguallab/files/plurilinguallab/plurilingual

Galante, A. (2020). The moment I realized I am plurilingual": Plurilingual tasks for creative representations in EAP at a Canadian university. *Applied Linguistics Review, 11*(4), 551–580. Advance online publication. DOI: 10.1515/applirev-2018-0116

Galante, A. (2022). Plurilingual and pluricultural competence (PPC) scale: The inseparability of language and culture. *International Journal of Multilingualism, 19*(4), 477–498. Advance online publication. DOI: 10.1080/14790718.2020.1753747

Galante, A., Okubo, K., Cole, C., Elkader, N. A., Carozza, N., Wilkinson, C., Wotton, C., & Vasic, J. (2019). Plurilingualism in Higher Education: A Collaborative Initiative for the Implementation of Plurilingual Pedagogy in an English for Academic Purposes Program at a Canadian University. *TESL Canada Journal, 36*(1), 121–133. Advance online publication. DOI: 10.18806/tesl.v36i1.1305

Gallegos-Rejas, V. M., Thomas, E. E., Kelly, J. T., & Smith, A. C. (2023). A multi-stakeholder approach is needed to reduce the digital divide and encourage equitable access to telehealth. [sagepub.com]. *Journal of Telemedicine and Telecare, 29*(1), 73–78. DOI: 10.1177/1357633X221107995 PMID: 35733379

Gaon, A., & Stedman, I. (2019). A Call to Action: Moving Forward with the Governance of Artificial Intelligence in Canada. *Alberta Law Review*, 1137. Advance online publication. DOI: 10.29173/alr2547

García, O. (2011). *Bilingual education in the 21st century: A global perspective*. John Wiley & Sons.

García, O., & Otheguy, R. (2020). Plurilingualism and translanguaging: Commonalities and divergences. *International Journal of Bilingual Education and Bilingualism, 23*(1), 17–35. Advance online publication. DOI: 10.1080/13670050.2019.1598932

Garg, S., & Sharma, S. (2020). Impact of artificial intelligence in special need education to promote inclusive pedagogy. *International Journal of Information and Education Technology (IJIET), 10*(7), 523–527. Advance online publication. DOI: 10.18178/ijiet.2020.10.7.1418

Garlinska, M., Osial, M., Proniewska, K., & Pregowska, A. (2023). The influence of emerging technologies on distance education. Electronics. mdpi.com

Gatsiou, C., Fragkou, E., Hatzidaki, A., & Korda, D. (2024). Artificial Intelligence (AI) in Translation and Interpreting: Exploring AI's Potential in Translation and Interpreting Profession and Pedagogy in the Medical Context and its Ethical Implications

Gedeon, M. M., Samantaray, S., & René, K. B. (2024). Changing the Trajectory: Preserving the Linguistic Diversity of Shi Language Using AI and NLP (pp. 57–69). DOI: 10.1007/978-981-97-1987-7_5

Genç Ersoy, B., & Belet Boyacı, Ş. D. (2021). Devising gamification for vocabulary development and motivation: An experimental, mixed-model study. *International Technology and Education Journal*, *5*(1), 32–49.

Georgieva, V. (2025). Embracing the inevitable: Tips for EFL and ESP learning with AI. *E-Learning Innovations Journal*, *3*(1), 89–115. DOI: 10.57125/ELIJ.2025.03.25.05

Getachew, S., & Yayeh, Y. (2023). Gex'ez-English Bi-Directional Neural Machine Translation Using Transformer. 2023 International Conference on Information and Communication Technology for Development for Africa (ICT4DA), 160–164. DOI: 10.1109/ICT4DA59526.2023.10302254

Getman, Y., Phan, N., Al-Ghezi, R., Voskoboinik, E., Singh, M., Grosz, T., Kurimo, M., Salvi, G., Svendsen, T., Strombergsson, S., Smolander, A., & Ylinen, S. (2023). Developing an AI-Assisted Low-Resource Spoken Language Learning App for Children. *IEEE Access : Practical Innovations, Open Solutions*, *11*, 86025–86037. Advance online publication. DOI: 10.1109/ACCESS.2023.3304274

Ghafar, Z. N., Salh, H. F., Abdulrahim, M. A., Farxha, S. S., Arf, S. F., & Rahim, R. İ. (2023). The role of artificial intelligence technology on English language learning: A literature review. *Canadian Journal of Language and Literature Studies*, *3*(2), 17–31.

Ghazal, L. (2007). Learning vocabulary in EFL contexts through vocabulary learning strategies. *NOVITAS-ROYAL*, *1*(2), 84–91.

Ghosh, R. K., Ghosh, M., Roy, D., Gupta, B., Chakraborty, S., Biswas, A., & Basu, M. (2025). Personalized Financial Services through NLP and AI-Driven Innovations in FinTech. In *IGI Global eBooks* (pp. 371–420). DOI: 10.4018/979-8-3693-9944-6.ch019

Ghosh, S. (2025). Developing artificial intelligence (AI) capabilities for data-driven business model innovation: Roles of organizational adaptability and leadership. *Journal of Engineering and Technology Management*, *75*, 101851. DOI: 10.1016/j.jengtecman.2024.101851

Ghufron, M. A. (2019). Exploring an automated feedback program 'Grammarly' and teacher corrective feedback in EFL writing assessment: modern vs. traditional assessment. The 3rd English Language and Literature International Conference, ELLiC, Semarang, Indonesia.

Giannakos, M., Azevedo, R., Brusilovsky, P., Cukurova, M., Dimitriadis, Y., Hernandez-Leo, D., Järvelä, S., Mavrikis, M., & Rienties, B. (2024). The promise and challenges of generative AI in education. *Behaviour & Information Technology*, •••, 1–27. DOI: 10.1080/0144929X.2024.2394886

Giri, A. (2024). Revolutionizing student evaluation. In *Advances in educational technologies and instructional design book series* (pp. 333–362). DOI: 10.4018/979-8-3693-6170-2.ch012

Gkinko, L., & Elbanna, A. (2022). Hope, tolerance and empathy: Employees' emotions when using an AI-enabled chatbot in a digitalised workplace. *Information Technology & People*, *35*(6), 1714–1743. Advance online publication. DOI: 10.1108/ITP-04-2021-0328

Gligorea, I., Cioca, M., Oancea, R., Gorski, A. T., Gorski, H., & Tudorache, P. (2023). Adaptive learning using artificial intelligence in e-learning: A literature review. [mdpi.com]. *Education Sciences*, *13*(12), 1216. DOI: 10.3390/educsci13121216

Godwin-Jones, R. (2018). Contextualized vocabulary learning. *Language Learning & Technology ISSN*, *22*(3), 1–19. https://scholarspace.manoa.hawaii.edu/server/api/core/bitstreams/fe8e9343-3e0c-4bfb-858f-c47c4f36ff41/content

Godwin-Jones, R. (2019). Future directions in informal language learning. *The handbook of informal language learning*, 457-470.

Godwin-Jones, R. (2024, March 29). Distributed agency in second language learning and teaching through generative AI. arXiv.org. https://arxiv.org/abs/2403.20216

Goh, C. C. M. & Vandergrift, L. (2021). Teaching and learning second language listening: Metacognition in action. [HTML]

Goncalves, A., Ray, P., Soper, B., Stevens, J., Coyle, L., & Sales, A. P. (2020). Generation and evaluation of synthetic patient data. *BMC Medical Research Methodology*, *20*(1), 108. Advance online publication. DOI: 10.1186/s12874-020-00977-1

González, A. S., & Rampino, L. (2024). A design perspective on how to tackle gender biases when developing AI-driven systems. *AI and Ethics*. Advance online publication. DOI: 10.1007/s43681-023-00386-2

González-González, C. S., Muñoz-Cruz, V., Toledo-Delgado, P. A., & Nacimiento-García, E. (2023). Personalized gamification for learning: A reactive chatbot architecture proposal. [mdpi.com]. *Sensors (Basel)*, *23*(1), 545. DOI: 10.3390/s23010545 PMID: 36617143

Google. (2021, May 5). Woolaroo: A new tool for exploring indigenous languages. Google Arts & Culture Blog. https://blog.google/outreach-initiatives/arts-culture/woolaroo-new-tool-exploring-indigenous-languages/

Gozcu, E., & Caganaga, C. K. (2016). The importance of using games in EFL classrooms. *Cypriot Journal of Educational Sciences*, *11*(3), 126–135. DOI: 10.18844/cjes.v11i3.625

Graham, C. R. (2011). Theoretical considerations for understanding technological pedagogical content knowledge (TPACK). *Computers & Education*, *57*(3), 1953–1969. DOI: 10.1016/j.compedu.2011.04.010

Green, K. J. (2024). AI-Driven programming education for Black, Latinx, and Afro-Caribbean communities. *Deep Blue (University of Michigan)*. DOI: 10.7302/23676

Grimes, D., & Warschauer, M. (2010). Utility in a fallible tool: A multi-site case study of automated writing evaluation. *The Journal of Technology, Learning, and Assessment*, *8*(6), 1–43.

Gu, X., Chen, S., Peng, Y., & Qin, Y. (2024). One mind, two languages: researching language and cognition in bilinguals The Study of Bilingual Language Processing: by Nan Jiang, Oxford, Oxford University Press, 2023, ix+ 273 pp.,£ 35.00 (paperback), ISBN 9780198852513.

Guerrettaz, A. M., & Engman, M. M. (2023). Indigenous Language Revitalization. In *Oxford Research Encyclopedia of Education*. Oxford University Press., DOI: 10.1093/acrefore/9780190264093.013.559

Guo, A., Kamar, E., Vaughan, J. W., Wallach, H., & Morris, M. R. (2020). Toward fairness in AI for people with disabilities SBG@a research roadmap. *ACM SIGACCESS Accessibility and Computing*, *125*(125), 1. Advance online publication. DOI: 10.1145/3386296.3386298

Guo, Q., Feng, R., & Hua, Y. (2022). How effectively can EFL students use automated written corrective feedback (AWCF) in research writing? *Computer Assisted Language Learning*, *35*(9), 2312–2331. DOI: 10.1080/09588221.2021.1879161

Guo, X., & Chen, Y. (2024). Generative AI for Synthetic Data Generation: Methods, Challenges and the Future. https://arxiv.org/abs/2403.04190

Gupta, R., Agarwal, U., & Helen Victoria, A. (2024, January). Multilingual Communication: NMT-Based On-Call Speech Translation for Indian Languages. In International Conference on Multi-Strategy Learning Environment (pp. 113-127). Singapore: Springer Nature Singapore. [HTML] DOI: 10.1007/978-981-97-1488-9_9

Gu, X., Yu, T., Huang, J., Wang, F., Zheng, X., Sun, M., Ye, Z., & Li, Q. (2023). Virtual-Agent-Based Language Learning: A Scoping Review of Journal Publications from 2012 to 2022. *Sustainability (Basel)*, *15*(18), 13479. Advance online publication. DOI: 10.3390/su151813479

Gyonyoru, K. I. K., & Katona, J. (2024). Student Perceptions of AI-Enhanced Adaptive Learning Systems: A Pilot Survey. *2024 IEEE 7th International Conference and Workshop Óbuda on Electrical and Power Engineering (CANDO-EPE)*, 93–98. DOI: 10.1109/CANDO-EPE65072.2024.10772884

Hagendorff, T. (2020). The ethics of AI ethics: An evaluation of guidelines. *Minds and Machines*, *30*(1), 99–120. https://link.springer.com/article/10.1007/S11023-020-09517-8. DOI: 10.1007/s11023-020-09517-8

Håkansson, A., & Hartung, R. L. (2020). *Artificial Intelligence-Concepts, Areas, Techniques and Applications*. Studentlitteratur.

Håkansson, A., & Phillips-Wren, G. (2024). Generative AI and large language models - benefits, drawbacks, future and recommendations. *Procedia Computer Science*, *246*, 5458–5468. DOI: 10.1016/j.procs.2024.09.689

Haleem, A., Javaid, M., Qadri, M. A., & Suman, R. (2022). Understanding the role of digital technologies in education: A review. *Sustainable Operations and Computers*, *3*, 275–285. DOI: 10.1016/j.susoc.2022.05.004

Hale, K. (1992). Endangered languages: On endangered languages and the safeguarding of diversity. *Language*, *68*(1), 1–42. DOI: 10.1353/lan.1992.0052

Halkiopoulos, C. & Gkintoni, E. (2024). Leveraging AI in e-learning: Personalized learning and adaptive assessment through cognitive neuropsychology—A systematic analysis. Electronics. mdpi.com

Halpin, E., Prishker, N., & Melzi, G. (2021). The Bilingual Language Diversity of Latino Preschoolers: A Latent Profile analysis. *Language, Speech, and Hearing Services in Schools*, *52*(3), 877–888. DOI: 10.1044/2021_LSHSS-21-00015

Hamari, J. (2017). Do badges increase user activity? A field experiment on the effects of gamification. *Computers in Human Behavior, 71*, 469–478. DOI: 10.1016/j.chb.2015.03.036

Han, A., & Cai, Z. (2023). Design implications of generative AI systems for visual storytelling for young learners. Proceedings of IDC 2023 - 22nd Annual ACM Interaction Design and Children Conference: Rediscovering Childhood, 470–474. DOI: 10.1145/3585088.3593867

Han, Y. C. & Reber, P. J. (2022). Implicit sequence learning using auditory cues leads to modality-specific representations. Psychonomic bulletin & review. springer.com

Hanna, M., Pantanowitz, L., Jackson, B., Palmer, O., Visweswaran, S., Pantanowitz, J., & Rashidi, H. (2024). Ethical and Bias Considerations in Artificial Intelligence (AI)/Machine Learning. [sciencedirect.com]. *Modern Pathology*, •••, 100686. PMID: 39694331

Hanus, M. D., & Fox, J. (2015). Assessing the effects of gamification in the classroom: A longitudinal study on intrinsic motivation, social comparison, satisfaction, effort, and academic performance. *Computers & Education*, *80*, 152–161. DOI: 10.1016/j.compedu.2014.08.019

Haoming, L., & Wei, W. (2024). A systematic review on vocabulary learning in AR and VR gamification context. *Computers and Education: X Reality, 4*. DOI: 10.1016/j.cexr.2024.100057

Harry, A., & Sayudin, S. (2023). Role of AI in Education. [INJURITY]. *Interdiciplinary Journal and Hummanity*, *2*(3), 260–268. Advance online publication. DOI: 10.58631/injurity.v2i3.52

Harunasari, S. Y. (2023). Examining the Effectiveness of AI-integrated Approach in EFL Writing: A Case of ChatGPT. *International Journal of Progressive Sciences and Technologies*, *39*(2), 357. Advance online publication. DOI: 10.52155/ijpsat.v39.2.5516

Hashemi, A. (2021). The effects of using games on teaching vocabulary in reading comprehension: A case of gifted students. *Journal for the Education of Gifted Young Scientists*, *9*(2), 151–160. DOI: 10.17478/jegys.846480

Hashmi, E., Yayilgan, S. Y., Hameed, I. A., Yamin, M. M., Ullah, M., & Abomhara, M. (2024). Enhancing multilingual hate speech detection: From language-specific insights to cross-linguistic integration. *IEEE Access : Practical Innovations, Open Solutions*, *12*, 121507–121537. DOI: 10.1109/ACCESS.2024.3452987

Hassan, M. M., & Mirza, T. (2021). The digital literacy in teachers of the schools of Rajouri (J&K)-India: Teachers' perspective. *International Journal of Education and Management Engineering*, *11*(1), 28–40. DOI: 10.5815/ijeme.2021.01.04

Haßler, B., Major, L., & Hennessy, S. (2016). Tablet use in schools: A critical review of the evidence for learning outcomes. *Journal of Computer Assisted Learning*, *32*(2), 139–156. DOI: 10.1111/jcal.12123

Hasumi, T., & Chiu, M. S. (2024). Technology-enhanced language learning in English language education: Performance analysis, core publications, and emerging trends. *Cogent Education*, *11*(1), 2346044. Advance online publication. DOI: 10.1080/2331186X.2024.2346044

Hatipoğlu, Ç., Delibegović Džanić, N., Gajek, E., & Miloshevska, L. (2022). Crowdsourcing and language learning habits and practices in Turkey, Bosnia and Herzegovina, the Republic of North Macedonia and Poland in the pre-pandemic and pandemic periods. Slovenščina 2.0: Empirical. *Applied and Interdisciplinary Research*, *10*(2), 132–183. DOI: 10.4312/slo2.0.2022.2.132-183

Heath, M. K., Gleason, B., Mehta, R., & Hall, T. (2024). More than knowing: Toward collective, critical, and ecological approaches in educational technology research. *Educational Technology Research and Development*, *72*(5), 2519–2541. DOI: 10.1007/s11423-023-10242-z

Hebert, Y., Guo, Y., & Pellerin, M. (2008). New Horizons for Research on Bilingualism and Plurilingualism: A Focus on Languages of Immigration in Canada. *Encounters in Theory and History of Education*, *9*, 57–74. Advance online publication. DOI: 10.24908/eoe-ese-rse.v9i0.647

Heift, T., & Schulze, M. (2007). Errors and intelligence in computer-assisted language learning: Parsers and pedagogues. *Computational Linguistics*, *34*(1), 1–283.

Hennebry, M., & Gao, X. (2021). Interactions between medium of instruction and language learning motivation. [HTML]. *International Journal of Bilingual Education and Bilingualism*, *24*(7), 976–989. DOI: 10.1080/13670050.2018.1530190

Heo, K., Cheng, S., Joos, E., & Joharifard, S. (2024). Use of innovative technology in surgical training in resource-limited settings: A scoping review. [HTML]. *Journal of Surgical Education*, *81*(2), 243–256. DOI: 10.1016/j.jsurg.2023.11.004 PMID: 38161100

Herrera-González, B. D., Gelbukh, A., & Calvo, H. (2020). Automatic Story Generation: State of the Art and Recent Trends (pp. 81–91). DOI: 10.1007/978-3-030-60887-3_8

Hervieux, S., & Wheatley, A. (2021). Perceptions of artificial intelligence: A survey of academic librarians in Canada and the United States. *Journal of Academic Librarianship*, *47*(1), 102270. Advance online publication. DOI: 10.1016/j.acalib.2020.102270

Heugh, K., French, M., Arya, V., Pham, M., Tudini, V., Billinghurst, N., Tippett, N., Chang, L.-C., Nichols, J., & Viljoen, J.-M. (2022). Multilingualism, translanguaging and transknowledging: Translation technology in EMI higher education. *AILA Review*, *35*(1), 89–127. DOI: 10.1075/aila.22011.heu

Hew, K. F., Huang, W., Du, J., & Jia, C. (2023). Using chatbots to support student goal setting and social presence in fully online activities: learner engagement and perceptions. Journal of Computing in Higher Education. springer.com

He, X. S., & Loewen, S. (2022). Stimulating learner engagement in app-based L2 vocabulary self-study: Goals and feedback for effective L2 pedagogy. [HTML]. *System*, *105*, 102719. DOI: 10.1016/j.system.2021.102719

Historica Canada. (2023, November 28). AI-powered preservation of endangered languages. https://www.historica.org/blog/ai-powered-preservation-of-endangered-languages

Ho, C. C. (2024). Using AI-Generative Tools in Tertiary Education: Reflections on Their Effectiveness in Improving Tertiary Students' English Writing Abilities. *Online Learning : the Official Journal of the Online Learning Consortium*, *28*(3), 33–54. DOI: 10.24059/olj.v28i3.4632

Hooda, M., Rana, C., Dahiya, O., Rizwan, A., & Hossain, M. S. (2022). Artificial intelligence for assessment and feedback to enhance student success in higher education. [wiley.com]. *Mathematical Problems in Engineering*, *2022*(1), 5215722. DOI: 10.1155/2022/5215722

Hopp, H., & Thoma, D. (2021). Effects of Plurilingual Teaching on Grammatical Development in Early Foreign-Language Learning. *Modern Language Journal*, *105*(2), 464–483. Advance online publication. DOI: 10.1111/modl.12709

Hossain, K. I. (2024). Reviewing the role of culture in English language learning: Challenges and opportunities for educators. Social Sciences & Humanities Open. sciencedirect.com

Hou, R., Fütterer, T., Bühler, B., Bozkir, E., Gerjets, P., Trautwein, U., & Kasneci, E. (2024, July). Automated assessment of encouragement and warmth in classrooms leveraging multimodal emotional features and ChatGPT. In *International Conference on Artificial Intelligence in Education* (pp. 60-74). Cham: Springer Nature Switzerland. DOI: 10.1007/978-3-031-64302-6_5

Huang, J.-X., Kwon, O.-W., Lee, K.-S., & Kim, Y.-K. (2018). Improve the chatbot performance for the DB-CALL system using a hybrid method and a domain corpus. In P. Taalas, J. Jalkanen, L. Bradley & S. Thouësny (Eds.), *Future-proof CALL: Language learning as exploration and encounters – short papers from EUROCALL 2018* (pp. 100–105). Research-publishing.net. DOI: 10.14705/rpnet.2018.26.820

Huang, C., Zhang, Z., Mao, B., & Yao, X. (2023). An Overview of Artificial Intelligence Ethics. *IEEE Transactions on Artificial Intelligence*, *4*(4), 799–819. Advance online publication. DOI: 10.1109/TAI.2022.3194503

Huang, L. (2023). Ethics of Artificial Intelligence in Education: Student Privacy and Data Protection. *Science Insights Education Frontiers*, *16*(2), 2577–2587. Advance online publication. DOI: 10.15354/sief.23.re202

Huang, W., Hew, K. F., & Fryer, L. K. (2022). Chatbots for language learning—Are they really useful? A systematic review of chatbot-supported language learning. [wiley.com]. *Journal of Computer Assisted Learning*, *38*(1), 237–257. DOI: 10.1111/jcal.12610

Huang, X., Zou, D., Cheng, G., & Xie, H. (2021). A Systematic Review of AR and VR Enhanced Language Learning. *Sustainability (Basel)*, *13*(9), 4639. DOI: 10.3390/su13094639

Huang, Y., & Wilson, J. (2021). Using automated feedback to develop writing proficiency. *Computers and Composition*, *62*, 102675. DOI: 10.1016/j.compcom.2021.102675

Huertas-Abril, C. A., & Hà, T. A. (2025). Opportunities and challenges of using artificial intelligence in language education: Perspectives from Vietnam. *Computer-Assisted Language Learning in the Global South*, 81-98.

Humble, N., & Mozelius, P. (2022). The threat, hype, and promise of artificial intelligence in education. *Discover Artificial Intelligence*, *2*(1), 22. Advance online publication. DOI: 10.1007/s44163-022-00039-z

Hutahaean, B., Telaumbanua, S., Tamba, L., Hutabarat, R. G. N., & Sumani, S. (2024). Analysis of Innovative and Adaptive Higher Education Curriculum Development to Education 5.0 Based Challenges in Indonesia. *International Journal of Learning. Teaching and Educational Research, 23*(4), 76–98.

Idrissi, M., El Morabit, N., & El Kandoussi, M. (2024). Bridging Technology and Language Learning: A Comprehensive Analysis of CALL Integration within Second Language Acquisition. International Journal of Linguistics [al-kindipublisher.com]. *Literature and Translation, 7*(4), 60–65.

Imamguluyev, R., Hasanova, P., Imanova, T., Mammadova, A., Hajizada, S., & Samadova, Z. (2024). AI-POWERED EDUCATIONAL TOOLS: TRANSFORMING LEARNING IN THE DIGITAL ERA. *International Research Journal of Modernization in Engineering Technology and Science, 6*(12). Advance online publication. DOI: 10.56726/IRJMETS65040

Incelli, E. (2025). Exploring the Future of Corpus LInguistics: Innovations in AI and Social Impact. *International Journal of Mass Communication, 3*, 1–10. DOI: 10.6000/2818-3401.2025.03.01

Irzawati, I. (2023). The integration of Duolingo into EFL learning. *ESTEEM: Journal of English Study Programme, 6*(2), 328–337. DOI: 10.31851/esteem.v6i2.12317

Jafary, M., & Shakib Kotamjani, S. (2025). *Enhancing Linguistic Accessibility and Academic Inclusion through AI Tools: A Pilot Study on Plurilingual Graduate Students at McGill University.*

Jafarzade, S. (2020). Culture has an impact on a language. *Science Bulletin, 2*, 12–18. DOI: 10.54414/lbsc1457

Jane, O. C., Ezeonwumelu, C. G., Barah, C. I., & Jovita, U. N. (2024). Personalized Language Education in the Age of AI: Opportunities and Challenges. *NEWPORT INTERNATIONAL JOURNAL OF RESEARCH IN EDUCATION, 4*(1), 39–44. DOI: 10.59298/NIJRE/2024/41139448

Jang, E. E., Lajoie, S. P., Wagner, M., Xu, Z., Poitras, E., & Naismith, L. (2017). Person-oriented approaches to profiling learners in technology-rich learning environments for ecological learner modeling. *Journal of Educational Computing Research, 55*(4), 552–597. DOI: 10.1177/0735633116678995

Jasmine. (2024, November 15). *Rosetta Stone Review: Learning Made Easier*. Language Throne. https://www.languagethrone.com/rosetta-stone-review/

Javed, F. (2024). The Evolution of Artificial Intelligence in Teaching and Learning of English Language in Higher Education: Challenges, Risks, and Ethical Considerations. In *The Evolution of Artificial Intelligence in Higher Education: Challenges, Risks, and Ethical Considerations* (pp. 249-276). Emerald Publishing Limited.

Jaworski, R., Seljan, S., & Dunđer, I. (2023). Four Million Segments and Counting: Building an English-Croatian Parallel Corpus through Crowdsourcing Using a Novel Gamification-Based Platform. *Information (Basel)*, *14*(4), 226. Advance online publication. DOI: 10.3390/info14040226

Jia, F., Sun, D., Ma, Q., & Looi, C. K. (2022). Developing an AI-Based Learning System for L2 Learners' Authentic and Ubiquitous Learning in English Language. *Sustainability (Basel)*, *14*(23), 15527. Advance online publication. DOI: 10.3390/su142315527

Jiang, L., Yang, S., Zhou, M., Liu, X., & Zhu, Q. (2009). Mining Bilingual Data from the Web with Adaptively Learnt Patterns. In *ACL and AFNLP*. http://cul.beelink.com/20060205/2021119.shtml

Jiang, N., Liu, X., Liu, H., Lim, E. T. K., Tan, C. W., & Gu, J. (2023). Beyond AI-powered context-aware services: The role of human–AI collaboration. *Industrial Management & Data Systems*, *123*(11), 2771–2802. DOI: 10.1108/IMDS-03-2022-0152

Jing, W. (2024). Speech recognition sensors and artificial intelligence automatic evaluation application in English oral correction system. *Measurement. Sensors*, *32*, 101070. DOI: 10.1016/j.measen.2024.101070

Jose, J., & Jayaron Jose, B. (2024). Educators' Academic Insights on Artificial Intelligence: Challenges and Opportunities. *Electronic Journal of E-Learning*, 00–00. DOI: 10.34190/ejel.21.5.3272

Jose, L. (2025, January). *Harnessing Artificial Intelligence for Language Learning: A Mixed-Methods Study on ChatGPT Integration in Secondary Education*. DOI: 10.21203/rs.3.rs-5703952/v1

Joshi, R., Singla, K., Kamath, A., Kalani, R., Paul, R., Vaidya, U., Chauhan, S. S., Wartikar, N., & Long, E. (2024). Adapting Multilingual LLMs to Low-Resource Languages using Continued Pre-training and Synthetic Corpus. https://arxiv.org/abs/2410.14815

Joyner, J. (2007, September 19). Dying Languages – Cause for Concern? Outside The Beltway. https://outsidethebeltway.com/dying_languages_-_cause_for_concern/

Juan, A. Y. S., & Murai, Y. (2022). Turning frustration into learning opportunities during maker activities: A review of literature. *International Journal of Child-Computer Interaction*, *33*, 100519. DOI: 10.1016/j.ijcci.2022.100519

Jurafsky, D., & Martin, J. H. (2024). Speech and Language Processing: An Introduction to Natural Language Processing, Computational Linguistics, and Speech Recognition. Retrieved from https://web.stanford.edu/~jurafsky/slp3/ed3book.pdf

Kabudi, T., Pappas, I., & Olsen, D. H. (2021). AI-enabled adaptive learning systems: A systematic mapping of the literature. *Computers and Education Artificial Intelligence*, *2*, 100017. DOI: 10.1016/j.caeai.2021.100017

Kaiss, W., Mansouri, K., & Poirier, F. (2023). Effectiveness of an Adaptive Learning Chatbot on Students' Learning Outcomes Based on Learning Styles. *International Journal of Emerging Technologies in Learning*, *18*(13), 250–261. Advance online publication. DOI: 10.3991/ijet.v18i13.39329

Kamal, A. (2022). Critical appraisement of Monitor Model. *Research Journal in Advanced Humanities*, *3*(1). Advance online publication. DOI: 10.58256/rjah.v3i1.766

Kandasamy, S., & Cherukuri, A. K. (2020). Query expansion using named entity disambiguation for a question-answering system. *Concurrency and Computation*, *32*(4), e5119. DOI: 10.1002/cpe.5119

Kang, B. O., Jeon, H. B., & Lee, Y. K. (2024). AI-based language tutoring systems with end-to-end automatic speech recognition and proficiency evaluation. *ETRI Journal*, *46*(1), 48–58. Advance online publication. DOI: 10.4218/etrij.2023-0322

Kan, M. S., & Ito, A. (2020). Language Cognition and Pronunciation Training Using Applications. *Future Internet*, *12*(3), 42. DOI: 10.3390/fi12030042

Kanoksilapatham, B. (2020). Local Culture Preservation through Southern Thainess-Based English Lessons. *KEMANUSIAAN The Asian Journal of Humanities*, *27*(2), 179–199. DOI: 10.21315/kajh2020.27.2.10

Karakas, A. (2023). Breaking down barriers with artificial intelligence (AI). In *Advances in educational technologies and instructional design book series* (pp. 215–233). DOI: 10.4018/978-1-6684-9893-4.ch012

Kasepalu, R., Prieto, L. P., Ley, T., & Chejara, P. (2022). Teacher artificial intelligence-supported pedagogical actions in collaborative learning coregulation: A wizard of Oz study. *Frontiers in Education*, *7*, 1–15. DOI: 10.3389/feduc.2022.736194

Kasirzadeh, A., & Gabriel, I. (2023). In conversation with artificial intelligence: Aligning language models with human values. *Philosophy & Technology, 36*(2), 27. DOI: 10.1007/s13347-023-00606-x

Kasneci, E., Sessler, K., Küchemann, S., Bannert, M., Dementieva, D., Fischer, F., Gasser, U., Groh, G., Günnemann, S., Hüllermeier, E., Krusche, S., Kutyniok, G., Michaeli, T., Nerdel, C., Pfeffer, J., Poquet, O., Sailer, M., Schmidt, A., Seidel, T., . . . Kasneci, G. (2023). ChatGPT for good? On opportunities and challenges of large language models for education. In *Learning and Individual Differences* (Vol. 103). DOI: 10.1016/j.lindif.2023.102274

Katemba, C. V. (2022). Vocabulary enhancement through multimedia learning among grade 7th EFL students. *MEXTESOL Journal, 46*(1), 1–13. DOI: 10.61871/mj.v46n1-8

Katiyar, P. D. N., Awasthi, M. V. K., Pratap, D. R., Mishra, M. K., Shukla, M. N., Singh, M. R., & Tiwari, D. M. (2024). *Ai-Driven Personalized Learning Systems: Enhancing Educational Effectiveness*. Educational Administration Theory and Practices., DOI: 10.53555/kuey.v30i5.4961

Kato, M. (2024). Scoring Difficulty in Summary Writing Assessment: Toward the Reconstruction of Analytic Rubric. *Journal of Education and Learning, 14*(2), 74. DOI: 10.5539/jel.v14n2p74

Katsarou, E., Wild, F., Sougari, A. M., & Chatzipanagiotou, P. (2023). A Systematic Review of Voice-based Intelligent Virtual Agents in EFL Education. *International Journal of Emerging Technologies in Learning, 18*(10), 65–85. Advance online publication. DOI: 10.3991/ijet.v18i10.37723

Kaur, P., Kumar, H., & Kaushal, S. (2023). Technology-Assisted Language Learning Adaptive Systems: A Comprehensive Review. In *International Journal of Cognitive Computing in Engineering* (Vol. 4). DOI: 10.1016/j.ijcce.2023.09.002

Kavitha, R., Fathma, S. S., & Vinitha, V. (2023). AI: a catalyst for language Preservation in the digital era. *Shanlax International Journal of English, 12*(S1-Dec), 102–106. DOI: 10.34293/rtdh.v12iS1-Dec.39

Kayyali, M. (2025). Ethical implications of generative AI in education: Privacy, bias, and integrity. In *Ethical AI in Education* (pp. 185–202). IGI Global. DOI: 10.4018/979-8-3693-8744-3.ch008

Kazu, İ. Y., & Kuvvetli, M. (2023). The influence of pronunciation education via artificial intelligence technology on vocabulary acquisition in learning English. *International Journal of Psychology and Educational Studies, 10*(2), 480–493. DOI: 10.52380/ijpes.2023.10.2.1044

Kazu, I. Y., & Kuvvetli, M. (2024). Improve speaking skills with Duolingo's mobile game-based language learning. *Asian Journal of Education and Training, 10*(1), 62–75. DOI: 10.20448/edu.v10i1.5488

Kehinde-Awoyele, A. A., & Adeowu, A. W. (2024). Exploring students' perceptions, academic outcomes, and ethical implications of AI in Social Studies education. *Social Science and Humanities Journal, 8*(12), 6003–6013. DOI: 10.18535/sshj.v8i12.1490

Kessler, M., Marino, F., & Farrell, S. (2025). Computer-Assisted Language Learning and Teaching: Emerging trends, challenges, and solutions in ELT. Adaptable English Language Teaching, 228-244. [HTML]

Kessler, M., Loewen, S., & Gönülal, T. (2023). Mobile-assisted language learning with Babbel and Duolingo: Comparing L2 learning gains and user experience. *Computer Assisted Language Learning*, •••, 1–25. DOI: 10.1080/09588221.2023.2215294

Khan, N. D., Khan, J. A., Li, J., Ullah, T., & Zhao, Q. (2025). Leveraging Large Language Model ChatGPT for enhanced understanding of end-user emotions in social media feedbacks. *Expert Systems with Applications, 261*, 125524. DOI: 10.1016/j.eswa.2024.125524

Khan, S., Mazhar, T., Shahzad, T., Khan, M. A., Rehman, A. U., Saeed, M. M., & Hamam, H. (2025). Harnessing AI for sustainable higher education: Ethical considerations, operational efficiency, and future directions. *Discover Sustainability, 6*(1), 23. Advance online publication. DOI: 10.1007/s43621-025-00809-6

Khasawneh, M. A. S. (2023). The potential of AI in facilitating cross-cultural communication through translation. *Journal of Namibian Studies, 37.*

Khasawneh, M. A. S., Ismail, S. M., & Hussen, N. (2024). The blue sky of AI-assisted language assessment: Autonomy, academic buoyancy, psychological well-being, and academic success are involved. *Language Testing in Asia, 14*(1), 47. DOI: 10.1186/s40468-024-00318-9

Kherazi, A., & Bourray, M. (2024). Gamification and m-learning: An innovative approach to sustainable language learning. *E3S Web of Conferences, 477*. DOI: 10.1051/e3sconf/202447700066

Khlaif, Z. N., Ayyoub, A., Hamamra, B., Bensalem, E., Mitwally, M. A., Ayyoub, A., Hattab, M. K., & Shadid, F. (2024). University teachers' views on the adoption and integration of generative AI tools for student assessment in higher education. *Education Sciences*, *14*(10), 1090. DOI: 10.3390/educsci14101090

Khogali, H. O., & Mekid, S. (2023). The blended future of automation and AI: Examining Some long-term societal and ethical impact features. *Technology in Society*, *73*, 102232. DOI: 10.1016/j.techsoc.2023.102232

Kholis, A. (2021). Elsa Speak App: Automatic Speech Recognition (ASR) for Supplementing English Pronunciation Skills. *Pedagogy: Journal of English Language Teaching*, *9*(1), 1–14. DOI: 10.32332/joelt.v9i1.2723

Khuman, P. (2024). The Navigation Of The English Language Teaching And Learning Ecosystem Using Digital Tools. HEMCHANDRACHARYA INTERNATIONAL E JOURNAL OF RESEARCH. hemchandracharyaejournal.com

Kik, A., Adamec, M., Aikhenvald, A. Y., Bajzekova, J., Baro, N., Bowern, C., Colwell, R. K., Drozd, P., Duda, P., Ibalim, S., Jorge, L. R., Mogina, J., Ruli, B., Sam, K., Sarvasy, H., Saulei, S., Weiblen, G. D., Zrzavy, J., & Novotny, V. (2021). Language and ethnobiological skills decline precipitously in Papua New Guinea, the world's most linguistically diverse nation. *Proceedings of the National Academy of Sciences of the United States of America*, *118*(22), e2100096118. Advance online publication. DOI: 10.1073/pnas.2100096118

Kilag, O. K., Marquita, J., & Laurente, J. (2023). Teacher-Led Curriculum Development: Fostering Innovation in Education. *Excellencia: International Multi-disciplinary. Journal of Education*, *1*(4), 223–237.

Kılıç, M. (2019). Vocabulary knowledge as a predictor in writing and speaking: A case study of Turkish EFL Learners. *PASAA*, *57*, 133–164. DOI: 10.58837/CHULA.PASAA.57.1.6

Kim, J., Lee, H., & Cho, Y. H. (2022). Learning design to support student-AI collaboration: Perspectives of leading teachers for AI in education. Education and Information Technologies. springer.com

Kim, D., & Gilman, E. (2021). Implementing AI tools in the classroom: Teacher perspectives and experiences. *Educational Technology Research and Development*, *69*, 409–428.

Kim, H. S., & Cha, Y. (2023). The Role of AI Translators on Reading Comprehension. *Korean Journal of English Language and Linguistics*, *23*, 38–58. Advance online publication. DOI: 10.15738/kjell.23..202301.38

Kim, H., Yang, H., & Ho Lee, J. (2022). Design principles and architecture of a second language learning chatbot. *Language Learning & Technology*, *26*(1), 1–18. http://hdl.handle.net/10125/73463. DOI: 10.64152/10125/73463

Kitcharoen, P., Howimanporn, S., & Chookaew, S. (2024). Enhancing Teachers' AI Competencies through Artificial Intelligence of Things Professional Development Training. *International Journal of Interactive Mobile Technologies*, *18*(2), 4–15. Advance online publication. DOI: 10.3991/ijim.v18i02.46613

Klimova, B., Pikhart, M., Benites, A. D., Lehr, C., & Sanchez-Stockhammer, C. (2022). Neural machine translation in foreign language teaching and learning: A systematic review. *Education and Information Technologies*, *28*(1), 663–682. DOI: 10.1007/s10639-022-11194-2

Klitgaard, R., & Gardner, H. (1984). Frames of Mind: The Theory of Multiple Intelligences. *Journal of Policy Analysis and Management*, *3*(4), 627. Advance online publication. DOI: 10.2307/3324560

Knox, J. (2020). Artificial Intelligence and education in China. *Learning, Media and Technology*, *45*(3), 1–14. DOI: 10.1080/17439884.2020.1754236

Kohnke, L., Moorhouse, B. L., & Zou, D. (2023). ChatGPT for Language Teaching and Learning. In Journal, R. E. L. C. (Ed.), *Issue 2* (Vol. 54, pp. 537–550). SAGE Publications Ltd., DOI: 10.1177/00336882231162868

Kohnke, L., Moorhouse, B. L., & Zou, D. (2023). Exploring generative artificial intelligence preparedness among university language instructors: A case study. *Computers and Education: Artificial Intelligence*, *5*, 100156. DOI: 10.1016/j.caeai.2023.100156

Kohnke, L., & Ulla, M. B. (2024). Embracing generative artificial intelligence: The perspectives of English instructors in Thai higher education institutions. *Knowledge Management & E-Learning*, *16*(4), 653–670. DOI: 10.34105/j.kmel.2024.16.030

Koivisto, J., & Hamari, J. (2019). The rise of motivational information systems: A review of gamification research. *International Journal of Information Management*, *45*, 191–210. DOI: 10.1016/j.ijinfomgt.2018.10.013

Koka, N. A. (2024). Exploring Insights from Undergraduates on the Use of Artificial Intelligence (AI) Tools to Enhance Proficiency in Tense and Aspect in Foreign Language Instruction. [PJLSS]. *Pakistan Journal of Life and Social Sciences*, *22*(2). Advance online publication. DOI: 10.57239/PJLSS-2024-22.2.001440

Koltovskaia, S. (2020). Student engagement with automated written corrective feedback (AWCF) provided by Grammarly: A multiple case study. *Assessing Writing*, *44*, 100450. DOI: 10.1016/j.asw.2020.100450

Kondic, A. (2021). Data collection for a documentation project: South Eastern Huastec (Mayan, Mexico). In Strategies for Knowledge Elicitation: The Experience of the Russian School of Field Linguistics. DOI: 10.1007/978-3-030-79341-8_14

Kooli, C., & Yusuf, N. (2024). Transforming educational assessment: Insights into the use of ChatGPT and large language models in grading. *International Journal of Human-Computer Interaction*, •••, 1–12. DOI: 10.1080/10447318.2024.2338330

Krahnke, K. J., Krashen, S. D., & Terrell, T. D. (1985). The Natural Approach: Language Acquisition in the Classroom. *TESOL Quarterly*, *19*(3), 591. Advance online publication. DOI: 10.2307/3586280

Kramsch, C. (1995). The cultural component of language teaching. *Language, Culture and Curriculum*, *8*(2), 83–92. DOI: 10.1080/07908319509525192

Kramsch, C. (2014). Language and Culture. *AILA Review*, *27*, 30–55. DOI: 10.1075/aila.27.02kra

Krashen, S. (1989). We acquire vocabulary and spelling by reading: Additional evidence for the Input Hypothesis. *Modern Language Journal*, *73*(4), 440–463. DOI: 10.1111/j.1540-4781.1989.tb05325.x

Krashen, S. D. (1982). *Principles and practice in second language acquisition*. Pergamon Press.

Kremer, M., & Pinto, S. (2025). Exploring the interconnectedness between English-medium instruction and intercultural competence: A systematic literature review. *International Journal of Instruction*, *18*(1), 193–214. DOI: 10.29333/iji.2025.18111a

Krisbiantoro, B., & Ashari, I. A. (2024). Evaluating the SAMR model for enhancing ICT integration in English language teaching at the tertiary level: A systematic literature review. *Frasa: English Education and Literature Journal*, *5*(2), 108–115. DOI: 10.47701/frasa.v5i2.4027

Kubota, R., & Bale, J. (2020). Bilingualism—But Not Plurilingualism—Promoted by Immersion Education in Canada: Questioning Equity for Students of English as an Additional Language. *TESOL Quarterly*, *54*(3), 773–785. Advance online publication. DOI: 10.1002/tesq.575

Kucherbayeva, D., & Smagulova, J. (2023). Language Revitalization: Challenges for Kazakh in Higher Education. *Journal of Eurasian Studies*, *14*(2), 166–178. DOI: 10.1177/18793665231189326

Kuddus, K. (2022). *Artificial intelligence in language learning: Practices and prospects*. Advanced Analytics and Deep Learning Models. [HTML]

Kujundziski, A. P., & Bojadjiev, J. (2025). Artificial Intelligence in Education: Transforming Learning Landscapes. In *Reimagining Intelligent Computer-Assisted Language Education* (pp. 1-54). IGI Global.

Kukulska-Hulme, A., & Lee, H. (2020). Intelligent assistants in language learning: An analysis of features and limitations. *Research-publishing.net*.

Kulkarni, P., Mahabaleshwarkar, A., Kulkarni, M., Sirsikar, N., & Gadgil, K. (2019). Conversational AI: An overview of methodologies, applications & future scope. 2019 5th International Conference on Computing, Communication, Control and Automation, pp. 1-7.

Kumar, A., & Nagar, D. K. (2024). AI-Based Language Translation and Interpretation Services: Improving Accessibility for Visually Impaired Students. As the editors of Transforming Learning. *Power and Education*, •••, 178.

Kurakin, A., Ponomareva, N., Syed, U., MacDermed, L., & Terzis, A. (2023). Harnessing large-language models to generate private synthetic text. https://arxiv.org/abs/2306.01684

Kushnina, L. V., Kudritskaya, M. I., & Bermukhambetova, A. A. (2024). Foreign Language Student Linguistic Personality as a Vector for the Professional Bilingualism. *Вестник Нижневартовского государственного университета*, (3), 65-76.

Kusumadewi, H., & Widyastuti, M. (2018). The effects of using Duolingo towards students' vocabulary mastery. [Indonesian Journal of English Teaching]. *IJET*, *7*(2), 172–186. DOI: 10.15642/ijet2.2018.7.2.172-186

Lai, K.-W. K., & Chen, H.-J. H. (2023). A comparative study on the effects of a VR and PC visual novel game on vocabulary learning. *Computer Assisted Language Learning*, *36*(3), 312–345. DOI: 10.1080/09588221.2021.1928226

Lam, S. L. (2014). Use of gamification in vocabulary learning: A case study in Macau. *Center for English Language Communication*, *13*, 90–97.

Lane, P. (2023). From Silence to Silencing? Contradictions and tensions in language revitalization. *Applied Linguistics*, *44*(5), 833–847. DOI: 10.1093/applin/amac075

Lastrucci, A., Wandael, Y., Ricci, R., Maccioni, G., & Giansanti, D. (2024). The Integration of Deep Learning in Radiotherapy: Exploring Challenges, Opportunities, and Future Directions through an Umbrella Review. *Diagnostics (Basel)*, *14*(9), 939. DOI: 10.3390/diagnostics14090939

Latief, A. D. Yuyun, Uliniansyah, M. T., Nurfadhilah, E., Komariah, K. S., Isnaeni Nurul Afra, D., Gunarso, Sampurno, T., Jufri, N., Gusnawaty, Rosvita, I., Kaharuddin, M. N., Muis, A., & Hazriani. (2024). Enhancing Bugis Language POS Tagging Using Recurrent Neural Networks and Semi-Supervised Self-Training. 2024 International Conference on Computer, Control, Informatics and Its Applications (IC3INA), 219–224. DOI: 10.1109/IC3INA64086.2024.10732738

Laufer, B., & Hulstijn, J. (2001). Incidental vocabulary acquisition in a second language: The construct of task-induced involvement. *Applied Linguistics*, *22*(1), 1–26. DOI: 10.1093/applin/22.1.1

Lau, W. S., & Shea, M. (2024). Empowering English learners in the classroom through culturally responsive social-emotional teaching practices. [HTML]. *Journal of Multilingual and Multicultural Development*, *45*(7), 2880–2897. DOI: 10.1080/01434632.2022.2078337

Lawrance, J. C., Sambath, P., Shiny, C., Vazhangal, M. S. P., & Bala, B. K. (2024). Developing an AI-Assisted Multilingual Adaptive Learning System for Personalized English Language Teaching. *2024 10th International Conference on Advanced Computing and Communication Systems (ICACCS)*, 428–434. DOI: 10.1109/ICACCS60874.2024.10716887

Lawrance, J. C., Sambath, P., Shiny, C., Vazhangal, M., & Bala, K. (2024). Developing an AI-Assisted Multilingual Adaptive Learning System for Personalized English Language Teaching," 2024 10th International Conference on Advanced Computing and Communication Systems (ICACCS). *Coimbatore*, 428–434.

Lee, J. S., & Hudson, J. (2024). Digital education in teaching English as an international language. In *The Routledge Handbook of Teaching English as an International Language*. Routledge. DOI: 10.4324/9781003203261-21

Lee, J., Hicke, Y., Yu, R., Brooks, C., & Kizilcec, R. F. (2024). The life cycle of large language models in education: A framework for understanding sources of bias. *British Journal of Educational Technology*, *55*(5), 1982–2002. DOI: 10.1111/bjet.13505

Lee, S. M., Yang, Z., & Wu, J. G. (2024). Live, play, and learn: Language learner engagement in the immersive VR environment. [HTML]. *Education and Information Technologies*, *29*(9), 10529–10550. DOI: 10.1007/s10639-023-12215-4

Lee, S. S., & Moore, R. L. (2024). Harnessing Generative AI (GenAI) for Automated Feedback in Higher Education: A Systematic Review. *Online Learning : the Official Journal of the Online Learning Consortium*, *28*(3). Advance online publication. DOI: 10.24059/olj.v28i3.4593

Lepage-Richer, T., & McKelvey, F. (2022). States of computing: On government organization and artificial intelligence in Canada. *Big Data & Society*, *9*(2), 20539517221123304. Advance online publication. DOI: 10.1177/20539517221123304

Létourneau, A., Deslandes Martineau, M., Charland, P., Karran, J. A., Boasen, J., & Léger, P. M. (2025). A systematic review of AI-driven intelligent tutoring systems (ITS) in K-12 education. *NPJ Science of Learning*, *10*(1), 29. Advance online publication. DOI: 10.1038/s41539-025-00320-7

Lewington, A., Vittalam, A., Singh, A., Uppuluri, A., Ashok, A., Athmaram, A. M., . . . Liu, Y. (2024). Creating a Cooperative AI Policymaking Platform through Open Source Collaboration. *arXiv preprint arXiv:2412.06936.*

Lewis, A. A. (2025). Unpacking Cultural Bias in AI Language Learning Tools: An Analysis of Impacts and Strategies for Inclusion in Diverse Educational Settings. *International Journal of Research and Innovation in Social Science*, *IX*(I), 1878–1892. DOI: 10.47772/IJRISS.2025.9010151

Li, B., Lowell, V. L., Wang, C., & Li, X. (2024). A systematic review of the first year of publications on ChatGPT and language education: Examining research on ChatGPT's use in language learning and teaching. *Computers and Education: Artificial Intelligence*, 100266.

Liang, W., Yuksekgonul, M., Mao, Y., Wu, E., & Zou, J. (2023). GPT detectors are biased against non-native English writers. In *Patterns* (Vol. 4, Issue 7). Cell Press. DOI: 10.1016/j.patter.2023.100779

Liang, M. Y. (2024). Transcreation on social media through translingual English. *Asian Englishes*, •••, 1–18.

Liang, W., Tadesse, G. A., Ho, D., Fei-Fei, L., Zaharia, M., Zhang, C., & Zou, J. (2022). Advances, challenges and opportunities in creating data for trustworthy AI. [HTML]. *Nature Machine Intelligence*, *4*(8), 669–677. DOI: 10.1038/s42256-022-00516-1

Li, D., & Wang, H. (2024). Natural language processing in language learning: Personalized and adaptive English language teaching using artificial intelligence. *Applied Mathematics and Nonlinear Sciences*, *9*(1), 20243290. Advance online publication. DOI: 10.2478/amns-2024-3290

Li, J. (2014). Examining genre effects on test takers' summary writing performance. *Assessing Writing*, *22*, 75–90. DOI: 10.1016/j.asw.2014.08.003

Lijie, D. (2024). A Review of Research in Translation Technology Based on Citespace. *International Journal of Education and Humanities*, *4*(2), 137–146. DOI: 10.58557/(ijeh).v4i2.222

Li, L., Ma, Z., Fan, L., Lee, S., Yu, H., & Hemphill, L. (2024). ChatGPT in education: A discourse analysis of worries and concerns on social media. *Education and Information Technologies*, *29*(9), 10729–10762. DOI: 10.1007/s10639-023-12256-9

Lin, H. & Chen, Q. (2024). Artificial intelligence (AI)-integrated educational applications and college students' creativity and academic emotions: students and teachers' perceptions and attitudes. BMC psychology. springer.com

Linguistics News. (2023, December 19). How Globalization is Impacting Language Extinction Rates. Linguistics News. https://linguisticsnews.com/insight/how-globalization-is-impacting-language-extinction-rates/

Link, S., Mehrzad, M., & Rahimi, M. (2022). Impact of automated writing evaluation on teacher feedback, student revision, and writing improvement. *Computer Assisted Language Learning*, *35*(4), 605–634. DOI: 10.1080/09588221.2020.1743323

Lin, P. (2023). ChatGPT: Friend or foe (to corpus linguists)? *Applied Corpus Linguistics*, *3*(3), 100065. Advance online publication. DOI: 10.1016/j.acorp.2023.100065

Li, R. (2021). Does game-based vocabulary learning APP influence Chinese EFL learners' vocabulary achievement, motivation, and self-confidence? *SAGE Open*, *11*(1), 1–12. DOI: 10.1177/21582440211003092

Lisagor, M. (2025, April 10). Language preservation efforts get an AI boost. Dartmouth News. https://home.dartmouth.edu/news/2025/04/language-preservations-efforts-get-ai-boost

Lissitz, A. (2025). Insights Unleashed: Harnessing AI for learning Analytics. In *WORLD SCIENTIFIC eBooks* (pp. 155–196). DOI: 10.1142/9789811296475_0009

Liu, M. (2023). Exploring the Application of Artificial Intelligence in Foreign Language Teaching: Challenges and Future Development. *SHS Web of Conferences*, *168*, 03025. DOI: 10.1051/shsconf/202316803025

Liu, X., Li, Y., & Huang, Y. (2021). A model of teachers' excellent teaching behaviors based on natural language processing. In *Lecture notes in computer science* (pp. 303–311). DOI: 10.1007/978-3-030-92836-0_26

Liu, Y., Sahagun, J., & Sun, Y. (2021). An adaptive and interactive educational game platform for english learning enhancement using AI and chatbot techniques. In 10th international conference on natural language processing (NLP 2021). Academy and Industry Research Collaboration Center (AIRCC). DOI: 10.5121/csit.2021.112308

Liu, Z., Richardson, C., Hatcher, R., Jr., & Prud'hommeaux, E. (2022). Not always about you: Prioritizing community needs when developing endangered language technology. arXiv preprint arXiv:2204.05541. https://arxiv.org/abs/2204.05541 DOI: 10.18653/v1/2022.acl-long.272

Liu, J., Shindo, H., & Matsumoto, Y. (2019). Development of a computer-assisted Japanese functional exression learning system for Chinese-speaking learners. *Educational Technology Research and Development*, *67*(5), 1307–1331. DOI: 10.1007/s11423-019-09669-0

Liu, L. (2024). Impact of AI gamification on EFL learning outcomes and nonlinear dynamic motivation: Comparing adaptive learning paths, conversational agents, and storytelling. *Education and Information Technologies*. Advance online publication. DOI: 10.1007/s10639-024-13296-5

Liu-Thompkins, Y., Okazaki, S., & Li, H. (2022). Artificial empathy in marketing interactions: Bridging the human-AI gap in affective and social customer experience. [springer.com]. *Journal of the Academy of Marketing Science*, *50*(6), 1198–1218. DOI: 10.1007/s11747-022-00892-5

Liu, Z. (2022). Effective Transfer Learning for Low-Resource Natural Language Understanding. https://arxiv.org/abs/2208.09180 DOI: 10.14711/thesis-991013106358603412

Li, Z., Li, J. Z., Zhang, X., & Reynolds, B. L. (2024). Mastery of Listening and Reading Vocabulary Levels in Relation to CEFR: Insights into Student Admissions and English as a Medium of Instruction. *Languages (Basel, Switzerland)*, *9*(7), 239. Advance online publication. DOI: 10.3390/languages9070239

Li, Z., Zhu, H., Lu, Z., & Yin, M. (2023). Synthetic Data Generation with Large Language Models for Text Classification: Potential and Limitations. *Proceedings of the 2023 Conference on Empirical Methods in Natural Language Processing*, 10443–10461. DOI: 10.18653/v1/2023.emnlp-main.647

Lokare, V. T., & Jadhav, P. M. (2024). An AI-based learning style prediction model for personalized and effective learning. [HTML]. *Thinking Skills and Creativity*, *51*, 101421. DOI: 10.1016/j.tsc.2023.101421

Long, M. H. (1981). Input, interaction, and second language acquisition. *The New York Academy of Sciences, 379*(1), 259–278. DOI: 10.1111/j.1749-6632.1981.tb42014.x

Lotherington, H., Thumlert, K., Boreland, T., & Tomin, B. (2022). Redesigning for mobile plurilingual futures. *OLBI Journal, 11*, 141–172. Advance online publication. DOI: 10.18192/olbij.v11i1.6179

Luo, B., Lau, R. Y., Li, C., & Si, Y. W. (2022). A critical review of state-of-the-art chatbot designs and applications. *Wiley Interdisciplinary Reviews. Data Mining and Knowledge Discovery*, *12*(1), e1434. DOI: 10.1002/widm.1434

Lyanda, J. N., Owidi, S. O., & Simiyu, A. M. (2024). Rethinking Higher Education Teaching and Assessment In-Line with AI Innovations: A Systematic Review and Meta-Analysis. *African Journal of Empirical Research*, *5*(3), 325–335. DOI: 10.51867/ajernet.5.3.30

Ma, L. (2021). An immersive context teaching method for college English based on artificial intelligence and machine learning in virtual reality technology. Mobile Information Systems. wiley.com

Maatouk, Z., & Payant, C. (2022). The pertinence and feasibility of implementing a plurilingual approach in Quebec, Canada: The beliefs of pre-service ESL teachers. *International Journal of Bilingual Education and Bilingualism*, *25*(10), 3685–3697. Advance online publication. DOI: 10.1080/13670050.2022.2072681

MacFarlane, E., & Spring, R. (2024). Automated feedback on fluency and complexity measures for L2 academic paragraphs: Student perspectives and impacts on human-rater scores. *Technology in Language Teaching & Learning*, *6*(3), 1536. DOI: 10.29140/tltl.v6n3.1536

Madan, A., & Lohani, V. J. (2024). Leveraging Event Gamification for Event Planning and Creating a Memorable Experience. In *New Technologies in Virtual and Hybrid Events* (pp. 198–227). IGI Global. [HTML] DOI: 10.4018/979-8-3693-2272-7.ch011

Madhavi, E., Sivapurapu, L., Koppula, V., Esther Rani, P. B., & Sreehari, V. (2023). Developing Learners' English Speaking Skills using ICT and AI Tools. *Journal of Advanced Research in Applied Sciences and Engineering Technology*, *32*(2), 142–153. Advance online publication. DOI: 10.37934/araset.32.2.142153

Mageira, K., Pittou, D., Papasalouros, A., Kotis, K., Zangogianni, P., & Daradoumis, A. (2022). Educational AI chatbots for content and language integrated learning. [mdpi.com]. *Applied Sciences (Basel, Switzerland)*, *12*(7), 3239. DOI: 10.3390/app12073239

Maher, B., Polezzi, L., & Wilson, R. (2024). *The Routledge Handbook of Translation and Migration*. DOI: 10.4324/9781003287797

Mahmood, R. Q., & Bui, H. P. (2024). EFL learners' perceptions of pronunciation corrective feedback: insights from synchronous high variability phonetic training. In *Innovations in technologies for language teaching and learning* (pp. 95–119). Springer Nature Switzerland. [HTML] DOI: 10.1007/978-3-031-63447-5_6

Maimaiti, M., Liu, Y., Luan, H., & Sun, M. (2022). Data augmentation for low-resource languages NMT guided by constrained sampling. *International Journal of Intelligent Systems*, *37*(1), 30–51. DOI: 10.1002/int.22616

Maity, S., & Deroy, A. (2024). *Generative AI and Its Impact on Personalized Intelligent Tutoring Systems*. DOI: 10.36227/techrxiv.172954174.48041095/v1

Malyuga, E. N. (2024). *The Language of Corporate Communication: Functional, Pragmatic and Cultural Dimensions*. Springer Nature. DOI: 10.1007/978-3-031-58905-8

Manire, E., Kilag, O. K., Cordova Jr, N., Tan, S. J., Poligrates, J., & Omaña, E. (2023). Artificial Intelligence and English Language Learning: A Systematic Review. *Excellencia: International Multi-disciplinary Journal of Education (2994-9521)*, *1*(5), 485-497.

Mao, Y., Tao, D., Zhang, S., Qi, T., & Li, K. (2025). *Research and Design on Intelligent Recognition of Unordered Targets for Robots Based on Reinforcement Learning*. https://arxiv.org/abs/2503.07340 DOI: 10.1109/ICETCI64844.2025.11084189

Marouf, A. M., & Abu-Naser, S. S. (2019). Intelligent Tutoring System for Teaching Computer Science I in Al-Azhar University, Gaza. [IJAAR]. *International Journal of Academic and Applied Research*, *3*(3), 31–53. http://ijeais.org/wp-content/uploads/2019/03/IJAAR190306.pdf

Marques-Cobeta, N. (2024). Artificial Intelligence in Education: Unveiling Opportunities and Challenges. Innovation and Technologies for the Digital Transformation of Education: European and Latin American Perspectives, 33-42. [HTML]

Marrahí-Gómez, V., & Belda-Medina, J. (2022). The application of augmented reality (AR) to language learning and its impact on student motivation. International Journal of Linguistics Studies, 2(2), 07-14. al-kindipublisher.com

Marras, M., Boratto, L., Ramos, G., & Fenu, G. (2022). Equality of learning opportunity via individual fairness in personalized recommendations. [springer.com]. *International Journal of Artificial Intelligence in Education*, *32*(3), 636–684. DOI: 10.1007/s40593-021-00271-1

Marshall, S., Moore, D., & Himeta, M. (2021). French-Medium Instruction in Anglophone Canadian Higher Education: The Plurilingual Complexity of Students and Their Instructors. *Canadian Journal of Applied Linguistics, 24*(1), 181–204. Advance online publication. DOI: 10.37213/cjal.2021.29345

Martin Doherty. (2025, January 24). *Bridging the Gap: Democratizing Access to Quality Education with AI.*

Martin-Alguacil, N., Avedillo, L., Mota-Blanco, R., & Gallego-Agundez, M. (2024). Student-Centered Learning: Some Issues and Recommendations for Its Implementation in a Traditional Curriculum Setting in Health Sciences. [mdpi.com]. *Education Sciences, 14*(11), 1179. DOI: 10.3390/educsci14111179

Martin, F., Chen, Y., Moore, R. L., & Westine, C. D. (2020). Systematic review of adaptive learning research designs, context, strategies, and technologies from 2009 to 2018. *Educational Technology Research and Development, 68*(4), 1903–1929. Advance online publication. DOI: 10.1007/s11423-020-09793-2

Martyushev, N., Shutaleva, A., Malushko, E., Nikonova, Z., & Savchenko, I. (2021). Online communication tools in teaching foreign languages for education sustainability. [mdpi.com]. *Sustainability (Basel), 13*(19), 11127. DOI: 10.3390/su131911127

Marzuki, W., Widiati, U., Rusdin, D., Darwin, , & Indrawati, I. (2023). The impact of AI writing tools on the content and organization of students' writing: EFL teachers' perspective. *Cogent Education, 10*(2), 2236469. Advance online publication. DOI: 10.1080/2331186X.2023.2236469

Mauidloh, N. H., Anam, S., & Widyastuti. (2024). The correlation between students' engagement and reading comprehension while using Quizlet gamification for vocabulary learning. *JORER: International Journal of Recent Educational Research, 5*(4), 1013–1025.

Maximova, M. V., Frolova, O. V., Etuev, Kh. Kh., & Aleksandrova, L. D. (2023). Adaptive personalized learning: Implementation of emerging technologies in higher education. *Informatics and Education, 38*(4), 14–27. Advance online publication. DOI: 10.32517/0234-0453-2023-38-4-14-27

McCarthy, J. (2007). What is artificial intelligence? Retrieved from https://www-formal.stanford.edu/jmc/whatisai.pdf

McCarty, T. L., Romero-Little, M. E., & Zepeda, O. (2006). Native American Youth Discourses on Language Shift and Retention: Ideological Crosscurrents and Their Implications for Language Planning. *International Journal of Bilingual Education and Bilingualism, 9*(5), 659–677. DOI: 10.2167/beb386.0

McCrocklin, S. (2019). Learners' feedback regarding ASR-based dictation practice for pronunciation learning. *CALICO Journal, 36*(2), 119–137. DOI: 10.1558/cj.34738

McCrocklin, S. M. (2016). Pronunciation learner autonomy: The potential of automatic speech recognition. *System, 57*, 25–42. DOI: 10.1016/j.system.2015.12.013

McGeachie, J., & Dingel, J. (2007). Translate One, Analyze Many: Leveraging the Microsoft Intermediate Language and Source Code Transformation for Model Checking. *Electronic Notes in Theoretical Computer Science, 190*(1), 3–18. DOI: 10.1016/j.entcs.2007.02.057

Mcgovern, R. J., Garcia, O., Lin, A. M. Y., May, S., & Hornberger, N. (2017). *Encyclopedia of Language and Education Series Editor: Bilingual and Multilingual Education Third Edition*. https://www.springer.com/series/15111

McLaughlin, B. (1990). Restructuring. *Applied Linguistics, 11*(2), 113–128. DOI: 10.1093/applin/11.2.113

Meadows, E. (2024). *Exploring Classroom Teachers' Experiences of PD About Emergent Bilinguals: An Interpretative Phenomenological Analysis* (Doctoral dissertation, George Mason University).

Meara, P. (1980). Vocabulary acquisition: A neglected aspect of language learning. *Language Teaching, 13*(3-4), 221–246. DOI: 10.1017/S0261444800008879

Mecartty, F. (2000). Lexical and grammatical knowledge in reading and listening comprehension by foreign language speakers of Spanish. *Applied Language Learning, 11*(2), 323–348.

Meelen, M., O'Neill, A., & Coto-Solano, R. (2024). End-to-End Speech Recognition for Endangered Languages of Nepal. Proceedings of the Seventh Workshop on the Use of Computational Methods in the Study of Endangered Languages, 83–93. https://aclanthology.org/2024.computel-1.12/

Metwally, A. A., & Bin-Hady, W. R. A. (2025). Probing the necessity and advantages of AI integration training for EFL educators in Saudi Arabia. *Cogent Education, 12*(1), 2472462. DOI: 10.1080/2331186X.2025.2472462

Meyer, J., Jansen, T., Schiller, R., Liebenow, L. W., Steinbach, M., Horbach, A., & Fleckenstein, J. (2024). Using LLMs to bring evidence-based feedback into the classroom: AI-generated feedback increases secondary students' text revision, motivation, and positive emotions. *Computers and Education: Artificial Intelligence, 6*, 100199. Advance online publication. DOI: 10.1016/j.caeai.2023.100199

Miceli, M., Yang, T., Alvarado Garcia, A., Posada, J., Wang, S. M., Pohl, M., & Hanna, A. (2022). Documenting data production processes: A participatory approach for data work. arXiv: 2207.04958 Documenting Data Production Processes: A Participatory Approach for Data Work

Michel-Villarreal, R., Vilalta-Perdomo, E., Salinas-Navarro, D. E., Thierry-Aguilera, R., & Gerardou, F. S. (2023). Challenges and opportunities of generative AI for higher education as explained by ChatGPT. [mdpi.com]. *Education Sciences*, *13*(9), 856. DOI: 10.3390/educsci13090856

Min, A. (2023). Artifical Intelligence and Bias: Challenges, Implications, and Remedies. *Journal of Social Research*, *2*(11), 3808–3817. Advance online publication. DOI: 10.55324/josr.v2i11.1477

Mirek-Rogowska, A., Kucza, W., & Gajdka, K. (2024). AI in Communication: Theoretical Perspectives, Ethical Implications, and Emerging Competencies. *Communication Today*, 16–29. DOI: 10.34135/communicationtoday.2024.Vol.15.No.2.2

Mishara, P. (2024). The ethical implications of AI in education: Privacy, bias, and accountability. *Journal of Informatics Education and Research*, *4*(2), 1–14.

Mishra, P., & Koehler, M. (2006). Technological pedagogical content knowledge: A framework for teacher knowledge. *Teachers College Record*, *108*(6), 1017–1054. DOI: 10.1111/j.1467-9620.2006.00684.x

Mohamed, Y. A., Khanan, A., Bashir, M., Mohamed, A. H. H. M., Adiel, M. A. E., & Elsadig, M. A. (2024). The Impact of Artificial Intelligence on Language Translation: A Review. *IEEE Access : Practical Innovations, Open Solutions*, *12*, 25553–25579. Advance online publication. DOI: 10.1109/ACCESS.2024.3366802

Mohanta, S. K., Mohapatra, A. G., Mohanty, A., & Nayak, S. (2024). Deep Learning is a State-of-the-Art Approach to Artificial Intelligence. In *Deep Learning Concepts in Operations Research* (pp. 27–43). Auerbach Publications. DOI: 10.1201/9781003433309-3

Mohanty, R. N., Thomas, A., & Kori, A. (2024). Next-Generation Innovative Teaching Ecosystems for Futuristic Management Education. In *Global Higher Education Practices in Times of Crisis: Questions for Sustainability and Digitalization* (pp. 5-28). Emerald Publishing Limited. DOI: 10.1108/978-1-83797-052-020241002

Monika, M., & Suganthan, C. (2024). A Study on analyzing the role of Chatgpt in English acquisition among ESL learners during English language classroom. *Bodhi International Journal of Research in Humanities, Arts and Science, 8*(2).

Morales, A., Ono, K., & Kim, S. (2025). Generative AI and large language models in language preservation: Opportunities and challenges. arXiv. https://arxiv.org/abs/2501.11496v2

Morley, J., Kinsey, L., Elhalal, A., Garcia, F., Ziosi, M., & Floridi, L. (2023). Operationalising AI ethics: Barriers, enablers and next steps. *AI & Society*, *38*(1), 411–423. Advance online publication. DOI: 10.1007/s00146-021-01308-8

Morris, R., Perry, T., & Wardle, L. (2021). Formative assessment and feedback for learning in higher education: A systematic review. Review of Education. wiley.com

Moulieswaran, N., & Kumar, P. N. S. (2023). Investigating ESL Learners' Perception and Problem towards Artificial Intelligence (AI) -Assisted English Language Learning and Teaching. *World Journal of English Language*, *13*(5), 290. Advance online publication. DOI: 10.5430/wjel.v13n5p290

Moussalli, S., & Cardoso, W. (2020). Intelligent personal assistants: Can they understand and be understood by accented L2 learners? *Computer Assisted Language Learning*, *33*(8), 865–890. DOI: 10.1080/09588221.2019.1595664

Müller, F. A. & Wulf, T. (2024). Differences in learning effectiveness across management learning environments: A cognitive load theory perspective. Journal of Management Education. sagepub.com

Mumpande, I., & Barnes, L. (2022). Obstacles and Challenges Confronting Tonga Revitalisation in Zimbabwe. *Language Matters (Pretoria)*, *53*(3), 25–46. DOI: 10.1080/10228195.2022.2125553

Munday, P. (2015). The Case for Using Duolingo as Part of the Language Classroom Experience. *RIED Revista Iberoamericana de Educación a Distancia*, *19*(1). Advance online publication. DOI: 10.5944/ried.19.1.14581

Muñoz-Basols, J. (2019). Going beyond the comfort zone: Multilingualism, translation and mediation to foster plurilingual competence. *Language, Culture and Curriculum*, *32*(3), 299–321. Advance online publication. DOI: 10.1080/07908318.2019.1661687

Muñoz-Basols, J., Craig, N., Lafford, B. A., & Godev, C. (2023). Potentialities of Applied Translation for Language Learning in the Era of Artificial Intelligence. *Hispania*, *106*(2), 171–194. Advance online publication. DOI: 10.1353/hpn.2023.a899427

Murtaza, M., Ahmed, Y., Shamsi, J., Sherwani, F., & Usman, M. (2022). AI-based personalized e-learning systems: Issues, challenges, and solutions. *IEEE Access : Practical Innovations, Open Solutions*, *10*, 81323–81342. DOI: 10.1109/ACCESS.2022.3193938

Muslimin, A. I., Mukminatien, N., & Ivone, F. M. (2023). TPACK-SAMR digital literacy competence, technostress, and teaching performance: Correlational study among EFL lecturers. *Contemporary Educational Technology*, *15*(2), ep409. DOI: 10.30935/cedtech/12921

Muthmainnah, M., Al Yakin, A., Seraj, P. M. I., Darmawati, B., Elngar, A. A., & Obaid, A. J. (2024, April). Integrating Robot-Based Resources to Foster Computational Thinking and Communication Skills in EFL Education: A Path Towards Sustainable Development. In *International Conference on Sustainable Development through Machine Learning, AI and IoT* (pp. 70-80). Cham: Springer Nature Switzerland.

Nacimiento-García, E., Díaz-Kaas-Nielsen, H. S., & González-González, C. S. (2024). Gender and Accent Biases in AI-Based Tools for Spanish: A Comparative Study between Alexa and Whisper. *Applied Sciences (Basel, Switzerland)*, *14*(11), 4734. DOI: 10.3390/app14114734

Nagy, L., & Hortobagyi, I. (2023). Novel approaches to contemporary minority language revitalization. Bulletin of the Transilvania University of Brasov. Series IV: Philology and Cultural Studies, 85–100. DOI: 10.31926/but.pcs.2023.65.16.1.6

Nasution, A. (2022). The effect of Memrise application on students' vocabulary mastery at seventh grade of MTs PAB 1 Helvetia. *Bright Vision: Journal of Language and Education*, *2*(1), 32–44.

Nath, S., Marie, A., Ellershaw, S., Korot, E., & Keane, P. A. (2022). New meaning for NLP: The trials and tribulations of natural language processing with GPT-3 in ophthalmology. *The British Journal of Ophthalmology*, *106*(7), 889–892. ucl.ac.uk. DOI: 10.1136/bjophthalmol-2022-321141 PMID: 35523534

Naveen, P. & Trojovský, P. (2024). Overview and challenges of machine translation for contextually appropriate translations. Iscience. cell.com

Na-Young, K. (2020). *Chatbots and language learning: Effects of the use of AI chatbots for EFL learning*. Eliva Press.

Negia, M. K., Tamiru, R. M., & Meshesha, M. (2022). Amharic-Kistanigna Bi-directional Machine Translation using Deep Learning. 2022 International Conference on Information and Communication Technology for Development for Africa (ICT4DA), 61–65. DOI: 10.1109/ICT4DA56482.2022.9971194

Nekoto, W., Marivate, V., Matsila, T., Fasubaa, T., Fagbohungbe, T., Akinola, S. O., . . . Adelani, D. I. (2020). Participatory research for low-resourced machine translation: A case study in African languages. Findings of EMNLP 2020, 2144–2160. https://aclanthology.org/2020.findings-emnlp.195

Neumann, A. T., Yin, Y., Sowe, S., Decker, S., & Jarke, M. (2024). An LLM-Driven Chatbot in Higher Education for Databases and Information Systems. *IEEE Transactions on Education.*

Neuman, S. B., & Dwyer, J. (2009). Missing in action: Vocabulary instruction in Pre-K. *The Reading Teacher*, *62*(5), 384–392. DOI: 10.1598/RT.62.5.2

Ng, D. T. K., Leung, J. K. L., Su, J., Ng, R. C. W., & Chu, S. K. W. (2023). Teachers' AI digital competencies and twenty-first century skills in the post-pandemic world. *Educational Technology Research and Development*, *71*(1), 137–161. DOI: 10.1007/s11423-023-10203-6

Ngoc Le, T., & Sadat, F. (2020). Revitalization of Indigenous Languages through Pre-processing and Neural Machine Translation: The case of Inuktitut. *Proceedings of the 28th International Conference on Computational Linguistics*, 4661–4666. DOI: 10.18653/v1/2020.coling-main.410

Nguyen, A., Ngo, H. N., Hong, Y., Dang, B., & Nguyen, B. P. T. (2023). Ethical principles for artificial intelligence in education. [springer.com]. *Education and Information Technologies*, *28*(4), 4221–4241. DOI: 10.1007/s10639-022-11316-w PMID: 36254344

Nguyen, T. S., Nguyen, T. D. T., Hoang, N. Q. N., & Do, T. K. H. (2025). How AI-Powered Voice Recognition Has Supported Pronunciation Competence among EFL University Learners. *CALL-EJ*, *26*(3), 64–83. DOI: 10.54855/callej.252634

Niess, M. L., Sadri, P., & Lee, K. (2013). Technology-based instruction (TbI) model: A structured approach to integrating AI in EFL classrooms. *World Journal of English Language*, *12*(6), 304–320. DOI: 10.5430/wjel.v12n6p304

Nitzberg, M., & Zysman, J. (2022). Algorithms, data, and platforms: The diverse challenges of governing AI. *Journal of European Public Policy*, *29*(11), 1753–1778. Advance online publication. DOI: 10.1080/13501763.2022.2096668

Noels, K. A. (2023). Self-Determination Theory and Language Learning. In Ryan, R. M. (Ed.), *The Oxford Handbook of Self-Determination Theory* (1st ed., pp. 619–637). Oxford University Press., DOI: 10.1093/oxfordhb/9780197600047.013.31

Novak, E., McDaniel, K., & Li, J. (2023). Factors that impact student frustration in digital learning environments. Computers and Education Open. sciencedirect.com

Novák, A., Barcza, B., & Horváth, D. (2024). LLMs for extremely low-resource Finno-Ugric languages. arXiv. https://arxiv.org/abs/2410.18902

Nova, M. (2018). Utilizing Grammarly in evaluating academic writing: Narrative research on EFL students' experience. *Premise: Journal of English Education and Applied Linguistics*, *7*(1), 80–96.

Ntouvlis, V., & Geenen, J. (2023). "Ironic memes" and digital literacies: Exploring identity through multimodal texts. *New Media & Society*. Advance online publication. DOI: 10.1177/14614448231189801

Nurfauziah, D. H., Murtiningsih, T., & Al Farhan, M. (2024). Learning English Vocabulary Strategies for Non-English Department Students at Intensive English Class. IALLTEACH (Issues In Applied Linguistics & Language Teaching), 6(2), 210-218. uib.ac.id

Nurhasanah, S., & Nugraha, M. S. (2024). The future of learning: Ethical and philosophical implications of AI integration in education. *Indonesian Journal of Multidisciplinary Research*, *4*(2), 341–352. DOI: 10.17509/ijomr.v4i2.78038

Nursuhaniah, N. (2025). Improving Students' Speaking Skill And Interest Through Duolingo As Gamification Application. *Indonesian Journal Learning and Instruction*, *8*(1), 23–32. DOI: 10.25134/ijli.v8i1.11625

Nwakaego, A. M. (2024). Selection of Instructional Materials for Efficiency in Teaching and Learning English Language. Educational Research (IJMCER). ijmcer.com

O'Neill, R., & Russell, A. M. T. (2020). Grammarly: Help or hindrance? Academic learning advisors' perceptions of an online grammar checker. *Journal of Academic Language and Learning*, *13*(1), A88–A107.

Office of the Privacy Commissioner of Canada. (2022). *PIPEDA and AI: Principles for the ethical use of artificial intelligence in education.*

Ofosu-Asare, Y. (2024). Cognitive imperialism in artificial intelligence: Counteracting bias with indigenous epistemologies. *AI & Society*, *40*(4), 3045–3061. DOI: 10.1007/s00146-024-02065-0

Orosoo, M., Goswami, I., Alphonse, F. R., Fatma, G., Rengarajan, M., & Bala, B. K. (2024, March). Enhancing Natural Language Processing in Multilingual Chatbots for Cross-Cultural Communication. In *2024 5th International Conference on Intelligent Communication Technologies and Virtual Mobile Networks (ICICV)* (pp. 127-133). IEEE. DOI: 10.1109/ICICV62344.2024.00027

Ortega, L. (2019). SLA and the Study of Equitable Multilingualism. *Modern Language Journal*, *103*(S1), 23–38. Advance online publication. DOI: 10.1111/modl.12525

Ouald Chaib, S., Merrahi, M., & Khoulji, S. (2024, April). Enhancing Language Learning Personalization Through Deep Learning-Driven Chatbot Assistance. In International Conference On Big Data and Internet of Things (pp. 837-851). Cham: Springer Nature Switzerland. [HTML] DOI: 10.1007/978-3-031-74491-4_65

Ouariach, S., Khaldi, M., Mohamed, E., & Khaldi, M. (2023). The Flipped Classroom: From Passive Information Absorption to Active Learning. In Handbook of Research on Language Teacher Identity (pp. 269-293). IGI Global. [HTML]

Ouyang, F., & Jiao, P. (2021). Artificial intelligence in education: The three paradigms. *Computers and Education: Artificial Intelligence*, *2*, 100020. DOI: 10.1016/j.caeai.2021.100020

Owan, V. J., Abang, K. B., Idika, D. O., Etta, E. O., & Bassey, B. A. (2023). Exploring the potential of artificial intelligence tools in educational measurement and assessment. *Eurasia Journal of Mathematics, Science and Technology Education*, *19*(8), em2307. Advance online publication. DOI: 10.29333/ejmste/13428

Oxford, R. L. (1990). *Language learning strategies: What every teacher should know* (1st ed.). Heinle & Heinle.

Paap, K. R., Mason, L., & Anders-Jefferson, R. (2021). Predictions about the cognitive consequences of language switching on executive functioning inspired by the adaptive control hypothesis fail more often than not. Brain Sciences. mdpi.com

Panagiotidis, P. (2024). *LLM-Based Chatbots in Language Learning*. *7*(1).

Pan, K., Zhang, X., & Chen, L. (2024). Research on the training and application methods of a lightweight agricultural domain-specific large language model supporting Mandarin Chinese and Uyghur. *Applied Sciences (Basel, Switzerland)*, *14*(13), 5764. DOI: 10.3390/app14135764

Panmei, B., & Waluyo, B. (2023). The pedagogical use of gamification in English vocabulary training and learning in higher education. *Education Sciences*, *13*(1), 1–22. DOI: 10.3390/educsci13010024

Papadopoulos, D., & Hossain, M. M. (2023). Education in the Age of Analytics: Maximizing Student Success Through Big Data-Driven Personalized Learning. *Emerging Trends in Machine Intelligence and Big Data*, *15*(9), 20–36. https://orientreview.com/index.php/etmibd-journal/article/view/19

Park, N., Regenbrecht, H., Duncan, S., Mills, S., Lindeman, R. W., Pantidi, N., & Whaanga, H. (2022). Mixed Reality Co-Design for Indigenous Culture Preservation Continuation. Proceedings - 2022 IEEE Conference on Virtual Reality and 3D User Interfaces, VR 2022, 149–157. DOI: 10.1109/VR51125.2022.00033

Parmaxi, A., & Demetriou, A. A. (2020). Augmented reality in language learning: A state-of-the-art review of 2014–2019. In Journal of Computer Assisted Learning (Vol. 36, Issue 6, pp. 861–875). Blackwell Publishing Ltd. DOI: 10.1111/jcal.12486

Paulsen, L., & Lindsay, E. (2024). Learning analytics dashboards are increasingly becoming about learning and not just analytics - A systematic review. *Education and Information Technologies*, *29*(11), 14279–14308. DOI: 10.1007/s10639-023-12401-4

Pawar, S., Park, J., Jin, J., Arora, A., Myung, J., Yadav, S., Haznitrama, F. G., Song, I., Oh, A., & Augenstein, I. (2024). Survey of Cultural Awareness in Language Models: Text and Beyond. *arXiv (Cornell University)*. https://doi.org//arxiv.2411.00860DOI: 10.48550

Pawlicka, A., Pawlicki, M., Kozik, R., Andrychowicz-Trojanowska, A., & Choraś, M. (2024). AI vs linguistic-based human judgement: Bridging the gap in pursuit of truth for fake news detection. *Information Sciences*, *679*, 121097. DOI: 10.1016/j.ins.2024.121097

Pedersen, B. S. (1999). Systematic Verb Polysemy in MT: A Study of Danish Motion Verbs with Comparisons with Spanish. *Machine Translation*, *14*(1), 35–82. DOI: 10.1023/A:1008183205171

Pedro. (2019). Challenges and Opportunities for Sustainable Development Education Sector United Nations Educational, Scientific and Cultural Organization. https://en.unesco.org/themes/education-policy-

Peng, H., Ma, S., & Spector, J. M. (2019). Personalized adaptive learning: An emerging pedagogical approach enabled by a smart learning environment. *Smart Learning Environments*, *6*(1), 1–14. DOI: 10.1186/s40561-019-0089-y

Peng, H., & Zhou, P. (2024). Evolution and Development of Artificial Intelligence Interpretation Technology in the Age of Large-scale Language Models. *Journal of Electrical Systems*, *20*(2), 1988–1996. DOI: 10.52783/jes.1646

Pennycook, A. (2010). *Language as a local practice*. Routledge. DOI: 10.4324/9780203846223

Pereltsvaig, A. (2012, January 25). Obituary: The Ubykh Language. Languages of The World. https://www.languagesoftheworld.info/geolinguistics/obituary-the-ubykh-language.html

Pessach, D., & Shmueli, E. (2022). A Review on Fairness in Machine Learning. *ACM Computing Surveys*, *55*(3), 1–44. Advance online publication. DOI: 10.1145/3494672

Pfeiffer, J., Gutschow, J., Haas, C., Möslein, F., Maspfuhl, O., Borgers, F., & Alpsancar, S. (2023). Algorithmic Fairness in AI: An Interdisciplinary View. In *Business and Information Systems Engineering* (Vol. 65, Issue 2). DOI: 10.1007/s12599-023-00787-x

Piccardo, E. (2020). "We are all (potential) plurilinguals": Plurilingualism as an Overarching, Holistic Concept. *OLBI Working Papers, 10*. DOI: 10.18192/olbiwp.v10i0.3825

Piduru, B. R. (2023). The Role of Artificial Intelligence in Content Personalization: Transforming User Experience in the Digital Age. *Journal of Artificial Intelligence & Cloud Computing*. DOI: 10.47363/JAICC/2023(2)193

Pierres, O., Christen, M., Schmitt-Koopmann, F. M., & Darvishy, A. (2024). Could the Use of AI in Higher Education Hinder Students With Disabilities? A Scoping Review. *IEEE Access : Practical Innovations, Open Solutions*, *12*, 27810–27828. Advance online publication. DOI: 10.1109/ACCESS.2024.3365368

Pikhart, M. (2020). Intelligent information processing for language education: The use of artificial intelligence in language learning apps. *Procedia Computer Science*, *176*, 1412–1419. DOI: 10.1016/j.procs.2020.09.151 PMID: 33042299

Piñeiro-Martín, A., García-Mateo, C., Docío-Fernández, L., & Del Carmen López-Pérez, M. (2023). Ethical challenges in the development of virtual assistants powered by large language models. *Electronics (Basel)*, *12*(14), 3170. DOI: 10.3390/electronics12143170

Pinhanez, C., Cavalin, P., Storto, L., Finbow, T., Cobbinah, A., Nogima, J., Vasconcelos, M., Domingues, P., De Souza Mizukami, P., Grell, N., Gongora, M., & Gonçalves, I. (2024, July 17). Harnessing the power of artificial intelligence to vitalize endangered Indigenous languages: technologies and experiences. arXiv.org. https://arxiv.org/abs/2407.12620

Pisica, A. I., Edu, T., Zaharia, R. M., & Zaharia, R. (2023). Implementing Artificial Intelligence in Higher Education: Pros and Cons from the Perspectives of Academics. *Societies (Basel, Switzerland)*, *13*(5), 118. Advance online publication. DOI: 10.3390/soc13050118

Pitura, J., Kaplan-Rakowski, R., & Asotska-Wierzba, Y. (2024). The VR-AI-assisted simulation for content knowledge application in pre-service EFL teacher training. *TechTrends*, *68*(6), 734–749. DOI: 10.1007/s11528-024-01022-4

Plakans, L., & Gebril, A. (2017). Exploring the relationship of organization and connection with scores in integrated writing assessment. *Assessing Writing, 31*, 98–112. DOI: 10.1016/j.asw.2016.08.005

Poe, M., & Elliot, N. (2019). Evidence of fairness: Twenty-five years of research in Assessing Writing. *Assessing Writing, 42*, 100418. DOI: 10.1016/j.asw.2019.100418

Polyakova, O., & Galstyan-Sargsyan, R. (2021). Sustainable Higher Education via Telecollaboration: Improving Plurilingual and Pluricultural Competence. *Integra Educativa, 25*(4), 544–561. Advance online publication. DOI: 10.15507/1991-9468.105.025.202104.544-561

Prabhakaran, V., Qadri, R., & Hutchinson, B. (2022). *Cultural Incongruencies in Artificial Intelligence*. https://arxiv.org/abs/2211.13069

Prasetyo, G. A., Martono, & Suparno. (2018). The use of Rosetta Stone as teaching media to improve students' vocabulary mastery. *English Education Journal, 6*(3), 304–311.

Prieto Ramos, F. (2024). Revisiting translator competence in the age of artificial intelligence: The case of legal and institutional translation. *The Interpreter and Translator Trainer, 18*(2), 148–173. DOI: 10.1080/1750399X.2024.2344942

Prieto, J., Martinez, C., Robles, M., Moreno, A., Palacios, S., & Manrique, R. (2024). Translation systems for low-resource Colombian Indigenous languages, a first step towards cultural preservation. *Proceedings of the 4th Workshop on Natural Language Processing for Indigenous Languages of the Americas (AmericasNLP 2024)*, 7–14. DOI: 10.18653/v1/2024.americasnlp-1.2

Priya, S. S., Manivannan, D., Kujani, T., & Bharathi, S. (2024, August). Cross-Language Connect: A Chat App for Smooth Multilingual Communication. In *2024 Second International Conference on Intelligent Cyber Physical Systems and Internet of Things (ICoICI)* (pp. 159-164). IEEE. DOI: 10.1109/ICoICI62503.2024.10696715

Procter, T., & Joshi, A. (2022). Cultural Competency in Voice Evaluation: Considerations of Normative Standards for Sociolinguistically Diverse Voices. *Journal of Voice, 36*(6), 793–801. DOI: 10.1016/j.jvoice.2020.09.025 PMID: 33060004

Puentedura, R. R. (2006). Transformation, technology, and education in the state of Maine [Web log post]. https://www.hippasus.com/rrpweblog/archives/2006_11.html

Qassem, M. (2020). Translations of Stylistic Variations in the Noble Qur'an into English: Stylistic and Exegetical Perspectives. *Journal of Intercultural Communication Research, 50*, 1–19.

Qiao, H., & Zhao, A. (2023a). Artificial intelligence-based language learning: Illuminating the impact on speaking skills and self-regulation in Chinese EFL context. *Frontiers in Psychology*, *14*, 1255594. Advance online publication. DOI: 10.3389/fpsyg.2023.1255594

Qin, L., Che, W., Ni, M., Li, Y., & Liu, T. (2021). Knowing Where to Leverage: Context-Aware Graph Convolutional Network with an Adaptive Fusion Layer for Contextual Spoken Language Understanding. In *IEEE/ACM Trans. Audio Speech Lang. Process., 29* (pp. 1280–1289). IEEE. DOI: 10.1109/TASLP.2021.3053400

Qin, L., & Zhong, W. (2024). Adaptive System of English-Speaking Learning Based on Artificial Intelligence. *Journal of Electrical Systems*, *20*(6s), 267–275. DOI: 10.52783/jes.2637

Qiu, X. Y., Chiu, C. K., Zhao, L. L., Sun, C. F., & Chen, S. J. (2023). Trends in VR/AR technology-supporting language learning from 2008 to 2019: A research perspective. [HTML]. *Interactive Learning Environments*, *31*(4), 2090–2113. DOI: 10.1080/10494820.2021.1874999

Quynh, P. T. (2022). Maximizing vocabulary retention with gamification tools. *Scientific Journal of Tan Trao University*, *8*(4), 5–15.

Rabbianty, E. N., Azizah, S., & Virdyna, N. K. (2023). AI in academic writing: Assessing current usage and future implications. *INSANIA : Jurnal Pemikiran Alternatif Kependidikan*, *28*(1a), 14–35. Advance online publication. DOI: 10.24090/insania.v28i1a.9278

Rachels, J. R., & Rockinson-Szapkiw, A. J. (2018). The effects of a mobile gamification app on elementary students' Spanish achievement and self-efficacy. *Computer Assisted Language Learning*, *31*(1–2), 72–89. DOI: 10.1080/09588221.2017.1382536

Rad, H. S., Alipour, R., & Jafarpour, A. (2024). Using artificial intelligence to foster students' writing feedback literacy, engagement, and outcome: A case of Wordtune application. *Interactive Learning Environments*, *32*(9), 5020–5040. DOI: 10.1080/10494820.2023.2208170

Radhika, A., Bhasin, N. K., Sabareesh, R., Raju, Y. R., Satyanarayana, K. N. V., & Raj, I. I. (2024, March). Optimization of Natural Language Processing Models for Multilingual Legal Document Analysis. In *2024 Third International Conference on Intelligent Techniques in Control, Optimization and Signal Processing (INCOS)* (pp. 1-6). IEEE. DOI: 10.1109/INCOS59338.2024.10527598

Rafikha, H., Ula, N., Rahmah, H., Khaira, N., Fitri, K., Ulfa, P. R., & Rasikhah, P. A. (2024). *Seven Innovative Ways to Learn English for Non-Native Speaker*. USK Press. [HTML]

Rahali, A., & Akhloufi, M. A. (2023). End-to-End Transformer-Based Models in Textual-Based NLP. In *AI (Switzerland)* (Vol. 4, Issue 1). DOI: 10.3390/ai4010004

Rahman, M. H., & Nor, H. (2024). Unveiling The Role of Artificial Intelligence on Reading Processes. *PRIMACY Journal of English Education and Literacy, 3*(1), 18–27. DOI: 10.33592/primacy.v3i1.4877

Rahman, N., Wahyuddin, W., & Fariza, M. N. (2024). La Galigo: Representation and Reference in Bugis Culture. *International Journal of Religion*, *5*(10), 3635–3644. DOI: 10.61707/xwc7fr98

Raiaan, M. K., Mukta, M. S. H., Fatema, K., Fahad, N. M., Sakib, S., Mim, M. M. J., Ahmad, J., Ali, M. E., & Azam, S. (2024). A review on large language models: Architectures, applications, taxonomies, open issues and challenges. *IEEE Access : Practical Innovations, Open Solutions*, *12*, 26839–26874. DOI: 10.1109/ACCESS.2024.3365742

Rajagopal, A., Nirmala, V., Jebadurai, I. J., Vedamanickam, A. M., & Kumar, P. U. (2023). Design of Generative Multimodal AI Agents to Enable Persons with Learning Disability. *ACM International Conference Proceeding Series*. DOI: 10.1145/3610661.3617514

Rajak, L., Chauhan, S., & Bara, S. (2024). Transforming English Pedagogy with Artificial Intelligence: Enroute to Enhanced Language Learning. In *Artificial Intelligence: A Multidisciplinary Approach towards Teaching and Learning* (pp. 216-241). Bentham Science Publishers.

Rajak, L., Chauhan, S., & Bara, S. (2024). Transforming English Pedagogy with Artificial Intelligence: Enroute to Enhanced Language Learning. In Artificial Intelligence: A Multidisciplinary Approach towards Teaching and Learning (pp. 216-241). Bentham Science Publishers. [HTML]

Rajaram, K. (2023). Future of learning: Teaching and learning strategies. In Learning Intelligence: Innovative and Digital Transformative Learning Strategies: Cultural and Social Engineering Perspectives (pp. 3-53). Singapore: Springer Nature Singapore. [HTML]

Raj, N. S., & Renumol, V. G. (2021). A systematic literature review on adaptive content recommenders in personalized learning environments from 2015 to 2020. *Journal of Computers in Education*, *9*(1), 113–148. DOI: 10.1007/s40692-021-00199-4

Ramadhan, S., Sukma, E., & Indriyani, V. (2019). Teacher competence in utilizing digital media literacy in education. *Journal of Physics: Conference Series, 1339*(1), 012111. DOI: 10.1088/1742-6596/1339/1/012111

Rameshkumar, R., & Bailey, P. (2020). Storytelling with Dialogue: A Critical Role Dungeons and Dragons Dataset. *Proceedings of the 58th Annual Meeting of the Association for Computational Linguistics*, 5121–5134. DOI: 10.18653/v1/2020.acl-main.459

Rapaka, A., Dharmadhikari, S. C., Kasat, K., Mohan, C. R., Chouhan, K., & Gupta, M. (2025). Revolutionizing learning– A journey into educational games with immersive and AI technologies. [HTML]. *Entertainment Computing*, *52*, 100809. DOI: 10.1016/j.entcom.2024.100809

Razali, N. N. F. M., & Ismail, R. (2017). The use of simulation and role-play in enhancing speaking skills in learning English language. *Journal of Education and Social Sciences*, *6*(2), 72–78.

Razem, R. J. (2024). Codeswitching Among Arabic-English Bilingual Children: An Autoethnographic Case Study in Dubai. *International Journal of Information Technology and Language Studies*, *8*(2).

Rebolledo Font de la Vall, R., & González Araya, F. (2023). Exploring the Benefits and Challenges of AI-Language Learning Tools. *International Journal of Social Sciences and Humanities Invention*, *10*(01), 7569–7576. Advance online publication. DOI: 10.18535/ijsshi/v10i01.02

Reinhardt, J. (2019). *Gameful Second and Foreign Language Teaching and Learning*. Springer International Publishing., DOI: 10.1007/978-3-030-04729-0

Renacido, J. M. D., & Biray, E. T. (2025). Enhancing Peer Engagement and Student Motivation Through AI-Gamified Interactive Learning Tools. In Advancing Sustainable Development Goals With Educational Technology (pp. 277-342). IGI Global Scientific Publishing. [HTML]

Resyadi, H. (2025). Integrating AI in language teaching: Challenges and opportunities for novice EFL teachers. *Edukasi: Jurnal Pendidikan dan Pengajaran, 12*(1), 124–134. http://jurnal.radenfatah.ac.id/index.php/edukasi

Review, A. I. (2023). *ELSA: Price, Pros & Cons, Alternatives, App Reviews*. https://www.ai-review.com/

Ribeiro, R. V., Bieski, I. G. C., Balogun, S. O., & Martins, D. T. de O. (2017). Ethnobotanical study of medicinal plants used by Ribeirinhos in the North Araguaia microregion, Mato Grosso, Brazil. *Journal of Ethnopharmacology*, *205*, 69–102. DOI: 10.1016/j.jep.2017.04.023

Robles, M., Martínez, C. A., Prieto, J. C., Palacios, S., & Manrique, R. (2024). Preserving Heritage: Developing a Translation Tool for Indigenous Dialects. *Proceedings of the 17th ACM International Conference on Web Search and Data Mining*, 1200–1203. DOI: 10.1145/3616855.3637828

Roebuck, R. (1998). *Reading and recall in L1 and L2: A sociocultural approach.* Ablex Publishing Co.

Roever, C., & Kasper, G. (2018). Speaking in turns and sequences: Interactional competence as a target construct in testing speaking. *Language Testing*, *35*(3), 331–355. DOI: 10.1177/0265532218758128

Rusmiyanto, R., Huriati, N., Fitriani, N., Tyas, N. K., Rofi'i, A., & Sari, M. N. (2023). The Role Of Artificial Intelligence (AI) In Developing English Language Learner's Communication Skills. *Journal of Education*, *6*(1), 750–757. DOI: 10.31004/joe.v6i1.2990

Sadeghi, K., & Farzizadeh, B. (2013). The effect of visually supported vocabulary instruction on beginner EFL learners. *MEXTESOL Journal*, *37*(1), 1–12. PMID: 24902323

Sadeghi, K., & Richards, J. C. (2021). Professional development among English language teachers: Challenges and recommendations for practice. *Heliyon*, *7*(9), e08053. DOI: 10.1016/j.heliyon.2021.e08053 PMID: 34622060

Safder, I., Abu Bakar, M., Zaman, F., Waheed, H., Aljohani, N. R., Nawaz, R., & Hassan, S. U. (2024). Transforming language translation: A deep learning approach to Urdu–English translation. *Journal of Ambient Intelligence and Humanized Computing*, *15*(10), 3651–3662. DOI: 10.1007/s12652-024-04839-2

Sailer, M., Hense, J. U., Mayr, S. K., & Mandl, H. (2017). How gamification motivates: An experimental study of the effects of specific game design elements on psychological need satisfaction. *Computers in Human Behavior*, *69*, 371–380. DOI: 10.1016/j.chb.2016.12.033

Sajja, R., Sermet, Y., Cikmaz, M., Cwiertny, D., & Demir, I. (2024). Artificial intelligence-enabled intelligent assistant for personalized and adaptive learning in higher education. Information. mdpi.com

Sakkir, G., & Syamsuddin, N. A. (2023). Students' Perceptions of Duolingo Mobile Assisted Language Learning (MALL) in Learning English Vocabulary. *EduLine: Journal of Education and Learning Innovation*, *3*(3), 381–388. Advance online publication. DOI: 10.35877/454RI.eduline1970

Saleh, A. M., & Althaqafi, A. (2022). The effect of using educational games as a tool in teaching English vocabulary to Arab young children: A quasi-experimental study in a kindergarten school in Saudi Arabia. *SAGE Open*, *12*(1), 1–10. DOI: 10.1177/21582440221079806

Sales, A., Marzà, A., & Torralba, G. (2023). "Daddy, Can You Speak Our Language?" Multilingual and Intercultural Awareness through Identity Texts. *Journal of Language, Identity, and Education*, *22*(6), 510–526. Advance online publication. DOI: 10.1080/15348458.2021.1901586

Samala, A. D., Rawas, S., Wang, T., Reed, J. M., Kim, J., Howard, N. J., & Ertz, M. (2024). Unveiling the landscape of generative artificial intelligence in education: A comprehensive taxonomy of applications, challenges, and future prospects. *Education and Information Technologies*, •••, 1–40.

Samantray, K., İZGİ, F. D., Ocampo, M. B., Dehghan, M., Mohammadpour, S., Siriphaprapagon, Y., ... & Babu, S. D. (2024). *The Power of Words in AI-Driven World: Exploring the Interplay of Language, Culture, and Communication*. SKET-SAMEDIA.

Sambamurthy, P. (2024). The Intersection of AI and Human Intelligence. [IJCET]. *International Journal of Computer Engineering and Technology*, *15*(4), 251–264. https://iaeme.com/Home/article_id/IJCET_15_04_021

Samuel, C., & Ali, I. T. (2024). Batak Toba language-Indonesian machine translation with transfer learning using no language left behind. *International Journal of Advances in Applied Sciences*, *13*(4), 830. DOI: 10.11591/ijaas.v13.i4.pp830-839

Sandu, I., Wiersma, M., & Manichand, D. (2022). Time to audit your AI algorithms. *Maandblad Voor Accountancy en Bedrijfseconomie*, *96*(7/8), 253–265. Advance online publication. DOI: 10.5117/mab.96.90108

Saptiany, S. G., Hadi, S., Hardian, B. A. N., & Nashir, M. M. (2024). Artificial intelligence-moderated gamification apps: Elevating Gen-Z's English vocabulary mastery. *Al-Ishlah Jurnal Pendidikan*, *16*(4), 4969–4983. DOI: 10.35445/alishlah.v16i4.5957

Sargazi Moghadam, T., Darejeh, A., Delaramifar, M., & Mashayekh, S. (2024). Toward an artificial intelligence-based decision framework for developing adaptive e-learning systems to impact learners' emotions. *Interactive Learning Environments*, *32*(7), 1–21. Advance online publication. DOI: 10.1080/10494820.2023.2188398

Sarker, I. H. (2021). Machine learning: Algorithms, real-world applications and research directions. SN computer science. springer.com

Sarker, I. H. (2022). AI-based modeling: techniques, applications and research issues towards automation, intelligent and smart systems. SN Computer Science. springer.com

Savela, N., Pellert, M., Latikka, R., Bergdahl, J., Garcia, D., & Oksanen, A. (2025). Affective, cognitive, and contextual cues in Reddit posts on artificial intelligence. *Journal of Computational Social Science*, *8*(1), 6. Advance online publication. DOI: 10.1007/s42001-024-00335-x

Sawaki, Y. W. (2019). Meneropong Tipologi Bahasa-bahasa di Papua: Suatu Tinjauan Singkat. *Linguistik Indonesia*, *36*(2), 129–143. DOI: 10.26499/li.v36i2.79

Scarino, A. (2008). Community and culture in intercultural language learning. *Australian Review of Applied Linguistics*, *31*(1), 5.1–5.15. Advance online publication. DOI: 10.2104/aral0805

Scherer, R., Siddiq, F., & Tondeur, J. (2019). The technology acceptance model (TAM): A meta-analytic structural equation modeling approach to explaining teachers' adoption of digital technology in education. *Computers & Education*, *128*, 13–35. DOI: 10.1016/j.compedu.2018.09.009

Schmidt, T., & Strasser, T. (2022). Artificial intelligence in foreign language learning and teaching. *Anglistic: International Journal of English Studies*, *33*(1), 165–184. DOI: 10.33675/ANGL/2022/1/14

Schmitt, N. (2000). *Vocabulary in language teaching* (1st ed.). Cambridge University Press.

Schorr, I., Plecher, D. A., Eichhorn, C., & Klinker, G. (2024). Foreign language learning using augmented reality environments: a systematic review. In *Frontiers in Virtual Reality* (Vol. 5). Frontiers Media SA. DOI: 10.3389/frvir.2024.1288824

Sebastian, G. (2023). Privacy and Data Protection in ChatGPT and Other AI Chatbots. *International Journal of Security and Privacy in Pervasive Computing*, *15*(1), 1–14. Advance online publication. DOI: 10.4018/IJSPPC.325475

Seliger, H. W., & Shohamy, E. (1989). *Second language research methods*. Oxford University Press.

Selvam, D. C., Devarajan, Y., & Raja, T. (2025). Exploring the potential of artificial intelligence in nuclear waste management: Applications, challenges, and future directions. *Nuclear Engineering and Design*, *431*, 113719. DOI: 10.1016/j.nucengdes.2024.113719

Selwyn, N. (2024). On the Limits of Artificial Intelligence (AI) in Education. *Nordisk Tidsskrift for Pedagogikk Og Kritikk*, *10*(1). Advance online publication. DOI: 10.23865/ntpk.v10.6062

Şenel, M., & Akman, D. B. (2016). Fun teaching! Fun tech-ing! Interactive educational games for young learners. *Participatory Educational Research*, *2016*(1), 12–21. DOI: 10.17275/per.16.spi.1.2

Serban, I. V., Sankar, C., Germain, M., Zhang, S., Lin, Z., Subramanian, S., Bengio, Y. (2017). A deep reinforcement learning chatbot. *arXiv preprint arXiv:1709.02349*.

Seyfeddinipur, M., Krifka, M., Ameka, F., Kung, S., Bolton, L., Monroig, M., Blumtritt, J., Neba, A. N., Carpenter, B., Nordhoff, S., Cruz, H., Pakendorf, B., Drude, S., von Prince, K., Epps, P. L., Rau, F., Ferreira, V., Rice, K., Galucio, A. V., & Woodbury, T. (2019). Public access to research data in language documentation: Challenges and possible strategies. *Language Documentation and Conservation*, *13*, 545–563. http://hdl.handle.net/10125/24901

Shadiev, R., & Feng, Y. (2023). Using automated corrective feedback tools in language learning: A review study. *Interactive Learning Environments*, •••, 1–29. DOI: 10.1080/10494820.2022.2153145

Shadiev, R., Liu, T., & Hwang, W. (2020). Review of research on mobile-assisted language learning in familiar, authentic environments. *British Journal of Educational Technology*, *51*(3), 709–720. DOI: 10.1111/bjet.12839

Shahid, S., & Paul, J. (2021). Intrinsic motivation of luxury consumers in an emerging market. [HTML]. *Journal of Retailing and Consumer Services*, *61*, 102531. DOI: 10.1016/j.jretconser.2021.102531

Shahin, I., Nassif, A. B., Thomas, R., & Hamsa, S. (2023). Novel Task-Based Unification and Adaptation (TUA) Transfer Learning Approach for Bilingual Emotional Speech Data. *Information (Basel)*, *14*(4), 236. Advance online publication. DOI: 10.3390/info14040236

Shahmerdanova, R. (2025). Artificial Intelligence in Translation: Challenges and Opportunities. *Acta Globalis Humanitatis et Linguarum*, *2*(1), 62–70. DOI: 10.69760/aghel.02500108

Shakib Kotamjani, S., Shirinova, S., & Fahimirad, M. (2023). Lecturers' perceptions of using Artificial Intelligence in Tertiary Education in Uzbekistan. *Proceedings of the 7th International Conference on Future Networks and Distributed Systems*, 570–578. DOI: 10.1145/3644713.3644797

Shao, S., Alharir, S., Hariri, S., Satam, P., Shiri, S., & Mbarki, A. (2022). AI-based Arabic Language and Speech Tutor. *2022 IEEE/ACS 19th International Conference on Computer Systems and Applications (AICCSA)*, 1–8. DOI: 10.1109/AICCSA56895.2022.10017924

Shareef, S. M. & Nithyanantham, V. (2022). Fundamentals of educational technology. [HTML]

Sharma, D., Sood, A. K., Darius, P. S., Gundabattini, E., Darius Gnanaraj, S., & Joseph Jeyapaul, A. (2022). A study on the online-offline and blended learning methods. Journal of The Institution of Engineers (India): Series B, 103(4), 1373-1382. springer.com

Sharples, M. (2023). Towards social generative AI for education: Theory, practices and ethics. *Learning: Research and Practice*, *9*(2), 159–167. Advance online publication. DOI: 10.1080/23735082.2023.2261131

Sheldon, L. (2020). *The multiplayer classroom: Designing coursework as a game* (2nd ed.). CRC Press., DOI: 10.1201/9780429285035

Shelestova, T. Y., Kalizhanova, A. N., & Bedelbayeva, M. V. (2024). Personality-based intercultural awareness in undergraduate translation students via postcrossing. *Cogent Arts & Humanities*, *11*(1), 2313839. DOI: 10.1080/23311983.2024.2313839

Shengquan, Y., & Yu, L. (2021). *An Introduction to Artificial Intelligence in Education*. Springer.

Shi, H., & Aryadoust, V. (2024). A systematic review of AI-based automated written feedback research. *ReCALL*, *36*(2), 187–209. DOI: 10.1017/S0958344023000265

Shohieb, S. M., Doenyas, C., & Elhady, A. M. (2022). Dynamic difficulty adjustment technique-based mobile vocabulary learning game for children with autism spectrum disorder. *Entertainment Computing*, *42*, 100495. DOI: 10.1016/j.entcom.2022.100495

Sholekhah, M. F., & Fakhrurriana, R. (2023). The Use of ELSA Speak as a Mobile-Assisted Language Learning (MALL) towards EFL Students Pronunciation. *JELITA: Journal of Education, Language Innovation, and Applied Linguistics*, *2*(2), 93–100. Advance online publication. DOI: 10.37058/jelita.v2i2.7596

Shorten, C., Khoshgoftaar, T. M., & Furht, B. (2021). Text Data Augmentation for Deep Learning. *Journal of Big Data*, *8*(1), 101. Advance online publication. DOI: 10.1186/s40537-021-00492-0

Shortt, M., Tilak, S., Kuznetcova, I., Martens, B., & Akinkuolie, B. (2021). Gamification in mobile-assisted language learning: A systematic review of Duolingo literature from public release of 2012 to early 2020. *Computer Assisted Language Learning*, *36*(3), 517–554. DOI: 10.1080/09588221.2021.1933540

Siau, K., & Wang, W. (2020). Artificial intelligence (AI) Ethics: Ethics of AI and ethical AI. In *Journal of Database Management* (Vol. 31, Issue 2). DOI: 10.4018/JDM.2020040105

Sindermann, C., Sha, P., Zhou, M., Wernicke, J., Schmitt, H. S., Li, M., Sariyska, R., Stavrou, M., Becker, B., & Montag, C. (2021). Assessing the attitude towards artificial intelligence: Introduction of a short measure in German, Chinese, and English language. *KI- Künstliche Intelligenz, 35*, 109–118. DOI: 10.1007/s13218-020-00689-0

Singh, A. K. (2021). Legal Protection of Endangered Languages in India with Reference to Meghalaya. *IARS International Research Journal*, *11*(1), 25–30. DOI: 10.51611/iars.irj.v11i1.2021.152

Singh, J., Evans, E., Reed, A., Karch, L., Qualey, K., Singh, L., & Wiersma, H. (2022). Online, hybrid, and face-to-face learning through the eyes of faculty, students, administrators, and instructional designers: Lessons learned and directions for the post-vaccine and post-pandemic/COVID-19 world. [sagepub.com]. *Journal of Educational Technology Systems*, *50*(3), 301–326. DOI: 10.1177/00472395211063754

Singh, M., Kumar, R., & Chana, I. (2021). Machine translation systems for Indian languages: Review of modelling techniques, challenges, open issues and future research directions. *Archives of Computational Methods in Engineering*, *28*(4), 2165–2193. DOI: 10.1007/s11831-020-09449-7

Singh, V., & Ram, S. (2024). Impact of Artificial Intelligence on Teacher Education. *Shodh Sari-An International Multidisciplinary Journal*, *03*(01), 243–266. Advance online publication. DOI: 10.59231/SARI7669

Sivakumar, A. & Vanitha, V. (2024). Multilingualism in Global Education and Language Learning. Digital Skill Development for Industry 4.0. [HTML]

Skille, E. Å., Pedersen, S., & Skille, Ø. (2023). Friluftsliv and olggonastin – multiple and complex nature cultures. *Journal of Adventure Education and Outdoor Learning*, •••, 1–13. DOI: 10.1080/14729679.2023.2254862

Slaughter, Y., & Cross, R. (2021). Challenging the monolingual mindset: Understanding plurilingual pedagogies in English as an Additional Language (EAL) classrooms. *Language Teaching Research*, *25*(1), 39–60. Advance online publication. DOI: 10.1177/1362168820938819

Smets, W., & Struyven, K. (2018). Aligning with Complexity: System-Theoretical Principles for Research on Differentiated Instruction. *Frontline Learning Research*, *6*(2), 66–80. DOI: 10.14786/flr.v6i2.340

Smirani, L., & Yamani, H. (2024). Analysing the Impact of Gamification Techniques on Enhancing Learner Engagement, Motivation, and Knowledge Retention: A Structural Equation Modelling Approach. *Electronic Journal of e-Learning*, *22*(9), 111–124. DOI: 10.34190/ejel.22.9.3563

Smith, B., Jiang, X., & Peters, R. (2024). The effectiveness of Duolingo in developing receptive and productive language knowledge and proficiency. *Language Learning & Technology*, *2024*(1), 1–26. https://hdl.handle.net/10125/73595. DOI: 10.64152/10125/73595

Snyder, B. (2010). Unsupervised multilingual learning [Doctoral dissertation, Massachusetts Institute of Technology, Massachusetts Institute of Technology]. http://dspace.mit.edu/handle/1721.1/7582

Soliman, M. M., Ahmed, E., Darwish, A., & Hassanien, A. E. (2024). Artificial intelligence powered Metaverse: Analysis, challenges and future perspectives. *Artificial Intelligence Review*, *57*(2), 36. Advance online publication. DOI: 10.1007/s10462-023-10641-x

Solsona-Puig, J., Muñoz-Muñoz, E., & Rodriguez-Valls, F. (2024). Reimaging Bilingual Education in California: A Critical Analysis of Bilingual Teacher Performance Expectations (BTPE). *Journal of Latinos and Education*, •••, 1–13.

Song, C., Shin, S., & Shin, K. (2023). Optimizing Foreign Language learning in Virtual Reality: A comprehensive theoretical framework based on Constructivism and Cognitive Load Theory (VR-CCL). *Applied Sciences (Basel, Switzerland)*, *13*(23), 12557. DOI: 10.3390/app132312557

Song, C., & Song, Y. (2023). Enhancing academic writing skills and motivation: Assessing the efficacy of ChatGPT in AI-assisted language learning for EFL students. *Frontiers in Psychology*, *14*, 1260843. Advance online publication. DOI: 10.3389/fpsyg.2023.1260843

Song, Y., Weisberg, L. R., Zhang, S., Tian, X., Boyer, K. E., & Israel, M. (2024). A framework for inclusive AI learning design for diverse learners. In *Computers and Education* (Vol. 6). Artificial Intelligence., DOI: 10.1016/j.caeai.2024.100212

Son, J.-B., Ružić, N. K., & Philpott, A. (2025). Artificial intelligence technologies and applications for language learning and teaching. *Journal of China Computer-Assisted Language Learning*, *5*(1), 94–112. Advance online publication. DOI: 10.1515/jccall-2023-0015

Soon, G. Y., Abdullah, N. A. C. B., Suyan, Z., & Yiming, C. (2024). Integrating AI Chatbots in ESL and CFL Instruction: Revolutionizing Language Learning with Artificial Intelligence. *LatIA*, *2*, 23–23. DOI: 10.62486/latia202423

Soylu, D., & Şahin, A. (2024). The Role of AI in Supporting Indigenous Languages. *AI and Tech in Behavioral and Social Sciences*, *2*(4), 11–18. DOI: 10.61838/kman.aitech.2.4.2

Spada, N., & Lightbown, P. M. (2022). In it together: Teachers, researchers, and classroom SLA. [HTML]. *Modern Language Journal*, *106*(3), 635–650. DOI: 10.1111/modl.12792

Srinivasa, K. G., Kurni, M., & Saritha, K. (2022). Harnessing the Power of AI to Education. In *Learning, teaching, and assessment methods for contemporary learners: pedagogy for the digital generation* (pp. 311–342). Springer Nature Singapore. [HTML] DOI: 10.1007/978-981-19-6734-4_13

Ssemugabi, S. (2025). The Role of AI in Modern Language Translation and Its Societal Applications: A Systematic Literature Review. In *Southern African Conference for Artificial Intelligence Research* (pp. 390-404). Springer, Cham. DOI: 10.1007/978-3-031-78255-8_23

Stephenson, P., & Rumley, G. (2005). Inclusive work at a European level: A case study. *Support for Learning*, *20*(3), 141–145. DOI: 10.1111/j.0268-2141.2005.00378.x

Stibel, J. M., & Barrett, H. C. (2023). How cultural framing can bias our beliefs about robots and artificial intelligence. In *Behavioral and Brain Sciences* (Vol. 46). DOI: 10.1017/S0140525X22001686

Strang, B. (2020, January 15). Duolingo app to add te reo Māori course for beginners. RNZ (Radio New Zealand). https://www.rnz.co.nz/news/te-manu-korihi/407379/duolingo-app-to-add-te-reo-maori-course-for-beginners

Strasser, T. (2023). Narrow AI-powered visualization facilitation tools in foreign language learning: a visual approach promoting equal opportunities in foreign language grammar teaching. In *Facilitating Visual Socialities: Processes, Complications and Ethical Practices* (pp. 85–98). Springer International Publishing. DOI: 10.1007/978-3-031-25259-4_5

Streit, J. M. K., Felknor, S. A., Edwards, N. T., & Howard, J. (2021). Leveraging Strategic foresight to advance worker safety, health, and well-being. *International Journal of Environmental Research and Public Health*, *18*(16), 8477. DOI: 10.3390/ijerph18168477 PMID: 34444224

Strielkowski, W., Grebennikova, V., Lisovskiy, A., Rakhimova, G., & Vasileva, T. (2024). AI-driven adaptive learning for sustainable educational transformation. Sustainable Development. wiley.com

Strielkowski, W., Grebennikova, V., Lisovskiy, A., Rakhimova, G., & Vasileva, T. (2024). AI-driven adaptive learning for sustainable educational transformation. *Sustainable Development*. Advance online publication. DOI: 10.1002/sd.3221

Su, F., & Zou, D. (2022). Technology-enhanced collaborative language learning: Theoretical foundations, technologies, and implications. [HTML]. *Computer Assisted Language Learning*, *35*(8), 1754–1788. DOI: 10.1080/09588221.2020.1831545

Suhail, F., Adel, M., Al-Emran, M., & AlQudah, A. A. (2024). Are students ready for robots in higher education? Examining the adoption of robots by integrating UTAUT2 and TTF using a hybrid SEM-ANN approach. *Technology in Society*, *77*, 102524. DOI: 10.1016/j.techsoc.2024.102524

Su, J., Guo, K., Chen, X., & Chu, S. K. W. (2024). Teaching artificial intelligence in K–12 classrooms: A scoping review. *Interactive Learning Environments*, *32*(9), 5207–5226. DOI: 10.1080/10494820.2023.2212706

Su, J., & Yang, W. (2024). Artificial Intelligence (AI) literacy in early childhood education: An intervention study in Hong Kong. *Interactive Learning Environments*, *32*(9), 5494–5508. DOI: 10.1080/10494820.2023.2217864

Sumakul, D. T., Hamied, F. A., & Sukyadi, D. (2022). Artificial intelligence in EFL classrooms: Friend or foe? *LEARN Journal: Language Education and Acquisition Research Network*, *15*(1), 232–256.

Sundari, M. S., Penthala, H. R., & Nayyar, A. (2024). Transforming Education through AI-Enhanced Content Creation and Personalized Learning Experiences. In *Impact of Artificial Intelligence on Society* (pp. 98–118). Chapman and Hall/CRC. [HTML]

Sun, W. (2023). The impact of automatic speech recognition technology on second language pronunciation and speaking skills of EFL learners: A mixed methods investigation. *Frontiers in Psychology*, *14*, 1210187. Advance online publication. DOI: 10.3389/fpsyg.2023.1210187

Suriano, R., Plebe, A., Acciai, A., & Fabio, R. A. (2025). Student interaction with ChatGPT can promote complex critical thinking skills. *Learning and Instruction*, *95*, 102011. DOI: 10.1016/j.learninstruc.2024.102011

Susnjak, T., Ramaswami, G. S., & Mathrani, A. (2022). Learning analytics dashboard: A tool for providing actionable insights to learners. *International Journal of Educational Technology in Higher Education*, *19*(1), 12. Advance online publication. DOI: 10.1186/s41239-021-00313-7

Swain, M. (2000). *The output hypothesis and beyond: Mediating acquisition through collaborative dialogue* (Lantolf, J. P., Ed.). Oxford University Press.

Syamkumar, A., Tseng, N., Barron, K., Yang, S., Karumbaiah, S., Uppal, R., & Hu, J. (2024). Improving Bilingual Capabilities of Language Models to Support Diverse Linguistic Practices in Education. *arXiv preprint arXiv:2411.04308*.

SYSTRAN. (2025). Our history. Retrieved from https://www.systransoft.com/systran/

Tai, T. Y. (2024). Effects of intelligent personal assistants on EFL learners' oral proficiency outside the classroom. [HTML]. *Computer Assisted Language Learning*, *37*(5-6), 1281–1310. DOI: 10.1080/09588221.2022.2075013

Tai, T. Y., & Chen, H. H. J. (2023). The impact of Google Assistant on adolescent EFL learners' willingness to communicate. *Interactive Learning Environments*, *31*(3), 1485–1502. DOI: 10.1080/10494820.2020.1841801

Tai, T. Y., & Chen, H. H. J. (2024). Improving elementary EFL speaking skills with generative AI chatbots: Exploring individual and paired interactions. [HTML]. *Computers & Education*, *220*, 105112. DOI: 10.1016/j.compedu.2024.105112

Tang, F. (2024). … technology in educating the students of english language: does it promote critical thinking and self-directed learning for achieving sustainability in education with the …. BMC psychology. springer.com

Tang, C. M., & Chaw, L. Y. (2016). Digital literacy: A prerequisite for effective learning in a blended learning environment? *Electronic Journal of e-Learning, 14*(1), 54–65. https://www.ejel.org/

Tangsakul, S., & Poonpon, K. (2024). Aligning Academic Reading Tests to the Common European Framework of Reference for Languages (CEFR). *Reflections: The SoL Journal, 31*(2), 614–638. DOI: 10.61508/refl.v31i2.275057

Tao, Y., Viberg, O., Baker, R. S., & Kizilcec, R. F. (2024). Cultural bias and cultural alignment of large language models. *PNAS Nexus, 3*(9), pgae346. Advance online publication. DOI: 10.1093/pnasnexus/pgae346

Tapalova, O., & Zhiyenbayeva, N. (2022). Artificial intelligence in education: AIEd for personalized learning pathways. *Electronic Journal of e-Learning, 20*(5), 639–653. DOI: 10.34190/ejel.20.5.2597

Tapia, J. (2021). *Puzzles to foster A1 vocabulary retention in teenagers (Master's Thesis).* Pontificia Universidad Catolica del Ecuador.

Tariq, M. U. (2024). AI-powered language translation for multilingual classrooms. In *Integrating Generative AI in Education to Achieve Sustainable Development Goals* (pp. 29–46). IGI Global., DOI: 10.4018/979-8-3693-2440-0.ch002

Te Hiku Media. (2018). Papa Reo: Sovereign Māori data and the future of language technology. https://www.tehiku.nz/te-hiku-media/te-reo/27153/papa-reo-maori-data-and-language-tech

Te Hiku Media. (2024, September 5). Thousands of Indigenous languages face extinction, but AI provides hope. Time Magazine. https://time.com/6321970/ai-indigenous-languages-preservation/

TeenVogue. (2023). Indigenous youth are using coding and AI to save Native languages. https://www.teenvogue.com/story/these-coding-camps-are-teaching-indigenous-youth-to-save-native-language-through-ai

Tegon, R. (2021). Toward the 4th Agenda 2030 Goal: AI Support to Executive Functions for Inclusions. In Handbook of Research on Teaching With Virtual Environments and AI (pp. 591-615). IGI Global. [HTML]

Thiagarajah, K., Ng, M. M., Jeyaraja, S. S. B., Gunasehgaran, V., & Maniam, M. (2022). Effectiveness of gamification tool in teaching vocabulary. *International Journal of Academic Research in Business & Social Sciences, 12*(9), 1046–1063. DOI: 10.6007/IJARBSS/v12-i9/14604

Thornbury, S. (2002). *How to teach vocabulary* (1st ed.). Pearson Education Limited.

Thukroo, I. A., Bashir, R., & Giri, K. J. (2022). A review into deep learning techniques for spoken language identification. [HTML]. *Multimedia Tools and Applications*, *81*(22), 32593–32624. DOI: 10.1007/s11042-022-13054-0

Thurairasu, V. (2022). Gamification-Based Learning as the Future of Language Learning: An Overview. *European Journal of Humanities and Social Sciences*, *2*(6), 62–69. DOI: 10.24018/ejsocial.2022.2.6.353

Tian, X. (2024). Personalized translator training in the era of digital intelligence: Opportunities, challenges, and prospects. Heliyon. cell.com

Tian, X. (2024). Personalized translator training in the era of digital intelligence: Opportunities, challenges, and prospects. *Heliyon*, *10*(20), e39354. DOI: 10.1016/j.heliyon.2024.e39354

Tiddi, I., Lécué, F., & Hitzler, P. (2020). *Knowledge Graphs for eXplainable Artificial Intelligence: Foundations, Applications and Challenges* (Vol. 47). IOS Press.

Tilmes, N. (2022). Disability, fairness, and algorithmic bias in AI recruitment. *Ethics and Information Technology*, *24*(2), 21. Advance online publication. DOI: 10.1007/s10676-022-09633-2

Time. (2024a). Peter-Lucas Jones. https://time.com/7012841/peter-lucas-jones/

Time. (2024b). Endang Aminudin Aziz. https://time.com/7012839/endang-aminudin-aziz/

Timotheou, S., Miliou, O., Dimitriadis, Y., Sobrino, S. V., Giannoutsou, N., Cachia, R., Monés, A. M., & Ioannou, A. (2023). Impacts of digital technologies on education and factors influencing schools' digital capacity and transformation: A literature review. [springer.com]. *Education and Information Technologies*, *28*(6), 6695–6726. DOI: 10.1007/s10639-022-11431-8 PMID: 36465416

Tondeur, J., van Braak, J., Ertmer, P. A., & Ottenbreit-Leftwich, A. (2017). Understanding the relationship between teachers' pedagogical beliefs and technology use in education: A systematic review of qualitative evidence. *Educational Technology Research and Development*, *65*(3), 555–575. DOI: 10.1007/s11423-016-9481-2

Tour, E., Turner, M., Keary, A., & Tran-Dang, K. L. (2024). Bringing plurilingual strategies into linguistically diverse classrooms: Affordances of digital multimodal composing. *Language and Education*, *38*(3), 465–481. Advance online publication. DOI: 10.1080/09500782.2023.2203124

Tran, T. T. H. (2024). AI Tools in Teaching and Learning English Academic Writing Skills. *Proceedings of the AsiaCALL International Conference, 4*, 170–187. DOI: 10.54855/paic.23413

Trinh, E., de Oliveira, L. C., & Selvi, A. F. (Eds.). (2024). *Multilingual Leadership in TESOL.* Taylor & Francis. DOI: 10.4324/9781003396079

Trust, T., Whalen, J., & Mouza, C. (2023). Editorial: ChatGPT: Challenges, Opportunities, and Implications for Teacher Education. *Contemporary Issues in Technology & Teacher Education*, *23*(1).

Trzaskawka, P. (2020). Selected Clauses of a Copyright Contract in Polish and English in Translation by Google Translate: A Tentative Assessment of Quality. *International Journal for the Semiotics of Law*, *33*(3), 689–705. DOI: 10.1007/s11196-020-09680-2

Tseng, H., Jurafsky, D., & Manning, C. (2005). Morphological features help POS tagging of unknown words across language varieties. SIGHAN@IJCNLP 2005 - 4th SIGHAN Workshop on Chinese Language Processing, Proceedings of the Workshop, 32–39. https://aclanthology.org/I05-3005.pdf

Tseng, J. J., Chai, C. S., Tan, L., & Park, M. (2022). A critical review of research on technological pedagogical and content knowledge (TPACK) in language teaching. [HTML]. *Computer Assisted Language Learning*, *35*(4), 948–971. DOI: 10.1080/09588221.2020.1868531

Tsvilodub, P., Chevalier, E., Klütz, V., Oberbeck, T., Sigetova, K., & Wollatz, F. (2023). Improving a Gamified Language Learning Chatbot Through AI and UX Boosting. *Lecture Notes in Networks and Systems, 581 LNNS*. DOI: 10.1007/978-3-031-21569-8_52

Tulgar, A. T., Yilmaz, R. M., & Topu, F. B. (2022). Research Trends on the Use of Augmented Reality Technology in Teaching English as a Foreign Language. *Participatory Educational Research*, *9*(5), 76–104. DOI: 10.17275/per.22.105.9.5

Turkle, S. (2016). *Reclaiming Conversation: The Power of Talk in a Digital Age.* Penguin Press.

Ugwu, E. O. (2020). English Language, Globalisation and the Future of the Nigerian Indigenous Languages. *European Scientific Journal*, *16*(14), 38. Advance online publication. DOI: 10.19044/esj.2020.v16n14p38

Ul Hassan, M. N., Yu, Z., Wang, J., Li, Y., Gao, S., Yang, S., & Mao, C. (2024). LKMT: Linguistics Knowledge-Driven Multi-Task Neural Machine Translation for Urdu and English. *Computers, Materials & Continua*, *81*(1), 951–969. DOI: 10.32604/cmc.2024.054673

Uliniansyah, M. T., Santosa, A., & Perdana, R. A. (2024). Enhancing OCR Accuracy for Bugis Language to Bahasa Indonesia Dictionary Conversion through Image Pre-processing and Scaling Techniques. 2024 International Conference on Computer, Control, Informatics and Its Applications (IC3INA), 452–457. DOI: 10.1109/IC3INA64086.2024.10732090

Ulla, M. B., Perales, W. F., & Busbus, S. O. (2023). ChatGPT in Language Education: How To Use It Ethically? *PASAA*, *67*(1), 361–377. Advance online publication. DOI: 10.58837/CHULA.PASAA.67.1.12

Ulutaş, N. K., Durmaz, M. E., Elbuğa, N., Sezgin, S., Kaya, K., & İsmailoğulları, B. (2025). The Use of Augmented Reality (AR), Virtual Reality (VR), and Artificial Intelligence (AI) in Language Education: A Systematic Literature Review. *Reimagining Intelligent Computer-Assisted Language Education*, 401-430.

UNESCO. (2010). Reaching the marginalized | EFA Global Monitoring Report. UNESCO Publishing. https://www.unesco.org/gem-report/en/reaching-marginalized

UNESCO. (2023, November 28). National consultation on Indigenous languages: A call for preservation and technology integration. https://www.unesco.org/en/articles/national-consultation-indigenous-languages-call-preservation-and-technology-integration

Uysal, H. (2023). Multilingualism and identity: Interdisciplinary perspectives. *Journal of Multilingual and Multicultural Development*, 1–2. Advance online publication. DOI: 10.1080/01434632.2023.2222973

Vallejo, C., & Dooly, M. (2020). Plurilingualism and translanguaging: Emergent approaches and shared concerns. Introduction to the special issue. *International Journal of Bilingual Education and Bilingualism*, *23*(1), 1–16. Advance online publication. DOI: 10.1080/13670050.2019.1600469

Van Dijk, J. (2020). *The Digital Divide*. John Wiley & Sons.

van Doremalen, J., Boves, L., Colpaert, J., Cucchiarini, C., & Strik, H. (2016). Evaluating automatic speech recognition-based language learning systems: A case study. *Computer Assisted Language Learning*, *29*(4), 833–851. DOI: 10.1080/09588221.2016.1167090

Varghese, E. B., Qaraqe, M., & Al-Thani, D. (2024). Utilizing Artificial Intelligence to Support Autism Research. In The Impact of Artificial Intelligence on Societies: Understanding Attitude Formation Towards AI (pp. 87-108). Cham: Springer Nature Switzerland. [HTML]

Vashishth, T. K., Sharma, V., Sharma, K. K., Kumar, B., Panwar, R., & Chaudhary, S. (2024). AI-driven learning analytics for personalized feedback and assessment in higher education. In *Using traditional design methods to enhance AI-driven decision making* (pp. 206–230). IGI Global. [HTML] DOI: 10.4018/979-8-3693-0639-0.ch009

Vassilakopoulou, P. & Hustad, E. (2023). Bridging digital divides: A literature review and research agenda for information systems research. Information Systems Frontiers. springer.com

Velander, J., Taiye, M. A., Otero, N., & Milrad, M. (2024). Artificial Intelligence in K-12 Education: Eliciting and reflecting on Swedish teachers' understanding of AI and its implications for teaching & learning. *Education and Information Technologies, 29*(4), 4085–4105. DOI: 10.1007/s10639-023-11990-4

Verga, L., & Kotz, S. A. (2017). Help me if I can't: Social interaction effects in adult contextual word learning. *Cognition, 168*, 76–90. DOI: 10.1016/j.cognition.2017.06.018 PMID: 28658646

Vikas, S. & Mathur, A. (2022). An empirical study of student perception towards pedagogy, teaching style and effectiveness of online classes. Education and Information Technologies. springer.com

Vinall, K., & Hellmich, E. A. (2022). Do you speak translate? Reflections on the nature and role of translation. *Journal of Linguistics and Language Teaching, 14*(1), 4–25.

Virtanen, T., Lindén, M., & Haaranen, A. (2021). AR/VR solutions for Sámi language learning. *Nordic Journal of Indigenous Studies, 3*(2), 45–60. DOI: 10.7557/13.6461

Viterbi Conversations in Ethics. (2025). Preserving the past: AI in Indigenous language preservation. https://vce.usc.edu/weekly-news-profile/preserving-the-past-ai-in-indigenous-language-preservation/

Vlachopoulos, D., & Makri, A. (2017). The effect of games and simulations on higher education: A systematic literature review. *International Journal of Educational Technology in Higher Education, 14*(1), 22. DOI: 10.1186/s41239-017-0062-1

Voinov, V. (2010). Words should be fun: Scrabble as a tool for language preservation in Tuvan and other local languages 1. 4, 213–230. https://scholarspace.manoa.hawaii.edu/items/2157ea03-e476-4f15-bd96-fe3422a46610

Vu, D. V. & Peters, E. (2021). Vocabulary in English language learning, teaching, and testing in Vietnam: A review. Education Sciences. mdpi.com

Vu, N. N., Hung, B. P., Van, N. T. T., & Lien, N. T. H. (2022). Theoretical and instructional aspects of using multimedia resources in language education: A cognitive view. [HTML]. *Multimedia Technologies in the Internet of Things Environment, 2*, 165–194. DOI: 10.1007/978-981-16-3828-2_9

Vygotsky, L. S. (1980). *Mind in society: The development of higher psychological processes*. Harvard University Press. DOI: 10.2307/j.ctvjf9vz4

Waer, H. (2021). Using gamification in EFL vocabulary learning and learners' attitudes towards gamification use. *Journal of Scientific Research in Education, 22*(2), 547–570.

Wald, M. (2021). AI Data-Driven Personalisation and Disability Inclusion. *Frontiers in Artificial Intelligence, 3*, 571955. Advance online publication. DOI: 10.3389/frai.2020.571955

Waluyo, B., & Bucol, J. L. (2021). The impact of gamified vocabulary learning using Quizlet on low-proficiency students. *Computer-Assisted Language Learning Electronic Journal, 22*(1), 158–179.

Wang, J., Hwang, G.-W., & Chang, C.-Y. (2021). Directions of the 100 most cited chatbot-related human behavior research: A review of academic publications. *Computers and Education: Artificial Intelligence, 2*, 100023. DOI: 10.1016/j.caeai.2021.100023

Wang, S., Christensen, C., Cui, W., Tong, R., Yarnall, L., Shear, L., & Feng, M. (2020). When adaptive learning is effective learning: Comparison of an adaptive learning system to teacher-led instruction. *Interactive Learning Environments, 31*(2), 793–803. DOI: 10.1080/10494820.2020.1808794

Wang, Y. F., & Petrina, S. (2013). Using learning analytics to understand the design of an intelligent language tutor- Chatbot Lucy. [IJACSA]. *International Journal of Advanced Computer Science and Applications, 4*(11), 124–131. DOI: 10.14569/IJACSA.2013.041117

Wang, Y., Deng, Y., Wang, G., Li, T., Xiao, H., & Zhang, Y. (2025). The fluency-based semantic network of LLMs differs from humans. *Computers in Human Behavior: Artificial Humans, 3*, 100103. DOI: 10.1016/j.chbah.2024.100103

Wang, Y., Zhou, J., Li, Z., Zhang, S., & Han, X. (2024). Automatically Difficulty Grading Method for English Reading Corpus With Multifeature Embedding Based on a Pretrained Language Model. *IEEE Transactions on Learning Technologies, 17*, 474–484. DOI: 10.1109/TLT.2023.3319582

Wan, N., & Cumming, T. M. (Eds.). (2015). *Sustaining Mobile Learning*. Routledge., DOI: 10.4324/9781315766553

Wark, N. (2018). Shifting paradigms: A critical pragmatic evaluation of key factors affecting learner-empowered emergent technology integration.

Warschauer, M. (2003). *Technology and Social Inclusion*. The MIT Press., DOI: 10.7551/mitpress/6699.001.0001

Wei, L. (2023). Artificial intelligence in language instruction: impact on English learning achievement, L2 motivation, and self-regulated learning. Frontiers in Psychology. frontiersin.org

Wei, J. (2025). Philosophical Examination of Conflict and Integration: English Education Policies and Cultural Values in the Age of Globalization. *Cultura. International Journal of Philosophy of Culture and Axiology*, *22*(1).

Wei, L. (2023). Artificial intelligence in language instruction: Impact on English learning achievement, L2 motivation, and self-regulated learning. *Frontiers in Psychology*, *14*, 1261955. DOI: 10.3389/fpsyg.2023.1261955 PMID: 38023040

Wei-Xun, L., & Jia-Ying, Z. (2024). Impact of AI-driven language learning apps on vocabulary acquisition among English learners. *Journal of Research Studies in English Language Teaching and Learning*, *2*(1), 2–10. DOI: 10.62583/rseltl.v2i1.32

Weng, X. & Chiu, T. K. F. (2023). Instructional design and learning outcomes of intelligent computer assisted language learning: Systematic review in the field. Computers and Education: Artificial Intelligence. sciencedirect.com

Weng, X., & Chiu, T. K. F. (2023). Instructional design and learning outcomes of intelligent computer assisted language learning: Systematic review in the field. *Computers and Education: Artificial Intelligence, 4*.

Werdiningsih, I., Marzuki, N., & Rusdin, D. (2024). Balancing AI and authenticity: EFL students' experiences with ChatGPT in academic writing. *Cogent Arts & Humanities, 11*(1), 2392388. Advance online publication. DOI: 10.1080/23311983.2024.2392388

Wertsch, J. V. (1985). *Vygotsky and the social formation of mind*. Harvard University Press.

Wiesinger, M. (2024). ChatGPT and its Implications for EFL Learning: Issues with AI-driven language systems in undergraduate language degree programmes. *New Pathways in Teaching English*, *4*, 187–210.

Wijekumar, K. K., Harris, K. R., Graham, S., & Lei, P. (2022). A teacher technology tango shows strong results on 5th graders persuasive writing. *Educational Technology Research and Development*, *70*(4), 1415–1439. Advance online publication. DOI: 10.1007/s11423-022-10117-9

Wikipedia. (2024). *Rosetta Stone (software)*. Wikipedia. https://en.wikipedia.org/wiki/Rosetta_Stone_(software)

Wilder, B. T., O'Meara, C., Monti, L., & Nabhan, G. P. (2016). The Importance of Indigenous Knowledge in Curbing the Loss of Language and Biodiversity. In BioScience (Vol. 66, Issue 6, pp. 499–509). Oxford University Press. DOI: 10.1093/biosci/biw026

Wilkins, D. A. (1972). *Linguistics in language teaching*. MIT Press.

Williamson, B. (2017). *Big Data in Education: The digital future of learning, policy and practice*. SAGE Publications Ltd., DOI: 10.4135/9781529714920

Wiltshire, B., Bird, S., & Hardwick, R. (2024). Understanding how language revitalisation works: A realist synthesis. *Journal of Multilingual and Multicultural Development*, *45*(9), 3946–3962. DOI: 10.1080/01434632.2022.2134877

Wired. (2021, June 24). Māori are trying to save their language from Big Tech. Wired. https://www.wired.com/story/maori-language-artificial-intelligence/

Wise, G., Dickinson, C., Katan, T., & Gallegos, M. C. (2020). Inclusive higher education governance: Managing stakeholders, strategy, structure and function. *Studies in Higher Education*, *45*(2), 339–352. Advance online publication. DOI: 10.1080/03075079.2018.1525698

Woo, J. H., & Choi, H. (2021). Systematic review for AI-based language learning tools. *arXiv preprint arXiv:2111.04455*.

Wood, J. (2022, January 5). 1,500 endangered languages could disappear by the end of the century. World Economic Forum. https://www.weforum.org/stories/2022/01/languages-endangered-diversity-loss-spoken/

Woodruff, E. (2024). AI Detection of Human Understanding in a Gen-AI Tutor. *AI*, *5*(2), 898–921. DOI: 10.3390/ai5020045

Woo, J. H., & Choi, H. (2021). Systematic Review for AI-based Language Learning Tools. *Journal of Digital Contents Society*, *22*(11), 1783–1792. DOI: 10.9728/dcs.2021.22.11.1783

Woolf, B. P., Lane, H. C., Chaudhri, V. K., & Kolodner, J. L. (2013). AI Grand Challenges for Education. *AI Magazine*, *34*(4), 66–84. DOI: 10.1609/aimag.v34i4.2490

Wu, N. (2018, October 9). Hawaiian language course now available on Duolingo. Star Advertiser. https://www.staradvertiser.com/2018/10/09/breaking-news/hawaiian-language-course-now-available-on-duolingo/

Wu, Y. (2024). Exploring the Influence of Large Language Models (LLMs) on English Learners and their Teachers. In *Journal of Education, Humanities and Social Sciences IEMB* (Vol. 2023).

Wu, D., Chen, M., Chen, X., & Liu, X. (2024). Analyzing K-12 AI education: A large language model study of classroom instruction on learning theories, pedagogy, tools, and AI literacy. *Computers and Education: Artificial Intelligence*, *7*, 100295. DOI: 10.1016/j.caeai.2024.100295

Wu, L. (2024). AI-based Writing Tools: Empowering Students to Achieve Writing Success. *Advances in Educational Technology and Psychology*, *8*(2). Advance online publication. DOI: 10.23977/aetp.2024.080206

Wulandari, F., Astuti, M. T., & Marhamah, M. (2024). Enhancing Writing Literacy Teachers' through AI Development. *Jurnal Onoma: Pendidikan, Bahasa. Dan Sastra*, *10*(1), 246–256. DOI: 10.30605/onoma.v10i1.3175

Wu, Y. (2024). Exploring the Influence of Large Language Models (LLMs) on English Learners and their Teachers. *Journal of Education. Humanities and Social Sciences*, *27*, 530–535.

Wu, Y., Albornoz-De Luise, R. S., & Arevalillo-Herráez, M. (2025). On improving conversational interfaces in educational systems. [sciencedirect.com]. *Computer Speech & Language*, *89*, 101693. DOI: 10.1016/j.csl.2024.101693

Wu, Y., Schuster, M., Chen, Z., Le, Q. V., Norouzi, M., Macherey, W., Krikun, M., Cao, Y., Gao, Q., Macherey, K., Klingner, J., Shah, A., Johnson, M., Liu, X., Kaiser, Ł., Gouws, S., Kato, Y., Kudo, T., Kazawa, H., & Dean, J. (2016). Google's Neural Machine Translation System: Bridging the Gap between Human and Machine Translation. https://arxiv.org/abs/1609.08144

Wu, Z., Abdul Halim, H., & Mohd Saad, M. R. (2024). Artificial Intelligence (AI) and Gamification in Blended Learning: Enhancing Language and Literacy in Shanxi, China. [MJSSH]. *Malaysian Journal of Social Sciences and Humanities, 9*(12), e003159. DOI: 10.47405/mjssh.v9i12.3159

Wu, Z., Qi, S., & Zuo, L. (2024). Learning endangered languages in LLMs with in-context linguistic descriptions. arXiv. https://arxiv.org/abs/2402.18025v2

Xiao, Y., Zhang, T., & He, J. (2024). A Review of Promises and Challenges of AI-Based Chatbots in Language Education through the Lens of Learner Emotions. Heliyon. cell.com

Xia, Y., Shin, S. Y., & Kim, J. C. (2024). Cross-Cultural Intelligent Language Learning System (CILS): Leveraging AI to Facilitate Language Learning Strategies in Cross-Cultural Communication. *Applied Sciences (Basel, Switzerland), 14*(13), 5651. Advance online publication. DOI: 10.3390/app14135651

Xu. (2010). The effects of glosses on incidental vocabulary acquisition in reading. *Journal of Language Teaching and Research, 1*(2), 117–120. DOI: 10.4304/jltr.1.2.117-120

Xu, Y., Liu, Y., Meng, F., Zhang, J., Xu, J., & Zhou, J. (2021). *Bilingual Mutual Information Based Adaptive Training for Neural Machine Translation.* https://arxiv.org/abs/2105.12523 DOI: 10.18653/v1/2021.acl-short.65

Yadav, S. (2024). Advancing education with AI-Driven education for diverse learners. In *Advances in educational technologies and instructional design book series* (pp. 49–80). DOI: 10.4018/979-8-3693-6130-6.ch003

Yadav, S. (2025). *Advancing Education With AI-Driven Education for Diverse Learners: Integrating AI Into Pedagogical Practices*. Integrating AI Into Pedagogical Education. [HTML]

Yakkala, K. K.Krishna Kashyap Yakkala. (2024). AI-powered assessment tools for E-learning: Enhancing feedback and grading systems. *World Journal of Advanced Engineering Technology and Sciences, 13*(1), 792–802. DOI: 10.30574/wjaets.2024.13.1.0497

Yandex Translate. (2025). Translator for 100+ languages. Retrieved from https://translate.yandex.com/en/

Yang, I., Ma, W., & Vosoughi, S. (2024). NüshuRescue: Revitalization of the endangered Nüshu language with AI. CoRR, abs/2412.00218.

Yang, F. C. O., Lo, F. Y. R., Hsieh, J. C., & Wu, W. C. V. (2020). Facilitating communicative ability of EFL learners via high-immersion virtual reality. *Journal of Educational Technology & Society*, *23*(1), 30–49.

Yang, H., Gao, C., & Shen, H. Z. (2024). Learner interaction with, and response to, AI-programmed automated writing evaluation feedback in EFL writing: An exploratory study. *Education and Information Technologies*, *29*(4), 3837–3858. Advance online publication. DOI: 10.1007/s10639-023-11991-3

Yeşilçınar, S. (2023). Personalized Learning Through Gamification: A ChatGPT Approach to English Language Learning. In Kartal, G. (Ed.), (pp. 44–64). Advances in Educational Technologies and Instructional Design. IGI Global., DOI: 10.4018/978-1-6684-9893-4.ch003

Yilmaz, R., Yurdugül, H., Yilmaz, F. G. K., Şahin, M., Sulak, S., Aydin, F., & Ömer, O. R. A. L. (2022). Smart MOOC integrated with intelligent tutoring: A system architecture and framework model proposal. [sciencedirect.com]. *Computers and Education: Artificial Intelligence*, *3*, 100092. DOI: 10.1016/j.caeai.2022.100092

Young, R. F. (2011). Interactional competence in language learning, teaching, and testing. In Hinkel, E. (Ed.), *Handbook of research in second language teaching and learning* (2nd ed., pp. 426–443). Routledge.

Younis, H. A., Ruhaiyem, N. I. R., Ghaban, W., Gazem, N. A., & Nasser, M. (2023). A systematic literature review on the applications of robots and natural language processing in education. [mdpi.com]. *Electronics (Basel)*, *12*(13), 2864. DOI: 10.3390/electronics12132864

Yowaboot, C., & Sukying, A. (2022). Using digital flashcards to enhance Thai EFL primary school students' vocabulary knowledge. *English Language Teaching*, *15*(7), 61–74. DOI: 10.5539/elt.v15n7p61

Yu, H. (2024). The application and challenges of ChatGPT in educational transformation: New demands for teachers' roles. Heliyon. cell.com

Yuan, L., & Liu, X. (2025). The effect of artificial intelligence tools on EFL learners' engagement, enjoyment, and motivation. *Computers in Human Behavior*, *162*, 108474. DOI: 10.1016/j.chb.2024.108474

Yu, H., Yao, N., Zhang, J., & Gao, B. (2019). Time-course of attentional bias for culture-related cues in Mongolian-Chinese bilingual children. *The International Journal of Bilingualism*, *23*(6), 1483–1501. DOI: 10.1177/1367006918808047

Yu, S., Androsov, A., Yan, H., & Chen, Y. (2024). Bridging computer and education sciences: A systematic review of automated emotion recognition in online learning environments. *Computers & Education, 220*, 105111. DOI: 10.1016/j.compedu.2024.105111

Yuxiu, Y. (2024). Application of translation technology based on AI in translation teaching. *Systems and Soft Computing, 6*, 200072. Advance online publication. DOI: 10.1016/j.sasc.2024.200072

Yuyun, Y., Prakasa, E., Uliniansyah, M. T., Latief, A. D., Karsanti, H. T., Jarin, A., Munawirah, M., Hazriani, H., Zahrani, Z., & Gunarso, G. (2024). Enhancing Neural Machine Translation Model for Low-Resource Languages: A Case Study of Indonesian to Mamuju. DOI: 10.2139/ssrn.4872856

Zabetian, F. (2024, April 1). 10 stats & breakthroughs in AI speech translation in 2024. KUDO. https://kudo.ai/blog/the-10-most-important-statistics-breakthroughs-in-ai-speech-translation-from-2024/

Zagouras, C., Egarchou, D., Skiniotis, P., & Fountana, M. (2022). Face to face or blended learning? A case study: Teacher training in the pedagogical use of ICT. [springer.com]. *Education and Information Technologies, 27*(9), 12939–12967. DOI: 10.1007/s10639-022-11144-y PMID: 35729873

Zamri, M. T., & Mohamad, S. N. A. (2024). Technology integration in education: A review and analysis of SAMR model. *International Journal of Research and Innovation in Social Science, 8*(3), 6195–6200. DOI: 10.47772/IJRISS.2024.803463S

Zhai, C. & Wibowo, S. (2023). A systematic review on artificial intelligence dialogue systems for enhancing English as foreign language students' interactional competence in the university. Computers and Education: Artificial Intelligence. sciencedirect.com

Zhai, C., & Wibowo, S. (2022). A systematic review on cross-culture, humor and empathy dimensions in conversational chatbots: The case of second language acquisition. *Heliyon, 8*(12), e12056. Advance online publication. DOI: 10.1016/j.heliyon.2022.e12056

Zhai, C., & Wibowo, S. (2023). A systematic review on artificial intelligence dialogue systems for enhancing English as foreign language students' interactional competence in the university. *Computers and Education: Artificial Intelligence, 4*, 1–26. DOI: 10.1016/j.caeai.2023.100134

Zhang, & Hasim, Z. (2023). Gamification in EFL/ ESL instruction: A systematic review of empirical research. *Frontiers in Psychology, 13*, 1–12. DOI: 10.3389/fpsyg.2022.1030790

Zhang, Z., Zhou, Y., Li, C., Zhao, B., Liu, X., & Zhai, G. (2024). Quality assessment in the era of large models: A survey. *arXiv preprint arXiv:2409.00031.*

Zhang, A., & Zhu, X. (2023). Analysis of english translation of corpus based on blockchain. *International Journal of Web-Based Learning and Teaching Technologies*, *18*(2), 1–14. Advance online publication. DOI: 10.4018/IJWLTT.332767

Zhang, C., & Lu, Y. (2021). Study on artificial intelligence: The state of the art and future prospects. [HTML]. *Journal of Industrial Information Integration*, *23*, 100224. DOI: 10.1016/j.jii.2021.100224

Zhang, F. (2024). Globalisation and Minority Languages: A Critical Analysis of the Impact of Globalisation on Minority Languages. *International Journal of Frontiers in Sociology*, *6*(4). Advance online publication. DOI: 10.25236/IJFS.2024.060404

Zhang, K., & Aslan, A. B. (2021). AI technologies for education: Recent research & future directions. *Computers and Education: Artificial Intelligence*, *2*, 100025. DOI: 10.1016/j.caeai.2021.100025

Zhang, R., Du, H., Liu, Y., Niyato, D., Kang, J., Sun, S., Shen, X., & Poor, H. V. (2024). Interactive AI with retrieval-augmented generation for next generation networking. *IEEE Network*, *38*(6), 414–424. DOI: 10.1109/MNET.2024.3401159

Zhang, S., Liu, Y., Meng, F., Chen, Y., Xu, J., Liu, J., & Zhou, J. (2022). *Conditional Bilingual Mutual Information Based Adaptive Training for Neural Machine Translation*. https://arxiv.org/abs/2203.02951 DOI: 10.18653/v1/2022.acl-long.169

Zhang, Y., Wu, M., Tian, G. Y., Zhang, G., & Lu, J. (2021). Ethics and privacy of artificial intelligence: Understandings from bibliometrics. *Knowledge-Based Systems*, *222*, 106994. DOI: 10.1016/j.knosys.2021.106994

Zhao, X. (2023). Leveraging Artificial Intelligence (AI) Technology for English Writing: Introducing Wordtune as a Digital Writing Assistant for EFL Writers. *RELC Journal*, *54*(3), 890–894. DOI: 10.1177/00336882221094089

Zheng, X., & Fan, H. (2024). Exploration of the Effectiveness and Experience of AI-Assisted Academic Reading. *Proceedings of the Association for Information Science and Technology*, *61*(1), 447–456. DOI: 10.1002/pra2.1041

Zhou, Y., Zhang, M., Jiang, Y. H., Liu, N., & Jiang, B. (2024, June). A Study on Educational Data Analysis and Personalized Feedback Report Generation Based on Tags and ChatGPT. In *Conference Proceedings of the 28th Global Chinese Conference on Computers in Education (GCCCE 2024). Chongqing, China: Global Chinese Conference on Computers in Education* (pp. 108-115).

Zhu, B., Chau, K. T., & Mokmin, N. M. (2024). Optimizing cognitive load and learning adaptability with adaptive microlearning for in-service personnel. *Scientific Reports, 14*(1), 25960. Advance online publication. DOI: 10.1038/s41598-024-77122-1

Zhui, L., Yhap, N., Liping, L., Zhengjie, W., Zhonghao, X., Xiaoshu, Y., Hong, C., Xuexiu, L., & Wei, R. (2024). Impact of large language models on medical education and teaching adaptations. *JMIR Medical Informatics, 12*(1), e55933. DOI: 10.2196/55933

Zhu, J., Zhang, X., & Li, J. (2024). Using AR filters in L2 pronunciation training: Practice, perfection, and willingness to share. [HTML]. *Computer Assisted Language Learning, 37*(5-6), 1364–1396. DOI: 10.1080/09588221.2022.2080716

Zhumatayeva, Z. N., Mametkarim, Z. M., & Dosanova, A. M. (2024). THE ROLE OF ARTIFICIAL IN LIGENCE IN THE FORMATION OF COMMUNICATIVE COMPETENCE IN FOREIGN LANGUAGE LESSONS. *THE BULLETIN, 412*(6). Advance online publication. DOI: 10.32014/2024.2518-1467.858

Zohrabi, M., Tadayyon, P., & Dobahkti, L. (2018). The effects of rote and contextualized memorization on Iranian immediate EFL learners' vocabulary development. *Iranian Journal of English for Academic Purposes, 7*(2), 16–31.

Zou, B., Du, Y., Wang, Z., Chen, J., & Zhang, W. (2023). An Investigation Into Artificial Intelligence Speech Evaluation Programs With Automatic Feedback for Developing EFL Learners' Speaking Skills. *SAGE Open, 13*(3), 21582440231193818. Advance online publication. DOI: 10.1177/21582440231193818

About the Contributors

Ali Sorayyaei Azar is an Assistant Professor at the Department of Language and Literacy Education within the Faculty of Education, University of Malaya (UM), Malaysia. He also got his Ph.D. in Applied Linguistics from the Faculty of Languages and Linguistics, University of Malaya, Malaysia. In a career spanning 27 years, he has worked as an EFL/ESL senior lecturer, researcher, and curriculum developer in Iran, Turkey, Qatar, and Malaysia. He has published and presented research papers on his topic of interest namely Academic Discourse Analysis, Genre Analysis, Corpus Linguistics, TESL, Educational Technology, and English Language Teaching Strategies in several prestigious journals including GEMA Online@ Journal of Language Studies (UKM, Malaysia), Asian ESP Journal, Asian EFL Journal, Studies in English Language and Education, World Journal of English Language, and Education and Information Technologies (Springer). He is the head of MAAL- SIG (Research Methods in Applied Linguistics). He is also the Editor of three books, including 'Reconceptions of Policies, Strategies, and Challenges in Education 5.0.', 'Innovations in Educational Robotics: Advancing AI for Sustainable Development', and 'Smart Education and Sustainable Learning Environments in Smart Cities'. IGI Global- Publisher, USA has published the three edited volumes. Besides, Dr. Azar has been appointed as a member of the Editorial Board for several journals, including the Asian Journal of University Education (AJUE) indexed in Scopus- Q2, established by Universiti Teknologi MARA, Shah Alam, Malaysia; the International Journal of Modern Languages and Applied Linguistics (IJMAL), established by Akademi Pengajian Bahasa (APB), Universiti Teknologi MARA, Shah Alam, Malaysia; Education Quarterly Reviews- indexed in ERIC, established by the Asian Institute of Research, Indonesia; and the journal of Pragmatics and Discourse Research- indexed in Sinta 3, established by Perkumpulan Pengelola Jurnal Bahasa Sastra dan Pengajarannya (PPJBSIP), Indonesia. Scopus Author: 55561989000

Sedigheh Shakib Kotamhani (Nahid) holds a doctoral degree from the University Putra Malaysia in the field of Teaching English as a Second Language. She works as an associate professor and the deputy head of research in the ELT department of English Education at Central Asian University where she teaches academic writing, linguistics, and methodology to undergraduate students and research skills to staff and students and supervises PhD students. She also holds Cambridge Delta Module 2. Her research interests are applied linguistics, language learning technology, academic writing, collocation, and corpus linguistics. She has authored and co-authored several journal papers.

Marine Milad is the Local Dean of the Faculty of Language Studies & Associate Professor of Applied Linguistics/TEFL at Arab Open University in Kuwait. She is the General Course Chair for the TEFL course and Exploring Grammar in Contexts I & II courses across AOU's eight branches. She is TESOL Kuwait's Past President. Dr. Marine Milad has PhD in TEFL, Curriculum and Instructions from Cairo University with a grade of distinction. She also attained a Master Level Course in ESL/EFL Assessment Techniques from Indiana University, Bloomington, U.S.A. Currently, she is an assistant professor at the Arab Open University (AOU), Kuwait Branch. She is the General Course Chair for three courses: Reading Comprehension, Academic Writing and Composition, and Methods of Teaching English language across eight AOU branches. She has worked in both the governmental and private sectors as well as NGOs in reputable entities In the MENA reign like Arab Open University, Egypt Branch & Kuwait Branch (accredited by Open University, OU, UK), Ain Shams University, Center for Developing English Language Teaching (CDELT), Mansoura University, Sinai University, Misr University for Science and Technology (MUST), and Education Reform Program (ERP), a USAID program and Human Network International, Dubai, UAE. Through her teaching/training sessions, she has facilitated the professional development and career advancement of teachers, managers, and employees of some reputable organizations. She has delivered several academic and technical presentations in local and international conferences in the field of Language Learning, E-Learning, Blended Learning, Multiple Intelligences and Brain Color, Constructivism, Learning by Doing, educational reform, and soft skills. Her sessions are student-centered and consider different brain colors, learning styles, and multiple intelligences through employing authentic real-life situations and activities. Dr. Marine was elected as the president of TESOL Kuwait 2020/2022 affiliated with TESOL International and currently serving as the past TESOL Kuwait president.

Shanina Sharatol Ahmad Shah has been a Senior Lecturer at the Language and Literacy Education Department, Faculty of Education, University of Malaya since 2015. She is also currently serving as the Head of Department of Language and Literacy Education at the same faculty. Her responsibilities include teaching language education courses which include English Phonetics and Phonology, Linguistics for Language Teachers, Foundation of Language Teaching Methodology, Teaching of Reading, Syllabus Design and Material Development, and Simulated Teaching. On top of that, she also teaches Qualitative Research Methods and Educational Philosophy; as well as supervising postgraduate and undergraduate students' research. She holds a doctoral degree in Education (TESL) from University of Malaya, a master of education degree (TESL) from the University of Malaya, and a bachelor of education degree (TESOL) from the University of Surrey, United Kingdom. Her current research interests include English Language teaching methodology and second language teacher education. Shanina's main research has focused on qualitative research methods and teacher's cognition in Pronunciation instruction. She has also written numerous book chapters and journal articles on research related to language teacher education. For the past 25 years, her work has also revolved around working with pre-service and in-service teachers in improving and enhancing English Language literacy among students at various levels and the community through various projects under several research grants. Shanina has supervised her undergraduate students on various reading projects specifically on extensive reading. Some of the extensive reading programs designed have been conducted with secondary school students under her supervision.

***

Dian Isnaeni Nurul Afra is a researcher at the National Research and Innovation Agency (Badan Riset dan Inovasi Nasional – BRIN), Indonesia. She holds a Bachelor's degree in Informatics Engineering from Universitas Brawijaya and a Master's degree in Information Technology from Universitas Indonesia. She is currently pursuing a Doctoral degree in Computer Science at Universitas Indonesia, focusing on natural language processing.

Nurul Aini, a researcher, a reviewer, an English teacher, is currently pursuing a Ph.D at Universitas Negeri Malang (UM), Indonesia. She is an experienced English teacher at the English Department, State Islamic Institute (IAIN) of Kediri, Indonesia, where she teaches a variety of courses including Research Review: Academic Speaking, Advanced Academic Speaking, Public Speaking, Advanced Public Speaking, Grammar in Media Discourse, Grammar in Academic Discourse, Translation, and Thesis and Publication. Nurul Aini is an active researcher and author of numerous research articles. Her research interests include Technology in English teaching and learning, Artificial Intelligence in Education (AIEd), English

Teaching Methodology for EFL. She serves as the Managing Editor of the Journal of English Education and Linguistics Studies (JEELS) at IAIN Kediri, Indonesia. and American Research Journal of Humanities & Social Science (ARJHSS), USA Nurul Aini is a reviewer for several Scopus-indexed journals, including the Journal of Language Education (JLE), National Research University, Russia. Education Journal, University of New Delhi, India. She is a member of TEFLIN (The Association of Teaching English as a Foreign Language in Indonesia) and ASIA TEFL and has participated in International Conferences in Korea, Malaysia, and Singapore. Nurul Aini is a part of the translation agency lokabahasa.com and is also an active freelance translator and proofreader for academic research articles. Nurul Aini has experience working with an American non-governmental organization, which has enhanced her cultural integration.

Ahmad Al Yakin, Universitas Al Asyariah Mandar Sulawesi Barat, Indonesia

Yasir Ahmed Mohammed Alsbbagh is a dedicated academic professional with extensive experience in teaching, research, and leadership. He holds a Bachelor of Arts in English, a Master of Business Administration in Marketing, a Master's degree in Semantics from UKM – Malaysia, and a Doctor of Philosophy in Linguistics. Recognized for pioneering research on the semantics of Arabic particles in Quranic texts, Yasir has offered groundbreaking insights into Arabic grammar and Quranic interpretation. His scholarly work also delves into artificial intelligence and political discourse, examining AI influences on teaching and communication. With innovative teaching methodologies and significant contributions to linguistics, particularly in epistemic modality, Yasir has demonstrated leadership excellence through his roles at Al-Iraqia University, fostering academic growth and advancing interdisciplinary research.

Safia E. Aming is a faculty member of the College of Criminal Justice Program of the Western Mindanao State University in Philippines. She is a graduate of Bachelor of Laws, a graduate in Accounting Management, a graduate of Certificate in Governmental Management, and Master of Public Administration.

Eka Apriani, M.Pd. is an English Lecturer at English Tadris Study Program of the Faculty of Tarbiyah in Islamic State Institute of Curup. She is a Editor in Chief in Journal of English Franca and International Journal of Education Research and Development. She is also the secretary of Corolla Education Centre Foundation, Indonesia. She Received her Master Degree (Master of Language Education) from Sriwijaya University in 2013 and Doctor of Education in Bengkulu University 2022. She has published some researchs in international journal and national journal. She has Scopus Id and WOS Id. She is a member of profession organisation: ADRI,

TEFLIN, PDPI and ELITE. She is treasurer of ADRI in Bengkulu Province. Her research interest is in Writing skill and ICT in learning English. She write some books: The beauty of Rejang Lebong, Semantics Crossword, Metode Pengajaran BIPA, Drama Manuscript: The Marriage of Siti Zubaidah. She has also some Intelektual Property Right: Semantics Crossword, The beauty of Rejang Lebong, The Marriage of Siti Zubaidah, Metode Pengajaran BIPA, etc.

Andi Asrifan is an accomplished educator and academic leader with a Doctorate in Education, specializing in English Language Education from Universitas Negeri Makassar. With a strong academic foundation, he holds a Master's degree in the same field and a Bachelor's degree in Secondary Education. His dissertation focused on developing bilingual educational materials, reflecting his commitment to enhancing language education. Dr. Asrifan has extensive experience in various educational roles, including serving as the Head of the International Affairs Office at Politeknik Negeri Nunukan and as the Head of the Institute for Student Development and Alumni at Universitas Muhammadiyah Sidenreng Rappang. He is also an active member of several professional organizations, including the Linguistics Society of Indonesia and TEFLIN. In addition to his administrative roles, Dr. Asrifan is a passionate advocate for educational innovation and has participated in numerous international conferences and webinars, sharing his insights on language teaching and curriculum development. His dedication to professional development is evident through his participation in various training programs.

Selami Aydin is a full professor in the Department of English Language Teaching at Istanbul Medeniyet University, Istanbul, Turkey. He researches on EFL writing, testing, affective states, technology use and social media effects on language learning and teaching processes. Currently, he teaches ELT related courses at BA and MA programs.

Luis Miguel Cardoso is Former Dean of Higher School of Education and Social Sciences (8 years) Adjunct Professor Researcher at C3I - Polytechnic Institute of Portalegre and CEC - Lisbon University (Portugal)

Sandip Chakraborty is an Assistant Professor at Brainware University, specializing in subjects like Operating Systems and Web Design. He holds an M.Tech in Computer Science and Engineering from Pondicherry University and a B.Tech in Computer Science and Engineering from Adamas Institute of Technology. Qualified in UGC NET for Computer Science, Sandip has two years of teaching experience and is adept at fostering engaging learning environments. His research interests include Algorithms, Cloud Computing, and Machine Learning. Sandip has participated in multiple faculty development programs on AI, Blockchain, and IoT, and is actively pursuing certifications in AWS and React.

Gourab Dutta, an Assistant Professor at Brainware University, seamlessly Integrates academic prowess with practical expertise. He earned his B.Tech in Computer Science and Engineering in 2007 from Narula Institute of Technology, followed by a Masters in Computer Science and Engineering in 2013 from the Institute of Engineering and Management, Kolkata. Currently pursuing a Ph.D. in Computer Science and Engineering at the University of Kalyani, Mr. Dutta's research encompasses the Impact of Cloud-Based Smart Food Service Inventory Management Systems on Business Applications. With over 10 years of experience in academia, he has authored 6 research papers in prestigious journals and holds 4 patents, showcasing his significant contributions to the field.

Radhiyatul Fajri is a researcher at the Research Center for Data and Information Sciences, National Research and Innovation Agency (BRIN), Indonesia. She obtained her Bachelor's degree in Informatics Engineering from Universitas Putra Indonesia "YPTK" (2013) and her Master's in Computer Science from IPB University (2022). Since 2021, her research has centered around artificial intelligence (AI), particularly in the areas of natural language processing (NLP), large language models (LLMs), and computer vision. Her work includes projects on sentiment analysis, facial recognition, and AI-driven applications for automation and data insight generation. She is passionate about advancing AI technologies to develop innovative solutions that address complex challenges in data science and digital communication.

Rahul Kumar Ghosh is an esteemed academic and assistant professor at Brainware University, Kolkata. With a rich history in computer science and education, he holds a Master of Science (M.Sc.) in Applied Statistics and Analytics from Maulana Abul Kalam Azad University of Technology, West Bengal, another Master's degree in Information Technology and a Doctor of Philosophy (Ph.D.) from Seacom Skills University, West Bengal. His thesis, titled "Digitalization of Education Credentials Using PERMANENT EDUCATION NUMBER: An Empirical Approach Towards Greener Environment" reflects his interests in the intersection of education, technology, and environmental sustainability. He has also qualified for NET-UGC in the subject of computer science and application, earning the Junior Research Fellowship (JRF) position. Dr. Ghosh is a Microsoft Certified Technology Specialist (Database Administrator) and has completed various courses in database management systems and programming. His dedication to research and academia is reflected in his numerous publications in esteemed journals and conferences. He has presented research papers on various topics, including knowledge management, digital

Magna Anissa A. Hayudini is a graduate of Post-Doctor in Strategic Management and Leadership, a graduate of Doctor of Public Administration, a graduate of Master of Public Administration, a graduate of Master of Arts in Nursing, a graduate of Bachelor of Science in Nursing, and a graduate of Associate in Health Science Education. They also have academic units in Doctor of Philosophy in Educational Management and Bachelor of Science in Secondary Education. They published 2 papers indexed in Scopus and published several papers in non-Scopus indexed. They authored 5 books and published by Lulu Housing Publication in USA and Yawman Publication House in the Philippines. They are an international speaker, a faculty, a research mentor, and panel.

Sedar Hoser was born in Yalova, Turkey. He graduated from ELT department at İstanbul Medeniyet University and got his MA degree. He has been working as an English teacher in Turkey.

Mohamadreza Jafary earned his Ph.D. in Educational Studies from Universiti Putra Malaysia (UPM) and has been dedicated to the fields of English Language Teaching (ELT) and writing studies since 2002. He is currently a full-time researcher in the Language Acquisition Program (LAP) within the Department of Integrated Studies in Education at McGill University, where he also lectures on a contractual basis at both undergraduate and graduate levels. In addition to his academic research, Dr. Jafary holds certifications as a Cambridge language assessor and serves as an official IELTS examiner in Canada. He is a member of the editorial board of the Canadian Center of Science and Education and has contributed to the McGill Language Policy and Planning (LPP) Conference as both a program building committee member and peer reviewer. His research interests include academic writing, AI-integrated writing modules, machine learning, applied and corpus linguistics, critical pedagogy, language assessment, international exit exam preparation, writing assessment, and written feedback in second language acquisition

Juvrianto Chrissunday Jakob is a dedicated English lecturer at the Civil Engineering Department of Ambon State Polytechnic, Indonesia. With a strong academic background and a passion for education, his areas of expertise encompass Teaching English as a Foreign Language (TEFL), integrating Technology in Language Learning, Discourse Analysis, and English for Specific Purposes (ESP). These fields reflect his commitment to equipping students with language skills tailored to their professional and academic needs. He holds a master's degree in English Education from Universitas Negeri Makassar, Indonesia, where he honed his skills in pedagogy and research. His scholarly pursuits focus on exploring innovative teaching methodologies and the application of modern tools in language instruction, ensuring his teaching methods align with the evolving demands of education in the digital era. Beyond his role as a lecturer, He is an active contributor to academic communities. He serves as a tutor and language instructor, helping learners enhance their English proficiency. His dedication to academic excellence is further evident in his role as a reviewer for several local and international journals, where he evaluates and supports the dissemination of research in his field. His professional journey is driven by his belief in lifelong learning and his desire to foster effective communication skills in students and professionals alike. His contributions to the intersection of language, technology, and education underscore his impact as an educator and scholar.

Fareeha Javed is an Associate Professor of English with 28 years of experience in higher education. She earned her PhD from Massey University, New Zealand, where she also completed a Postgraduate Diploma in Teaching and Learning. Her academic background further includes a Master's degree in English Literature and Educational Planning & Management. Dr. Javed's research interests lie in language education, digital pedagogy, curriculum design, learner motivation, and educational policy. Dr. Javed remains committed to inclusive and transformative education and considers herself a lifelong learner. She values collaboration and is continually inspired by her students, colleagues, and the evolving landscape of education.

Andi Djalal Latief began his career as an engineer in the field of computer applications at Indonesia's Agency for the Assessment and Application of Technology (BPPT) in 1986. In 2021, he joined the Center for Data Science and Information at the National Research and Innovation Agency (BRIN) as a researcher. His current research focuses on artificial intelligence, particularly natural language processing (NLP), with an emphasis on developing NLP technologies for low-resource and endangered languages.

Amal Metwally is an Assistant Professor of Linguistics and Translation at the College of Languages and Translation, King Khalid University, Saudi Arabia. She has been teaching undergraduate and postgraduate courses in linguistics, translation, and research methodology since 2013. She is currently the coordinator of the Master in Translation Program and previously headed Graduate Studies and Scientific Research Unit (2021–2023) and Translation Unit (2024). She also served as a Consultant to the Scholarship Administration (2020–2022). Dr. Metwally holds PhD from the Department of English Language, Literature, and Simultaneous Interpretation at Al-Azhar University in Cairo, focusing on linguistic markers of metaphor in the Qur'an, and an MA in Translation, specializing in the translation of culture-specific expressions. Her research interests include translation strategies, corpus linguistics, and digital pedagogy.

Elvira Nurfadhilah is a researcher at the Research Center for Data and Information Sciences, National Research and Innovation Agency (BRIN), Indonesia dibidang NLP dan computer vision (biometrik data sidik jari, mata, iris dll). She obtained her Bachelor's degree in Computer Science (2011) and her Master's degree in Computer Science (2015) from IPB University. She began her professional career as an engineer at the Agency for the Assessment and Application of Technology (BPPT) in 2014 before joining BRIN. Since 2021, she has been an active researcher in the field of artificial intelligence (AI), focusing on speech and natural language processing (NLP). Her research covers speech recognition, speech analytics, sentiment analysis, machine translation, and NLP for low-resource languages.

Ahmed J. Obaid, is a Asst. Professor at the Department of Computer Science, Faculty of Computer Science and Mathematics, University of Kufa, Iraq. Dr. Ahmed holds a Bachelor in Computer Science, degree in – Information Systems from College of Computers, University of Anbar, Iraq (2001-2005), and a Master Degree (M. TECH) of Computer Science Engineering (CSE) from School of Information Technology, Jawaharlal Nehru Technological University, Hyderabad, India (2010-2013), and a Doctor of Philosophy (PhD) in Web Mining from College of Information Technology, University of University of Babylon, Iraq (2013-2017). He is a Certified Web Mining Consultant with over 14 years of experience in working as Faculty Member in University of Kufa, Iraq. He has taught courses in Web Designing, Web Scripting, JavaScript, VB.Net, MATLAB Toolbox's, and other courses on PHP, CMC, and DHTML from more than 10 international organizations and institutes from USA, and India. Dr. Ahmed is a member of Statistical and Information Consultation Center (SICC), University of Kufa, Iraq.

Siska Pebiana is an AI enthusiast who are focused on Natural Language Processing Research.

Kokoy Siti Komariah received her Ph.D. in AI Convergence from Pukyong National University, South Korea, in 2023. She is currently a researcher at the National Research and Innovation Agency (BRIN), Indonesia. Her research focuses on text processing, information retrieval, and natural language processing, with particular interest in developing AI-driven solutions for language understanding and knowledge discovery.

Prabu Kresna Putra is a researcher at the Center for Data Science and Information Research within the National Research and Innovation Agency (BRIN). He holds a Bachelor's degree in Informatics Engineering and a Master's degree in Information Technology. He began his career at the Center for Natural Resource Inventory Technology within the Agency for the Assessment and Application of Technology (BPPT). His research interests include data mining, social media analytics, remote sensing, environmental studies, GIS, terrestrial and marine resource studies, data analytics, and related fields. He has been actively involved in various research projects, including large language models, resource inventory, modeling, and natural resource accounting.

Like Raskova Octaberliana, M.Ed, stands out as a distinguished educational figure, particularly in English language teaching. With an impressive educational background that includes a Master's degree from Monash University, Australia, and a Doctorate from the State University of Malang, Indonesia, she brings a wealth of knowledge and expertise to her profession. Prof. Like Raskova Octaberliana is recognized for her academic achievements and dynamic involvement in various capacities, such as a speaker, trainer, and keynote speaker at national and international platforms. Her contributions extend to numerous conferences, workshops, and seminars, where she shares her insights on English language teaching, education, and motivation training. Her professional journey is marked by a strong foundation in English linguistics, literature, and language teaching methodologies, complemented by her publications in several esteemed journals. Prof. Like Raskova Octaberliana's dedication to the field is further evidenced by her active participation in international conferences and research projects and her commitment to teaching English. As a member of various professional organizations, she has enriched her experience by working across different educational institutions, fostering an environment of learning and growth. Moreover, Prof. Like Raskova Octaberliana's expertise is not limited to language teaching; she is also highly skilled in public speaking, human resource development, and personality character building. Her motivational training sessions are particularly noteworthy, as she has earned numerous awards and scholarships. This recognition is a testament to her impactful contributions to education and her ability to inspire and cultivate the minds of learners and educators alike. Prof. Dr. Like Raskova Octaberliana, M.Ed, embodies the essence of a dedicated educator and mentor whose work continues to influence English language teaching and beyond.

Hammam Riza, M.Sc., is a distinguished academic and technologist renowned for his pioneering contributions to Artificial Intelligence (AI), cybersecurity, and digital transformation in Indonesia. He is principal engineer of BRIN the National

Research and Innovation Agency. Prof. Riza holds a Doctor of Engineering degree in Electrical Engineering (cum laude) from the Bandung Institute of Technology (ITB), where he conducted groundbreaking research at the Computing Research Laboratory (CRL), New Mexico State University, USA. He also earned a Master of Science in Computer Science from the University of Kentucky, USA, and a Bachelor's degree in Electrical Engineering, with a major in Electronics and Control Systems, from ITB. Currently, Prof. Riza serves as a Professor of AI at Syiah Kuala University (USK), where he leads initiatives in AI research, education, and public engagement. His academic pursuits are deeply interwoven with practical applications, fostering innovation in AI-driven solutions for public services and industrial competitiveness.

Agung Santosa received the BSEE from University of Toledo, USA, in 1992 and Master of Computer Science from University of Indonesia, Indonesia, in 2015. He is an associate researcher at the Research Center for Data and Information Sciences, affiliated with the National Research and Innovation Agency (BRIN) in Indonesia. Since 2021, he has been an active researcher in the domain of artificial intelligence, specifically focusing on speech and natural language processing. His research includes speech recognition, speech analytics, sentiment analysis, and natural language processing. He can be contacted at email: agun006@brin.go.id.

Mohammad Uliniansyah has an Education Bachelor Degree, Telecommunication Engineering, Shibaura Institute of Technology, Japan (1991) Master Degree, Computer Science, Oklahoma State University, USA (1998) Doctoral Degree, Media Governance, Keio University, Japan (2007)

Nimas Untariyati is a researcher with areas of expertise in IT, namely information systems, e-government, data science and application auditing.

Raveenthiran Vivekanantharasa is a distinguished academic and researcher in the fields of educational management, leadership, and technology-enhanced learning. He currently serves as a Senior Lecturer at the Faculty of Education, The Open University of Sri Lanka. Holding a PhD in Educational Management, an MSc in Management, and a Bachelor of Education, Dr. Vivekanantharasa has extensive experience in higher education, curriculum development, and teacher training. With a strong international presence, he has been a keynote speaker, panelist, and resource person at numerous global conferences, contributing to discussions on AI in education, inclusive learning, and digital transformation in pedagogy. Additionally, he serves as a peer reviewer and editorial board member for several international academic journals. Beyond academia, Dr. Vivekanantharasa is actively involved in research focusing on online learning, school-based management, and special needs education. His dedication to advancing educational practices has earned him recognition, including multiple international awards for excellence in teaching and research.

WabulaYuyun Wabula is a senior researcher in National Research and Innovation Agency, Indonesia. His research interest includes NLP, LLM, Machine Learning, and regional language processing.

Muthmainnah Yakin is a senior lecturer at Universitas Al Asyariah Mandar in West Sulawesi, Indonesia. She has extensive experience as a lecturer, global speaker, and international leader. Muthmainnah has held numerous positions at her university, including Chairman of the Indonesian Language Department, Public Relations Officer, Director of Women's Centre Studies, Deputy Director of Quality Assurance Unit, and currently, Deputy Director of the Language and Character Development Institute. Muthmainnah is also an accomplished author, having written 90 national and International books, published by esteemed publishers such as IGI Global, Springer, Emerald, Wiley, Taylor and Francis. She serves as an international board member for various scientific innovation research groups, adjunct faculty of MAAUN Nigeria, adjunct faculty at Buriram Rajabhat university (BRU) Thailand and adjunct faculty at MANIPAL Global Ntx Malaysia Muthmainnah has won over 100+ international awards, including Outstanding Professor, Outstanding Leadership, Best International Influencer, Best Emerging Professor of the Year, International Award for Working Women, and SDGs Warrior. She is also an honorary doctorate degree holder from Layahe University and the recipient of the Doctor of Excellence award from the Philippines. Moreover, Muthmainnah is a member of the United Nations volunteers' roster and the advisory board of Indonesian education share to care volunteers. Her research interests include developing literary work, instructional teaching material, assurance of learning (Assure), TESOL (Teaching English to Speakers of Other Languages), ICT in education, digital education, GenAI and cybergogy. Muthmainnah is an outstanding scholar with a Sinta (Indonesian Ministry of education and culture) score overall of 4680 and h-index 17 Her position as External examiner for PhD students at 3 A+ accredited campuses in India, Malaysia, Florida, USA, Cyprus Europe and Australia. She is a strong believer in international collaboration and teamwork, making her an ideal candidate for various academic and leadership roles. With her extensive experience and outstanding track record, Muthmainnah is open to international collaborations and teamwork.

Ambar Yoganingrum is a senior researcher at the Research Center for Data and Information Sciences, National Research and Innovation Agency (BRIN), Indonesia since 2019. She was a researcher in Center for Scientific Documentation and Information, Indonesian Institute of Sciences (PDII LIPI) for 18 years. She obtained her bachelor degree in Pharmaceutical Sciences from University of Padjadjaran, Indonesia in 1990. She earned a Master's degree in Health Informatics from the University of Indonesia in 2003 and a Doctorate in Information Systems from the same university in 2015. Ambar Yoganingrum's research interests include issues in the field of informetrics, information system, and digital media.

Index

Symbols

A

B

C

D

E

G

P

R

S

T

V

www.ingramcontent.com/pod-product-compliance
Lightning Source LLC
LaVergne TN
LVHW061532290926
849162LV00004B/763
* 9 7 9 8 3 3 7 3 0 2 7 5 1 *